Employee Relations Management

Employee Relations Management

P. N. SINGH
NEERAJ KUMAR

Delhi • Chennai

Senior Acquisitions Editor: Praveen Tiwari
Development Editor: Soma Banerjee
Assistant Production Editor: Barun Kumar Sarkar
Compositor: Glyph International
Printer: Shree Maitrey Printech Pvt. Ltd

ISBN 978-81-317-2601-3

First Impression, 2011

Published by Pearson India Education Services Pvt.Ltd,CIN:U72200TN2005PTC057128.
Formerly known as TutorVista Global Pvt Ltd, licensees of Pearson Education in South Asia

Head Office: 7th Floor, knowledge Boulevard, A-8(A) Sector-62, Noida (U.P) 201309, India

Registered Office: Module G4, Ground Floor, Elnet Software City, TS -140,Block 2 & 9
Rajiv Gandhi Salai, Taramani, Chennai, Tamil Nadu 600113.,Fax: 080-30461003,
Phone: 080-30461060, www.pearson.co.in email id: companysecretary.india@pearson.com

Digitally printed in India by Saurabh Printers Pvt. Ltd. in the year of 2016.

To my loving, departed wife, Usha.

P. N. Singh

To my parents, Kusum and Balram Thakur.
I would be nothing, but for your constant support and the encouragement for learning that you provided throughout my life.

Neeraj Kumar

about the authors

P. N. Singh, a postgraduate in labour and social welfare from Patna University, started his career in 1962 with NMC as a management trainee. Two years later, in 1964, he joined the Bokaro Steel Plant which was then at the project stage. He worked there for 29 years, rising through the ranks to head the human resource management function during the last three years of his service as Executive Director (Personnel and Administration). From there, he moved to the State Trading Corporation as Personnel Director for a short while before joining SAIL in 1994 as Director, Personnel. Having worked in the industry for nearly three-and-a-half decades, he switched to academia in 1996 when he joined the Institute of Management Technology, Ghaziabad as a professor in the area of organizational behaviour and human resources. Concomitantly, he also served as Vice Chairman, Appeals Committee, ONGC for three years. In 2004, he shifted to the FORE School of Management as Senior Professor, OB and HR. He taught there for three years before joining the Army Institute of Management in 2008.

An excellent negotiator, Professor Singh is credited with having established numerous systems relating to human resources management at the Bokaro Steel Plant. He has led path-breaking settlements with unions on issues of redeployment of surplus in line with business requirement. As a member, and later Convenor of the National Joint Consultative Committee for Steel Industry, he managed to settle the wage agreements for the Indian steel industry through collective bargaining with representatives of the central trade union organizations. At a policy-making level, he has been instrumental in many strategic initiatives including human resources planning for modernization, managing change through people and the turnaround of SAIL. From shop floor to board room, he has handled the entire range of issues relating to human resources management in general, and employee relations in particular. He has also been a member of tripartite committees on contract labour.

Having headed the HR functions of two very prominent PSUs in India, P. N. Singh is experienced in successfully resolving industrial conflicts and establishing systems and procedures for handling employee relations issues in a multi-union environment. He uses this rich experience to provide an industry perspective to aspiring managers in the classroom. Besides teaching, he also works as a consultant and conducts management development programmes in both public and private sector organizations.

Neeraj Kumar holds a bachelors degree in physics from the University of Delhi and a postgraduate diploma in Labour and Social Welfare from the University of Calcutta. He started his career with the SAIL in 1981 as a management trainee. In his 23-year career with SAIL, he handled all the functions of HR including industrial and employee relations, performance management, strategic HRM and organization development. In the early phases of his career, he handled employee-related issues at various shop floors in the highly unionized environment of the Durgapur Steel Plant. He successfully introduced many productivity and discipline improvement measures at the shop floor through discussions and negotiations with the employees and their unions. Later, he moved to corporate HR where he was closely associated with the change management and turnaround initiative at SAIL.

Professor Kumar quit SAIL in 2004 to work as a freelance consultant in areas pertaining to HRM, management of discipline, negotiations and collective bargaining, leading, teaming, communicating and other soft skills (such as inter and intrapersonal effectiveness, handling conflicts, managing emotions, negotiating and adapting to change). He used his long industry experience to design and deliver management development programmes in leading private and public enterprises including Xansa, SAIL, Bharti Airtel, BALCO, HINDALCO,

METSO Minerals, Punj Lloyd, Daewoo Motors, NTPC, Motherson Sumi Systems Limited, Capgemini, PGCIL, GAIL India, Engineers India Limited, Wockhardt, Maruti Udyog Limited, Siemens and Perot Systems.

Neeraj Kumar has been a part of academia since he joined the FORE School of Management as an associate professor in the area of organizational behaviour and human resources management in 2008. He teaches HRM, industrial relations, performance and compensation management, labour legislations and organization design and change.

contents

foreword

While knowledge management is increasingly considered significant for business success and there is increasing use of technology in knowledge management, books written by practitioners has been an age-old effective form of knowledge management. I feel honoured to be asked to write a foreword for this new book on Employee relations management authored by two very experienced managers codifying their decades of experience.

When I was doing my Ph.D. in England on Industrial Relations, often, there was talk about approaching the subject as "employee relations" rather than "industrial relations". Employee relations has become both a reality and a necessity in the wake of globalization, increasing competition, demographic changes, and increased levels of education and awareness through the spread of print and electronic media. While the growth of human resource management as a discipline altered the way one looked upon and managed white-collar employees, our way of addressing the issues of grass-root employees, who often rely on physical labour and manual skills, remained relatively unchanged. The turbulent decade of the 1980s led to the questioning of the traditional tools and techniques of labour management. As often happens, this seeking of solutions also led to the searching of souls. It dawned on practitioners and theoreticians alike that it was not just a question of tools and techniques but a fundamental change of mindset and approach that was required to elicit productive response from employees to enhance competitiveness. Discretionary contribution of employees was not dependent on the management exercising its discretion; rather the management realization that true exercise of discretion meant a newer approach to addressing traditional relationships.

I am glad that two experienced professionals, P.N. Singh and Neeraj Kumar have chosen to capture certain facts of this new movement in the Indian context in their new book. Both of them worked for decades in various capacities with the illustrious Steel Authority of India Limited, a well-known public-sector *navratna* which at one time had the distinction of employing more than 160,000 employees. Despite the constraints of being a public-sector organization, SAIL pioneered many leading employee relations practices and often worked as a laboratory for experimenting with new innovations in this difficult area. The geographic spread of its plants in diverse climatic and cultural environments often challenged the best human resource managers and their skills in creating productive employer–employee relationships. The authors were nurtured in this environment and undoubtedly developed a point of view on how employee relations can be effectively managed in the Indian context and in the context of large manufacturing corporations.

The book, divided out into eighteen chapters, focuses on each area of employee relations and covers both the legal and the contextual factors that impact the framework of such relationships. I am confident that this book will be an important additional source of knowledge and insight for both practitioners and researchers of employee relations in India. I wish the book great success.

Dr Santrupt B. Misra
Director
Aditya Birla Management Corporation Limited

preface

Employee Relations Management is a textbook for students and practitioners of HRM (both beginners and specialists) who wish to learn the concepts, their applications and the latest trends in the field of industrial relations (IR). Based on our experiences as managers and instructors, we have attempted to write a textbook that is practical, contemporary and application-oriented. This book attempts to link actual happenings in industry with the existing body of knowledge that exists in this field. In our opinion, a clear understanding of both is necessary for developing an interest in the subject.

The Motivation for This Book

Having spent several decades in the industry and in academia, we have been acutely aware of the need for a textbook in the area of employee relations/industrial relations that clearly establishes the link between classrooms and workplaces. We sorely felt the need for a textbook that could make abstract concepts real, for both practising and aspiring managers and students. Since the subject matter of industrial relations is largely country-specific, we found that the available titles either leaned towards concepts and research or focused on wider coverage of the syllabuses.

As instructors at the postgraduate level, we needed a textbook that would cover the theoretical topics in the field of industrial relations; correlate the concepts to prevalent industry practices and real events; and pose probing, thought-provoking questions to enable students and instructors explore the topics. Further, we felt that a textbook should bring to life a few difficult areas in labour legislations. We believed that illustrations highlighting different situations inviting the application of various legislations, calculation of workmen's compensation, PF contributions, gratuity and bonus, etc. would be immensely helpful in a textbook.

From Industrial Relations to Employee Relations

We witnessed the profound effects of liberalization and other policy changes on industrial relations. We needed a textbook that would explain the concepts against the background of these changes in the economy and industry, describing the consequences of these changes on industrial relations and related concepts. So when we began working on this book, we made a conscious decision to emphasize the shift that is taking place as a result of liberalization and globalization. These two factors have forced employers, governments and trade unions to align to new realities. There is an ongoing paradigm shift from conflict resolution in traditional industrial relations to collaborative partnerships through employee relations management. Hence, the title of the book.

The Organization of the Book

Employee Relations Management is divided into four parts and comprises 18 chapters in all.

Part I covers the broad context, evolution, conceptual framework of industrial relations. It essentially deals with topics that were traditionally covered in a textbook of industrial relations. This is essential for a student new to the subject: it lays the conceptual foundation on which to build. However, here too, we have tried to establish their relevance to extant practices in industry, wherever possible. The evolution and growth of IR, IR in India and major economies of the world, trade unionism and trade unions in India are discussed in this part.

Part II focuses on the shift that is taking place in organizations, from the legacy practices of managing relationships through formal bodies of employees to a more direct, strategic approach.

Part III takes the readers through different aspects of labour administration and legislation. In this part, we have ensured that readers comprehend the laws instead of merely committing them to memory. The nature of conflicts and disputes, the measures for resolving them, process of bargaining and industrial discipline, wage and labour administration machinery have been covered in this part in detail.

Part IV covers the soft skills for a professional in the area of HRM/ERM, with special emphasis on negotiation skills.

Features

The book incorporates several pedagogical features that have been designed to foster the ability to question, correlate and analyse events from the real-world in the context of employee relations.

Chapter Outlines

Chapter outlines capture the major topics that are discussed within the chapter.

CHAPTER OUTLINE

5.1 The Concept of Trade Unionism
5.2 Politics and Trade Unions
5.3 Rights of Trade Unions
5.4 Roles, Functions and Objectives of Trade Unions
5.5 Features of an Effective Trade Union
5.6 The Classification of Trade Unions
5.7 Strategies for the Achievement of Trade Union Objectives
5.8 The State of Trade Unions in the World

Learning Objectives

Learning objectives capture the salient points that students need to focus on while studying the chapter.

LEARNING OBJECTIVES

After reading this chapter, you will be able to:

- Describe the concept of trade unionism
- Identify the factors that led to the origin and the growth of trade unions
- Define the principles underlying trade unionism
- Understand the various approaches to the study of trade unions
- Understand the structure, functions and activities of trade unions

Tata's Takeover of Jaguar and Land Rover[1]

The takeover of Jaguar and Land Rover, emblems of the British auto, by Tata Motors in March 2008 was greeted with approval but regret by Unite, Britain's largest trade union formed by the merger of Amicus and the Transport and General Workers' Union on 1 May 2007.

Unite, though not happy about the impending ownership change, in early July 2007, sent a five-point charter to Ford demanding, among other things, that the union be involved in the sale process. The union members were present in the early stages of presentations and negotiations between Ford and the bidders. Despite the lack of unanimity among the rank and file of Unite, the union's preference helped Tata Motors to emerge the front-runner, leaving the other bidders behind.

In November 2007, Unite issued a public statement saying that, of all the bidders, Tata Motors, with an established presence and background in manufacturing, was its preferred buyer for Jaguar and Land Rover. Tata Motors, realizing how critical it was going to be for them to take Unite along for both the acquisition and post-acquisition support, during the various stages of discussion and negotiation with Ford, reiterated through various channels that the jobs of the workers at Jaguar and Land Rover would remain secure and post-takeover, the 160,000-odd jobs across the various Ford sites in Britain would continue untouched.

In January 2008, about three months prior to the actual closing of the deal, Tony Woodley, General Joint Secretary, Unite, said in a press release that detailed meetings focusing on the job security of the workers in Jaguar, Land Rover and other Ford plants in the UK were necessary. Other crucial issues around wages, terms and conditions and pension also needed to be addressed before the final decision could be taken.

In March 2008, the takeover was formalized, but only after Tata Motors issued an undertaking that jobs would be saved. Tata Motors also committed to long-term supply agreements for components from Ford units in the UK.

Opening Vignettes

Opening vignettes present snapshots of real-world scenarios. These give a practical flavour to the concepts discussed in the chapter.

Policies and Procedures

- Need to be written in a language easily understood
- Should be widely circulated
- Consulted for guidance
- Set standards of workplace behaviour and practices
- Define the scope and limits of the influence of the workplace

Margin Definitions and Notes

Margin definitions and notes capture the definitions and salient points from each page.

The features of an effective trade union are:

- Internally democratic
- Have a strong leadership
- Exhibit a responsibility towards their worker members
- Committed to promote industrial peace and harmony
- Inclined towards collective bargaining that is collaborative and not competitive.
- Possess financial security
- Adaptable to change

BOX 12.4 FOR CLASS DISCUSSION

Nandigram in East Midnapur district of West Bengal is one of the seven SEZs sanctioned in West Bengal. The proposed SEZ (now scrapped) was to develop a mega-chemical hub. The choice of this mega-chemical hub in the Haldia region was the result of a long exercise undertaken by the Government of India where this venue was chosen along with four other sites in the country. With the existing petroleum refinery of the IOC, the petrochemical plant at Haldia in the joint sector and the huge facility of Mitsubishi chemicals, this decision to have the mega-chemical hub located here made business sense. The Haldia petrochemicals have led to 700 units in the downstream providing an employment to over 1 lakh people. The Government of West Bengal had signed a Memorandum of Understanding with the Indian Oil Corporation to be an anchor investor for the project, while the Salim group would have been the promoter for building the infrastructure.

The Chief Minister of West Bengal had stated no progress on the project would take place until consultations were held with elected representatives in the panchayat and the people of the area. As there had been no survey done and consultations held, the question of land acquisition did not arise before these processes took place.

The demand was that land acquisition would only take place if a credible plan for improving the quality of life and livelihood could be put forth. This was the overall approach of the left.

To add to the unrest, a number of other political forces had come together at Nandigram. There were cases of legitimate protests and also cases of planned violence disrupting the peace at Nandigram. The compelling reason for any such project in the state will be premised on the question of employment generation and improving the lot of the poor and disadvantaged sections. The Left Front had anticipated the need for such a project on the eve of the last elections. Therefore, the Left Front election manifesto had clearly stated: "Industrial parks have been decided to be set up in the task of modernizing the traditional labour-intensive industries, and to make them competitive. Parks will be set up for foundry, jute, rubber, garments, textile, iron and steel, chemicals polymer, light engineering, and food" and "a minimum of four big industrial taluka and special economic zones will be set up in the state".

The industrial conflict here was with regard to the nature of the industry and the manner in which it took place. The difference in perception was with regard to the private corporate's way of viewing industries and that of the Left. Will this have an effect on workplace IR?

"For Class Discussion" Boxes

"For Class Discussion" boxes contain topics for exploring and analysing issues from different perspectives, leading to a better understanding of the subject matter.

SUMMARY

- Unions are organizations designed to promote and enhance the social and economic welfare of their members.
- The unions emerged to protect worker interests, and, gradually, started playing an important role in the social and political affairs of a country.
- Trade unions are part of the fabric of industrial democracy and can play a constructive role in improving production and productivity, and the resolution of conflicts.
- Trade unionism had initially grown in order to:

Security: The security of employment of their members must be safeguarded.

- Trade unions have the following main objectives:
  - Ensure the security of workers
  - Obtain better economic returns
  - Improve working conditions
  - Power to influence management
  - Power to influence the government

Summary

The summary recapitulates the key concepts, definitions and points from the chapter. It serves as a ready reference for students who want to revise the concepts learned in a chapter

REVIEW QUESTIONS

1 What are the characteristics of trade unions?

2 What is a trade union and how are they generally formed? Trace the genesis of trade unions.

3 Explain the following:

i. the objectives of a trade union

ii. characteristics of trade unionism

iii. classification of trade unions

iv. strategies for the achievement of objectives of a trade union

Review Questions

Review questions included at the end of each chapter are designed to help students check their comprehension of concepts.

Questions for Critical Thinking

Questions for critical thinking, presented at the end of each chapter, are designed to foster analysis and application of concepts to solve problems.

QUESTIONS FOR CRITICAL THINKING

1 The growing internationalization of business and workforce has its impact on HRM in terms of problems of unfamiliar laws, languages, practices, attitudes, management styles, work ethics and more. HR managers face a challenge to deal with more and more heterogeneous sets of workers and more involvement in the employee's personal life. Discuss these changes in the light of industrial relations management.

2 Liberalization has led to large-scale reorganization of businesses in terms of expansions, mergers and acquisitions, joint ventures, takeovers, and internal restructuring of organizations. In circumstances as dynamic and as uncertain as these, it is a challenge to manage the employees' anxiety, uncertainties, insecurities and fears. Discuss probable employer response and union response to these changes. Give examples to support your answer.

3 There are signs of changing demographics of the workforce reflected in age and qualification mix, dual career couples, large chunk of young blood with contrasting ethos of work among old superannuating employees, growing number of women in workforce, working mothers, more educated and aware workers, etc. Thus, the changing demography of workforce has its own implications for industrial relations. Discuss these implications and the strategies required to cope with the same.

DEBATE

1 The second National Commission on Labour has recommended the enactment of a general law relating to hours of work, working conditions, annual leave, welfare, contract labour and others applicable to various categories of establishments alike. In a competitive environment, such provisions would further erode the competitiveness of Indian business.

2 Is the Shops and Establishments Act, as it obtains today, an impediment to 24 × 7 customer service?

3 Read the box-item below. What could be the arguments from each side?

The Karnakata government's plan to ban night shifts for women is ruffling feathers in Bangalore.

Women employees in the hotel Industry have to work late night shifts. And the number is substantial. But that might soon change. The Karnataka Assembly has passed a new Bill that seeks to ban night shifts for women in firms that come under the Karnataka Shops and Establishments Act.

The IT industry and hospitals, however, will be exempted. Women's groups are already protesting saying this is not a progressive step. It may hinder progress of women, they say. The employers say that in the world of business today one cannot have a segregated and isolated approach towards women workforce.

The government says it is the only way to ensure protection for women and will target the hotel industry, shopping malls and recreation centres. The recent incident of the murder of a woman employee returning from late night shift has prompted government concerns regarding women's safety.

4 Rather than abolish contract labour, we need to regulate it by protecting equality of wages, workers' health, safety, welfare and access to various amenities at the workplace.

5 Trade unions and workers' organizations can focus on "equal pay for equal work", rather than on the absorption of contract labour.

Debate

Topics for debate have been included to encourage students to understand and appreciate the various aspects of a problem.

Case Analysis

Each chapter concludes with two cases for analysis. Based on recent incidents in the industry, the discussion of these cases can be open ended, though the questions at the end help the instructor direct the discussion to relevant issues in the case.

CASE ANALYSIS

Labour Trouble in Nepal

A soft-drink manufacturing unit of a New Delhi-based businessman, N. K. Mishra, ran into labour trouble with angry workers protesting outside the NKM office trouble in Nepal. The NKM, which has interests in real estate, retailing, hospitality and education, also has stakes in the XYZ beverages industry. Although Maoist guerrillas have made their peace with the government, giving a respite to businessmen who had been bearing the brunt of bomb blasts, extortion and shutdowns, the beverages industry has come under attack from the labour union affiliated to the Communist Party of Nepal. The communist union, in a bid to nip the growing popularity of the Maoists, is asking NKM Beverages to give permanent employment to seasonal workers who have been employed for over 240 days, with sick leave and other facilities. The protest was reportedly triggered by the company's directive to the temporary employees to go on "unpaid leave" during off-season.

What would be your advice to deal with this IR problem?

Industrial Relations at McDonald's

McDonald's is basically a non-union company.

Collect information on the industrial relations practice followed by McDonald's in different countries where it operates.

The Teaching and Learning Package

A full range of resources that support teaching and learning is available with this book. The resources may be downloaded from **www.pearsoned.co.in/pnsingh**

For Instructors

PowerPoint Lecture Slides comprising chapter outlines, major concepts, diagrams, chapter summaries are available for each chapter.

For Students

The *Study Card* captures key concepts and definitions from each of the chapters. It is designed to enable the reader to browse through the salient points of each chapter quickly.

Acknowledgements

This book is all that we have learned as practitioners and instructors in our combined journey as HRM professionals and instructors. We have tried to keep the book simple, for students, practitioners and instructors.

We acknowledge with thanks the encouragement provided by the managements of FORE School of Management and IMT Ghaziabad towards the completion of this book.

We had several rounds of enriching discussions with several practitioners and academicians and we will be failing in our duty if we do not acknowledge their contribution. K. S. Sethi, Dean, MDI and former professor at IIM Calcutta; Santrupt Mishra, Director, Aditya Birla Group of Industries; D. N. Pandey, Professor, British University, Dubai; M. K. Kushwaha, Director, Army Institute of Management; A. K. Malkani, Professor, Ranchi University; and B. D. Singh, Director, KRIBHCO have helped enhance the book. We would also like to express our thanks to A. K. Sinha, President–HR (Aluminium Group) and K. K. L. Das, Chief People's Officer at the Aditya Birla Group of Industries. A. K. Sharma, Chairman and Managing Director, Amrapali Group has been a source of immense inspiration to us for which we are grateful to him.

We also acknowledge the reviewers who made valuable suggestions and critical comments, which helped in polishing the manuscript further. We wish to thank the members of the consultant board for their timeless dedication and commitment—Aijaaz Mattoo, Dean, School of Business Studies, Islamic University of Science and Technology, Kumar Mohit Spring, Professor, Xavier Institute of Social Service and Nandini Bajaj, Assistant Professor, Sri Bhagwan Mahaveer Jain College of Engineering, Bangalore. The consultant board's critical analysis of each chapter and their feedback on the entire book helped us create a lucid and student-friendly text.

Thanks are due to the staff of Pearson Education, particularly to Praveen Tiwari and Soma Banerjee, whose unstinted support, encouragement, help and faith made the book possible. Their patience and faith has been extraordinary.

P. N. Singh
Neeraj Kumar

part i

context

chapter one

CHAPTER OUTLINE

1.1 The Evolution of Industrial Relations
1.2 Definitions of Industrial Relations
1.3 The Scope of Industrial Relations
1.4 Objectives of Industrial Relations
1.5 Essential Features of Industrial Relations
1.6 Participants of Industrial Relations System and Dynamics of Their Participation
1.7 Industrial Relations: Perspective and Approach

LEARNING OBJECTIVES

After reading this chapter, you should be able to:

- Trace the necessity and evolution of approaches to the study of industrial relations
- Identify and explain the components that have been used to define industrial relations
- List the main actors of industrial relations and their respective roles in maintenance of industrial relations
- Identify the factors that shape the environment for industrial relations

A Complex Web of Relationships[1]

In 2008, in a move that earned it the wrath of worker unions, New Zealand's largest bank, ANZ National, decided to move up to 500 jobs from New Zealand to Bangalore by 2009. The jobs were in processing and operational functions, and did not involve any contact centre work.

In a statement, ANZ had said, "We are proposing to move 1 per cent of our New Zealand work to ANZ Bangalore this calendar year, and up to 5 per cent by 2009." The bank has a technology business called ANZ Operations and Technology in Bangalore since 1989. In 2008, it employed about 1,800 people in information technology development roles (about 1,100) and back office and support roles (about 700).

Saying it will redeploy all employees affected by the move, ANZ National had said it was confident of doing so as it adds 800 employees every year in New Zealand. "The staged shift of work over the next 18 months will also help staff [members] who wish to be redeployed to find a suitable alternative role within the bank. As a result, none of our staff needs to lose their job," it had added in its statement. It also clarified that all customer contact roles, including call centre roles, will remain in New Zealand and Australia.

However, the worker unions were not happy about it. FINSEC, the union representing workers in New Zealand's finance industry, had said that ANZ was putting billion-dollar profits ahead of its Kiwi customers and staff. "ANZ National is leading the race to the bottom for cheap labour in India by proposing to send these jobs offshore," FINSEC Campaigns Director Andrew Campbell was quoted as saying in a FINSEC statement.

The Union has asked the bank to make commitments on several fronts, including guaranteeing all affected staff jobs with pay and conditions equivalent to their previous ones, providing jobs for at least three years, guaranteeing that there will be no further off shoring in the next three years.

ANZ had said that the rationale behind the job transfers was to ensure better customer service and increased competitiveness. The customers, it said, would benefit from a longer 15-hour work window, with Bangalore's eight hours added to New Zealand's eight. "For ANZ, it will ensure we will remain competitive in an increasingly globalized marketplace through our access to a large pool of high calibre staff," it had said in a statement.

Industrial Relations: Evolution and Growth

Industrial relations is a major supporting subsystem of the overall management system. It constitutes an integral part of human resource development activity of any organization. The study of industrial relations has evolved over a period of time and has been shaped by the interplay of a number of forces and actors. The study of industrial relations requires a multi-disciplinary approach.

ANZ is one of the many global corporations dealing with interface relationships within the organization as well as outside. These relationships become more complex, yet vital for growth and performance, as the world progressively moves towards free trade. These relationships have evolved over a period of time, from simple production units of the post–Industrial Revolution era to the modern transnational corporations of today. Many players and forces have taken part in shaping the relationships and these will continue to do so. The unprecedented oil-price hike from around USD 50 to approximately USD 150 per barrel by OPEC in the year 2007–2008 sent the aviation industry into a tizzy, forcing domestic airlines to cut costs and announce job cuts. And, within six months, the international oil price dropped from USD 150 to around USD 40, forcing an altogether different economic scenario that took the industry some time to decipher and, amongst other things, forced the oil marketing companies in India to face a strike from its managerial staff demanding a hike in wages. The State and the political party in power had to take stern action to break the strike.

Such measures affect the employers, employee bodies (trade unions), the political parties, the government and, eventually, the employees themselves. Economic, political and social changes in any part of the world are now easily transmitted across borders and eventually invade business entities, socio-political institutions and individual lives in quick time. Against this complex and dynamic environment, it may be instructive to look at the meaning of industrial relations afresh, trace its evolution and identify the underlying changes in the emerging response patterns. We shall also work with different approaches, frameworks and tools to help us understand the actors, factors and dynamics that shape relationships between employers and employees.

1.1 The Evolution of Industrial Relations

The term *industrial relations* is generally associated with relations between the employer and the workmen in a unit or industry. The evolution of the concept is linked to industrialization and the growing complexity of work organization. As industrial enterprises grew in size and technological processes initiated a socio-technical dependence, there emerged certain peculiar characteristics that required an institutionalized rather than an individualized employer–employee relationship. Let us take a brief look at a few of the special features associated with these changes:

- **Segmentation (Blue-collar and White-collar Roles):** Mass-scale production required that repetitive tasks be performed with greater efficiency and competence. Work, therefore, got fragmented into smaller tasks. Those performing these fragmented and repetitive tasks needed supervision and, thus, the nature of roles within the workplace got classified as those of operatives, supervisors, managers, etc. This segmentation led to what later was classified as "blue-collared" and "white-collared" workers.

> **The changes at workplace relationships include:**
> - Increase in capital–labour ratio
> - Work specialization
> - Fragmentation of work
> - Repetitive work to increase efficiency
> - Fragmentation of work led to formation of groups and employees and employers
> - New perspective of an inter-group relationship
> - Growing sense of insecurity required a collective effort to counter any management initiative for retrenchment, dismissal, etc.

- **Specialization (Horizontal Differentiation):** Workers were further classified on the basis of groups that specialized in a small but distinct nature of task grouping (for example, fitters, riggers, riveters and painters). The differentiation, from an organizational point of view, was horizontal, and later led to what, in modern terms, could be akin to departments or sections. This horizontal differentiation also enabled workers to organize themselves on the basis of specialization or special skill sets at an enterprise level or even at the industry level. This kind of organization had its own impact on work relationships not only amongst the members but also with the employer and the industry.
- **Hierarchical Levels (Vertical Differentiation):** As the differentiation on the horizontal dimension increased, there was need for supervision and coordination, which resulted in a vertical hierarchy or vertical differentiation. The different levels thus created vertically were responsible and accountable for different tasks in terms of output, targets, costs, resource utilization, etc. With differentiations along both vertical and horizontal dimensions, work relationships became increasingly complex.
- **A New Relationship Interface:** The fragmentation of work and the resulting differentiations—both vertical and horizontal—resulted in increasing complexity in the relationship between employees and employers, and amongst different groups. A range of interfaces emerged Having maximized the production up to a given level with the technological resources available, the factor multiplication process of gaining through economies of scale was reached. The focus, then, shifted to technological transformation and innovations. Newer methods of production through newer technologies demanded different and new knowledge and skill sets. This impacted the security of the existing job holders because of knowledge and skill obsolescence and their redundancy. A collective effort for protecting their interests, thus, became a necessity.

The roots of the modern concept of industrial relations can be traced to the immediate aftermath of the Industrial Revolution and the problems that arose due to the growth in industries in terms of size, variety and volume of production. Employers adopted a mechanistic approach to work and began to view labour as one of the factors of production. The industries grew from small competitive business units to business corporations employing thousands of workers. The relationship between an employer and an employee changed from informal and personal to a formal and regulated one, and the nature of the employee–employer relationship changed from a private and individualized relationship to a standardized one.

With the employer–employee relationship entering the public domain and impacting society, formal institutions emerged to regulate the relationship. Trade unions, as mentioned above, emerged out of a necessity to restore some balance in the relationship between powerful capital and weak labour. Thus, trade unions (and also employers' associations) flourished, and with it, work relationships moved out of the realms affecting the enterprise or the labour alone. The complexity of issues relating to the social costs of industrial growth became increasingly apparent.

Industrial relations was no longer confined to the relation between an employer and an employee. The collective of workers necessarily had to be factored in, and it became a power to be dealt with; more so because the interests of employers and employees were largely conflicting. The conflict was natural since workers were dissociated from the ownership of the instruments, materials and other means of production. The origins of the concept of industrial relations lie here. This genesis of the term influenced the general perception for many years. Conflicting interests and ideological orientations conveyed an adversarial and strife-torn relationship. Industrial relations, therefore, conveys a subject matter largely related to the handling of conflicts in the industrial domain. State intervention became necessary for the creation and maintenance of good relations between workers and the management once the relationship crossed the purely two-party domain comprising the employer and the employee, and entered the domain of social and public welfare. The State sought to gain the cooperation of the two partners in industry supporting economic growth and development through an improvement in the quality of work life. The State had an obvious stake in this relationship as an instrument of socio-economic progress.

Gradually, the term industry was extended beyond economic activity to include all gainful employment, including service under the State. The relationship between the State and its employees also acquired the characteristic features of the employer–employee relationship in the industry. This is evident from the strike by government employees to demand better wages and benefits. Thus, employment in government and public sector enterprises, where ownership is vested with the State, also came within the scope of industrial relations.

1.2 Definitions of Industrial Relations

The simplest way to explore a subject is to start by looking at ways in which it has been defined. The reader is advised not to try and memorize the definitions. Rather, the focus should be on looking at the definitions from the perspective of the players, processes, structures and dynamics that each of the definitions emphasize. The bottom-line is to look at the relationship between the employers and the employees and the forces in environment that shape this relationship. As we go along, we should try to bring out the unique perspective of each definition so we can assemble our own working definition in the end.

More Players Get Associated

- Industrial relations originally implied employer–employee relations.
- When trade unions started espousing the cause of workers, their activities also came to be included in the scope of industrial relations.
- With the State stepping in to regulate the relationship for public interest and social welfare, these activities too got included within the ambit of industrial relations.

- The *Merriam-Webster Dictionary* defines industrial relations as "the dealings or relationships of a usually large business or industrial enterprise with its own workers, with labour in general, with governmental agencies, or with the public". This definition appears to point to relationships from the perspective of an organization and limits it to an industrial or business organization. It suggests a descriptive point of view relating to an entire range of relationships that an industrial organization may have with the stakeholders, including its employees. Does the inclusion of only industrial organizations in the definition mean that the central government employees protesting the anomalies in the Pay Commission report is not a subject matter of industrial relations? If we expand the scope here to include all organizations, should not a term such as employee relations be more appropriate?
- The *Encyclopaedia Britannica*[2] defines industrial relations as the "study of human behaviour in the workplace, focusing especially on the influence such relations have on an organization's productivity". This simple definition points to the existence of only two players operating in the industry and narrows down the scope from the previous definition to only relationships between employer and employees. It does not include anything about the dynamics and context of the relationship. The simplicity of the definition leaves out vital players and processes of the IR.
- Dale Yoder, in his definition, worked on the above premise but focused on issues emanating out of employment, describing "industrial relationship to be the designation of a whole field of relationships which exist because of the necessary collaboration of men and women in the employment process of an industry"[3]. Industrial relations describe the "relationship between managements, employees or among employees and their organizations that characterize or grow out of employment". Here, the emphases are on all kinds of relationships that come into existence because of employment. By implication, trade unions, employers' associations, State regulation and their impact on and from the basic employer–employee relationship would all get included in the definition.

IR Is

- A study of the relationship between employers and employees
- At an organization, industry or a nation level
- State's role
- Societal, economic, political and technological forces as context
- It includes:
    - *players, their objectives*
    - *structures*
    - *conflicts (origins and resolutions)*
    - *contexts and their impact*
    - *processes and their outcomes.*

1.2.1 A Working Definition

From all the above definitions, we may try to piece together a working definition for ourselves. Our working definition must take the following into account:

- IR is about relationships.
- The origin is in the relationship of employment.
- Employer–employee relationship pertains to all kinds of organizations.

Figure 1.1

Industrial relations—a pictorial representation.

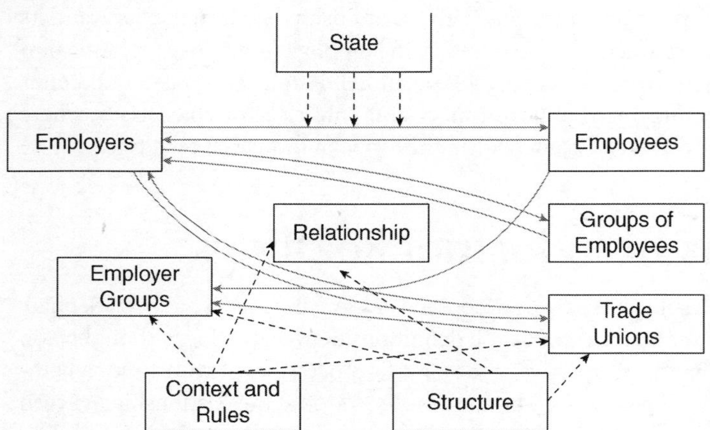

- There are actors other than the employer and the employees who influence the relationship.
- The relationships are shaped by the actors, structures, rules, law, technology, etc.
- The impact of social, economic, political and technological features of the context on the shaping of these relationships.

Industrial relations, therefore, at its core, is a discipline, that concerns itself with the study of the relationship between employers and employees at an organization, industry or a nation level. It also concerns itself with the two-way interaction that the State may have in influencing the relationship(s). These relationships are shaped in a larger context of societal, economic, political and technological forces that are in existence. The study encompasses the players and their objectives, the structures and their functions, the conflicts and their origins and resolutions, the contexts and their impact, the "processes" and their outcomes.

Figure 1.1 is a visual representation of our working definition. While this may not be a rigorous definition of a social scientist, it does capture the essence for a student or a practising manager. At this stage, keep the visual representation of the definition in mind. We will explore it further in the later part of the text.

1.3 The Scope of Industrial Relations

Key Elements in IR

- Relations existing in industry
- Relations between:
  - unions and management
  - unions themselves, management and the government, and unions and government
  - employers and employees
- conflicts in relationship
- regulation by the State

Different definitions of industrial relations provide different perspectives from which the term IR has been looked at. The scope of IR, therefore, should encompass an examination of these perspectives. The scope of industrial relations would include:

- Relations between employee groups/association or unions and management, management and the government, unions and government, or between employers and unorganized employees. It would also include collective relations among trade unions, employers' associations and the government.
- The activities relating to the above relationship would entail:
  - Structuring of labour-management relations and its regulation
  - Labour legislative compliance
  - Negotiating work-related contracts

Management of industrial relations does not confine itself only to the immediate actions arising out of the interfaces between the players but may also include a range of proactive measures for creating synergies in the coming together of capital, labour and technology. It,

BOX 1.1 **FOR CLASS DISCUSSION**

In October 2008, Jet Airways announced that it would lay-off around 1,000 employees due to rising international fuel prices. The decision to "lay-off" was triggered due to the economic environment facing the aviation industry. Jet Airways claimed this to be a necessary step to retain the economic viability of the company. The protesting employees got support from the political parties (MNS). The local political parties threatened not to let Jet Airways fly through Mumbai. The government too expressed its views opposing the move by the airlines. All this led to a rethink on the action by Jet Airways. The move by Jet Airways was able to force the government to announce concessions for the aviation industry.

Analyse the antecedents of the IR climate in the story; the abstractions in the passage above will come alive in a real-life situation. You may, for example, ask the following questions:

- Why did Jet Airways announce retrenchments?
- What was the immediate reaction in the environment?
- Was this reaction different from a reaction in USA over job losses in the Citi Group? Why?
- Why is retrenchment/lay-off such a big issue in India but not in USA/UK?
- Does it have something to do with the state of development of society/economy in the two countries?
- Does it have something to do with the respective values in the two cultures?
- Do we have different laws? Why? Who or what gives shape to legislation?
- Does our history have any role in shaping the kind of labour legislations that we have?

therefore, goes much beyond the restrictive interpretation that IR concerns itself mainly with smoothening the friction at interfaces. Industrial relations is mainly a part of social relations arising out of employer–employee relationship in organizations. These interactions and the resultant relationship are, to an extent, regulated by the State. The degree of State intervention would depend on the influence of organized social forces on the prevailing institutions regulating the employer–employee relationship. Box 1.1 brings to life the points that we have mentioned here, providing a better appreciation of the subject matter in real life.

Industrial relations must address:

- Maximizing individual development
- Relationship between employer and employees
- The best fit between the human resources and the environment

A literature survey on industrial relations shows that the scope is so broad as to be of little practical use at the working level. Or, it narrows down the field to such an extent that environmental and contextual factors get left out. It would be immodest to claim that this book straddles across the two extremes and provides *the* scope for IR. However, since the book is biased towards action, after introducing the complexities initially, it gets down to the business of interpreting these complexities at the field level. At the narrow end, therefore, scope of IR could be restricted to the following domains:

- Management–union relationship
- Employer–employee relationship
- Relationships amongst various groups of employees
- Effects of extraneous factors (State, socio-political-economic factors) on workplace relationships.

Factors influencing IR

- Economic: socialist, capitalist or mixed economy, per capita income of workers
- Social: nature and composition of workforce and their status and power in society
- Institutional: Government policy, labour legislations, trade unions, and employer organizations.
- Political: ideologies and policies
- Technological: modernization, automation and capital structure

1.3.1 Factors Shaping the Industrial Relations Climate

The industrial relations climate in a country, sector, industry or unit arises from a set of interdependent determinants involving historical, geographical, economic, social, political, legal and cultural variables. Therefore, an interdisciplinary approach needs to be taken for promoting good industrial relations climate. The various factors could further be categorized as either institutional or economic. Institutional factors would include industrial policy of the State, labour laws, social institutions (community, caste, religion, etc.) and systems operating in the cultural milieu with regard to power and status. Economic factors would be the State's level of economic growth, its economic activities, per capita income and human development indices that determine the quality of workforce.

1.4 Objectives of Industrial Relations

Objectives of industrial relations would have a different focus at different levels, namely, at the level of an enterprise, an industry or at the level of the State. At another level of analysis, different actors of the IR equation would provide primacy to their respective perspectives while spelling out their objectives. As an illustration, objectives of IR at the industry and at the State level could be as described below:

1.4.1 At the Industry or Enterprise Level

The objectives of industrial relations at the enterprise level appear rather obvious. Let us try and list them down. These could be:

- A healthy relationship between employees and employers
- Due regard to interests of labour and management by securing mutual understanding and trust
- An environment free from dysfunctional conflict between the parties
- Gains in productivity for mutual benefit
- Full utilization of available manpower through minimizing loss of man-hours due to accidents, strife or absenteeism
- Creation of a work environment that reduces attrition
- Participative working on principles of industrial democracy
- Enhancement in the quality of life of employees

These are only by way of example and we can go on adding to this list. However, instead of trying to memorize these, it would be useful if the reader asked "why" against each of the objectives. For example, "why is it important for the industry to ensure participative working principles of industrial democracy"? Is it there only because it appears a noble idea? Or is it out of some practical reason? Why should it matter to the enterprise to improve the quality of life of its employees? Reflecting on these questions will give the reader a practical flavour of industrial relations at work. As a prospective or practising manager, the reader should try and develop this ability to focus on the relevant.

"Why"–"Why" Analysis?

Why is it important for the industry to ensure participative working principles of industrial democracy?
Is it because it appears a noble idea?
Is it out of some practical reason? Why should it matter to the enterprise to improve the quality of life of its employees?

1.4.2 At the State Level

The objectives of the State in industrial relations do not appear to be so direct. However, the State is concerned with the wholesome socio-economic development of the nation. Industry, in that sense, becomes a microcosm of the entire nation. State has a stake in industrial relations in as much as it must be in consonance with the larger policies of the State. Industrial relations, in that sense, have a direct contribution to the economic progress and social development. Due to the flux of time and changes in technology, markets, policy regime, etc., distortions may occur in the socio-economic order, and these may directly impact the industrial relations because of the changes in relationships. The State may have to step in to restore balance. The State may also seek to facilitate resolution of problems created due to conflicting interests of the management and the working class through protectionist legislations or restraining indiscipline and exploitation through a legal system for settlement of disputes. Conversely, to give boost to economic growth and spur investments so that opportunities for employment get created, the State may step aside for creation of business-friendly regulations. The IT and ITES industry are an example where flexibility has been allowed to employers. The process of establishment of special economic zones (SEZs) could also be a case in point. Should the State intervene to regulate the IR framework in SEZs? Or allow laissez-faire till its attention is attracted towards distortions that may creep in the absence of State intervention?

The objective of State intervention in promoting industrial harmony and peace through good industrial relations is to:

- safeguard rights of both labour and management;
- enlist cooperation and collaboration from both parties to contribute to industrial growth;
- improve the economic conditions of workers through legislations prescribing minimum guaranteed wages, welfare benefits and social security through labour legislations; and
- control industrial establishments through regulations in terms of engaging and disengaging employees.

Industrial relations in a country are also determined by the form of political economy. The USA, Cuba, Japan, European Union and India may all give shape to a particular IR regime driven, in a large measure, by the forms of political government that each has. The objectives of the IR for State in each of these countries may have many similarities, but also significant differences. We will take a detailed look at this in Chapter 3.

1.5 Essential Features of Industrial Relations

The ratio of discussions so far throws up certain features of industrial relations that are common from any of the perspectives. Let us consolidate this learning before we wade deeper.

i) Industrial relations arise out of an employment relationship.

ii) The IR system sets complex rules and regulations for the participants, viz. employers, workers and the State to ensure industrial peace and harmony.

iii) The relationship hinges on a cooperative spirit between all partners, thereby emphasizing the need for adjustment and accommodation in the interest of growth and development.

iv) State intervention to prevent and control industrial conflicts and distortions in socio-economic order by stipulating rules with regard to terms and conditions of employment through enactment of labour laws and also creation of structures and institutions to resolve them, in case they arise.

v) Participants in industrial relations include employees and their organizations, employers and their associations, and the government.

In essence, industrial relations is the relationship *between* and *among* three players or actors—employers and/or their representatives, employees and the employee organization and the State. It is applicable to all organizations that gainfully employ human capital. Employee organizations or trade unions build a collective relationship with the employer's organization referred to as "management". The State machinery, through legislations and interventions, regulates this relationship. The government agencies influence and condition industrial relations through statutes (laws), rules and awards of the courts.

1.5.1 Conditions for Congenial Industrial Relations

Features of IR

- Arise out of an employment relationship
- Complex rules and regulations for the participants
- Cooperative spirit between all partners
- State intervention to control industrial conflicts and distortions in socio-economic order
- Participants include employers or management, employees, employees' organizations, the State

Healthy Industrial relations at the workplace, in the main, are a function of a problem-solving attitude on the part of both the unions and the management. Robust HRM policies and effective implementation create the foundation on which such attitudes can rest. To a large extent, openness in communication and confidence in dealing with mutual problems successfully determine the health of industrial relations. The maintenance of smooth industrial relations, therefore, should depend on:

- The existence of strong, well-organized and democratic employees' unions to ensure equal bargaining power for protection of employees' interests relating to wages, benefits, job security, etc. Interestingly, a few organizations in the post-liberalization economy have shown preference for a "union-less" organization.
- The existence of strong and well-organized employers' unions to facilitate promotion and the maintenance of uniform personnel policies among various organizations
- Belief in the process of settlement of conflicts through negotiation and consultation and cultivating a spirit of collective bargaining
- Sound personnel policies that emanate from the business strategy and guide the decision-making process in the eventuality of any employee relations problem
- Top management support for industrial relations function and support staff
- Creating systems and machineries for employee engagement
- Well-trained supervisors who understand the implications of building harmonious relations at the workplace, and avoidance of any managerial practice that could stimulate conflicts
- A systematic effort to institutionalize a culture of mutual trust, respect and understanding

1.5.2 Principles for Promoting Healthy Industrial Relations

Sound industrial relations will be based on the following fundamental principles:

The maintenance of sound IR needs:

- Strong, well-organized and democratic unions for balance of power
- Strong employers' organization
- Belief in cooperative collective bargaining
- Sound HR policies
- Sound preventive systems
- Management support to IR function
- Well-trained IR staff/supervisors
- Systematic effort at building a collaborative culture

i) Basic competence on the part of the employers and the trade unions to deal with their mutual problems freely, independently and responsibly.

ii) The employees and their organizations (trade unions) and the employers and their organizations must have faith in resorting to collective bargaining and, if necessary, should seek help from State agencies in resolving conflicts and disputes. There should be an underlying faith in the effectiveness of the "process", structure and the system.

iii) Employees (and trade unions) and employers (and their associations) must have the realization that they are interwoven into the larger socio-economic fabric of the nation/society and must be willing to associate with the State and its agencies while evaluating the general, social, public and economic measures affecting the employers and the workers.

1.6 Participants of Industrial Relations System and Dynamics of Their Participation

The "actors" in the industrial relations are one set of variables. These actors are not monolithic structures but have sub-structures within them. For example, "employer" may comprise managers at different hierarchical levels or functional areas or divisions. Similarly, "employees" may be seen as comprising those belonging to a department, grade, craft or skill. Or, they may be represented by their union or unions affiliated to different political ideologies. The State may be represented by the various agencies of legislature, executive and the judiciary.

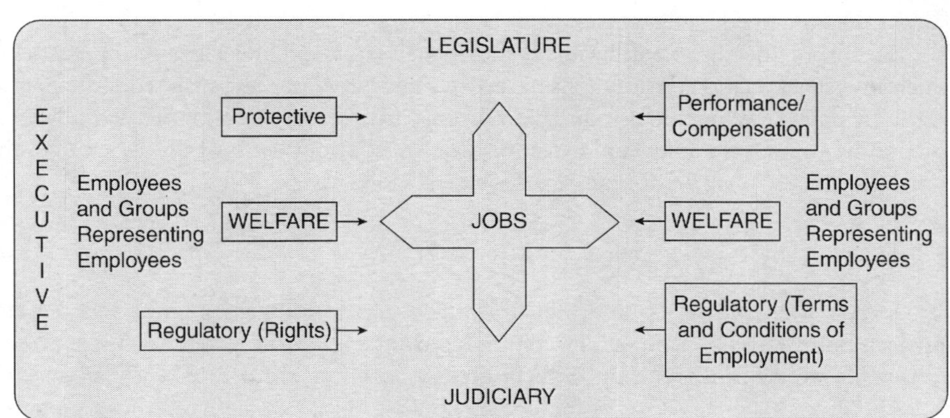

Figure 1.2

A schematic interplay amongst the main variables in IR.

The industrial relations system comprises different sets of participants or actors, which influence one another and the system. The degree of influence that each has is a variable. So, if we look at each of the three actors as variables, this is how they may influence the system:

i) **Workers and Their Organizations (Trade Unions or Associations):** The trade unions have a protective role of safeguarding workers' interests, regulatory function of ensuring implementations of statutes and non-violation of their rights. The Trade Unions Act, through an enabling process of registration, provides status and authority for the power vested in them through support of member co-workers. This power is used for negotiating wage increases, better benefits and service conditions, concessions, more amenities and welfare schemes. The structure of workers' organization or trade unions differs from country to country.

ii) **Employers' Organization:** The organization is represented through officials designated in the organization structure for coordination of activities relating to administering employment benefits, regulating terms and conditions of employment and providing welfare and social security benefits. This coordination is done through a graded, hierarchical structure through a formal communication channel of orders and directives. The style and manner in which employer organizations get work and regulate the terms and conditions of employment affects the industrial relations of the unit.

iii) **Government:** The government or State machinery regulates the relationship between workers' organizations and employers' organizations through statutes or legislations, the judiciary—labour courts and industrial tribunals—and an executive machinery that lays down rules, procedures, gives awards and monitors them.

The dynamics of participation and inter-relationships amongst the three variables is depicted in Figure 1.2.

The economic structure and policies, and also the political ideology of the government in power determine the role and influence of the three participants stated above. For example, with liberalization and globalization of the Indian economy, the trade unions (in the organized sector) appear to be less active than before. This issue would be discussed at length in the subsequent chapters.

1.7 Industrial Relations: Perspective and Approach

By now, we have had glimpses of the complexity of industrial relations—the participants, contextual factors, objectives and dynamics of relationships. From purely an academic point of view, the subject has been approached from different perspectives in order to provide a comprehensive framework for studying it. It is important to know the various approaches so that the breadth, depth and complexity of the subject are appreciated.

The purpose here is to outline and compare main academic theories and approaches by which industrial relations institutions, structures and processes are analysed. The theories that individuals develop about industrial relations are attempts to construct logically consistent ways of understanding and explaining social behaviour and real-life activities in this complex field. The main approaches are discussed below.

1.7.1 The Unitary Approach

The essence of the unitary approach of IR is that every work organization is an integrated and harmonious whole, existing for a common purpose. It is assumed, under this approach, each employee identifies with the aims of the organization and with its ways of working. Those holding this view aver that there is no conflict of interest between those supplying financial capital and their representatives on the one hand, and those contributing their labour and skills on the other. By definition, the owners of capital and labour are joint partners to the common aim of efficient production, good profit and high pay in which everyone in the organization has a stake. There cannot, therefore, be two sides in the industry. Managers and employees are the part of the same team. This "team" is provided strong leadership from the top to keep it working and to ensure commitment to the tasks.

> Under the unitary approach to industrial relations, work organizations are viewed as:
>
> - Unitary in structure
> - Unitary in purpose
> - Having a single source of authority
> - Having a cohesive set of participants

This implies a paternalistic approach towards the employee or an authoritarian one. It assumes team spirit across the organization and, at the same time, recognizes managerial authority. In short, work organizations are viewed as:

- Unitary in structure
- Unitary in purpose
- Having a single source of authority
- Having a cohesive set of participants

As a result, industrial relations is viewed as based on mutual cooperation and harmony of interest between the management and the employees within the organization. Collective bargaining and trade unions are, therefore, perceived as being anti-social and anti-managerial mechanisms, since acceptance of two opposed and competing interest groups within the enterprise, in the persons of management and union representatives, only precipitates and crystallizes unnecessary and destructive industrial conflict between what in effect are viewed as two non-competing, cooperative parties.

The unitary approach of industrial relations is predominantly managerially oriented in its inception, in its emphasis and in its application. Indeed, it is a theoretical perspective with which many managers and employers identify because it reassures them in their roles as organizational decision makers and legitimizes the acceptance of their authority by subordinate employees.

The Neo-unitary Approach. A variant of the Unitary Theory, Neo-Unitary Theory, appears to have emerged in some organizations since the 1980s. It builds on existing unitary concepts but is more sophisticated in the ways it is articulated and applied within enterprises. Its main aim seems to be to integrate employees, as individuals, into the companies in which they work. Its orientation is distinctly market-centred, managerialist and individualist. By gaining employee commitment to quality production, customer needs and

> BOX 1.2 **FOR CLASS DISCUSSION**
>
> Many post-liberalization organizations prefer to have a "union-less" environment. In fact, one of the KRAs of the HR manager is to prevent unionization. Discuss and arrive at a consensus regarding the management's philosophy in this case. List down all pros and cons that implementation of this philosophy may have on the relationships within the organization.

job flexibility, employers embracing this frame of reference have expectations of employee loyalty, customer satisfaction and product security in increasingly competitive market conditions. Companies adopting a neo-unitary approach try to create a sense of common purpose and shared corporate culture—they emphasize to all employees the primacy of customer service, they set explicit work targets for employees, they invest heavily in training and management development, and they sometimes provide employment security for their workers.

The personnel management techniques used to facilitate employee commitment, quality, output and worker flexibility include performance-related pay, profit sharing, harmonization of terms and conditions, employee involvement, and an HRM function, rather than a personnel management function. The emphasis of neo-unitary approaches to industrial relations (also, sometimes referred to as "employee relations") is that committed, motivated and well-trained people are the key to corporate success.

1.7.2 Systems Approach: The Dunlop Model

John T. Dunlop is credited with the application of the Systems Approach to industrial relations. Systems essentially comprise four processes: input acquisition, input transformation, output and feedback. When a system is self-contained with these processes, it is termed as a "closed system", that is, it has nothing to do with the environment in which it exists. An "open system" (see Figure 1.3), in contrast to a "closed system", exists in the context of its environment. If we consider an organization to be an "open system", then we recognize the fact that this exists in a context called environment. The organization influences its environment as well as gets influenced by the environment. The environment may comprise factors like social, political, technological and others. It (the organization) depends on the environment for essential supplies and it also depends on the environment to receive the outputs. The environment also influences the various processes for acquisition, transformation and delivery of outputs.

Dunlop visualized industrial relations to be a systemic construct, that is, industrial relations systems as a sub-system of society. "An industrial relations system, at any one time in its development, is regarded as comprised of certain actors, certain contexts, an ideology, which binds industrial relations systems together and body of rules created to govern the actors at the workplace and work community."[4]

Let us try to understand the Dunlop's System Model (see Fig. 1.4) from the output that industrial relations seeks to deliver. "Creation of rules", according to Dunlop, is the "output" that an IR "system" seeks to create. "Rules", in this context, comprise:

- Rules governing all forms of compensation
- The duties and performances expected of workers including rules for maintaining discipline
- Rules defining rights and duties of employers and employees (including legislations, terms of collective agreements)

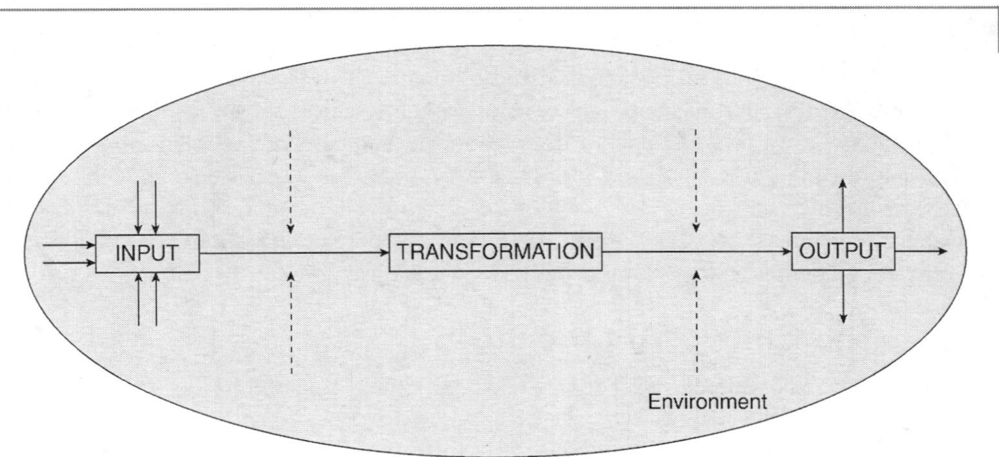

Figure 1.3

An open system.

- Procedures for establishing rules
- Procedures for application of rules, etc.

If this be the output from the IR system, then what would be the "input", "transformation" and "feedback" processes and how do they interact with each other?

The IR system involves three groups of "actors":

1. Managers and their organizations
2. Workers and their organizations
3. "State" and its agencies concerned with "workplace"

The actors function not in isolation but in an environmental context:

1. The technical context of the workplace, e.g., how the work is organized, what the state of technology is, whether it is labour or capital intensive
2. The market context or the revenue-related context, e.g., product demand, market growth, number of competitors, margins, profits, etc.
3. The "power" context, that is, how "power" is distributed amongst the three "actors"

The actors engage with each other on the basis of some common ideology; there is a minimum common denominator to the respective ideologies. The workers may hold a common belief that they must strive to have a greater say in the running of business or to improve the standard of living. The employer's ideology may include the cost-effective use of resources, continuous growth, a productive work force, etc. In an IR system, it is the common denominator of ideologies that binds and integrates the system. For example, all three hold a belief that employees are entitled to demand for a minimum quality of living, that discussion and bargaining must be the preferred way to solve disputes, that the State does have a limited but clear role as an arbiter in certain matters.

The actors, in given contexts, establish rules for the workplace and the work community including those governing the contacts among the actors in an industrial relations system. This network of rules and procedures decides their application in particular situations. The systems approach of Dunlop emphasizes the concern for order through systems, procedures, rules and regulations for containment of conflict.

Dunlop's System Approach and model has had its share of criticism, the most important one being that it focuses more on the structural aspects of the model and leaves out the processes leading to conflict. It also does not dwell upon the human aspects of the actors and their behaviour. The approach is predominantly an analytical one rather than a descriptive one, in the process, leaving out the genesis, handling and resolution of conflict. Fifty years since, when the model was proposed, perhaps the industrial landscape has changed and there may be need to include new actors to the model.

Nevertheless, Dunlop's Model has been one of the most popular theoretical frameworks. It helps explain why particular rules are established in particular IR systems and how and why they change in response to changes affecting the system. Changes can be brought about through historical, political, sociological and economic changes. Given this framework, we can appreciate the interlinks between the actors, and how rules that govern their actions are set in place. The actors do not operate in isolation. The emphasis of the systems model on the diverse forms of industrial relations rules that exist, the different rule-making methods, and the ways in which rules are applied is a useful contribution to the understanding of industrial relations practices. Thus, the industrial relations in a labour-intensive industry would be different from that in a capital-intensive or knowledge industry.

1.7.3 The Conflict Approach

There are two major approaches that have tried explaining industrial relations based on conflict inherent in the society.

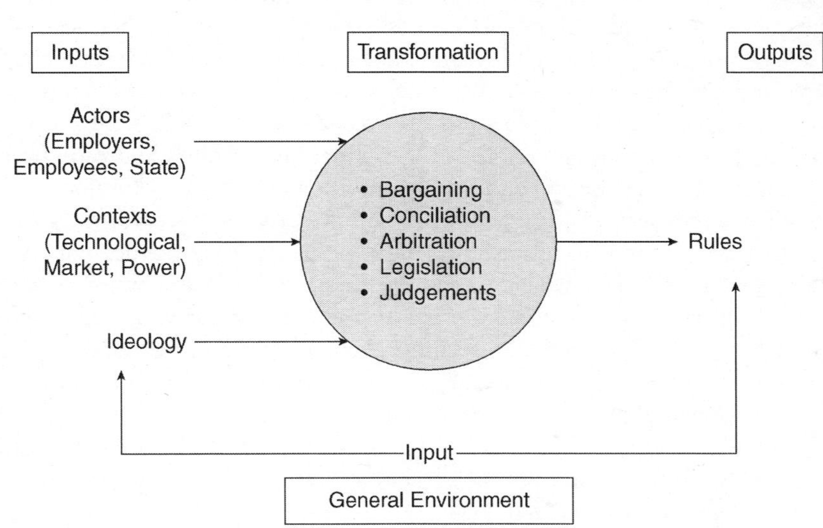

Figure 1.4

Dunlop's model. Reproduced with permission from J. T. Dunlop, *Industrial Relations Systems* (Boston, MA: Harvard Business Press, 1958).

PLURALISM. It is the existence of more than one ruling principle. The pluralist approach to IR accepts conflict as inevitable but containable through various institutional arrangements. Work organizations are microcosms of society. Since society comprises a variety of individuals and social groups, each having their own social values and each pursuing their own self-interests and objectives, it is argued that those controlling and managing work enterprises, similarly, have to accommodate the differing values and competing interests within them. It is only by doing this that enterprises can function effectively. Industrial relations between employers and unions and between managers and trade unionists, by this view, are an expression of the conflict and the power relations between organized groups in society in general. As such, it is claimed, industrial conflict between managers and their subordinates has to be recognized as an endemic feature of work relationships and has to be managed accordingly. This approach, called "pluralism", according to Clegg, "emerged as a criticism of the political doctrine of sovereignty—that somewhere in an independent political system, there must be a final authority whose decisions are definitive. Not so, said the pluralist. Within any political system, there are groups with their own interests and beliefs, and the government itself . . . depends on their consent and cooperation. There are no definitive decisions by final authorities: only continuous compromises"[5].

> **Pluralism**
>
> Pluralism is a belief in the existence of more than one ruling principle, giving rise to a conflict of interests. The pluralist approach to IR accepts conflict as inevitable but containable through various institutional arrangements.

A plural society, in other words, has to accommodate to different and divergent pressure groups to enable social and political changes to take place constitutionally. This is achieved through negotiation, concession and compromise between pressure groups, and between many of them and the government. Witness the Nano controversy in West Bengal with many interest groups negotiating with each other. This negotiation of conflicting interests was acceptable and expected.

> A plural society has to accommodate to different and divergent pressure groups to enable social and political changes to take place constitutionally. This is achieved through negotiation, concession and compromise between pressure groups, and between many of them and the government. Industry can be visualized as a microcosm of society with conflict inherent between different groups.

It is from this analysis of political pluralism that industrial relations pluralism is derived. Just as society is perceived as comprising a number of interest groups held together in some sort of loose balance by the agency of the State, so are work organizations viewed as being held in balance by the agency of management.

The pluralist and post-capitalist analyses of industrial relations emphasize the virtues of collective bargaining as separate but conflict-resolving and rule-making processes.

Critics of pluralism point out that those working within the pluralist framework implicitly accept the institutions, principles and assumptions of the social and political *status quo* as unproblematic.

POST-CAPITALISM. Further, another (sub) approach within the conflict theorists proposes that the nature of class conflict has substantially changed from that suggested by Marx in his nineteenth-century analysis. In Marxist theory, class conflict is perceived as being synonymous with industrial conflict and political conflict. Under market capitalism, Marxists argue, the capitalists or the owners of the means of production are identical with the ruling class in industry and politics, while wage-earners, owning only their labour resources, are relatively powerless in industrial relations and in politics. Capitalists are the social elite and the proletariat are the socially weak. What, then, has changed according to post-capitalist analysis? It is argued, we now live in a more open and socially mobile society compared with the class-based social divisions associated with nineteenth-century and early twentieth-century capitalism. The widening of educational opportunity, the democratization of politics, and the growth of public sector industry, for instance, have opened up recruitment to a whole range of sought-after roles in society, including those within industry, politics, education, the professions, the arts and so on, which would have been inconceivable a hundred years ago.

The distribution of authority, property and social status in society is more widely diffused than it was in the past. The positions that individuals occupy in the authority structure of industry, for example, do not necessarily correlate with their positions in the political structure or with their social standing in the community.

Above all, these theorists believe that the institutionalization of conflict in industry not only has decreased in intensity but also has changed its form. Several changes seem to be of particular importance in this respect:

- The organization of conflicting interest groups itself
- The establishment of representative negotiating bodies in which these groups meet
- The institutions of mediation and arbitration
- Formal representations of labour within the individual enterprise
- Tendencies towards and institutionalization of workers' participation in industrial management

Thus, it is argued, the emergence of trade unionism, employers' organizations and collective bargaining, together with union representation at enterprise and workplace level, now effectively regulating the inevitable social conflicts seems improbable; third-party intervention, usually through State agencies providing conciliation and arbitration services, is not available to provide workable remedies. By this analysis, extending worker participation in managerial decision making, as happens in board-level worker representation in countries like Denmark, the Netherlands and Germany, is seen as a logical progression in institutionalizing the power relations between managers and subordinates at work. Post-capitalist society, in short, is viewed as an open society in which political, economic and social power is increasingly dispersed and in which the regulation of industrial and political conflict are of necessity dissociated.

Post-capitalist society is viewed as an open society in which political, economic and social power is increasingly dispersed and in which the regulation of industrial and political conflict are of necessity dissociated.

Industrial conflict theory remains a major theoretical approach to industrial relations. Yet, whilst collective bargaining fits easily into a pluralist theory, consultation or joint problem solving does so to a lesser extent. For this reason, it is useful to distinguish between "hard" pluralism and collective bargaining, which are conflict centred, and "soft" pluralism and joint consultation, which are problem centred.

1.7.4 Weber's Social Action Approach

Social action theory in industrial relations emphasizes the individual responses of the social actors, such as managers, employees and union representatives, to given situations. It contrasts with systems theory, which suggests that behaviour in an industrial relations system is explicable in terms of its structural features. Social action theory is pre-eminently associated with the studies of Max Weber. According to Weber, action is social "by virtue of the subjective meaning attached to it by the acting individual . . . it takes account of the behaviour of others and is thereby oriented in its course". He insists that in order for social actions to be explained, they must be interpreted in terms of their subjectively intended meanings, not their objectively valid ones. If only observable behaviour is examined, it is argued, the significance and the value that individual actors place upon their behaviour are likely to be misinterpreted.

Social action, then, is the behaviour having subjective meaning for individual actors, with social action theory focusing on understanding particular actions in industrial relations situations rather than on just observing explicit industrial relations behaviour. This contrasts with systems theory, which regards behaviour in industrial relations as reflecting the impersonal processes external to the system's social actors over which they have little or no control.

Social action is behaviour having subjective meaning for individual actors, with social action theory focusing on understanding particular actions in industrial relations situations rather than on just observing explicit industrial relations behaviour control.

The fundamental point is that social action emerges out of the meanings and circumstances attributed by individuals to particular social situations, thereby defining their social reality. Through interaction between actors, such as that between personnel managers and union officers; line managers and personnel specialists; and union representatives and their members, individuals as well as those having an element of choice in interpreting their own roles and in acting out their intentions, also modify, change and transform social meanings for themselves and for others. The major difference between a social action approach in examining behaviour in industrial relations and a systems approach is this: the action theory assumes an existing system where action occurs, but cannot explain the nature of the system, "while the systems approach is unable to explain satisfactorily why particular actors act as they do". The first views the industrial relations system as a product of the actions of its parts; the other aims to explain the actions of its parts in terms of the nature of the system as a whole.

1.7.5 The Gandhian or Trusteeship Approach

Mahatma Gandhi was the main proponent of the trusteeship approach with truth, non-violence and non-possession as ideologies. Basically, a business enterprise has the inherent responsibility to its consumers, workers, shareholders and the community. The responsibilities are mutual. A business enterprise is meant for good for all and not just for profits. According to Gandhi, conflicts are inevitable in an industrializing society, but labour and capital must learn to peacefully coexist for mutual benefit, and for the community at large. He, however, recognized the worker's right for a strike (peaceful non-cooperation) subject to the following conditions:

i) Workers should seek redress of just and reasonable demands through collective action.

ii) Trade unions should decide to go on strike taking ballot authority from all workers, and remain peaceful using non-violent methods.

iii) Workers should avoid strikes to the extent possible.

iv) Strikes are to be the last resort.

v) Workers should avoid formation of philanthropic organizations.

vi) Workers should take recourse to voluntary arbitration where direct settlement fails.

1.7.6 The Marxian or Radical Approach

The Marxist interpretations of industrial relations are not strictly theories of industrial relations *per se*. Marxism is, rather, a general theory of society and of social change with implications for the analysis of industrial relations within capitalist societies.

The starting points for the Marxist analysis of a society are the assumptions that: social change is universal; class conflict is the catalytic source of such change; and these conflicts, which arise out of differences in economic power between competing social groups, are rooted in the structures and institutions of the society itself. The conceptual method by which Marxists examine the dynamic character of social relations is described as "dialectical materialism".

The contradictions that persist between those who privately own the means of production in the pursuit of profit, on the one hand, and those who have to sell their labour for wages to survive, on the other, are perceived as being irreconcilable in the context of a class-based bourgeois society.

The contradictions that persist between those who privately own the means of production in the pursuit of profit, on the one hand, and those who have to sell their labour for wages to survive, on the other, are perceived as being irreconcilable in the context of a class-based bourgeois society.

For Marxists, moreover, unlike pluralists and unitarists, political and class conflicts are synonymous with industrial conflict since "the capitalist structure of industry and of wage-labour is closely connected with the pattern of class division in society". Thus, the conflict

BOX 1.3 **INDUSTRIAL RELATIONS IN ASIA PACIFIC**

Industrial relations in countries, sub-regions and regions have been influenced by a variety of circumstances and actors such as political philosophies, economic imperatives, and the role of the State in determining the direction of economic and social development, the influence of unions and the business community, as well as the legacies of colonial governments. Over several decades, IR in many industrialized market economies of the West, and also in Australia and New Zealand, in the Asia-Pacific as well as in the South Asian countries paid less attention to competitiveness than did the younger "discipline" human resource management. IR fulfilled the function of providing employees with a collective voice, and unions with the means to establish standardized terms and conditions of employment not only within an enterprise but also across an industry, and, sometimes, across an economy. This was achieved through the freedom of association, collective bargaining and the right to strike. Similar results were achieved in the South Asian sub-region where political democracy, and, sometimes, socialist ideology, provided enormous bargaining power and influence on legislative outcomes to even unions with relatively few members. A different IR regime emerged in some of the Southeast and East Asian economies driven by competition in export markets and different political systems bearing little resemblance to the values underpinning Western-style democracies.

During the past decades, labour relations were often viewed by Asian governments as a means of minimizing conflict, preventing union agitation, or as in the case of India and Sri Lanka, of controlling employers and winning votes. Conflict resolution was achieved through dispute prevention and settlement mechanisms external to the enterprise, such as conciliation, arbitration and labour courts. In South Asia, the objective was also achieved through restrictions and prohibitions on the freedom of action of employers in matters such as termination of employment, closures and even transfers of employees. On the other hand, several Southeast Asian countries resorted to measures to restrict trade-union action and to control unions, as well as to avoid union multiplicity. In South Asia, while the focus of IR was on equity from the point of view of workers and unions, in Southeast Asia, the emphasis was on economic efficiency and less on worker-protection laws. Low unionization in many Asian countries, strong governments in Southeast Asian countries and the Republic of Korea, and perceptions that unions can be potential obstacles to a particular direction of economic development, led to a relative neglect of IR. Moreover, hierarchical management systems and respect for authority, which have mirrored the external social system, have been inconsistent with consultation, two-way communication, and even with the concept of negotiating the employment relationship. Japan, however, was an exception where, since the 1960s, workplace relations and flexibility facilitated by enterprise unionism dominated IR in the larger enterprises. Australia and New Zealand have traditionally focused on centralized IR, though the emphasis has radically changed in New Zealand during this decade, and is changing in Australia.

Globalization has led employers to push for less regulation of IR, less standardization of the employment relationship, and a greater focus on the workplace as the centre of gravity of IR. Employers as well as some governments are viewing IR from a more strategic perspective, i.e., how IR can contribute to and promote workplace cooperation, flexibility, productivity and competitiveness. It is increasingly recognized that how people are managed impacts on an enterprise's productivity and on the quality of goods and services, labour costs, the quality of the workforce and its motivation.

Source: Sriyande Silva, "The Changing Focus of Industrial Relations and Human Resource Management", paper presented at the *ILO Workshop on Employers' Organizations in Asia-Pacific in the Twenty-First Century,* Turin, Italy, 5–13 May 1997.

taking place in industrial relations between those who buy labour and those who sell it is seen as a permanent feature of capitalism.

Class conflict permeates the whole of society and is not just an industrial phenomenon. In the same way, trade unionism is a social as well as an industrial phenomenon. Trade unions are, by implication, challenging the property relations whenever they challenge the distribution of the national product. They are challenging all the prerogatives, which go with the ownership of the means of production, not simply the exercise of control over labour power in industry.

There are both short-term and long-term implications in the Marxist analysis of bourgeois society and of the class-based structure of capitalist industrial relations. Within society, for example, the class struggle between capital and labour is regarded as being continuous—even where trade unions are absent. It takes place, it is argued, because capitalists and proletarians seek to maintain and to extend their relative positions in the economic power structure enabling "surplus value" to be distributed between them. Such conflict is seen to be unremitting and unavoidable. Neither employees individually nor trade unions collectively can be divorced from the realities of these power relations, either by disregarding them or by succumbing to the manipulative techniques of employer persuasion.

A trade union organization is viewed as the inevitable consequence of the capitalist exploitation of wage labour. The vulnerability of employees as individuals invariably leads them to form collective groups or unions in order to protect their own class interests. Collective bargaining and militant trade unionism, however, cannot resolve the problems of industrial relations in a capitalist society. They merely accommodate temporarily the contradictions inherent within the capitalist mode of production and social relations. Indeed, "the starting point of any realistic analysis must be the massive power imbalance between capital and labour. This derives from the very fact that the productive system is, in the main, the private property of a tiny minority and that profit is the basic dynamic, Confronting this concentrated economic power, the great majority who depend on their own labour for a living are at an inevitable disadvantage"[6].

More significantly, industrial relations become not ends in themselves, but a means to an end—the furtherance of the class war between capital and labour towards establishment of a classless society. Trade unionism and industrial relations conflict are merely symptoms of the inherent class divisions within capitalism.

The article in Box 1.3, by Silva, briefly traces the evolution of industrial relations regime in various regions of the Asia Pacific. You can see how the multitude of factors go into shaping and the evolution of industrial relations. Transition towards a free trade regime and a clamour for "inclusive growth" in growing economies like India, social and cultural factors all combine to provide a melting pot for continuous evolution of industrial relations.

SUMMARY

- In the process of managing human resources in industry, certain relationships get established between employers and employees.
- These relations are generally known as industrial relations, which, due to its complexity and differing perceptions and interest, are also associated with State intervention.
- Industrial relations refer to the interrelations between three main actors—employees and their organizations, management and the government.
- The primary objective of industrial relations is to establish and maintain good and healthy relations between the two partners in industry—labour and management.
- Industrial relations are influenced by the existing and emerging economic, institutional and political factors in the region in which it is located.
- The scope of industrial relations includes labour relations, employer–employee relations, group relations, and community or public relations.
- Industrial relations are shaped by socio-economic, psychological and political factors. These relations are complex and multifaceted, and to understand them from differing perspectives, a multi-disciplinary approach is desirable.
- The various industrial relations perspectives include the systems model of Dunlop, the pluralist approach, Weber's social action approach, the Marxian radical and the Gandhian approach of peaceful coexistence.
- Dunlop analysed industrial relations systems as a sub-system of society. The actors, in given contexts, establish rules for the workplace and the work community, including those governing the contacts among the actors in an industrial relations system.

- Weber's perspective focused on the power struggle in which all the actors in the industrial relations system are caught up.
- The unitary perspective emphasizes the organization as a coherent and integrated team unified by a common purpose. The pluralist perspective emphasizes organization as an amalgamation of separate homogeneous groups—a miniature democratic State composed of sectional groups with divergent interests over which the government tries to maintain some kind of dynamic equilibrium.
- The radical perspective emphasizes the organization as a microcosm and replica of the society within which it exists; and industrial conflict and trade union actions are just a means towards the establishment of a classless society.

KEY TERMS

- employers' organizations 11
- industrial relations 3
- pluralism 15
- post-capitalist society 16
- social action theory 16
- systems model of IR 13
- trusteeship 17
- unitary theory 12
- workers' organizations 11

REVIEW QUESTIONS

1 Considering different definitions attributed to industrial relations, which definition in your opinion is most appropriate in the current context of global organizations?

2 How does the concept of industrial relations differ from the concept of human resource management?

3 Explain the roles of the different participants in the industrial relations system.

4 What are the functions of the industrial relations department of an organization and the activities to be taken up by the IR specialists in the department?

5 In the current day industrial scenario, what, according to you, are the necessary conditions for a healthy industrial climate?

6 Taking into consideration different perspectives and approaches advocated for industrial relations, can you advocate or build a theoretical model for industrial relations? Give reasons and arguments to support your answer.

7 What, in your opinion, is the future of industrial relations?

QUESTIONS FOR CRITICAL THINKING

1 Critically examine the role of three main players of IR in the current Indian context. How do you think their roles would evolve in the coming years? What major challenges do you think is there before each one of them?

DEBATE

1 State intervention/regulation in industrial relations must be removed to enable the industry to become internationally competitive.

2 Theories of industrial relations do not really matter. It is the reality of the workplace that determines the outcome of industrial relations.

CASE ANALYSIS

Increase in Working Hours

Amitabh Saha is Regional Personnel Manager (North) of Indian Steel Company. Indian Steel Company is an integrated steel manufacturer that manufactures 5 million tones of finished steel per annum at its plant located in Jharkhand. The finished steel products are then dispatched to the countrywide steel warehouses from where they are delivered to customers against orders.

The northern region of ISC has warehouses in the states of J&K, Haryana, Punjab, Himachal, Delhi, Rajasthan. These warehouses are managed by a branch manager and around 40 staff members. Every branch has a recognized union. The region is headed by a regional manager and Amitabh reports to him administratively.

The regional manager calls Amitabh and tells him that there is a need to extend the working hours from the existing 7 hours to 8.5 hours. This is necessary because of increased competition and, therefore, need for a customer service better than competitors. He also wants to reduce the number of holidays in all the branches from the existing 12 days to 4 days.

1. How do you propose that Amitabh go about his talks?
2. Who are the people and agencies with whom he would need to interact?
3. What has forced this change? Can you identify the contextual factors here?
4. Do you think this move of the management is justified? Why? Will the workers look at the issue in the same way? Will the government be involved?

Violence at Honda Motorcycles and Scooters, India

The workers' struggle at the Honda Motorcycles and Scooters India Ltd (HMSI) in Gurgaon, capped by an extraordinarily brutal attack on them by the Haryana police, constitutes the first labour landmark of the twenty-first century in India. The police action of 25 July has brought labour issues—absent from the media's radar-screen for a decade or more—back into the national limelight in ways not seen for a long time. Perhaps, the only comparable events are the Mumbai textile workers' strike of 1982–1983, one of the longest strikes in the world, and the 1995 self-immolation in Delhi by a textile-mill worker driven to despair by prolonged unemployment and near-starvation.

However, there are two major differences. First, the earlier episodes ended in both personal tragedies and setbacks to the labour movement. But the Gurgaon event spurred corrective action on the part of the state government, itself goaded by an acutely embarrassed United Progressive Alliance (UPA) leadership, as well as public opinion. HMSI was forced to take back all the workers, including those dismissed and suspended. Although it is true that the workers had to give an undertaking that they would raise no fresh demands for a year, but the management implicitly conceded the illegitimacy of its own anti-worker actions during May and June, by agreeing to pay the full salary for that period.[4]

1. Please do a background research to bring out full facts of the case.
2. Discuss the following:
   - The main players in the episode
   - The "issues" from the perspectives of each of the players
   - Which of the various approaches to industrial relations, in your opinion, best describes the dynamics of the episode? Why?
   - Discuss the systemic failure with focus on the three actors of the industrial relations system.

NOTES

1 Adapted from Deepshikha Monga, "ANZ National to move 500 processing jobs to Bangalore Worker Unions Slam Move, Set Slew of Conditions", *The Economic Times*, 19 April 2008, http://www.articlearchives.com/company-activities-management/company-strategy-outsourcing/1716320-1.html.

2 *Encyclopædia Britannica Online*, 15th ed., s. v. "industrial relations".

3 Dale Yoder, *Personnel Principles and Policies: Modern Manpower Management*, Englewood Cliffs:Prentice-Hall, 1959.

4 J. T. Dunlop, *Industrial Relations System*, Cambridge, Mass.: Harvard Business Press,1958.

5 H. A. Clegg, "Pluralism in Industrial Relations", *British Journal of Industrial Relations*, November 1975, pp. 309.

6 R. Hyman and R. H. Fryer, "Trade Unions—Sociology and Political Economy, Processing People—Cases in Organizational Behaviour" in John B. Mckiunlay, Holt, Rinchart and Winston <publishing details>,1975, pp 160.

7 Adapted from: Praful Bidwai, "For a 'New Deal' on Labour", *Frontline*, 22: 17, 2005 http://www.flonnet.com/fl2217/stories/20050826003310900.htm

SUGGESTED READING

Clegg, H. A. *The Changing System of Industrial Relations in Great Britain* (Oxford, UK: Blackwell, 1979).

Dunlop, J. T. *Industrial Relations Systems* (Boston, MA: Harvard Business Press, 1958).

ILO 2004, "A Fair Globalization—Creating Opportunities for All" in *Report of the World Commission of Social Dimensions of Globalization*, Vol. 27, Issue 1, pp 9–23. Report of the World Commission of Social Dimensions of Globalization

Jerome, Joseph. *Industrial Relations, Towards a Transformational Process Model* (New Delhi: Global Business Press, 1995).

Kuruvilla, S. and C. S. Venkatratnam. "Economic Development and Industrial Relations: The Case of South and Southeast Asia", *Industrial Relations Journal*, March 1996.

Reports of the First and the Second National Commission on Labour (1969, 2002)

Venkatratnam, C. S. *Industrial Relations* (New Delhi: Oxford University Press, 2006).

Yoder, Dale. *Personnel Management and Industrial Relations* (New Delhi: Prentice Hall of India, 1967).

chapter two

CHAPTER OUTLINE

LEARNING OBJECTIVES

After reading this chapter, you should be able to:

- Trace the evolution of the system of industrial relations in India
- Appreciate the context of the ongoing paradigm shift from industrial relations to employee relations
- Identify the concerns that need to be addressed by employers, unions and the government in the current competitive global environment
- Have a better understanding of the problems related to labour reforms

From Industrial Relations to Employee Relations

Raman Shenoy has recently taken over as Assistant Vice President (People Engagement) of a large ITES organization in Delhi. The company is the global hub for the management of business processes for clients from across the world. Raman's company employs more than 20,000 people and has won several major awards for employee and customer satisfaction. When queried on how he managed industrial relations or industrial action or trade-union activism in the company, this is what Raman had to say:

"Because of our proactive policies towards employees, we almost do not face any industrial relations issues. Trade unions are non-existent. Most of our employees, because of their excellent compensation, "job content" and working conditions, do not fall within the purview of any labour legislation. Gone are the days of the old-economy companies where you had to deal with unionized employees, industrial action, compliance with labour legislations. In the new economy, we cannot afford to function with the legacies of the old economy."

A few of the proactive measures towards employee relations that Raman listed out for his organization are:

- Employee relations SPOCs (single points of contact) are aligned to each process and provide touch points for employees.
- All issues, grievances and concerns of employees are accorded top priority by respective managers and the ER team.
- Regular and scheduled one-on-one, skip meetings, both by operations and ER, help to address the issues as soon as possible.
- Open houses are held for each process once every quarter wherein the top management presents highlights of performance, policies, and answers questions.
- Reward and recognition is a part of the work life of all employees. Almost every month, R&R schemes are rolled out, offering attractive prizes and gifts for better performance and productivity.
- There are annual budgets assigned to facilitate critical employee-related activities—ER, R&R, team fund, parties, celebrations, etc.
- The retention of employees is the key challenge for management. Even employees are aware of this and try to exploit this.

Raman says the above covers the entire range of issues pertaining to employee relations. He says it is a sea change from his previous company, an aluminium-manufacturing company with the legacy "IR system" of management. There is no union to deal with and hardly any regulatory compliance. The state government, in order to ensure that the new industry thrives in a globally competitive environment, is very flexible with granting exemptions if the provision exists in the law. The market forces have ensured that very good care is taken of the employees.

Industrial Relations in India

The system of industrial relations in India has evolved since the early part of the twentieth century. The State has played an important part in this evolution, both directly and indirectly. The colonial history, International Labour Organization, economic policies, political movement, etc. have helped shape the industrial relations system in India.

While Raman's experience may not be true across different sectors of the industry, it does indicate the coexistence of totally different frameworks of relationships amongst the players of IR across different industries/regions across the country. On the other extreme, there have been instances where the relationship deteriorated to the extent of widespread and brutal violence. Since the diversification of the economy post 1991, it is but to be expected that the future trends would reflect heterogeneity of workplace contexts. Some parts of the Indian economy are still rural/agricultural, some dominated by traditional manufacturing, while the others comprise high-tech manufacturing and modern service sector[1]. Is this how relationships will be managed across the organized industries? How is it different from the other periods in our development history? What are the forces and initiatives that have helped shape relationships at the workplace, and have these forces changed over a period of time? Will there be some kind of homogenization in the quality of employer–employee–State relationship shaped by the prevailing economic and social forces? Will the State leave the industries in the organized sector to regulate their own relationships and focus its attention on the unorganized sector? From a colonial past to the Freedom struggle, to the building of a nation and an economy, the industrial relations system has crossed many bends in the road. In this chapter, we trace the journey of the industrial relations system in India to understand the nuances of the current set up, and go on to answer these questions.

"The Indian government considers its responsibility to maintain industrial peace and harmony in order to safeguard the interests of workers and employers. The State has, therefore, assumed powers to regulate labour relations. It has, since Independence, encouraged mutual settlement, collective bargaining, conciliation, voluntary arbitration and adjudication as the principal means of resolving industrial conflicts. It has also recognized trade-union rights of workers and their promotion through democratic means and has intervened through legislative action for enhancing living and working conditions of workers and promoting social security".[2] This statement captures the approach of the State, so far, towards industrial relations in the country since Independence. In going through the chapter, we will familiarize ourselves with the evolution and meaning of the various terms that have been used in the statement. The statement provides a useful reference for examining the mosaic of industrial relations in the country through history, and for creating a platform from which one can attempt to comprehend how the future may unfold.

2.1 The System of Industrial Relations in India

The institutional framework of the industrial relations system in India has been largely influenced by its colonial history. The government's role has been primarily to control industrial conflict; and, hence, has been regulatory and predominated by labour legislations. The legislations provide the preventive machinery that attempts to avoid sources of conflict by prescribing safety, hygiene, occupational-health-related provisions to be ensured by employers in addition to compliance with the specified procedures regarding leave, dismissal and layoffs. The Industrial Disputes Act (1947) puts checks in place relating to layoffs, retrenchments and closures—potential sources of major conflicts. The trade unions have strong political affiliations and have the right to strike, provided due notice (where required) is given. The industrial disputes *settlement machinery* includes conciliation, arbitration and adjudication. Strikes could be called off if a request for third-party intervention through conciliation officers is sought by either party. The failure to resolve conflicts through either conciliation or mediation may lead to the parties either seeking voluntary arbitration or referring to the government for resolution through compulsory arbitration or adjudication by courts or tribunals. The labour legislations, thus, follow a protectionist philosophy to reduce potential sources of conflict, while the dispute settlement mechanism attempts to resolve conflicts.

Industrial Dispute

Industrial dispute has been defined under the Industrial Disputes Act, 1947. Stated simply, it is a dispute between an employer and (a group of) employees on matters relating to employment or conditions of employment.

The industrial relations policy of India has, by and large, been worker centric, driven by the socialist principles of the economic policy that predominated the post-Independence period till the 1980s. Social security provisions were made mandatory for all employers through provident fund schemes, thereby making them bear some part of the social-policy costs.

Settlement Machinery

Once an industrial dispute arises, the ID Act (1947) has provisions for a three-tier machinery (conciliation, arbitration and adjudication) for the settlement of the dispute.

The industrial policy and import substitution controls provided by the government protected both public- and private-sector firms from international competition. However, this protectionism led to inefficiencies and workforce rigidities, reflected in the preference for employment in public sectors and the government, and reluctance towards labour-displacing technologies, rationalization of labour, labour-cost-control strategies and productivity-based incentive schemes.

Forces Shaping the IR System in India

- The colonial history
- The government's role in IR—preventive and regulatory
- India being a founder member of ILO
- The political movement for Freedom and labour participation
- "Worker-centric" State policies
- The protection of domestic industries—import substitution
- Multiplicity of TUs and political affiliation of TUs
- Labour in Concurrent List

The Trade Unions Act of 1926 provided a means to organize labour, and recognized that need of labour organizations by the State. This provided a fillip to the growth of trade unions in the country, more so after Independence. The unionization of the work force, however, has been largely restricted to the organized sector.[3] A large number of unions are affiliated to regional or national federations, the major ones being the Indian National Trade Union Congress, the All-India Trade Union Congress, the Centre of Indian Trade Unions, the Indian Workers' Association, and the United Trade Union Congress. These federations, in turn, have affiliations to various political parties. Political affiliations, many times, have led to industrial action in furtherance of larger political goals rather than immediate enterprise or industry-level issues agitating the minds of the workforce. The political affiliation of trade unions led to the multiplicity of unions and leaders, often emerging from outside the labour force.

With no legal provision requiring a *sole bargaining agent*, the participatory system of industrial relations that should have emerged, given the above-mentioned practices and a democratic political system, have not yet been strongly established. Labour is in the Concurrent List, which allows different states to enact their own industrial relations laws, required also because of the differing institutional histories of different states. For example, trade unions in Mumbai (Bombay) have historically been quite different in their orientation towards collective bargaining relative to trade unions in comparison to states such as West Bengal, which have a strong CITU influence. The MPIR Act requires a sole bargaining agent and, hence, Madhya Pradesh has had a more successful collective-bargaining practice than other states. In addition, there are also institutional differences across industries.

Sole Bargaining Agent

A provision making it binding for a recognized union alone to bargain on behalf of all employees

Some of the basic characteristics of the industrial relations system in India are as follows:

i) The industrial relations climate is controlled through the regulatory provisions in labour laws and the settlement machinery comprising conciliation officers and boards, voluntary arbitration and labour courts and industrial/national tribunals for adjudication.

ii) The regulation of labour relations by the State has been primarily through legislations that have been greatly influenced by the British labour laws. Though the laws promulgated are extensive, they are confounded with serious ambiguities and gaps such as procedures for the recognition of unions and collective bargaining with the sole bargaining agent or the recognized union.

iii) Indian unions are restricted to the organized sector of industry. Most unions have political affiliations. This has generated multiplicity of unions operating in an industry, which has fostered external leadership rather than encouraging the emergence of leaders from the rank and file of workers.

iv) State intervention has continued to prevail since the time of Independence, although in the last decade, it has shown a declining trend.

v) There is a marked difference in the labour management relations in different states and also between organized and unorganized sectors, public and private enterprises, multinationals and domestic companies.

vi) There is no national industrial relations policy. The Industrial Relations Bill and the report of the National Commission on Labour were just steps in this direction. Similarly, there is no national wage policy, and also no clear evidence of a pattern in terms of the operation of the industrial relations institutions.

vii) Collective bargaining is more a matter of optional practice with no statutory backing.

viii) The changes brought in by the new economic policy have resulted in changes in the industrial relations structure. The heterogeneity of the emerging workforce has made it difficult to establish standards or uniform IR practices in the Indian industry.

2.1.1 The Role of the State

In a developing country like India, State intervention has been deemed necessary because:

i) The labour organizations, however numerous, were relatively weak. The relationship has been one of profound distrust and, hence, the government has to play a major role in taking an interventionist role in maintaining industrial relations.

ii) Labour situations, at times, lead to lawlessness, making it necessary for the State to intervene through industrial relations policies, which are likely to ensure social justice and industrial peace.

iii) The federal nature of the constitution has made it imperative for the State to intervene in labour matters to ensure smooth and continuing production. The fact that labour and industrial relations is on the Concurrent List means that the centre has to enact certain laws that are applicable to certain sections of labour throughout the country.

iv) The Directive Principles of the State policy enjoins upon the State to establish a welfare State and to look after the interests of the weakest sections of the society, including the handicapped.

> The policy on various aspects of industrial relations has traditionally evolved through a consensual approach involving all the three players—the State, the employers and the employees. Several institutions for tripartite consultations have been created.

2.1.2 The Labour Policy

The labour policy in India has evolved from the needs expressed in the policy objectives in relation to industrial development. Policies and practices have been created, modified and developed on the basis of joint consultations, at different levels, amongst the three players—the employers, the employees and the government. A measure of consensual outcome of these consultations found expression in legislation and other measures of the government. The common denominator of the views of the three parties, in a way, came to represent the national policy on labour and industrial relations, operating on a voluntary basis.

2.1.3 Tripartism in India's Industrial Relations System

Consultations amongst the three actors of industrial relations namely employer, employee and the State, has since the beginning years, has been a cornerstone of the IR Policy in India. To give shape to this element of policy, a number of bodies and fora were created. 'Tri-Partism', therefore, is an important feature of the IR System and Policy in India.

Consultations amongst the three actors of industrial relations, namely, the employer, the employee and the State, since the initial years, have been the cornerstone of IR policy in India. To give shape to this element of policy, a number of bodies and fora were created. Every major piece of policy initiative has emerged out of consultations amongst the three parties. The consultative machinery has been operationalized through a large number of tripartite bodies set up by the government to provide a forum to discuss and deliberate upon labour issues, policies and legislations. Notable among these are:

i) Indian Labour Conference (ILC)

ii) Standing Labour Committee (SLC)

iii) Committee on Conventions

iv) The Industrial Committees

The need and evolution of these tripartite bodies are based on the recommendations of ILO (itself tripartite in nature) and the Royal Commission on Labour (Whitley Commission) in 1931. The rules and procedures of the Indian tripartite consultative machinery are largely in tune with the recommendations of the ILO Committee on Consultation and Cooperation. The Indian Labour Conference (ILC) and Standing Labour Committee (SLC) are the most important constituents of tripartite bodies that play a vital role in shaping the IR system of the country. The representatives of the workers and employers are nominated to these bodies by the central government in consultation with the all-India organization of workers and employers.

The important tri-partite bodies are:

- Indial Labour Conference
- Standing Labour Committee
- Committee on Conventions
- Industrial Committees

The highest tripartite mechanism in the country, the Indian Labour Conference and the Standing Labour Committee, were set up in 1942 "to advise the Government of India on matters brought to its notice". The objectives set before these two tripartite bodies at the time of their inception were:

i) to promote uniformity in labour legislation;

ii) to lay down a procedure for the settlement of industrial disputes; and

iii) to discuss all matters of all-India importance as between employers and employees.

The union labour minister is the ex-officio chairperson of the ILC and the SLC. The agenda for the ILC and the SLC meeting is finalized by the labour ministry after taking into account all the issues raised before it by the member bodies. The demand that the conference should frame its agenda and have an independent secretariat was not accepted by the government.

India, being a founder member of the ILO, has been influenced in a large measure by the deliberations at the ILO. The Committee on Conventions, a tri-partite body, examines the ILO conventions and recommendations for ratification by India.

According to the National Commission on Labour, these two bodies have immensely contributed to the attainment of the objectives set before them. The tripartite deliberations helped to reach a consensus on the statutory minimum wage fixation (1944), the introduction of health insurance (1945), the enactment of the Employment Standing Order Act, 1946, the Industrial Disputes Act, 1947, Minimum Wages Act, 1948, the Employees' State Insurance Act, 1948, the Employees' Provident Fund Scheme, 1950, and the Employees' Provident Fund Act, 1947, to name a few. The range of subjects discussed at the forums of ILC/SLC has been large ranging from social, economic and administrative matters concerning labour policy. Apart from these, other subjects under their purview include workers' education, workers' participation in management, training within the industry, wage policy, wage boards, the code of discipline, criteria and procedures for the recognition of unions. Though the recommendations of the tripartite bodies are of an advisory nature, the government, the workers and the employers attach considerable weight to their recommendations. Though the government is one of the three parties with the union labour minister being the ex-officio chairperson of ILC, the government has made it clear that the recommendations of the ILC are nothing more than just that—recommendations—and, therefore, not binding on the government.

When initially constituted, it was expected that the ILC would meet at least once a year and the SLC whenever necessary. The ILC met regularly till the early 1970s. Thereafter, the meetings have become few and far between, almost one meeting in three to four years. A major reason for infrequent meetings can be attributed to the question of representativeness of the three participants, namely, the government, the employers and the employees.

The Committee on Conventions is a three-member tripartite committee set up in 1954 with the objective:

i) to examine the ILO conventions and recommendations for ratification, which will be discussed in the last section of this chapter, and

ii) to make suggestions for implementation of ILO standards

The industrial committee was set up to discuss specific problems of industries and also deliberate on the legislative proposals that are put forth by different parties.

2.1.4 The Impact of the ILO on Indian Labour Relations

The impact of the activities of the ILO on the Indian labour scene is two-fold. First, the ILO was the principal source for the labour legislation in India through the ratification of the ILO standards. The principles of these standards are incorporated into the existing labour laws. Second is the effect of Article 3 of the Constitution of the ILO, which provides for the nomination of non-government delegates and advisors to the International Labour Conference. The nomination of these non-government delegates from amongst employers and employees meant an effort at organizing the employers and employees' bodies so that they may represent in the annual events at the ILO.

RATIFICATION PROCEDURES OF THE ILO STANDARDS. The ILO standards are analogous to treaties requiring competent national authority within a period of one year or eighteen months. In India, the treaty-making power is within the competence of the government of India. The power to enact and implement legislation lies in the hands of the parliament. The Director General of the ILO sends a certified copy of the convention to all member States. Since labour is in the Concurrent List of the constitution, the government of India dispatches the convention to the state governments, to the ministers of labour of the union, as well as to the all-India organizations of workers and employers, inviting their views regarding the desirability and practicability of giving effect to these standards. A statement of action is drawn up; taking into account the comments received, it is considered by the union cabinet and is placed before the parliament, where the proposals are discussed from all aspects. Copies of the statements are forwarded to the International Labour Office, the state government, and the workers' and the employers' organizations. Follow-up action, by way of ratification of conventions, is taken up subsequently.

The Tripartite Committee of India was set up to draw up a programme of implementation of the ILO conventions. This committee makes a detailed scrutiny of these ILO conventions. It is on the recommendation of this committee that India ratifies conventions and recommendations. In case where the committee has not ratified a particular instrument, it focuses on the reasons for non-ratification.

> The ILO has made a total of eight conventions as Core Conventions or Human Rights Conventions. India has ratified four of these conventions, namely:
>
> - Forced Labour Convention (No. 29)
> - Equal Remuneration Convention (No. 100)
> - Abolition of Forced Labour Convention (No. 105)
> - Discrimination (Employment Occupation) Convention (No. 111)

THE RATIFICATION OF CONVENTIONS BY INDIA. There was no important labour legislation in India up to 1919. But the establishment of the ILO and the continuous association of our country with its organization have greatly influenced labour legislation. India has so far ratified 30 conventions. According to these conventions, the labour legislations have been adopted or amended in our country. Of the 30 conventions ratified by India, 11 were ratified prior to 1930, 4 between 1930 and Independence, and 15 after Independence.

The eight Core Conventions of the ILO (also called "fundamental/human rights conventions") are:

1. Forced Labour Convention (No. 29)
2. Abolition of Forced Labour Convention (No.105)

3. Equal Remuneration Convention (No.100)
4. Discrimination (Employment Occupation) Convention (No.111)

The above four have been ratified by India.

5. Freedom of Association and Protection of Right to Organized Convention (No.87)
6. Right to Organize and Collective Bargaining Convention (No.98)
7. Minimum Age Convention (No.138)
8. Worst Forms of Child Labour Convention (No.182)

These four are yet to be ratified by India[4]

Consequent to the World Summit for Social Development in 1995, the above-mentioned conventions (Sl. No. 1 to 7) were categorized as the Fundamental Human Rights Conventions or Core Conventions by the ILO. Later on, Convention No. 182 (Sl. No. 8) was added to the list.

The government of India has its own compulsions in not having ratified all the ILO conventions. For one, ratifying would mean taking action to give effect to the conventions through bringing out suitable legislations.

2.2 The Historical Perspective

Prior to Independence, during the early part of the twentieth century, the industrial relations philosophy was mainly laissez-faire and selective intervention (National Commission on Labour, 1969). The main driver was to allow the industry to produce, and any interventions by the government were largely in furtherance of this objective. Growing unrest of labour, the Bolshevik Revolution in Russia and the formation of the ILO were stimuli to usher in a few changes through legislation. The Trade Disputes Act (1929) was, therefore, enacted and it provided for government intervention in industrial disputes. The Royal Commission on Labour (1931) recommended a few changes in the Act. In the mean time, the Bombay Trade Disputes (Conciliation) Act was enacted in the year 1934. This Act provided for:

- A compulsory recognition of the union by the employer
- The right of the workers to get represented by a union or a government official
- The setting up of industrial courts
- The certifying of standing orders
- The prohibition of strike/lock outs in certain circumstances

On recommendations of the Royal Commission and lessons drawn from the Bombay Trade Disputes Act, the Trade Disputes Act was amended in 1938.

The Government of India Act of 1935 put labour in the Concurrent List, which meant both the centre and the state were competent to legislate. With a view that a modicum of uniformity in legislations of the centre and different states was desirable, a need was felt for a tripartite consultation at an apex level. Indian Labour Conference and Standing Labour Committee were a response to this felt need of the employer, the employees and the government.

The period during the World War II witnessed turbulence in the industrial relations situation. The exploitation of labour for furthering the war effort, a fall in earnings due to price rise, political influence of the Freedom struggle, all combined to make a volatile labour situation. The Defence of India Rules, at this time, introduced a structure for resolution of industrial disputes through the process of adjudication. Many of the provisions of the Defence of India Rules were later incorporated in the Industrial Disputes Act of 1947.

The policy objectives of the elected government after Independence were to protect the labour of exploitation and to ensure industrial peace and harmony. The initial phase was a paternalistic protective phase.

2.2.1 The Protective Phase (1947–1956)

This phase of industrial relations was characterized by providing "rights" to citizens by the adoption of the constitution and the Industrial Truce Resolution to restrain from work stoppages. The constitutional provisions provided for certain rights that ensured every citizen be treated equally on principles of economic and social justice. The articles in the constitution that are relevant for initiation of the protective phase of industrial relations are outlined in Box 2.1:

The protective phase witnessed the enactment of the Industrial Disputes Act (1947), the Constitutional Provisions, the Industrial Truce Resolution, the First Five Year Plan, etc.

The reader would do well to go through the constitutional provisions relating to labour. This would help in understanding the genesis of various legislations and government-led initiatives.

The Industrial Truce Resolution, which was the outcome of the ILC of 1947, required labour and management to agree to maintain industrial peace and prevent any work stoppage during the next three years to facilitate industrial development. The implementation of this truce resolution was facilitated by a central advisory council covering the entire field of industry with committees under each for each industry, supported by provincial advisory boards and committees for each major industry at the state level. The Industrial Policy Resolution of 1948 reserved the government right to undertake new development in six basic industries, viz, coal, iron and steel, aircraft and shipbuilding, telephone and telegraph, mineral and oil production, which were taken up in the public sector. In addition, arms and ammunition, atomic energy and rail transport were made state monopolies.

On the legislative front, the legal provisions for regulating industrial relations were embodied in the Industrial Disputes Act, 1947, which sought the prevention and the settlement of industrial disputes in all industries through conciliation, arbitration and adjudication. The act also provided for the establishment of permanent machinery for settlement of disputes by the appointment of conciliation officers, industrial tribunals, labour courts and making settlement/awards given by them binding on both parties. In addition, the Labour Relations Bill of 1950 introduced the principle of compulsory collective bargaining, but lapsed with the dissolution of the parliament. However, the concept introduced a movement towards a non-legal industrial relations of voluntary bipartite negotiations and collective bargaining, which later came to be known as the Giri Approach as it was advocated by V. V. Giri, the then labour minister.

The principle of protectionism was followed through in the First Five Year Plan, which, aimed at bringing about an all-round development of the country, set certain targets to be achieved in the field of production. It was, therefore, considered essential that industrial/economic development should progress smoothly during the planning era. The implementation of the targets necessitated industrial peace, that is, no strikes, no lockouts, no stoppages of work so that production can go on unhampered. Even though the focus of the First Five Year Plan was agriculture, as far as industry was concerned, it spelled out the following:

i) Workers' right of association, organization and collective bargaining to be recognized as the basic premise on which mutual relationship could be built.

ii) Employer–employee relationship to be based on satisfaction of mutual economic needs

iii) Closer association between trade unions and employers' representatives at various levels—unit, industry, regional and national level

iv) Strengthening the legal machinery for settlement of disputes by arbitration or adjudication in the form of tribunals and courts manned by experts

v) Setting up norms and standards to govern the relations and dealings between employers and employees and for the settlement of industrial disputes through tripartite bodies like the Indian Labour Conference, the Standing Labour Committee and the Industrial Committees for particular industries

vi) In case of differences between management and labour, the Plan recommended that the board of directors must have a few people who understand labour problems and understand their point of view.

BOX 2.1 **CONSTITUTIONAL PROVISIONS RELATING TO LABOUR**

Fundamental Rights

Article 14: The State shall not deny to any person equality before the law or the equal protection of the laws.

Article 19: All citizens shall have the right:

(*a*) to freedom of speech and expression;
(*b*) to assemble peaceably and without arms;
(*c*) to form associations or unions;

subject to some reasonable restrictions laid down by the law.

Article 21: No person shall be deprived of his life or personal liberty except according to procedure established by law.

Directive Principles of State Policy

Article 38: (1) The State shall strive to promote the welfare of the people by securing and protecting as effectively as it may a social order in which justice, social, economic and political, shall inform all the institutions of the national life.
(2) The State shall, in particular, strive to minimize the inequalities in income, and endeavor to eliminate inequalities in status, facilities and opportunities, not only amongst individuals but also amongst groups of people residing in different areas or engaged in different vocations.

Article 39: The State shall, in particular, direct its policy towards securing:

(*a*) that the citizens, men and women equally, have the right to an adequate means of livelihood
(*b*) that the ownership and control of the material resources of the community are so distributed as best to subserve the common good
(*c*) that the operation of the economic system does not result in the concentration of wealth and means of production to the common detriment
(*d*) that there is equal pay for equal work for both men and women
(*e*) that the health and strength of workers, men and women, and the tender age of children are not abused and that citizens are not forced by economic necessity to enter avocations unsuited to their age or strength

Article 41: The State shall, within the limits of its economic capacity and development, make effective provision for securing the right to work, to education and to public assistance in cases of unemployment, old age, sickness and disablement, and in other cases of undeserved want.

Article 42: The State shall make provision for securing just and humane conditions of work and for maternity relief.

Article 43: The State shall endeavour to secure, by suitable legislation or economic organization or in any other way, to all workers, agricultural, industrial or otherwise, work, a living wage, conditions of work ensuring a decent standard of life and full enjoyment of leisure and social and cultural opportunities and, in particular, the State shall endeavour to promote cottage industries on an individual or cooperative basis in rural areas.

Article 43A: The State shall take steps, by suitable legislation or in any other way, to secure the participation of workers in the management of undertakings, establishments or other organizations engaged in any industry.

In terms of systems, the First Five Year Plan prescribed:

i) A need for a systematic "grievance procedure" to be helped by having elected shop stewards

ii) The importance of work committees as the "key to the system of industrial relations".

iii) A need for a single bargaining agent over as large an area of industry as possible.

iv) The public sector to set itself as a model employer, in terms of wages, working conditions and welfare facilities

The First Five Year Plan Prescribed:

- A systematic grievance procedure
- Work committees as the key
- A single bargaining agent
- The public sector to be a model employer

The protectionism phase was marked with the provision of minimum wages and conditions of labour, uniformity in labour laws, initiation of facilitative machineries like grievance procedures and work committees to deal with man-management issues.

2.2.2 The Consolidation Phase (1956–1965)

While the first phase saw a number of legislative interventions by the State, the second phase saw a host of initiatives based on "moral" exhortations. This was also the period of the Second Five Year plan with the focus shifting to rapid industrialization. Under the stewardship of Gulzari Lal Nanda, a slew of Codes was introduced in industrial relations as a non-statutory moral regulation for a better relationship between labour and management. This was based on the Gandhian trusteeship approach discussed in Chapter 1, with three important contributions made in the forms of the Code of Conduct, the Code of Discipline, and the Draft Code of Efficiency and Welfare.

THE CODE OF DISCIPLINE IN INDUSTRY. When the government shifted its emphasis from legislation to voluntary agreements, it tried to bring home to the parties (the government, the workers and the employers) an awareness of their obligations under the labour legislations, and also create in them an attitude of willing acceptance of their responsibilities. It was in this context that the question of discipline in the industry was discussed at length by the Indian Labour Conference held in July 1957. The following general principles were laid down:

- There should be no lockout or strike without notice.
- No unilateral action should be taken in connection with any industrial matter.
- There should be no recourse to go-slow tactics.
- No deliberate damage should be caused to plant or property.
- Acts of violence, intimidation, coercion, or instigation should not be resorted to.
- The existing machinery for settlement of disputes should be utilized.
- Awards and agreements should be speedily implemented.
- Any action that disturbs cordial industrial relations should be avoided.

In order to consider these aspects and the relevant matters, a tripartite sub-committee was appointed, on whose report, recommending a code of discipline was accepted with certain modifications. The Code of Discipline in Industry, thus evolved, was accepted in March 1958 after due discussion, and came into force on 1 June 1958 (The full Code of Discipline in Industry is given in Appendix III).

The Code of Discipline is a set of self-imposed and mutually agreed voluntary principles of discipline and relations between the management and the workers in the industry. It is a code of conduct both for the workers and the management, and provides for the voluntary and mutual settlement of disputes, through mutual negotiations, voluntary arbitrations and conciliations without the interference of an outside agency. While it refrains both the parties from unilateral action, it induces them to make the best use of the existing machinery for the settlement of disputes. Thus, the code compels both the parties not to indulge in any strike or lockout without exploring the avenues for voluntary, mutual settlement of any possible misunderstanding or disputes. In a nutshell, it lays emphasis on the atmosphere of mutual regard and respect.

The fairly successful results of the planning process initiated after Independence created a need for the consolidation of the process of economic growth and development through implementation, for better results. The consolidation process was done by laying greater emphasis on bipartism and tripartism for increased association between labour and management. The Second Five Year plan recommended the following:

i) The avoidance of disputes at all levels, including the last stage of mutual negotiations and conciliation

ii) The importance of preventive measures for achieving industrial peace

iii) An increased association between management and trade unions through formation of joint councils and a proper demarcation of the functions of workers' committees and trade unions

iv) A need for the avoidance of indiscipline in industry for which a Code of Discipline was agreed upon in 1958

v) Suggested restrictions on the number of outsiders who serve as office bearers of unions

vi) A need for union recognition to make collective bargaining effective, and the representative union to have the sole right to take up matters with the management

vii) The use of voluntary arbitration in case of unresolved disputes rather than compulsory adjudication

The central government amended the Industrial Disputes Act accordingly to include a new provision, Section 10 A, providing for such a reference of disputes to voluntary arbitration. On the social security front, the EPF Act was extended to cover industries and commercial establishments having 10,000 workers or more and the contribution enhanced from 6.25 to 8.33 per cent. The ESI Act proposed to extend coverage to the workers' families.

This phase can, therefore, be characterized by a consolidation process wherein worker interests were retained and the government's control initiated through the philosophy of bipartism and tripartism.

During the Second Plan period, two more initiatives were started, that of Joint Management Councils and Worker's Training. Joint Management Councils were introduced in 23 units, with a purpose to jointly discuss issues related to production and productivity.

At the time of the Chinese aggression, the second Industrial Truce Resolution was passed on 3 November 1962, which emphasized:

- The need to maximize production and the need to exercise restraint by employers and workers
- That no interruption of work be allowed
- That all disputes should be settled by voluntary arbitration, especially those related to dismissal, discharge and retrenchment of workers
- That unions should discourage absenteeism, and negligence on the part of the workers
- Joint emergency production committees to be set up

The policy initiatives during the second and the third plant periods can, thus, be summarized as follows:

- The introduction and improvement of the three codes introduced in 1958, to give a more positive orientation to industrial relations

- Active implementation of workers' education programmes
- Enlarging the coverage of the ESI scheme to 3 million workers' families by extending the coverage of the Act to establishments employing 20, from the earlier 150
- A national safety council set up in 1966
- Model Grievance Procedure based on the principle of bipartite forums
- Scheme for workers' participation through joint councils
- The resolution of conflicts by voluntary arbitration
- Central Wage Boards
- The establishment of norms for wage determination

Thus, the approach for the consolidation used was through bipartite and tripartite machinery promoted by the State.

The second phase had two Five Year Plans. The policy initiatives taken up in this period reflected a new labour policy that aimed towards the prevention and settlement of disputes. Prevention was facilitated by modifications in labour legislation and the creation of mutually beneficial relations through workers' participation and joint councils. This established the bipartism spirit in the industrial relations climate.

2.2.3 The Conflict-ridden Interventionist Phase (1966–1976)

The fragmentation of the Indian polity made it difficult for tripartite agreements to be arrived at by consensus. Political affiliations of trade unions brought interference of political parties to a state level. This resulted in labour turbulence, and with non-Congress governments in most states, the practice of tripartism declined. The much greater polarization in national politics resulted in clearer conflict lines being drawn not only among the unions, but also between labour and management. The spirit of cooperation that was sought to be introduced through the various voluntary arrangements (Code of Discipline et al.) all disappeared from the IR scenario; they were but a faint memory. "When these arrangements were discussed in the tripartite fora, the actors could not disagree openly with such lofty ideals. The moral appeal, though outstanding, soon waned. In retrospect, it appears the actors agreed to these because they were merely voluntary and non-adherence did not entail any sanctions."[5] In the 1970s, the government was forced to increasingly step in for securing industrial peace since the machinery in existence was proving to be inadequate.

The political uncertainty created economic insecurities and the declaration of emergency created a more volatile industrial relations climate. Despite the decline in industrial activity and social militancy, this period was crucial in labour history as it created a platform to evaluate and initiate labour reforms that would facilitate economic revival and growth. An important development during this phase was the appointment of National Commission on Labour in 1967, with Justice P. B. Gajendragadkar as its chairman. Although the recommendations could not be implemented, but till date, there has not been a more comprehensive assessment of the industrial relations, and the recommendations are valid even today.

The Fourth Five Year Plan (1969–1974) came after three years of a plan holiday and coincided with the emergency period. This was a period when labour rights and privileges were withdrawn and the right to strike suspended from June 1975. The employers' rights to closure were restricted but not that of lockouts. A national apex body was set up as a bipartite consultative forum to resolve industrial relations problems supported by similar bodies at the state level. This forum issued guidelines to resolve industrial relations problems that affected production and productivity, but in practice, were not very successful. In addition, national industrial committees were set up for some major industries to deal with their specific problems. The Fourth Plan continued with the industrial policy of the previous years and made only a brief reference to industrial relations, according importance to the growth of a healthy trade-union movement for better labour-management relations. Renewed emphasis was placed on collective bargaining and settlement of disputes through voluntary arbitration. It recommended summary powers to labour courts and that workers' participation through joint councils be extended to the plant level.

The third phase or the conflict-ridden phase was precipitated by the fragmentation of political parties, different parties in power in the centre and in the states and the onset of the emergency. This period also saw the report of the first National Commission on Labour in 1960. With increasing strife, the government's role became increasingly interventionist.

2.2.4 The Directionless Phase (1977–1980)

Despite the change in the political supremacy of non-Congress parties and the government being composed of those non-aligned to the Congress, there were no fresh initiatives taken in the field of labour relations, although they were brought to power by pro-labour campaigns. The bottled-up grievances of the emergency period opened up floodgates of industrial disputes; strikes and indiscipline were rampant. As a result of this, the government was constrained to introduce a legislation to restrict strikes and lockouts in essential services. The national-level apex body discussed above was discontinued. Tripartism was given a fillip with a labour conference inviting 10 major central trade-union organizations (CTUO), some of whom were never invited earlier for consultations on creating a comprehensive law on industrial relations. The conference led to the introduction of an industrial relations bill in the parliament, which was never passed. Thus, the net result was nothing concrete for either labour or the industrial relations climate. The Janata government, however, introduced the Industrial Policy Statement that envisaged decentralization of the industrial structure.

The Fifth Five Year Plan (1975–1980) made only a brief reference to industrial relations focusing once again on conciliation machinery, enforcement of labour legislations, research in labour relations, imparting training to labour officers, undertaking studies on wages and productivity. Special attention was given to improving productivity in all spheres of the economy.

This directionless phase was, however, too short-lived to make any impact either ways.

2.2.5 The Productivity-, Efficiency-, Quality-orientation Phase (1981–1990)

The post-1980s period, around the world, emphasized quality and productivity. The Industrial Policy Resolution of 1980 was a reassertion of the 1956 resolution recalling the socialist principles, employment generation and correction of regional imbalances, but with a leaning towards productivity and efficiency. The IMF credit added to the prioritization for higher productivity and cost efficiency.

Certain changes were made in the ID Act in 1982, under which "go slow" and "gherao", the typical work stoppage tactics of the Indian workforce, were declared as unfair labour practices. The rationalization of manpower was attempted by a few private-sector industries. By and large, a lot of structural changes were witnessed. Employment in public sector reduced, thereby reducing the trade-union strength.

The Sixth Five Year Plan (1980–1985) emphasized industrial harmony and advocated an internal mechanism within units to promote this. The measures suggested included suggestion schemes, grievance redress machinery, participative joint councils at the unit level. Workers Participation in Management Scheme was formulated in 1983, which was made applicable to all public-sector undertakings.

The Seventh Five Year Plan (1985–1990) emphasized efficiency, capacity utilization and productivity, and envisaged greater competition within the industry. Interestingly, this plan, while highlighting that there was considerable scope to improve industrial relations, admitted that the existence of inter- and intra-union rivalry created industrial relations problems. It stated that "if adequate consultative machinery and grievance procedures are evolved and made effective, strikes and lockouts would become redundant. Effective arrangements should be made for the settlement of inter-union disputes and to discourage unfair practices and irresponsible conduct".

2.2.6 *The Competitive Phase*

The adoption of the liberalization programme with the New Economic Policy (NEP) in 1991 brought with it a paradigm shift in the concept of industrial relations. The shift to employee relations has been the focus of this book to prepare students for the same. There have been, interestingly, no explicit changes in the labour policy but the worker-centric State approach has shown a greater leaning towards pro-management positions. The NEP introduced a competitive phase through the process of liberalization and globalization. The focus shifted to gain competitive advantage, which more often than not was not in favour of labour, with the rationalization of manpower, automation, restructuring, reengineering, etc. To get around retrenchment, employers have experimented with novel ways such as the VRS or a "golden handshake" to shed surplus labour. Employer practices clearly show more aggression while promoting one-to-one employer–employee relationship. To circumvent the provisions of labour laws, more and more organizations are re-designating the workmen as "supervisors" or "executives". This also helps with low unionization of the workplace and thereby reduces chances of workplace conflicts and disputes. The worker-centric State role has seen a shift towards being more neutral. The government–labour coalition has weakened considerably, given the State's enthusiastic support for economic liberalization.

The period of 1980s saw a shifting emphasis on productivity and quality enhancement. The Industrial Policy Resolution of 1980, while maintaining the earlier socio-political-economic orientation, leaned towards the enhancement of productivity in the industry. The plan document also emphasized industrial harmony for greater productivity.

With a view to inducting an element of dynamism in the Indian economy, a new industrial policy was announced by the government in 1991. The said policy has brought about a drastic change in the organization and working of the industrial system of the country that, in turn, considerably influenced its labour policy. With a view to safeguarding the interest of labour, the industrial policy has stated that the "government will fully protect the interests of labour, enhance their welfare and equip them in all respects to deal with the inevitability of technological change. [The] government believes that no small section of society can corner the gains of growth, leaving workers to bear its pains. Labour will be made an equal partner in progress and prosperity. Workers' participation in management will be promoted. Workers cooperatives will be encouraged to participate in packages designed to turn around sick companies. Intensive training skill development and ungradation programmes will be launched".

The decade 1995–2005 has seen a clearer shift to pro-management position of the government, reflected in lesser control of the labour ministry in policy making, lesser labour inspectors employed in the states and a kind of disengagement with industrial relations climate. With employment in the public sector reducing, the role of the State and its control has also declined. The Eighth, Ninth and Tenth Five Year Plans have focused on competitive advantage, manpower planning and reduction in losses due to industrial unrest. There has been a decline in the number of strikes and lockouts and also the number of man-days lost due to work stoppages.

"A review of industrial relations in the pre-reform decade (1981–1990) reveals that as against 402.1 million man-days lost during the decade (1981–1990), that is, in the pre-reform period, the number of man-days lost declined to 210 million during 1991 to 2000, that is, the post-reform period. But more man-days have been lost in lockouts than in strikes . . ."

Extract from a Report on Second National Commission on Labour

2.3 Trends in Industrial Relations Management

Fundamentally, liberalization requires a laissez-faire policy, reducing the government interference to the minimum. Competition is the key to market regulations in a capitalist economy. This leads to the important question of how the principles of socialism, inbuilt in our constitution, can be integrated in this scenario. Globalization has imposed a need to make our labour laws adaptable to the new reality. Without a change in the constitution and, with an increasingly globalized economy, as far as the labour policy is concerned, a stalemate of sorts has arrived with the three actors unable to come to a consensus on the way ahead. A fractured polity does not help the matter much.

2.3.1 The Inclusion of the Needs of Unorganized Labour

Today, the unorganized sector contributes 93 per cent of our workforce. An IR and labour policy directed at only 7 per cent of the working population will be farcical. Any policy on labour must take into account the vast unorganized sector, many of which comprise what is called the SME sector. The second NCL suggests a separate set of labour legislation just for the SMEs. The UPA government, in its Common Minimum Programme, is committed to the extension of the social-security net to cover workers from the unorganized sector. Maybe, it is time to let the organized sector regulate itself through the progressive human resources management approach, while the government focuses its attention on the upliftment of employees in the unorganized sector.

2.3.2 Labour Laws

The second NCL has discussed in detail the competitiveness of the Chinese industry when compared to that of India. An oft-repeated point cited in favour of China's competitiveness is their labour laws (read labour market and employment flexibility, to put it crudely, the right of employer to hire and fire). This restriction in India is said to be the major impediment to a level of FDI, which is much less when compared to that of China. This may be taking an overtly simplistic view of a complex issue and putting the blame where it may not be due. Nevertheless, even without comparisons, inherent in the prevailing labour legislative schemes are distortions that manifest themselves in the form of dissatisfaction expressed by both the employers and the employees. The employees face the problem of employment security, while the industry is faced with the problems of absenteeism, indiscipline and labour mobility. While all parties feel that changes may be required, such changes should take into consideration problems faced by both workmen and industries.

The existing labour laws are tilted in favour of labour due to historical reasons, and rightly so. However, the forces in the environment are not the same as obtained 50 years back. At least in the organized sector, despite laments from the labour, the situation has changed. In acknowledgement of these changes, the government has become neutral (where the inclination was pro-labour earlier), though it has not been able to push forth with reforms due to lack of consensus. In the existing labour laws, the emphasis is more on rights. A result of this is the tendency of trade unions to raise demands without due regard to financial implication in a competitive environment. To strike a balance, the Second National Commission on Labour has made certain suggestions[6]:

- The existing set of labour laws should be broadly grouped into four or five groups of laws pertaining to (i) industrial relations, (ii) wages, (iii) social security, (iv) safety and (v) welfare and working conditions, and so on.
- The coverage as well as the definition of the term "worker" should be the same in all groups of laws, subject to the stipulation that social-security benefits must be available to all employees including administrative, managerial, supervisory and others.
- Simple, common definitions of terms that are in constant use; such terms include "worker", "wages" and "establishment"
- The Commission has given considerable thought to the number of employees that should be fixed as the threshold point for the organized sector. The Commission feels that a limit of 19 workers should be accepted.
- Instead of having separate laws, it may be advantageous to incorporate all the provisions relating to employment relations, wages, social security, safety and working conditions, etc., into a single law, with separate parts in respect of establishments employing less than 20 persons.
- The government may lay down a list of such highly paid jobs, which are presently deemed as workmen category as being outside the purview of the laws relating to workmen and included in the proposed law for the protection of non-workmen. Another alternative is that the government may fix a cut-off limit of remuneration, which is substantially high enough, in the present context, such as INR 25,000 per month, beyond which employees will not be treated as ordinary "workmen".
- Keep all the supervisory personnel, irrespective of their wage/salary, outside the rank of the worker, and keep them out of the purview of the labour laws meant for the workers.
- It is necessary to provide a minimum level of protection to managerial and other (excluded) employees too, against unfair dismissals or removals. This has to be through adjudication by labour court or Labour Relations Commission or arbitration.

- There should be an enactment of a special law for small-scale units. The reasonable threshold limit will be 19 workers. Any establishment with workers above that number cannot be regarded as small.
- Provisions must be made in the law for determining negotiating agents, particularly on behalf of the workers.
- Changes in the labour laws should be accompanied by a well-defined, social-security package that will benefit all workers, regardless of whether they are in the "organized" or the "unorganized" sector, and should also cover those in the administrative, managerial and other categories, which have been excluded from the purview of the term "worker".
- There is no need for different definitions of the phrase "appropriate government", and there must be a single definition of the phrase, applicable to all labour laws.
- The provisions of all these laws (related to labour management relations, e.g. ID Act, Trade Unions Act and Industrial Employment Standing Orders Act) should be judiciously consolidated into a single law called the Labour Management Relations Law or the Law on Labour Management Relations.
- New and effective legislation involving workers in the grievance-settlement machinery is necessary.
- A system of legal aid to the workers must be designed so that they are not handicapped due to their inability to afford a lawyer's fee.
- A clause naming an arbitrator or a panel of arbitrators may be added in every settlement so that any dispute arising out of interpretation of a settlement, or any other dispute can be referred to arbitration immediately without delay.
- ESMA should be withdrawn.

Recommendations of the Second National Commission on Labour

- Defining the organized sector
- Uniformity in definitions
- Fewer streamlined labour laws
- A separate law for small-scale sector
- Social-security package for all
- Withdrawal of ESMA
- Supervisors and highly paid categories to be kept out of "worker" category

2.4 Conclusion

There have been substantial changes in the economic environment. Fifty years of development have brought about changes in both the employers and the employees. There have been no systemic shifts in the management of industrial relations. The country is poised to make its presence felt amongst the comity of nations. However, multiplicity of trade unions, employers' organizations, political parties and different parties in power at the centre and the states, a coalition government during times of change have all contributed to a state where a consensus on facing the challenges ahead is proving to be elusive. The time has come, perhaps, to forge a consensus amongst the three actors of IR for heralding a completely new paradigm of industrial relations.

SUMMARY

- The industrial relations system of India has its origins in the colonial past.
- The movement for Independence, too, influenced the evolution of the industrial relations system in India.
- The constitution embodies certain rights to prevent any form of discrimination or exploitation.
- The State role has been interventionist and labour policies have been pro-labour, being enacted through a consultative process of involving major trade unions, government representatives and employer representatives.
- Industrial relations in India has been shaped largely by principles and policies evolved through tripartite consultative machinery at the industry and the national levels.
- The ILO guidelines have a great influence in promoting uniform standards in the field of labour policy and industrial relations.

- The historical evolution of the industrial relations system can be categorized under six phases (i) The Protective Phase (1947–1956) (ii) The Consolidation Phase (1957–1965) (iii) The Conflict-ridden Interventionist Phase (1966–1976) (iv) The Directionless Phase (1977–1980) (v) The Productivity-, Efficiency-, Quality-orientation Phase (1981–1990) (vi) The Economic Growth Competitive Phase (1991 onwards).
- The current scenario points to a shift in the relative bargaining power in industrial relations, away from the workers to the employers.
- It is argued that the labour laws are restrictive to the extent that they impose restrictions on closure of units, firing of employees and rationalization of manpower.
- A dichotomy exists, where the economic objective is global competitiveness and the social objective is employment security. Resolving this would require substantial underwriting of a large part of social-security costs by the State, which is possible only with an interventionist government providing for higher rates of public-resource mobilization and public expenditure.

KEY TERMS

REVIEW QUESTIONS

1 The first phase of unionism represented a period of State-driven industrialization that possibly required government support and control of the labour movement. Elaborate.

2 The growth and transitions in the industrial relations scenario in India have been closely connected with the economy and the Five Year Plans or with the political changes. Bring out the features of the Five Year Plans that had a significant impact on the industrial relations in India.

3 Which phase in the Indian industrial history contributed most to the development of a congenial industrial climate? Give reasons for your answer.

4 The mid-1990s were characterized by a union-movement shift from those of "rights" to those of "interest". Elucidate.

QUESTIONS FOR CRITICAL THINKING

1 Why should one study industrial relations? What should be the focus and the expected outcomes of this study?

2 The structural changes of the economy had an effect on union activity, collective bargaining practices and labour relations in general. Elaborate.

DEBATE

1 With globalization, the labour law provisions should be as liberal in India as they are in the advanced economies.

2 The industrial relations system in India caters to the elite 7 per cent of labour in the organized sector. The remaining 93 per cent in the unorganized sector has largely been ignored by the State, trade unions and employers alike. There should be no protective labour legislation in the organized sector and it should be left to the market to regulate human resources.

3 Since labour is one of the factors of production, free movement of labour should encourage the efficient use of global resources.

CASE ANALYSIS

1. There were a few incidents of labour unrest during the year 2005. Brief reports from a few newspapers are reproduced here. Gather the relevant details regarding these incidents. On the basis of this, discuss the direction that the system of industrial relations in India should be allowed to take to address such issues on a long-term basis. Do you think incidents like these would impact India's global competitiveness? Why?

S Kumar's, nationwide: The company's worsted fabrics plant at Thandavapura, near Mysore, closed on 31 May 2005 as the workers resorted to an illegal strike. It was announced on 27 June that the issue was resolved and production back on track. The financial-loss estimate is unavailable.

Omax Auto, Gurgaon: Along with group company Speedomax (both with units in Haryana), it was faced with labour problems that lasted for a month between June and July, but were resolved a day before the police–protesters clash broke out in Gurgaon over the HMSI issue. It cost the company close to INR 5 crore (INR 50 million) in production losses.

Hitachi Electric, Gurgaon: It lost two-and-a-half days' production in May 2005, but differences were kept within company walls. The financial-loss estimate is unavailable.

Toyota Kirloskar Motor, Bangalore: There was minor spat between the workers and the management over wage hike in April-May 2005. The issue was settled for the time being with a management truce in the form of a 15 per cent wage hike. The shaken company is considering setting up its second plant in a location that is relatively peaceful.

Apollo Tyres, Limbda, Gujarat: Operations at its plant were temporarily suspended on 31 May on account of an "illegal strike" by one section of trade unions in the factory. A week later, the issue was resolved. The financial-loss estimate is unavailable.

Tata Motors, Jamshedpur: A minor flash strike took place on 7 June. Three hundred workers attached to the transport section struck work for four hours against the suspension of a union member. Management revoked its plans to outsource general transportation from a contracting firm. No financial loss has been reported.

2. Read the news report[7] given below. Why do you think the employees did not seek government intervention? There have been employee-related issues such as shift-working for women, employee safety, occupational diseases and payment for over time in the "new economy" industries including IT, BPO and financial services. Discuss what the State should do to handle such issues. Should the State intervene at all?

There's trouble brewing in India's BPO paradise. For the first time, the shadow of labour strife appears to be looming over the outsourcing industry.

WNS Global Services, one of India's biggest BPOs, experienced this first-hand at its Nashik unit when a section of workers agitated over pay earlier this week and then turned to local politicians for help. Till date, attempts to unionise employees in the BPO industry have not been successful.

While the upheaval in Nashik has been quelled for now, independent local sources in Nashik said the employees stayed away from work for two days and returned after only repeated assurances from the management. The signs are ominous for the sunrise industry, which is estimated to clock revenues of $11 billion for 2007–08.

A WNS spokesperson denied there was a strike at the Nashik centre, but admitted some workers were asking for payment of additional bonus and that it was in talks with them.

"In October 2007, the government passed a notification which required the industry to retrospectively change its bonus payouts for employees from April 1, 2006. We have complied with this notification and paid bonuses accordingly. On account of additional payment of statutory bonus for 2006–07, the difference in bonus payouts, for that period, among certain high-performing and average performing employees of WNS has reduced. As a result, some of our employees were asking for payment of additional bonus over and above statutory/performance incentive bonus for 2006–07. We are in discussions with these employees and hope to resolve the issue soon," the spokesperson told ET in an email.

The Nashik unit of Maharashtra Navnirman Sena appears to have played a minor role in the matter.

NYSE-listed WNS has other problems to contend with. It saw net profit fall 23.1% to $5.5 million in the third quarter to December 2007 due to the rise in rupee. US economic woes and high employee turnover are eroding the profitability of the sector.

WNS employs about 1,800 people in two centres in Nashik, where it mainly gets data processing work done. The spokesperson said there has been no disruption in client service. The town, about 130 km northeast of Mumbai, has developed into tier-II BPO destination, where wages and property prices are much lower than in frontline cities such as Mumbai and Pune.

In fact, in recent months, a lot of public debate over wage levels has taken place in Nashik, where a BPO employee typically gets Rs 4,000 ($100) or less per month. About low wages, the WNS spokesperson said the compensation was also a matter of location.

"The compensation for a Mumbai or Delhi-based employee would definitely be more than cities like Pune or Nashik," he told ET over the phone.

NOTES

1 C. S. Venkatratnam, "New Paradigm in Labour Management Relations", in *Globalization and Labour Management Relations—Dynamics of Change* (New Delhi: Response Books, 2001), pp. 304.

2 P. D. Shenoy, Labour Secretary, Government of India, as quoted in a PIB release titled "Towards Harmonious Industrial Relations", 17 January 2003. http://pib.nic.in/feature/feyr2003/fjan2003/f170120031.html.

3 In India, the organized sector refers to the sector comprising public and private enterprises, which are registered and come under the purview of any, some, or several Act(s), and maintain annual accounts and balance sheets. C. S. Venkatratnam, "A Historical Analysis of Industrial Relations" in *Globalization and Labour Management Relations* (New Delhi: Response Books, 2000), pp. 20.

4 India and the ILO', Ministry of Labour, Government of India (http://labour.nic.in/ilas/indiaandilo.htm)

5 C. S. Venkatratnam, "A Historical Analysis of Industrial Relations in India", in *Globalization and Labour Management Relations—Dynamics of Change* (New Delhi: Response Books, 2001), pp. 28.

6 Report of the Second National Commission on Labour (2002)

7 Ritwik Donde, "Bonus Blues Stir up Labour Unrest at WNS' Nashik Unit", *The Economic Times,* 12 April 2008.

SUGGESTED READING

Johri, C. K. (ed.), *Issues in Indian Labour Policy* (New Delhi: Shriram Center for Industrial Relations,).

Mathur, K. and N. R. Seth *Tripartism in Labour Policy: The Indian Experience* (New Delhi:

Report of the Second National Commission on Labour (2002).

Sarkar, Santanu "Trade Unionism in Indian BPO-ITES Industry—Insights from Literature", *Indian Journal of Industrial Relations,* Vol. 44, No 1, July 2008.

Sheth, N. R. "Labour Relations in New Economic Environment", *Vikalpa,* Vol. 18 (3), 1993.

Shriram Center for Industrial Relations, 1969).

Sodhi, J. S. and S. P. S. Ahluwalia (eds.), *Industrial Relations in India: The Coming Decade* (New Delhi: Shri Ram Center for Industrial Relations, 1992).

Venkatratnam, C. S. (ed.), *Paradigm in Labour Management Relations* (New Delhi: Response Books, 2001).

Venkatratnam, C. S., *Industrial Relations* (New Delhi: Oxford University Press, 2006).

APPENDIX I

Observations of the Second National Commission on Labour (2002) on Changes in the Industrial Relations

"A review of industrial relations in the pre-reform decade (1981–1990) reveals that as against 402.1million man-days lost during the decade (1981–1990), that is, in the pre-reform period, the number of man-days lost declined to 210 million during 1991 to 2000, that is, the post-reform period. But more man-days have been lost in lockouts than in strikes . . . A large number of workers have lost their jobs as a result of VRS, retrenchment and closures both in the organized and the unorganized sector. The exact number is not available. According to our information, no data on this subject has been compiled by any State government . . . We have received a large number of complaints on VR schemes. We have also been told of elements of indirect compulsion, pressure tactics, innovative forms of mental harassment, compelling employees to resign by seeking to terminate them, and in some cases, physical torture and threats of violence against themselves or dependents.

"We shall make a few other general observations on matters that have come before us about the industrial relations scenario: i) it is increasingly noticed that trade unions do not normally give a call for strike because they are afraid that a strike may lead to the closure of the unit; ii) service-sector workers feel they have become outsiders and are becoming increasingly disinterested in trade-union activities; iii) there is a trend to resolve major disputes through negotiations at a bipartite level. The nature of disputes or demands is changing; iv) the attitude of the government, especially of the central government, towards workers and employers seems to have undergone a change. Now, permissions for closure or retrenchment are more easily granted; v) the conciliation machinery is more eager to consider problems of employers and today consider issues like increase in productivity, cost reduction, financial difficulties of the employer, competition, market fluctuations, and so on; vi)recovery proceedings against employers who could not pay heavy dues of workers are not being seriously pursued by the industrial relations machinery, if the financial position of the employer is very bad; vii) the labour adjudication machinery is more willing to entertain the concerns of industry."

APPENDIX II

Main Recommendations of National Commission on Labour on Industrial Relations Policy

Collective Bargaining: While realizing the fact that the collective bargaining agreements have not made much headway in India, the NCL has recommended compulsory recognition of a union as a sole representative for the purpose of bargaining.

The commission has suggested various measures to encourage the growth of collective bargaining which, according to it, enjoys an important place in maintaining peaceful industrial relations. It has observed that:

1. In the absence of arrangements for statutory recognition of unions, except in some states and provisions, which require employers and workers to bargain in "good faith", it is no surprise that reaching of collective bargaining agreements has not made much headway in India. Nonetheless, the record of reaching collective agreements has not been as unsatisfactory, as is popularly believed. Its extension to a wider area is certainly desirable.
2. There is a case for a shift in emphasis and increasingly greater scope for and reliance on collective bargaining. Any sudden change replacing adjudication by a system of collective bargaining has to be gradual. A move should be made towards collective bargaining in such a way that it may acquire primacy in the procedure for settling industrial disputes.

The Commission also observed that:

1. An essential step to facilitate collective bargaining process is the *compulsory recognition of a union as sole representative* for the purpose of bargaining with the management.
2. In order to enable employees to effectively participate in the process of collective bargaining, they should be well-organized and trade unions must become strong and stable.
3. The place which strike/lockout should have in the overall scheme of industrial relations needs to be defined. Collective bargaining cannot exist without the right of strike or lockout.

The Recognition of Unions: A trade union seeking recognition as a bargaining agent from an individual employer should have a membership of at least 30 per cent of workers in the establishment. The minimum membership should be 25 per cent if the recognition is sought for an industry in a local area.

The Commission is of the view that statutory recognition should be granted to the union as a sole bargaining agent. In this connection it recommends:

1. Recognition should be made compulsory under a Central Law in all undertakings employing 100 or more workers or where the capital invested is above a stipulated size. A trade union seeking recognition as a bargaining agent from an individual employer should have a membership of at least 30 per cent of the workers in the establishment. The minimum membership should be 25 per cent if the recognition is sought for an industry in a local area.
2. The Industrial Relations Commission is to certify the union as a representative union on the basis of either verification of membership of the contending unions or by a secret ballot open to all workers in the establishment. The Commission will deal with various aspects of union recognition such as: (i) determining the level of recognition—whether plant, industry, centre-cum-industry to determine which the majority union is; (ii) certifying the majority union as a recognized union for collective bargaining; and (iii) generally dealing with other related matters.
3. The recognized union should be statutorily given certain exclusive rights and facilities, such as the right of sole representation; the right to enter into collective agreements on terms of employment and conditions of service; the right to collect membership subscriptions within the premises of the undertaking; the right of check-off, holding discussions with departmental representatives within factory premises; inspecting, by prior agreement, the place of work of any of its members; and nomination of its representatives on works/grievance committees and other bipartite committees to represent cases of dismissal and discharge of their members before the Labour Court.
4. The unions should be made strong organizationally and financially. Multiplicity of unions and intra-union rivalries should be discouraged by:

   a. Providing compulsory registration of unions

   b. Raising the minimum number required for forming a union

   c. Raising the minimum membership fee

   d. Reduction in the number of outsiders

   e. Taking steps to build internal leadership

5. The minority unions should be allowed only the right to represent cases of dismissal and discharge of their members before the Labour Court.
6. To represent cases of dismissal and discharge of their members before the Labour Court.
7. The compulsory registration of employers' association has also been recommended.

Strikes/Lockouts and *Gheraos*: The NCL has categorized industries as "essential" and "non-essential" for the purpose of strikes and lockouts, and observed that every strike/lockout should be preceded by a notice.

It has made the following recommendations:

1. In essential industries/services, where a cessation of work may cause harm to the community, the economy or the security of the nation itself, the right to strike may be banned, but with the simultaneous provision of an effective alternative like arbitration or adjudication to settle disputes.
2. In non-essential industries, a maximum period of one month has to be fixed for the continuance of a strike or lockout. After the lapse of this period, the dispute has automatically to go before the IRC for arbitration. In essential industries, the right to strike/lockout should be made redundant by requiring the IRC to adjudicate when mutual negotiations fail and parties do not agree to arbitration.
3. Every strike/lockout should be preceded by a notice. A strike notice to be given by a recognized union should be preceded by a strike ballot open to all the members of the union, and the strike decision must be supported by two-thirds of the members present and voting. *Gherao* cannot be treated as a form of labour unrest since it involves physical coercion rather than economic pressure. It is harmful to the working class, and in the long, run may affect national interest.
4. The penalties, which have been provided for unjustified strikes/lockouts, would ultimately discharge these and would, in due course, persuade the parties to sit round the table earnestly and settle their disputes by negotiation.
5. To restrain the outbreak of unnecessary strikes/lockouts, compensation and forfeiture of wages for a strike/lockout should be provided for.

Conciliation: The Second National Commission on Labour observes that "the functioning of conciliation machinery has not been found satisfactory due to the delays involved, the casual attitude of one or the other party to the proceedings, lack of adequate background in the officer himself for understanding the major issues involved, the ad hoc nature of the machinery and the discretion vested in the government in the matters of reference to disputes. It has, therefore, pointed out:

1. Conciliation can be more effective if it is freed from outside influence and the conciliation machinery is adequately staffed. The independent character of the machinery will alone inspire greater confidence and will evoke greater cooperation of the parties. The conciliation machinery should, therefore, be a part of the proposed Industrial Relations Commission. This transfer will introduce important structural, functional and procedural changes in the working of the machinery as it exists today.
2. Officers using the machinery would function effectively if there is proper selection adequate pre-job training and period in-service training.

Arbitration: The Commission has observed that with the growth of collective bargaining and the general acceptance of recognition of representative unions and improved management attitudes, settlement of disputes through voluntary arbitration will be accepted.

Unfair Labour Practices: The Commission recommends that "unfair labour practices" on the part of both employers' and workers' unions should be detailed and suitable penalties prescribed in the industrial relations law for those found guilty of committing such practices. Labour Court will be the appropriate authority to deal with complaints relating to unfair labour practices."

Works Committees and Joint Management Councils: As per NCL, works committees should be set up in units which have a recognized union. The union should be given the right to nominate the worker-members of the Works Committee.

> "A clear demarcation of the functions of the Works Committee and the recognized union, on the basis of mutual agreement between the employer and the recognized union, will make for a better working of the Committee".
>
> About joint management councils, the Commission says:
>
> "When managements and unions are willing to extend cooperation in matters they consider to be of mutual advantage, they may set up a joint management council. In the mean time, wherever the management and the recognized trade union in a unit so desire, they can by agreement enhance the powers and scope of the Works Committees to ensure a greater degree of consultation/cooperation. The functions of the two in this latter situation can as well be amalgamated."

The Settlement of Industrial Disputes: According to the Commission, the best way to settle industrial disputes for the parties is to talk over their differences across the table and settle them by negotiation and bargaining. A settlement so reached leaves no rancour behind and helps to create an atmosphere of harmony and cooperation. There should be a shift to collective bargaining. Disputes between employers and workers, the Commission observes, have been taking a legalistic turn, mainly because of the emphasis on adjudication through industrial tribunals and courts.

The Commission has laid down the procedure for the settlement of disputes. It observes:

After negotiations have failed and before the notice of a strike/lockout is served, the parties may agree to voluntary arbitration. The IRC will help the parties in choosing a mutually acceptable arbitrator or may provide an arbitrator from among its members/officer if the parties agree to avail of such services.

In essential services/industries, when collective bargaining fails and parties do not agree to arbitration, either party may notify the IRC of the failure of negotiations, whereupon the IRC shall adjudicate on the dispute.

The Grievance Procedure: The Commission has observed that "statutory backing should be provided for the formulation of an effective grievance procedure, which should be simple, flexible, less cumbersome and more or less on the lines of the present Model Grievance Procedure. It should be time-bound and have a limited number of steps, say, approach to the supervisor, then to the departmental head, and thereafter a reference to the Grievance Committee consisting of management and union representatives. The Commission has, therefore, recommended that:

1. Grievance procedure should be simple and have a provision for at least one appeal. The procedure should ensure that it gives a sense of (a) satisfaction to the individual workers (b) reasonable exercise of authority to the manager, and (c) participation to unions. A formal grievance procedure should be introduced in units employing 100 or more workers.
2. A grievance procedure should normally provide three steps: (a) submission of a grievance by the aggrieved worker to his immediate superior, (b) appeal to the departmental head/manager, (c) appeal to a bipartite Grievance Committee representing the management and the recognized union. In rare cases, where unanimity eludes the Committee, the matter may be referred to an arbitrator.

The Discipline Procedure: After the views of both the employers and the workers have been heard, the Commission has suggested the following changes in the discipline procedure:

1. Standardization of punishment for different types of misconduct
2. Inclusion of workers' representatives in the domestic enquiry committee; an adequate show-cause opportunity to a workman
3. Presence of a union official to represent the case of a workman during the enquiry proceedings
4. Supply of the record of proceedings to the aggrieved workman
5. Payment of a subsistence allowance during the suspension period
6. Right of appeal to administrative tribunals set up for the purpose
7. Fixing a time limit for tribunal proceedings and giving unfettered powers to it to examine the case de novo, modify or cancel a punishment ordered by the employer.

To make the procedure more effective, the Commission has made the following recommendations:

1. In the domestic enquiry, the aggrieved workers should have the right to be represented by an executive of the recognized union or a workman of his choice
2. A record of the domestic enquiry should be made in a language understood by the aggrieved employee or his union
3. The domestic enquiry should be completed within a prescribed time, which should be necessarily short
4. Appeal against the employer's order of dismissal should be filed within a prescribed period
5. The worker should be entitled to subsistence allowance during the period of suspension as per agreement
6. Supply of the record of proceedings to the aggrieved workman
7. Payment of a subsistence allowance during the suspension period
8. Right of appeal to administrative tribunals set up for the purpose
9. Fixing a time limit for tribunal proceedings and giving unfettered powers to it to examine the case de novo, modify or cancel a punishment ordered by the employer
10. Having an arbitrator to give his decision in a domestic enquiry

Industrial Harmony: While industrial peace calls for both a negative and positive approach, the attainments of industrial harmony necessarily calls for a positive and constructive approach to the solution of industrial disputes. Therefore, the Commission laid emphasis on the freedom of industrial relations machinery from "political partisan" influence. This was necessary in view of the multi-party governments that were emerging in the country.

The Commission has referred to certain weaknesses in the working of the existing industrial relations machinery, namely, the delays involved, the expenditure, the largely ad hoc nature of the machinery and the discretion vested in the government in matters of reference for disputes. Therefore, to make the industrial machinery more effective and more acceptable, suitable modification in the existing machinery should be made.

Industrial Relations Commission: The Commission has recommended—

"The constitution of an Industrial Relations Commission, on a permanent basis, both at the state level and the centre. The state IRC will deal with disputes in respect of industries for which the state government is the appropriate authority, while national IRC will deal with disputes involving questions of national importance or those likely to affect or interest establishments situated in more than one state. One of the principal reasons for suggesting these Commissions is the desire to eliminate the possibility of political influence disturbing or distorting industrial peace in the country.

"The Commission will have both judicial and non-judicial members. The judicial member as well as the President of the National/State IRE are to be appointed from among persons eligible for appointment as judges of High Courts. Non-judicial members need not have qualifications to hold judicial posts, but should be otherwise eminent in the field of industry, labour or management.

The IRC will be high-powered bodies independent of the executive. The main functions of these IRCs will be (a) adjudication in industrial disputes, (b) conciliation, and (c) certification of unions as representative unions.

"The conciliation wing will consist of a conciliation officer with the prescribed qualifications and status.

"The functions relating to certification of unions will rest with a separate wing of the National/State IRC.

"The Commission may provide arbitrators from among its members/officers, in case parties agree to avail of such services.

"All collective agreements should be registered with the IRC.

"An award made, by the IRC in respect of a dispute raised by recognized union should be binding on all workers in the establishment(s) and the employer(s)."

Labour Courts: The Commission recommended for—

1. The setting up of Labour Courts in each state. The strength and location of such courts is to be decided by the appropriate government.
2. Members of the Labour Court will be appointed by the government on the recommendation of the High Court.
3. Labour Courts will deal with the disputes relating to rights, obligations, interpretation and implementation of awards and claims arising under the relevant provisions of laws or agreements, as well as with disputes relating to unfair labour practices.
4. Labour Courts will thus be courts where all the disputes specified above will be tried and their decisions implemented. Proceedings instituted by parties asking for the enforcement of rights falling under the aforesaid categories will be entertained in that behalf.
5. Appeals over the decisions of the Labour Court in certain clearly defined matters may be with the High Court within whose jurisdiction/area the court is located.

APPENDIX III

Code of Discipline

Managements and Unions agree:

1. That no unilateral action should be taken in connection with any industrial matter and that disputes should be settled at an appropriate level
2. That the existing machinery for settlement of disputes should be utilized with the utmost expedition
3. That there should be no strike or lockout without notice
4. That affirming their faith in democratic principles, they bind themselves to settle all future differences, disputes, grievances by mutual negotiation, conciliation and voluntary arbitration
5. That neither party will have recourse to (a) coercion (b) intimidation (c) victimization or (d) go-slow
6. that they will promote constructive cooperation between their representatives at all levels and as between workers themselves that they will establish upon mutually agreed basis, a grievance procedure, which will ensure a speedy and full investigation leading to settlement
7. That they will promote constructive cooperation between their representatives at all levels and as between workers themselves and abide by the spirit of agreements mutually entered into
8. That they will establish upon mutually agreed basis, a grievance procedure, which will ensure a speedy and full investigation leading to settlement
9. That they will abide by various stages in the grievance procedure and take no arbitrary action, which would bypass this procedure
10. That they will educate the management personnel and workers regarding their obligations to each other

Managements agree:

1. Not to increase workloads unless agreed upon or settled otherwise
2. Not to support or encourage any unfair labour practice such as (a) interference with the right of employees to enrol or continue as union members (b) discrimination,

restraint, or coercion against any employees because of recognized activity of trade unions and (c) victimization of any employee and abuse of authority in any form

3. To take prompt action for (a) settlement of grievances and (b) implementation of settlements, awards, decisions and orders
4. To display in conspicuous places in the undertaking the provisions of this code in the local language(s)
5. To distinguish between actions justifying immediate discharge and those where discharge must be preceded by a warning, reprimand, suspension or some other form of disciplinary action, and to arrange that all such disciplinary action should be subject of an appeal through normal grievance procedure
6. To take appropriate disciplinary action against its officers and members in cases where enquiries reveal that they were responsible for precipitate action by workers leading to indiscipline
7. To recognize the union in accordance with the criteria (Annexure I) evolved at the 16th Session of the Indian Labour Conference in May 1958.

Unions agree:

1. Not to engage in any form of physical duress
2. Not to permit demonstrations, which are not peaceful and not to permit rowdyism in demonstrations
3. That their members will not engage or cause other employees to engage in any union activity during working hours, unless as provided for by law, agreement or practice
4. To discourage unfair labour practices such as (a) negligence of duty (b) careless operation (c) damage to property (d) interference with or disturbance to normal work and (e) insubordination
5. To take prompt action to implement awards, agreements, settlements and decisions
6. to display in conspicuous places in the union offices, the provisions of this code in the local languages, and
7. to express disapproval and to take appropriate action against office bearers and members for indulging in action against the spirit of this code

chapter three

CHAPTER OUTLINE

LEARNING OBJECTIVES

After reading this chapter, you should be able to:

- Understand the complexities in comparing the IR systems across countries
- Design a framework for a meaningful comparison of IR systems in major economies of the world
- Identify the international trends in industrial relations

National Steel Limited

National Steel Limited is the flagship company of the National Group—an industrial conglomerate with diverse interests. With around 20,000 employees, it is seen as one of the best employers in the country. It enjoys an unblemished record in having a distinctive culture and maintaining industrial peace. National Steel, with a plant in Jharkhand that has the capacity to produce 5 million tonnes of steel per annum, is the lowest-cost steel producer in the world, up to the crude steel stage. It has around 20 per cent of the domestic market share in products such as coils, bars, merchant products and structurals. It has recently started supplying sheets to the automobile sector but weak R&D has prevented it from accessing the high-end international market. Currently ranked as the 52nd largest steel producer in the world, National is looking to sufficiently grow through acquisitions so as to feature in the global top ten. To do so successfully, it will have to add an additional capacity of around 20 million tonnes. National wants to add this excess capacity within India (closer to the raw-material source) for crude-steel production, and procure finishing mills closer to the global high-end markets (Europe and North America).

National has located a reputed steel group in Europe with a sizeable presence in the North American and European markets. Though National, conscious of its corporate image and its contribution to the brand value, does not intend to tarnish its image, yet, it wants to leverage this advantage in global acquisitions. However, to maintain cost advantage and maximize the synergy of the two companies, issues such as manpower rationalization, rotation, and systematic people development have to be considered before making a decision. The whole range of regulatory bodies, trade unions, wage policy, etc. may be quite different in the EU than in India.

Raman Seth is the head of corporate HR of the National Group and also a part of the core group that has been constituted to make an in-depth study on the proposed acquisition. Raman must plan well in advance and give his inputs well before the bidding process starts. Till now, he had no reasons to learn about employee- and employment-related issues outside India.

Industrial Relations in Major Industrialized Economies: A Comparative Study

The formulation of labour-management relations policy is one of the significant tasks at the national level, and its successful formulation and implementation can influence the labour-relations climate at the industry and enterprise levels. Such policy formulation is generally done at the national level and is, thus, influenced by the socio-economic and political climate of the country and also practices adopted by neighbouring countries. However, the effectiveness of the industrial relations system is dependent largely on the respective strengths of the employers' and the workers' organizations.

As India Inc. globalizes, issues that face Raman Seth become common. Indian managers are expected to be nimble on their feet as they modernize, acquire and expand. The world is fast becoming their playground. HR-related issues are one of the defining factors that determine the success or the failure of mergers and acquisitions. The cultural assimilation of two diverse populations to derive synergies require sensitive appreciation of how the different industrial systems have evolved, what the driving forces are and where they are heading. It would be useful to take a look at one aspect of the industrial systems, that is, industrial relations system, and how they have shaped up in a few representative economies of the world.

The need to understand and appreciate differences in perspective and approach to industrial relations in different countries emerges from the internationalization of business. It is a difficult task to compare industrial relations systems, structure and processes across countries since there is no framework for such comparison. Unlike other functional areas such as production, marketing or accounting standards, the area of industrial relations is woven into the socio-political, cultural and economic fabric of a nation. From a purely practical point of view, setting up a unit in another country may require a relationship and a structure completely different from what obtains in the home country, unlike operations or production systems. There are appreciable differences in concepts and context across nations. The labour legislations may be completely different and so may be the structure of trade unions.

A framework for such comparison, therefore, may be necessary. For the purpose of this chapter, we may take a look at a few industrialized economies and examine the industrial relations with particular reference to: evolution, trade unions, collective bargaining and legislations.

3.1 Industrial Relations: A Historical Perspective

At its inception, the management of industrial relations emphasized the economic perspective, labour being a factor of production and the employment terms predominated by demand-and-supply economics. The classical-economics view predominated the labour–management relationship, advocating free and unregulated labour markets. As discussed in Chapter 1, the laissez-faire approach led to an exploitative regime as far as capital's treatment of labour was concerned. Industrial relations, therefore, initially took on a regulatory role to correct this unequal bargaining power. Subsequently, industrial relations broadened its scope taking on a protectionist role, addressing the problems that came to the fore during the laissez-faire phase. The laissez- faire essentially resulted in complete one-sidedness of a power relationship between the employers and the employees, almost always loaded against the employee because of market imperfections. With external factors and market imperfections coming into focus, State intervention had to be initiated to address these issues. Legislations to protect the rights of the employees and an institutional mechanism to handle conflicts were the products of this phase. The employees organized themselves into trade unions and fought for legitimization of the same, thus restoring some balance in the power equation between the employers and the employees. The right to associate was an important one and was duly recognized as such, thus providing a major force in shaping the trend of industrial relations. With this emerged the bargaining role of the industrial relations system and the demarcation of the role of the State, the employers and the employee organizations/ trade unions.

State intervention brought the focus of industrial relations outside the industrial enterprise through bargaining at a pan-industry level and sometimes even on the national level. To a large extent, labour ceased to be a factor of production that could give competitive advantage on account of cost differential. Conflicts moved out of the workplace and, hence, State intervention was welcomed by the employers. Unions got the advantage of an influential base outside the workplace. This, however, led to the politicization of industrial relations in general and trade unions in particular.

The State intervention and the labour-related regulations, however, failed to address labour-related problems such as low productivity, absenteeism, attrition, employment security, working conditions in terms of safety and occupational health. The above concerns led to the emergence of the human-resource-management perspective in the 1980s; that it is not factors external to the enterprise, but ineffective human-resources strategies, policies and practices that create labour problems. With the pressure on enterprises to adapt and change, employers started concentrating on issues at the enterprise level.

3.1.1 The International Factors

A major thrust for all parties to IR is to establish a robust system of IR so as to ensure economic and social imperatives. To do so, a few contemporary issues have to be taken into account by the actors of an IR system so as to factor these in, while trying to arrive at that robust system.

> Sound labour relations are built up from within an organization. The environment external to the enterprise is and should be facilitative, or "protective" in terms of prescribing basic standards and norms relating to areas like social security, safety and health, freedom of association, weekly and other holidays and rest periods, etc.

- The globalization of business and the resultant competition, changes in technologies, scales of operation and the widening of markets are forcing all enterprises to cut flab and become nimble. All factors of production have ceased to be the source of permanent competitive advantage. It is the competence of the employees, and their motivation and involvement on which the enterprise has to rely for a sustainable competitive advantage.
- Information technology has had and is having a huge impact on organization structures, work processes, working conditions, geographical spread, the nature of supervision, communications, performance measurement, compensation strategies and the management of people. The demographic profile of workers has also changed with greater women and older worker's participation.
- The restructuring of industrial enterprises and business organizations is taking place across a majority of countries as they adapt to the forces unleashed by globalization. In many cases, this has resulted in situations that have a big impact on industrial relations and socio-political fronts. Privatization and divestment of State-owned companies have resulted in redundancies that cause a strained relationship amongst the actors of IR.
- Another feature is the changes occurring in the workforces, to varying degrees, in both industrialized market economies and developing economies. The new worker/ employee, by and large, is better educated and is different in outlook when compared to his blue-collared predecessor. And this proportion is rising, which means a complete change in the approach to managing this lot. Knowledge economies and an increasing

service sector (comprising almost 55 per cent in India) will see a complete shift in employee profile. Perhaps, the skill and knowledge of an employee may be one area where the interests of all actors merge leading to an increasing shift towards participative management and employee involvement, both in development and production.

- With the emphasis on cost efficiency and product quality, more and more of non-core activities may get outsourced to those who specialize in some non-core aspect of work. There may be different sub-groups of employees to be managed. The era of "one consolidated workforce" may be a thing of the past.
- The role of unions is changing. The unions seem to be in disarray, trying to define a role in the changing environment. Unionization is on a decline and they have not yet adapted themselves to the new realities of fundamental shifts in the work and business environment. In the interim, there is a growing realization that, perhaps, the employees, too, need to lend a hand in competency development for sustained advantage and survival. However, there are many issues on which they may have formulated a position but not the wherewithal to forge ahead; for example, collectively challenging the issues facing the knowledge and service workers, outsourcing, etc. And, maybe, there is a growing a realization that their contribution may be more effective in managing workplace relations.

The main factors driving changes in industrial relations are:

- Increasingly competitive environments caused by the integration of world markets
- The direction of the change towards decentralization of bargaining
- A movement towards increased flexibility in wages, labour deployment, and workplace practices

Judging from the attention paid by researchers, it would seem that the 1980s and the 1990s were periods of change, turmoil, and even transformation in industrial relations systems all over the world. Researchers, by and large, agree that factors driving these changes are:

- Increasingly competitive environments caused by the integration of world markets
- The direction of the change: decentralization of bargaining, and a movement towards increased flexibility in wages and labour deployment at the workplace level

The changing perspective of IR may be attributed to:

- The internationalization of business, intense competition and rapid changes in technology, products and markets
- Information technology, and its impact on the structure of organizations, the nature of work and the way it is organized
- The changing workforce profile
- The tendency towards outsourcing
- The changing role of unions

Relatively less attention has been paid to how industrial relations systems have changed in the developing nations of Asia. Given that countries have seen considerable changes in their industrial relations systems, we need to understand the nature of these changes.

3.1.2 The Political Factors

Labour Relations, by most governments, were viewed as a means to prevent workplace conflicts or to contain such conflicts so that the production doesn't suffer and consequences of conflict don't spill over to the other domains of political-social-economic realms. In the South and Southeast Asian countries, this was largely achieved through the creation of dispute-settlement and conflict-resolution machineries established by the government, that is, outside the purview of the workplace alone. In a few industrialized economies of the West, the employer–employee relationships were largely controlled through enactments and legislations. The objective of the State in industrial relations in Asian countries was keep a control on the freedom of the employer for such actions that may affect employment, especially termination, closures, dismissals. At the same time, they also resorted to restrict trade-union action and control unions, to keep proliferation of unions in control. The Asian countries emphasized efficiency; and the protection of employment was subservient to this overall objective. The cultural factors represented by a strong hierarchical structure, paternalistic management systems, respect for authority were hindrances to a negotiation and communication, based on equality, between the employers and the employees. Japan, however, maintained a different culture of workplace flexibility, strong enterprise identity and enterprise unions. Australia and New Zealand, on the other hand, had centralized IR models, but things are changing now even there.

The industrial relations systems in a few countries are discussed in the next sections. The historical evolution of industrial relations system primarily originated from Britain and, hence, has been elaborated in detail. The framework for comparison mainly comprises trade unionism, the role of employer organizations and the legislative framework.

3.2 Industrial Relations in the UK

Britain was the first country to industrialize and also the first country to set up industrial relations institutions. The history of IR in Britain has been eventful, and it is necessary to discuss this evolution, especially in the twentieth century, in some detail.

3.2.1 The Evolution

Britain is regarded as the place where modern industrial relations came into existence and matured. Any serious study of industrial relations will remain incomplete (and may not even make sense), unless one has some appreciation of the developments during the years of industrialization and the years following it in Great Britain.

PRIOR TO 1990. During the early part of the twentieth century, the IR was largely shaped around the challenges of the staple industry, with the twin concerns of containing industrial conflict because of wages and also with a view to regulating the industry because of intense competition. This resulted in an industry-level collective bargaining to take care of the twin problems. The next major change was ushered in the time after the World War, when the concern was an increased productivity in a war-ravaged economy as well as new capital-intensive technology. The lack of firm-level bargaining was acutely felt, and increasingly, it was pointed out that due to this lack, there was little scope for firms to take measures for improvement in productivity and introduce changes or/and reorganize changes in work. This concern was articulated by the Donovan Commission that submitted its report in 1968 mainly saying that the trade unions and the employers' organizations were so focused on industry-level bargaining that not enough resource and attention was being paid at the firm level, where most of the changes were to take place. There was little control over the unionized employees and also an absence of institutions for regulating, at the firm level. The legislative measures based on the recommendations could not be pushed through due to large-scale protests. It was only in 1974 when, gradually, reforms to introduce discussions at the firm level were introduced. The main provisions were:

> There is a balance of social power in the workplace, a largely unitarist view of industrial relations, and, most fundamentally, an emphasis upon individual rather than collective regulation of social relations.

i) A statutory right to trade-union recognition

ii) Workers were granted a set of individual rights designed to encourage and improve collective bargaining, including funding for shop-steward training, time off for shop stewards, and rights to information and consultation

iii) A new form of extension procedure was created, which permitted trade unions to use legislation to drive the employers to the bargaining table and grant them recognition

> **Post-1979**
>
> With the collapse of the institutions of collective regulation, there was a shift in the balance of class power in Britain, with the shrinking of trade unionism. The autonomous strength of British trade unionism was overcome by a combination of the scale and the scope of State activism and legislations and also the willingness of governments to endure industrial conflict.

This resulted in facilitating decentralized bargaining and a proliferation of bargaining into industries and firms hitherto unexplored. However, instead of promoting peace, the reforms plunged Britain into an era of widespread industrial conflict, threatening to affect competitiveness of the UK and also affecting its economic power. The unions, at most places, brought the management to its knees.

The era of "Thatcherism" (which largely implied actions based on Margaret Thatcher's political and economic philosophy of reduced State intervention, free markets, and entrepreneurialism) and the Employment Relations Act (1979) were reactions to the era of industrial chaos and strong-arm tactics of the trade unions. The above Act made revisions in the trade-union recognition and modified/removed a number of other rights. The thrust of the government was to restore a balance in the relationship through taming the unions. Recession in the early 1990s further weakened the trade unions, thus paving the way for a fundamental restructuring of the industrial relations. There has been a sharp decline in trade unionism since then. A new individualized kind of relationship has emerged where a large proportion of workers are not members of any trade union and are not covered under collective bargaining.

RECENT CHANGES. There have been a few changes to protect the rights of the workers, including regulations on minimum wages, working hours, more protection against unfair termination, rights for working women, etc., but the emphasis remains towards weakening collectivism in the management of industrial relations. The regulation of the labour market has taken the form of individual legal rights, enforceable through labour courts and State agencies, not collective rights designed to strengthen trade unions, which could then take on the role of regulating social relations through collective bargaining.

Thatcherism

Margaret Thatcher's political and economic philosophy of reduced State intervention, free markets, and entrepreneurialism

3.2.2 Trade Unions in the UK

Three characteristics distinguish the British industrial relations system. First and foremost is the tradition of voluntarism. The second feature is the representation of workers through trade-union officers at workplaces in the form of shop stewards. Shop stewards are members who occupy an official position in the union hierarchy and who are also employees of an organization. Third, the organization of trade union-membership is on occupational rather than industrial lines. So, there is a "formal system", originating from institutions created through the agency of the State and the other is the informal system created by actual behaviour of trade unions and employers' associations, managers, shop stewards and workers. The formal and informal systems are generally in conflict, as the informal system undermines the regulative effect of industry-wide agreements. The formal system, however, still exerts a powerful influence in the industrial climate of the UK.

The trade unions function with a focus on primarily three sets of objectives:

i) Maintaining and improving wages, hours and conditions of work, and also what wages can buy, increasing the size of real and net income and the share accruable to the working class

ii) Providing and improving opportunities for the advancement of the workers for full employment

The three distinctive characteristics of trade unions in Britain:

- The tradition of voluntarism
- The representation of workers through trade-union officers at workplaces in the form of shop stewards
- The organization of trade-union membership being on occupational rather than industrial lines

Shop Stewards

Shop stewards are members who occupy an official position in the union hierarchy and who are also employees of an organization.

BOX 3.1 **FOR CLASS DISCUSSION**

The "It's About Time" Campaign aims to put long hours and work–life balance at the top of the workplace agenda. It builds on the growing evidence of long hours, greater pressure at work, and the need to introduce more flexibility to UK workplaces.

The EU Working Time Directive sets a 48-hour average limit to the working week. The UK introduced the directive in 1998, but secured an opt-out for certain workers and industries. The European Parliament wants the UK to be compelled by the European Commission to "come into line" with the rest of Europe.

In 2002, the Department for Trade and Industry (DTI) found that twice as many UK employees would rather work shorter hours than win the lottery. The 2003 Labour Force Survey (LFS) found that 4,000,000 people work more than 48 hours a week on an average. That is 700,000 more than in 1992, when there was no long-hour's protection. A TUC (Trade Union Congress, an umbrella organization comprising a federation of trade unions in the UK) poll in 2003 found that only one in three people at work know that there is a 48-hour average working-week limit. The 2003 TUC survey found that one in three of those who have signed an opt-out say they were given no choice. Nearly two out of three people who say they work regularly for more than 48 hours a week say they have not been asked to opt out of the working-time regulations. The TUC believes that either the law is being ignored, or the loopholes and exceptions are so great that few workers enjoy protection.

In what way do you think the unions have changed their approach? What could be the factors responsible for this change in approach?

Source: http://www.bized.co.uk/compfact/tuc/tuc19.htm

iii) Extending the influence of the working class over the industry and arranging for their participation in management

The trade unions of Britain, not only defend or improve the wages and conditions of labour, but also raise the status of the workers in the industry and society. They extend the area of social control of the nation's economic life. Trade unions in England have provided benefits for themselves and have also worked for the development of social services in the State. They recognize the needs of individuals and are, to a large extent, taking responsibility for the whole community. Read and discuss the issue raised in Box 3.1.

3.3 Industrial Relations in the European Union

For the purpose of industrial relations, the European Union cannot be considered as an integrated whole as of today and the traditional framework for studying IR may not be applicable. Nevertheless, as the efforts to integrate are on, at this point of time, we may take a look at the important institutions, laws and trade unions as obtains in member countries. The European Commission has been attempting a pooling of research on the IR structures, processes, laws and practices in member countries with a view to bring in gradual uniformity on larger policy matters pertaining to industrial relations, but it is early days yet.

3.3.1 The Trends in the EU

In this section, we identify a few trends across the member States[1]

Trade Unions:

- Unions in most of the member countries are organized on a sectoral or occupational basis.
- Blue-collar unions are losing influence and the white-collar unions gaining significance.
- In most countries, there is more than one peak organization or confederation, with divisions on occupational, religious or political lines.
- Large differences in trade-union density—the ratio of actual to potential membership—continue to exist between the member States, ranging from 80 per cent in Denmark to 8 per cent in France.
- The density rate is high in the Nordic countries, while Spain, France and most of the new Central and Eastern European member States have comparatively low rates.
- The overall weighted-average-density rate in the EU is now between 25 per cent and 30 per cent of wage earners, and the trend in union density is clearly downward across Europe.
- Most of the EU member states experienced a fall in density over the period from 1995 to 2004, with unions in Central and Eastern Europe facing dramatic membership losses.

Collective Bargaining:

- Collective bargaining, almost across all the member States, has moved towards decentralization, although wide variations exist in practice.
- For example, in Spain, works councils operate with a clear mandate and sign 74 per cent of plant agreements.
- In Austria, commentators observe "organized decentralization", a phenomenon linked to "delegation" or "opening" clauses, enabling some flexibility on certain economic and working conditions.

Workplace Representation:

- Workplace representation has been legally established and formally installed in most of the EU countries and is a distinctive feature of the EU industrial relations system.
- There is, however, a great range of forms of representation, reflecting the specific characteristics of industrial relations in particular countries.
- The most significant European legislation on workplace representation is the framework directive of the minimum standards for informing and consulting employees at the company level in all the member States (Directive 2002/14). However, the directive is drafted in very broad terms, leaving considerable scope for individual States to implement its terms. Thus, it creates a general framework for informing and consulting employees, without harmonizing representation.

Despite the variations, there appears to be a conscious effort to build a pan-European framework on industrial relations. Regular exchanges of reports and research at the commission level have been taking place over the past few years and have resulted in a few directives for the constituents. Therefore, despite this diversity in country-specific practices in TUs, collective bargaining and employee representation, there is a progressive unity and coherence at the European level. The European Trade Union Confederation (ETUC) brings together virtually all major confederations and centres in the current member States (with a number of gaps in coverage filled in recent years). Also affiliated to ETUC are major European-industry federations, grouping almost all major EU trade unions in their respective sectors, along with many from the new member States.

There is a distinct movement towards trade-union organization at the pan-EU level. Though some diversity prevails at national levels, efforts are on at some sort of integration. The ETUC is a step in that direction.

3.4 Industrial Relations in the USA

3.4.1 Trade Unions in the USA

Industrial relations in the USA parallels the development of trade unions, organized labour and labour legislations, as it does elsewhere. The first major landmark in the history of modern US industrial relations was the founding of the American Federation of Labour (AFL) by Samuel Gompers in the year 1886. The AFL, at its time during the late nineteenth and the early twentieth century, was the largest federation of unions in the USA. It was organized on the basis of "craft unions" and was conservative in approach in as much as it did not challenge "capitalism" but was more concerned with the bread and butter issues of workers, such as improvements in the working conditions. Being basically an association of crafts-based unions, AFL failed to prevent dissension in ranks when it could not organize itself into industrial unions, when important sectors like auto, steel, etc. started growing. The Congress of Industrial Organizations (CIO) was another federation formed in 1935 and took the industrial-union approach, mostly comprising dissenters from the AFL. Both unions saw growth during the years when the economy was slack and competed with each other, sometimes violently. The CIO, in 1955, merged with the AFL to form AFL-CIO.

Today, approximately 60 unions in the USA and Canada are affiliated with the AFL-CIO (American Federation of Labour-Congress of Industrial Organizations) and it represents close to 10 million employees. The AFL-CIO has little direct control over the affairs of its members. Rather, it works as an umbrella organization for trade unions at the policy level.

Craft Unions

Craft union refers to organizing a union in a manner that seeks to unify workers along the lines of the particular craft or trade that they work in.

AFL-CIO

The American Federation of Labour and Congress of Industrial Organizations, commonly known as the AFL-CIO, is a national trade-union centre. It is the largest federation of unions in the United States. It was formed in 1955 with the merger of two large federations named AFL and CIO.

- The AFL was the first Federation of Trade Unions in the USA.
- The AFL promoted the craft-union strategy and generally saw its role within a capitalist philosophy.
- The CIO was formed later, in the 1930s, and followed an industrial-union pattern.

3.4.2 Labour Legislations in the USA

The first major piece of legislation pertaining to labour relations was the Norris La Guardia Act, 1932. Prior to this Act, employers were not required to enter the collective bargaining process, had free hand in hiring and firing, and enforcing unfair employment contracts. One such unfair condition was forcing an undertaking from employees of not joining a union as a precondition to employment. These employment contracts were known as "yellow dog

The major pieces of labour legislation governing the relationship issues were:

- The Norris La Guardia Act, 1932
- The Wagner Act, 1935
- The Taft Hartley Act, 1947
- The Landrum Griffin Act, 1959

contracts". The Norris La Guardia Act (1932) made these contracts illegal, thus allowing employees to form and join unions. This was followed by the National Labour Relations Act (1935), also known as the Wagner Act, which provided for the employees:

1. Protection of their rights to organize
2. The right to engage in collective bargaining and
3. The right to strike in furtherance of their demands
4. Striking of certain unfair labour practices by employers as illegal
5. Secret ballot elections for representative unions
6. The creation of National Relations Board for enforcing certain provisions of the Act

These two Acts gave fillip to the unions, and their activities increased both under the AFL and the CIO. The balance of power shifted towards the unions and this period (till 1947) witnessed an increase in strikes and pressure tactics by the unions.

The Taft Hartley Act of 1947, also known as the Labour-Management Relations Act, put curbs on the activities of the unions in order to restore a balance in the relationship between the management and the workers. The significant provisions included:

- The addition of a list comprising "unfair labour practices" on the part of the employees' union
- The prohibition of certain kinds of strikes and industrial action on the part of the union, e.g., wildcat strikes
- The prohibition of "closed shop" and severe restriction on "union shops"
- The injunction on strikes affecting national health or safety

The Landrum Griffin Act of 1959 aimed at protecting the union members from possible wrong-doing and also empowering the members to terminate the right of the union to represent through decertification elections.

While the Wagner Act and the Taft Hartley Act concern the workers and the unions in the private sector, the provisions on the same have been extended to the government employees through the Executive Orders and also the Civil Services Reform Act.

3.5 Industrial Relations in Australia

Just as in India, both the federal and the state governments can legislate on labour matters. Though the federal law, in order of precedence, is at a higher level, even the state laws and systems have a significant influence on most matters relating to industrial relations. The federal system is largely based on conciliation and arbitration. An important institution that plays a role in IR in Australia is the Industrial Tribunal as a compulsory third-party arbitration in matters involving disputes and conditions of employment.

3.5.1 The Evolution

The oldest piece of legislation in Australia is the Conciliation and Arbitration Act, 1904. This Act has seen many amendments over the years. The principal aim of arbitration was to prevent any form of industrial action. The matters of dispute could be referred to a court for settlement or award through arbitration, which would be binding. The Act also encouraged the employers to recognize a representative union. By and large, the State has intervened consistently and vigorously in matters pertaining to IR in Australia. The Conciliation and Arbitration Act, 1904, was replaced by the Industrial Relations Act, 1988. The IR Act, 1988, required the federal trade unions to register themselves with a registrar to be able to take assistance of the arbitration process and other legal rights flowing from the Act.

3.5.2 The Recent Changes

There has been a change in the IR framework in Australia with a distinct movement towards decentralization and encouragement for the employers and the employees to settle at the enterprise level without third-party intervention. The most significant instrument of the workplace-relationship-reform process was the Workplace Relations Act 1996 (WR Act) with the objective to the settlement of conflicts and disputes at the workplace itself. The government itself intervenes only in settling issues like minimum wages and working conditions, but other matters pertaining to wages and working conditions are left to the parties to settle between themselves. Another feature is the freedom to negotiate collectively or to arrive at the Australian Workplace Agreement (AWA) that permits agreement between the employer and a single employee through a bargaining agent of choice. The freedom of association (including a choice not to associate) has also been provided in the Act.

3.5.3 Trade Unions in Australia

There is only one major trade union federation in Australia, The Australasian Council of Trade Unions (ACTU). Formed in 1927, it was an attempt to consolidate the unions into one big body. However, the objective of ACTU has not been fully met since, instead of becoming one coherent whole, it remains a lose collection of trade-union organizations. It represents a majority of trade unions, but not all. The ACTU was primarily a union of blue-collar employees, and subsequently, the white-collar and government employees have mainly been covered under bodies that emerged later. The ACTU has a close relationship with the Labour Party.

The trend now is towards amalgamation into larger unions. The number of unions with smaller numbers (1,000 and below) has decreased, whereas, those with larger numbers (50,000 or more) have increased their percentage of total union membership.

BOX 3.2 **FOR CLASS DISCUSSION**

The Australian government is bringing about reforms in the area of workplace relations continuously since 1996. The extract below is the latest in a series of such proposed reforms. Discuss the reasons that you think are behind these changes and how it would impact business and the employees. You may also discuss the similarities and differences with the provisions that obtain in India.

A New Workplace Relations System

The Australian government began to develop a new workplace relations system with the introduction of its transitional reform measures in March 2008. These measures initiated the award modernization process and removed the power to make new Australian Workplace Agreements (AWAs).

The government was drafting a new legislation, which was expected to be introduced into the parliament in late 2008, enabling the commencement of a simpler, fairer and more flexible workplace relations system by the start of 2010.

The key elements of the government's new workplace relations system were:

- Collective enterprise bargaining, with no provision for statutory individual agreements
- A safety net of legislated minimum employment standards and modern awards
- The right to freedom of association and genuine workplace representation
- Grievance-and-dispute-settlement procedures and freedom from discrimination
- A new independent umpire—Fair Work Australia
- Balanced laws that provide protection from unfair dismissal in a way which addresses the particular circumstances and concerns of small businesses
- A uniform national workplace relations system for the private sector

---

Source: Australian Government: Department of Foreign Affairs and Trade; http://www.dfat.gov.au/facts/workplace_relations.html.

3.6 Industrial Relations in China

3.6.1 The Historical Perspective

China's industrial relations system is deeply entrenched with its economic and political organization. The All-China Federation of Trade Unions was set up as early as 1925; its incorporation into the Chinese communist party defined the labour movement's role within a State-dominated, import-substitution industrialization policy in a centrally planned closed economy[2]. The main characteristics of the system included State ownership of industrial enterprises, the implicit guarantee of employment for workers, centralized wage structure, a rigid labour market with little inter-enterprise or inter-regional mobility, and the absence of price- or efficiency-driven controls over the industry. Thus, employment was permanent, and the enterprise was responsible for the provision of housing, and for all welfare, medical, and retirement benefits, as well as for social and entertainment needs. Thus, the enterprise shouldered the responsibility for national social security. A sense of identity for the industrial worker was based on cradle-to-grave welfare benefits. The term "iron rice bowl" is used to describe this inclusive IR system. Within this system, industrial relations consisted of a dualistic structure of co-determination.

PRIOR TO 1990. The combination of administrative labour allocation and the "iron rice bowl" produced a rigid and inflexible system within the enterprise, and outside as well. The absence of numerical flexibility was further reinforced by the absence of labour mobility, given the household registration system (which only permitted workers to be permanently employed in their area of residence). The objectives of industrial relations policy were to support the economic and social structure that communism built, through mobilization of the mass of workers behind economic policies. However, it needs to be noted that trade unions rights and roles were banned during the Cultural Revolution (restored under the modernization period of Deng. By and large, however, the need for flexibility in the IR system was absent, given the absence of competitive pressures in the system.

THE RECENT CHANGES. The Chinese industrial relations system has been in considerable ferment since the opening up of the Chinese economy post-1978, and, in particular, post-1983. Decentralization in the State sector implied changes in industrial relations and human-resource practices, with new practices that are increasingly focused on getting a higher degree of numerical and functional flexibility. The contract system emerged to replace the lifetime employment system. The joint ventures brought with them flexible IR and HR practices from abroad. Further, as part of these reforms, the Chinese government enacted a new labour law in 1994 that essentially sought to create a new industrial relations system within the socialist market economy, but the implementation of this law has not been uniform. In terms of industrial relations legislation, the government's focus in the foreign-investment sector is to keep basic labour protection and welfare laws as similar as possible to the State-owned sector.

The industrial relations system in China is struggling to adapt to the fundamental economic changes post-1978. From a rigid system in the pre-1978 era to the gradual adjustment to global practices has left the system in a state of flux.

3.6.2 Trade Unions in China

The trade union constitution's preamble states the role of the union rather clearly: "The Trade Unions of China are the mass organization of the working class led by the party and are the transmission belts between the party and the masses"[3]. Therefore, although the unions played a variety of economic and political roles, their role as a communication channel between the party and workers was the most central. The trade union focused on day-to-day shop-floor problems, educating the workers, ensuring the success of the enterprise, and ensuring that the management of the enterprise did not exploit workers. They dealt with matters such as grievances and decisions regarding social activities. Workers congresses (composed of representatives of workers) met about four times a year and had the responsibility for decisions on enterprise funds for welfare activities, changes in organizational structure and payment systems, and the election of the enterprise director and other key management personnel.

3.7 Industrial Relations in Japan

The Japanese industrial relations system is an institutionalized one and has historically included workplace-focused enterprise unions, lifetime-employment systems, broad-based training, and seniority-based wages. One of the key outcomes of the Japanese IR system, when examined in conjunction with related Japanese institutions such as the keiretsu system and the system of production organization (sub-contracting and quality-focused, team-based work) is the simultaneous achievement of stability in labour-market terms and considerable functional flexibility in workplace-level industrial relations through the development of internal labour markets.

3.7.1 The Historical Perspective

PRIOR TO THE 1990S. The institutionalization of the Japanese industrial relations system can be assumed to have originated as early as the late 1800s in the silk industry where employers, forced to compete for scarce labour, instituted lifetime employment to create stable employment conditions. However, it was the large-scale conflict between labour and capital in the early post-war years, partly in response to many workers being made redundant as the war industries shut down coupled with the revolution in production management, that encouraged the institutionalization of lifetime-employment practice in the Japanese industry. The institutional structures that provided stable internal labour markets also provided Japanese employers a high degree of functional flexibility in the use of human resources, as lifetime employment, firm specific training, and enterprise-based unionism became widespread. Thus, the Japanese industrial environment became characterized by highly functionally flexible IR systems within firms, in a context of a fair degree of rigidity in the labour market. The development of internal labour markets and lifetime-employment systems created a highly segmented labour force, with little inter-segment mobility.

The concept of lifetime employment is changing in Japan too. Globalization has had its impact on many employment-related practices, for example, hiring practices, limited-term employment, employment contracts and outsourcing. Japan is no exception.

THE RECENT CHANGES. The recession of the 1990s led to the questioning of the lifetime-employment concept, with severe declines in job security on an unprecedented scale. Changes were seen in the hiring practices with a dramatic increase in outsourcing strategies, the introduction of limited-term-employment contracts for some occupations, increased wage flexibility, and some degree of union restructuring. These changes suggested a gradual adaptation of the economic circumstances. There was evidence of a sudden and dramatic increase in outsourcing within Japan, termed "work commissioning". This resulted in an increase in wage flexibility, resulting in reducing the power of the trade unions.

3.7.2 Trade Unions in Japan

Trade Unions in Japan are mostly organized at the enterprise level. These enterprise unions, in turn, are affiliated to a federation of unions relevant to the same industry. The third level is the organization of such federations into a national confederation. Apart from this, there are two other independent federations covering respectively metallurgy, and chemical and energy sectors.

Enterprise unions are mostly autonomous. One of the two major federations in Japan, based on size, is Japanese Trade Union Confederation (Rengo). It was a result of efforts at restructuring the federations that were in existence then. Rengo was formed

Industry Union

In this form of organization, the workers in the same industry are organized into the same union, irrespective of their skills.

in 1987 after efforts of several years starting 1982. It covers round about 65 per cent of unionized workers. The initial membership of Rengo was 5.6 million, mostly comprising employees from the private sector. Later, in 1989, many public-sector units joined Rengo. The second confederation, the National Confederation of Trade Unions (Zenroren), represents only around 9 per cent of all unionized workers. Although reorganizations within the federations are going on, the overall membership of unions has been steadily declining.

COLLECTIVE BARGAINING. As seen in the above paragraph, in Japan, the unions are organized at enterprise, industry and national levels. At present, there is no legislation in place that governs the process of collective bargaining in Japan. However, traditionally, it has been taking place at the enterprise level and has become a practice. Normally, most of the issues concerning working conditions, wages and personnel policies are discussed and negotiated at the enterprise level. However, the industry union, at its level, decides on a wage level to be negotiated, based on the best pay levels in the industry. The industry-level unions also take a more strategic role in deciding the overall industry-level targets on wages, industrial action plan, etc. so as to strengthen the collective bargaining strength. In an indirect way, this helped in maintaining a kind of industry-level parity across different enterprises. In recent years, however, with increasing competition and sluggish growth, the unions have not been very successful in maintaining parity as the wage increase is dependent on the performance of the individual enterprise.

3.8 Industrial Relations in South Korea

3.8.1 The Historical Perspective

The Korean industrial relations system evolved primarily after the 1953 legislation regarding trade unions after the war. The rights granted to trade unions, however, were revoked during the 1960s period and thereafter. During the 1945–1960 period, workplace industrial relations in the major conglomerates known as the "chaebol" was closely modelled on the Japanese system, and were either paternalistic or authoritarian. The primary characteristics of the system were paternalistic where the interests of the State and the employer were assumed to also take care of the interests of the workers. This was aimed towards the prevention of industrial conflict that might threaten the prosperity of the chaebol and, thus, economic development. The State also mandated labour-management councils in every enterprise, introduced tripartite commissions at provincial (district) levels to resolve disputes (these commissions grew out of the 1953 legislation), and promulgated laws that restricted direct action by labour.

PRIOR TO 1990. 1981 witnessed a change in economic-development strategy towards higher value-added exports, which resulted in more changes in industrial relations legislation. Legal changes mandated the formation of enterprise unions, although it was made mandatory for these enterprise unions to be a part of FKTU, a union confederation created under the mandate of the government. This ensured a kind of indirect control over the enterprise unions. Chaebols, thus, continued with the paternalistic management and the stated objective of conflict avoidance was achieved. Although there were some efforts to introduce some labour-protection laws and regulate vocational and skills training, the primary focus was political control of IR activity, i.e., stability. During this period, therefore, conflict prevention and conflict avoidance became the stated objective, and all actions purported to achieve that as part of the overall goal of maintaining stability in industrial relations for economic development (e.g., in particular, the government's efforts to control wage costs), and political control.

THE RECENT CHANGES. With democratization in 1987, industrial relations legislation and practice have changed substantially. With the liberalization of labour law, the trade-union movement mushroomed, with a sharp increase in union density and strikes during the 1987–1989 periods.

The scope of bargaining expanded substantially, and trade unions, confronted with a management unused to collective bargaining, have been able to use their economic power to win substantial nominal wage increases Bargaining power, thus, appeared to be with the unions in the years immediately following democratization. Given the erosion of their competitive position, Korean chaebol reacted to the militant union demands by following a mixture of suppressive policies and progressive HR practices, although these practices were introduced by only some of the chaebol (e.g., LG promoting labour-management collaboration.). These changes happened in the early 1990s, despite the employers calling for the need to cut labour, given the increases in costs. The State initially tried to inject some wage moderation through the articulation of wage norms with little success, as different chaebols adopted different strategies of dealing with the union.

The erosion in competitive position in the mid-1990s saw the increase in Korean investment abroad in low-cost areas, particularly in Asia and Latin America. As Korean exports and profits started to decline during the 1994–1995 period, employers began to step up their demands for industrial relations restructuring, to make workplaces more flexible, and to get rid of the implicit lifetime-employment contract (or norm) that existed in the large chaebol. The diversity of employer strategies increased as they sought to restructure IR and HR. The government in 1996 introduced a few labour reforms to tackle union militancy. It allowed union participation in politics and multiple unions; no new federation was to be recognized till the year 2000. This increased the authority of the employers to lay off employees. These changes resulted in widespread labour agitation and strikes. In general, the nine years following democratization can be characterized as a period of experimentation and diversification in industrial relations practice and regulation.

From the paternalistic and totalitarian orientation during the dictatorship, South Korea experienced a greater need for participation by the employees. Competitive forces forced employers to demand restructuring in the IR system. The Asian Currency Crisis hastened the process for fundamental changes with tripartite involvement in the policy. The IR system in Korea is still in the transition phase, adapting to the global practices.

However, the Korean industrial relations continue to be in a period of transition, witnessing a lot of experimentation with institutions, and a high degree of diversity in practices. The transition to democracy in Korea coincided with, and to some extent hastened the need for, increased flexibility in industrial relations, as Korean competitiveness in several sectors eroded.

3.8.2 Trade Unions in South Korea

The early 1990s witnessed the breaking down of the hegemony of the FKTU, as new independent unions formed and some of them created the KCTU in opposition to the FKTU. In the late 1990s, however, there were several divisions in the unionized set up. On the one hand, some unions, notably those affiliated with the FKTU, advocated moderation, given the needs of Korean competitiveness, but the independent unions that started forming around 1991 and finally grew into the KCTU in 1995 (which was illegal and continued to be so until 1999), were not in agreement with the policies of the FKTU.

As a consequence of the 1997 legislation permitting the formation of new unions, the number of industrial unions is growing, even though industrial-level bargaining has been resisted by the employers. Clearly, however, numerical flexibility has become a key aim for the Korean employers, while job security has become a key goal of the Korean unions, during the decade of the 1990s.

3.9 Industrial Relations in Singapore

Singapore's industrial relations system is well known for its distinctive tripartite features, and is considered both functional and flexible. Upon adoption of its export-oriented industrialization programme, based on foreign investment in the 1960s, the focus of industrial relations policy in Singapore was to provide foreign investors with a "stable, cheap, and flexible industrial relations system". Low cost of labour was a big advantage in the 1960s, as was stability. The twin factors were to attract foreign investments initially. Carefully thought out institutional support were put in place so as to promote stability and industrial peace. A tripartite industrial relations structure with joint decision making on all aspects of economic and social development helped usher in an environment of stability. The State provided funds and training on development issues so as to lay the foundation for "responsible" unionism. To ensure that disputes did not result in strikes, the legislation provided for secret ballots on strikes, a notice period, and withdrawal of strikes once the dispute was under mediation or conciliation proceedings. An industrial arbitration court was established to deal with disputes not settled through discussions or mediation. Strikes were prohibited in industries deemed essential for economic development. To create stability in wage negotiations, the tripartite National Wages Council recommended standard wage increases across the industries. At the workplace level, a few contentious issues that impacted the operational flexibility and efficiency were kept out of the bargaining (transfers, promotions, termination, hiring, etc.). Besides reducing scope for disputes, this also provided to the employer flexibility and substantial control over the operational decisions. The State has been making continuous and focused efforts towards competence building of the working population through labour enactments and the setting up of institutions for the same.

3.10 International Trends

Globalization and free trade have witnessed three major industrialized hubs and economic powerhouses, namely, North America (USA), the European Union and Japan. These key regions have become kinds of benchmarks for industrial systems, including the industrial relations systems. Their economy, state of employment and social-development outcomes are key areas for benchmarking for the countries in other regions. Apart from nation-specific factors that shape the differences in industrial relations, there are forces such as globalization, industrial peace and the desire to protect employment and income that are common across geographies and economies. An interplay between these forces have thrown up a few distinctive trends:

Emerging International Trends in IR

- The decline of union membership and union density
- Consolidation and merger of trade unions
- Variations in collective-bargaining practices
- A shift in the relationship from the employers' organizations and trade unions to the employer and an individual employee
- Organization restructuring the emergence of "atypical" forms of employment

- The decline in union membership across the industrialized-market economies. This could be because of the fall in employment in the traditional high-employment sector like manufactuting. Manufacturing, traditionally, had high unionization, whereas the unionization in the service sector has been low. The union density, too, has declined.
- Trade unions, to offset their decline, are increasingly trying to consolidate and merge.
- A variation exists across nations in collective bargaining practices. These practices, in a large measure, are determined by the political economy and the ideology of the political party in power.
- The focus of the employer is now on individual employee involvement rather than collective involvement, which means reaching the employee directly rather than through trade unions.
- Increasing corporate restructuring through mergers, acquisitions, outsourcing of processes, divestments, joint ventures, closures, etc. This structural change could be the industry's coping mechanism to the forces of globalization and fierce competition. These structural changes impact the employment, both in the number of jobs and the nature of jobs. The outsourcing of CRM has created

a large number of jobs in India and has also brought in many issues relating to conditions of employment due to the change in the nature of jobs. Globalization has also, in its wake, strengthened a movement for globalization in labour standards too. These issues are being addressed by different countries in different ways depending on the existing system in place and the local political processes for managing change. In many places, including India, the regulatory framework for adapting to these changes is under transition, and this transition period may throw up issues that may impact future IR systems.

- Competition is forcing employers to restructure the nature and forms of employment. Contractual, part-time work, flex-times, work-from-home, virtual office, professional service are a few such emerging trends that have impacted the industrial relations already.

SUMMARY

- In most of these countries, the initial primary goal of the industrial relations system was to maintain labour peace and, more generally, industrial stability. The stated rationale for the need for stability varied from nation to nation. For example, in India, the rationale was to channel conflict away from strikes to third-party-dispute-settlement mechanisms, given that strikes were seen to hinder economic development. In Singapore, industrial conflict was seen as a deterrent to foreign investment, while in South Korea, there were apparent political imperatives for industrial relations stability.
- In many countries, the industrial relations system began to be institutionalized only in the post-war period, coinciding with independence for some of the countries.
- The IR systems of these countries experienced long periods of stability before the dramatic and, in some cases, fundamental changes of the 1980s and 1990s. Most of the major changes in the industrial relations systems have been in the last decade. In some countries, the changes in IR and HR can be seen in legislative changes, but often, change is manifested in the strategies of the political parties leading the government. The underlying compulsion inevitably has been increased competition on account of globalization generating a need for greater numerical and functional flexibility.

KEY TERMS

- AFL-CIO 53
- craft union 53
- industry union 58
- shop stewards 51
- Thatcherism 50
- trade union congress 51

REVIEW QUESTIONS

1 European firms have tended to deal with labour unions at the industry level (frequently via employer associations) rather than at the firm level. Give reasons based on your knowledge of the industrial relations system in the EU countries.

2 The United States has one of the lowest union-density rates in the Western world. What impact would this have on industrial relations? Discuss other aspects of the industrial relations system in the USA.

3 Compare the industrial relations scenario in Asian countries and those in the European Union.

4 Explain how the national history and culture influence in creating the industrial relations system of the country.

5 Discuss the emerging global trends in industrial relations. What are some of the factors driving these changes?

QUESTIONS FOR CRITICAL THINKING

1. Critically evaluate the statement—'"Workers of the world unite!' is a slogan which was never so relevant as it is today!"
2. Multinationals generally delegate the management of labour relations to their foreign subsidiaries because national differences in economic, political, and legal systems produce markedly different labour relations systems across countries. Do you think it ia an appropriate strategy? How can they ensure a congruency with their corporate labour relations strategy?
3. Make a comparative chart bringing out the salient features relating to the IR systems of the major economies of the world. What common features do you find?
4. With the onslaught of internationalization, globalization and competition, soon there would be a globalization of industrial relations practices too. Discuss why or why not this is possible.

DEBATE

1. Time has come for forcing uniformity in the industrial relations structures in all industrialized countries. This is essential for promotion of free trade amongst nations. In the light of what you have learned till now, bring out arguments for and against the statement.
2. Trade unions in India have become largely redundant in the organized sector. This is a welcome development. Discuss.

CASE ANALYSIS

Labour Trouble in Nepal

A soft-drink manufacturing unit of a New Delhi-based businessman, N. K. Mishra, ran into labour trouble with angry workers protesting outside the NKM office trouble in Nepal. The NKM, which has interests in real estate, retailing, hospitality and education, also has stakes in the XYZ beverages industry. Although Maoist guerrillas have made their peace with the government, giving a respite to businessmen who had been bearing the brunt of bomb blasts, extortion and shutdowns, the beverages industry has come under attack from the labour union affiliated to the Communist Party of Nepal. The communist union, in a bid to nip the growing popularity of the Maoists, is asking NKM Beverages to give permanent employment to seasonal workers who have been employed for over 240 days, with sick leave and other facilities. The protest was reportedly triggered by the company's directive to the temporary employees to go on "unpaid leave" during off-season.

What would be your advice to deal with this IR problem?

Industrial Relations at McDonald's

McDonald's is basically a non-union company.

Collect information on the industrial relations practice followed by McDonald's in different countries where it operates.

NOTES

1. Industrial Relations in Europe (2006), European Commission, Directorate-General for Employment, Social Affairs and Equal Opportunities (http://ec.europa.eu/social/keyDocuments.jsp).
2. Greg O'Leary, "The Contemporary Role of Chinese Trade Unions" in Sukhan Jackson (ed.), *Contemporary Developments in Asian Industrial Relations,* UNSW Studies in Human Resource Management and Industrial Relations in Asia, No. 3 (Sydney: University of New South Wales Press, 1994).
3. Frederick C. Teiwes, "The Chinese State During Maoist Era," in David Stanbaugh (ed.) *The Modern Chinese State* (Cambridge: Cambridge University Press, 200): 105–160.

SUGGESTED READING

Annual Reports of European Industrial Relations Observatory (EIRO), 2008, 2007, 2006 (http://www.eurofound.europa.eu/eiro/annualreports.htm).

Brown, Clair, Yoshifumi Nakata, Michael Reich, and Lloyd Ulman, *Work and Pay in the United States and Japan* (New York: Oxford University Press, 1997).

Chew, S. B. and Rosalind Chew, "Impact of Development Strategy on Industrial Relations in Singapore" in Anil Verma, Thomas A. Kochan, and Russell Lansbury (eds.) *Employment Relations in the Growing Asian Economies* (London: Routledge, 1995), pp. 158–193.

DeSousa, Valerian "Colonialism and Industrial Relations in India", in Sarosh Kuruvilla and Bryan Mundell (eds.), *The Institutionalization of Industrial Relations in Developing Nations,*

Erickson, Christopher L. and Sarosh Kuruvilla, "Industrial Relations Implications of the Asian Economic Crisis", *Perspectives on Work*, Vol. 2, No. 2., 1998, pp. 42–48.

Gordon, Andrew *The Evolution of Labor Relations in Japan: Heavy Industry, 1853–1955* (Cambridge, MA: Harvard University Press, 1985).

Industrial Relations in Japan 2003–2004, European Industrial Relations Observatory Online

Kaufmann, B. *The Global Evolution of Industrial Relations* (Geneva: ILO, 2004).

Leggett, C. "Korea's Divergent Industrial Relations", *New Zealand Journal of Industrial Relations,* Vol. 22, No. 1, April 1997.

Venkatratnam, C. S. *Globalization and Labour Management Relations: Dynamics of Change* (New Delhi: Sage Publications, 2002). Questions for Critical Thinking

chapter four

CHAPTER OUTLINE

LEARNING OBJECTIVES

After reading this chapter, you will be able to:

- Describe the changing characteristics of the Indian labour force over a period of time
- Appreciate the need for maintaining industrial relations for production, productivity and performance management from the employer's perspective
- Understand the reason behind the paradigm shift towards employee relations
- Relate the changes in industrial relations with economic and social changes
- Identify the concerns in the context of the trade union's role in the current economic scenario
- Understand the different forces that have led to the changes in industrial relations in India
- Identify approaches for smooth, harmonious and healthy employee relations

Go, Get a Life

Technological innovation has speeded up bank transactions, in the process, reducing human drudgery and the possibilities of human error. Banking operations have become more customer-friendly and flexible. Approaching the concerned bank branch has become multi-channelled, and more and more customers are finding little need to visit the bank. The employees today would not even remember the earlier 10-to-5 routine of a bank and dealing with harried customers during "public hours" from 10 a.m. to 2 p.m. Instead of dedicated tellers earlier, the bank staff must multi-task between front desk, a teller's job and maybe a few others. Go to any of the modern banks today and look at the long hours of monotonous jobs being performed by the employees just because wafer-thin margins have made it necessary to raise productivity. On the other hand, the aspiring employee, today, is largely from generation X or generation Y, from a nuclear, urban family, and with aspirations of much more than just being a wage earner from the "traditional" or "baby boomer" generation. He would not like to be slotted as an industrial worker, but would like to be a part of the mainstream hierarchy. Work–life balance, enough earning to satisfy an urban lifestyle, a meaningful and flexible job, good work environment, scope for training and learning, quick promotions may be what they look for.

Recently, the HDFC Bank exhorted its employees to "go, get a life". The bank does not want its employees to spend too much time in the office. All employees have been told to shut down their computers about two hours after close of banking. They are encouraged to leave early also so that they spend quality time with their family and friends. Those who stay back late have to give an explanation![1]

While the concern of the bank for its employees is laudable, is it entirely for altruistic purpose? Alternatively, is it some kind of balancing the bank is attempting, to cope with increasing productivity and to prevent attrition? Apart from the changes in the business environment, has the profile of the employees changed too?

The Changing Characteristics of Industry and Workforce in India

The changes in social and economic environment, demographics, globalization and technological developments have thrown up new challenges for employee relationship management.

The banking industry in India has undergone a sea change within a decade. So have many other industries in manufacturing and service sectors. Information and communication technologies have fundamentally transformed the business processes and work practices and generated demand for a labour force much different in age, knowledge, skills and attitude profiles. Many new industries have emerged. The service sector now comprises approximately 55 per cent of the economy. The mixes in the mixed economy have undergone change. Global practices are sweeping the industry bringing in their wake wholesale changes in work practices, employee profiles, working conditions, benchmarks for performance and individual aspirations. The industry has been assimilating these changes and, in the process, the interface dynamics amongst the players, namely, the employer, the employees, their organizations, and the government, too, have been adjusting.

The characteristic features of industrial employment determine the industrial relations climate.

4.1 The Changing Characteristics of Industries

Technology changes, more so in the last two decades, have resulted in mechanization, automation, information-based services and disintermediation in most industries.

This has led to:

i) The rationalization of manpower

ii) Labour substitution in the case of automation

These changes impact the work and task design, enabling people to improve the work procedures, which indirectly have an impact on the social and the economic status. The use of more sophisticated machineries or tools and techniques leads to a reduction or substitution of labour deployed for want of a higher-level skill. Taking an adversarial approach in the implementation of such labour-displacing initiatives resulted in industrial relations problems and conflicts.

Technological changes are brought about in industries to enable them to compete through improved efficiency and productivity, and at times, it may be a means of survival of an enterprise. Social implications and priorities do not have much role to play when deciding on technological changes. Technological changes in organizations, therefore, are almost always viewed with apprehension by the employees who fear for job security, retraining capabilities and career prospects. The effect on employees is both social and economic. Obviously, therefore, changes in technology have a powerful impact on the industrial relations front in the following manner:

i) Work intensification and more output and productivity demands

ii) Absence from work not only entails loss of man-days but also cost of idle capacity

ii) Rationalization of manpower and the consequent reduction in employment levels

Result of Changes in Technology:

- Mechanization
- Automation
- Information-based Services
- Disintermediation, which, in turn, has led to:
  - rationalization of manpower, and
  - labour substitution in the case of automation.

Disintermediation

In the current context, it means the removal of an employee's role between the customer and the product or service. ATMs, for example, enable the customer to avail of the service without going through a bank teller. Information technology has enabled organizations to adopt disintermediation in a big way.

Rationalization of Manpower

Strictly, it means bringing the manpower requirements of a firm to optimum levels. In practice, however, it largely means measures to reduce redundant manpower through redeployment, voluntary separation schemes, outsourcing, etc.

Technological changes affect labour in two ways—social and economic, thereby affecting the quality of life in all spheres.

iv) Changes in work organization and structural relationships
v) The size of work groups
vi) The length of job cycles
vii) Changes in work environment and occupational adjustment to the same
viii) Retraining and redeployment potential of existing employees
ix) Skill requirement—more multi-skilling
x) Resistance to transfers and job rotation
xi) The level of job satisfaction—with individual differences

Technological changes, therefore, impact both quality of work-life and quality of life. It is bound to create apprehensions, and a resistance to change the old order. It appears logical that participation and consultation with labour would be the way to go for a smooth introduction of changes in technology. Wherever management refrained from transparent and open communication, the transition has not been smooth. Major forces driving the changes in the last decade and a half can be discussed under the following heads.

THE IMPACT OF COMPUTERIZATION. Revolutionary changes in information technology, telecommunication and a marriage of the two have resulted in complete transformation and re-engineering of business processes, and industries have exploited this development. In the process, industries and businesses have adapted to more efficient processes and a different kind of division of labour. There has been a change in the demand of skill sets with greater requirements of knowledge workers and technology specialists. To fill this demand, there has been a movement towards skill enhancement for categories such as engineering, sciences, solicitors, pharmacists, economists, computer-hardware and software technicians. With a booming service sector and service being recognized as a differentiator, there has also been an increasing demand for skills at the delivery end, e.g., logistics specialists, drivers, CRM specialists, service engineers, security specialists, and air and ground crew. It is the generalist, middle-level, white-collar category that has taken a beating. "Whole Jobs" have been broken into "tasks" and each of these tasks de-criticalized. When computerization resulted in elimination of jobs or replacement of manpower for want of computer skills, trade unions were aggressive in their approach demanding redeployment through training, instead of replacing existing labour. This situation led to the tripartite discussions of 1966 and 1967 in the 24th and 25th session of the ILC (Indian Labour Conference). As no conclusion could be reached, computerization was a controversial issue among trade unions for quite some time. In January 1983, the government of India came up with a Technology Policy Statement (TPS) that emphasized on the dual objective of technology—to provide maximum gainful and satisfying employment to all strata of society and steps to reduce drudgery. The Seventh Plan, however, was more emphatic in stating the need for modernization, but emphasized the need to explore how this could be achieved without affecting the industrial relations climate.

THE IMPACT OF AUTOMATION. Automation in India emerged as part of the modernization of industries. Its impact was determined by the extent of labour augmentation or labour displacement. The new industries, starting off with automation, faced with little or no resistance. The central trade unions opposed automation only if it would affect employment. Automation of housekeeping services in the airports as part of the global tendering process by Airport Authority of India was faced with stiff resistance by the trade unions, who struck work to raise this issue.

THE IMPACT OF RATIONALIZATION OF MANPOWER. The need for rationalization of manpower emerged as a consequence of the comparatively low labour-productivity levels in Indian industries. The aspect of carrying "surplus labour" to cope with absenteeism was making most industries burdened with additional labour costs. When rationalization was introduced, there was opposition on the part of the workers and trade unions for the fear of losing jobs. The Planning Commission and the Ministry of Labour imposed safeguards in the form of fixing work loads, recruitment freeze, voluntary retirement schemes, and facilitating productivity-sharing gains for workers through higher wages. The Second Five Year Plan and the Model Agreement adopted in the 15th session of the ILC in 1957 introduced some regulations that made rationalization possible only if it did not lead to unemployment. The emphasis, therefore, was to identify redeployable surplus and provide redeployment training to engage them in suitable jobs.

Automation

It is the use of control systems or computers used to control industrial machinery or processes replacing human operators. Automation greatly reduces the need for human *sensory* and *mental* requirements.

THE IMPACT OF GLOBALIZATION. The process of globalization and the opening up of the economy, post the economic reforms, focused the need to gain competitive advantage. Competitive advantage through people was an important dimension. Essentially, it meant flexibility in employing labour as per requirement (shorn of all jargon, this meant freedom to hire and fire). For PSUs, it immediately meant a need to assess the requirement of manpower as per business needs and, as a reaction, a complete recruitment freeze. Downsizing in the best of times is difficult; more so, in a PSU. In perpetually loss-making PSUs, the unions leant a passive support to "voluntary" retirement schemes. It must be acknowledged that with the onset of economic liberalization, there were sincere efforts to find a solution through tripartite discussions.

The choice to adopt a new technology is least governed by social priorities. Hence, the initial reaction of employees to the introduction of new technology is one of apprehension about job security, retraining capabilities and career prospects.

4.2 The Changing Characteristics of the Industrial Workforce

The changing face of the Indian industry has an obvious impact on the labour market, more so in India, which has serious unemployment issues to deal with. The dynamics of the above changes and its impact on labour need to be understood against the historical characteristics of the labour force, which have been discussed in the next few sections to facilitate understanding the changing face of the Indian workforce.

The major forces in the last decade and a half driving the changes can be categorized as:

- Computerization
- Automation
- Rationalization
- Globalization

4.2.1 The Indian Workforce Prior to the Recent Changes

The Indian labour force has been traditionally characterized in the following ways:

i) Driven by unemployment, willing to work for low wages in organized or unorganized sector

ii) Heterogeneous in composition but spontaneously divided by religion, caste, communities, ethnic groups and language

iii) Initiation from migrant and displaced population from the rural areas, mainly the uneducated and those low in the social strata

iv) Mine workers predominantly from tribal areas

v) Neither organized nor stable working class, as they continued to go back to their rural roots by taking breaks in employment

vi) Primarily male-dominated; women workers employed in unorganized sectors where skill requirement and wages were low

vii) Working class undifferentiated by industry or sectoral origin

viii) A high rate of absenteeism and turnover, as more importance given to partaking in family, social and religious activities at the cost of their responsibility towards production and productivity

ix) Low on commitment

Globalization

It refers to economic integration of national economies into the international economy through trade, foreign direct investment, capital flows, migration, and spread of technology.

The industrial change has affected the labour market in the following ways:

- Changed occupational structure
- Changed nature of work
- Integrated job markets leading to a global occupational structure
- Improved education facilitating economic growth

4.2.2 The Impact of Industrial Change on the Workforce

THE CHANGING OCCUPATIONAL STRUCTURE. Technological changes, automation and computerization have resulted in a change in the occupational structure. The information revolution, communication technology and automation have brought in wholesale changes in the nature of occupations, a shift of occupations, primarily manual or clerical in nature, to those involving intellectual work. The end result is the emergence of a global occupational structure with an increasingly integrated labour market.

THE CHANGING NATURE OF WORK. Technical changes in the last decade have placed an increasing demand on multi-skilling and have also necessitated specialized skills, adapting to the industrial requirements and technical changes. The skill-biased technical change has altered work environment. It has transformed the nature of work and its content. The changes are at individual as well as organizational level, and this impacts employment structures and labour markets. Flexi-work schedules, outsourcing jobs and the creation of boundary-less and virtual organizations are new emerging trends. This has also led to an increase in "service"-oriented and "knowledge"-oriented jobs. Unskilled, manual jobs have declined. The work content of jobs has changed leading to new demands in terms of knowledge, skills and behaviour. In view of rapid technical changes, in many cases, the focus is now on attitudes and the behaviour of people with technical capabilities, renewed continually through training provided by the company.

INTEGRATED JOB MARKETS LEADING TO GLOBAL OCCUPATIONAL STRUCTURE. An integrated global economy has increased the supply of labour significantly. Productivity gains due to technological changes have created higher wages and incomes. The resultant cost increases have led to offshore outsourcing of data-intensive work. The intense competition has resulted in the integration of job markets.

HIGHER EDUCATION AND ECONOMIC GROWTH. Technological changes, automation and industrial restructuring have made knowledge the key factor in economic development. The emerging workforce will be the knowledge technologist creating competitive advantage as human capital. This transformation has both increased and updated the skills required in an economy. This implies that the education system has to be attuned to the development of vocational skills. This is being experienced at the industry level where the employers lament the unavailability of "employable" labour, despite the availability of "qualified" labour. This means although people may have the required academic qualifications, they may not have sufficient technical or soft skills, so essential for employment. As a consequence, the skilled manpower is exercising multi-entry and multi-exit options. The industry is taking the lead in providing training opportunities for skill development to retain talent, thereby increasing employee involvement. An employee–employer relationship is getting established eliminating the need for a collective representation of employees. Indirectly, this has moved trade unionism to the periphery and the concept of "industrial relations" is being substituted by "employee relations".

4.2.3 The Factors Facilitating Adaptation to Changes

The adaptability of the Indian workforce to the changing characteristics of the Indian industry was facilitated by the following factors:

i) Indian workers, today, are more urbane than the previous generations
ii) The obligatory link with the place of origin (village) has reduced and, hence, they are more stable than transitory
iii) Workers are more focused on the present occupation than on the land-related, economic interests in their places of origin

iv) Workers prefer domiciliary to State citizenship and, hence, more stable in employment

v) Workers are more skilful and educated

vi) Women employment is on the rise

vii) Workers are high on job commitment for self-interest and growth

viii) They are more mobile and on the lookout for better opportunities within and outside the country

Further, the emerging situation as regards employment makes it very clear that individuals have to also train and develop themselves to gain competitive edge, and the collective strength of trade unions will no longer be the push factor that can ensure their employability for long. The unions have also been appreciative of the economic growth and its effect on the standards of living and, hence, have not been raising demands that could affect growth and development of the country.

4.2.4 The Current Employment and Unemployment Situation

A report prepared for the Planning Commission[2] observes that any vision of the future has to be rooted in the current reality, and policies and processes have to be identified to bridge the gap between the current reality and the future vision. The current reality regarding labour and employment is summarized as:

- In the year 1999–2000, 7.32 per cent of the labour force was unemployed. In absolute terms, the number of unemployed stood at 26.58 million.
- Among the employed, the proportion of poor is as high as in the population at large, suggesting a large proportion of workers engaged in subsistence employment.
- Only about 8 per cent of the total employment is in organized sector. More than 90 per cent are engaged in informal sector activities, which are largely outside the reach of any social-security benefits, and also suffer from many handicaps in the form of limited access to institutional facilities and other support facilities.
- The educational and skill profile of the existing workforce is very poor.

How will the above reality impact the current industrial relations, especially in the organized sector?

Subsistence Worker/ Employment

Subsistence workers are those who hold a self-employment job, and in this capacity, produce goods or services that are predominantly consumed by their own household, and constitute an important basis for its livelihood.

4.2.5 The Composition and the Demographic Features of the Workforce

There have been changes in the composition and the demographics of the workforce, and this will have a bearing on the industrial relations, may be the beginning of a new course.

AGE. The proportion of different age groups (as measured by Participation Rate, which is the proportion of people in the labour force out of total cohort population) has undergone a change. The dynamics created by the labour-force composition impacts production, productivity and innovative transformations in the industry. There has been a decline in participation rates observed during 1993–94 to 1999–2000. As shown in Table 4.1, there is maximum decline in participation rates for younger age groups (20–29) in 1999–2000, but it has climbed back to more or less the 93–94 level in 2004–2005. On the other hand, with an extension of retirement age to 60 in the organized sector, older people are active participants in the labour force. Participation rates across all age groups have remained the same since 1993–1994 level except for a minor dip in 1999–2000 in the younger age groups.

Participation Rate

The proportion of people in the labour force out of total cohort population

- In 1999–2000, 7.32 per cent of the labour force, i.e. 26.58 million, were unemployed
- A large proportion of those employed are in subsistence employment
- Only 8 per cent of those employed are in the organized sector
- The education and the skill profile of the current work force is poor

Table 4.1

Workforce participation rate according to age group (WFPR).

Age Group	Urban					
	Male			Female		
Year	1993-94	1999-00	2004-05	1993-94	1999-00	2004-05
5-9	4	3	3	4	2	3
10-14	71	52	53	47	37	35
15-19	404	366	381	142	121	144
20-24	772	755	769	230	191	250
25-29	958	951	957	248	214	261
30-34	983	980	987	283	245	308
35-39	990	986	984	304	289	340
40-44	984	980	983	320	285	317
45-49	976	974	976	317	269	269
50-54	945	939	939	287	264	259
55-59	856	811	832	225	208	218
60 & Above	443	402	366	114	94	100
All (0+)	542	542	570	164	147	178

Source: Ministry of Statistics and Programme Implementation, Government of India

The main changes in labour demographics include:

- The decline in participation rates across age groups
- The entry of the younger age groups into the labour force
- More active participation of older people in the labour force
- A reduction in differentials between male and female participation
- Relatively low education and skill levels
- An attitudinal change towards technical and vocational courses

GENDER. Females are closing the gap with respect to males in labour participation. Table 4.1 also shows an increase in participation rate for females up to the age of 40. One implication of this on IR could be arising out of the fact of low mobility of women and their reluctant participation in trade-union activities. With progressive lowering of the gap, the issues taken up by employees' organizations may undergo a change, and so would the workplace practices.

SKILLS. It is generally accepted and borne out by data that education level of labour in India is low. The Economic Survey of 2007 revealed that about 44.0 per cent of all workers in 1999–2000 were illiterate and another 22.7 per cent had schooling only up to the primary level[3]. For an effective industrial relations system to prevail, the working groups need to be educated and mature to establish a productive and collaborative relationship with management. In the earlier passage, we have noted the changes in the demanded profile of labour due to changes in the nature of business and industry in India. More and more jobs today demand educated and skilled workers. The level of craft or occupational unionization in India is low, it being more dictated by the nature of the industry, geography or even ideology. To meet the new demands of the job, the level of education and skill formation must increase. The inability to bridge this gap will create its own dynamics. The NSSO estimates of skilled labour is given in Table 4.2.

Though very old, the figures would not have undergone any significant change. They reveal an abysmally low level of skill formation. Perhaps, the preference is for a generalist orientation due to the fact that a government job requires academic qualification rather than vocational skills. There is some change in this perception in the recent years due to a clamp down on such recruitments by the government and the PSUs, and opportunities opening for skilled labour in the "new economy" industries.

Table 4.2

The percentage distribution of persons by possession of skills (1993–1994).

	Rural		Urban	
Possessing	**Male**	**Female**	**Male**	**Female**
No skill	89.9	93.7	80.04	88.8
Some Skill	10.1	6.3	19.6	11.2
Total	100.0	100.0	100.0	100.0
Sample persons	(183464)	(172835)	(109067)	(99283)

Source: NSSO Report No. 409 on Results of 50th Round (1993–1994) Survey on Employment and Unemployment

4.3 The Demand for Labour

The current demand for labour is directed towards vocational skills and the need for knowledge workers. This gap in demand and supply of labour may require some structural tweaking during transition, but in the industrial relations context, the larger question may be to enhance the productivity levels of existing workers and those who are likely to enter the labour force.

4.3.1 Employment Distribution

The result of the changes discussed in Section 4.2 has brought about distinctive changes in sectors with employment opportunities. It is now different from the traditional sectors of industrial employment, namely, organized sector including the government and the PSUs, manufacturing, etc. These changes are discussed in the subsequent paragraphs, and it is important for the readers to proactively debate the consequences of these changes on the scope and coverage of industrial relations.

ORGANIZED–UNORGANIZED. The growth of employment in the organized sector has not kept pace with that in the unorganized sector. A major reason for this could be the near freeze in employment opportunities in the PSUs and the government. The data in Table 4.3 is revealing:

Table 4.3

The organized-sector employment.

Sector	**Employment (in million)**				**Growth Rate (per cent per annum)**	
Organized Sector	1983	1988	1994	1999–2000	1983–1994	1994–2000
Employment	24.01	25.71	27.18	28.11	1.13	0.56
Public Sector	16.46	18.32	19.30	19.41	1.46	0.10
Private Sector	7.55	7.39	7.88	8.70	0.39	1.64

Note: The organized sector employment figures are as reported in the Employment Market Information System of Ministry of Labour and pertain to 1 March of 1983, 1988, 1994 and 1999

Employment in the organized sector has virtually stagnated post 1993–1994. More than 90 per cent of employment in 2001 (Census 2001) was in the unorganized sector. Typically, due to reasons such as dispersal, small and scattered size, lack of opportunity to forge a commonality of objectives and limited accessibility to protection of labour laws, the labour in such employments comprise the unorganized sector or unorganized labour. The implication of this distribution will largely keep this labour force outside the purview of any industrial relations system due to the following reasons:

- Poor bargaining power
- The lack of continuity of employment due to seasonality, and the economic viability of the unit to continuously employ such persons through ups and downs of a business cycle
- Outside the coverage of industrial/labour law
- The casual nature of employment and the lack of formal relationship with the employer
- Outside the welfare coverage due to discontinuity of employment, number not being large enough to collectively raise the issue, general apathy of the employer towards welfare
- Non-unionization due to small numbers and also the reluctance of main TUs to stretch themselves and reach these workers; there is not enough "pay-off" to unionization effort
- Out of reach of the major social-security schemes, since the enforcement of the schemes is geared towards larger organized sectors

The major trends in the unorganized sector include:

- Ninety-three per cent of employees in the unorganized sector
- The absence of an institutionalized IR system
- Labour regulations not for smaller establishments
- Social security being out of reach
- The absence of unions does not provide any opportunity for collective bargaining

It is paradoxical that the section of labour most in need of the protection of labour legislation, trade unions, labour enforcement machinery, social security schemes draws the least. The knee-jerk reaction to this state of affairs may be to immediately bring the entire population under the above-mentioned protection, but that may kill the flexibility and business viability of the small sector. And finding innovative measures to find the balance is where the challenge lies for the employers, the employees and the State and their respective organizations. This sector, in the coming years, is going to grow, and there is no way but to prepare for tomorrow's battle with tomorrow's weapons, rather than tinkering with outdated weapons. The alternative could be an adhocracy in the industrial relations management with occasional road bumps. An approach could be:

- A tripartite consensus on labour and employment flexibility with a viable social-security net
- A creative solution to equitable sharing of the social-security burden
- The shifting of labour to the organized sector, either through expansion or increasing the coverage of labour legislations and effective enforcement
- Some kind of institution to promote union security for increasing the participation of unions in the hitherto unattended areas; unions must commit to focus their attention to areas other than the organized sector

- Profit and market leadership are the prime drivers, not social objectives.
- Changes in market and technology are throwing up newer competency requirements.
- There are large employment opportunities in the private sector.
- Public-sector employment faces stagnation and decline.
- More opportunities are there in tertiary sectors.

THE PUBLIC–PRIVATE SECTOR. The public enterprises were set up in India with the dual objective of social development and infrastructure development. Till mid-1991, the government policy was based on socialist principles. As a consequence, employment opportunities in the public sector were far more than those in private sectors. The public sector had a monopoly of basic and heavy industries, and employed a large number of people. Despite liberalization, employment in public sectors continues to be greater than the private sector, but the growth in this sector has shown a decline, while the private sector is opening up large employment opportunities for the youth.

It needs to be understood that in the competitive environment in which a global economy functions, profit and market leadership are the prime drivers, not social objectives that public sectors are associated with. The social objective of private industries comes by way of the corporate social responsibility that a particular company may choose to associate with. Competition being the driver, competence of individuals becomes the criterion for employment. Furthermore, it is not just competence, but a competence that matches with the competency required for the job, which also undergoes changes keeping pace with the changing market and technological environment in the industry.

INDUSTRY-WISE DISTRIBUTION. The distribution of workers by the industry category has also shown a dramatic rise in the tertiary sector. The shift in working population from the primary sector, like agriculture, to the secondary sector—manufacturing and allied industries—to the now-emerging tertiary sector is similar to the trend witnessed by several developed economies. This places a greater demand on skills and attitude in addition to updated knowledge to match the job competencies. The employment potential sectors have shifted from factories, mines and plantations to finance, commercial, IT and ITES and community services.

4.3.2 The Impact on Labour Deployment, Utilization and Productivity

The benefits of economic growth as a result of globalization have, however, been restricted mainly to the educated and/or skilled urban population. The main beneficiaries of globalization in the region have been skilled labour, especially workers in the information/communication technology sector. That the firms today operate in a fiercely competitive environment is a clichéd statement but a reality. The response to this competition has to be nimble-footed changes in structures and strategies, with one of the aims being to reduce competition itself. This may involve acquisitions, mergers, alliances that give breathing space to the entity facing competition. However, these measures throw up their own challenges of adjustments. And, to make these adjustments, organizations need flexibility. The private-sector companies have adjusted well through labour-deployment strategies to optimize human-capital utilization, but the public sector needs to think out of the box to be more responsive to change, more so with regard to the pace of change. The large-scale employment, however, does prove to be a bottleneck, but a change in strategy oriented towards employee relations can have a catalytic effect on change.

BOX 4.1 FOR CLASS DISCUSSION

"There must be a consensus on social partnership (between employers and unions) to avoid chaos and street riots in the present situation of widespread downsizing of workforce, outsourcing, casualization of labour and deindustrialization as a result of economic reform."

W. R. Varadrajan of CITU, in a CII-sponsored seminar in the year 2001

These were the words spoken by a senior left-union representative almost 10 years after liberalization. In the light of the happenings since, do you think such statements are exaggerated? What was he referring to as "social partnership" and why has it become necessary?

Source: Quoted in R. Gopalakrishnan, "Industrial Relations: Towards Social Partnership," *The Hindu*, 26 July 2001

4.4 The Challenges to IR

The change in industry and business brought on by progressive integration of the Indian economy to the world economy on the one hand, and the change in demand profile for labour and the changing demographics, on the other, throw their own challenges. The effort to address these challenges may, perhaps, lead to a new paradigm in the management of industrial relations in India. The following issues need to be examined for a new perspective to emerge.

Ways for expanding the coverage of collective bargaining must be found to bring the large, uncovered population (almost 93 per cent of labour force) in the main system. Economic and social justice, a prerequisite for industrial peace, can be delivered only through this process.

Evolving mechanisms and the environment for collective bargaining to yield long-term agreements for stability amidst fluctuations in the business cycle and the environment are necessary, more so, since the emerging trend is for bargaining to take place at local/plant levels, specific to local requirements and in response to local realities.

Genuine democratization of the industrial relations system to give representation to diverse interests within the labour is imperative. Questionable attempts at democratization and strengthening of the democratization, representation and empowerment through secret ballot must be looked at with a view to arrive at consensus and innovative solutions. Recognition, single bargaining agent, the right to strike and dispute resolution must all be looked at with a view at ground realities.

Almost 50 years of existence of the above essential components of industrial relations system have, at best, been a "band aid" kind of solution to the problem, not a complete "health-care system". There has been a fundamental shift in the structure and processes, and the system now in place appears so inadequate that it has been left to stagnate where it was. All the protagonists recognize the problem but refuse to take the bull by the horn.

Modern HRM practices have significantly altered the framework of industrial relations in certain sectors that have come up post liberalization. Many companies have insisted upon, and have developed "union-less" organizations. What are the merits of these, and are there any hidden issues? Surely, these need to be examined dispassionately, for experiments such as these may provide insights for a future paradigm.

Labour management relations have witnessed regional variations with the advent of reforms. These may increase over the years with differential industrialization of regions. Instead of trying to get into the cause-and-effect cycle, perhaps, legislative compliance and enforcement across regions may be necessary to iron out discrepancies. If this is not done, then the distortions in investments may accentuate further, bringing with it consequences on the labour–management relationship front.

The impact on the industrial relations needs to be considered from the perspectives of (i) the employer (ii) the employees and (iii) the government.

4.4.1 The Employer's Perspective

There is a perceptible shift with employers veering towards the employee relations approach, giving adequate emphasis on the softer view of HRM concerned with facilitating optimum utilization of human resources/capital. They have taken over the union's role of ensuring that "hygiene" factors do not act as impediments to performance. Employee involvement, participation and engagement programmes, which would be discussed in subsequent chapters, are being introduced to increase commitment and generate organizational commitment. A shift from the creation of employment contracts to psychological contracts is slowly emerging.

Compensation structures have shifted from seniority/tenure based to pay for performance/skill/competence. HR strategies of employers aim towards motivating employees for quality, customer orientation and innovation. The new HRM model is composed of policies that promote mutuality of goals to elicit commitment. Employer initiatives provide greater flexibility and multi-skilling, thereby leading to removal of union demarcation by craft or industry. As we had discussed in Chapter 1, there appears to be a distinct shift towards a "unitary" approach or, more appropriately, a "neo-unitary" approach.

4.4.2 The Employee's/Union's Perspective

The new market-driven economy has moved trade unions from the centre to the periphery. HRM strategies focus on motivating manpower for customer delight, which can come only from enthusiasm and initiative. This requires commitment at each individual level in the organization. Commitment is a unitarist concept and not the spirit of collectivism that trade unions advocate. Dual commitment to both the employer and the trade unions is a misnomer and employees understand its consequences in a cost-driven competitive market.

The union's response to these changes has been politically motivated and influenced. In most cases, they have resisted whenever there is a linkage to reduced deployment of manpower, or the existing skill sets of labour cannot be upgraded for redeployment. It is the management's responsibility to create confidence and build up momentum, whenever such organizational restructuring is attempted, and facilitate learning and training opportunities for existing employees to adopt the technological changes. It is time that trade unions strategize their role as internal-change agents for the organization, and thereby contribute to organizational success.

The union has now been clearly motivated by ensuring clear benefits for workers, more welfare facilities and single table bargaining. The management needs to be proactive in ensuring their provision and be careful to avoid inequalities in pay.

Unions need to involve themselves in preparing the workers for the new-millennium competitive skills, and broaden the scope and coverage of content in communication with management. They need to take on the role of a facilitator, giving friendly counsel and advice to the workers, and aim at improving the quality of work life.

The unions must confront the reality of competition, technological changes, changes in industrial structures and processes brought about by competition and a changing workforce profile. They must acknowledge that to cope with these wholesale changes, organizations need to be flexible in their responses. "The consumer is the king" is a reality that the unions must accept from within, and not just pay lip service to it. Unions, perhaps, must focus more on the vulnerable areas where the workers need to organize, that is, the informal sector. This may also help them redeem their utility as a potent force for social development and reduce their increasing marginalization from the organized sector. Perhaps, the trade-union organizations, themselves, may undergo structural changes by the merging of ideologies.

4.4.3 The Government's Perspective and the Labour Laws

The existing legislative framework is not conducive to the creation of more opportunities for absorption of labour into industry. These are purported to be pro-labour, but end up discouraging the industry to employ more labour due to very restrictive and rigid provisions. It is generally recognized that the framework served the purpose in an exploitative colonial regime and, to an extent, in a protective and insulated economy. There is a need for a fundamental change today. Perhaps, with a slight tilt in the favour of employment, the structural problem of gap in supply and demand may be reduced. This issue is glaring at everybody in the face, but the consensus to do something about it is elusive. The government has to take the initiative to hammer out a consensus and usher in legislative reforms. It should not be impossible to find a balance between the incentive for greater intake of labour by the industry and the concern for labour welfare.

It needs to be appreciated that adopting stringent labour laws affects the bottom line, more so in the Indian context, where legislation is very labour oriented. Restructuring and changing work and task designs with technological changes impact the employment of labour in terms of quantity as well as skill requirements, but their impact must be related to productivity improvements. Wages must be linked to productivity and made competitive.

The role of the trade union in terms of not just rights but also obligations must be reinforced through a code of discipline. A similar code for management should be created to balance the roles and make both interdependent players in the market, and not create islands of wealth.

The communication between the employers and the employees needs to be transparent and direct. This would enable a better appreciation of the cyclical trends in business, and ensure a greater sense of involvement and participation.

SUMMARY

- The changing characteristics of the labour market have placed a greater demand for skilled labour on account of technological development.
- There is an emerging problem of maintaining continued employability of labour force, especially in community services, which placed a greater demand on multi-skilling.
- With globalization and liberalization, the industrial sector is adapting to the competitive market environment by gaining competitive advantage through technology, automation, rationalization and costs.
- It is time for the trade-union organizations to reinvent their strategic objectives and act as facilitators of change.
- The role of protecting rights of workers needs to be ensured.
- The employers, on their part, are moving towards employee relations rather than industrial relations, by having a one-to-one relationship with the employees.
- New economic reforms brought changes in legislation relating to trade, finance, and industrial policy, but none in labour laws.
- Many labour laws and judgements stay as impediments to our competitive status in the arena of global industry.
- The government needs to take the initiative to facilitate the process of economic growth by revisiting the labour legislations in the current context of a global economy.
- The following are important issues that need examination and debate:

  i. An endeavour to shift as much of labour force as possible from the unorganized to the organized sector. This would give workers a better deal in terms of wages. This is possible only if the rigidities in the labour market are relaxed, and wage determination begins to reflect the resource endowment in the country. This would encourage establishments to adopt labour-intensive technologies.

  ii. Employment creation in small establishments will have to be promoted by incentives linked with jobs created, rather than capital invested.

  iii. A strategy to raise the wage levels will have to be linked with a programme for the development of vocational skills. This requires a timely investment in skill development and training at an enhanced level, the enhancement of education and the skill level of the workers, and a responsive training system.

  iv. A simple, but broad-based, social-security system will have to be developed to improve the quality of employment, especially for the informal sector. Such a social-security system, coupled with better labour incomes, based on better productivity of trained manpower, will facilitate the conversion of emerging work opportunities into meaningful jobs, where chances of extreme exploitation of labour get eliminated. There is a need for an effective partnership of all stakeholders.

KEY TERMS

- automation 65
- disintermediation 65
- globalization 67
- participation rate 69
- rationalization 65
- subsistence worker/employment 69

REVIEW QUESTIONS

1 Discuss the changing characteristics of the Indian worker. In what way has the opening up of the economy influenced the changing workforce profile?

2 How has globalization affected industrial relations in India? Discuss the possible responses to the changes from the perspectives of each of the main players of industrial relations.

3 What has been the union response to automation and mechanization in India? Elucidate your answer with examples.

QUESTIONS FOR CRITICAL THINKING

1 The growing internationalization of business and workforce has its impact on HRM in terms of problems of unfamiliar laws, languages, practices, attitudes, management styles, work ethics and more. HR managers face a challenge to deal with more and more heterogeneous sets of workers and more involvement in the employee's personal life. Discuss these changes in the light of industrial relations management.

2 Liberalization has led to large-scale reorganization of businesses in terms of expansions, mergers and acquisitions, joint ventures, takeovers, and internal restructuring of organizations. In circumstances as dynamic and as uncertain as these, it is a challenge to manage the employees' anxiety, uncertainties, insecurities and fears. Discuss probable employer response and union response to these changes. Give examples to support your answer.

3 There are signs of changing demographics of the workforce reflected in age and qualification mix, dual career couples, large chunk of young blood with contrasting ethos of work among old superannuating employees, growing number of women in workforce, working mothers, more educated and aware workers, etc. Thus, the changing demography of workforce has its own implications for industrial relations. Discuss these implications and the strategies required to cope with the same.

DEBATE

1 Workforce demographics are changing and it is becoming more diverse in today's global village. Tapping synergies of a diverse workforce is crucial for innovations in a competitive environment. This would require a global corporate culture, and standardized policies and procedures. Industrial relations, therefore, will have no role to play, as unions and State intervention will become irrelevant.

2 The forces of globalization will never be able to address the main socio-economic issue of unemployment in India. It is inadvisable to open up the economy without a strong social-security system in place.

CASE ANALYSIS

The Airport Authority Strike Against Privatization

In February 2006, the employees of the Airport Authority of India struck work in protest against the privatization of the airport. AAEU also protested the development of Greenfield airports at Hyderabad and Bangalore, which meant closing down the old airports run by AAI. The Indian government's ambitious plan to privatize the modernization of the country's two biggest airports—at Mumbai and Delhi—sparked off another major controversy, leading to strikes, protests, threats, complaints and accusations.

Thousands of Airport-Authority-of-India employees went on an "indefinite" strike against the government's privatization plans, and a bidder who lost out, moved the court, challenging the airport bids.

The issues relating to the strike are summarized below:

- The government awarded the modernization contract for the Delhi and Mumbai airports—the country's two busiest airports—to two private consortia. GMR-Fraport clinched the modernization bid for the Delhi airport, while GVK-South African Airports bagged the Mumbai airport.
- This led to nationwide protests by the employees of the Airport Authority of India.
- The unions raised a fundamental question—were the airports in India so badly maintained that they needed to be modernized?
- There are, in fact, 449 airports/airstrips in the country. Among these, the AAI owns and manages 5 international airports, 87 domestic airports and 28 civil enclaves at defence airfields, and provides air-traffic services over the entire Indian airspace and adjoining oceanic areas. Some 35 million domestic and international passengers travel through these airports every year. But the infrastructure at all the airports has remained much below international benchmarks. This was stated to be the government's rationale for modernizing/privatizing the Mumbai and Delhi airports (to be followed by others).
- The government invited technical bids and financial tenders from private companies/consortia to build and maintain the two airports. The government finally selected two bidders and awarded the contracts to them.
- The airport employees protested as they feared they will lose jobs if the government went ahead with the modernization and eventual privatization plan. There were nearly 22,000 employees with the AAI, working across all the airports in the country. They feared that the private companies that were going to rebuild these airports would throw them out.
- The government says the charges were baseless. It says it had taken care of the welfare of the employees in the airport-modernization process. Both bidders had agreed to absorb 60 per cent of the employees. About 10 per cent of the employees would continue to work for AAI in these airports, and 7 to 8 per cent were expected to retire by 2009. The rest would be absorbed by the AAI and posted at other airports.

  One of the major political parties supporting the strike said they were not protesting against the "modernization" of these airports. They argued that all the airports in the country, especially the biggest ones like the Mumbai and Delhi airports, should be modernized and made world-class. "But in the name of modernization, what the government has done is to virtually sell the airport to a consortium of companies. We are all for modernization of airports; but we are dead against their privatization," said one of the Central Trade Union leaders.
- The alternative suggestion from the employees' unions was that instead of awarding the contract for modernizing the airports to private companies, the government should allow the AAI to build world-class airports. They had been arguing that the AAI is a profit-making company with reserves and surplus funds of INR 30,000 crore (INR 300 billion) and almost zero-debt status, which could meet the anticipated expenditure for the development of the airports.
- The AAI Employees' Union had, in fact, submitted an airport-modernization plan to the government. But the government said their plan was evaluated and it scored less than 50 per cent in the technical evaluation, not making the cut even after revisions by the bid document.

Questions

1. Discuss the above case and bring out the issues from an industrial relations perspective.
2. What would have reduced the confrontation with the unions?
3. Critically examine the stand of the unions.
4. How should the "consortia" handle the employee relations for a smooth project implementation?

NOTES

1 Adapted from A. B. Manju, "No More Late Hours for HDFC Bank Employees," *Financial Chronicle*, 9 June 2009, http://www.mydigitalfc.com/companies/no-more-late-hours-hdfc-bank-employees-302.

2 Employment (Vision 2020), pp. 1–2, http://planningcommission.nic.in/reports/genrep/bkpap2020/32_bg2020.pdf.

3 Ministry of Finance, Government of India, "Union Budget and Economic Survey", *Economic Survey* 2007–2008.

SUGGESTED READING

Deya, F. C. *Beneath the Miracle: Labour Standards in the New Asian Industrialism* (Berkley: University of California Press, 1989).

Government of India, *Report of the Working Group of Labour Policy, 9th 5 Year Plan* (New Delhi: Ministry of Labour, 1996).

Kuruvila, S. and C. S. Venkatratnam, "Economic Development and Industrial Relations in South and Southeast Asia: Past Trends and Future Developments", *Industrial Relations Journal (UK),* Vol. 27(1), March 1996.

Sengupta, A. K. "New Generation of Organized Workforce in India: Implications for Management and Trade Unions", in J. S. Sodhi and S. P. S. Ahluwalia (eds.), *Industrial Relations in India: The Coming Decades* (Delhi: Sriram Center for Industrial Relations, 1992).

Tulpule, B. "New Industrial Policy, Employment and Structural Adjustment in India", *Indian Worker,* Mumbai,1993.

Venkatratnam, C. S. (ed.) "Labour Management Relations and World in Transition", in *Globalization and Labour Management Relations* (New Delhi: Response Books, 2001).

Venkatratnam, C. S. and Anil Verma, *Challenge of Change: Industrial Relations in Indian Industy* (New Delhi: New Global Press, 1997).

chapter five

CHAPTER OUTLINE

LEARNING OBJECTIVES

After reading this chapter, you will be able to:

- Describe the concept of trade unionism
- Identify the factors that led to the origin and the growth of trade unions
- Define the principles underlying trade unionism
- Understand the various approaches to the study of trade unions
- Understand the structure, functions and activities of trade unions

Tata's Takeover of Jaguar and Land Rover[1]

The takeover of Jaguar and Land Rover, emblems of the British auto, by Tata Motors in March 2008 was greeted with approval but regret by Unite, Britain's largest trade union formed by the merger of Amicus and the Transport and General Workers' Union on 1 May 2007.

Unite, though not happy about the impending ownership change, in early July 2007, sent a five-point charter to Ford demanding, among other things, that the union be involved in the sale process. The union members were present in the early stages of presentations and negotiations between Ford and the bidders. Despite the lack of unanimity among the rank and file of Unite, the union's preference helped Tata Motors to emerge the front-runner, leaving the other bidders behind.

In November 2007, Unite issued a public statement saying that, of all the bidders, Tata Motors, with an established presence and background in manufacturing, was its preferred buyer for Jaguar and Land Rover. Tata Motors, realizing how critical it was going to be for them to take Unite along for both the acquisition and post-acquisition support, during the various stages of discussion and negotiation with Ford, reiterated through various channels that the jobs of the workers at Jaguar and Land Rover would remain secure and post-takeover, the 160,000-odd jobs across the various Ford sites in Britain would continue untouched.

In January 2008, about three months prior to the actual closing of the deal, Tony Woodley, General Joint Secretary, Unite, said in a press release that detailed meetings focusing on the job security of the workers in Jaguar, Land Rover and other Ford plants in the UK were necessary. Other crucial issues around wages, terms and conditions and pension also needed to be addressed before the final decision could be taken.

In March 2008, the takeover was formalized, but only after Tata Motors issued an undertaking that jobs would be saved. Tata Motors also committed to long-term supply agreements for components from Ford units in the UK.

Trade Unionism and Trade Unions

> *". . . .I do believe that the trade union movement has played a very important role in our national development. Trade unions are an integral part of the functioning of our social democracy. I seek their cooperation in taking our nation forward. I do urge our trade union leadership to recognize that in a world where demand and technology are undergoing rapid change and firms must adjust or perish, we need reasonable flexibility in markets and in public policy and our public policy must respond to such needs with speed. I do sincerely believe that such an approach will be in the best interests of promoting the growth of employment opportunities. . . . ."*
>
> **Prime Minister's Address to the 40th Indian Labour Conference (New Delhi: 9 December, 2005)**

Trade unions have come a long way since the middle of the eighteenth century to the present when they influence business decisions and even national policy. Taking the unions into confidence is one of the strategic necessities when companies pursue their strategies for growth. Just like Tata Motors, Hindalco, an Aditya Birla Group Company, also made an elaborate presentation to the trade unions of a Canadian Aluminium plant that it acquired in 2007. On-boarding of unions is now a part of the due diligence process before mergers and acquisitions. Alongside, companies also adopt a host of other corporate strategic moves. The journey of the trade unions up to this stage, as an important stakeholder in business, has been an eventful one as we learn in the following sections.

5.1 The Concept of Trade Unionism

Trade unions are an important institution in the realm of industrial relations. A trade union is an organization of workers or employees that is formed mainly to negotiate with the employers on various employment-related issues. This is a simplistic definition of a trade union; just to introduce the term, trade unions play a major role in representing interests of its members (employees) and in regulating labour-market relations with the employers. "Trade unionism", developed as an effort of the labour to organize during the Industrial Revolution era, promoted the Factory System of production and a laissez-faire approach of the State towards participants of the Factory System.

Put simply, the initial days of industrialization resulted in a kind of work organization where the employers, in their effort to extract maximum from the resources at hand (including labour), developed an exploitative regime as far as labour was concerned. An individual worker was powerless in the face of the employer and could do little for amelioration of his conditions of work. A collective might not be as powerless. Besides, an individual worker may be dispensable for an employer, a collective may not be. The genesis of modern trade unionism lies here. At the fundamental level, unionism binds the workers together into a common action, with "strike" as their ultimate weapon. This collectivism was aimed at restoring some kind of a balance in the employer–employee relationship. Trade unionism refers to that movement from the labour that has progressively sought to protect jobs and real earnings, secure better conditions of work and life, and fight against exploitation and

BOX 5.1 **FOR CLASS DISCUSSION**

"Globalization is too important a phenomenon to be left as unmanaged as today. The need is for stronger governance to preserve the advantages of global markets and competition to ensure that globalization works for the people, and not just for profits . . ."

INTUC in 21st Century

Do you think unions will have any role to play in meaningful governance of globalization?

Strike

"Strike" refers to a collective refusal to work by the workers with a view to bring pressure on the management to accede to a demand. This is the meaning in its simplest form, although an elaborate definition has been given in the Industrial Disputes Act, 1947.

arbitrariness to ensure fairness and equity in employment. In short, trade unionism had initially grown in order to:

- Respond to a clear demarcation between capital and labour
- Laissez-faire policy of the State in matters relating to labour and capital
- Provide bargaining power to the workers

But the journey of trade unions and trade unionism has been full of challenges.

5.1.1 Characteristics of Trade Unionism

The institution of trade unions has evolved over a few centuries and has undergone changes over the years. They (TUs) vary individually in their structure, types and activities, yet they also demonstrate certain similarities as organizations and institutions. Many trade unions have a long history. It may be necessary to understand the history of these trade unions to appreciate their responses to contemporary issues facing them. It may appear paradoxical that to tackle contemporary issues, many of the trade unions take recourse to early actions taken by early leaders and members.

Trade Union

It is an organization of workers or employees that is formed mainly to negotiate with the employers on various employment-related issues.

One of the earliest definitions of "trade unions" was given by Sidney and Beatrice Webb, and it is still valid in essential parts: "TU is a continuous association of wage earners for the purpose of maintaining or improving the conditions of their working lives."[2] This classical definition of trade union remains valid in as much as it is a person's work as an employee that determines his or her potential eligibility for membership. However, it needs to be recognized that trade unionism is not something that either exists or does not exist at a given point of time and space. It can exist along a continuum of varying strength. Union density is one of the measures of the strength of unionization. There are qualitative measures, too, which indicate the strength of unionization; for example, the extent of commitment to the principles and ideologies of trade unionism (whether the body declares itself to be a trade union, whether it is independent of employers for the purpose of negotiations, whether it recognizes bargaining as one of its major functions, and so on).

In a nutshell, the concept of trade unionism emerges from the need for a constant organization or a permanent association that is engaged in securing economic benefits for employees while protecting their interests.

5.1.2 The Origin of Trade Unionism

Industrialization brought about a new social order in societies. The distinction between capitalists and labour created a class distinction. The capitalist economic order is based upon the notion that the pursuit of self-interest by every individual leads to the establishment of an economic and social order that serves best the interests of all concerned. The capitalist economic system is an order that is supposed to accommodate all-pervading, conflicting interests. The trade union emerged as a result of the industrialization in the new social order, as a power-equating institution. That means the trade union checks the power of the management over individual workers.

The philosophy of economic liberalism and laissez-faire prevented the State from coming to the rescue of the exploited class of labour. The aggrievement of labour in a capitalist society stimulated the formation of unions and associations, which took up the cause of the working class. As an individual, the worker had no bargaining power and could easily be replaced. The collective power of association, therefore, provided cover, as collectively dispensing with a group of workers was a far more difficult proposition. The common problems and sentiments of the working class became the catalyst for organizing themselves into associations to meet and counter the employers.

5.1.3 The Impact of Trade Unions

Trade unionism owes its influence to industrialization and capitalism. Trade unionism from its inception has been assertive in fighting for the rights of workers and securing higher wages and benefits. In industrially advanced countries, trade unionism has also made a great impact on the social, political and economic life.

Trade unions have also, sometimes, led the movement for ameliorating the conditions of the weaker sections of the society. They have worked towards improving especially the working conditions for women and children, and abolishing child labour. In addition, they have constantly spearheaded the movements for general economic betterment of the working class, humane working hours, safety and other welfare measures pertaining to labour and dependants.

5.1.4 Principles of Trade Unionism

There are a few fundamental principles on which trade unionism hinges, the prominent ones being:

1. ***Unity***: Unity is strength.
2. ***Equality***: Workers must not be discriminated against on the basis of caste, creed or sex. In regard to pay, each worker must get equal pay for equal work.
3. ***Security***: The security of the employment of their members must be safeguarded.

5.1.5 Theories for the Emergence of Trade Unionism

A few important theories that have attempted to describe the emergence of trade unionism are discussed in the following sections.

Basic Theories of Trade Unionism

- Revolutionary-ownership based
- Industrial-democracy-rights based
- Business-economic power
- Socio-psychological-belongingness

REVOLUTIONARY THEORY. Credited to Marx and Engels and included in *Manifesto of the Communist Party*, this theory propounds that the means of production must belong to the workers[3]. Trade unions are instruments for a revolution in which the capitalists must be destroyed and the workers (proletariat) must take over the industry and, in turn, the government. Trade unions were a means towards the achievement of a classless society. With this approach, trade unions were regarded as a component in the larger political process for the establishment of a classless society. The events in the USSR and the erstwhile communist states proved disastrous to the movement of communism and their ideas of revolution.

INDUSTRIAL DEMOCRACY. Largely credited to Sidney and Beatrice Webb, this approach compares democracy in the government wherein "State power" is prevented from inflicting injury to individual citizens by means of elected representatives and people's power. Similarly, through unions, the workers protect themselves from the power and influence of the owners, as the individual workers are no match for the owners in these aspects. Unions are organizations where industrial democracy is established so that exploitation of any kind by the owners on the workers is prevented. All sets of rules and regulations are developed including industrial jurisprudence, which protect workers just as the public law protects citizens from the arbitrariness of the State.

BUSINESS THEORY. Here, the economic power of the workers' association—the union—is emphasized. Samuel Gompers, the advocate for this line of reasoning, emphasized that the primary objective of the union is to protect the economic interest of the workers.

SOCIO-PSYCHOLOGICAL THEORY. According to this theory, the workers make use of the union to meet their socio-psychological needs—physiological, security, companionship, ego, etc.

5.1.6 Reasons for Joining a Trade Union

It becomes increasingly important for us to examine the reasons for joining a trade union as we observe the shift from industrial relations to employee relations with a redundant role of trade unions. The workers join a union for the following reasons:

To attain economic security

- To be able to improve bargaining power
- For the ventilation of worker grievances
- For an information medium
- To protect unexpected economic needs
- To satisfy social needs
- For securing power

These needs are relevant even today in an era of "hire and fire", downsizing and redesigning of jobs. But the management takes on the role of negotiating individually with the worker on issues, concerns and aspirations of the workers. This makes the medium of the worker redundant. The trade unions can still play an important role by facilitating the economic transition by making workers adapt to the changes through training and personal upgradation of skills to suit the dynamics of the environment. Their success would add to their credibility with the management, which can provide the much-needed bargaining power for collective agreements to be drawn out concerning workers' interests.

5.1.7 Tools of Trade Unionism

Trade unions mostly use four methods for furthering their objectives:

Tools of Trade Unionism

- Mutual insurance
- Collective bargaining
- Legal enactment
- Direct action

- ***Mutual Insurance:*** In exchange for the fees that the members pay to the union, the union renders certain services, which are more functional in nature.
- ***Collective Bargaining:*** Unions attain most of their requirements through collective bargaining.
- ***Legal Enactment:*** Unions mainly advocate on changing and introducing legislation favourable to labour through legal enactment.
- ***Direct Action:*** Resorting to strikes and agitations to pressurize employers is an example of direct action.

Unions change their methods over periods of time and rarely use any one method even at a single point of time. The method used depends on the issues involved and the circumstances.

The "direct action" method could be any of the following:

Strike is the most common method, which is the collective withdrawal of work by the members of a union acting in concert. The strike may take place in an entire industry, or be confined to a single enterprise or even department. It may also be called by one or several unions jointly. Variations of the strike include "sit-in" or "work-in" strikes or "tool-down" or "pen-down" strikes. The sit-in strike is not only a work stoppage but also a refusal by strikers to vacate the premises. A work-in strike is one where the workers do not stop work but continue the production in defiance of management, who may have stopped production or declared a closure. It is, thus, the opposite of a usual strike—not a withdrawal of work but continuation of work to defy management. This type of strike was evolved by workers to protest closures of different plants during recessionary periods, and was particularly common in the ship-building yards of Britain in the late 1960s and early 1970s.

Other methods of withdrawal of work include mass casual leave, "pen down", etc. The problem with these types of agitation is that management may not know exactly how to deal with them. While there may be clear legislative guidelines for handling a strike, there are often no clear ways of dealing with strikers who take mass casual leave, or where it may be difficult to prove that the strikers have acted in concert.

Direct action also includes the "wildcat strike" or "walk-out", which is usually by a small section of workers who may be defying even their own union leaders, and could be in response to a small shop-floor issue, or an argument between a manager and a single employee. These are usually of short duration.

Some types of action taken by unions function as accessories to the main action or strike. These are picketing and boycott. Picketing is the action taken by unionists to prevent employees from attending work after a strike has been called. This activity is usually carried out at the gate or entrance, but may also be done at any other location near or far from the factory or a section of it. Picketing is a legitimate activity in some countries, although not specifically allowed in India. Generally, by convention, peaceful picketing is allowed, but once picketers turn violent or use force on the workers who want to work, it becomes banned. Boycott means the rejection by workers of specific activities, products or services provided by management. It may include pay boycott in case of unsatisfactory pay, food boycott in case of poor canteen facilities, and the boycott of goods supplied by a company. A secondary boycott includes the boycott of related items. This could mean the boycott of rail services during an airlines strike. Hunger strike is an activity where employees carry their protest by putting moral pressure on management.

The methods by which unions partially withdraw work or reduce output are "work-to-rule", and "go-slow". Under these methods also, the unions may not officially stop work, but work only at a slower pace or specifically refuse to do certain tasks, which have the effect of reducing the total output, or disrupting the work process.

Some coercive methods are used by unions or employees to make their displeasure or protest known to management, with the objective of getting unfavourable decisions reversed or modified. These include mass insubordination (the concerted refusal or defiance of management orders), demonstration, *gherao* (the confinement of managerial personnel within a small space till a more favourable decision is given, which may continue for even 48 hours), postering, and blockade. Blockade may not involve any stoppage of passage at a certain point or of certain goods. They do not, however, disturb the production process. The problem with these methods is that the management often does not know how to deal with these methods of strike. They may not know whether pay can be cut or disciplinary action taken.

Wildcat Strike

This type of strike is conducted usually by a small section of workers who may defy even their own union leaders and could be in response to a small shop-floor issue or an argument between a manager and a single employee.

Picketing

The action taken by unionists to prevent willing employees from attending work after a strike has been called "picketing". This activity is usually carried out at the gate or entrance, but may also be done at any other location near or far from the factory or a section of it.

Direct Action

Strike, tool-down, wild-cat strike, go-slow, sit-in, pen-down, walk-out, work-to- rule, work-in, mass leave, picketing, boycott, *gherao*, demonstration, postering, refusal, hunger-strike

Work-to-Rule and Go-Slow

Under these methods, unions may not officially stop work but work only at a slower pace or specifically refuse to do certain tasks, which have the effect of reducing the total output, or disrupting the work process.

5.2 Politics and Trade Unions

For decades, every problem of the labour movement, especially in India, has been attributed to a single cause—the political links of trade unions. This has been the case in several developing societies, although its peculiarity is distinctive to some former British colonies such as India and Sri Lanka. British unions that were created have sustained the Labour Party, and in this sense, they are as political as Indian unions. Marxists consider politicization essential. Marx criticizes the preoccupation of some unions with local and immediate struggles, and the resultant aloofness from general and political movements. The Marxian view on the role of trade unions has been commented upon by Dr Jerome Joseph. "Workers form unions to struggle against capitalist employers. However, trade unions have to transcend these limited aims. The capitalist system has created this capitalist class and the working class. Workers' organizations have to organize the working class not only to maintain and enhance the wage levels, but also to carry out a class

Link Between Politics and Trade Unions

- There is a link between politics and unionism.
- The politically committed members account for 15–20 per cent of total membership in a union, but their influence is high.
- Political parties and unions function in close cooperation, but there is an essential difference between the two.
- The TUs in India are fragmented due to their allegiance to different political parties.

struggle against the capitalist class."[4] An attempt to obtain shorter working hours in a single company by putting pressure on an individual employer may be a purely economic function of a union, but as soon as the same union acts on a national level or joins forces with others to obtain legislation to reduce working hours, it becomes a political movement. But politics seeks the advantages of linking with labour unions as a facilitator to capture mass vote banks of labour in industry-based constituencies. Even in the USA, the links between the AFL-CIO and the Democratic Party are quite close, as becomes apparent during the time of election.

It is generally recognized that unions use industrial and political action, and the latter implies political connection. The unions in the developing countries of Asia, Africa and Latin America are not alone in maintaining close links with political parties. There is an intimate link between a union and a party in every country in Europe. The politically committed members do not constitute a numerical majority, not even a large minority. They account for about 15–20 per cent of the total membership in every union. But their influence in the union is vastly superior to what their size would suggest. Research students have often ignored this question on the assumption that workers cannot be interested in politics.

While parties and unions function in close cooperation, there is an essential difference and even opposition between the two. The fundamental purpose of a party is to govern, while that of a union is to protest. All parties hope to wield the reins of power and run a government. In contrast, a union is an instrument of protest, not a government, neither an industry nor a nation.

5.3 Rights of Trade Unions

The International Labour Organization (ILO) recognized the right of association through the Freedom of Association and Protection of the Right to Organize Convention (Convention No. 87)[5]. Excerpts from the Convention are given in Box 5.2.

In 1987, the ILO then representing 97 member countries, 145 trade-union centres and 85 million workers, at its 73rd Conference, reiterated that many of the participating governments

BOX 5.2 **FREEDOM OF ASSOCIATION: EXTRACTS FROM THE CONVENTION 87 OF ILO**

Article 2

Workers and employers, without distinction whatsoever, shall have the right to establish and, subject only to the rules of the organization concerned, to join organizations of their own choosing without previous authorization.

Article 3

1. Workers' and employers' organizations shall have the right to draw up their constitutions and rules, to elect their representatives in full freedom, to organize their administration and activities and to formulate their programmes.
2. The public authorities shall refrain from any interference, which would restrict this right or impede the lawful exercise thereof.

Article 4

Workers' and employers' organizations shall not be liable to be dissolved or suspended by administrative authority.

Article 5

Workers' and employers' organizations shall have the right to establish and join federations and confederations and any such organization, federation or confederation shall have the right to affiliate with international organizations of workers and employers.

Article 6

The provisions of Articles 2, 3 and 4 hereof apply to federations and confederations of workers' and employers' organizations.

had not ratified this Convention. This warning was the result of a survey that the ILO had been conducting on member countries from 1983, and the violators mentioned were:

- Pakistan, where legislation restricted unionization in civil services, export processing zones, some public enterprises, schools, hospitals, and public transport
- Bangladesh, where authorities had extensive powers to supervise internal affairs of unions and could ban bargaining in public enterprises
- Indonesia, where the law required government permission before strikes and which was never given
- South Korea, where law restricted the right to associate itself
- Canada, where restrictions had been imposed on bargaining in public services in three provinces
- United Kingdom, where legislation seriously restricted the internal autonomy of unions and unionization in the communications centre at Cheltenham from 1984
- East Europe, USSR, Czechoslovakia, Poland, etc., where previous restrictions had not been removed

This report was even more candid about the repression on unionists. In 1986 alone, 200 union activists had been murdered, of which 190 were in Brazil. Of the 4,500 imprisonments in that year, 3,400 were from South Africa alone. This also indicates that union activism is inextricably linked with politics, even if we do not want to acknowledge it or would prefer to exclude it.

5.4 Roles, Functions and Objectives of Trade Unions

The role of trade unions is interpreted differently by different stake holders. The most widely recognized role of trade unions is that of a protector. Their primary effort throughout their existence has been in ameliorating the working conditions, protecting and enhancing wages and earnings, protecting employment and fighting discrimination, unfairness and exploitation of workers. However, with time, other roles of trade unions have also emerged and gained prominence although the primary role remains the raison d'etre of the TUs. By and large, in their protective role, the TUs have been instrumental in forging out collective agreements. The legislative regimes in various countries have also affected and have been affected by the trade-union roles and efforts. For example, in many countries, wage levels are largely determined by the government, whereas in others, it is left to market forces and collective bargaining. Different legislative regimes in different countries modify the role of the trade unions to that extent.

In short, the role of a trade union is to protect and promote and regulate the relations between workers and employers, or between workers and workers through collective bargaining. They play an important role in moulding the industrial relations.

5.4.1 Objectives of Trade Unions

The following are the broad objectives of trade unions:

1. **Ensure Security of Workers:** This involves continued employment of workers, preventing retrenchment, layoffs or lockouts; restricting the application of "fire" or "dismissal or discharge", etc.
2. **Obtain Better Economic Returns:** This involves wage hike at periodic intervals, bonus at higher rates, other admissible allowances, subsidized canteen and transport facilities, etc.

The major objectives of trade unions are the following:

- Ensure security of workers
- Obtain better economic returns
- Improve working conditions
- Power to influence management
- Power to influence the government

3. **Improve Working Environment and Welfare Measures:** This involves better workplaces, ventilation, lighting, safety, healthcare, sanitation, less pollution, welfare measures for working ladies, maternity facilities, children's education, housing, insurance, social-security schemes, old-age covers, etc.
4. **Secure Power to Influence Management:** This involves the worker's participation in management, decision-making, the role of unions in policy decisions affecting workers, etc.
5. **Secure Power to Influence the Government:** This involves influence on the government to pass labour legislation that improves working conditions; safety, welfare, security and retirement benefits of the workers and their dependents; curbing the power of punishment by employers; seeking redress of grievances, etc.

5.4.2 Functions of Trade Unions

According to Punekar, the most basic function of trade unions is to build up its own organization and to give weight to its collective actions. Once this is accomplished, other functions follow—economic (or the attainment of the financial interests of workers) as well as political, legal and welfare functions. The social function is not what is meant by social purpose usually. The social purpose may be the object of a changing society. But there is a paradox in it. The social purpose of yesterday, once accomplished, becomes the social function of today. For example, the social purpose after the Great Depression was to establish the position of the trade unions in the industry on a firmer foundation, in terms of union security and recognition. After the Depression was over and the economy had recovered, that social purpose did not remain, but the unions continued to discharge social functions of obtaining recognition. In recent years, the social purpose of unions appears to be to help the industry achieve higher levels of productivity.

Broadly speaking, the functions of trade unions are:

- Organizational
- Economic
- Political-legal
- Welfare

Broadly speaking, the functions of a modern trade union are very comprehensive, much more so than those of their counterparts in the past; it has, moreover, a clearer perception of its ultimate aims and objectives. Its functions are generally classified into those that are militant or protective, and those that are fraternal, ministrant or positive. Under the former group of functions, a trade union is primarily concerned with obtaining better conditions of work and of employment for its members through such militant activities as strikes and boycotts, which are generally resorted to when efforts at collective bargaining fail to bear results. The latter functions relate to the provision of such benefits as sickness and accident payments. A trade union also offers financial support to its members during strikes and lock-outs and during periods of temporary unemployment.

PROTECT ECONOMIC INTERESTS. Arguably, the economic function of a trade union is the most significant one. A trade union, once organized, revolves around the economic demand of its members, which manifest themselves in the following forms:

- Improved economic status
- Shorter working day
- Improvement in working and living conditions
- Better health and safety standards
- Upgrading welfare facilities
- Promoting internal and external equity

SOCIAL. The power of management within an enterprise can be kept in check through strong unionism. In addition, unions affect nearly every other measurable aspect of the operation of workplace and the enterprises, from top line to the enhancement of productivity to the compensation structure. The absence of strong unionization in the unorganized sector is reflected in the behaviour of workers and firms, which differ substantially from the organized sector. On the balance, unionization appears to improve rather than to harm the social and economic system. It is with this belief that the First Five Year Plan encouraged trade unions to:

i) Present plans to workers so as to create enthusiasm in implementing them

ii) Exercise utmost restraint in regard to work stoppage

iii) Formulate wage demands that are attuned to the requirements of economic development and are in keeping with considerations of social justice

iv) Assume greater responsibility for the success of productive effort

POLICY AND LEGISLATIVE. Initially, unions were successful in correcting arbitrary conditions of work and service, often through legislation. They made their presence felt in the area of personnel policy within undertakings by including recruitment, transfer and promotion in collective bargaining. But today, there may be very little left to fight for. For instance, many organizations under business compulsions have ceased to exploit their workforce and offer not only good wages but ample welfare and comfortable working conditions. To a great extent, these have rendered trade unions superfluous. In developed countries, unions devote more time to issues other than wages and working conditions. Even in developing countries, unions in large, well-established firms have few of the traditional conflicts with management. In today's context, however, the questions of employment and the work process itself occupy more time and energy of the unions. In most countries, unions find themselves increasingly concerned with economic policies at the national level.

REDRESS INEQUALITY. If we get back to the basics of unionism, we see that there is unequal distribution of money and power in all organizations. The job of any union is to redress this inequality; that is, to make the distribution of money and power less unequal than it is. They may negotiate with management the terms and conditions under which their members are employed. This may bring pressure to bear on the government to enact legislation for the same.

Functions of Trade Unions:

- Protect economic interests of the members
- Influence social relationships at the workplace
- Influence policies at the national level
- Collective action for sectional interest
- Collaboration for productivity and gain-sharing
- Enhancing professional status
- Research
- Communication, welfare and education

PRECIPITATE COLLECTIVE WITHDRAWAL IN THE PURSUIT OF SECTIONAL INTEREST. But their most important weapons and one that unions have fiercely clung on to throughout history is the collective withdrawal of labour, otherwise called the strike. Through union organization, workers bring pressure to bear on enterprise management and the ruling elite.

PRODUCTIVITY. Also, the establishment of union–industry conferences have facilitated the collaboration between unions and management, which has been necessitated by the fact that power, wherever it lies, cannot be dissociated from responsibility, in the long run. And this collaboration serves the purpose of industry as well as labour.

ENHANCE PROFESSIONAL STATUS. Unions have also assumed a role of enhancing professional competence of their members through providing expert knowledge, raising the standard of competency in their occupation, improving the professional equipment of their members, educating them and endeavouring by every means to increase their status in public estimation. Enlarging opportunities for promotion and training is a function that has the most congruence with the business objectives of an enterprise.

PREPARATION FOR BARGAINING. Monappa adds research functions to trade-union activities.[6] Research on wages, working conditions, effects of work on their members' health and safety or even on the management performance in an enterprise (which

Philips' workers did in Bombay once) would be an inevitable part of the activities of any efficient union.

To summarize then, unions perform numerous functions to preserve, protect and advance the interests of their members, and to maintain the association itself.

ANCILLARY

Communication: Many large unions bring out newsletters clarifying the union's policy or stand on certain principal issues. It is also used as a channel of communication on the management activities as well as union activities.

Welfare Activities: They include self-employment opportunities for women or spouse of workers, education facilities for worker children, organizing medical camps, sports activities, etc. Some unions also set up housing and cooperative societies.

Education: This involves organizing adult literacy classes, promoting the government's worker-education schemes and information-driven seminars on aspects concerning their rights and responsibilities.

In India, the trade unions have been focusing on the following functions:

- Achieving higher wages and living standards/working conditions by entering into agreements through negotiations/collective bargaining
- Acquiring the control of industry by workers, especially in major public services and utilities such as railways, air traffic and transport
- Resisting job insecurities, helplessness and victimization, which was clearly evident during the Airport Authority strike in 2005
- Grievance identification and devising a procedure for its redress
- Raising the status of workers as an important constituent of economic growth and development
- Enhancing morale and self-confidence and thereby enlarging opportunities for growth
- Educational, cultural and recreational facilities in townships or at the workplace
- Promoting the identity of interests of workers with their industry
- Ancillary-communication, welfare, education, etc.; basically organizing and guiding workers
- Intervening to promote worker interests during the formulation of HR policies
- At the national level, serve as an agency for industrial democracy advocating workers' rights and protecting against arbitrary and unfair treatment of their jobs

5.4.3 Activities of Trade Unions

The functions discussed in Section 5.4.2 can be broken down into the following activities:

ECONOMIC. Exercising pressure for protecting and promoting economic interests of workers, such as:

i) Improved economic status

ii) Shorter working day

iii) Improvement in working and living conditions

iv) Better health and safety standards

v) Upgrading welfare facilities

vi) Reducing inequalities—both internally within the organization and outside

POLITICAL

i) Seeking/obtaining political power through political affiliations

ii) Lobbying activities to influence the cause of labour and legislations for the same

iii) Participating in, and representing the workers on bipartite forums

iv) Developing revolutionary ideologies among the workers

v) Protesting against governmental decisions that may be detrimental to the interest of workers; *bandhs* called by political parties)

SOCIAL

i) Initiating and developing workers' education scheme

ii) Organizing welfare and recreational activities such as mutual insurance

iii) Providing monetary and other help during periods of strikes and economic distress

iv) Running cooperative welfare schemes and societies

v) Facilitating housing needs

vi) Community-development work

vii) Organizing cultural functions

viii) Associating with the government's social-welfare programmes

NATIONAL/INTERNATIONAL LEVEL

i) Representing workers at the national level on advisory committees

ii) Associating with national federations for the purpose of building working-class unity and solidarity

iii) Raising funds in case of national/international calamities or tragedies

5.5 Features of an Effective Trade Union

Trade unions are basically a consequence of democratic institutions and, hence, must be formed through an elected consensus. This implies that trade unions must be internally democratic with a strong leadership that safeguards worker interests and their need to participate in the management's decision-making process. External leadership or leaders with political aspirations would provide the referral support of the State to bargain, but this dependency would create far more insecurities than consolidation of gains. The democratic nature would be through regularity in participation in meetings and actively contributing to workers' interests.

Trade unionism has a responsibility to national growth and development. Working on collective needs of the workers should not delineate them from the macro-perspective of achieving productivity gains for the economy. This implies that trade unions have a responsibility towards their worker members and also the State to promote industrial peace and harmony essential for growth. Collective bargaining should be collaborative, and not competitive.

Financial security should be ensured by the initiation of activities that can raise funds and put the union on a strong foundation. The union should operate with honesty and integrity of purpose with clearly defined objectives, coherent and well-conceived policies and organizational methods.

The features of an effective trade union are:

- Internally democratic
- Have a strong leadership
- Exhibit a responsibility towards their worker members
- Committed to promote industrial peace and harmony
- Inclined towards collective bargaining that is collaborative and not competitive.
- Possess financial security
- Adaptable to change

Trade unions should accept change as a part of the growth cycle and view all types of changes, be it technological, structural, systemic or cultural in a macro-perspective, while also preparing workers to adapt to the changes required. In fact, a trade union is effective and also desirable by the management if it acts as an internal-change agent that stimulates competitive advantage gains on all fronts.

5.6 The Classification of Trade Unions

The classification of trade unions emerges from the interests of the workers. Thus, over a period of time, the union structure has evolved through various interests, sometimes, protective, sometimes regulatory, and at times revolutionary, in the given socio-political environment. They can either be classified by their purpose, which could be protective and regulatory, reformist or revolutionary. They may also be categorized on the basis of how they are organized, which could be on the basis of some trade, skill or craft (e.g. Welder's Union or Diploma Engineers Union); as a mix across different skills or trades, more on the lines of a general union; or an attempt to organize all workers within a particular industry resulting in industrial unionism. These may further have local branches and unite centrally with a national federation. Table 5.1 gives a simple structure for classification on the basis of purpose or membership.

BY PURPOSE

(a) **Regulatory Unions:** They protect workers' rights, fight against victimization and exploitation. They function on the ideology of economic and social justice, and regulate any decision or policy that violates the "rights" of workers.

(b) **Reformist Unions:** They aim at preservation of the capitalist economic structure through the maintenance of employer–employee relationship. They do not seek to change the existing social, economic or political structure of the State or the business strategy of the industrial unit. A further subdivision of this classification could be (a) business unionism, where employees enter into successful business relationships with employers or (b) friendly or uplift unions, where they aspire to elevate the moral, intellectual and social life of the workers.

(c) **Revolutionary Unions:** They aim at destroying the present structure and replacing it with a new order that is regarded as preferable to the working class. They could be anarchist or political in nature. A variant of this is called "predatory union", which does not subscribe to any revolutionary ideology but ruthlessly pursues an expedient objective.

BY MEMBERSHIP

(d) **Craft Unions:** These unions are formed by the membership only of those employed in a particular craft or trade or related trades/craft. The earliest unions were generally craft unions, with members from just one craft or trade, such as weavers or engine drivers. The craft unions proved to be stable unions by virtue of their collective craft or specialization power. The skill level of the members was usually at par and the union operated purely for the sectional interests of their craft. Membership is restricted to persons belonging to a particular skill level in a particular trade. The union may operate

Craft Union

Craft union is a trade union that comprises workers who are engaged in a particular craft or skill but who are not all working for the same employer; e.g. Welder's Union, Cabin Crew Association.

Table 5.1

The classification of unions.

Basis of Classification	Types
Purpose	Regulatory, Reformist, Reactionary
Membership	Craft, Staff, Industrial, General

in a single enterprise or in a particular industry and may be small or large. A modern equivalent is the pilots' guild, which has been able to bring air-traffic movement to a standstill on many occasions. The members of this union are conscious of their rights as key-category professionals and their strategic role to the business objectives.

(e) **Staff Union:** These include all workers or staff of the unit/enterprise, the specialized or craftsmen included. Their organization is based on common concerns, needs or aspirations and derives strength from their solidarity. Being multidisciplinary in composition, the issues of concern are wide ranging and keep changing with the changing dynamics of the industrial society. Participation is greater as membership is greater and power is derived from the strength of membership.

(f) **Industrial Union:** This is similar to the staff union except that it extends beyond one unit or enterprise and is collectively concerned with the industry as a whole. It, therefore, focuses on the industry-specific concerns. Examples include Textile Labour Association of Ahmedabad, and Rashtriya Mazdoor Sangh, Bombay.

Industrial Union

This is a trade union that combines all workers, both skilled and unskilled, who are employed in a particular industry.

Craft unions provide stable leadership, training and have strong bargaining power; whereas industrial trade unions have joint, collective bargaining power and can ensure uniformity in service conditions and coordinate sectional claims. Too many craft unions would help the employer play one union against another.

(g) **General Unions:** These unions cover various industries and workers/labour of different types and skills. The issues are generic and their source of strength is the membership and solidarity among them for a purpose.

5.6.1 The Evolution of the Trade Union Structure

As industry became more complex and the differentiation within the workforce grew, the craft union began to federate, or join with other craft unions to form larger pressure groups in order to gain more power. This forced them to shed many of their exclusive demands peculiar only to one craft or trade and push more general issues, which would satisfy most or all of their members. The more common issues had to be pressed first. In certain cases, sectional interests were contrary to general interests of workers and had to be abandoned. This led ultimately to the general or industrial union, the commonest form today in large industry. The membership of a general or industrial union is open to any worker or employee either in an enterprise or in an industry operating also at either level. Usually, the size of general unions is larger than that of craft unions.

The location of a union may thereafter determine the level of its operation or functioning. For instance, we refer to plant or enterprise-level unions, which operate at the factory level, industry-level unions, which operate at the industry level comprising several or many factories or enterprises. In addition, we also refer to federations, which are combinations of two or more plant-level unions operating either at the company level or at the industry level.

There are also central union bodies or apex organizations, which function as the mouthpiece of the labour movement, in general. In the USA, the AFL-CIO, and in the UK, the Trade union Congress (TUC) serve this purpose. In India, there are also central unions or forums, which are not registered under the Trade Unions Act, but which act as the apex bodies of politically oriented unions. Thus, all types of unions owing allegiance to one political party are affiliated to the central forum of that party and are easily identifiable in India and in other countries like Germany or France where political links are close.

5.6.2 Determinants of the Growth of Trade Unions

Moving on from the evolution of trade unions and what makes them effective and attracts workers to become members, one can identify the factors that affect the growth of trade unions as given in Box 5.3.

BOX 5.3 **THE FACTORS DETERMINING THE GROWTH OF TRADE UNIONS**

- The growth of group attitude based on common concerns, interest and aspirations
- Separate distinction based on class—workers and management or labour and management—that precludes certain rights and facilities to the workers
- Dissatisfaction with the current economic and welfare benefits
- The realization of the strength of collectivism against the individual's insecurity and dispensability on the job
- The degree of industrial commitment of workforce—the less mobile the worker, the greater would be the forces driving for unionization
- The composition of workforce—the greater the number of skilled/key category workers, the greater would be the unionization
- The introduction of labour-displacing technology has an inherent potential for unionization on account of the fear of losing jobs
- Leadership can be a driving force drawing workers to join a particular union.
- The attitude of employers towards unions—the more restrictive, lower the growth but greater the intensity of resistance put forth by the existing union
- Political and legal framework—the political affiliations with the political party in power provide an impetus to the growth of such unions. The legal sanctity accorded to trade unions also furthers the pace of growth.
- Public opinion with regard to trade unions is dependent on the political and social ideology prevailing at a point of time. If the opinion views trade unions to be counter-productive, it can retard the pace of growth of trade unionism.

5.7 Strategies for the Achievement of Trade Union Objectives

Trade unions use a combination of strategies for achieving their objectives. A few basic ones are listed below, although these are not exhaustive:

i) Organizing on the basis of craft or skill and using the union's power of collective indispensability to bargain

ii) Getting recognized as the sole bargaining agent to advocate the interest of the members. The recognition could be voluntary, coming from the management or gained through secret ballot elections.

iii) Associating with national federations to get political support to their cause

iv) Collective bargaining of terms and conditions of employment, thereby entailing concerted action on the part of the employees and employers on the basis of a common agreement

v) Union security achieved through closed shop or union shop or an agency-shop arrangement

(vi) Channelizing the procedures that involve the processing and handling of grievances

vii) Negotiating agreements with the management on wages, hours of work and other terms and conditions of employment

viii) Arbitration by which unsettled or unresolved disputes can be settled by an outside agency

ix) Political pressure through local legislations or political affiliations

x) Mutual insurance through common contributions to meet financial needs of workers; the method of mutual insurance focuses only on welfare benefits provided by trade unions to its members for improving their conditions. It may involve the creation of a common fund to which every member contributes. This induces workers to join the union, improves their financial position and also helps in maintaining discipline among the members.

xi) Legal enactments—trade unions send their representatives to legislatures so that protective labour legislations may be enacted to secure better working and living conditions for workers.

The trade unions, at the present juncture, are undergoing a transition and groping for an approach that would be relevant to this reality. Everyone agrees that labour-market flexibility in some form is inevitable under the current forces, but there is no consensus on how this flexibility is to be achieved. Trade unions find this transition threatening since it would have a social cost, which will question the very purpose of their existence. There is no easy answer for them under the present framework except to approach it as a shared problem amongst the affected players and their needs.

5.8 The State of Trade Unions in the World

The general perception about the trade unions today is negative, mainly owing to the functioning rather than the results that they are able to achieve. The underlying principles for the existence of trade unions are generally acceptable, but the chequered history sometimes puts a question mark on their methods and morality. This, however, is true of any public institution to some extent, so it would be unfair to single out the TUs for such perception.

There has been a decline in union membership across the world.

Union structures and dynamics, to a large extent, are shaped by the socio-political-legal framework of a country and, therefore, the structure and dynamics are not uniform all over the world. They vary, depending upon the legal framework that obtains in that country.

We will learn about "union security" in Chapter 6. Different laws about "closed shop" in different countries affect the manner in which a trade union goes about its business. In

Closed Shop

Closed Shop employs only people who are already union members, and in this case, the employer must recruit directly from the union.

Table 5.2

Trade unions in different countries: A comparison.

Country	Structure	Functions
USA	A single main national centre, the American Federation of Labour and Congress of Industrial Organization (AFL-CIO), made up of a relatively large number (currently 64) of industrial and occupational unions	Protecting wages of workers against capitalist exploitation Increasing wages Reducing hours of work Securing just and human working conditions Improving the sanitary and safety conditions at workplace Increasing workers' share in national income Introducing working rules Democratizing labour management Achieving equal opportunity Safeguarding the labour movement from communists, fascists Encouraging the sale of union-made goods through the use of union label Participating in various community activities

(Continued)

Table 5.2 (cont.)

Trade unions in different countries: A comparison.

Country	Structure	Functions
Former USSR	State socialist trade unions acting as a "transmission belt" between the party and the masses. The organizational structure of the trade unions mirrored that of the party-State, the majority of their functions were party-State functions and their authority derived from the party-State.	Raising labour productivity Improving the quality of production Participation in planning Regulation of wages Assisting in techno-structural changes Collective agreements on wages and working conditions Participation in settlement of disputes Concluding agreements on the utilization of funds allotted for social and industrial security Striving for better organization of medical assistance and the protection of the health of women and children Developing artistic mass activity Promoting culture and sports Helping attract women into public, productive and social life Drafting, issuing, implementation and the supervision of labour legislation Maintenance of labour discipline Provision of housing and other welfare amenities
UK	Tradition of voluntarism; the representation of workers through trade-union officers at workplaces in the form of shop stewards; organization of trade-union membership is on occupational rather than industrial lines	Maintaining and improving wages, hours and conditions of work Providing and improving opportunities for the advancement of workers to obtain "full employment" Extending the influence of the working class on policy issues Extending social control on the nation's economic life Avoiding inequalities between different sectors
China	Mass organization of the working class led by the party, and are the transmission belts between the party and the masses	Organizing workers to launch labour-emulation drives, strengthening labour discipline and ensuring fulfilment of plans Improving material and cultural standards of the workers' lives and supervising the managements with a view to implement various targets Organizing political, educational and technical studies as well as cultural and sports activities Ensuring equal pay for equal work Guaranteeing material assistance to the workers in old age/illness Providing recreational activities Protecting women and children from exploitation Working for the improvement of living conditions Entering into collective agreements with management on wages, labour norms, welfare and social security

Germany, for example, closed shops are illegal, that is, there can be no discrimination on the basis of membership to a particular union. Germany also encourages greater participation and decision-making than in other industrialized countries. Margaret Thatcher introduced a series of changes in the UK in the 1980s, which gave freedom to employees to either join or not join a union. A union's functioning also depends, to an extent, on the degree to which it shares the ideology with political parties. In many countries, unions and political parties are close and even share leadership. The Labour Party in the UK is a case in point. CITU is a part of the CPI(M) and almost all the central TU organizations in India are closely aligned with a political party.

Some differentiating variables of the unions in different countries have been covered in Chapter 3. The summary table in Table 5.2 below gives a snapshot of the differences.

SUMMARY

- Unions are organizations designed to promote and enhance the social and economic welfare of their members.
- The unions emerged to protect worker interests, and, gradually, started playing an important role in the social and political affairs of a country.
- Trade unions are part of the fabric of industrial democracy and can play a constructive role in improving production and productivity, and the resolution of conflicts.
- Trade unionism had initially grown in order to:
  - Respond to a clear demarcation between capital and labour
  - Laissez-faire policy of the State in matters relating to labour and capital
  - Provide bargaining power to the workers
- Trade unionism is not something that either exists or does not exist at a given point of time and space. It can exist along a continuum of varying strength.
- There are a few fundamental principles on which trade unionism hinges, the prominent ones being:

  Unity: Unity is strength.

  Equality: Workers must not be discriminated against on the basis of caste, creed or sex. In regard to pay, each worker must get equal pay for equal work.

  Security: The security of employment of their members must be safeguarded.
- Trade unions have the following main objectives:
  - Ensure the security of workers
  - Obtain better economic returns
  - Improve working conditions
  - Power to influence management
  - Power to influence the government
- Broad functions of TUs can be clubbed under the following heads:
  - Organizational
  - Economic
  - Political-Legal
  - Welfare
- The union classification can be done on the basis of their interests, sometimes, protective, sometimes regulatory, and at times revolutionary, in the given socio-political environment.
- They can either be classified by their purpose, which could be protective and regulatory, reformist or revolutionary. They may also be categorized on the basis of how they are organized, which could be on the basis of some trade or skill.

KEY TERMS

- craft union 92
- closed shop 94
- industrial union 93
- picketing 85
- "sit-in" strike 84
- strike 82
- trade unions 82
- union shop 94
- wildcat strike or walk-out 85
- work-to-rule and go-slow 85

REVIEW QUESTIONS

1. What are the characteristics of trade unions?
2. What is a trade union and how are they generally formed? Trace the genesis of trade unions.
3. Explain the following:
   i. the objectives of a trade union
   ii. characteristics of trade unionism
   iii. classification of trade unions
   iv. strategies for the achievement of objectives of a trade union

QUESTIONS FOR CRITICAL THINKING

1. What are the functions of trade unions? Examine whether the trade unions in India have been able to fulfil these functions.
2. In the current-day competitive environment, has the role of trade unions changed? Do you think, in the present environment, the trade unions need to reinvent themselves?
3. Discuss the changing role of trade unions and the resultant impact of union–management relations consequent to globalization and technological breakthroughs in industry.

DEBATE

1. The days of trade unions are over. With an increase in the knowledge workers and knowledge economy, the conditions that prevailed in the Factory System are no longer present.
2. Trade unions cannot be effective unless they back their actions with militancy or industrial action.

CASE ANALYSIS

The Value of Unions to UK Businesses

A joint statement setting out the positive contribution that modern union representatives can make to the workplace has been launched by the Department for Business, the TUC and the CBI.

Featuring real-life examples where well-known companies have worked with union representatives to bring about changes that have been in the best interests of the employer and the workforce, the case studies show that union representatives can be a major resource in the workplace.

Reps in Action shows how modern union representatives and company managers have worked together to deal with situations that can occur in any workplace and as a result have, for example, improved working practices, enhanced workplace training provision or lead to greener workplaces.

According to research conducted by BERR in 2007, union reps are worth between £3.4bn and £10.2bn to the UK economy, on the basis that their presence in a workplace brings about a combination of productivity gains, reduced staff turnover, less time off as a result of sickness, improved health and safety and better training for staff.

TUC General Secretary Brendan Barber said: "This joint publication reveals the positive contribution that union reps can make in the workplace. In these tough times, Britain's businesses need as much support as possible. Union reps can be a vital resource not only for unions and their members, but also for the companies and organizations that employ them.

"The business benefits of a union presence at work add further weight to the case for union equality reps and union green reps being given new legal rights to paid time off to do their duties and to undertake training related to their union work.

"At the moment, union equality reps and green reps—unlike shop stewards, learning and safety reps—often have to carry out union work in their own time, and as a result, are not nearly as effective as they could be, if they had paid time off to carry out their union duties. That's why the TUC is campaigning hard for statutory rights for these reps."

(Source: Trade Unions Congress, UK - http://www.tuc.org.uk/organizationorganization/tuc-16456-f0.cfm)

If there is such complete cooperation between management and trade unions, don't you think the very purpose of forming a trade union is defeated?

Do you think the union has a role in contributing to what are regarded as totally management functions, e.g., increasing productivity, reducing absenteeism and improving workplace safety?

NOTES

1 "Tata Closes in on Jaguar Takeover", BBC News, 3 January 2008 http://news.bbc.co.uk/2/hi/business/7169681.stm. "British Union Regrets Ford's Jaguar Exit, Welcomes Tata Takeover", 26 March 2008, http://economictimes.indiatimes.com/articleshow/2902057.cms. Bill Koening and Gopal Ratnam, "Tata in Talks to Buy Ford's Jaguar, Land Rover Units", 3 January 2008, http://www.bloomberg.com/apps/news?pid=20601087&sid=aBdsVtn_7HuU&refer=home. Nandini Sen Gupta and Sudeshna Sen, "Tata Group Emerges Front-runner for Jaguar Land Rover", *The Economic Times*, 23 November 2007, http://economictimes.indiatimes.com/India_Inc_in_top_gear_Tata_takes_lead/articleshow/2563247.cms.

2 Sidney and Beatrice Webb, *The History of Trade Unionism* (New York: Augustus Kelley, 1965), p 1.

3 Manifesto of the Communist Party available online at www.marxists.org/archive/marx/workers/1848/communist-manifesto/index.htm.

4 Jerome Joseph, Industrial Relations: Towards a Transformational Process Model, (Delhi: Global Business Press, 1995) 7.

5 International Labour Organization, "Freedom of Association and Protection of the Right to Organize Convention, 1948", Convention No. 87, http://www.ilo.org/ilolex/cgi-lex/convde.pl?C087.

6 Arun Monappa, *Industrial Relations* (New Delhi: Tata McGraw-Hill, 1985), pp. 56.

SUGGESTED READING

Beaumont, Phil *Change in Industrial Relations* (London: Routledge, 1990).

Deodhar, S. B., S. D. Punekar and Saraswathi Sankaran, *Labour Welfare Trade Unionism and Industrial Relations,* Fifteenth edition, (New Delhi: Himalaya Publishing House, 2003).

Gaur, G. L. *Trade Unionism and Industrial Relations* (New Delhi: Deep and Deep Publications, 1986).

Monappa, Arun *Industrial Relations* (New Delhi: Tata McGraw-Hill, 1985).

Waddington, Jeremy and Paul Edwards (eds.), *Trade Union Organization in Industrial Relations—Theory and Practice* (Oxford: Blackwell Publishing, 1995).

chapter six

CHAPTER OUTLINE

LEARNING OBJECTIVES

After reading this chapter, you will be able to:

- Trace the evolution of the trade-union movement in India
- Understand the structure and political affiliations of the major trade unions
- Understand the problems of Indian trade unions
- Know the provisions of the Trade Unions Act,1926

A Show of Strength

The Dwarkapur Steel Plant, established in the year 1956 with technical collaboration from the UK, employed around 20,000 workers and 1,200 managers. Set up at a time when the foundation of the country was being laid through the creation of infrastructure, the plant managed to attain its rated capacity of 1 million tonne per annum by the early 1960s. Most workers in the plant were members of the union that was affiliated to the ruling party—the Indian National Congress. The government at the centre as well as in the State were from the same party. In the late 1960s, and early 1970s, changes in the political landscape saw the rise of the left parties in the State. The rising influence of these left parties encouraged the unions affiliated to these parties to make their presence felt in the Dwarkapur Steel Plant. To show that it was a force to reckon with, the newly created union encouraged protests including work stoppages, *gheraos* and demonstrations, wherever it had pockets of influence. The management, however, continued dealing with the Congress-affiliated trade union, as it was the "recognized" union and, as far as records went, the union with a "majority". The left-affiliated union, in a bid to demonstrate its hold over the workers in the plant, challenged the management to verify the union membership of all the workers to ascertain which union had a majority. The management was in a fix, since sensing a threat to its status, the Congress-affiliated union was opposing the move for verification, threatening industrial action if the management even formally held discussions with the other union that was not recognized in the first place. In the mean time, a change in the ruling party at the State level increasingly pressurized the management to undertake the verification process. Both the unions, to establish their strength, started competing with each other completely vitiating the industrial relations atmosphere in the plant. Dwarkapur Steel Plant was a central PSU, with the Ministry of Steel, Government of India being the administrative ministry. On the other hand, the appropriate government under various labour laws was the state government. This further complicated the issues.

Trade Unions in India

> *"Our trade-union movement today is fragmented. Everyone talks of the value of unity, the imperative need of unity today, but in practice, hardly anyone seems to be willing to give up separate identities."*
>
> **National Commission on Labour**

The opening case highlights one phase of the development of the trade-union movement in India. Although today, the influence of trade unions seems to have waned to a large extent, it may be because they are in the process of evaluating a coherent response to the forces unleashed by liberalization, privatization and globalization. To reach this stage, trade unions have travelled a long distance—both chronologically and conceptually. This chapter traces the genesis of the trade-union movement in India, and examines the issues and challenges that face them in present times.

The trade-union movement in India is over a century old and the trade unions in this country are generally regarded as too fragmented. Since at least the middle of the twentieth century, trade unions have split on ideological, political, craft, caste and even on personality bases. These splits have often resulted in bitter rivalry, and in a few cases, many unions at a workplace have competed for the allegiance of the same set of workers.

6.1 Phases in the Growth of Trade Unions in India

The growth of trade unions in India has passed through a few distinctive phases, paralleling the political and economic developments in the country.

6.1.1 The Pre-independence Phase

India being an agricultural country, trade unionism was largely restricted to industrial areas. The earliest known trade unions in India were the Bombay Millhand's Association formed in 1890, the Amalgamated Society of Railway Servants of India and Burma formed in 1897, the Printers' Union formed in Calcutta (now Kolkata) in 1905, the Bombay Postal Union which was formed in 1907, the Kamgar Hitwardhak Sabha, Bombay formed in 1910. The trade-union movement began in India after the end of the First World War. After a decade following the end of the First World War, the pressing need for the coordination of activities of the individual unions was recognized. Thus, the All India Trade Union Congress was formed in 1920 on a national basis; the Central Labour Board, Bombay and the Bengal Trades Union Federation were formed in 1922. The All India Railwaymen's Federation was formed in the same year, and this was followed by the creation of both provincial and central federations of the unions of post-and-telegraph employees. The origin of the passing of a Trade Unions Act in India was the historic Buckingham Mill case of 1940 in which the Madras High Court granted an interim injunction against the Strike Committee of the Madras Labour Union forbidding them to induce certain workers to break their contracts of employment by refusing to return to work. The trade-union leaders found

> Some interesting facts about trade unions in India:
>
> - The trade-union movement in India is over a century old.
> - Indian trade unions are very fragmented.
> - Early splits in Indian trade unions tended to be on ideological grounds.
> - Recent fragmentations have centred on personalities and, occasionally, on regional and caste considerations.
> - Trade-union activities are restricted to industrial areas.
> - The AITUC was formed in 1920 on a national basis.
> - The Trade Union Act was passed in 1926.

that they were liable to prosecution and imprisonment for bona fide union activities and it was felt that some legislation for the protection of the trade union was necessary. In March 1921, Shri N. M. Joshi, then General Secretary, All India Trade Union Congress, successfully moved a resolution in the Central Legislative Assembly, recommending that the government should introduce legislation for the registration and protection of trade unions. The opposition from the employers to the adoption of such a measure was, however, so great that it was not until 1926 that the Indian Trade Unions Act was passed. The Indian Trade Unions Bill, 1925 was introduced in the Central Legislative Assembly to provide for the registration of trade unions, and in certain respects, to define the law relating to registered trade unions in provinces of India.

A trade union in India is the primary instrument for promoting the trade-union movement and championing the cause of the working class in India. The Indian government passed the Trade Unions Act in 1926, which legalized the registered trade unions in India. The Act also gives protection to these trade unions against certain civil and criminal cases. There are at present many trade unions in India, which regulate the aspirations of the working classes. The All India Trade Union Congress (AITUC) is the oldest trade union in India, and till 1945, it remained the central trade-union organization in India. The trade unions in India could be grouped under two main categories, i.e., the politically affiliated unions and the independent ones. The affiliated unions (those having links with one or the other political parties) have federated themselves industry-wise as also geographically. There are almost 70,000 registered trade unions in India and the BMS is the most representative national union.

The evolution of trade unionism, post-Independence, is described below, in terms of the "four phases of unionism" corresponding to the structural changes in the economy that impacted the labour market and industrial relations scenario.

6.1.2 The First Post-independence Phase

The first decade (1950–mid-1960s) corresponds to an era of State planning and import substitution, when public-sector employment and public-sector unionism rose phenomenally. Unions and bargaining structures were highly centralized; the two main federations were the nationalist Indian National Trade Union Congress (INTUC) and the communist All India Trade Union Congress (AITUC). State interventionz in the determination of wages and working conditions was the norm, and "state-dominated pluralism" prevailed. There was a spurt in union membership and also an increase in labour fragmentation with new political parties/break-away groups emerging in the fore front of national politics. The Hind Mazdoor Sabha (HMS), launched in 1948, emerged stronger with its focus on the nationalization of key industries, securing effective recognition to bargain collectively, workers' participation for the regulation of industries and advocating the cooperative movement.

> The first post-independence phase of the growth of trade unions was characterized by:
>
> - An era of State planning and import substitution
> - The rise in public-sector employment and public-sector unionism
> - Centralized union structures and bargaining
> - INTUC and AITUC main federations
> - State intervention in wage determination and working conditions
> - State-dominated pluralism
> - A spurt in union membership and labour fragmentation

6.1.3 The Second Post-independence Phase (Mid-1960s–1980)

The two-decade period (1960s–1980) was a period of economic stagnation and political turmoil. Many more unions emerged in various parts of India, based on local political support. Indian politics also became more heterogeneous with dissident groups emerging. Employment slowed down, there were massive inter-union rivalries, and industrial conflict increased. Centralized bargaining institutions now started feeling the pressure of dissent from below, and both the Hind Mazdoor Sabha (HMS) and the Centre of Indian Trade Unions (CITU) made significant progress in the labour movement. The crisis culminated in the May 1974 railway strike that was followed by the 1975–1977 Emergency Regime of Mrs Gandhi. An "involuted" pluralism dominated Indian labour relations during this second phase.

6.1.4 The Third Post-independence Phase (1980–Pre-liberalization Era)

The third phase (1980–1991) corresponds to a period of segmented and uneven economic development. Decentralized bargaining and independent trade unionism enter the stage in a significant way. Two major strikes (the 1980–1981 Bangalore public-sector strike and the 1982 Mumbai textile workers' strike) marked this phase, and inter-state and inter-regional variations in the nature of labour–management regimes became much wider. In the more profitable economic sectors, the unions gained, but in the unorganized and declining sector, workers lost out and the unions were left with few strategies.

The 1960s to the 1980s represented the second post-Independence growth phase of trade unions, characterised by:

- A period of economic stagnation and political turmoil
- The emergence of many more unions
- Heterogeneity of politics
- Employment slow down
- Inter-union rivalry
- An increase in industrial conflicts
- Pressure on centralized bargaining
- The railway strike of 1974 and severe curbs during Emergency

6.1.5 The Fourth Post-independence Phase (Post-liberalization Era)

Finally, the fourth phase of unionism represents the post-economic reform period. The stabilization and structural-adjustment programmes led to demands for increased labour-market flexibility, especially employment flexibility. This has led to a recruitment freeze in many public-sector sites, and the unions in these sectors now have to cope with competition at the local level. In non-viable public enterprises, unions are coming to terms with "voluntary" retirement schemes. In the early years of economic reform, there were sincere attempts by all parties to engage in tripartite consultations, but there now seem to be several barriers to this form of engagement.

The pre-liberalization era from 1980 to 1991 represented the third major phase in the growth of trade unions:

- Period of segmented and uneven economic growth
- Decentralized bargaining and independent trade unionism
- Bangalore PSU strike and Mumbai textile workers' strike
- Inter-state and inter-regional variations in labour–management relations

6.2 The Structure of Trade Unions in India

In India, in general, the structure of trade unions consists of three levels: the plant/shop or local level, the state and the centre. The ideology at the central level percolates to the state and plant/unit level. Every national federation of labour in India has state branches, state committees or state councils, from where its organization works down to the local level. There are two types of organizations to which the trade unions in India are affiliated:

i) National federations

ii) The federation of unions

National federations have all trade unions, irrespective of the industry, as their affiliated members. Such federations are the apex of trade-union structure and coordinate activities of all trade unions to give trade-union policies a national character. All central unions discussed in Section 6.1.2 are national federations based on different political ideologies and have different positions on labour-related issues. The characteristic features of these national federations are:

- Trade-union leadership provided by politicians
- Political leanings determine whether to follow policy of cooperation/militancy/continuous strife/litigation based on the party's affiliation to the ruling party
- Empowered to decide jurisdiction of local and state councils
- Allow unit/state-level bargaining with employers
- Nominate delegates to represent in the ILO/International Confederation of Free Trade Unions' conferences

The liberalization of the economy in 1991 posed new challenges for the growth of trade unions further:

- Post–economic reform period
- Stabilization and structural adjustments
- Demands for labour-market flexibility
- Recruitment freeze in public sector
- Right sizing of manpower through VRS
- Reducing the role of unions

The Federation of Unions is a combination of various unions for the purpose of gaining strength and solidarity. Such federations may be local, regional, state, national or even international. Examples of local federations of unions include Bharatiya Kamgar Sena; Labour Progressive Federation, Chennai; The National Front of Indian Trade Unions; and the

Coordinating Committee of Free Trade Unions. Most of these unions are affiliated to the central unions.

The National Commission on Labour in India (1969) points out, "The growth of industry-cum-centre has been facilitated by the provisions in the industrial relations legislation in certain states permitting recognition of industry-wise unions in a given area. The setting up of institutions like wage boards and tripartite industrial committees have provided greater scope for formal and informal consultations in the formulation and implementation of policy at the all-India level."[1] Stating that the unions in India are not distinctive by craft or category and in view of the advantages enjoyed by industry unions, the NCL has recommended that:

i) The unions operating in a unit/industry should be encouraged to amalgamate into an industrial union.

ii) Where an industrial union covering all categories of workers in an enterprise has been recognized as the sole bargaining agent, it would be desirable for such a union to set up committees for important craft/occupations so that the problems peculiar to them receive adequate attention.

6.3 Union Security

Union security is gained through membership that is sought by providing benefits only to those who remain their members. The union derives its meaning and strength from the number of members it has. The unions, therefore, look for measures that enhance security, i.e., maintaining a healthy membership in comparison to others. These measures may include:

- Recognition as the sole bargaining agent, whereby the union is accepted as a bargaining agent for all employees in the unit, irrespective of whether they are members or not
- Maintenance of membership
    - **Preferential Union Shop:** wherein additional recognition by agreement is accorded by management to give the first chance to union members in recruitment
    - **Union Shop:** employs non-union workers as well, but sets a time limit within which new employees must join the union
    - **Closed Shop:** employs only people who are already union members, and in this case, the employer must recruit directly from the union
    - **Open Shop:** does not discriminate based on union membership in employing or keeping workers. Where a union is active, the open shop allows those workers to be employed who do not contribute to a union or the collective bargaining process
    - **Agency Shop:** requires non-union workers to pay a fee to the union for its services in negotiating their contract
- Check-off, where an employer deducts union dues directly from pay and hands over the same to the union as a lump sum.

The National Commission on Labour (1969) in India, while discussing the advantages and disadvantages of union security measures, made the following recommendations:

i) A closed shop is neither practicable nor desirable. A union shop may be feasible, although some compulsion is in-built in the system also.

ii) Neither should be introduced by the State. The union security measure should be allowed to evolve as a natural process of trade-union growth.

iii) An enabling provision to permit check-off on demand by a recognized union would be adequate.

In fact, most countries are unfavourably inclined towards closed shops or union shops.

6.4 Political Affiliations of Trade Unions

At present, there are nine central unions, all affiliated to a major political party. The major and important ones are discussed below (see Table 6.1):

1. **AITUC** (All India Trade Union Congress) was established in 1920 as an outcome of the resolution passed by the organized workers of Bombay, and its first President was Lala Lajpat Rai. The AITUC endeavours to achieve its objectives through legitimate, peaceful and democratic methods such as legislation, education, propaganda, demonstrations, and only as a last resort, opts for strikes or other methods of protest. The AITUC is affiliated with the World Federation of Trade Unions (WFTU).
2. **INTUC** (Indian National Trade Union Congress) was established in 1947 as an outcome of the resolution by Central Board of the Hindustan Mazdoor Sevak Sangh, a labour organization working under the direction of the National-Congress-minded labour leaders on the Gandhian philosophy of Sarvodaya. S. C. Banerjee was the first President of INTUC. The INTUC stands for the gradual transformation of the existing social order and it attempts to instil a sense of responsibility in the workers. INTUC is associated with the ILO since 1949 and is one of the founding members of the International Confederation of Free Trade Union Congress (ICFTU).
3. **UTUC** (United Trade Congress) was formed in 1949 with the aim of establishing a "pure" trade union, free from the control of political parties. The leadership was dominated by various left-wing political groups.
4. **HMS** (Hind Mazdoor Sabha) came into being in 1948 and espouses the socialist philosophy, having linkages with socialist parties. However, there has been a division within the socialist ranks with the emergence of the Hind Mazdoor Panchayat, another federation with socialist leanings.
5. **BMS** (Bharatiya Mazdoor Sabha) was the outcome of a decision taken by the Jana Sangh in its convention in 1954 and is viewed as a productivity-oriented, non-political trade union based on a triple ideology—(i) nationalize labour (ii) labourize the industry and (iii) industrialize the nation.
6. **CITU** was established in 1971 as a result of the split in the AITUC, which was a sequel to the split in the CPI, a new centre, owing to its allegiance to the CPI (M).

Table 6.1

The structure and stated objectives of the major trade unions in India.

	Structure	Objectives
AITUC	i) Affiliated unions (unit/plant) ii) Provincial bodies (state level) iii) General council—Central	i) Establish a socialist state and the nationalization of the means of production, distribution and exchanges as far as possible ii) Improve economic and social conditions of the working class, by securing better terms and conditions of employment iii) Safeguard and promote the workers' right to free speech, freedom of association/assembly and the right to strike
INTUC	i) Affiliated unions (unit/plant) ii) Industrial federation	i) Establish an order of society free from hindrances to an all-round development of its individual members, which fosters the growth of human personality in all its aspects

(Continued)

Table 6.1 (cont.)

The structure and stated objectives of the major trade unions in India.

	Structure	Objectives
	iii) Regional branches/ councils iv) Assembly of delegates v) General council—working committee	ii) Place industry under national ownership and control in a suitable form iii) Secure increasing association of workers in the administration of industry and full participation in that control iv) Organize society in such a manner as to ensure full employment and their full participation in that control v) Promote social, civic and political interest of the working class vi) Establish just industrial relations vii) Secure redress of grievances without stoppage of work first by conciliation and thereafter arbitration and adjudication viii) Make necessary arrangement for the efficient control and satisfactory and speedy conclusion of unauthorized strikes or *satyagraha* ix) Foster the spirit of solidarity, service, brotherhood, cooperation and mutual help x) Develop a sense of responsibility among the workers xi) Raise the standard of efficiency and discipline
HMS	i) Affiliated organization ii) General council ii) Working of general council	i) Promote the economic, political and social interest of the workers and to improve their terms and conditions of employment ii) Form a federation of unions from the same industry or occupation at the national level iii) Promote the formation of cooperative societies and to foster workers' education
CITU	i) Central committee (national level, general council) ii) State committee iii) Affiliated unions	Organizing workers to further their interests in economic, social and political matters
BMS		i) Establish *Bharatiya* order of a classless society ii) Assist workers in organizing themselves as trade unions as a medium of service to motherland irrespective of faiths and political affiliations iii) Right to strike iv) Inculcate in the minds of workers the spirit of service, cooperation and dutifulness v) Establish a socialist society vi) Establish a workers' and peasant state in India vii) Nationalize and socialize the means of production, distribution and exchange viii) Safeguard and promote the interest, rights and privileges of all workers in all matters, social cultural, economic and political

Table 6.1 (cont.)

The structure and stated objectives of the major trade unions in India.

Structure		Objectives
		ix) Secure and maintain the workers' freedom of speech, freedom of press, freedom of association, freedom of assembly, right to strike, right to work and social security x) Bring about unity in the trade-union movement
UTUC	i) General body ii) General council iii) Working committee	

Box 6.1 describes the structure and the stated objectives of the major trade-union organizations in India.

The ideologies of the different TUs can be described briefly as under:

- **AITUC:** Opposed to adjudication, but also agrees that everything should not be left to the two parties to sort out without State intervention
- **UTUC:** Favours conciliation and adjudication but resents the government's discretion in the matter of reference of disputes to adjudication
- **HMS:** Favours collective bargaining and is strongly opposed to compulsory adjudication. It is, however, open to State intervention in case conciliation fails and also favours the right to strike as a weapon for bargaining
- **INTUC:** Condemns strike and has played the conventional role of raising the issues of labour welfare and working conditions
- **CITU:** Objectives have a socialistic flavour with a demand for public ownership of industry

6.5 The Problems of Trade Unions in India

A lot has been written and discussed in various forums about the problems of trade unions in India, but very little has been done in this regard. India has the largest number of trade unions, yet their growth and effectiveness have not been very significant. The reasons and problems that have been detrimental are enumerated below and then discussed briefly to prepare ground for understanding the trade union's role in the current context of employee relations management.

6.5.1 The Politicization and Proliferation of Unions

Even though the stimulus to form trade unions was the economic hardship of the workers, the influence of various historical and institutional factors and the social, economic and political developments in the country made the trade unions assume a political character. The political affiliations of the national federations and the local unions taking protective cover under these federations resulted in a lot of political interference in the union activities. Most of their activities could be better explained in political terms, rather than on worker-interest concerns. As unions are closely aligned to political parties, political leaders continue to dominate the unions even now. The use of political methods and using labour groups to create vote banks has made the trade-union movement in India more political than labour-inspired or labour-driven. This has resulted in trade unions being grossly misused by politicians to serve their own narrow, political aspirations.

BOX 6.1 **RECOMMENDATIONS OF THE SECOND NATIONAL COMMISSION ON LABOUR**

- We strongly believe in the role that bilateral interaction, dialogue and negotiations can play in promoting harmonious industrial relations. In a sense, bilateralism is the recognition of the stake that workers and the management have in the viability and success of the undertaking. Our Trade Union movement today is fragmented. Everyone talks of the value of unity, the imperative need of unity today, but in practice, hardly anyone seems to be willing to give up separate identities. One of the ways to strengthen the incentives for consolidation can lie in the field of registration and recognition, where the criteria for eligibility can be upgraded or at least proportionately upgraded.
- Negotiating agent should be selected for recognition on the basis of the check-off system, with 66 per cent entitling the union to be accepted as the single negotiating agent, and if no union has 66 per cent support, then unions that have the support of more than 25 per cent should be given proportionate representation on the college.
- The question of the method that should be used to identify the bargaining agent has been the subject of discussion and debate for many decades now.
- The Commission carefully considered the advantages and disadvantages of the relevant options. In dealing with this issue, we had to keep in view our belief that collective negotiations require a strong trade-union movement, which, in its turn, demands an increasing degree of unionization. Any formula which militates against increasing unionization should, therefore, ab initio be avoided.
- Secret ballot even on a restricted basis is logistically and financially a difficult process in industries like railways, banks, post offices, coalmines and other undertakings operating in a number of states.
- Check-off system has the advantage of ascertaining the relative strengths of trade unions based on continuing loyalty reflected by the regular payment of union subscription. The argument advanced against the check-off system is that it exposes the loyalty of the worker, and this may make him vulnerable to victimization by the management or persecution by members of other unions.
- Check-off system in an establishment employing 300 or more workers must be made compulsory for members of all registered trade unions.
- Though the check-off system will be preferred in the case of establishments employing less than 300 persons too, the mode of identifying the negotiating agent in these establishments may be determined by the LRCs. Any union in such smaller enterprises may approach the LRCs for conducting a secret ballot. We are recommending a slightly different dispensation for units employing less than 300 as we feel that it is in such units that the possibility of victimization has to be provided against.
- We would also recommend that recognition, once granted, should be valid for a period of four years, to be co-terminus with the period of settlement. No claim by any other trade union/federation/centre for recognition should be entertained till at least four years have elapsed from the date of earlier recognition. The individual workers' authorization for check-off should also be co-terminus with the tenure of recognition of the negotiating agent or college.

The multiplicity of trade unions is also an outcome of dissident groups and break-away political parties emerging in the Indian polity. A split in political ideology results in a split in the trade union professing the same ideology. With proliferation of a large number of unions, the multiplicity character at the plant level provides little or no bargaining power to a union. Further, with so many unions operating at the unit level, their size is considerably reduced. Besides, there are ambiguities of dual membership, wherein names are repeated in the member lists of two or more unions. The divide-and-rule syndrome has only reduced the solidarity of the workers and given more bargaining power to the management.

6.5.2 Outside Leadership

The Indian trade-union movement, from the very inception, was closely associated with the Freedom struggle and, thus, led by national leaders. Post-Independence, every political party patronized a particular union and provided the much-desired leadership. It needs to be appreciated that the worker community at the time of Independence was illiterate and migratory in nature, having come from agricultural regions, and taking breaks, during the harvesting season, to go back to their original roots. The social status between the management and the workers, and their educational and communication levels being different, this intermediary external leadership was beneficial to both workers and management. Further, the resource-starved unions got some financial support from the national federations in times of need.

6.5.3 Inter-union Rivalry

The multiplicity of unions emerging from political affiliations and led by external political leaders brought to fore the politics of many and the dynamics associated with it. Unions became competitive, and the survival of the fittest led to inter-union conflicts and mutual accusations being traded freely. This became advantageous for the management, which followed the policy of "divide and rule". The predominance of inter-union rivalry has entered the very roots of trade unionism in India, and is one of the most significant factors that has pushed them to the periphery in the current global economic environment.

The major problems faced by trade unions in India are:

- Outside or political leadership
- Multiplicity of unions and inter-union rivalry
- Small size of the unions
- Low membership
- Uneven growth
- Poor financial position
- Low level of knowledge of labour legislation
- Fear of victimization

6.5.4 Intra-union Rivalry

Indian trade unionism has also demonstrated the intra-union rivalry coming to the forefront and hampering production and industrial relations. The National Commission on Labour remarked that while healthy rivalry and opposition are necessary within the democratic structure of any trade union, it can have pernicious effects when motivated by personal considerations. The NCL recommended that intra-union rivalries should best be left to the central workers' organizations concerned to settle disputes, and that labour courts should step in at the request of either group or on a motion by the appropriate government in cases where a central organization was unable to resolve the dispute.

6.5.5 Small Size

The small size of trade unions is an outcome of the Indian Trade Unions Act of 1926, which allows a large number of small unions to be registered. With multiple unions operating, the size gets reduced and with inter-union rivalry taking centre stage, new employees shy away from becoming members. It also needs to be noted that women employees, who now account for a large section of the workforce, refrain from joining any union, and this has also impacted the size and growth of unions in India.

6.5.6 Financial Insecurity

The membership fee, which is the major source of revenue for the Indian trade unions, is low, given the low per capita income of the workers. More often than not "ad hoc" payments are made rather than regular payments. They do not get any financial support from any agency, as opposed to the situation in America, where the National Federation of Central America makes regular contributions. The insufficiency of funds affects their working, and their organization is dependent on honorary workers whose time availability to focus exclusively on workers' interests is limited.

6.5.7 The Changing Demography of Workforce

Apart from the low membership coverage and fragmentation of the trade unions, there is evidence of a decline in membership, growing alienation between trade unions and membership, particularly due to changing characteristics of the new workforce and the waning influence of national federations over the enterprise unions. The new pattern of unionization points to a shift from organizing workers in a region or industry to the emergence of independent unions at the enterprise level, whose obsession is with enterprise-level concerns with no forum to link them with national federations that could secure for them a voice at national policy-making levels. The shift in employment from the organized to the unorganized sector discussed in the earlier chapters adds to the fragmentation of the unions. To sum up, the Indian trade-union movement is closely affiliated to political parties, and has narrow support base on account of small-sized multiple unions operating at the unit level. The centralized decision-making, ad hoc management, obsolete strategies, external and over-aged leadership that is more personalized and power-oriented makes it less labour-oriented and more politically motivated. The confrontationist attitude, non-existent second-tier leadership, and negligible women representation dilute its credibility and, hence, do not provide motivation for the new workforce to become members of a union.

6.6 The Recognition of Unions

One of the critical problems in industrial relations facing trade unions, government and employers for a long time is to evolve a satisfactory and acceptable way to settle the competitive claims of rival unions for being declared the sole bargaining agent. This is essential for collective bargaining to be successful. There is no uniform law covering the entire country stipulating the employer to recognize a union, nor any spelt-out procedure for the recognition of a union; managements either refrain from doing so or recognize a union of their choice. Recognition is the process whereby the management accepts a particular trade union as having a representative character and, hence, willing to conduct discussions with them pertaining to workers' interests. A union, once recognized, continues to enjoy the powers associated with it, irrespective of their current membership or credibility among the workers. As workers are unsure about which union holds a key to management lobbying, they become members of more than one union. The Bombay Industrial Relations Act, 1946; The Madhya Pradesh Industrial Relations Act, 1960; and the Industrial Disputes Act (Rajasthan Amendment), 1958 provide for the registration of unions as the representative union, subject to their fulfilling certain conditions.

There are two issues with regard to recognition—one is recognition in an un-unionized situation and in a multi-union situation, and second is the verification process. The verification process based on membership creates ambiguity as the same names are found in the membership list of rival unions. Secret ballot is a solution that can be taken up by the State machinery on the request of the management. There is no legislation in this regard and ad-hocism prevails. In Gujarat and Maharashtra, unions are classified as representative, qualified and primary. Recognition requires 15 per cent of employee strength, qualified union should have membership of over 5 per cent of industry employment and primary union 15 per cent or more employees enrolled at the plant level. The relevant provisions regarding union recognition in the Mumbai IR Act are as under:

1. Where there is more than one union, a union claiming recognition should be functioning for at least one year after registration. Where there is only one union, this condition would not apply.
2. The membership of the union should have over at least 15 per cent of the workers in the establishment concerned. Membership would be counted only for those who

paid subscriptions for at least three months during the six months immediately preceding the reckoning.

3. For a union operating in an industry in a local area, the prescribed membership was fixed at 25 per cent.
4. A union recognition would be binding for a period of two years.
5. Where there are several unions, the one with the largest membership should be recognized. Only the unions observing the Code of Discipline would be recognized, provided other conditions are fulfilled.

6.7 Rights of Recognized Unions

Most of the cases of inter-union rivalry/disputes relate to the issue of recognition of a second or a third union. In many similar establishments, the managements refuse to recognize any union at all. See Box 6.2. This is especially true of attempts to unionize the informal sector of industry.

Suggesting a remedy to this problem, the first National Commission of Labour observed that "this situation can only be set right by a proper demarcation of the rights and functions of the industry/area of recognized unions and plant-wise unions, and by ensuring that recognition at the industry/area level is conferred subject to certain well-defined conditions. We consider that industry-wise recognition is desirable, wherever possible. A union recognized as the representative union under any procedure should be statutorily given, besides the right of sole representation of the workers in any collective bargaining, certain exclusive rights and facilities to enable it to effectively discharge its functions."[2] These rights, in the Commission's opinion, would include:

a) The right to raise issues with the management
b) The right to collect membership fees within the premises of the organization
c) The ability to demand check-off facility
d) The ability to put up a notice board on the premises for union announcements
e) The ability to hold discussions with employees at a suitable place within the premises
f) The right to discuss members' grievances with the employer
g) The ability to inspect beforehand a place of employment or work of its members
h) The nomination of its representatives on committees formed by the management for industrial relations purposes as well as in statutory bipartite committees.

These rights largely repeated the Right of Recognized Unions incorporated in the Code of Discipline at the 20th session of the ILC in 1962. For minority or non-recognized unions (shelved by the ILC), the Commission suggested that they be allowed only the right to represent the cases of dismissal and discharge of their members before the labour court (NCL, 1969, Para 23.61). Most of these rights were available under the Bombay Industrial Relations Act, 1946, some under the Madhya Pradesh Act, 1960, and only the collective bargaining right under the Industrial Disputes Rajasthan (Amendment) Act, 1958. But the first two also had provisions of unfair labour practices.

BOX 6.2 FOR CLASS DISCUSSION

Should we have a uniform law requiring the management to "recognize" a union? Is it desirable? Can you discuss the practicalities of having or not having such a law?

6.8 Unfair Labour Practices with Regard to Trade Unions

The main concept of unfairness in labour practices relate to management interference in the relations between a union and its members or between two unions, or the freedom of employees to choose a union. The unfair labour practices of the unions are rarely discussed in negative terms and are considered methods of protest. In the USA, unfair labour practices are a long list of don'ts for the unions. For instance, the primary unfair labour practices to be avoided are the refusal of a recognized union to bargain in good faith, coercive activities, union instigation or active support for an illegal strike, physical prevention of willing employees from joining work during a strike, intimidation of employees or managerial staff during a strike, go-slow or squatting on work premises after working hours, forced confinement of managerial staff and demonstrations at the residence of employers.

The Bombay IR Act provides that "management cannot dismiss, discharge or reduce any employee of such union or punish him in any order manner merely because he is an officer or member of the registered union or a union which has applied for recognition under the Act" (Section 101). This provision is necessary to protect union activists from being victimized by managers for their union activities. Without this protection, the right to association becomes hollow.

The Industrial Disputes Act, 1947, includes amendments made in 1982 to Chapter V, containing provision against unfair labour practices. The Fifth Schedule of the Act details the specific practices considered illegal. Primarily, the management's victimization of trade unions by such activities as the denial of promotion or punitive transfers, management intervention in trade-union affairs, union coercion of workers to join a union, or threats for not joining, or the use of violence have all been included as unfair practices. Box 6.1 lists a few important recommendations of the Second National Commission on Labour pertaining to the issue of recognition.[3]

6.9 Trade Unionism in India Today

Unions today do not show any distinctive pattern. Unionization is different in different industries and also their impact varies from state to state. The key industries had industry-level unions dominated by external leadership with unit- or plant-level issues dealt with by the unit leadership. Collective bargaining was at the industry level in core sectors of the economy like steel and coal. Plant-level bargaining existed in BHEL, HMT, etc. The private-sector industries, as a practice, discouraged the formation of unions, and wherever they existed, collective bargaining was at the plant level. Union density is directly proportional to the size of the industry in India. In small units, unions are practically non-existent.

The multi-union rivalry and the competition among the different trade unions have effectively diluted the power base of the unions. Though unionization is in recession the world over, and India is no exception, but the reassertion of capitalism under the New Economic Policy has been the major reason for the decline in the unionized workforce. In addition, worker mobility, and the changing demography and aspiration level of the new workforce dispel the pluralistic principle of unionization.

By and large, unionization in different industries and sectors has followed different patterns. The traditional industries exhibited a pattern of industry-level unions, whose leadership was largely external, with plant-level industrial relations taken care of by plant-level leadership. Collective bargaining in industries like jute, tea, coal and banking take place at the industry level. Many public-sector industries, particularly in the core areas like steel and coal, also follow this pattern. However, there are also several public-sector undertakings where unions were formed at the plant level, but combined thereafter for bargaining purposes. Examples of this type may be observed in Bharat Heavy Electricals, Hindustan Machine Tools, and so on.

The private sector, other than traditional industries, has exhibited a different pattern again. Generally, enterprises with multinational origins, had plant-level unions, which were discouraged from forming federations with other unions, either in the region or in the other plants of the same company. Bargaining takes place at the plant level with separate agreements for different plants or units. This practice, while making the unions quite powerful in their respective domains, prevents large-scale concerted action. In the government transport sector, like airlines or railways, powerful craft unions operate.

Compared to this, there is hardly any unionization at all in the medium- or small-scale sector. If present at all, they are usually small, divided and weak, and unable to stand up to management, either in bargaining or in other spheres. Union density in India, being directly proportional to the size of the organization, is thus becoming almost zero in small units. The problems of organizing this sector are related to the uncertainty of jobs and personnel. Unionists or workers trying to organize unions may be dismissed promptly, and since there is no job security, they are treated with suspicion by workers. It is only when major crises confront such workers that they turn to unionism or welcome regular organizers. Even if an organization starts, regular unions find it difficult to keep track of workers in these units, since they are laid off, or the unit is closed, or shifted to some other location. Union density is, therefore, related to the lack of organizing freedom in India.

Trade unions today are facing more and more competition among themselves. At the same time, they are also facing a much more determined management response. They are, thus, fighting on both fronts. But this is a common feature in many countries of the world and not confined to India alone.

Unionism is in recession today. The decades of the 1980s and the1990s have been bad years for trade unionism all over the world. Union membership has been declining in most developed countries, with the USA and the UK leading, and even Japan not far behind. Unions need to understand the three sets of forces working against them. But trade unions, even today, consider themselves as the sole representatives of the working class in India. The Indian Trade Unions Act of 1926 has undergone a number of minor amendments, but the overall framework of the Act has remained unaltered. According to the Act, any group of seven persons could form a union. There are, however, discussions to bring in amendment to raise the number to 100 or 10 per cent of the employees as minimum required for the registration of a trade union.

The Indian Trade Union Movement (ITUM) held its centenary celebrations in 1992. The ITUM membership has remained stagnant, and its activities have been more or less confined to the organized sector, more so to the public-sector enterprises—from where over 70 per cent of its membership is drawn. Since the focus of ITUM was the workers in the organized sector, particularly, those employed in the government-owned establishments, the concerns of the unorganized workforce sector has remained out of its focus. The trade unions, too, are now trying to penetrate the unorganized sector. This has been evident in tobacco, construction, fisheries, forestry and film industries. It needs to be examined whether the enrolment for union membership has led to alleviating the concerns of the workers in these industries, as the techniques used in organized employment may not easily work in the unorganized sector, since the government controls are weaker in this sector. The five central trade-union organizations accorded recognition of being national centres of trade unions are the BMS, with maximum verified membership, followed by INTUC, CITU, HMS and AITUC. In addition, there are a large number of non-affiliated/independent unions functional particularly in the unorganized sector and private/joint-venture companies. Then there are other forms of workers' organizations, such as Morcha, labour cooperatives, NGOs, etc. performing the role of promoting workers' welfare.

During over a century of its existence, the trade unions in India have grown in size and strength, despite the fact that their membership account for no more than 2 per cent of the Indian workforce. As of now, the trade-union movement in India comprises over 70,000 registered unions and an unaccountable number of non-registered organizations engaged on the issue of promoting and protecting workers' interests. The politically affiliated unions have consolidated themselves by establishing a well-developed federal structure. They have

Trade Unionism in India today

- Unionization according to industry/region/state
- 70,000 registered TUs, many not registered
- 2 per cent of the workforce unionized
- PSUs: Industry-level collective bargaining in coal/steel; enterprise level elsewhere
- Private Sector—Plant-level collective bargaining
- Union density according to the size of industry
- Craft unions in the government transport sector
- Low unionization in SMEs
- Twin battle against inter-union competition and assertive management
- Like global trend, unionization in India under recession

established their federations at the state and the district levels as also industry-wise. The unions that are not politically affiliated, on the other hand, are fragmented, despite being very professional, financially sound and effective. Their involvement in policy-making bodies is almost negligible.

In spite of these weaknesses, the trade unions occupy a significant position in India, more so in matters relating to labour policies. Politically, almost every political party patronizes the trade unions as they have a strong influence in garnering labour votes, in the key industries such as cement, iron and steel, coal, heavy electrical, transportation, textile, dock, banking, etc. Thus, in India, the working class in the organized sector exercises political and economic power far in excess of what their number warrant.

A concluding assessment of Indian trade unions could be made in the context of legal rights that they have. This legal framework depends on the following factors:

- The immunity of trade unions and the degree of such immunity
- The rights and obligations of unions towards employers, the community and their members
- The access trade unions have to information
- Settlement machinery
- Consultation with management
- Relations of unions with their members and the rights of rank and file
- Procedures regarding funds, financing, use of funds, elections and duties of office-bearers
- Status vis-à-vis management or claims against management or against other unions (this is particularly important in a multi-union situation)
- Limitations on industrial action such as restrictions on strikes or lockouts

The main laws that allow or restrict the unions are the Trade Unions Act, 1926 and the Industrial Disputes (ID) Act, 1947. The provisions under The Trade Unions Act are discussed in the following paragraphs. Under the ID Act, trade unions have considerable degree of freedom to strikes in small organizations (employee strength below 100). For larger organizations, unions have to follow certain sets of procedures by giving the notice before a strike. There are also restrictions on strikes or direct industrial action during and for some time after conciliation or arbitration proceedings.

There are no provisions in either of the two acts, which lay down guidelines for relations with their own members. Except for the need to call annual general meetings, which is common for any type of organization in all types of situations, there is very little that union members can do against their own leadership. The procedures for removing a leader are so much a matter of political and group dominance, that members have little power to do anything. This may be one of the reasons why there is so much dissidence within unions, leading ultimately to splits and fragmentation. Political affiliation helps to fan dissidence. There is no provision on strike ballot, a basic tool in many countries, which gives rank and file members some control over the most decisive tool in the hands of the unions. This implies that union leaders can take a decision on strike without really consulting many of its members.

6.10 The Trade Unions Act, 1926

The Trade Unions Act, 1926 provides for the registration of trade unions with a view to render lawful organization of labour to enable collective bargaining. It also confers on a registered trade union certain protection and privileges.

6.10.1 Scope and Coverage

The Act extends to the whole of India and applies to all kinds of unions of workers and associations of employers, which aim at regularizing labour–management relations. A trade union is a combination, whether temporary or permanent, formed for regulating the relations not only between workmen and employers, but also between workmen and workmen or between employers and employers.

6.10.2 Objectives

The main objectives of the Act are to:

i) Provide for the registration of trade unions and

ii) To accord registered trade unions a legal and corporate status, immunity to office bearers and members from civil and criminal liability in respect of legitimate trade-union activities. This protection is provided for under Section 120 B, sub-section 2 of The Indian Penal Code.

6.10.3 Provisions

The Act, therefore, stipulates the following:

- The Trade Unions Act, 1926 was enacted mainly in deference to the ILO convention, the recognition of the right of workers to organize and also to strengthen the bargaining power of the workers.
- The Act aims to provide for the registration of trade unions and, in certain respects, to define the law relating to registered trade unions. The objective of the Act is to:
    - Lay down conditions governing the registration of TUs
    - Define obligations of a registered TU
    - Prescribe rights and liabilities of a registered trade union

DEFINITION. Trade Union: It means a combination, whether temporary or permanent, formed primarily for—the purpose of regulating the relations between workmen or employers for imposing restrictive conditions on the conduct of any trade or business, and includes any federation of two or more unions.

REGISTRATION. Any trade union formed with at least seven members may apply for registration to the Registrar with the following documents:

i) A copy of the rules of the trade union

ii) Names, occupation and addresses of members making the application

iii) Name of the trade union and address of its office

iv) Designation, names, age, addresses and occupation of the office

v) Bearers of the trade union

vi) In case already in operation—submit statement of accounts/assets and liability statement

RULES. The rules of trade union require constitution of its executive with the following:

- The name of the trade union
- Objectives for which it is established
- The membership list in a form that can be made available for inspection
- The purpose for which funds shall be applicable
- Members to be persons actually working in the unit/industry
- Honorary/temporary office bearers in the executive
- Payment of subscription to be less than 25 paise
- Conditions under which members entitled to any benefit/fines to be imposed
- The manner in which rules shall be amended, varied or rescinded
- The manner in which office bearers shall be appointed
- Safe custody of funds
- The manner in which the trade union may be dissolved

The Registrar, if satisfied with the requirements, shall register the trade union by entering the information in a register, to be maintained in a prescribed form. In case all terms of the Act are complied with, it is obligatory upon the Registrar to register the union, and he has no discretion in this matter.

Registration may be cancelled if the Registrar, at any point during verifications, is certain that the registration was obtained by fraud or mistake, or it ceased to exist, or has contravened any provisions in the Act.

ON REGISTRATION. A trade union, after registration, acquires the following characteristics:

- It becomes a body incorporate by the name under which it is registered, and it becomes a legal entity distinct from its members of which it is composed.
- It has perpetual succession and a common seal.
- It has the power to acquire and hold both movable and immovable property.
- It has the power to contract.
- It can, by the name under which it is registered, sue and be sued. Under the present law, registration is not compulsory. Unregistered trade unions are not illegal either.

But the benefits conferred by the law on registered unions will not be available to unregistered trade unions. An unregistered union has neither corporate existence nor legal entity.

RIGHTS AND LIABILITIES OF REGISTERED TRADE UNIONS. Section 15 of the Act provides for certain obligations and liabilities of registered unions and also stipulates the purpose for which funds can be utilized.

THE AMALGAMATION OF TRADE UNIONS. Any two or more registered trade unions may become amalgamated together as one trade union, with or without dissolution for division of funds of such trade unions, or either or any of them, provided that (a) the votes of at least half of the members of each or every such trade union is entitled to vote are recorded; and (b) at least 60 per cent of the votes recorded are in favour of the proposal.

DISSOLUTION. When a registered trade union is dissolved, the notice of the dissolution signed by seven members and by the secretary of the trade union is required to be submitted within 14 days of the dissolution to the Registrar for verification as to whether the dissolution has been effected as per rules of the union. In case the rules do not provide for distribution of funds consequent to the dissolution, the Registrar shall divide the funds among the members in such manner as prescribed. The members can alternatively form another society under the Societies Registration Act, 1869, for the purpose of recovering the said properties.

6.11 Managerial Trade Unionism

In India, we have unions in the executive cadre as well, such as civil services, doctors, electricity board, bank officers, merchant navy officers, etc. These associations among white-collared workers are more pronounced in the public sector. In the private sector, officers' associations (not unions) exist in Grasim, Tata Electric, ITC, Glaxo, etc. The white-collar unionism in India today has brought into its fold even professionals like college and university teachers, engineers and resident doctors. The characteristic difference between the worker unions and these associations are that they are loosely knit, focus on few issues and have a narrower perspective. Most of them are registered under the Societies Registration Act rather than the Trade Unions Act, even though their activities and functions are more on the lines of a union. The reasons for their unionization are the same as that of trade unions but are more protective than regulatory. The emergence of these unions has invariably been attributed to the erosion of their social status and the treatment from the employer on their issues and concerns; the management reaction to these associations has not been considered very positive either.

SUMMARY

- The Indian trade-union movement is over a century old but is still coping with problems of small membership and financial insecurities.
- The political affiliations have resulted in external leadership, and politicization created break-away factions and multiplicity of unions.
- The inter-union rivalries and dynamics associated with it have made trade unionism in India ineffective, and post–New Economic Policy, they have been pushed to the periphery.
- The provisions of the Trade Unions Act, though comprehensive in terms of registration and deregistration, make the formation of unions even with mere seven members possible, thereby creating a large number of trade unions in the country.
- The Act is, however, silent on statutory recognition of trade unions, which is the essential foundation on which collective bargaining can be made successful.
- As in the rest of the world, in India too, there has been a decline in the growth of trade unionism as a consequence of the process of globalization and liberalization.

KEY TERMS

- agency shop 104
- check-off 104
- closed shop 104
- open shop 104
- preferential union shop 104
- sole bargaining agent 104
- trade unions 101
- union shop 104

REVIEW QUESTIONS

1 Define the following terms:

a. Trade unions

b. Check-off

c. Registered trade union

d. Recognized trade union

e. Preferential shop

f. Agency shop

g. Closed shop

h. Open shop

i. Sole bargaining agent

j. Union security

2 Describe briefly how trade unions are registered and certificates of registration issued.

3 What are the rights of a registered trade union?

4 What are the characteristics of trade unions?

5 Why do you think the recognition of trade unions in every establishment should be done? What are the disadvantages for the employer?

6 What is a trade union and how is it generally formed?

7 When can the registration of a trade union be cancelled or withdrawn?

8 Is the amalgamation of two or more trade unions possible? How can this be done?

9 Define the scope and objectives of The Trade Unions Act, 1926.

10 Differentiate between

i. Craft and industrial unions

ii. Preferential union shops and closed shops

iii. Registered and recognized unions

QUESTIONS FOR CRITICAL THINKING

1 Discuss some of the problems of trade unions in India and the recommendations of the National Commission of Labour in this regard.

2 What are the functions of trade unions? Examine whether the trade unions in India have been able to fulfil these functions.

3 Taking into consideration the existing problem of trade unionism in India, suggest measures for strengthening trade unionism and give reasons for the same.

4 In the current day competitive environment, has the role of trade unions changed? Explain and describe its impact on the industrial relations climate.

5 Discuss some of the problems of trade unions in India and suggest steps that can be taken to improve the same in the current-day context of multinationals and a growing unorganized workforce. Are the National Commission of Labour recommendations still applicable?

6 Discuss the changing role of trade unions and the resultant impact of union–management relations consequent to globalization and technological breakthroughs in industry.

DEBATE

1 Does India's booming information technology and information-technology-enabled-services (IT/ITES) industry, which employs almost one million professionals, require a trade union to fight for its rights?

2 Though India has the largest number of trade unions, their contribution to industrial work life has not been phenomenal.

CASE ANALYSIS

Inter-union Rivalry

Given below is an extract of a news item relating to Bajaj[4] Auto Ltd. Analyse the legal issues emanating out of this and the alternatives available to the management to cope with this problem.

The stalemate between workers, unions and the management of the two-wheeler manufacturer Bajaj Auto Ltd took an unexpected turn with the Pune industrial court declaring the automaker's biggest workers' group, Vishwa Kalyan Sanghatana or VKS as the "recognized" union at the firm's Akurdi mother plant since it had support of the majority of the workers.

The court simultaneously revoked the recognized union status accorded to another worker group Bharatiya Kamgar Sena or BKS, backed by the Shiv Sena party, partly on whose support company chairman Rahul Bajaj got elected to the Rajya Sabha last year.

The Bajaj Auto management has been negotiating workers' issues such as wages only with BKS in the last two years. VKS insists that it will hold talks with the firm's management only after it allows workers into the premises of the Akurdi factory that has been shut down since 1 September. Some 1,400 workers have been striking work since then demanding that Bajaj Auto bring back production of two-wheelers shifted out to units at Aurangabad and Uttarakhand. VKS, which is fighting the BKS union recognition since November 2005, says it has the support of more than 1,600 of the 2,700 workers at Akurdi, while BKS has a following of just a few hundred.

The IT industry and Trade Unions

Read the following news item[5] and then discuss the questions below:

The Leftist trade unions insist that it is high time the massive industry, which contributes more than 4.5 per cent to the country's national economic output, had a trade union to protect their jobs.

The Indian ITES-BPO (business process outsourcing) industry aggregated revenues to the tune of $5.2 billion in 2004–05.

The proposal to forge a union for IT workers has now come from the Centre for Indian Trade Unions (CITU)—the trade-union wing of the Communist Party of India (Marxist)—the largest Left party in the country.

So why do white-collar IT professionals need a trade union?

"A union for IT workers is the urgent need of the hour. I would call the IT professionals 'the labourers of the information age'. They toil long hours; they work at night; and some of them still get meagre salaries. So a labour union for them would help fight for their rights," according to the CITU president. To begin with, CITU, in collaboration with other Left-unions—like the All India Trade Union Congress—wants the Union government to enact a law separately to deal with the labour issues of the IT industry.

"Yes, there is an urgent need for a labour law exclusively for the IT industry. It is the one sector that is booming across India, and we need to frame a legislation for IT workers. We are going to take up the issue with the Manmohan Singh government soon," said the Community Party of India national secretary.

How are the Left trade unions going ahead to form the unions for IT workers?

"It is not going to be easy. Already, we have begun the process to hold consultations with many senior IT employees in places like Kolkata, Bangalore, Chennai and Trivandrum (Thiruvananthapuram). We do hope to establish a proper union soon," a Union Leader of CITU pointed out.

Left leaders say there is also already tremendous backing from the Union of Network International, a global alliance of 900 trade unions, to forge an IT industry workers' union in India.

"IT industry professionals in India are 'cyber coolies'. We are trying to organize them and convince them on the need to form a union to fight for their rights and job protection," said Narayan Ram Hegde, who works for the Union of Network International in India.

But Hegde says the task is not going to be easy because young IT professionals always have a negative image of trade unions in India.

A number of organizations for IT professionals now exist at the state level in Hyderabad (in Andhra Pradesh) and Bangalore (in Karnataka).

Left leaders say the idea now is to broad base this forum into a politically empowered union that can demand and stand up for the rights and protection of IT workers.

Here is what some of the employers from the industry have to say about unionization of the workforce:

Kiran Karnik, President, National Association of Software and Services Companies (Nasscom): "Employees in IT and ITES sector do not need any external intervention as they are looked after very well. It is not a good move and I don't think it would succeed. The employees who think of themselves as the CEOs of the future may not support it."

R. Vidyasagar, Director (HR), Philips Software India: "There is no need for a third-party intervention and it did not augur well for the industry. I feel that unionism will not take off as employees will not like to be led by somebody else. We need to maintain our pre-eminence in the IT and ITES sector as countries such as China are fast catching up."

Raman Roy, ex-CEO, Wipro BPO: "I have no problems with a union in the BPO industry, as long as it guarantees that no employee will leave the organization before one year. The union should work with the BPO industry to control the menace of attrition."

Prosenjit Ganguly, Head (HR), HTMT, a BPO firm: "The move to unionize workers is a retrograde step and would spell disaster for the industry. After having reached this level, any attempt to unionize the workers would set us back."

1. What do you think are the reasons of non-unionization in the emerging sectors like IT/ITES?
2. Look at the reasons from the business as well as the socio-psychological perspective. Why do you think trade unions have failed to make inroads?
3. Make out a comprehensive case from the management side as to why it is not a good idea for allowing unionization in this sector.
4. What kind of workplace regulatory mechanism do you foresee in the coming years in this sector? On what do you base your analysis?

NOTES

1 Ministry of Labour and Employment, Government of India, "Chapter XX" Report of National Commission on Labour, 1969: para 20.17.

2 Report of the National Commission on Labour (1969), Government of India Press, para 23.58

3 "Recommendations", Report of the National Commission on Labour, p. 41.

4 Sudha Menon, "Bajaj Auto Workers Union Gets Court Recognition," *Mint,* 17 October, 2007.

5 George Iype, *Does the IT industry Need a Trade Union?* 6 October 2005. Available on *www.Geojit.comhttp://202.54.124.133/money/2005/oct/06bspec.htm*

SUGGESTED READING

Ramaswamy, E. A. "Managerial Trade Unionism", EPE, Vol. 21, 1985.

Reports of the National Commission on Labour (1969 and 2002), Government of India.

Sharma, B. R. *Managerial Unionism: Issues in Perspective* (New Delhi: Shriram Center for Industrial Relations, 1993).

part ii

paradigm shift

chapter seven

CHAPTER OUTLINE

LEARNING OBJECTIVES

After reading this chapter, you should be able to:

- Appreciate the need and relevance of the change from "industrial relations" to "employee relations"
- Differentiate between employee relations and industrial relations in terms of influencing factors, operating principles, scope, objectives and its linkage to other HR functions
- Identify the preconditions for good employee relations management
- Differentiate the line and staff role in employee relations
- Understand the practical implications of the paradigm shift from industrial relations to employee relations in terms of the role of the line and HR manager

They Also Produce Steel

The Tata Group's relationship with its employees has changed from the patriarchal to the practical, but this is a bond that continues to be nourished with compassion and care. The focus, clearly, is on the relationship with employees, which is both individualized and also has a collective approach.

The Tata Group touches and moulds the everyday lives of more people than any private-sector employer in the country. The richness of this relationship, fashioned by a tradition of benevolence and empathy, represents a workplace culture that goes way beyond work.

As any "Tata person" will tell you, there is something positively distinctive, something less than completely explainable, about working for the group—the experience is cast in a hue quite different from the ordinary. This view continues to hold despite the changes that have altered the way the Tatas interact with their people, moving from the paternalistic philosophy of yore to bringing the group in line with the ever-evolving, human-resource methodologies.

The transition from then to now has not eroded what remains a central theme with the group—providing its employees more than mere jobs. Workers and their welfare were of utmost importance to the group founder Jamsetji Tata, who, writing to his son Dorab Tata in 1902, five years before a site for his proposed steel enterprise had been decided, stated: "Be sure to lay wide streets planted with shady trees, every other of a quick-growing variety. Be sure that there is plenty of space for lawns and gardens. Reserve large areas for football, hockey and parks. Earmark areas for Hindu temples, Mohammedan mosques and Christian churches."

To understand the dynamics of the present, it is necessary to peep into the past. The Tatas pioneered a slew of employee benefits that would later be mandated through legislation in India and elsewhere in the world. The eight-hour working day, free medical aid, welfare departments, grievance cells, leave with pay, provident fund, accident compensation, training institutes, maternity benefits, bonus and gratuity—all of these and more were introduced by the group before any legal rules were framed on them. To give but one example of how far ahead of the times the Tatas were—while their first provident-fund scheme was started in 1920, the government regulation on this issue came into force in 1952.

These workplace measures were complemented by what Tata companies created to enable their employees to live fuller lives away from their offices and factories, and to realize their vocational potential. The management-training programmes conducted by dedicated group institutions are devised to help employees give expression to their talent. Driving every one of the group's initiatives in the wide sphere of employee relations is a value system that, slowly but surely, percolates to each person looking to craft a career in the Tatas.

From Industrial Relations to Employee Relations

There is a gradual shift in focus at the enterprise level, from collective to the individual, from the containment of conflict to the creation of enabling systems and structure that promote partnership, from "industrial relations" to "employee relations".

Industrial relations (IR), as discussed in Chapter 1, refers to a collective relationship between "employers" and "employees", and is generally referred to as labour-management relations or union-management relations. Industrial relations takes a collective approach and, therefore, deals with relations between groups, and regards an organization as a collective unit managed by representative officials who represent and deal with collective issues of workers/employees. Such relations function at various levels of the concerned organization, dictated by the complex and diverse needs, aspirations, attitudes and aptitude of both the employer(s) and the employees and is regulated by the State. This signifies an inter-group/intra-group relationship spectrum based on functional interdependence arising from industrial activity. Industrial relations are essentially contingent upon the economic, political and social conditions within which the industrial unit operates. On the other hand, the discipline of human resources management has addressed the issues of "competitiveness" more often than those of industrial relations. Industrial relations, a function, as it has been specifically described as such in the organization structure, has provided employees with a collective voice and has ensured standardization in the terms and conditions of employment in industries and nations as well.

In India, the politicization of trade unionism has made the State machinery focus on minimization of employer–employee conflict through conciliation and arbitration and by exercising active control over employers to prevent any action detrimental to the interest of the working class—considered to be valuable "vote banks".

With increasing competition and the process of globalization spreading its roots the world over, most organizations have realized that competitive advantage can only be gained through people. Strategic management of human resources requires leveraging skill, scale and technology. Leveraging skill and scale demand a "capital" approach to the utilization of human resources that gives a "rate of return". Organizations today, therefore, prefer using the term "human capital" to "human resource" to differentiate and inculcate the practice of gaining competitive advantage through people. The concept and practice of industrial relations and its associated legislative and regulatory machinery are claimed not to facilitate this process.

Over the years, the HR function has evolved itself into two distinctive roles—the operational day-to-day activities required for the maintenance of human resources, and the strategic one for creating organizational capabilities and inventing new ways to gain sustainable and distinct competitive advantage. The employees, on the other hand, are more knowledgeable and aware of their rights and responsibilities and do not seem to require a collective forum to voice their concerns.

A paradigm shift indicating a radical change from the reactive or preventive industrial relations approach to a proactive strategic employee relations approach is the new flavour, eroding the regulatory and legislative machinery for accommodating fresh demands and evolving equations between the employer and the employee. It has also resulted in shifting focus from "employment contracts" to "psychological contracts".

Drivers for the Shift in Focus

- Changing political ideologies dictated by concerns for economic growth
- Trying to achieve sustained competitive advantage through people
- Changing characteristics of workforce
- Fast-paced changes in technology reducing dependence on industrial workforce
- The declining credibility of unions

7.1 A Shift in Focus

If the aim is to build a collective relationship through a regulatory mechanism between labour and management instead of being restricted only to "industrial activity", a more appropriate term would be "employee relations". This relationship can be between the employer(s) and a single employee, the employer(s) and a group of employees or even between the employee(s) and more than one union. Strictly speaking, industrial relations, as a term, should concern itself only with collective relationship issues between employers and employees only in an industrial set up. Governments, educational institutions, autonomous bodies, etc. should, therefore, not be within the purview of IR. IR also need not necessarily work towards conflict resolution; it can work towards building meaningful, collective partnerships instead. This book aims to take a more strategic approach to relationship management with employees, and hence, "industrial relations" is discussed with the primary thrust on the individual "employee" and the "employer", keeping in mind the regulatory mechanism of the State.

The key shift in focus has been in perceptible narrowing down of areas of conflict and greater convergence towards efficiency and competitiveness. This requires collaborative teamwork and the least external interference of any kind. Political parties, at the same time, could no longer ignore economic growth and development as the means of improving quality of work-life and life itself. This could only be achieved through the growth in industrial activity in terms of quantity and quality. Quantitative approaches require leveraging economies of scale and technology. Qualitative improvements can only be made by leveraging skill through people, which requires a unitary approach rather than a collective one.

Opening up of the markets and other liberalization measures have forced employers to demand less rigidity/more flexibility in regulations, less standardization of the employment relationship, and a greater focus on individual aspirations and workplace efficiency. Every function within an enterprise and every activity are now necessarily viewed to evaluate the strategic contribution. In this context, IR must contribute to increase competitiveness through ensuring cooperation, flexibility, adaptability, productivity, etc. Gaining competitive advantage by shifting the focus on people is the new diktat.

With the growth in the service sector and the increasing pool of technically skilled workers, the traditional concepts of "fair wages" and standard terms and conditions of employment for all are giving way to competence-based variable pay, outsourcing jobs and flexible working options. With the growing aggressiveness of competition and increasingly consumerist ethics, the State's interest in intervention in the name of maintaining harmonious industrial relations has also reduced. In these circumstances, over-regulation, neither practical nor advisable, has lost its relevance, as it only serves to reduce the flexibility employers require to compete with the dynamics prevailing in the industry.

The advent of new technology and industrial automation has further reduced dependency on industrial workforce. The relationship of man and machine is now associated with the quantity and quality that it produces. A collective spirit that promotes quality consciousness, and enhances productivity and customer satisfaction requires a participative model, where not representatives of workers but each individual employee of the workforce engages himself/herself in this mission. Principles and theories of motivation have gained prominence in designing compensation packages tailored to suit individual needs, innovating exciting individual and team incentives and introducing employee participation, involvement and engagement through a variety of schemes and programmes.

The workforce composition has also undergone a transformation in terms of demography and competence. The advent of an "informed" worker who is fully aware of his/her rights and responsibilities has reduced dependency of any kind on a collective forum to represent or fight for their cause. Further, an employee today is not looking for a long tenure in an organization, but for career growth and development and, hence, is far more mobile than before. The workforce is younger today, and at the same time, organizations are equally open to retaining older employees, if their competence provides them a strategic advantage. The percentage of female workforce has also increased, giving rise to a new set of gender-related issues that have been rarely taken up by the unionized workforce. The most important characteristic of the workforce composition, however, is the fact that no employee looks for a long tenure in one organization, if it does not fulfil his/her aspirations. The concept of unionization and collectivism has, therefore, been replaced by an individualized concept, wherein each employee tries to fend for himself. This has automatically put the focus of employee–employer relationship on "individuals" and has ensured the retention of human capital competency in organizations.

The technological revolution and its impacts on the industrial landscape coupled with the trade-union performance over the past couple of decades have led to the decline of trade unionism and its importance in India. Trade-union membership has reduced drastically, and the worker-interest in trade-union activities has also declined. The modern workplace is a vital part of the modern economy and trade unions must, therefore, operate in ways that best reflect these modern practices. The organizations today have sought alternative ways of gaining whatever advantages trade unions could provide them, through diversified channels of communication, flexible policies and transparency in working and one-to-one dealings with employees.

The Employee–Employer Relationship

- Individualized
- Proactive
- Development-oriented rather than maintenance driven
- Flexible rather than standardized
- Informal rather than institutionalized

7.1.1 The Employee–Employer Relationship

The term "industrial relations" is a legacy of the "industrial revolution". Labour, essentially, was perceived as a factor of production by entrepreneurship. This resulted in an informal and controlled relationship between the employer and the employees. Industrial growth spearheaded the employment of a larger workforce characterized as "wage earners". Gradually, as research and literature threw light on the disturbing "hygiene" and other factors at the workplace, the relationship between the "workers" and the "employer" moved beyond the private realm of an "employer–employee" relationship to the public domain and became one of social concern. Maintaining industrial peace became the essence of social welfare. Political ideologies emerged, and debates on the benefits and ills of a capitalist and socialist economy led to a struggle for power along with the voicing of the workers' rights. This resulted in problems in industrial relations, which were manifested through strikes, lockouts, retrenchments, etc. Industrial peace and its impact on public welfare led to the emergence of trade unions and State regulations in order to ensure harmonious "industrial relations".

With globalization and the large-scale adoption of capitalist-driven growth models in most countries, there has been a strategic shift away from "industrial relations" to "employee relations". This shift adopts a proactive rather than a reactive approach to the management of employee relations. It encompasses all matters that arise in day-to-day associations between employers, workers and managers. It, therefore, includes:

- Relations between managers and individual workers
- Collective relations between managers and workers
- The role of the government in the regulation of these relationships

The shift towards employee relations implied that the traditional regulatory activities such as monitoring compliance to legislative requirements, rules and procedures take a back seat, and such issues as employee selection, retention, performance management, employee communication and involvement come to the forefront. Therefore, HRM function has reinvented itself from the traditional maintenance function to a strategic one, wherein human-resource policies are devised to establish consistency with the "core values" of the organization. Earlier, changes were initiated by the strategic team at the top, and driven through change agents. Today, the HRM function has taken upon itself a strategic role in change-management initiatives through communication and culture-building workshops, and preparing employees to cope with change. Developing relations with employees is now considered the right way to build an organization culture, based on a foundation of common values among its employees. See Box 7.1.

Employee Relations

Employee relations may be defined as the relationship between the employer or the representative manager and the employees, aimed towards building and maintaining commitment, morale and trust, so as to create a productive and secure workplace environment.

BOX 7.1 **FOR CLASS DISCUSSION**

"Pfizer endeavours to develop a collaborative, constructive approach to deal with grievances and differences of opinion between colleagues. The key thrust is on developing and maintaining a climate of openness, trust and mutual respect, and ensuring the promotion of Pfizer values and the code of conduct in all aspects of business behaviour."

How do you think Pfizer can operationalize this statement? What effect should this statement have on the trade-union organization in Pfizer, if it has one?

7.1.2 Why ERM?

The need for an employee-relationship management within the enterprise is a sine quo non for every enterprise operating in a competitive environment. Although a cliché, this makes sense. ERM is a strategy that aims to personalize employee relations. Converting the strategy to ground-level execution is around which ERM, as a function, must be designed. An ERM policy statement like the ones adopted by Pfizer and Sony facilitates the translation of the strategic objectives to key areas and activities that lay the foundation of a productive employee relationship.

Employee relations aim to produce successful, world-class organizations through relationship-building with and amongst its employees. High-performing organizations have a few common employee relations practices, but this being an inexact science at best, a simple, do-it-yourself formula fitting all situations does not exist. There are also clearly identifiable organizational issues that are responsible for productivity gaps. Employee relations, therefore, tries to inculcate characteristics that render an organization a success, and at the same time, proactively sensitizes itself to the organizational issues that can retard productivity. It is a given that change is inevitable (and essential for survival and growth), and employee relations management is increasingly geared towards increasing productivity, returns and competitiveness. However, since people are involved, it (ERM) needs sensitive handling, especially during times of technological changes, market slump, cost-cutting and organizational restructuring. The ERM must address procedural and interactional equity, which means "people" involvement in all vital processes.

7.2 Employee Relations Management

Employee relations management (ERM) has a strategic focus, takes a proactive, long-term view rather than the preventive and curative (in terms of settlement of conflict), short-term, immediate solution that industrial relations is associated with. Employee-relationship management aims at building relationships, commitment and organizational loyalty, whereas industrial relations resolves conflicts and prevents disputes in terms of maintaining relationships, discipline and subordination. ERM works towards employee empowerment, while industrial relations management talks of consultation and participation through systems and committees. ERM is an informal, ongoing process that is beyond employee and employer organizations and State regulations.

Industrial relations may have been perceived as necessitating the delicate handling in view of the complexity of issues, but with the growing prosperity, increased wages, higher standard of living, sophistication of work and mobility of workforce, organizations have ceased to be owned by individuals and have become corporate enterprises. A new breed of a progressive, yet status-dominated working class, with higher levels of individual aspirations and lesser concerns for social equity now dominates the work-labour scenario. This calls for the individualistic handling of employees and an appreciation of individual differences and diversity in work values, beliefs, attitudes and levels of aptitude. Hence, ERM is what

BOX 7.2 **GOALS OF ERM**

- Establishing a link and congruency between employee contract and the employment relationship through a psychological commitment
- Terms and conditions of employment to be based on the principle of fairness and ensuring the organizational objectives as well as individual needs and aspirations are fulfilled
- Developing policies, procedures, rules and regulations that are fair, just and conform to the basic objectives and philosophy of labour legislation
- Defining and clarifying performance-management expectations and standards to enable employees to strategize and plan for the achievement of tasks and targets set for their job positions
- Developing effective communication channels and systems that ensure the information needs of employees are met

would ensure progress, discipline and cohesiveness that are essential for industrial peace. In contrast, industrial relations aim at ensuring industrial peace through discipline and good relations with groups of employees.

Employee relations may, therefore, be defined as the relationship between the employer or the representative manager and the employees aimed towards building and maintaining commitment, morale and trust so as to create a productive and secure workplace environment (See Box 7.2). The regulatory role of the government in ERM has, thus, almost been discounted. It is now contingent only upon the receipt of complaints and non-conformance with prescribed mandatory legislations.

7.3 Industrial Relations and Employee Relations: Differences in Perspectives

The differences in perspective, focus and strategy between industrial relations and employee relations have been discussed under different heads in the following sections.

7.3.1 Influencing Factors

THE FACTORS INFLUENCING INDUSTRIAL RELATIONS MANAGEMENT

Economic Factors: These factors are determined by the structure of the economy—socialist, capitalist or mixed. The demand and supply of labour, the nature and composition of workforce, and the organization of labour would determine the economic status of the working class and also the bargaining strength influencing industrial relations.

Institutional Factors: These factors include government policy, labour legislation, functioning of labour courts/industrial tribunals, trade unions, and employers' organizations. Social and religious institutions can also greatly influence the industrial-relations scenario through a prevailing value system and by attempting to ensure conformance to the same. This is exemplified by the gender bias observed in some countries and industries.

Technological Factors: Techniques of production, automation, modernization, etc. are the technological factors. Lesser the dependency on human capital, the lesser would be the bargaining strength of employee organizations. Further advancement in "technowledge" and the upgradation of competency profiles for jobs have also created a new class of workers termed "knowledge workers" whose needs and aspirations are different.

Political Factors: The political system in the country, political parties and their ideologies constitute the political factors. The growth and strength of political parties and the methods used in formulating and implementing policies affect the industrial-relations climate. Furthermore, the involvement of trade unions in the formulation of policies also plays an important role in tilting the balance towards the working class. However, if these parties find themselves to be dependent on financial support from the corporate entities, the political equation then would be completely different.

In countries where State capitalism is the main ideology, collective bargaining would not be encouraged, trade unions would just be tolerated and labour-management relations would be regulated with a fair degree of strictness.

In countries like the former USSR, where the prevailing political ideology is State socialism, trade unions are assigned well-defined roles and they function within the parameters of the overall political system.

India having adopted a mixed economy, conciliation, arbitration, workers' participation in management, collective-bargaining are parts of labour-management relations.

Social and Cultural Factors: These factors refer to prevalent social norms, values and beliefs. In countries like the USA, where a stable socio-political order exists, the government promotes a common ideology of free enterprise, or democratic capitalism. In such countries, "collective bargaining" is facilitated by legislation and government intervention. In places such as the Scandinavian countries and the UK, where democratic socialism prevails, collective bargaining is the standard norm with almost no government intervention.

THE FACTORS INFLUENCING EMPLOYEE RELATIONS MANAGEMENT

Economic Factors: The pressure to compete in the global market with cost-effective quality products has put pressure on the employers' organizations to extract performance and ensure that the employees deliver. The focus has shifted from regulating terms and conditions of employment to regulating performances. This has, at times, necessitated "downsizing" according to the employees and "rightsizing" according to the employers. Subcontracting, outsourcing and contractual forms of employment have replaced tenure employments. The humanistic welfare concern of the employer is based on labour reciprocity through performance and results. The employee–employer relationship is more unilateral than a collective one. From dealing with groups of workers defined by craft, unit, or level, the employers now talk of teams—self-managed or self-directed by the employees.

Further, the new wave of consumerism in the Indian society, a consequence of liberalization and the opening up of the economy, has led to changing values among the workforce, now more individualistic than collective. The emergence of MNCs has led to new workplace arrangements. The price war in compensation is not based on equity but on individual competencies and deliverance. The market forces have created a new employment arrangement and a new relationship between the employer and the employees—one of mutual delivery on performance. This relationship is, thus, clearly distinct from the "industrial relations" concept that had previously served to determine the work culture of an organization.

Institutional/Governmental Factors: The new economic policy brought changes in legislation relating to trade, finance and industrial policy while leaving the labour laws as they were.

Indian labour laws are perceived to be pro-labour. Many labour laws and court judgments are impediments to India's competitive status in the global economy.

Labour unions in India are laden with problems of funds, external leadership, political affiliations and multiplicity of unions with low membership and inter-union rivalry. In the present market-driven economy, the trade unions have been moved from the centre to the periphery. In an environment where competitive advantage is gained through cost-leadership, trade unions are viewed as excess baggage and a drain on resources. The focus, therefore, is on building a relationship with the employee rather than with trade unions.

Social and Cultural Factors: In the post liberalization phase of economic growth, India has promoted individualism, consumerism and a driving ambition among the working classes to motivate its workforce to strive and move up the hierarchical ladder through performance and the development of individual competencies. With greater opportunities, the possibilities of labour mobility are far greater; attrition, too, is higher, which prefers a one-to-one employee relations management more than a relationship favouring collective herding. Commitment has become a unitary concept and has become of core essence to HR strategies. This has made it difficult for workers to offer dual commitment to both the employer and the trade union. The employers have broadened their roles to include and fulfil the roles earlier performed by the unions. The employees, therefore, prefer to offer their commitment to employers rather than to trade unions.

Technological Factors: New techniques and methods of work have changed work patterns and descriptions of jobs. A new creed of skilled workers following new patterns of motivation and aspiration levels has changed the character, scope and coverage of relationship management.

Political Factors: These factors include the political system in support of the new economic policy and its consequences. The communist parties have been repeatedly expressing their concern over diversifications, mergers, acquisitions and the entry of foreign players in key sectors of the economy. The resistance is manifested in trade unions affiliated to the communist ideology staging demonstrations against such government initiatives. In such a scenario, dealing with the fears and insecurities of individual employees, rather than a participative collective body such as a trade union, can play a more important role.

Organizational Factors: The competitive environment has brought about a visible change in the employment arrangement and new staffing practices. Flextime, outsourcing, contractual jobs are the order of the day. Staffing has become a profession rather than a function. Electronic processing has made personnel administration far easier, quicker and more responsive through e-HR. Even the one-to-one contact has become "virtual". The focus once again has shifted to the employee rather than employee groups.

Global Factors: The success stories of global corporations and Fortune 500 companies and their unique people-management programmes show a process of centralization of the employee in the workspace. Diversity and individual differences are accepted and dealt with carefully. This has greatly influenced the shift to employee relations management from a strictly industrial-relations-management approach.

Psychological Factors: Especially in the present performance-driven culture that promises no outstanding job security, psychological factors have a far greater role to play in ERM. The role of coaching, counselling and mentoring has a greater role to play in ERM than they ever did in industrial relations. HR strategies aim at motivating employees for excellence, innovation and customer satisfaction. Psychological tools are more useful as they deal with individual needs and aspirations and, hence, the focus shifts to the employee rather than to any employee organization that claims representative roles.

The factors influencing employee relations management include:

- Economic
- Institutional/governmental
- Social and cultural
- Technological
- Political
- Organizational
- Global
- Psychological

7.3.2 Principles

THE PRINCIPLES OF INDUSTRIAL RELATIONS MANAGEMENT

Rights and Obligations Under the Constitution of India: It is important that every employer organization and its designated representative(s) recognize the individual employee's right to personal freedom and equal opportunity. Article 14 of the Constitution of India guarantees certain fundamental rights to all Indian citizens. Further, the provisions in Articles 39, 41, 42 and 43 incorporate the elements of labour legislation and social security to the working class. The judiciary, through its judgements, also ensures "social justice" ultimately aiming for socio-economic equality.

The Acceptance of Mutual Responsibilities and Obligations: Accepting responsibility for one's action as an employee or an employer and its impact on the operations of the organization is the key to smooth industrial relations. The labour legislations, being in favour of labour, prescribe rights only for workers and obligations for employers. Recognizing the constraints of such legislations, the National Commission of Labour recommended drafting an Unfair Labour Practices document by both employees and employers and imposing penalties for the same.

Seeking Mutual Understanding and Cooperation: Attempts at fostering mutual understanding between the employers and employees by gaining each other's respect should be an ongoing process that would lead to harmonious industrial relations.

The Establishment of Industrial Democracy: This can be achieved when labour has the right to be associated with the running of an industry.

THE PRINCIPLES OF EFFECTIVE EMPLOYEE RELATIONS MANAGEMENT The principles underlying the shift towards employee relations are:

- The recognition of individual differences in needs and aspirations
- Trusting the employees' competence and the ability to perform and, thus, empowering them
- Providing support through coaching, counselling and mentoring
- Facilitating individual development
- Creating a collaborative work environment
- Promoting a healthy work–life balance
- A transparent and open communication system
- Mutual trust and respect as a core value

7.3.3 Scope

THE SCOPE OF INDUSTRIAL RELATIONS Industrial relations deals with the management of relationships, mainly with and within the groups or agencies as mentioned below:

- Employees: The relationship among/between employees and their superiors
- Union–Management or Labour Relations: Collective relations between trade unions and the management
- Government–Management–Union: Collective relationship between various organizations of employers and employees who represent the management, the workers and the State
- Community or Public Relations: The relations between an industry and the society. This explains the importance of corporate social responsibility that most corporate enterprises have initiated as a part of their work culture.

The subject matter of such relationships includes:

- Desirable working conditions
- The establishment and the maintenance of good personnel relations
- Developing a sense of belonging by ensuring closer contact between persons from various rungs of the industrial hierarchy
- Developing a situation characterized by mutual concern and a sense of responsibility for improved performance

- The maximization of social welfare
- The maintenance of industrial peace and the avoidance of industrial disputes

THE SCOPE OF EMPLOYEE RELATIONS The focus here shifts to performance, growth and development for creating competitive advantage.

- Employee Relations: The relationship among, and between employees and their superiors
- Group Relations: The relations between various groups of workmen and between workmen of the same work groups
- Community or Public Relations: The relations between an industry and the society. This introduces the concept of organizational citizenship in partnering social welfare and progress through the employees. In public-sector undertakings in India, a lot of community-welfare programmes are initiated, which even include joint celebrations of festivals, organizing sports events for children of the employees.

Areas of the relationship include:

- An improvement in working conditions
- Effective administration of personnel policies
- Maintaining good relations among employees
- Creating a sense of belonging
- Creating cohesive teams based on principles of collaboration
- Creating a sense of mutual responsibility for improved performance and productivity
- Maximizing employee welfare and benefits
- Improving employee morale and organizational pride
- Employee development, empowerment and engagement

7.3.4 Objectives

THE OBJECTIVES OF INDUSTRIAL RELATIONS

- To promote and develop congenial labour-management relations
- To maintain industrial peace and avoid industrial conflicts and disputes
- To improve performance and productivity by minimizing losses on account of industrial strife and conflict, manifested in the form of strikes, go-slows, etc.
- To safeguard the interests of labour and management by securing the highest possible level of mutual understanding and respect
- To enhance the economic status of the worker by improving wages and benefits
- To establish industrial democracy by strengthening employee partnerships
- To ensure organizational discipline
- To boost the morale of the workers and create a sense of organizational pride
- To enable the workers to solve their problems through mutual negotiations and consultations with the management

- To encourage and develop trade unions in order to increase the workers' strength and to institutionalize the process of collective bargaining
- To correct imbalances in the socio-economic order arising out of industrial development associated with complex social relationships and conflicting interests

THE OBJECTIVES OF EMPLOYEE RELATIONS

- To promote and develop good employee–employer relations
- To minimize conflict at the workplace, at individual, inter-group/team and intra-group/team levels
- To improve the performance and the productivity of individuals and groups/teams by a process of continuous value addition of human capital and reductions in cost centres
- To ensure smooth administration of the terms and conditions of employment and to secure the highest possible level of mutual understanding and respect
- To provide motivational incentives and benefits and enhance the economic status of the workers
- To establish democratic systems seeking employee partnership through employee-empowerment and employee-engagement programmes
- To ensure discipline at the workplace and establish a constructive and congenial work culture
- To boost the morale of the workers and create a sense of organizational pride
- To reduce attrition of good performers
- To enable workers to solve their problems through coaching, counselling and mentorship programmes
- To encourage and develop workers to engage in quality improvements, technical and process innovations and brainstorming sessions for organizational excellence
- To improve the quality of work-life, minimizing stress at workplace and facilitating a healthy work–life balance for the enhancement in employee productivity

7.3.5 **Preconditions**

THE CONDITIONS FOR HEALTHY INDUSTRIAL RELATIONS

- The existence of a strong, well-organized democratic employees' union. This would provide bargaining power to negotiate and protect employee interests in terms of wages, benefits, job and social security.
- The existence of employers' associations to facilitate the promotion of uniform personnel policies and to initiate requisite reforms in labour legislation that would promote economic wellbeing
- The practice of collective bargaining through process consultations and negotiations between the employee organizations or trade unions and the employers' organizations. If issues still remain unresolved, even through consultative discussions and negotiations, they could then be referred for voluntary arbitration instead of resorting to adjudication in order to maintain intra-industrial harmony and congeniality.

THE CONDITIONS FOR HEALTHY EMPLOYEE RELATIONS

- The incorporation of democratic principles as an essential core of the work ethic
- The promotion of collaborative group interactions through work systems, norms, rituals and informal social interaction
- The institutionalization of work culture through practices that promote the core values of the company
- Communications, both formal and informal, which must be open and transparent in nature

7.3.6 Measures

THE MEASURES FOR EFFECTIVE INDUSTRIAL RELATIONS The preventive measures taken to promote industrial peace are discussed in detail in Chapter 15, and they include the following:

- Labour welfare
- Joint consultative bipartite and tripartite bodies such as the Industrial Labour Conference (ILC) and Standing Labour Committee (SLC)
- Standing orders
- Grievance redress procedure
- Code of Discipline
- Wage policy and regulation machinery
- Schemes of workers' participation in management
- Collective bargaining
- Code of conduct and rules
- Workers' participation in rule-framing
- Strengthening employees' organizations

Apart from the above, the Industrial Disputes Act, 1947, has provided for a machinery for the settlement of disputes between groups so that industrial peace is not threatened. We will discuss this in detail in the later part of this book.

THE MEASURES FOR PROMOTING EMPLOYEE RELATIONS The measures to develop employee relations are as follows:

- Employee-engagement programmes, such as the Employee Stock Options (ESOPs), gain-sharing and profit-sharing schemes
- Employee-empowerment by facilitating employees to take on a key role in decision making
- Employee-involvement programmes like suggestion schemes
- Facilitating employee participation through a formation of joint working committees in areas like safety, quality, employee welfare, etc.
- Multi-level communication channels and new communication methods and systems
- Self-learning opportunities about company products, services and customers in a single, personalized and easily accessible enterprise portal

7.3.7 Linkage Human Resource Management

Human resources management entails the design of formal systems in an organization to ensure an effective and efficient use of human talent to accomplish organizational goals. The field of "man management", as it used to be called earlier, has also undergone changes from being regarded simply as personnel management to HRM. The shift from Taylor's theory of "scientific management" to "hygiene" factors affecting motivation and morale of employees emphasizing on a human approach to work design ushered in one phase of change. With globalization and an increasingly competitive environment becoming a given, the industrial world has seen another shift from a purely human-relations approach to an attempt at the management of human resources. This shift is primarily responsible for the thrust of change from industrial relations to employee relations. The primary causes associated with this shift are as follows:

- The realization that a happy worker is a hard worker is an oversimplification of reality
- The human-relations approach did not take care of individual differences
- The industrial relations management did not recognize the need for a job structure, performance parameters and performance-behaviour standards
- The human-relations approach did not explore other motivational tools, such as performance appraisals and career development, and merely concentrated on developing human relations as a collective group entity

The current approach is a human-resource approach, where employees are treated as investments and the emphasis is on policies, programmes and practices leading to a productive work environment. The new concept of human-resources-management function is one that facilitates the most effective use of the human resource or human capital, to achieve organizational excellence. This entails the following functions with regard to human resources:

- Acquisition
- Coordination
- Maintenance
- Motivation
- Development
- Retention

The role of relationship management holds a special significance in terms of increasing per capita income, improving the human development index and, thereby, upholding national growth and interest. This macro-perspective is better managed through the operative function of employee relations than through the managerial function of industrial relations.

The current issues and challenges of human resources management such as downsizing, restructuring, productivity and quality improvements, technological innovation and knowledge management can be solved when an employee-relations-management approach is used instead of the industrial-relations-management approach.

7.3.8 Line or Staff Function

Industrial relations management has been viewed as a specialized function requiring knowledge of labour laws, its application and interpretations. The management of statutory and non-statutory welfare activities; the management of social-security programmes and schemes like gratuity and provident fund; the management of conflicts, grievance-handling and bipartite committees under the scheme of workers' participation fall within the ambit of activities assigned to an industrial relations officer/manager. The maintenance of health and safety, canteen, welfare amenities, communication and counselling, too, are activities that are part of industrial relations management. Therefore, even though direct dealing with people has always been considered to be an integral part of every line manager's responsibility, specialized assistance of a staff support is provided for handling industrial relations.

Employee relations, on the other hand, refer to the direct communication with employees on a day-to-day basis. The administration of the terms and conditions of employment is serviced by the HR department. Therefore, ERM is the responsibility of both line and staff functions. However, that only a small part of employee relations management is administrative needs to be appreciated. The majority of the activities are related to the formulation

BOX 7.3 **THE JOB DESCRIPTION OF A MANAGER (INDUSTRIAL RELATIONS)**

- Designing new employee-related policies
- Establishing and maintaining good relationships with the trade unions
- Acting as a consultant to line managers on the implementation of policies
- Assisting in the resolution of specific disciplinary or grievance cases, including acting as an arbiter between the employee and the line manager
- Carrying out formal consultation procedures on a variety of issues as required by law
- Advising others on the proper procedures for carrying out negotiations and on the special regulations relating to employment and salary agreements
- Negotiating with trade unions on issues relating to pay and working conditions
- Providing accurate advice on issues arising from employment contracts and legislation
- Preparing staff handbooks to ensure that the workforce is aware of company policies
- Ensuring that grievance-handling and disciplinary proceedings are carried out in line with company policies and national legislation

The Job Description of a Manager (Employee Relations)*

- Interviewing workers to gather information on worker attitudes towards work environment, to facilitate resolution of employee relations problems
- Explaining to the workers the company and governmental rules, regulations, and procedures, and the need for compliance
- Gathering information on the workers' feelings about the factors that affect worker morale, motivation, and efficiency
- Meetings with line managers to discuss possible actions to be taken
- Inspecting work stations to ensure required changes or actions are implemented
- Interviewing workers to determine reactions to specific actions taken
- Preparing reports on the workers' comments and the actions taken
- Enrolling eligible workers in company programmes, such as pension and savings plans
- Maintaining medical, insurance, and other personnel records and forms. May operate computer to compile, store, or retrieve worker-related information, such as medical, insurance, pension, and savings plans

---

Adapted from http://www.careerplanner.com/DOT-Job-Descriptions/EMPLOYEE-RELATIONS

of policies, systems and taking a proactive role in the prevention of workers' conflicts and grievances. Thus, the ER manager finds himself playing a strategic and innovative role unlike an IR manager, who deals with unions only. The employee relations manager deals with all employees and also with the external environment in a manner that helps to create a brand image for the organization as a model employer, which, in turn, attracts the best talent to the organization.

7.3.9 The Role of an HR Manager

Industrial relations management had a consultative and executive role, whereas employee relations management has a facilitative and service role. This shift makes the HR professionals strategic partners in business growth and development. From a staff function, HR needs to take a developmental perspective towards its role, creating desirable changes and initiating interventions to improve the performance of the employees. A sample job description of a manager designated as Manager (IR) and Manager (ER) shown in Box 7.3, explains the difference in the work design of these two HR specialists. It must be noted that employee relations is an approach, still in transition and, therefore, there would be many overlaps between the two functions. Rather than being distinctly different from each other, the two should be seen as a movement along a spectrum.

Compare the two job descriptions and note the change in competency profile in terms of knowledge, skill and attitude. Industrial relations managers need to have a strong knowledge base of labour legislations, whereas an employee relations manager has to have requisite skills in building sound relationships at work.

SUMMARY

- The term "employee relations" was conceived as a replacement for the term "industrial relations". "Industrial relations" is generally understood to refer to the relationship between the employers and the employees, collectively.
- "Employee relations" broadens the study of industrial relations to include wider aspects of the employment relationship, including non-unionized workplaces, personal contracts and psychological, rather than contractual arrangements.
- Employee-relationship management is at the forefront of HRM scene.
- Good employee relations not only help reduce absenteeism and attrition, and avoid costly disputes while harnessing goodwill, but also facilitate in enhancing performance, productivity, effectiveness and commitment.
- ERM focuses on a comprehensive merger of corporate, management and employee needs to increase efficiency, productivity and profitability.
- ERM takes into consideration the dynamics of the environment and draws upon innovative and best practices in employee involvement, participation, engagement and empowerment programmes to get the best return from human capital.
- Sound employee relations would be based on:
    - Effective mechanisms at all levels in the organization
    - Enlisting participation of the employees
    - Ensuring safe and effective work environment
    - Eliciting commitment and motivation of all staff
- The emphasis and shift are in the following:
    - From collective institutions such as trade unions and collective bargaining, to the relationship with individual employees
    - From "employment contract" to "psychological contract"
    - Competency development attempted through employee involvement, engagement and empowerment programmes
    - Strategic rather than the preventive maintenance concept of industrial relations

KEY TERMS

- employee empowerment 126
- employee engagement 137
- employee involvement 136
- employee participation 124
- employee relations 123
- human capital 123
- industrial relations 123
- psychological contract 123

REVIEW QUESTIONS

1 Differentiate between the following terms:
   i. Industrial relations and employee relations
   ii. Human relations management and employee relations management
   iii. Employee involvement and employee participation
   iv. Employee empowerment and employee engagement
   v. Human resource and human capital

2 Do you think there should be a separate section dealing exclusively with ER within the HR department? Why or why not?

3 What do you understand by the terms "employee involvement", "employee engagement", "employee empowerment" and "employee participation"? Explain with examples.

4 Discuss the major differences in scope and coverage of "industrial relations" and "employee relations".

5 Is ER a line function or an exclusive HR function?

6 How can ER be built in service organizations spread globally?

QUESTIONS FOR CRITICAL THINKING

1 Discuss the changing dynamics of the industrial relations scenario in India brought about by the globalization and liberalization of the economy. Has it resulted in any paradigm shifts in the management of human resources? If yes, what are the challenges ahead for HR professionals?

2 In the light of the challenges brought about by globalization, the introduction of new technology, methods and processes, has the employee–employer relationship changed *completely*? If so, describe these changes and their impact on organizations.

3 Organizations are constituted by individuals hired to perform certain tasks and key responsibilities with roles structured to be part of a working group or team. Relationship management aims to govern relationships among individual employees as well as between groups. How can this relationship be developed and maintained?

4 The management of industrial relations has slowly undergone a metamorphosis. Explain with special reference to the scenario after the economic liberalization and globalization in India. Has the employee–employer relationship changed *completely*? If so, describe these changes and their impact on organizations.

DEBATE

Read the following extract, which gives the practical reality of employee relations, and then debate on the issues.

> THE scene is an aspiring human relations (HR) professional's campus interview. The first question asked is "So, why did you choose HR?" Pat comes the reply, "I love interacting and being with people."
>
> Over a year thereafter, the young HR professional realizes he has spent more time in front of his PC than with the "people" he had dreamt of. In the age of "mentafacturing" and "manufacturing", front-line services, professional services and technology services, human capital and intellectual

capital, on-site and offsite work, temping and contracting, who manages Employee Relations (ER)?

In the preoccupation with process and performance, has there been a compromise on "relationships"? In trying to share the responsibility, have both the line manager and the HR manager let employee relations die a slow death? In the eagerness to shape strategy, have HR professionals dropped ER from their agenda rather than make it an integral part of their work?

Source: Ganesh Chella, "Employee Relations—Why It Should Be Kept Alive", www.thehindubusinessline.com/2003/12/09. (Ganesh Chella is the founder and CEO of Totus consulting.)

CASE ANALYSIS

Case 1: Team or Union—Who Has the Greater Potential to Influence?

Patil was all excited when he was given permission by the General Manager to implement a quality circle in one of the units he supervised. In the beginning, the employees were very sceptical, and only a few volunteered for the training. Patil was well versed with the concept and he sincerely believed that it was exactly what would keep the workers interested and motivated to generate a better-quality product.

In the first round of discussions, during the training programme, the circle members came up with some very useful suggestions, one of these suggestions resulted in a drastic improvement in the reject rate. The work atmosphere in this unit was all charged up and the absenteeism rate among the quality-circle members dropped by 40 per cent.

Enthused by the initial success, Patil decided to publicize it in the in-house journal of the company. Word spread around and other unit managers showed interest in understanding the process, and they started emulating it in their units. Patil was asked to prepare a report on the process and its evaluation. The General Manager toyed with the idea of spearheading 10 more voluntary initiatives for quality circles. This information had spread across the plant. The President of the union also sought the report prepared by Patil. His first reaction was "What the hell is the management up to this time?"

By the next morning, all union members were told that quality circles were just one more attempt by the management to extract more work from them with no additional compensation. To support this, the President of the union distributed copies of articles that stated that quality circles were a technique for enhancing the productivity of the workers. The net result was a gradual withdrawal of participation in quality circles. A gradual process of alienation from the company seeped in. In fact, even the one quality circle that was operating effectively was forced by peer pressure from union members to close down.

Where did Mr Patil go wrong as regards employee relations management?

Case 2 "We Are Shifting the Office"

Amtec Ltd. designed process and control systems software for the automobile sector. They started as a small group of eight employees designing software for one automobile company. Within a span of 5 years, they had 34 employees and 8 major automobile companies as their clients. The initial start-up was from the basement of Mr Khemka, the owner's residence. On the New-Year's-eve company gathering, Mr Khemka announced that the office would shift to Gurgaon from February. He gave details of the office space interiors and other improvised welfare facilities that would be available to employees at the new site. He also declared that transport arrangements would be worked out for employees, but also advised them to consider shifting residence to Gurgaon.

Though some employees had some inkling of the shifting of the office, but the location and other details were not known to anyone. There was an uproar, and what should have been an exciting proposition turned into a major issue of concern for all. Precious time was lost in raising demands, queries and concerns—both individual and collective. The shifting of the office had to be eventually postponed, pending discussions with the "representatives of employees", who were nominated through a signature campaign.

Discuss the genesis of the problem from both IR and ER perspectives, and suggest what should have been done.

SUGGESTED READING

Howard, A. *The Changing Nature of Work* (San Francisco: Jossey-Bass, 1995).

Virmani, B. R. "Redefining Industrial Relations", *Indian Journal of Industrial Relations*, October 1996.

Lawler, E. E. *The Ultimate Advantage: Building a High Involvement Organization* (San Francisco: Jossey-Bass, 1992).

ILO, "Towards Fair Globalization: Report of the World Commission on Social Dimensions of Globalization", 2004.

Dayal, Ishwar "HRD in Indian Organizations: Current Perspectives and Future Issues", *Vikalpa*, IIM Ahmedabad, October–December 1989.

de Silva, Sriyan "Employers' Organizations in Asia-Pacific in the Twenty-First Century", paper presented at the *ILO Workshop on Employers' Organizations in Asia-Pacific in the Twenty-First Century*, Turin, Italy, 5–13 May 1997.

chapter eight

CHAPTER OUTLINE

LEARNING OBJECTIVES

After reading this chapter, you will be able to:

- Understand the employee relations imperative in the changed business environment and context
- Understand the role of employee relations in the larger strategic framework
- Think of practical approaches to the design and the implementation of systems and processes from an ER perspective

"You Can Never, Ever, Do Enough for Your People"[1]

FedEx was started in April 1973 by Fred Smith. FedEx is the world's largest express transportation company with more than 145,000 employees worldwide, delivering more than 3.2 million packages daily. They command a fleet of 634 aircrafts and more than 42,500 vehicles. They log more than 2.7 million miles each day on the ground. FedEx's revenues in 2008 were more than 37 billion USD.

FedEx has maintained its profitable commitment to excellence by applying 11 management principles. One of these eleven principles underlies FedEx's unparalleled success—you can never, ever, do enough for your people. Here is how this management principle operates at the grass roots in FedEx.

> The rights and value of a single human life have become the central focus of social evolution in the industrialized world . . . FedEx, from its inception, has put its people first both because it is right to do so and because it is good business as well. (FedEx manager's training guide).

Fred Smith, the CEO of FedEx, put people first, knowing that service and profits would follow. The flat management structure minimizes the distance between leaders and the front-line workers, empowering employees and expanding their responsibilities. While there can be no honest unconditional commitment to a no lay-off policy, what FedEx has done is to make a commitment to reasonable employment security by cross-training employees for more flexibility and allowing for the redistribution of work during slow periods. Thoughtful and imaginative compensation schemes are at the heart of FedEx's human resources policies. FedEx may provide flexible work hours, leave of absence for family emergencies, and permanent part-time work. Benefit packages are also structured to accommodate age, health, career paths, and other personal preferences. Individual bonuses and awards are tailored towards individual preferences and not bestowed indiscriminately.

FedEx has a policy of promotion from within, a procedure for resolving employee grievances that can result in the problem ultimately being reviewed by the CEO, executive vice-president, chief personnel officer, and two senior vice-presidents.

Open communication plays such an important part in FedEx that they have set up their own internal broadcasting company, FXTV—their internal CNN which reports on everything from inclement weather, company goals, the previous night's service levels, what the competition is up to, and candid call-in programmes.

Employee Relations Management at Work

Employee relations is concerned with maintaining employer–employee relationships that contribute to satisfactory productivity, motivation and morale. Essentially, employee relations is concerned with preventing and resolving problems involving individuals, which arise out of or affect work situations.

In 2008, FedEx appeared on the 97th position on Fortune's list of top 100 "Best Companies to Work For". In fact, it has consistently found a place in this list over the years. What do we make out of FedEx way with people? FedEx must be complying with the numerous legislations concerning employees, yet in the opening passages, it appears that compliance issues must be redundant with FedEx having risen much above mere compliance and maintenance of relationships with groups of employees. There seems to be a real concern for individual employees, work groups and performance. The industrial relations approach, i.e., managing the employee collective does not seem to be critical to organizational processes at FedEx. It is something else.

The "management principles" of FedEx, as mentioned in the chapter-opening case, have shaped the employee relations approach at FedEx. It certainly has influenced the business performance of FedEx. There is a definite focus on individuals while shaping the larger "people policy"; definitely not a "one shoe fit all" mind-set that one associates with "rule making" for a collective. The primary relationship at the workplace is between the employer and an individual employee. The relationships between the employer/management and groups or unions are all secondary relationships, derived from the primary.

"Employee relations" (ER), in its original form, was a generic term used to describe the system by which workplace activities were regulated, the arrangement by which the owners, managers and staff of organizations came together to engage in productive activity. It concerned setting standards and promoting consensus for achieving objectives.

The genesis lies in the economic and social changes of the industrial revolutions and the urbanization of the nineteenth century, the inherent conflict between labour and the owners of the firms, the formation of collectives (combinations of groups of workers to look after their own interests) and the demarcation lines and restrictive practices that some occupations and trades were able to build up. The influence of these traditions remains extremely strong, particularly in long-established industries such as factory work, transport and mining.

However, recent years have seen a transformation in the way businesses are carried out and also a complete transformation of the context in which businesses are carried out. There is a felt need for a departure from the "control" and "direct" mode of managing employees, and many organizations have responded to this need worldwide. Direct engagement with the employee and seeking his wholehearted involvement with the objectives of the organization is the only means now visible to build lasting competitive advantage. This is at the core of the transition that we are witnessing and which loosely is termed as "employee relations". The reasons for this shift have been discussed in previous chapters, but globalization, fierce competition, fast-paced technological changes, demography of the working population are only few of the forces that are shaping the shift. The main actors of the employment equation, i.e., the employer, the unions and the State are all feeling the need to readjust and reorient their perspectives. A serious attempt to change and to generate a more positive and harmonious ethos is visible, although there are variations between the three players' levels of seriousness, efforts and response. Companies and their managers have come to recognize the importance of positive employee relations and the contribution that they make to profitable and effective performance. Given the high attrition rates in knowledge and service sectors, "employees relations" is now taking a predominant and objective role. Further, when the collectivist approach of dealing with employee organizations/trade unions is resorted to, the balance of bargaining power is affected by the economic, legal and technological environments. It would still not motivate people to create high-performance teams, if their individual needs and aspirations are not addressed. At the workplace, this is translating into:

- Large-scale changes in people-related strategies and processes
- Human resources management and development becoming an area of strategic concern
- The recognition that core-competence-building and the design of the organization are key differentiators and the sources of competitive advantage
- The motivation of the employees for higher productivity, problem-solving and creativity is a necessity for which the "direct" and "control" model of management is grossly inadequate and the only way ahead is to get commitment and cooperation from the employees.
- Trade unions have to look beyond the economic demands and the organized sectors (the organized sectors seem to have outgrown the need of union intervention for economic demands anyway), and focus on larger economic and social issues.
- The government must strive to be more nimble in responding to the changes, and at the same time, protect the interests of all concerned in the productive endeavour.

8.1 Employee Relations in a Strategic Framework

The strategy of an organization refers to "a specific pattern of decisions and actions that managers take to use competences to achieve a competitive advantage and outperform competitors."[2] In this context, employee relations may be thought of as a common layer that animates the related fields of HRD, HRM and industrial relations. It is that software that tints every action in these functional areas so as to gain employee commitment for enhanced performance. It is that difficult-to-define body of actions, attitudes, systems, policies and processes, which induce competence-building. And since the building of core competence is at the core of a company's strategy, an employee relations approach assumes critical importance in the overall strategic objectives.

As we have read in the previous chapters, employee relations have evolved through different perspectives at different times, and these perspectives would impact strategic intent and fulfilment differently.

UNITARISM. This assumes that the objectives of all involved are the same or compatible, and concerned only with the well-being of the organization and its products, services, clients and customers. The most successful of unitary organizations such as McDonald's and Virgin set very well-defined and distinctive work, performance and personal standards, to which anyone working in the company must conform. This is apparent in a few Japanese companies as far as the management of human resources is concerned. With a unitary approach, clear and unambiguous strategies may be considered the salient elements.

MISSION. The mission maybe considered to be reflecting and summarizing the purpose of the organization, and its ways of working, in a clear and unambiguous manner.

TERMS AND CONDITIONS. These are based on adequate and stable wage levels, fairness and equality of work practice, managerial openness and transparency, universal access to information, regular high-quality consultation, integrity of operations and activities.

CORE VALUES (REFLECTING EXPECTED BEHAVIOUR AND ATTITUDES). The core value of employee relations is positiveness in attitude, with the view to create harmony and remove the causes of conflict, by adopting high moral and ethical standards of fairness, equality, respect, value and esteem.

CULTURE-INTEREST AND COMMITMENT. These involve strategies for generating identity, loyalty and a mutuality of interest.

WORK COMPOSITION. This would mean including the ability of everyone to progress and achieve their potential, acknowledging limitations in work division and occupational definitions, giving a universality of the principle of opportunity.

PLURALISM. This admits to a variety of objectives, not all compatible, among the staff. In view of the existing conflict, rules, procedures and systems are established to manage dissent and limit its influence as far as possible. This is the approach taken especially in public services, the local government and many industrial and commercial activities, where diverse interests have to be reconciled to in order that productive work may take place. In the pluralist perspective, a divergence of loyalties, commitments, ambitions and expectations is admitted. This means knowing and understanding what these are and why they exist. The pluralist perspective, consequently, recognizes the inherent nature of the conflict between different groups of staff, between functions, and within groups of staff. It also admits divided loyalties—an individual, for example, may have professional, occupational, work-group, trade-union or professional-body loyalties as well as those to their organization. Very often, this is reinforced where there has been a strong trade-union presence, a recent history of conflict of objectives, or where the profession exerts a strong influence on work standards and practices.

There are three perspectives that could determine the employer–employee relationship:

- Unitarism
- Pluralism
- Radicalism

RADICALISM. This is the view that commercial and industrial harmony is impossible until the staff control the means of production, and benefit from the generation of wealth. Until very recently, this was the cornerstone of the philosophy of many trade unions and socialist activists in industry. The radical perspective arises from the Marxist premise that efficient and effective industrial activity could only be successful if the workers owned and controlled the means of production. This could be facilitated by the following ways:

- The promotion of employee-share-ownership schemes and profit-related pay schemes take the point of view that giving the employee this form of stake in the organization helps to gain a positive mutual identity, and that the employee's commitment is gained because they themselves share the risks and rewards.
- The promotion of the partnership concept
- Setting standards to which people are required to conform

ER strategies are also influenced by the nature of the enterprise—whether it is the public or the government that is serviced; especially, there could be variations along a continuum on the following dimensions:

CONFLICT. Conflicts in an organization can arise because of mistrust, divergence, irreconcilable aims and objectives; disparity of location; divergence and complexity of patterns of employment and occupations; and differences amongst professional, technical, skilled and unskilled staff.

CONFORMITY. The diversity of staff and technology may be (and often is) as great as in the above scenario, but where the ER strategy sets standards of behavioural and operational norms aimed at requiring the different groups to rise above their inherent differences.

CONSENSUS. The way of working is devised as a genuine partnership between the organization and its staff and their representatives. Genuine consensus or partnership is very rare. Discuss the story of the Brazilian company given in Box 8.1.

8.2 Employee Relations at the Workplace

Employee relations can be visualized as that common factor that orients the HR, IR and development functions towards building of competence within the organization. All tradeoffs within these functions and between players must be decided in long-term competitive advantage. Every function, system, policies and process would be geared towards eliciting full participation, cooperation and commitment to the achievement of the advantage. It discards the long-held belief that the management has the divine right to know "the one right answer" and that all wisdom rests with the management who needs to "direct" and "control" the employees.

8.2.1 Principles, Structures, Functions, Policies and Processes

The activities that are associated with the ER function are the following:

- The evolution of core values that determine the organization culture, attitudes and values, and also specify the standards of ethics, behaviour and attitude
- Standards of performance and the management of performance including competence development
- Organizational design
- Range of employee relations activity
- Organizational and managerial approaches to employee-management organizations and managerial approaches to the management of disputes, grievances, discipline and dismissal
- Procedures for the management of disputes, grievances and discipline
- Consultation, participation and communication structures
- Workplace climate

PRINCIPLES

The Equity Concept: This concept is based on an ethical stance that all employees should be treated equally, and that the same fundamental terms and conditions of employment are to apply to all. This implies a single staff handbook applying to all, where the terms and conditions of employment are uniform. The participation in profit-sharing and gain-sharing schemes would involve everyone.

Behavioural issues reinforce this concept of equality. Everyone is addressed in the same manner regardless of occupation. The work of each employee is valued and respected.

BOX 8.1 **FOR CLASS DISCUSSION**

Industrial Democracy at Work

Ricardo Semler is the CEO and majority owner of Semco SA, a Brazilian company. Semler is best known for his convictions on industrial democracy and a miraculous turnaround of his company. His radical management style has generated widespread interest amongst management practitioners as well as academicians. Here is an excerpt from an article about Ricardo Semler and SEMCO:

"To see Semco's approach in action, just visit the company's pump plant on the outskirts of Sao Paulo. This operation bears about as much resemblance to a traditional factory as the rainbow hues of its walls—the choice of the employees—do to industrial gray. Forget about foremen barking out orders to passive people. On any given day, a lathe operator may himself decide to run a grinder or drive a forklift, depending on what needs to be done. João Vendramin Neto, who oversees Semco's manufacturing, explains that the workers know the organization's objectives and they use common sense to decide for themselves what they should do to hit those goals. 'There's no covering your ass,' says Mr Neto. 'The intent is to get straight to specific targets.'"

Semco's 3,000 employees set their own work hours and pay levels. Subordinates hire and review their supervisors. Hammocks are scattered about the grounds for afternoon naps, and employees are encouraged to spend Monday morning at the beach if they spent Saturday afternoon at the office. There are no organization charts, no five-year plans, no corporate values statement, no dress code, and no written rules or policy statements beyond a brief *Survival Manual* in comic-book form that introduces new hires to Semco's unusual ways. The employees elect the corporate leadership and initiate most of Semco's moves into new businesses and out of old ones. Of the 3,000 votes at the company, Ricardo Semler has just one.

In Mr Semler's mind, such self-governance is not some soft-hearted form of altruism, but rather the best way to build an organization that is flexible and resilient enough to flourish in turbulent times. He argues that this model enabled Semco to survive not only his own near-death experience, but also the gyrations of Brazil's tortured politics and twisted economy. During his 23-year tenure, the country's leadership has swung from right-wing dictators to the current left-wing populists, and its economy has spun from rapid growth to deep recession. Brazilian banks have failed and countless companies have collapsed, but Semco lives on.

The ultimate hands-off leader, Mr Semler doesn't even keep an office at Semco. "Here's why: Our people have a lot of instruments at their disposal to change directions very quickly, to close things and open new things." Flexibility is the key, he says. "If we said there's only one way to do things around here and tried to indoctrinate people, would we be growing this steadily? I don't think so."

Those four words, "I don't think so," delivered with a Brazilian Portuguese lilt, represent Mr Semler's standard answer to corporate dogma, assertions that something he wants to do cannot be done, and even overly doctrinaire interpretations of the participative management concept. Mr Semler is not a particularly self-effacing or humble advocate of human potential; his assurance in argument is legendary. In conversation, in teaching, and in his books *Maverick* and *The Seven-Day Weekend*, he puts forth participative management as not just a pragmatic path to business success, but also a healthy and enjoyable way of life."

What kind of approach is Semco following? Do you think such approach is sustainable in the long run? Or is it just some kind of gimmick?

Source: Excerpt from Lawrence M. Fisher, "Ricardo Semler Won't Take Control", www.strategy-business.com/press.

Differentiation between groups and categories of employees is on the basis of work function only; there are no exclusive canteens, or car-parking spaces.

The Flexibility Concept: Related to single status is the concept of the "flexible workforce", where everyone concerned is both trained and available for any work that the organization may require of them. The employees would be oriented to this philosophy when they join the organization. This is a fundamental departure from traditional specialization, demarcation and restrictive practices. Implicit in this are obligations on the part of the employees to accept continuous training and development as part of their commitment to the organization.

The Extent of the Workers' Participation in Management: The extent of participation of the employees in the management of an enterprise is also a matter of principle that sets the tone for an approach to employee relations. Many organizations have established workers' councils in recent years. In India, the Scheme of Workers' Participation in Management even provides for having on the board of directors a representative looking after the employee interests. This will be dealt with in detail in the subsequent chapters.

- The ER staff must form an identity with the organization.
- Boundaries of performance and behaviour requirements must be established.
- ER staff must become role models in terms of employee behaviour.
- ER and HRM must be seen as continuous processes and an area for constant improvement.

STRUCTURE. We assume that considering the business and contextual imperatives, organizations will surely transit from a collectivist approach to an individual approach to the management of employees. In essence, this means that the basic approach would gradually shift towards employee relations, maybe at a pace dictated by the different pressures on different industries and establishments. However, there would remain common threads in establishing functional linkages with other departments. Organizations must appreciate the nature and strengths of the types of staff that they employ in ER/IR departments. They must recognize that there are divergences of aims, and different priorities that must be resolved if effective and profitable work is to take place. The nature of ER and related staff-management activities will vary accordingly, but at the outset, all staff must form an identity with the organization that is both positive and complementary to its purposes. Boundaries of performance and behaviour requirements must be established in order that these purposes are achieved effectively and successfully. In fact, ER staff must become role models in terms of employee behaviour as the issues they deal with impact the style of workplace regulation. Above all, ER and HRM must be seen as continuous processes and an area for constant improvement. If designed and conducted effectively by the organization, it will constitute a major return on the investment made in the workforce as a productive entity. In this context, it needs to be appreciated that even the use of the term "human resources" is slowly getting replaced by "human capital". Human resource can become human capital only if deployed on productive work and assures an optimal rate of return on the investment made in terms of recruitment, training, etc.

The ER strategy adopted must, therefore, be supportive of, and complementary to, the wider aims and objectives of the organization. This will depend on the competence of the workforce. But ultimately, the workforce must be tuned to the needs of the organization. Effective ER strategies start from this point. They may have highly trained or professional employees; however, the overall direction of ER will seek again to match these with organizational requirements.

In organizations where the staff has a very strong group identity—because of their profession, or because of sectoral traditions, or a long history of unionism—the organization must work to ensure the harnessing and commitment of the staff members to its own purposes. If such "group think" behaviour is generated, it ultimately leads to devising IR strategies that have a collectivist approach.

Furthermore, work cohort emerging from inter-group dynamics may result in major conflicts between the "professional" commitment to clients and that to the management. Employee relations in these situations are largely ineffective. This is because of the inability of the organizations to direct their professional staff in ways universally understood as effective, and because of their lack of regard for, or ability in, ER matters. It has been compounded by the perceived conflict of objectives between service managers and service professionals.

Labour-intensive enterprises that have easy access to cheap labour have traditionally taken the view that conflict is inherent, and have sought to devise "safety-valve" ER strategies, to ensure, as far as possible, that when conflict does blow up, it can be contained without serious disruption to the work in hand. The employees in such organizations join the union, which provides welfare, leisure and recreation facilities, support for families in case of death or injury, represent their disputes, and lobby for increased investment in safety and technology. This is practised in the coal-mining sector. The workers' loyalty has been first and foremost to the union and no managing organization, either private or nationalized, has been able to provide an identity equivalent to this.

The ER strategy adopted will have to be supported by personnel/staff handbooks and rule-books, the procedures used and the ways in which these are promulgated, and any formal structures that are devised and put in place.

PROCEDURES AND POLICIES. Conformist ER requires the subordination of divergent and conflicting interests at the workplace, in the interests of pursuing common and understood goals. These are clearly specified by the organization in advance through staff circulars/brochures and other forms of internal communications. The emphatic focus is that the organization must be successful, effective and profitable, and that the purpose of ER is to contribute to this. This approach places primary responsibility on the organization and its managers. Standards are preset and prescribed, and are not the subject of negotiation. Areas of managerial prerogative, matters for consultation, and aspects open to negotiation are all clearly defined. Conformity leaves much open to consultation, but very little to genuine negotiation.

The procedures have to be quick and direct. The conflicts are not assumed to be dysfunctional, and managers seek to solve problems and promote harmony. The conflicts of interest between groups are kept to a minimum, and the disputes are resolved within given deadlines. Staff identity with the organization must be strong and, hence, initiatives need to be taken to promote organizational citizenship. The position of trade unions or any other staff-representative bodies is clearly defined and limited at the outset. The basis of any agreement is set by the organization. The union or representative body is invited to work within it. A union unable to do this does not get recognized.

> ER strategy must be supportive of, and complementary to, the wider aims and objectives of the organization.
>
> Where staff has a very strong group identity, employee relations may evolve to harness the group commitment to the organization's purpose.
>
> Labour-intensive organizations may adapt a "safety valve" framework for managing ER.

This approach to ER is seen adopted especially by Japanese companies operating in the West. It is a conformist approach. The ER agreement is made between the company and one trade union, along the conformist lines indicated above, with the overriding concern of streamlining and ordering workplace and staff relations, to ensure that their operation is as effective and ordered as any other business activity. This implies that in case it is deemed fit to have a trade union, the organization recognizes one single union. Pre-designed and predetermined by the organization, agreements with the union are normally limited to a single site or operational division.

To be effective and successful, this strategy for the management of ER must have the following attributes:

- It must mirror the philosophy, ethos, style and values of the organization concerned; there must be a visible commitment to it.
- Managers and supervisors are trained to manage staff on a basis free from inherent conflict, and are encouraged to solve rather than institutionalize problems, when they occur.
- Wage levels tend to be competitive and revisions never backdated.
- There is one set of procedures, terms and conditions of employment only. The ER sphere is not a matter for joint negotiation or agreement.
- Disciplinary and grievance practices operate from the standpoint of resolution and prevention of the matters in hand rather than institutionalization.
- The aim is towards positive discipline. Policies and procedures are designed for the optimum speed of operation.

This style of ER, oriented to business needs, is designed as a part of the process of ensuring the success, continuity and profitability of the organization.

If the intention is to avoid unionization, then the reasons why people join unions must be removed. Trade unions grew to prominence in organizations to represent the employees' interests. So an approach to ER that precludes the need for outside representation is essential. This normally consists of adopting a welfare-driven, consultative and open mode of communication. Equity and fairness have to be the principal foundation of ER. The responsibility for the style and tone of employee relations rests entirely with the organization. The staff adopts the desired corporate attitudes, values and aspirations more through a strong internal drive towards organizational citizenship.

In the direction and management of organizational and workplace employee relations, it is necessary to translate both the background and the legal provisions into a policy statement for effective ER operations and activities. This means understanding:

- The culture and background of the employees
- The perspective of work
- The basis of the prevailing expectations and attitudes to work
- The legal requirements, both in broad terms and also their specific application to the particular organization, and the operation of its sector or sectors overall

> A blend of the following principles in varying proportions sets the tone for an ER policy of an organization:
>
> - Equity
> - Flexibility
> - Employee participation in management

Policies need to be written and widely circulated for the purpose of regulating workplace activities—general employment practices, standards and approaches, general standards of workplace conduct and activity, discipline, grievance, disputes, health and safety, internal opportunities and equality. They are used by managers in their pursuit of established, standardized operating procedures and the successful operation of different aspects of work. They are for guidance, and only where something requires precise operation (such as a safety procedure), or there is a legal restraint (such as with discipline), should they be adhered to strictly. Their purpose is to set standards of behaviour and practice at work. This also has implications for the more general standards of decency, ethics and staff treatment that are established at the workplace. The procedures also indicate and underpin the required attitudes, and let everyone know where they stand. More generally, they define the scope and limits of the influence of the workplace.

The procedures should always be in writing, and state precisely the scope and coverage. They should be written in the language of the receiver, so that they are easily and clearly understood and followed. This enables new employees to know at the outset the defined boundaries, the dos and the don'ts, expectations and obligations on the part of both themselves and the organization. The procedures should be reviewed after due consultation and updated regularly. The final responsibility of ER policy design and implementation remains with the organization.

> **Policies and Procedures**
>
> - Need to be written in a language easily understood
> - Should be widely circulated
> - Consulted for guidance
> - Set standards of workplace behaviour and practices
> - Define the scope and limits of the influence of the workplace

Typically, the policies and procedures must address the following standards:

- The desired attitude, approach, standpoint by which ER is to be conducted
- The ethics, standards, attitudes, values and beliefs necessary for effective conduct
- The composition, style and approach of ER and employee handbooks, manuals and procedures
- The specific attitude and standpoint from which organization discipline is to be established and implemented
- Specific organizational and operational management issues arising from the composition and mix of the workforce, the nature and location of the sector or sectors in which activities are carried out, technology used, and the ways in which work is designed
- Specific sectoral operational issues such as volatility, seasonality, poaching and attrition
- Specific sectoral psychological issues such as social respect and esteem
- Specific sectoral preconceptions, prejudices and behavioural prejudices

8.2.2 The Role of an Employee Relations Manager

Some of the important functions to be handled by an employee relations manager in a contemporary organization would include the following:

1. The maintenance of employee motivation. The managers must establish formal, semi-formal and informal chains of communication with workforce representatives and with employees at large.
2. Day-to-day handling of staff matters
3. Negotiations, dealing with disciplinary and grievance matters, handling disputes and other problem-solving activities
4. Balancing the conflicting demands of groups of employees
5. Facilitating HRM by creating an atmosphere of positivism and industrial harmony. In case an atmosphere of mistrust prevails, it is the responsibility of the ER manager to move from problem to problem to ensure the attainment of some desirable solutions. The ability to make any progress and shape a more positive and effective future for the staff in such circumstances will stem from an understanding of the status quo in the first place.
6. A general appreciation of the traditions, history and background of ER and creating opportunities for reviving or practising the same
7. Bargaining activities
8. The resolution of conflict or negotiations
9. Reform if required to be carried out, either globally or at the workplace, in relation to new systems devised and implemented

8.3 Culture and Employee Relations

Both the organization structure adopted and the culture demonstrated by collective beliefs, values and ethics must match the overall purpose of the organization. This must be done in ways that ensure the best possible return on investment for an effective employee relationship, which translates into performance, responsiveness and adaptability. It is necessary to recognize that no two organizations are exactly alike.

All organizations are different. They have different methods of operation and working, different ways of doing things, different values, attitudes, beliefs and norms—different personalities, in fact. They are as different from each other as people, yet can be defined by a set of features, which translate into organization culture.

- The age and history of the organization, the degree of prominence that it has established, its traditions, its reputation and how this has arisen, its image, its standing in its markets and communities. The history, traditions and reputation require managerial understanding and activity to develop them further and, where necessary, to take remedial action.
- The size of the organization and related elements of spans of control, degrees of centralization and decentralization, departmentalization and divisionalization, the balance of primary and support functions, the nature and style of all activities. It is also necessary to consider information systems, other control mechanisms, reporting relationships and systems for the monitoring and evaluation of performance.
- The nature of work, the mix of skills, knowledge, expertise, professionalism, technical capability and other activities. People who are highly professionalized or trained bring distinctive sets of values with them, which may rub against those of the organization.

Organization Culture and Employee Relations

- Age and history of the organization
- The size of the organization
- The nature of work
- Technology
- Location
- The environment
- People factors
- Mission
- Core values
- Management style

Particular approaches are required, therefore, to generate organizational and operational harmony. Potential differences must be recognized at an early stage. Highly ordered and regulated tasks and series of tasks are normally mirrored in the organization of people to carry them out. At the other extreme, projects that involve pioneering and innovative work often require little formal direction, leaving much to the self-motivation and self-organization of those involved.

- The relationship between culture, structure and technology is a critical feature of the operational aspects of ER management. Small-scale activities require a lower and more flexible organization than do those with large scale, permanent or semi-permanent and mass-output methods. In large, complex organizations, economies of scale and the ER implications have to be considered, alongside questions of production and work-group organization and departmentalization. From this, there are implications concerning alienation, dysfunction, and organized labour and representation. The speed at which technology changes or becomes obsolete must also be considered. Organizations cannot seek permanence or stability in an era of rapid technological change or innovation. Even where a particular technology is deemed to have a degree of durability, its permanence may easily be called into question through the invention of a substitute, or substitute method of working, for the activity in question. The investment made in technology by organizations also has implications for the culture (and, therefore, the management of ER). Organizations that continuously upgrade their technology must also regularly improve their expertise and capability to exploit it to its full potential.
- The ability to work in harmony with the prevailing local customs and traditions. This includes religious and ethical, as well as social, pressures. It is certain to include legal constraints. There are also population size and mixes, access to services, age and composition of the local workforce. There will be standards set by other employers in the area (especially large employers) that have implications for all those working close by.
- The relationship between the organization, its markets, customers and clients, its competitors and its broader environment. This includes confidence, expansion, and contraction, economic and social factors. It includes local reputation as an employer. The states of environmental flux, diversity and complexity require organizations that can cope with, respond to and exist in harmony with the changes. It is also necessary to note the degree of stability of the environment. This includes threats and dangers of organization collapse, expansion, contraction and takeover, the loss of markets or the gaining of new markets, and also gains and losses in standing and confidence. The overall ability of the organization to survive and prosper in relation to its environment, and to fight battles with it when necessary, must be considered.
- People factors constitute a broad understanding of those who come to work for the organization. Different kinds of relationships are formed between the people and their organizations on the basis of degrees of professional and technical expertise, personal characteristics and attributes of status, ambiguity, stability and identity, and also their appropriateness to the form of organization in question. For example, a person who has a desire for a senior designation will not get this in a small, flexible organization. Nor will he or she get the same measure of order and stability from this organization as from public service, the government, or a multinational establishment. On the other hand, people with high energy, enthusiasm and ability are more likely to get frustrated in slow-moving, highly formalized organizations than in those that are flexible and dynamic.
- The extent to which the mission is clear, articulated, understood and accepted by all concerned, and the simplicity or complexity of the goals. There are also likely

to be subordinate aims and objectives, which may, on the face of it, conflict with the main stated purpose. It is also necessary to recognize that organizations change their purposes and directions. This occurs for a variety of reasons—shifts in talents, qualities and technologies, new opportunities, market changes and technological advance.

- A clear positive set of values or direction given by the organization to its people, with which they can all identify. The adoption of shared values is central to the generation of high levels of commitment and motivation among the staff. Recognizing that people bring a diverse range of qualities, and their own attitudes; values and beliefs, is essential. Giving them a clear corporate purpose that is both above individual aspirations and capable of accommodating them is a key feature of effective ER management. It gives a clear indication of the prevailing ethics and morality of the organization.
- There is a close interrelationship between the management style, the work that is carried out and the way in which it is organized and directed. It is affected by the size, complexity, scale and scope of the organization. In turn, it is also affected by hierarchical considerations, nature and degrees of conformity, alienation, the nature and mix of work, the commitments, qualities, capabilities and attitudes of the staff carrying out the work, and the expertise and capacities of the managers and supervisors.

ER policies would be primarily influenced by the organization culture. As an example, let us take three distinctive cultures and see how the ER policies need to be devised to overcome the barriers that such cultures create.

People/person culture: is where a group in their own overriding interests band together to produce an organization for their benefit. It is to be found in certain research groups, family firms, and companies started by groups of friends. In ER terms, the emergence of people cultures would invariably cause conflict with the broader organization at some point in time. Thus, subcultures emerge as lobbies with vested interest groups and would lead to the emergence of ER policies that cater to the needs of the most powerful subgroup. The equity principle has to be predominant here.

ER Policy – Organization Culture Match

- People/Person Culture
- Task Culture
- Role Culture

Task culture: is found in project teams, marketing groups and market- and customer-oriented organizations. The emphases are on getting the job completed to the customer's satisfaction, maintaining levels of customer and client satisfaction and responding to, and identifying, new market opportunities. At their best, task cultures are flexible, dynamic, adaptable and responsive. They accommodate the movements of staff necessary to ensure effective project and development teams and continued innovation, and require a degree of personal, as well as professional, commitment in the pursuit of customer satisfaction. In the management of ER, task cultures are prone to conflicts caused by confusion and task ambiguity/overlap or overload problem. Conflicts may also be caused where a group or groups perceive their task identity as distinct from others. A few members who idle away the time while the others perform tasks (called social loafing) leading to group frustration over carrying passengers is also likely. ER policies must, therefore, ensure conformity and consensus.

Role culture: is found where organizations have gained a combination of size, permanence and departmentalization, and where the ordering of activities, preservation of knowledge and experience and stability are important. The roles are defined, described and ordered. The role culture reflects the bureaucratic concept of hierarchy and permanence. Role cultures operate most effectively where the wider environment is steady and a degree of permanence is envisaged and where the demand for products and services is known to be relatively permanent and certain. Role cultures are governed by procedures and rule books. Conflicts and disputes arise, in ER terms, when there are breaches (or perceived breaches) of the rules of procedures. When conflicts do arise, each step of the way is governed by procedures that must be adhered to. At their best, these forms of ER are orderly and proceduralized; at their worst, they institutionalize and prolong conflict, which leads to frustration and alienation on the part of those involved.

8.3.1 Culture Design for Employee Relations

Whatever is done must be positive and not simply allowed to emerge by default. The values, aspirations and direction of the organization must be conveyed to all those who come to work, so that they clearly understand the attitudes, values and beliefs of the organization. Concerning some staff, this may involve a mutual rejection—organizations accommodate dissenting staff to the extent that dissents can be harmonized or made productive; to go further requires a dilution of core purpose and values. Other organizations take the view that however expert an individual may be in their chosen field, their way of working might not harmonize with the particular requirements of the situation. Flexibility, fluidity, responsiveness and initiative are all essential components of the establishment of, and ordering of, the culture and also the structure of organizations. This, then, forms the basis for:

- **The Approach of ER:** Its purpose and direction, the fundamental approach and attitude, suitability for organizational purpose
- **ER Policy:** The attitude and approach to key issues—organization discipline, the issues concerning discipline and grievances, pay and rewards, improvements in working conditions, the management style, managerial attitudes, the expectations of trade unions and/or other employee representative bodies
- **The Content of ER Activities:** What is included and what is not, where managerial prerogative lies, those matters open for consultation, the constitution of committees, groups and other representative bodies
- **Compensation Policy:** The management of pay and rewards, the attitudes to pay and rewards, differentials, equality and inequality, factors such as gain-sharing and profit-sharing options
- **Problem Resolution Approaches:** The organizational points of view on issues concerning pay and rewards, discipline and grievances, health and safety
- **ER Systems:** Formal systems, informal systems, systems for the management of specific issues—especially discipline, grievance, pay and reward, and health and safety
- **Employee Communications:** The process of communications, the content of written and formal communications, the content of face-to-face communications and organization responsiveness to employee issues
- **Organization Development in ER:** Attitudes to staff and management training, priorities for staff and management training, approach and content of the training, especially in negotiating skills, problem-solving, health, safety and emergency procedures and communications
- **Decision-making Processes:** Organizational and managerial standards and standpoints, content of decision-making processes, the extent to which these are autocratic, consultative, participative or democratic
- **The Conduct of ER:** Including consultation and participation, collective bargaining, the constitution of committees, the agenda of committees, the remit of committees, the extent of value and importance placed on key issues through these meetings—especially concerning pay and the conditions of health and safety

Flexibility, fluidity, responsiveness and initiative determine the establishment and ordering of the culture and structure of organizations. This, in turn, determines:

- The approach to ER
- The broad ER policy
- Scope and coverage of ER activities
- Compensation strategy
- Communication approach and structure
- ER systems
- Approach to problem-solving
- Decision-making processes
- Organization development

8.3.2 Organizational Behaviour in Culture Design

Identity and commonality of purpose can only be achieved through an understanding of the people who work in the particular organization, their wants and needs, hopes, fears, desires and aspirations. The following would contribute to this understanding and, therefore, must be taken into account with the employee relations strategies:

- **Leadership:** Qualities and capabilities, and the roles and functions adopted in ER. The nature and style of leadership, in the particular field of ER, plays a critical role in the creation of human structures and systems, motivation and direction, the resolution of conflict, the creation of overall vision and direction and recognizing the obligations that go with this, including providing resources.
- **Communication:** An understanding of the processes, perception and the principles of effective communication. The style, type and language of communication, through absence or indifference, cause the generation of, and reinforcement of, attitudes and behaviour related to negativity, alienation, uncertainty and anxiety. In ER terms, oral communication is required for conducting discussions and briefings with the staff, conducting negotiations, consultations and effective interviews (especially grievance, dispute and discipline), conducting effective performance appraisal and handling staff and organizational problems.
- **Decision-making:** The processes by which effective decisions are achieved, their communication and promulgation, and their acceptance. The general objective of anyone in the position of having to take decisions must be to minimize risks and uncertainties, minimize negative consequences, and to maximize the chances of success and effectiveness. In order to stand the greatest chance of success, therefore, participation and consultation need to be considered.
- **Power and Authority:** Sources of power and authority, the use of power and authority in ER situations. In terms of the organization and management of ER, it is necessary to understand the following:
  - Power and influence reside in the hands of managers because of the confidence in which they are held, as well as the expertise that they hold.
  - Power and influence reside in the hands of supervisors and the employees' representative because of the extent of the support that they command.
  - It is essential to understand the extent of reward power present in particular situations—especially the capability of organizations and their managers to deliver things that have been agreed upon.
  - Authority and influence have strong behavioural connotations. Besides having legitimized positions and designations in the hierarchical structure, there has to be a measure of confidence and belief in the individuals, in the first place.
- **Conflict in Organizations:** Sources, existence, management and containment. An area where specialized employee relations departments and officials can make key contributions to organizational effectiveness is in the analysis of the potential for, and the reality of, conflict in their organizations.

Employee relations strategies must draw from findings in the following areas of organization behaviour:

- Leadership
- Communication
- Decision-making
- Power and authority
- Management of conflicts

8.4 The Future of Employee Relations

As discussed earlier, the paradigm shift from "industrial relations" to "employee relations" has created a change in the perceptions of what it is, what it constitutes and what it should achieve. In the UK, there has been a transformation in the status and influence of trade unions and, while in UK terms, this influence has declined, both the EU at large and different organizations from other parts of the world ascribe very distinctive directions and objectives to the institutions and practices of ER. In India, the trade unions are rather inactive in comparison to the aggressive stands that were taken by them earlier.

The transformation is driven by a combination of technological changes, globalization of operations and markets, advances in managerial expertise, advances in the understanding of human behaviour patterns, changes in aspiration and expectations in

Forces Driving Organizations Towards an ER Orientation

- Technological changes
- Globalization of operations and markets
- Advances in managerial expertise
- Advances in the understanding of human behaviour
- Changes in aspiration and expectations in work situations
- Changes in organization structures
- Specific initiatives such as privatization, cost-cutting measures, and shake-ups for gaining competitive advantage

work situations, and changes in organization structures compounded by specific initiatives such as privatization, cost-cutting measures, and shake-ups for gaining competitive advantage.

Organizations offering security provisions through lifetime employment are continuing to do so with training, retraining and redeveloping employees. There is also the recognition of the position of staff as legitimate and key stakeholders in organizations, and new forms of profit-sharing and gain-sharing options have emerged. The EU has institutionalized this approach of "social partnership", and embodied it in the social charter. This means that organizations are increasingly required to adopt positions of openness, honesty, employee participation and effective communication. This in itself becomes the means of focus for the development of the organization, and the generation of harmony and understanding necessary to benefit everybody who works within it.

New and current approaches are concerned to ensure that ER is both cost effective and suitable to the needs of the organization. Direct relationships are established to remove barriers of alienation and motivation. Current approaches to ER stem from an organization-wide belief that there is a contribution to be made to organizational performance, customer satisfaction, competitive edge and, above all, profitability if they are adopted.

The future of ER is, therefore, dependent on the following:

- Clearly established standards that are communicated well, and training provided for conformity
- Managers are trained to value and adhere to those standards
- Problem-solving, decision-making and the resolution of disputes, grievances and disciplinary issues are conducted both from the standpoint of equity and fairness, and with a view to enhancing total departmental performance.

8.4.1 Transition

If ER is to be used as an effective and profitable managerial and organizational activity, the first step is to identify the organizational barriers, which could be the following:

- **Tradition:** This is a problem where there has been a long history of successful work in specific, well-understood and widely accepted ways.
- **Success** (and perceived success): If the organization is known or perceived to be successful in its current ways of doing things, then there is resistance.
- **Failure:** This is a barrier to change where a given state of affairs has been allowed to persist for some time. Resistance occurs when someone determines to do something about it—again, upsetting an overtly comfortable and orderly status quo.
- **Technology:** It is often the driving force behind jobs, tasks, occupation and activities. Their disruption causes trauma to those affected by the consequent need for job and occupation change, retraining, redeployment—and often redundancy. Technological changes, in turn, cause changes to work patterns and methods.
- **Vested Interests:** Needs for change are resisted by those who are, or who perceive themselves to be, at risk and for whom the current order represents a clear and guaranteed passage to increased prosperity and influence.
- **Managerial:** The managerial barrier is a consequence of the divorce between ownership and control.
- **Bureaucracy:** The bureaucracy barrier occurs where patterns of order and control have grown over long periods in the recording and supervision of activities and in the structuring of organizational functions.

8.4.2 Employee Relations and the Management of Change

When changes are required, all methods of communication at the disposal of the organization are to be invoked. This includes statutory obligations to consult with trade unions and other recognized staff-representative bodies. Good practice also requires that many different channels of communication are used, paying special attention to those who do not have formal representation. When great changes are involved, it is also usual for there to be specific individual and group problems that cannot easily be resolved in the greater scheme of things. It follows from this that it would be necessary to offer individual and group counselling and support methods and mechanisms. These are for the purpose of reassurance, the continued addressing of lingering or persisting uncertainties, and the means of tackling individual cases. They also reinforce organizational concern for, and commitment to, the specific needs of individuals and groups.

Problems are fewer, become apparent earlier, and are easier to tackle, when a general stance of openness and assertiveness is adopted. It also emphasizes the concern that organizations have for all employees. It may also be necessary to tackle managerial and supervisory groups, in order to ensure their support for what is proposed.

The most serious problems arise when, for whatever reason, the employees do not believe the message that they are receiving on account of a history of bad employee relations. It may be necessary for organizations in this situation to acknowledge their failings of the past and constitute working parties to demonstrate integrity of purpose in this set of circumstances.

Trade union, if they still exist, need to be engaged as workplace social partners. If employee interests are to be given the same status and legitimacy as shareholder interests, then employee representatives have to be the subject of a distinctive and defined organizational approach. Discuss the issues raised in Box 8.2.

A streamlined approach to the organization and management is the key to continued development of effective ER. The main issue remains the continued development of awareness and expertise in the totality of employee relations, and the contribution that it makes to the effective, profitable and enduring management of organizations. Particular attention also needs to be paid to the following:

- **Technological Advance and Its Impact on Work Design and Task Design:** This necessitates continued investment in training and development.
- **Investment:** It is important to invest in the creation of high-quality work environments for employees, regardless of the length of service, hours of work, or occupation carried out. Investment is also required in flexibility, dynamism, creativity and responsiveness, each of which has a direct measurable effect in terms of reduced sickness, absence, turnover, and conflict and grievance, as they advance employment satisfaction and security.
- **Culture, Attitudes and Values:** Organizations need to develop and adopt specific attitudes and values to
  - Support the organization's core values
  - Be capable of accommodating the differing, and often conflicting, interests of the employees
  - Transcend local cultural pressures

BOX 8.2 FOR CLASS DISCUSSION

Discuss the reasons for the paradigm shift from industrial relations (IR) to employee relations (ER). In an employee relations framework, the intervention of State will reduce increasingly. Discuss with examples from contemporary developments in the Indian industry.

- Create a basis of long-term, mutual commitment, serving the interests of the organization, its customers and the wider community as well as its staff.

- **Business Across Cultures:** This especially applies to organizations operating in the global market. This means creating attitudes and values, and supporting these with managerial capability, so that cultural differences are transcended.
- **Strategy:** ER strategy is increasingly concerned with developing and reinforcing long-term clarity of employment purpose. This means:
    - Reconciling the range of conflict inherent in the mix of staff capabilities and expertise present
    - Investing in and committing to the long-term in terms of technology and the derived investment necessary in building competence
    - Generating staff loyalty and commitment through a corporate determination to have a long-term future

  Above all, this means attention to attitudes and values, training and development, and to the managerial expertise required for effective ER. It constitutes a mutual and continuous obligation.
- **Flexible Patterns and Methods of Work:** This is based on a combination of the demand to optimize investment in production and other technology, and the changing patterns of customer requirements. The fundamental shift in staffing patterns and methods of work that has arisen as a result implies having the corporate will, and managerial expertise and commitment, to ensure that whatever the pattern of work or hours worked, all staff members are treated with the same fundamental principles of equality and opportunity.
- **Ethics:** There is a realization that there is a much greater propensity for customers to choose organizations in which they have confidence and which they can trust.

All of this is only possible if there is a fundamental integrity of relationship between the organization and its staff and, arising from this, a mutual commitment to a long-term and enduring staff–management relationship based on openness, honesty and trust.

Employee relations involves the body of work concerned with maintaining employer–employee relationships that contribute to satisfactory productivity, motivation and morale. Essentially, employee relations is concerned with preventing and resolving problems involving individuals, which arise out of or affect work situations. The key to competent employee relations is in effective communications. For the mutual benefit of the employers and the employee, engaging in conversations and consultations rather than passing orders down the line will be the way companies will operate. Rigid labour legislations and controls will become less relevant and the government systems will have to look at the needs of the future. The paradigm shift from IR to ER has begun in Indian corporate organizations as they become important players in the global economy.

SUMMARY

- The general level of understanding and appreciation required of the managers if they are to be truly effective in employee relations management is deep and complex.
- They must create a harmonious and productive working environment so that effective work can be carried out.
- Factors that dilute behavioural boundaries and constraints have to be recognized and whichever perspective is adopted, they have to be managed actively and positively.
- A distinctive ER strategy is required, and organizations need to take direct and positive responsibility for creating

institutions, procedures and practices that are going to work in the particular set of circumstances, providing their managers and supervisors the necessary training and instilling the right attitude to ensure that this is successful.

- ER must be seen as a contribution to profitable and effective performance, rather than a function.
- The function of ER experts should be to ensure that organization perspectives, strategies, policies and institutions operate in harmony and that these are supported with managerial and supervisory expertise, staff awareness and understanding. In turn, the truly expert manager—in whatever field—must become an expert in daily employee management, employee relations activities, and must recognize that their contribution and expertise in this part of the job is as important as in the others.
- The essential prerequisites to the total understanding of ER from the organizational perspective are leadership, communication, decision-making, power and conflict.
- It is essential to remember that all employee relations are founded on the interactions of people, and, therefore, on their behaviour and approaches in different situations. In principle, it is essential to understand that all organization activities—of which ER is one—are dependent upon effective leadership, communication and decision-making. The absence of these causes ER problems, in exactly the same way as they cause production output and sales problems.
- Beyond this, it is essential to recognize the function of leadership, and the need for firm direction and authority in the management of ER and the potential for conflict and dysfunction that exists in all human situations.
- Only when the behavioural aspects of ER are recognized, can an effective approach to the establishment and management of organization discipline, conflict and motivation be contemplated and the establishment of effective institutions for the conduct of both strategic and operational ER be considered.

KEY TERMS

- employee relations 141
- pluralism 143
- radicalism 143
- unitarism 142

REVIEW QUESTIONS

1 What are the employee relations strategies used by employers?

2 What are the functions of employee relations management? How are they different from IR?

3 What are the prerequisites for ERM? Are they prevalent in the industry today?

4 Discuss the cultural dimensions of ERM.

5 In the context of a future in global trade and industry, what are the expected trends that are going to shape employee relations? What would be the main forces driving these changes?

QUESTIONS FOR CRITICAL THINKING

1 What steps do organizations need to take to develop an ERM framework? Discuss with examples.

2 ERM requires a congruence of conformity and consensus. Can this be effective using the psychological approach by ERM? Elucidate with examples.

DEBATE

1 ERM is here to stay and unions may no longer be required to protect the interest of the workers.

2 The ERM approach will work only in knowledge sectors or where the challenge is on retaining talent.

CASE ANALYSIS

Best Textile Company

BEST Textile Company had an eventful history of dynamic industrial relations and multi-union, arm-twisting tactics that had a detrimental effect on the organization's performance. The company has now been taken over by a French company wanting to establish itself in India. The new CEO has begun the transformation process by initiating some employee-friendly programmes enumerated below:

- Maternity Leave: Extended period up to one year, in case accumulated earned leave available
- Childcare-in-house Facility
- Pick-up–Drop: Even if the staff has his/her own vehicle
- Canteen Facility: A subsidized/no profit basis
- Free-Local-Phone Facility
- ATM Inside/Near the Office
- Cheque Drop Boxes

This in effect is a paradigm shift towards employee relations. But the CEO is also holding discussions with the four unions in the three mills taken over and is initiating a process of recognizing a union through secret-ballot elections with the help of the Chief Labour Commissioner of the State.

1. Do you think the new CEO's strategy would work? Give reasons.
2. Can you enumerate the problems the new CEO is likely to face with this strategy?
3. What suggestions can you provide to facilitate smooth industrial/employee relations at BEST Company?

Team Computers India

Attrition in Team Computers India Private Limited, an INR 300 crore IT infrastructure management company, has reached 40 per cent. The company is growing at the rate of almost 20 per cent per annum and the requirement for skilled and experienced manpower is pinching the company. The non-availability of right-profile software/hardware engineers will become the main differentiator. Team Computers is an ethical company and maintains the industry standards in respect of compensation and benefits. They adhere to all the statutory requirements as far as labour-law provisions are concerned. The human resources department spends most of its resources scouting for talent and maintaining an employee database. There is a virtual war in the marketplace for talent. Employees are bargaining for—and getting—impossible terms including a five-day week, flexi-timing, onshore deployment, full pay on bench, etc. The HR department has been dealing with a collective of staff periodically to get a feedback on their requirements, but these meetings turn out to be one-sided, economic demands from the staff. Recently, you have heard that certain national trade unions are making forays into the IT sector to lobby for the regulation of the working conditions. This would complicate matters and will have direct impact on the cost and flexibility of operations.

1. What, in your opinion, are the fundamental issues faced by the management?
2. What would be the correct long-term approach for handling these issues?
3. Do you think the entry of trade unions in the IT industry will make it less competitive?

NOTES

1 Center for Good Governance, Government of Andhra Pradesh, *Handbook on Service Excellence—A Guide to Service Excellence in Public Management with Lessons from Best Managed Companies*", available online at http://unpan1.un.org/intradoc/groups/public/documents/CGG/UNPAN026214.pdf.

2 John Gareth and Mary Mathew, *Organizational Theory: Design and Change, 5th Ed.* (Delhi: Pearson Education, 2009), pp. 211.

SUGGESTED READING

Dayal, Ishwar "HRD in Indian Organizations", *Vikalpa*, Oct–Dec, 1989.

Joseph, Jerome "Challenges and Opportunities in Democratization of IR", *Vikalpa*, Vol. 14, No. 1, Jan–March, 1989.

National Commission on Labour Report (Second), Government of India.

Raj, Aparna *Industrial Relations in India: Issues, Institutions and Outlook* (New Delhi: New Century Publications, 2003).

Venkatratnam, C. S. *Industrial Relations* (New Delhi: Oxford University Press, 2006).

part iii

legislations and administration

chapter nine

CHAPTER OUTLINE

LEARNING OBJECTIVES

After reading this chapter, you will be able to:

- Classify the existing pieces of labour legislations on the basis of their objectives
- Identify the employment-related legislations
- Describe the objectives, scope and coverage of the major employment-related legislations
- List the significant provisions of the act(s) and their applicability to work situations
- Appreciate the need for reforms in a few provisions

Labour Law Compliance in Karnataka

Rajeev Ranjan, Group HRM Manager for the Vardhan Engineering Group, was to oversee the people-related issues of 19 group companies ranging from design, consultancy, manufacturing and software applications to financial services.

The group, with a combined turnover of INR 70 billion had units spread over 5 states. The employee strength was 2,500 and these were all categories of employees—blue-collared, clerical, supervisory, executive and managerial. Many of the units also employed contractual and casual employees. Each of the group companies was operating in a highly competitive space. Rajeev, while introducing best practices in all the units, was also responsible for compliance issues in various units.

And, being an experienced HR Manager, he knew how enormous the task was—considering the range of businesses the group was into, at least 20 to 25 labour legislations got attracted to the group companies. From Factories Act to the Bonus Act and the Maternity Benefit Act. Of course, there were a few units where even the Contract Labour (Regulation and Abolition Act) was attracted. There was no way he could take risks with the compliance issues, nor did he want to, considering most of the laws were meant for the protection of the labour.

At times, however, he felt a few provisions of the laws had not kept pace with the changing times. A few laws had even become irrelevant, he thought. The recent report of the National Labour Commission had looked into these issues and recommended a streamlining of the plethora of laws keeping in tune with current realities. But a lack of consensus has prevented the implementation of any of the changes.

The challenge that this poses for Rajeev is to have a trained internal group that is well-versed with the provisions of all the laws applicable to the respective units, with special reference to all actionable provisions. The group prides itself on being perceived as one of the most preferred places to work at.

Labour Legislation in a Changing Context

The competition in the global market to produce cost-effective quality products or services has put pressure on organizations in India to drive employees to deliver. The focus has shifted from regulasting terms and conditions of employment to regulating performance. India is witnessing a subtle shift in paradigm as far as terms of employment contract are concerned. There are efforts to find a meaningful middle path between requirements of labour productivity that is closer to global benchmarks and, at the same time, within the requirements of employment-related legislations.

Post-reforms, there have been frequent news reports in favour of reforms in labour legislations in the country. This clamour, at least from the employers' side, is for the flexibility in hiring and firing, reduced burden on social security, the reduction of inspection regime (to be replaced by self-regulation), etc. While these issues have been debated, no headway has been made in terms of concrete legislative reforms.

Labour legislation in India comprises both central and state legislations. There are numerous such enactments that give the impression that the labour market is inflexible in India. Most of the enactments that are in force today took shape in an economy that was insulated from global forces. Although the industries that emerged in this insulated economy have had to adapt to the provisions of the existing labour laws, there is a pressing need to usher in labour-law reforms to make investments in India more attractive and the Indian industry more competitive in the new global economy. Now, this clamour is one-sided and may give an impression that the only way to competitiveness is through reforming the "restrictive" labour laws. The truth may be somewhere in between.

At this juncture, before we debate the need and direction of reforms, we need to develop a clear understanding of the relevant provisions. It is also necessary to know the provisions to facilitate compliance and appropriate decision-making. The ideal way to begin is to get straight into a myriad of shop-floor situations and get a feel of the application of labour legislations. Before proceeding further, read the caselets in Box 9.1 and discuss each of them with your peers and the instructor. After you read the entire textbook, revisit this box and check your understanding.

We now have a "flavour" of a variety of situations where compliance may be needed. To study labour laws, it would be sensible to follow the route map mentioned below:

i) Describe a logical framework for the classification of major pieces of legislations that are relevant to the industry.

ii) Define a scheme that would make it easy for us to look at the main provisions of these legislations in a structured manner.

iii) Relate the major provisions to actual application at the workplace.

It is not the purpose of this book to provide an exhaustive treatment of all the provisions of all the labour-related laws. There are publications that contain the various "bare acts". There are also very good publications, which deal exhaustively with all the provisions of legislation and go on to discuss the relevant case laws in detail. The purpose of this book is to enable an employee relations manager or student to appreciate the various provisions in terms of actual application and compliance.

BOX 9.1 **FOR CLASS DISCUSSION**

1. Amit is a bus conductor with DTC. He could not report for duty one day due to an emergency at home. He could not inform his supervisor also. As a result, the bus scheduling got disrupted causing a chain reaction and inconvenience to passengers. The next day, Amit's supervisor refused to allow him to resume his work. Instead, after asking him to wait for a couple of hours, the supervisor handed to him a signed order dismissing Amit from service (the order was signed by the supervisor). Is it alright?
2. Prabha has recently joined a BPO in Gurgaon as a customer-service agent. From next week, she has been asked to report for duty in the night shift from 10 p.m. to 6 a.m. Can this be done?
3. Balwant is a Grade I welder in an automobile-manufacturing factory at Manesar. His duty hours are from 8 a.m. to 12 noon and then again from 5p.m. to 9 p.m. He, therefore, works for eight hours during a day. Is this alright?
4. The linesmen of an electricity-distribution company in Delhi have gone on a flash strike. They have not given any notice. What action can management take? Does the government have any role to play in this?
5. Munnalal is a messenger in an auto-component plant in NOIDA. One day, due to some altercation, he slapped his supervisor. Other than slapping him back, what action can the supervisor take against Munnalal?
6. Mr Paranjpe is the branch manager of a PSU bank at Masoodpur. The normal office timing for the staff is from 10 a.m. to 5 p.m. with a 30-minute lunch break. The bank stops all public dealings after 2 p.m. However, with the increased competition in the banking sector, all the new banks have staggered working hours from 9 a.m. to 9 p.m. Mr Paranjpe wants to change the timings in his bank also as, otherwise, he will lose all business. Can he change the timings? How?
7. Can an employer sack a manager? How? Can he sack a worker? Can he ask a worker to leave after complying with the notice-period formalities?
8. The workers at a major automobile company in Gurgaon are very agitated regarding delays in the payment of their wages. Though they get their salaries every month, the payment sometimes get delayed beyond 10–15 days. The workers are not sure when they will receive their salaries. Can they do anything about it (other than going on strike)? Do they have a legal remedy?
9. V. Subramanyam, Chargeman Grade III at a steel factory at Jamshedpur, while supervising pouring of hot metal into ladles, suffered severe burn injuries when the molten metal accidentally spilled over the floor. One such metal fragment pierced one of his eyes causing complete damage to vision in that eye. Subramanyam was given alternative employment by the same employer without any loss in salary. Do you think he is entitled to any other compensation?
10. An aluminium-manufacturing unit in Renukoot, UP, employs labour on contract for unloading of their raw materials from the railway wagons. These workers have been working at the plant for the last nine years, although they are on the rolls of a contractor. Can these workers claim permanent employment with the aluminium-manufacturing unit? What would be the implications? Why do we employ people on contract?

9.1 The Classification of Labour Laws

The various labour legislations can be classified in a number of ways depending upon the object of study. For example, they can be classified on any one of the following arbitrary bases:

1. **Purpose:**
   a) Regulation of working conditions (terms of employment, procedure for employment, safety + health + welfare requirements)
   b) Social security (protection against loss in earning and risks)
   c) Regulation of wages and bonus
   d) Industrial relations and conflict prevention
2. **Legislature:** Central or state or both. A sample of central legislations relating to various labour and employment subjects is given at the end of the chapter in a tabular form.
3. **Period of Enactment:** Early days, pre-Independence, post-Independence

The National Labour Commission (Second), in its report (Chapter VIA) has also discussed the labour laws under the following classifications:

1. Employment Relations
2. Contract Labour
3. Laws on Working Conditions and Welfare
4. Laws Relating to Wages
5. Laws Relating to Social Security
6. Miscellaneous Matters

Since this book is largely aimed at aspiring or practising HR managers in the organized sector, it will be useful if we used the classification based on the purpose of the enactment. According to this classification, the main enactments roughly fall under the following heads:

9.1.1 The Regulation of Working Conditions

1. The Factories Act, 1948
2. The Shops and Establishments Act, 1953
3. The Contract Labour (Regulation and Abolition) Act, 1970

Other similar legislations include The Mines Act, 1952; The Employers' Liability Act, 1938; The Child Labour (Prohibition and Regulations) Act, 1986; The Plantation Labour Act, 1951; The *Beedi* and Cigar Workers (Conditions of Employment) Act, 1966; The Cine-Workers and Cinema Theatre Workers (Regulations of Employment) Act, 1981; The Indian Dock Labourers Act, 1934; The Inter-State Migrant Workmen (Regulation of Employment and Conditions of Service) Act, 1979; The Motor Transport Workers Act, 1961; The Sales Promotion Employees (Conditions of Service) Act, 1976; and The Working Journalists and Other Newspaper Employees (Conditions of Service) and Miscellaneous Provisions Act, 1955.

Of all these legislations, first three would provide a general overview of the genre and, therefore, have been taken up for detailed treatment. This chapter would focus on the objectives, scope, coverage, provisions and applications of these legislations.

9.1.2 Legislations Related to Social Security

1. Employees' State Insurance Act, 1948
2. Workmen's Compensation Act, 1923
3. The Payment of Gratuity Act, 1972
4. The Employee's Provident Fund and Miscellaneous Provisions Act, 1952

The above legislations are the main social-security provisions in India. These have been discussed in Chapter 10.

9.1.3 Legislations Related to Wage and Bonus

1. The Payment of Wages Act, 1936
2. The Minimum Wages Act, 1948
3. The Payment of Bonus Act, 1965

These are covered in Chapter 11.

The labour laws can be classified in many ways. In the scheme followed in the book, the major labour laws have been classified on the basis of purpose as under:

1. Regulation of Working Conditions
2. Furtherance of Social Security
3. Wages and Bonus Regulation
4. Industrial Relations and Conflict Prevention

9.1.4 Industrial Relations and Conflict Prevention

1. The Industrial Disputes Act, 1947
2. The Industrial Employment (Standing Orders) Act, 1946
3. The Trade Unions Act, 1926

The Trade Unions Act, 1926 has been discussed in detail in Chapter 7. The Industrial Disputes Act, 1947 shall be covered in detail in Chapters 12 and 13.

9.2 The Scheme for a Structured Study of the Acts

For a student and a practitioner, the most important aspects of the labour laws, in the opinion of the authors, are the applicability of the provisions in relation to:

i) the nature of the establishment and

ii) the category of employees covered by it (the definition of "worker", "workman", "employee" under the different Acts).

To study the labour laws in a structured way, it is necessary to have a thorough understanding of a few terms/concepts that have been used in different Acts. Specifically, care must be taken to understand the following:

1. The definition and coverage of "workman", "worker", "employee" in each of the Acts
2. The meaning of "factory", "establishment", "industry", etc. in the relevant Acts
3. The definition and judicial pronouncements on the "appropriate government".

More so, during the last 15 years, many new categories of establishments and employees have been added to the industry. To keep pace with the impact of globalization of business, many new working practices have been introduced—24 × 7 work, off-shoring and on-shoring, the reduction of human interface, flexi-time, remote log-in and work, distributed workplaces and mobile workforce, virtual offices, project-based assignments, extended business hours, etc. It is important to understand the applicability of the statutes under the changing context. Even though the legislations in existence have not undergone many changes, a conceptual understanding will help assess their applicability in a fast-changing business context. The focus, therefore, is on the conceptual framework rather than a detailed study of various provisions.

Two other concepts, which have been used in different Acts, have the potential to cause confusion. These concepts have been interpreted by various courts in the country, at different points of time. A thorough understanding of these terms is also essential in order to:

i) have clarity on the applicability of the laws, and

ii) get an insight into the direction of industrial jurisprudence and also into the thoughts of the different players of industrial relations on these concepts/issues.

These two concepts are those of "appropriate government" and "industry", both discussed exhaustively in different fora. A definition of "appropriate government" and "industry" are given in Chapter 12, The Industrial Disputes Act, 1947.

9.3 The Factories Act, 1948

The first Factories Act was enacted in 1881 and amended in 1891. There were major changes in the Act in 1934 on the basis of recommendations of The Royal Commission on Labour. The Factories Act, 1948 was the outcome of the investigation and recommendations of the Labour Investigation Committee appointed by the Government of India in February, 1944 to investigate conditions of employment in respect of various industries. The Act came into force on 1 April 1949. In 1987, certain provisions with regard to safety and occupational health were incorporated through an amendment.

There are similar and separate enactments for mines, plantations, and docks and ports where the working conditions are typical. Knowing about one of these major Acts (Factories Act) will provide familiarity and foundation for understanding the other Acts also.

9.3.1 Objectives

The beginning of modern legislation lies in factory legislation. The rapid industrialization and urbanization without any planning resulted in unsanitary, unhygienic, unsafe and crowded work and living places. Both quality of work-life and the quality of life itself were affected by the capitalist's quest for making quick bucks, unmindful of its social consequences. This led to excessive hours of work and also resulted in employing young children for more than twelve hours a day. The objective of this Act was to protect human beings from being subjected to unduly long hours of physical strain or manual labour. The Act provided that employees should work in healthy and sanitary conditions as far as the manufacturing process allowed and that precaution should be taken for their safety and the prevention of accidents. The main objectives of this Act are:

- To protect health, safety and welfare of the workmen
- Regulate hours of work, weekly offs and annual leave
- Regulate the employment of women and young persons

9.3.2 Coverage

The Factories Act is a Central Legislation and extends to the whole of India, including Jammu and Kashmir.

The provisions of this Act are applicable to all factories, including the factories that belong to the central government or any state government.

The provisions of this Act cover persons who are included within the meaning of the term "worker" as contained in the Act.

It would, therefore, be necessary to discuss the meaning and definition of the terms "factory" and "worker", and all other terms that are needed to explain these two terms.

9.3.3 Applicability

The applicability of the Act will become clear once we understand the main terms—"factory", "manufacturing process" and "worker". Please keep in mind that since this is a "beneficent" legislation, for the good of the "weaker section of society", historically the judiciary has been in favour of liberal interpretation of the terms. What this means is that benefit of doubt while interpreting a term has gone in favour of the workers.

What is a "factory"? A "factory" has been defined in Section 2(m) of the Act, and it means any premises including precincts thereof:

i) Where 10 or more workers are working or were working on any day of the preceding 12 months, and in any part of which manufacturing process is being carried out with the aid of power, or

ii) Where 20 or more workers are working or were working on any day of the preceding 12 months, and in any part of which manufacturing process is being carried out without the aid of power.

To understand the above, we need to be clear about the concepts of "premises" and "precincts", and "manufacturing process". In the normal parlance, "premises" denote a building where as "precincts" denote any space enclosed by walls. However, through a number of judicial pronouncements, the scope of precincts and premises of a factory has been expanded to include almost all buildings and spaces that fulfil the twin conditions of:

i) whether the manufacturing process is carried on or not, and

ii) whether 10 or 20 workers are working/have worked in any part of the premises where manufacturing process is carried on.

9.3.4 Definitions

Let us now define a few critical terms related to the Factories Act.

A MANUFACTURING PROCESS. A "manufacturing process" has been defined in Section 2(k). It means any process for:

- Making, altering, repairing, ornamenting, finishing, packing, oiling, washing, cleaning, breaking-up, demolishing, or otherwise treating or adapting any article or substance with a view to its use, sale, transport, delivery or disposal or
- Pumping oil, water sewage or any other substance, or
- Generating, transforming or transmitting power, or
- Composing types of printing letter press, lithography, photogravure or other similar process or book-binding, or
- Constructing, reconstructing, repairing or refitting, finishing or breaking-up of ships or vessels, or
- Preserving or restoring any article in the cold storage

The above covers a very wide range of activities that come under the manufacturing process. Without being stuck to the letter of Section 2(k), a very wide interpretation should be allowed depending upon specific circumstances. The Factories Act being a "beneficent" legislation, the interpretation has always been biased towards the inclusion of different activities under the manufacturing process. For example, the following have been held to be "manufacturing processes":

- Transmission of electrical power through supply lines for sale
- Dry-cleaning of garments
- Conversion of sea water into salt

The manufacturing process together with a prescribed number of workers would constitute the essential elements of a factory.

Mines, covered under The Mines Act, 1952, a mobile unit of the armed forces, railway running shed, hotels, restaurants and eating places are specifically excluded from the definition of a factory.

WHO IS A WORKER? It is very important to understand the terms "worker", "workman", "employee", "staff" in the context of specific Acts. The Factories Act has defined the term "worker", whereas the Industrial Disputes Act has defined the term "workman". This is one of the most critical parts that needs to be understood by a student and a practitioner. They should devote considerable time to understand the coverage and applicability of different Acts to different establishments and category of workmen. Clarity on these points will go a long way in facilitating practical application of these laws.

The Factories Act, 1948 has defined a "worker" in section 2(l):
A "worker" means

- A person employed
- Directly or by or through any agency
- With or without the knowledge of the principal employer (PE)
- He may be employed with or without remuneration

A worker must be employed in:

- The manufacturing process, or
- In cleaning some parts of machinery or premises used for the manufacturing process, or
- In some other kind of work incidental to or connected with the manufacturing process

The above description is not a verbatim copy of the definition as contained in the Act, but it captures all the essential components of the definition.

"Employment", in the context of labour laws, would mean the co-existence of an "employer" (one who engages the service of another person), an employee (one who works for another for hire) and a "contract of employment" (employment results from a "contract for service"). There should be a master–servant relationship between the employer and the employee. The employee agrees to serve the employer subject to his control and supervision.

The employment may be directly under the employer or through a "contractor". It would not make a difference to the employee falling within the definition of a "worker". The contractor, in this case, becomes the employer, whereas the employer is termed the "principal employer". For example, suppose a steel-manufacturing company has engaged a contractor for unloading of iron ore from railway wagons to the silos meant for the purpose of storing iron ore. For the employees of the contractor, the Steel Plant is the principal employer and the contractor is the employer. These employees would be deemed to be workers as per the meaning in the Factories Act. The employee, to be defined as a worker, must be engaged in the manufacturing process, or something incidental or related to the manufacturing process.

To sum up, the application of The Factories Act, 1948 can be schematically understood as given in Figure 9.1. A complete understanding of this scheme will facilitate an easy recall of all the important terms contained in the main definitions.

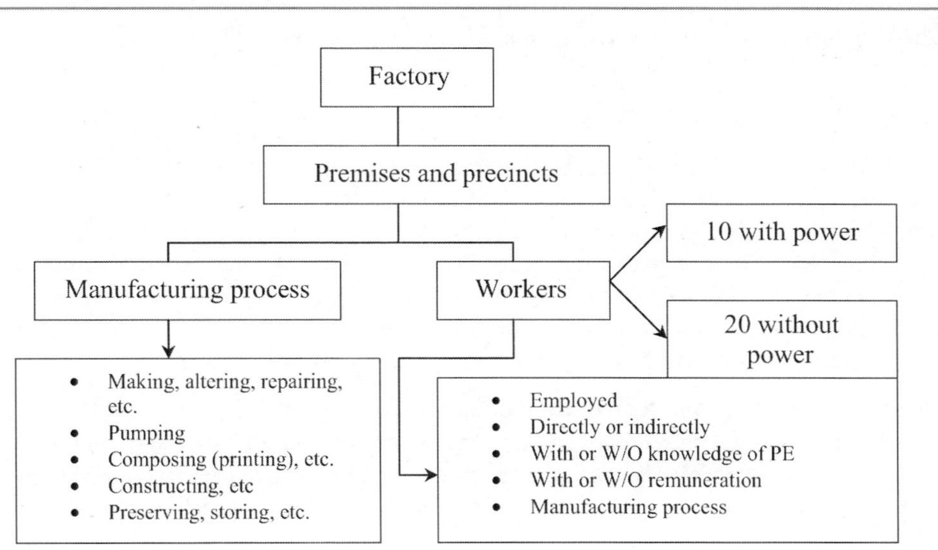

Figure 9.1
A schematic representation of the Factories Act.

BOX 9.2 **FOR CLASS DISCUSSION**

Based on the preceding discussion and a reading of the definition of "factory" in the Bare Act, discuss whether each of the following can be considered a "factory" or not (with reasons). Please look up reference to provisions relating to hotels and IT industries:

- NTPC Limited
- Durgapur Steel Plant (Works Area)
- Delhi International Airport
- ICICI Bank Limited
- New Delhi Railway Station
- A Cold Storage
- The Ashok Hotel
- NIIT Technologies

From the description, you can see that banks, BPO centres, corporate offices, etc. do not have any manufacturing process and would, therefore, normally be precluded from being called a factory.

A production foreman on the shop floor of a CD-manufacturing factory employing 100 people would be considered a "worker" as per the meaning in the Factories Act, 1948.

For every employee, therefore, you can test whether or not he/she is a worker according to the definition in the Factories Act and whether the relevant provisions would apply to them or not.

Another important definition is that of an "occupier" of the factory (Section 2(n)). An "occupier" refers to a person who has the ultimate control of the factory. In case of a partnership, any one partner shall be deemed as the "occupier". In case of a company, any one of the directors, and in case of a factory owned by the central or state government, the person appointed to manage the affairs of the factory shall be deemed as the "occupier".

The Bhopal Gas Tragedy led to significant changes in the provisions of The Factories Act in 1987, especially with respect to "hazardous processes" and the definition of an "occupier". The essence of the definition is the determination of the point as to who has the "ultimate control" of the factory. There have been various judicial pronouncements on the interpretation of the term "occupier". It is important because the "occupier" has significant obligations under the Factories Act. The "manager" of a factory can not be taken to be the "occupier" unless ultimate control has been passed on to him by a resolution of the company. A discussion on the applicability of the definition of "factory" to the entities mentioned in Box 9.2 will provide conceptual clarity.

9.3.5 Structure

The structure of the Factories Act, 1948 is diagrammatically shown in Figure 9.2.

9.3.6 Main Provisions

The Factories Act primarily aims at preserving the health, safety and welfare of the workers working in a factory. The Act also provides for regulating the working hours, weekly offs, leave with wages and the employment of young persons and women. For the workers, being the "weaker section of the society", the State has made elaborate provisions and institutional framework to ensure that exploitation of labour by the employer does not take place. Chapters 3 to 8 contain all the main provisions relating to health, safety, welfare and other working conditions of workers. The other significant provisions are:

Approval, Licensing, and Registration of Factories (Section 6): Details regarding the proposed factory along with schemes and drawings have to be submitted to the Chief Inspector of Factories for approval. The Chief Inspector of the appropriate government must respond within a defined time period. In the event of no response within the specified period, approval will deemed to have been granted.

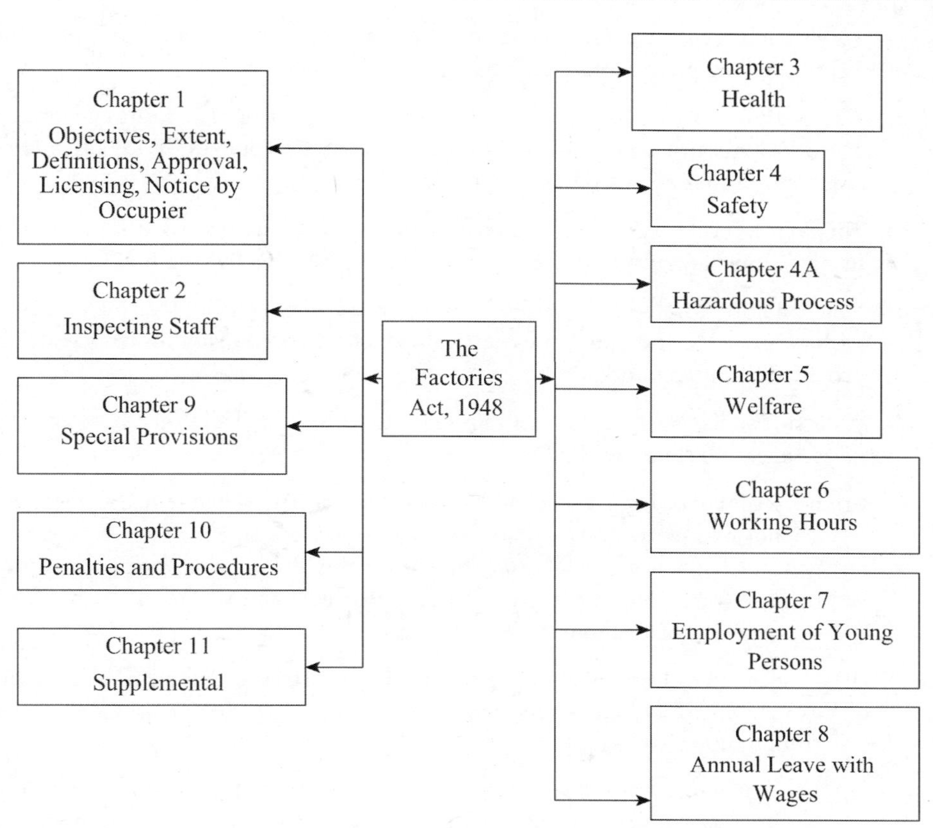

Figure 9.2

The Factories Act: A schematic representation of the contents.

Notice of "Occupation": Section 7(1) prescribes a notice to be sent to the Chief Inspector within 15 days before he begins to occupy or use any premises as a factory, detailing the name and situation of the factory, the name and address of the occupier and the owner of premises or building, the nature of manufacturing process and address for communication relating to the factory.

Section 7 A (discussed in Chapter 2) is very important since it lists down the General Duties of an Occupier, which are as follows:

1. Every occupier shall ensure (as far as is reasonably practicable), the health, safety and welfare of all workers while they are at work in the factory.
2. The matters to which such duty extends shall include—
   a) The provision and maintenance of plant and systems of work in the factory that are safe and without risks to health
   b) The arrangements in the factory for ensuring safety and absence of risks to health in connection with the use, handling, storage and transport of articles and substances
   c) The provisions of such information, instruction, training and supervision as are necessary to ensure the health and safety of all workers at work
   d) The maintenance of all places of work in the factory in a condition that is safe and without risks to health, and the provision and maintenance of such means of access to, and egress from, such places as are safe and without such risks

HEALTH AND HYGIENE. Sections 11 to 20 of The Factories Act, 1948 detail out the health provisions that need to be followed in "factories". In particular, provisions for health and hygiene comprise the following:

Section 11—Cleanliness:

Every factory shall be kept clean and free from effluvia arising from any drain, privy or other nuisance. The following precautions shall be taken in particular.

a) Accumulation of dirt and refuse shall be removed daily from the floors and benches of workrooms and from staircases and passages, by sweeping or by any other effective method, and disposed of in a suitable manner

b) The floor of every workroom shall be cleaned at least once every week by washing, using disinfectant, where necessary, or by some other effective method

c) Where a floor is liable to become wet in the course of any manufacturing process to such an extent as incapable of being drained, effective means of drainages shall be provided and maintained

d) All inside walls, partitions, all ceilings of tops of rooms and all walls, sides and tops of passages and staircases shall

   i) be repainted or revarnished at least once in every period of five years, where they are not painted with washable water paint or varnish; where they are painted with washable water paint, they shall be repainted with at least one coat of such paint at least once in every period of three years and washed at least once in every period of six months

   ii) be cleaned at least once in every period of fourteen months by such method as may be prescribed, where they are painted or varnished or where they have smooth impervious surfaces

   iii) be kept white-washed or colour-washed, and the white-washing or colour-washing shall be carried out at least once in every period of fourteen months, in any other case

e) All doors and window frames and wooden or metallic framework and shutters shall be kept painted or varnished and the painting or varnishing shall be carried out at least once in every period of five years

Section 12—Disposal of Waste and Effluents:

Effective arrangements shall be made in every factory for the treatment of wastes and effluents due to the manufacturing process carried on thereon, so as to render them innocuous and disposable.

Section 13—Ventilation and Temperature:

Effective and suitable provisions shall be made in every factory for securing and maintaining in every workroom:

a) Adequate ventilation by the circulation of fresh air, and

b) Such a temperature as will secure to workers therein reasonable conditions of comfort and prevent injury to any health hazard

Section 14—Dust and Fume:

This section prescribes effective measures, which should be adopted to keep the workrooms free from dust and fume. In every factory, which, due to the manufacturing process carried on, gives off any form of dust or fume or other impurity of such a nature and to such an extent as it is likely to be injurious or offensive to the workers employed therein, effective measures shall be taken to prevent its inhalation and accumulation in any workroom. If any exhaust appliance is necessary for the above purposes, it shall be applied as near as possible to the point of origin of dust, fume or other impurity and such points shall be enclosed as far as possible. Further, in any factory, no stationery internal combustion engine shall be operated unless the exhaust is conducted into the open air, and no other internal combustion engine shall be operated in any room unless effective measures have been taken to prevent such accumulation of fumes as are likely to be injurious to workers employed in the room.

Section 15—Artificial Humidification:
All factories in which humidity of the air is artificially increased, the state government may make rules—

a) Prescribing standards of humidification
b) Regulating the methods used for artificially increasing the humidity of the air
c) Directing prescribed tests for determining the humidity of the air to be correctly carried out and recorded
d) Prescribing methods to be adopted for securing adequate ventilation and cooling of the air in the workroom

Section 15(2) lays down that in any factory in which humidity of the air is artificially increased, the water used for the purpose shall be taken from a public supply or other source of drinking water, or shall be effectively purified before it is so used.

Section 16—Over-crowding:
No room in any factory shall be over-crowded to an extent injurious to the health of workers employed therein. There shall be in every workroom of a factory in existence on the date of commencement of this Act at least 14.2 cubic metres of space for every worker employed therein. No account shall be taken of any space, which is more than 4.2 metres above the level of the floor of the room, for the purpose (calculating the volume) of this provision.

Section 17—Lighting:
In every part of the factory, where workers are working or passing, the provision and maintenance of sufficient and suitable lighting—natural, artificial or both—should be ensured. All glazed windows and skylights used for lighting of the workrooms shall be kept clean on both the inner and outer surfaces and should be free from obstruction.

Effective provisions shall so far as practicable, be made for the prevention of—

a) glare either directly from a source of light or by reflection from a smooth or polished surface
b) the formation of shadows to such an extent as to cause eye-strain or the risk of accident to any worker

Section 18—Drinking Water:
In every factory, effective arrangements shall be made to provide and maintain at suitable points conveniently situated for all workers employed therein, a sufficient supply of wholesome drinking water. All such points are to be legibly marked as "drinking water" in a language understood by a majority of workers employed in the factory and no such point shall be situated within six metres of any washing place, urinal, latrine, spittoon, open drain carrying sullage or effluent or any other source of contamination unless a shorter distance is approved in writing by the Chief Inspector.

Section 18(3) provides that in every factory employing more than 250 workers, provision of cool drinking water during hot weather with effective distribution arrangements should be made.

Section 19—Latrines and Urinals:
In every factory—

a) Sufficient latrine and urinal accommodation of prescribed type shall be provided conveniently situated and accessible to workers at all times while they are at the factory
b) Separate enclosed accommodation shall be provided for male and female workers
c) Such accommodation shall be adequately lighted and ventilated, and no latrine or urinal, shall, unless specially exempted in writing by the Chief Inspector, communicate with any workroom except through an intervening open space or ventilated passage

d) All such accommodation shall be maintained in a clean and sanitary condition at all times

e) Sweepers shall be employed whose primary duty would be to keep clean latrines, urinals and workplaces

In every factory wherein more than 250 workers are ordinarily employed—

a) All latrine and urinal accommodation shall be prescribed sanitary types

b) The floors and internal walls up to a height of 90 cm of the latrines and urinals and sanitary blocks shall be laid in glazed tiles or otherwise finished to provide a smooth polished impervious surface

c) The floors, portions of the walls and blocks so laid or finished and the sanitary pans and urinals shall be thoroughly washed and cleaned at least once every day with suitable detergents or disinfectants or with both.

Section 20—Spittoons:
Section 20(1) lays down that in every factory, there shall be provided sufficient number of spittoons in convenient places, which are to be maintained in clean and hygienic conditions.

Figure 9.3 will aid recall of all the provisions related to health.

Health-related Provisions

- Section 11: Cleanliness
- Section 12: Disposal of Waste and Effluents
- Section 13: Ventilation and Temperature
- Section 14: Dust and Fume
- Section 15: Artificial Humidification
- Section 16: Over-Crowding
- Section 17: Lighting
- Section 18: Drinking Water
- Section 19 : Latrines and Urinals
- Section 20: Spittoons

SAFETY PROVISIONS. Elaborate provisions for the safety of workmen have been made in Chapter 4 of the Act. Subsequently, in 1987, Chapter 4A was added, which had further provisions related to hazardous processes. These provisions, contained in Section 21 to 41, are obligatory and further supplemented and elaborated by rules framed by each of the state governments. Briefly, the provisions of the Act are given below. In the end, the various safety-related provisions have been schematically described to enable easy recall and also an overall understanding of the provisions. Students, however, are advised to refer to the Bare Act for detailed provisions. Bare Acts are easily available on the Internet. The simplified provisions in the following paragraphs have been adapted from the Bare Act.

Section 21—Fencing of Machinery:
In every factory, the dangerous parts of every machine are to be securely fenced. The following have been stipulated:

i) Every moving part of a prime mover and every fly wheel connected to a prime mover, whether the prime mover or fly wheel is in the engine-house or not

ii) The headrace and tailrace of every water wheel and water turbine

Figure 9.3

Provisions relating to health.

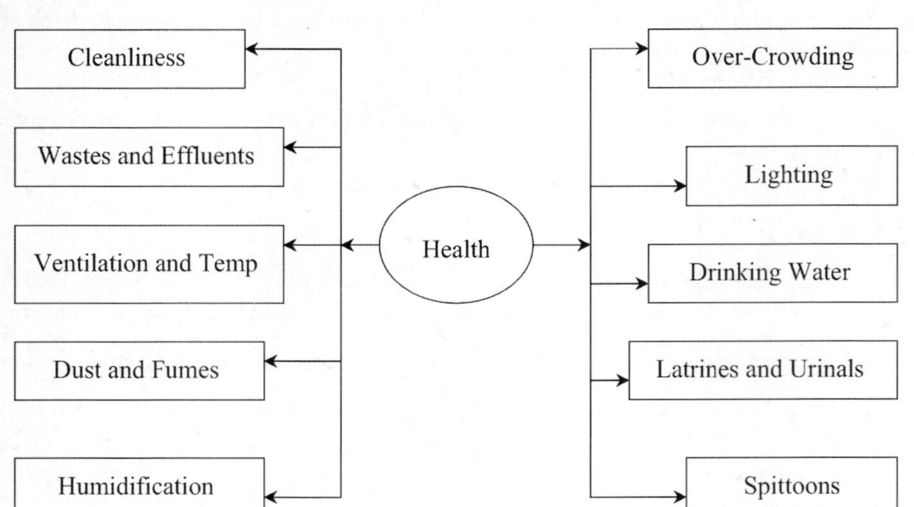

iii) Any part of a stock bar that projects beyond the head stock of a lathe

iv) Unless they are in such position or of such construction as to be safe to every person employed in the factory as they would be if they were securely fenced, the following, namely—

a) every part of an electric generator, a motor or rotary converter;

b) every part of transmission machinery; and

c) every dangerous part of any other machinery

shall be securely fenced by safeguards of a substantial construction, which shall be constantly maintained and kept in position while the parts of machinery they are fencing are in motion or in use. Sub-section 1 provides for examination or operation to determine whether any part of the machinery is in such position or such construction as to be safe.

Section 22—Work on or Near Machinery in Motion:
To take precautionary measures with regard to operational safety arising out of malfunctioning of machines and defects in functional mechanisms, Section 22 provides for lubrication or other adjusting operation carried out by a trained adult worker wearing tight-fitting clothing, which shall be supplied by the "occupier" of the factory. Sub-section 2 ensures special protection to women and young persons (below 18 years of age and above 15 years of age) against risk of injury from any moving part either of that machinery or an adjacent machinery by prohibiting engagement of women and young persons in the processes of cleaning, lubrication or adjusting operation of any part of a prime mover or any transmission machinery while these are in motion.

Section 23—Employment of Young Persons on Dangerous Machines:
No young person shall work at any machine (dangerous machines to be specified by the state government) unless he has been fully instructed as to the dangers arising in connection with the machine and the precautions to be observed and:

a) has received sufficient training in work at machine, or

b) is under adequate supervisions by a person who has a thorough knowledge and experience of the machine.

Section 24—Striking Gear and Devices for Cutting off Power:
In order to ensure further safety of the workmen, Section 24 provides for—
(i) striking gear (ii) cutting power and (iii) locking device as under:

i) Suitable striking gear or other efficient mechanical appliance to be provided, maintained and used to move driving belt to and from fast and loose pulleys, which form part of the transmission machinery

ii) Suitable devices to be provided, maintained and used for cutting off power in emergencies from running machinery

iii) Locking device to prevent accidental starting of transmission machinery

Section 25—Self-acting Machines:
Keeping in view the possible likelihood of accidents, no traversing part of a self-acting machine in any factory and no material carried thereon shall, if the space over which any person is liable to pass, whether in the course of his employment or otherwise, be allowed to run on its outward or inward traverse with a distance of 45 centimetres from any fixed structure that is not part of the machine.

Section 26—Casing of New Machinery:
Casing of any machinery driven by power is to be ensured to prevent danger of accidents. This includes:

i) Every screw, bolt or key on any revolving shaft, spindle wheel or pinion to be either so sunk, encased or guarded

ii) All spur, worm and other toothed or friction-gearing, which does not require adjustment while in motion, to be encased or so situated as if it were completely cased

Section 27—Prohibition of Employment of Women and Children near Cotton Openers:
In case the feed end is separated from the delivery end by a partition, the Chief Inspector may permit in writing the employment of women and children at the feed-end side of the partition.

Section 28—Hoists and Lifts:
Hoists and lifts should be of good mechanical construction, properly maintained and examined once in every six months. Protection by an enclosure fitted with glass, with safe working load indicated and gate fitted with interlocking or any other efficient device must be ensured.

Section 29—Lifting Machines, Cranes, Chains, Ropes and Lifting Tackles:
These should be of good construction and examined once every 12 months. Safe workload limits, at least six-metre distance from any other workplace of employees, needs to be ensured.

Section 30—Revolving Machinery:
In every room in a factory in which the process of grinding is carried on, there shall be permanently affixed to or placed near each machine in use a notice indicating the

- maximum safe working peripheral speed of every grindstone or abrasive wheel
- speed of shaft or spindle upon which taw heel is mounted and
- the diameter of pulley upon such shaft or spindle necessary to secure such safe working peripheral speed.

Section 31—Pressure Plant:
If in any factory, any part of the plant and machinery used in a manufacturing process is operated at a pressure above atmospheric pressure, effective measures shall be taken to ensure that the safe working pressure of such a part is not exceeded.

Section 32—Floors, Stairs and Means of Access:
In every factory, all floors, steps, stairs, passages and gangways shall be of sound construction and properly maintained and shall be kept free from obstruction and substances likely to cause persons to slip, so that safety is ensured.

Section 33—Pits, Sumps, Opening in Floors, etc.:
In every factory, fixed vessel, sump, tank, pit or opening in the ground or in a floor which, by reason of its depth, situation, construction or contents, is or may be a source of danger, shall be either securely covered or securely fenced.

Section 34—Excessive Weights:
No person shall be employed in any factory to lift, carry or move any load so heavy (the state government to prescribe weights specifically for adult men and women, adolescents and children) as to be likely to cause injury.

Section 35—The Protection of Eyes:
The state government is to prescribe rules regarding the use of effective screens or suitable goggles, which shall be provided for the protection of persons employed on or in the immediate vicinity of the process that is likely to involve (i) risk of injury to the eyes from particles or fragments thrown off in the course of the process, or (ii) risk to the eyes by reason of exposure to excessive light.

Section 36—Precaution Against Dangerous Fumes:
In any factory, no person shall enter or be permitted to enter any chamber, tank, vat, pit, pipe, flue or other confined space in which dangerous fumes are likely to be present to such an extent as to involve risk of persons, unless it is provided with a manhole of adequate

size or effective means of egress. Further, no person shall be required or allowed to enter such a space unless all measures have been taken to remove all such noxious substances. Persons entering such spaces need to have a written certificate from a competent authority, to grant permission for the entry in such places based on a test carried out by self. In such cases, workers must wear suitable breathing apparatus and the belt has to be securely attached to a rope.

Section 36 A—Precautions Regarding the Use of Portable Light:
Section 36 A stipulates that no portable electric light or any other electric appliance of voltage exceeding 24 volts shall be permitted for use inside any chamber, tank, vat, pit, pipe, flue or any other confined space. Lamps and light of flame-proof construction only are permitted for use in such cases.

Section 37—Explosive or Inflammable Dust, Gas, etc.:
In any factory, where any manufacturing process produces dust, gas, fume or vapour of such character and to such extent as to be likely to explode on ignition, all practicable measures shall be taken to prevent any such explosion by:

i) Effective enclosure or the plant of machinery used in the process

ii) Removal or prevention of the accumulation of such dust, gas, fume or vapour

iii) Exclusion or effective enclosure of all possible sources of ignition

Section 38—Precautions in Case of Fire:
This Section stipulates provision for means of escape in case of fire, exit doors to be constructed to open outwards, which should be easy to open and distinctly marked in a language understood by all. Clearly audible warning alarms also need to be provided.

Section 39—Power to Require Specification of Defective Part or Tests of Stability:
The Inspector of Factories has been authorized with powers to seek drawings, specifications and other particulars as may be necessary or to carry out such tests as prescribed in case any part of building, machinery is in such condition that it may be dangerous.

Section 40—Safety of Buildings and Machinery:
In the event of the Inspector finding any machinery or plant in a factory to be in such a condition that it is dangerous to human life, he may serve on the occupier an order in writing, specifying measures, which in his opinion should be adopted and carried out before a specific date.

Section 40 A—The Maintenance of Buildings:
In the event of the Inspector finding any machinery or plant in a factory to be in a state of disrepair as is likely to lead to conditions detrimental to the health and welfare of workers, he may serve a notice on the occupier specifying measures, which in his opinion need to be taken within a specified date.

Section 40 B—Safety Officers:
Safety Officers are required to be appointed in every factory through a state-government-gazette notification wherein:

i) One thousand or more workers are ordinarily employed

ii) Any manufacturing process or operation is carried on, which, in the opinion of the state government, involves any risk of bodily injury, poisoning or disease, or any hazard to health, to the persons employed in the factory.

Section 41—Grants Rule-making Power to States:
While it may not be necessary to know the detailed provision (we can always refer to the Act), it is desirable that an overall understanding of safety provisions be there. Figure 9.4 gives a big picture of the safety-related provisions of The Factories Act, 1948 (Chapter 4 of the Act, Sections 21 to 41).

Figure 9.4

Provisions relating to safety.

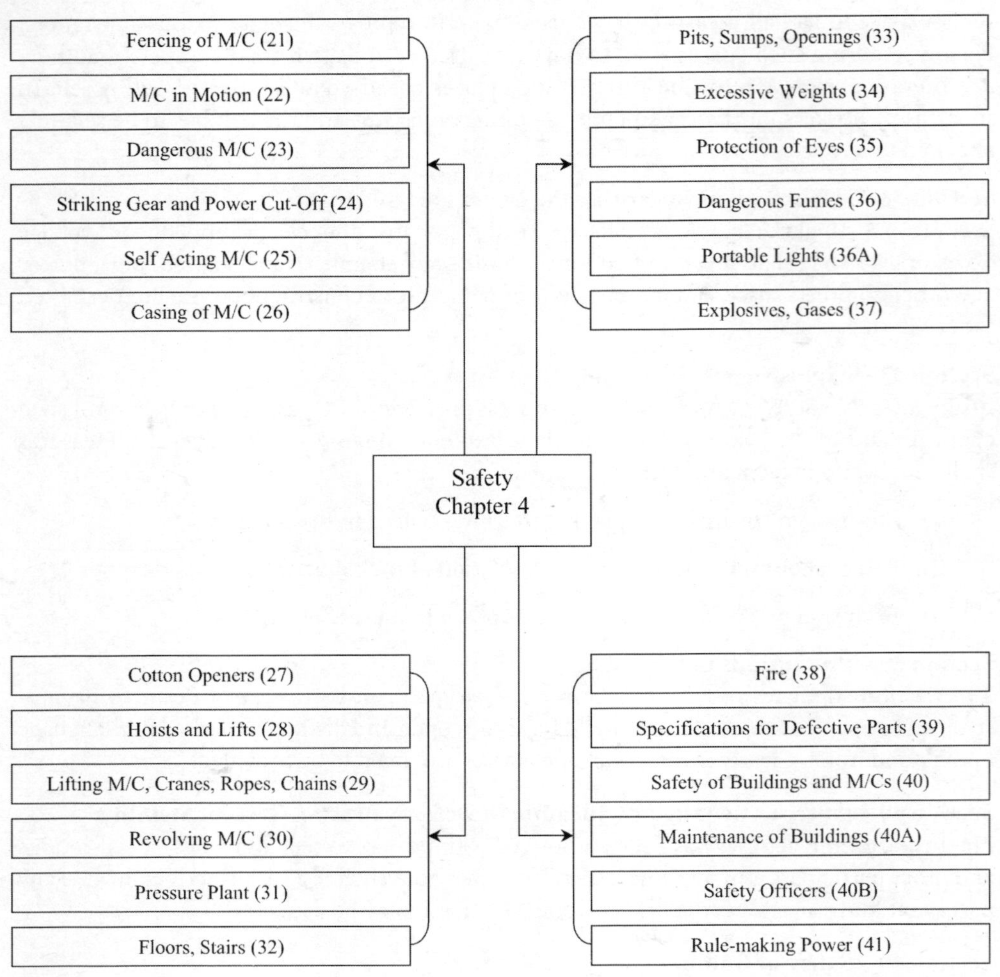

HAZARDOUS PROCESSES. As mentioned earlier, Chapter 4A has been added to The Factories Act to make provisions for factories employing hazardous processes. "Hazardous process" has been defined in Section 2(cb) of the Act. In essence, it implies such processes that may be carried out in an industry specified in Schedule 1 of the Act and the process may cause one of the following two (or both):

i) Cause material impairment to the health of the persons engaged in or connected with it

ii) Result in pollution of the general environment

The Bhopal Gas Tragedy was one of the reasons for special provisions being made for hazardous processes.

Sections 41 A to 41 H have been added to Chapter 4A dealing with provisions for hazardous process. The provisions, in brief, are as under:

- Constitution of site appraisal committees (41A)
- Compulsory disclosure of information by occupier (41B)
- Specific responsibility of occupier in relation to hazardous process (41 C)

- Power of central government to appoint Inquiring Committee (41D)
- Laying down emergency standards (41 E)
- Prescribing permissible limits of exposure of toxic substances (41 F)
- Workers' participation in safety management (41 G)
- Right of workers to warn about imminent danger (41 H)

WELFARE PROVISIONS. The welfare measures are contained in Chapter V of the Act. The concept of welfare of industrial workmen has been espoused by ILO. The Industrial Truce Resolution of 1947 also emphasized labour welfare to be essential for industrial peace. Labour welfare, therefore, finds mention in the Constitution of India too. The Factories Act has devoted one whole chapter to welfare provisions, in line with the ILO classification of the welfare measures for industrial workers.

Welfare facilities within the factory premises are supposed to provide mental peace to the workers so that they can devote their attention and energy to work at hand and not on looking for such facilities. Though each provision has been discussed below briefly, the student is advised to refer to the detailed and exact wording in the Bare Act. At the end, "a big picture" of the welfare provision has been given in Figure 9.5 to aid easy understanding and recall.

Section 42—Washing Facilities:
Clean and accessible washing facilities (separate and adequately screened for the use of male and female workers) shall be provided and maintained for the use of workers.

Section 43—Facilities for Storing and Drying Clothing:
Provision of a suitable place for keeping clothes not worn during working hours and for drying of wet clothing, in respect of any factory or class of factories may be made based on rules made in this regard by the state government.

Section 44—Facilities for Sitting:
In every factory, suitable arrangements for sitting shall be provided and maintained for all workers who are obliged to work in a standing position. If workers engaged in a particular manufacturing process or working in a particular room are able to do their work comfortably in a sitting position, the Chief Inspector may require the occupier of the factory to provide such seating arrangements, if practical.

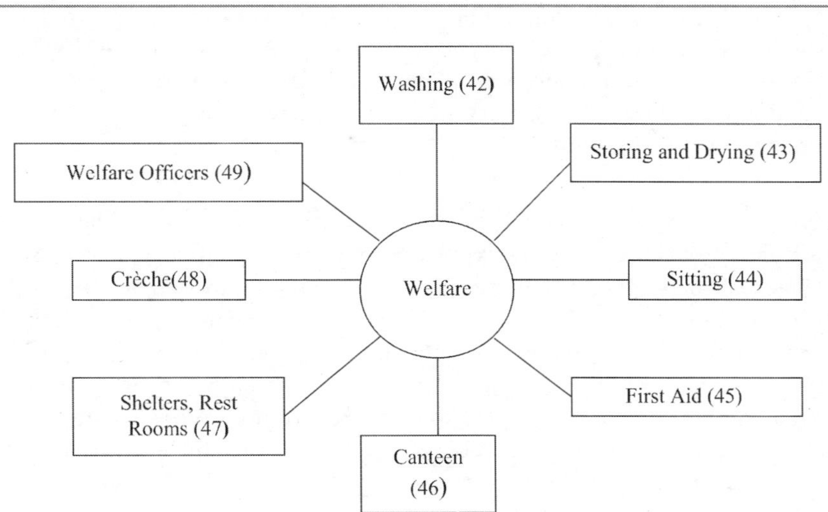

Figure 9.5
Welfare provisions under the Factories Act.

Section 45—First-Aid Appliances:
In every factory, first-aid appliances or first-aid boxes or cupboards equipped with the prescribed contents shall be provided and maintained so as to be readily available during all working hours. The boxes so provided shall not be less than one for every 150 workers ordinarily employed.

Section 46—Canteens:
The state government is empowered to make rules requiring that in any specified factory wherein more than 250 workers are ordinarily employed, a canteen or canteens shall be provided and maintained by the occupier for the use of workers. The state is also authorized to prescribe standards of food items, charges and also infrastructure requirements and management of the canteen.

Section 47—Shelters, Rest Rooms and Lunch Rooms:
In every factory, wherein more than 150 workers are ordinarily employed, adequate and suitable shelters or rest rooms and a suitable lunch room, with provisions of drinking water, where workers can eat meals brought by them, shall be provided and maintained for the use of the workers. But any canteen maintained in accordance with the provisions of Section 46 shall be regarded as part of the requirements of this sub-section, and where a lunch room exists, no worker shall eat any food in the workroom.

Section 48—Crèches:
Every factory employing more than 30 women workers must provide and maintain a suitable room or rooms for children below 6 years of age. Such rooms shall be clean, adequately lighted, ventilated and maintained in clean sanitary conditions, and be under the charge of a woman trained in the care of infants.

Section 49—Welfare Officers:
In every factory, wherein 500 or more workers are ordinarily employed, the occupier shall employ in the factory such number of welfare officers as may be prescribed. The state government may prescribe the duties, qualification and conditions of service of such officers.

Section 50:
This section empowers the state government to make rules regarding exemption of factories from a few of the provisions subject to compliance with alternative provisions. It also empowers the state government to make rules for the association of worker representatives to be involved in the management of welfare arrangements.

Figure 9.5 gives an overview of the range of welfare amenities to be provided for in a factory as per the Factories Act. Most of the modern manufacturing organizations have gone much beyond the minimum requirements prescribed by the Act. Instead of the legal requirements, these organizations have taken an employee relations approach to proactively cater to the needs of the employees. It is the unorganized sector and a few of the SMEs where the statutory minimum is the benchmark.

WORKING HOURS, WEEKLY OFFS AND SPREAD-OVERS. Chapters VI, VII and VIII contain provisions regarding regulation of work hours in a factory, weekly holidays, rest intervals between work, spread-over of working hours, employment of young persons and annual leave. These provisions are meant to prevent exploitation and ensure that excessive working hours are interspersed with adequate provisions for rest and holidays. These are very important provisions and there is currently a demand from industry to provide more flexibility in working hours in a continuous process industry. On the other hand, the government has proposed a few industries (e.g. the hotel industry) to be brought under the purview of the Factories Act to better regulate the working hours of the employees of this industry. The main provisions are explained below in a simple-to-understand manner.

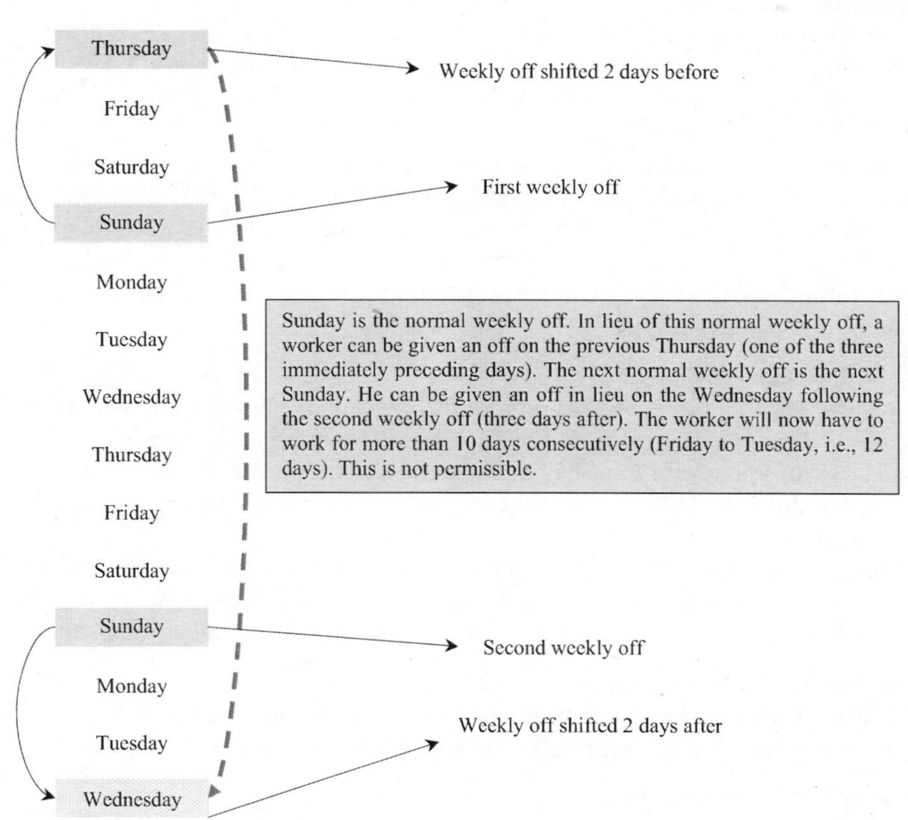

Figure 9.6

The scheme of weekly holidays under the Factories Act.

Weekly Hours (Section 51):
No adult worker shall be required or allowed to work in a factory for more than forty-eight hours in a week.

Weekly Holidays (Section 52):
No adult worker shall be required or allowed to work in a factory on the first day of the week (Sunday) unless given a full day's holiday on one of the three days immediately before or after the said day. This section also specifies that this substitution should not result in any worker working for more than ten days consecutively without a holiday for a whole day. Figure 9.6 makes the scheme simple to understand.

Compensatory holidays (Section 53):
In case Section 52 is not applied on account of any exemption, a worker deprived of any of the weekly holidays shall be allowed, within a month in which holidays were due to him or within the two months immediately following that month, compensatory holidays of equal number to the holidays so lost.

Daily Hours (Section 54):
No adult worker shall be required or allowed to work in a factory for more than nine hours in any day.

Intervals for Rest (Section 55):
The periods of work of adult workers in a factory each day shall be so fixed that no period shall exceed five hours and no worker shall work for more than five hours before he has had an interval for rest of at least half an hour. The state government, however, is empowered to exempt by a written order any factory from this provision only to the extent that the total number of hours worked by a worker without an interval does not exceed six.

Spread-over (Section 56):
The periods of work of an adult worker in a factory shall be so arranged that inclusive of his intervals for rest, they shall not spread over more than ten and a half hours in any day. The Chief Inspector may, however, increase the spread-over up to twelve hours by a special order in writing.

In simple terms, "spread-over" means the total duration of time (hours of work plus rest intervals). For example, a worker is asked to work from 8 a.m. to 12 p.m. and then again from 3 p.m. to 7 p.m., i.e., a total of 8 working hours in a day. However, the spread-over in this case is 11 hours (8 a.m. to 7p.m.). Even though the working hour and rest interval adhere to the provisions of the Factories Act, the total spread-over exceeds the stipulation of ten and a half hours.

Night Shifts (Section 57):
In case a worker in a factory works on a shift that extends beyond midnight, a holiday for a whole day shall mean a period of 24 consecutive hours beginning when his shift ends. The following day for him shall be deemed to be the period of 24 hours beginning when such a shift ends, and the hours he has worked after midnight shall be counted in the previous day.

If a worker has worked in a night shift from 10 p.m. to 6 a.m., the holiday for him will be 24 hours from 0600 hours and not from 0000 hours. There should be a clear 24-hour break (at least) between the end of his shift and the beginning of the next shift after a holiday.

The Prohibition of Overlapping Shifts (Section 58):
Work shall not be carried on in any factory by means of a system of shifts so arranged that more than one relay of workers is engaged in work of the same kind at the same time.

Extra Wages for Overtime (Section 59):
Where a worker works in a factory for more than nine hours in any day or for more than forty-eight hours in any week, he shall in respect of overtime work, be entitled to wages at the rate of twice his ordinary rate of wages. Ordinary rate of wages means basic wages plus allowances. In case of piece-rated workers, the time rate shall be deemed to be equivalent to the daily average of their full-time earnings.

Restriction on Double Employment (Section 60):
No adult worker shall be required or allowed to work in any factory on any day on which he has already been working in any factory, save in such circumstances as may be prescribed.

Notice of Periods of Work for Adults (Section 61):
No worker shall be required or allowed to work in any factory other than in accordance with the notice of periods of work for adults displayed in the factory and the entries made beforehand against his name in the register for adult workers of the factory. Notice is to be displayed, regarding periods of work on a daily basis and shift systems planned for the week.

Section 64:
This Section restricts the total number of work hours in a week including overtime to 60 and the total number of hours of overtime to 50 in a quarter. There is a demand from the industry to increase the total overtime hour from 50 to 150 hours in a quarter in a continuous-process industry.

The Employment of Women and Young Persons:
There are specific restrictions on employment of women and young persons in a factory.

Women: The employment of women in any factory is restricted to timings between 6 a.m. and 7 p.m. Women are not to be deployed on night shifts. The provision made in this section states that women cannot be exempted from the requirement that the maximum working day for adults is nine hours, and cannot work in factories between 7 p.m. and 6 a.m. (unless the factory falls within a specific exemption, but in any case, not between 10 p.m. and 5 a.m.). In relation to women, there must not be a change of shifts except after a weekly or other holiday. Periods of absence on maternity leave are included in calculating periods of service for the purposes of annual leave.

Table 9.1

Provisions relating to working days and holidays.

Item	Provision	Remarks
Working hours/day	9 hours maximum	Adult worker. Total working hours including overtime not to exceed 60 hours in a week.
Working hours/week	48 hours maximum	Adult workers
Overtime	Payable if working hours > 9 hours/day or 48 hours/week	Either of the two conditions. Subject to a maximum of 60 working hours in a week. Total overtime not to exceed 50 hours in a quarter.
Overtime rate	Double the ordinary rate of wages	
Rest interval	At least 30 minutes rest after a maximum of 5 hours' work	
Spread-over	10.5 hours	Extendable to 12 hours through approval in writing
Women workers' timings	Not to be deployed between 7 p.m. and 6 a.m.	Unless there is an exemption, but in no case between 10 p.m. and 5 a.m.
Weekly off	First day of the week	Can be shifted to any of the preceding or succeeding 3 days subject to condition that there should not be more than 10 working days between 2 weekly offs
Annual leave with wages (earned leave)	1 day for every 20 days' work subject to a qualifying 240 days' work in the qualifying year	

The Prohibition of Employment of Young Children (Section 67):
No child who has not completed his 14th year shall be required or allowed to work in any factory.

Annual Leave with Wages (Section 79):
Every adult worker who has worked for a period of 240 days or more in a factory during a calendar year shall be allowed during the subsequent calendar year one day of leave entitlement for every 20 days of work.

Table 9.1 summarizes the provisions relating to working hours, holidays, annual leave with wages, etc.

Conclusion:
The lacunae in The Factories Act can be related to its coverage as it does not have provision for some important places of work such as hotels, hospitals, fire stations, and others where serious health and safety risks may exist. Box 9.3 describes the government's intention of bringing the hotel industry within the definition of a factory. The process of automation and the information technology revolution, which has resulted in computer-based production methods, have totally transformed the workplace. Consequently, the role of labour inspection has also changed and needs reorientation. Inspectors need additional skills and

BOX 9.3 **THE HOTEL INDUSTRY**

The centre is considering to include the hotel industry under the Factories Act. A delegation representing reputed hotels recently met the Labour Secretary to demand hotel industries to be continued to be covered under the Shops and Establishments Act.

Hotels will have to change many rules once the industry is included under the Factories Act. Rules like fixed shifts of eight hours would have to be in place and employers would have to pay extra for overtime.

Hotels would also have to ensure health, safety and welfare facilities, employment of young persons and annual leave with wages.

The central government maintains that "the industry needs to discipline themselves a bit. It is about safety and security of people working in hotels. And that number is huge."

Defaulters can face a maximum punishment of two years' jail sentence or a fine of up to Rs one lakh, or both.

The hotel industry maintains that there is no need to include it under the purview of the Act, as high standards are already being maintained.

Adapted From: Press Trust of India, "Govt Sticks to Decision to Include Hotels Under Factories Act", *Times of India,* 17 February 2008.

expertise and a new approach when assessing and evaluating workplace conditions and hazards. This has not yet happened in India. The second National Commission on Labour has recommended the enactment of a general law relating to hours of work, working conditions, annual leave, welfare, contract labour and others applicable to various categories of establishments alike.

The industry has called for "an urgent shift from a 'persecution mind set' to a 'guidance-oriented mindset' to free the domestic manufacturing sector from the clutches of the 'Inspector Raj'. The industry has sought amendments to the Factories Act to make the licence-renewal requirement once in three years, inspections once in two years, easing of the restricted number of working hours, self-certification and prosecution only in case of glaring evidence of management callousness"[1]. There appears to be a case for thorough discussion and review since the law was enacted in 1948, where the ground realities and priorities have undergone a sea change with issues such as competitiveness, productivity, quality, change management, work–life balance, safety, health and environment, and human development coming to the fore.

9.4 The Shops and Establishments Act, 1953

The Shops and Establishments Act is a state legislation. Each state frames its own rules for the Act. The object of this Act is to provide statutory obligation and rights to employees and employers in the unorganized sector of employment, i.e., shops and establishments. A barber shop, a general store, corporate office of a company (not located within the manufacturing premises), etc. are all examples of shops and establishments. Since every state has its own enactment, it may not be practical to cover all of them. However, each of the Acts has certain common features. The explanation below is based on the common elements. These elements, state-wise, have minor variations.

9.4.1 Objectives

The objectives are to provide statutory obligation and rights to employees and employers in the unorganized sector of employment, i.e., shops and establishments.

9.4.2 Scope and Coverage

It is a state legislation; each state has framed its own rules for the Act. It is applicable to all persons employed in an establishment with or without wages, except the members of the employer's family.

9.4.3 Main Provisions

Under this Act, registration of shop/establishment is necessary within 30 days of commencement of work. Fifteen days of notice is required to be served before the closing of the establishment. In the main, the Act stipulates the following:

- Compulsory registration of shop/establishment within 30 days of commencement of work
- Communications of closure of the establishment within 15 days from the closing of the establishment
- Hours of work per day and week
- Guidelines for spread-over, rest interval, opening and closing hours, closed days, national and religious holidays, and overtime work
- Rules for employment of children, young persons and women
- Rules for annual leave, maternity leave, sickness and casual leave, etc.
- Rules for employment and termination of service
- Maintenance of registers and records and display of notices
- Obligations of employers
- Obligations of employees

It can be seen that the S&E Act is for shops and establishments what the Factories Act is for manufacturing concerns.

THE REGISTRATION OF AN ESTABLISHMENT. To register the establishment under the Shops and Establishments Act, certain documentary evidence in respect of rightful possession/occupation of the premises of the establishment needs to be obtained as prescribed under the Act. The following need to be kept in mind while seeking registration:

- The application for the registration of an establishment is not accepted prior to the commencement of business.
- The employer is obliged to get the establishment registered within 30 days from the date of commencement of his business by sending to the Inspector of his area an application with a statement in the prescribed form along with the requisite fees.
- This is merely a Registration Certificate and not a licence, and does not by itself bestow any legality on the structure in which the shop/commercial establishment is located.

RESTRICTIONS ON WORKING HOURS OF EMPLOYEES IN SHOPS AND ESTABLISHMENTS. The main restrictive provisions of the Act about the working hours of employees in shops and commercial establishment are as follows:

a) The general rule about the opening hours of shops is that they are not allowed to be opened earlier than 7 a.m. But shops selling such goods as milk, vegetable and fish. are allowed to be open from 5 a.m. onward. The exact timings, however, vary from state to state.

b) This general rule about the closing hours of shops is that they must be closed at the latest by 8.30 p.m. But shops selling goods such as pan and *beedi* are allowed to be kept open up to 11 p.m.

c) Commercial establishments are not allowed to be opened earlier than 8.30 a.m. and closed later than 8.30 p.m. in a day

d) An employee in a shop or commercial establishment cannot be required or allowed to work for more than 9 hours in a day and 48 hours in a week.

e) He/she must be allowed an interval of rest of at least one hour after five hours of continuous work.

f) Spread-over cannot exceed 11 hours in a day.

g) Every shop and commercial establishment must remain closed on one day of the week. No deduction can be made from the wages of any employee in a shop or commercial establishment on account of any day on which it has so remained closed.

Interestingly, most state governments have registered IT and ITES companies as public utility services and these have got exemption from some of the provisions of The Shops and Establishments Act. The new economy businesses have brought in different work practices such as 24 × 7 customer services and round-the-clock operations. The Shops and Establishments Act, like many other pieces of labour legislation, may need a review to keep up with the times from both labour and business point of view. Recently, a few call centres in Haryana got notices in terms of provisions of the Punjab Shops and Establishments Acts invoking the provision of non-deployment of women in the night shift where almost 50 per cent of employees in these call centres were women. On the other hand, inadequate security for employees has led to mishaps in Delhi and Bangalore, when women employees were being dropped home after performing duties late at night.

9.5 The Contract Labour (Regulation and Abolition) Act, 1970

The government has been concerned about the exploitation of workers under the contract labour system. With a view to removing the difficulties of contract labour and bearing in mind the recommendations of various commissions and committees and the decisions of the Supreme Court, the Contract Labour (Regulation and Abolition) Act was enacted in 1970. This Act seeks to regulate the employment of contract labour in certain establishments and to provide for its **abolition** under certain circumstances.

Contract labour, by and large, is neither borne on pay roll or muster roll, nor is paid wages directly. The establishments, which farm out work to contractors, do not own any direct responsibility in regard to their labourers. Generally, the wage rates to be paid and the observance of working conditions are stipulated in agreements, but in practice, they are not strictly adhered to.

9.5.1 Objectives

The objectives of the Act are to:

i) Abolish the system of contract labour wherever possible and practicable

ii) Improve service conditions of contract labour where abolition of the contract labour was not possible

iii) Regulate the working conditions of the contract labour so as to place it at par with labour employed directly

iv) Ensure timely payment of wages and provision of essential amenities

9.5.2 Scope and Coverage

The Act applies to every establishment/contractor in which 20 or more workmen are employed or were employed on any day in the preceding 12 months as contract labour and to every contractor who employs or who employed on any day of the preceding 12 months, 20 or more workmen. It does not apply to establishments where the work performed is of intermittent or seasonal nature. An establishment, wherein work is of intermittent and seasonal nature, will be covered by the Act if the work performed is more than 120 days and 60 days in a year respectively. The Act also applies to establishments of the government and local authorities as well.

9.5.3 Definitions

Principal Employer: The manager or occupier of a factory or head of the department of a government/local authority [Section 2(1) (g)].
Contract Labour: A workman is deemed to be employed as "contract labour" in or in relation to work of the establishment, if he/she is hired for such work by or through a contractor, with or without knowledge of the principal employer. [Section 2(1) (b)].
Appropriate Government: The jurisdiction of the central and state government has been laid down by the definition of the "appropriate government" in Section 2(1)(a) of the Act, as amended in 1986. The appropriate government, in respect of an establishment under the Contract Labour (Regulation and Abolition) Act, 1970 is the same as that in the Industrial Disputes Act, 1947.
Controlled Industry: Any industry the control of which by the union has been declared by any central Act to be expedient in public interest
Establishment: (i) Any office or department of the government or a local authority or (ii) any place where any industry, trade, business, manufacture or occupation is carried on.

9.5.4 Registration and Licensing

The establishments covered under the Act are required to be registered as principal employers with the appropriate authorities. Every contractor is required to obtain a licence and not to undertake or execute any work through contract labour, except under and in accordance with the licence issued in that behalf by the licensing officer. The licence granted is subject to conditions relating to hours of work, fixation of wages and other essential amenities in respect of contract as prescribed in the rules.

9.5.5 Duties of the Controlling Authorities

Control over contract labour will be exercised by the "appropriate government". An appropriate government means the central government in case of railways, docks, IFCI, ESIC, LIC, ONGC, UTI, Airport Authority, industry carried on by or under authority of central government. It would be the state in case of other industrial disputes [Section 2(1)(a)]. An appropriate government can make rules. It will appoint inspecting staff to ensure that the provisions of the Act are being followed (Section 28). The principal employer should maintain a register of contractors in the prescribed form (Section 29). He is required to ensure that the contractor makes adequate provision for canteen, rest rooms, supply of drinking water, latrines, urinals, wash rooms, etc. to a contract labour. If the contractor fails to do so within the prescribed time, the principal employer shall provide the amenities, and can recover from contractor the cost incurred by him in providing these amenities (Section 20).

BOX 9.4 **FOR CLASS DISCUSSION**

What happens if an inspector finds a contract labour working within a factory premise, which is not "registered" under the Contract Labour (R&A) Act, 1970?

Further, he finds that the "contractor" has not obtained a "licence". What would be the implications for the "principal employer"?

9.5.6 Duties of Contractors

The Act applies to every contractor who employs 20 or more workmen [Section 1(3)(b)]. The contractor shall be licensed (Section 12). The contractor is required to maintain muster roll and register of wages (Section 29). He is required to follow other provisions as may be contained in rules made by the appropriate government. The contractor is required to pay wages to workmen on time, in the presence of an authorized representative of the principal employer (Section 21). He should issue wage slips to a workman and obtain signature or thumb impression on the wage register. If the contractor fails to make payment of wages, the principal employer is liable to make payment of wages to the contract labour. He can recover this amount from the contractor [Section 21(4)]. The contractor is required to provide canteen facilities, first-aid, rest rooms, drinking water, latrines and washing facilities, as per rules made by the state government (Section 16 and 17).

OBLIGATIONS OF A CONTRACTOR

a) Grievance handling of contract labour must be done by the contractor only.

b) If the contractor has similar types of contracts in different concerns, then he should try to transfer the employees from one establishment to another establishment.

c) The contractor shall select and appoint the workmen without any interference of the principal employer.

d) The contractor shall determine the mode, method and manner of working. The principal employer shall not interfere in regard to the same.

e) The contractor shall employ the workforce, according to his requirement, but he shall not in any case exceed the number of workmen shown in the licence.

f) The contractor shall submit monthly printed bill to the company for payment of the work done by him by the 1st day of the following month.

g) The contractor should pay the wages to his workmen in the presence of the representatives of the company who shall also sign on the muster.

h) The contractor shall pay his own taxes as per the provisions of statutory Act.

i) Every contractor shall send a half-yearly return to the licensing officer within 30 days of the close of the half-year.

Obligations of a Contractor

- Grievance handling of contract labour
- Administrative control over labour without interference from the principal employer.
- Should not employ more labour than what has been allowed in the license
- Shall pay wages in the presence of the PE's representative
- Submit half-yearly returns to the licensing officer
- Pay taxes as per statutory provisions

9.5.7 Duties of the Principal Employer

The principal employer shall make an application to the registration officer of the area where the establishment is situated. Every contractor to whom the Act applies is required to obtain a licence. An application will be made in Form IV to the licensing officer of the area where the establishment is located. The application will be accompanied by a certificate of the principal employer to the effect that the applicant has been employed by him as a contractor in relation to the establishment. The licence will be granted in Form VI and has validity of one year from the date it is granted or renewed. Please note that for each "contract", a separate application has to be made even if the principal employer is the same.

OBLIGATIONS OF THE PRINCIPAL EMPLOYER

- The employer has to ensure that the contractor is paying wages to his workmen before expiry of the seventh day of every month if the number of workers employed in the company does not exceed a thousand, or before the expiry of the tenth day of every month if the number of workers employed in such Company are more than one thousand.

- Also, the employer has to ensure that minimum wages are paid to contract labour.
- The principal employer shall pay wages in full to the contract workmen in case the contractor fails to pay the same.
- The principal employer has a statutory obligation for the payment of wages to contract labourers including arrears, in case the contractor commits default, which he can recover from the contractor by deducting from any amount payable to him or as debt payable to him or as debt payable by him.
- The Act stipulates the obligation of the principal employer and the contractor employing contract labour to provide canteens facilities. In case of failure on the part of the contractor to provide such facilities, the principal employer is made liable to provide the amenities.
- The principal employer shall ensure while making payment to the contractor that the contractor has paid the employees' provident fund and ESI contributions deductions both of the contractor and employees on time.
- The Act enjoins obligation on every principal employer and every contractor to maintain the registers and records.
- The principal employer shall send the return annually so that it reaches the registering officer not later than 15th of February following the end of the year to which it relates.

Obligations of the PE

- Ensure that the contractor is paying wages to his workmen
- Ensure that minimum wages are paid
- Pay wages in full to the contract workmen in case the contractor fails to pay the same, which he can recover from the contractor
- Ensure that the contractor has paid the PF and ESI dues
- Ensure provision of amenities as provided for in the Act
- File annual returns to RO.

9.5.8 The Engagement of Contract Labour

Contract labour may be engaged for the following reasons:

a) For seasonal/occasional requirement/temporary increase of work

b) Need of expertise in a particular job

c) Economic and financial feasibility

9.5.9 The Prohibition of Employment of Contract Labour

Areas where contract labour should not be engaged:

i) All such jobs as notified by the appropriate government

ii) All processes, operations and other work incidental to, or necessary for, the industry, trade, business, manufacture, or occupation are carried on in the establishment for jobs of perennial nature, that is to say, of sufficient duration

iii) Jobs done ordinarily through regular workmen in the establishment

Apart from the regulatory measures provided under the Act for the benefit of contract labour, the appropriate government under Section 10 (1) of the Act is authorized, after consultation with the Central Board or State Board, as the case may be, to prohibit, by notification in the official gazette, employment of contract labour in any establishment in any process, operation or other work. This is one of the most controversial sections of the Act. It lays down sufficient guidelines for deciding upon the abolition of contract labour in any process, operation or other work in any establishment. The guidelines are mandatory in nature and are as follows:

- Conditions of work and benefits provided to the contract labour
- Whether the work is of a perennial nature
- Whether the work is incidental or necessary for the work of an establishment

- Whether the work is sufficient to employ a considerable number of whole-time workmen
- Whether the work is being done ordinarily through regular workmen in that establishment or a similar establishment

The central government, on the recommendations of the Central Advisory Contract Labour Board, has prohibited the employment of contract labour in various operations/category of jobs in various establishments. So far, 73 notifications have been issued since the inception of the Act.

Guidelines for the Prohibition/Abolition of Contract Labour Deployment

Work is of "perennial" nature

Work is incidental to or necessary for the work of the establishment

There is sufficient work to employ sufficient number of whole-time workers

Where a particular work is ordinarily being done through regular workmen

Where conditions of work and benefits for the contract labour are not alright

9.5.10 The Central and State Advisory Boards

The central government and state governments are required to set up Central and State Advisory Contract Labour Boards to advise the respective governments on matters arising out of the administration of the Act as are referred to them. The Boards are authorized to constitute committees as deemed proper. The Central and State Contract Labour Boards are tripartite bodies comprising members from employers, employees and the government. The Central Advisory Board comprises a Chairman (appointed by the Central Government), a Chief Labour Commissioner (ex-officio) and 11–17 members representing employers, contractors and workmen. The composition must be such that the number of workmen representatives is not fewer than the number of representatives of employers and contractors. The State Advisory Board is constituted along similar lines with the number of members ranging from 9 to 11. Among other things, the Boards make recommendations for abolition (or otherwise) of contract labour in certain jobs.

9.5.11 Facilities for Contract Labour

The Act has laid down certain amenities to be provided by the contractor to the contract labour for the establishment of canteens and rest rooms, latrines and urinals, washing facilities and first-aid facilities and arrangements for sufficient supply of wholesome drinking water have been made obligatory. In case of failure on the part of the contractor to provide these facilities, the principal employer is liable to provide the same.

9.5.12 Payment of Wages

The contractor is required to pay wages and a duty is cast on him to ensure disbursement of wages in the presence of the authorized representative of the principal employer. In case of failure on the part of the contractor to pay wages either in part or in full, the principal employer is liable to pay the same. The contract labour, who performs the same or similar kind of work as regular workmen, will be entitled to the same wages and service conditions as regular workmen as per the Contract Labour (Regulation and Abolition) Central Rules, 1971.

9.5.13 Other Laws Applicable to Contract Labour

Besides the Contract Labour (Regulation and Abolition) Act, various other Acts are applicable to contract labour—(a) the Factories Act: The Act makes no distinction between persons directly employed and employed through a contractor; (b) Employees' Provident Funds Act; (c) ESIC; (d) the Payment of Wages Act; (e) the Minimum Wages Act; (f) the Industrial Disputes Act; and (g) the Workmen's Compensation Act.

In India, contracting out various items of work to workers or to contractors has been common and wide-spread. Governments are the biggest contract-labour-employing agencies. Public and private sectors extensively use the services of contractors and in turn their workers. The engagement of contract labour provides flexibility, leads to efficient utilization of resources and improves productivity. Considering the need to regulate such employment and protect the interests of the workers, the Government of India brought in Contract Labour (Regulation and Abolition) Act, 1970.

This Act not only seeks to regulate the contract labour but provides for the abolition of industries where the nature of work is perennial.

Even though this Act has been in force for more than 35 years, its enforcement is far from satisfactory and has led to enormous litigation. The enforcement machinery is preoccupied more with the activity of abolition rather than regulation. The pressure on the public enterprises, the railways and the government, to abolish the contract labour and provide regular and permanent employment to the workers is much greater as compared to cases where private industry is involved.

Various judicial pronouncements in regard to the Contract Labour (R&A) Act, 1970, have made things much more difficult for the employers. Often, trade unions, working in tandem with the enforcement machinery, have harassed the employers and burdened them with manpower they do not need. With the globalization of business and trade, there is increasing competition among nations and industrial groups. In order to compete, it is important to streamline the operations and produce goods and services most efficiently and at the least cost. It is recognized widely that the enterprises should focus on their core activities and the rest be left to the agencies and outfits that can undertake the peripheral activities more efficiently and economically. Out-sourcing of various goods and services is the inevitable outcome. In this context, the engagement of contract workers, directly or through contractors, has not only assumed importance but is crucial. This has also attracted the attention of International Labour Organization with a view to regulate the same.

Most of the employers have demanded that the stringent provisions of the Act should be made easy so that the engagement of contract labour in certain areas where deployment of regular workers is not feasible or economical is not affected. The judicial pronouncement of the Supreme Court in Air India Corporations case places a heavy burden on the employers, which may affect the economic viability of industries. In view of changed scenario as a result of economic liberalization, there is a need to allow the industries to employ contract labour in support and peripheral services so that the industries can concentrate on core activities. Provisions of the Contract Labour (R&A) Act need to be amended suitably so that the appropriate government is empowered to withdraw, abrogate, and modify its own notification issued under Section 10, enabling industries to function with economic viability and greater competitiveness. The employers have been seeking a complete review of the Act and requesting the government to regulate contract labour and not abolish it. While employers want flexibility, the workers need security. If our industry and trade have to have the competitive edge in the international market, there should be flexibility in the labour market. The background in which the Act was promulgated has since undergone a complete change. Therefore, there is adequate justification for a complete review of the legislation and bringing out a new piece of legislation, which would provide the needs of both the employers and the workers in a balanced way.

SUMMARY

The Factories Act, 1948

- The Factories Act, 1948 is the principal legislation, which governs the health, safety, and welfare of workers in factories.
- The Act extends to the whole of India. Mine and railway workers are not included as they are covered by separate Acts.
- However, it was not until 1987 that the elements of occupational health and safety, and the prevention and protection of workers employed in hazardous processes, got truly incorporated in the Act (after the Bhopal Gas Tragedy).
- The Act does not permit the employment of women and young persons in a dangerous process or operation.
- There is provision for one weekly holiday, and an adult worker should work not more than 48 hours in a week.
- There is at least half-an-hour rest after a stretch of five hours of continuous work.
- No women should be employed between 7 p.m. and 6 a.m.
- No person less than 14 years of age should work in the factory. No child should work for more than 4 hours a day and should not work in the night between 10 p.m. and 6 a.m.

- One full-wage leave should be given to an adult worker for every 20 days of work and one for every 15 days to the child worker. Twelve weeks of maternity leave should be given to a woman.

The Shops and Establishments Act

- The Shops and Establishments Act, 1953 was enacted to provide statutory obligation and rights to employees and employers in the unorganized sector of employment, i.e., shops and establishments.
- It is applicable to all persons employed in an establishment with or without wages, except the members of the employer's family.
- It is a state legislation and each state has framed its own rules for the Act.
- The state government can exempt, either permanently or for a specified period, any establishments from all or any provisions of this Act.
- The Act provides for compulsory registration of shop/establishment within 30 days of commencement of work and all communications of closure of an establishment within 15 days from its closing.
- It also lays down the hours of work per day and week as well as the guidelines for spread-over, rest interval, opening and closing hours, closed days, national and religious holidays, overtime work, etc.

The Contract Labour (R&A) Act, 1970

- The Contract Labour (Regulation and Abolition) Act, 1970 applies to every establishment in which 20 or more workmen are employed or were employed on any day on the preceding 12 months as contract labour and to every contractor who employs or who employed on any day of the preceding 12 months 20 or more workmen.
- It does not apply to establishments where the work performed is of intermittent or casual nature. The Act also applies to establishments of the government and local authorities as well.
- The central government and the state governments are required to set up Central Advisory Board and State Advisory Boards, which are authorized to constitute committees as deemed proper. The Boards carry out the functions assigned to them under the Act.
- The establishments covered under the Act are required to be registered as the principal employer. Likewise, every contractor to whom the Act applies is required to obtain a licence and not to undertake or execute any work through contract labour except under and in accordance with the licence issued.
- The Act has provided for the establishment of canteens. For the welfare and health of contract labour, provision is made for restrooms, first-aid, wholesome drinking water, latrines and urinals. In case of failure on the part of the contractor to provide such facilities, the principal employer is made liable to provide the amenities.
- The contractor is required to pay wages and a duty is cast on him to ensure disbursement of wages in the presence of an authorized representative of the principal employer. In case of failure on the part of the contractor to pay wages either in part or in full, the principal employer is liable to pay the same. In case the contract labour perform same or similar kind of work as regular workmen, they will be entitled to the same wages and service conditions as regular workmen as per the Contract Labour (Regulation and Abolition) Central Rules, 1971.
- The appropriate government under Section 10 (1) of the Act is authorized, after consultation with the Central Board or State Board, as the case may be, to prohibit, by notification in the official gazette, employment of contract labour in any establishment in any process, operation or other work.
- The Act lays down sufficient guidelines for deciding upon the abolition of contract labour in any process, operation or other work in any establishment.

KEY TERMS

REVIEW QUESTIONS

1 Discuss the important provisions of the Factories Act, 1948.

2 What do you understand by the terms "worker", "manufacturing process" and "factory" under the Factories Act?

3 Does the Factories Act, 1948 apply to factories belonging to the central government? Give reasons for your answer.

4 What do you understand by a "young person"? Distinguish between "adult" and "adolescent" as defined in the Factories Act, 1948.

5 What are the working hours for children and women in a factory? Under the Factories Act, 1948, what are the main provisions of restrictions regarding the employment of young persons? How should the register of child workers be maintained in a factory?

6 What are the weekly and the daily hours for which an adult worker may be required or allowed to work in a factory?

7 What are the basic objectives of The Shops and Establishments Act?

8 Discuss some of the restrictions imposed on hours of work with regard to employees governed under the S&E Act.

9 Is it necessary for an employer to notify the closing of his establishment under the S&E Act?

10 How can a shop or establishment get an exemption under this Act?

11 Define the object of the Contract Labour (R&A) Act, 1970.

12 Explain the following terms used in the Contract Labour (R&A) Act:

a. Appropriate government

b. Contractor

c. Contract labour

d. Principal employer

13 When is registration of an establishment obligatory under the Contract Labour (R&A) Act?

14 What is the procedure followed for the abolition of contract labour in any process, operation or any other work in an establishment?

QUESTIONS FOR CRITICAL THINKING

1 Employers through their federations have been seeking amendments to some of the provisions to The Factories Act. One of them is to raise the total number of hours of overtime of workers from 50 to 150 (in a quarter) for a continuous process industry and also that the rate of overtime should be the same as ordinary rate of wages instead of the existing twice the ordinary rate. Do you agree? Give reasons.

2 A recent report said that "hotels will be classified as 'factories' and the definition of a 'hazardous industry' will be substantially broad-based if amendments proposed to the Factories Act of 1948 come through." What could be the possible implications of this move? Will it be good or bad for business? Will it be good or bad for the employees?

3 According to provisions of The Delhi Shops and Establishments Act, women employees are not allowed to work overnight and also those working on holidays are entitled to double wages and compensatory leave. Section 14 of the Delhi Shops and Establishments Act says, "no young person or woman shall be allowed, or required to work, whether as an employee or otherwise, in any establishment between 9 p.m. and 7 a.m. during the summer season and between 8 p.m. and 8 a.m. during the winter season". This provision, however, grants exemptions to air services companies, cloak-room attendants, girl telephone operators, ayaas, lady house keepers and artists in cabaret and entertainment shows except children in hotels, theatres and other places of public amusement.

i. What could be the implications of this provision?

ii. How do you think the BPO industry has managed to circumvent these provisions?

4 Services in the information technology (IT) and IT-related sectors are being brought under the ambit of the Contract Labour (R&A) Act. In these sectors, a lot of non-core activities are outsourced. What would be the implications of such a move.?

5 Given below are some of the jobs that are of perennial nature, and organizations are deploying contract labour for these jobs/activities:

- sweeping, cleaning, dusting and the collection and disposal of all kinds of wastes
- security services
- courier services
- maintenance, service and repair of equipment/machines
- loading and unloading of materials
- running canteen services
- house-keeping and laundry services

Do you think the government will allow registration of these establishments under the Contract Labour (R&A) Act? Why?

6 In the context of globalization, many clichéd terms such as "global quality" and "global competition" are being increasingly used. But what is being lost sight of is that global

competitiveness is achievable only if certain global benchmarks in relation to running of the business are also considered and accorded due importance. One such benchmark is the linking of productivity to man power. Over-staffing is something that no industry can afford. The practical advantage of outsourcing non-core activities to contractors is lost under the provisions of the Contract Labour (Regulation and Abolition) Act, 1970. Critically examine this statement in light of the current reality of the Indian industry and provisions of the Contract Labour (R&A) Act, 1970.

DEBATE

1 The second National Commission on Labour has recommended the enactment of a general law relating to hours of work, working conditions, annual leave, welfare, contract labour and others applicable to various categories of establishments alike. In a competitive environment, such provisions would further erode the competitiveness of Indian business.

2 Is the Shops and Establishments Act, as it obtains today, an impediment to 24 × 7 customer service?

3 Read the box-item below. What could be the arguments from each side?

The Karnakata government's plan to ban night shifts for women is ruffling feathers in Bangalore.

Women employees in the hotel Industry have to work late night shifts. And the number is substantial. But that might soon change. The Karnataka Assembly has passed a new Bill that seeks to ban night shifts for women in firms that come under the Karnataka Shops and Establishments Act.

The IT industry and hospitals, however, will be exempted. Women's groups are already protesting saying this is not a progressive step. It may hinder progress of women, they say. The employers say that in the world of business today one cannot have a segregated and isolated approach towards women workforce.

The government says it is the only way to ensure protection for women and will target the hotel industry, shopping malls and recreation centres. The recent incident of the murder of a woman employee returning from late night shift has prompted government concerns regarding women's safety.

4 Rather than abolish contract labour, we need to regulate it by protecting equality of wages, workers' health, safety, welfare and access to various amenities at the workplace.

5 Trade unions and workers' organizations can focus on "equal pay for equal work", rather than on the absorption of contract labour.

CASE ANALYSIS

Shifting of Weekly Off (Factories Act):

MK Manufacturers Ltd decided to shift their weekly off to Tuesday. The daily normal working hours of the workmen are 8 hours on all days except Sunday, when working hours are 4-3/4 hours only. Thus, the total working hours during the week comes to 44-3/4 hours. If piece rated workers were required to work beyond the aforesaid normal working hours, they were not given overtime payment for work up to 48 hours in a week. Overtime was paid only beyond the 48 hours in a week.

1. Is this a contravention to the provisions in The Factories Act?
2. Is the overtime payment justified?

Shifting of Weekly Off (Shops and Establishments Act)[2]:

In February, 2008, the Haryana government's labour department has notified the closing of all shops in the city on Tuesdays. This implies that the largely unorganized, semi-skilled and unskilled workers employed in many shops and malls in Gurgaon will get their weekly off on Tuesdays. However, the labour commissioner stated that that they would not mind allowing employers to keep their shops opened 24 × 7, only if they strictly adhere to labour laws. "They must follow the laws so far as following the outer limit for working hours in a week. They must give wage for extra time as laid down in the laws. At any cost, no employee should be exploited. In those conditions we can relax the opening of shops."

"This is a conscious decision. The earlier proposal of closing shops on Sunday was opposed by the stakeholders as they argued that their sale is much better on official holidays. Hence, from now onwards, our officials will initiate action against the violators," he said. "If the employers feel that Gurgaon is recognized globally, the citizens must follow the best practices," the Labour Commissioner said. He said this move is aimed at regulating the working of shops and not to discourage them.

Discuss the above decision with respect to the provisions of The Shops and Establishments Act. In case some shopkeepers decide to keep their shops open on Tuesdays, what are their obligations towards the employees? What are the likely restrictions?

The Absorption of Contract Labour:

JNK Plastics Ltd had been employing contract labour for loading and unloading of materials and finished goods on a regular basis. The contracts for this job were based on tender invitations for job contracts, and for the past five years, the same contractor has been awarded the job. This year, a mechanized system of loading has been introduced, which has done away with the need of contract labour. The union has been putting pressure on the management for absorption of the labour and deploying them on unskilled-level jobs in the manufacturing unit.

Due to intense pressure from the union, the management worked out a voluntary-retirement scheme for contract workmen, which were settled through a tripartite agreement. Forty per cent of the burden is being funded by the management out of its welfare fund.

Bring out the legal as well as industrial relations issues in the above case. Discuss the strategy adopted by the management within the constraints of law. Could there have been a better strategy?

NOTES

1 Bureau, "Industry Calls for Changes in Factory Act, Labour Laws", *The Hindu Business Line*, 6 December 2004.

2 Times News Network, "Thank God it's Tuesday in Gurgaon", *The Times of India,* 3 March, 2008.

chapter ten

CHAPTER OUTLINE

LEARNING OBJECTIVES

After reading this chapter, you will be able to:

- Understand the concept of social security
- List the major central legislations pertaining to social security
- Describe the major benefits and provisions of these legislations
- Explain the role of the government, employer and employees in the implementation of social-security measures

An Accident at the Workplace

Badrinath, a senior machinist with one of the major auto ancillaries in Gurgaon, liked to be punctual. No matter how troublesome the 15-km ride to the factory was, Badrinath made it a point to be on time. Of course, putting his two children through school meant that he needed every paisa of his salary each month. Badrinath had his priorities sorted out—good education for his children and a good standard of living for his family. Saving for a rainy day did not feature on his priority list. He was not unduly worried about his job. He was a skilled machinist in a market where trained local technicians were in short supply and the employers were many. Confident of his own professional abilities, Badrinath figured that the need to save for old age was still distant.

On the morning of that fateful day, Badrinath punched his card in the office at 0730 hours in the general shift, as was his wont. He immediately reported to the shop floor. Striding towards bay number 5, Badrinath, through his peripheral vision, vaguely sensed something rushing towards him. Before he could react, it hit him hard on the right side causing him to fall down. A momentary sense of excruciating pain was followed by numbness. Badrinath, lying crumpled on the floor, could see all the workers rushing towards him but he could not move at all—not even his neck. His vision faded as he slipped into unconsciousness.

Eyewitnesses of the accident described to the doctor that the tyre of the heavy dumper crushed his right leg and hit his back, probably damaging the backbone as well. The immediate medical attention that Badrinath received from the hospital he was rushed to could do no more than merely save his life. Badrinath—completely paralysed below his neck—had become a living vegetable with little or no hope of either recovering or finding gainful employment in the future.

Social-security Legislations

Social security is one of the key components of labour welfare. Labour welfare refers to all such services, amenities and facilities to the employees that improve their working conditions as well as their standard of living. Social security benefits provided by an enterprise should protect not only their employees but also their family members through financial security including healthcare. Social security envisages that the employees shall be protected against all types of social risks that may cause undue hardships to them in fulfilling their basic needs.

What would be the fate of the likes of Badrinath (and dependants) for the rest of their lives? Such accidents in the course of employment do happen more frequently than we would like to imagine.

Accidents, job losses, retirement, sickness, death while on duty—these are realities of working life and leave a person and/or his dependants vulnerable. Social security is an attempt by the employer and the State to institute measures that mitigate such social risks. The concept of social security, though old, was first enacted in the last century in the USA during the 1930s at the time of Great Depression. In India, too, there have been attempts to institute social-security measures in place even though it is still at a nascent stage.

10.1 Major Legislations

India, being a welfare State, has taken upon itself the responsibilities of extending various benefits of social security and social assistance to its citizens. The social-security legislations in India derive their strength and spirit from the Directive Principles of the State Policy as contained in the Constitution of India. Although the Constitution of India is yet to recognize social security as a fundamental right, it does require the State to promote the welfare of the people by securing and protecting a social order in which justice—social, economic and political—shall prevail in the institutions of national life. Article 41 of the Constitution requires that the State should, within the limits of its economic capacity, make effective provisions for securing the right to work, to education and to public assistance in case of unemployment, old age, sickness and disablement. While Article 42 requires that the State should make provisions for securing just and humane conditions of work and for maternity relief, Article 47 requires that the State should raise the level of nutrition and the standard of living of its people and improvement of public health as among its primary duties. The obligations cast on the State in the above Articles constitute social security.

A Social Security Division has been set up under the Ministry of Labour and Employment. The division deals with framing of social-security policy for the workers, administration of all the legislations relating to social security and the implementation of the various social-security schemes. In the context of labour, social security aims at mitigating risks against loss in earnings or earning capacity due to age, illness or work-related injuries.

Social security to the workers is provided, among others, through five major central Acts:

i) The Employees' State Insurance Act, 1948

ii) Employees' Provident Funds and Miscellaneous Provisions Act, 1952

iii) The Workmen's Compensation Act

iv) The Maternity Benefit Act

v) The Payment of Gratuity Act

In addition, there are a large number of welfare funds for certain specified segments of workers such as *beedi* workers, cine workers and construction workers.

The major thrust of social security relating to labour is two-pronged:

- Those relating to the medical facilities, compensation benefits and insurance coverage to the employees in case of accidents, incapacity, illness
- Those relating to the provident fund and gratuity provisions

It consists of preventive, promotional and protective measures for labour welfare.

10.2 The Employees' State Insurance Act, 1948

The Employees' State Insurance Act, (ESIC) 1948, is a piece of social-welfare legislation enacted primarily with the object of providing certain benefits to employees in case of sickness, maternity and employment injury and also to make provision for certain others matters. The Act is an effort at achieving the goal of socio-economic justice mentioned in the Directive Principles of State Policy under Part 4 of Constitution, in particular, Articles 41, 42 and 43, which enjoin the State to make effective provisions for securing the right to work, to education and public assistance in cases of unemployment, old age, sickness and disablement. Specifically, there is a scheme in the Act that makes provisions for the following benefits under different contingencies (see Figure 10.1).

It may be seen that the ESI Act aims to provide security (financial and medical) to employees (and their dependents) during contingencies that may affect their earning capacities, temporarily or permanently.

10.2.1 Scope, Applicability and Coverage

The Act extends to the whole of India. The ESIC Act applies to non-seasonal, power-using factories or manufacturing units employing 10 or more persons, and non-power using establishments employing 20 or more persons. Under the enabling provisions of the Act, a factory or establishment, located in a geographical area, notified for the implementation

Figure 10.1

The ESI Act.

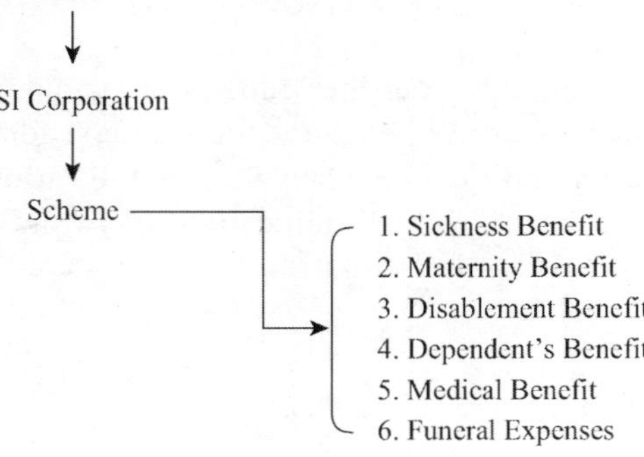

of the scheme, falls in the purview of the Act. Employees of the aforesaid categories of factories or establishments, but drawing wages only up to INR 10,000 a month, are entitled to health insurance cover under the ESI Act. The wage ceiling for the purpose of coverage is revised from time to time, to keep pace with the rising cost of living and subsequent wage hikes. The present ceiling of INR 10,000 has been revised recently. The appropriate government, state or central, is empowered to extend the provision of the ESI Act to various classes of establishment—industrial, commercial, agricultural or otherwise in nature. Under these enabling provisions, most of the state governments have extended the ESI Act to certain specific classes of establishments, such as shops, hotels, restaurants and cinemas, employing 20 or more persons. But no industry has the right to opt out of the scheme.

An employee who is covered at the beginning of a **contribution period** shall continue to remain covered till the end of that contribution period notwithstanding the fact that his wages may exceed the prescribed wage ceiling at any time after the commencement of that contribution period. Wage ceiling for the purpose of coverage is revised from time to time by the central government on the specific recommendation of the ESI Corporation.

The Act, in the first instance, was to be applicable to factories as defined in the Act. The government, however, could extend it to other establishments too. Over the years, the Act has been extended to all kinds of establishments. This is a "beneficient" Act and, therefore, the interpretation of its coverage has been very liberal. The following are excluded from the coverage of the Act:

i) Factories working with the aid of power wherein less than 10 persons are employed

ii) Factories working without the aid of power wherein less than 20 persons are employed

iii) Seasonal factories engaged exclusively in any of the following activities, viz. cotton ginning, cotton or jute pressing, decortication of groundnuts, the manufacture of coffee, indigo, lac, rubber, sugar (including *gur*) or tea or any manufacturing process incidental to or connected with any of the aforesaid activities, and including factories engaged for a period not exceeding seven months in a year in blending, packing or repackaging of tea or coffee, or in such other process as may be specified by the central government

iv) A factory that was exempted from the provisions of the Act as being a "seasonal factory" will not lose the benefit of the exemption on account of the amendment of the definition of "seasonal factory"

v) Mines subject to the Mines Act, 1952

vi) Railway running sheds

vii) Government factories or establishments, whose employees are in receipt of benefits similar or superior to the benefits provided under the Act

viii) Members of Indian navy, military and air force

Employee: This term includes any person who is engaged or employed for wages/salary in connection with the work of the establishment to which this Act applies. It does not include any person whose wages (excluding OT) exceed the limit prescribed by the central government—currently INR 10,000 per month.

Every employee (including casual and temporary employees), whether employed directly or through a contractor, who is in receipt of wages up to INR 10,000 is entitled to be insured under the ESI Act. However, apprentices engaged under the Apprentices Act are not entitled to the ESI benefits. Coverage of part-time employees under the ESI Act will depend on whether they have "contract of service" or "contract for service" with the employer. The former is covered, whereas the latter are not covered under the ESI Act.

Besides, in the following cases, the employees have been held to be covered under the Act:

i) Persons employed in a canteen of a club

ii) Drivers employed by the transport organization

iii) Persons engaged in distribution and sale of products

iv) Persons carrying administrative work of processing the orders and executing sales

v) Hawkers employed for the sale of products

vi) Employees of cycle stand and canteen run in cinema theatres by contractors

vii) Members of editorial and administrative staff of a printing press, publishing, newspaper

viii) A home worker rolling *beedis* at home

ix) Medical representative

x) Persons employed in a hospital attached to and maintained by factory

xi) Part-time doctor employed for ambulance room

xii) Book-binders engaged by a contractor

xiii) Sales clerk working in a factory

It can, once again, be seen that the interpretation regarding coverage is very liberal. As regards coverage of category of employees or type of establishment, in case of doubt, it will be prudent to err on the side of liberal and inclusive interpretation. More often that not you will be right!

Exemption from Maternity Benefit Act, 1961 and Workmen's Compensation Act, 1923: An employer/establishment covered under the ESI Act is exempt from the provisions of Maternity Benefit Act and Workmen's Compensation Act. It is specifically provided that when a person is entitled to any of the benefits provided by the ESI Act, then he/she shall not be entitled to recover any similar benefits admissible under the provisions of any other enactment.

10.2.2 Important Terms Used in the Act

Exempted Employee: An employee who is not liable under this Act to pay the employees' contribution

Family: All or any of the following relatives of an insured person:

i) A spouse

ii) A minor, legitimate or adopted child, dependent upon the insured person

iii) A child who is wholly dependent on the earnings of the insured person and who is (a) receiving education, till he or she attains the age of 21 years (b) an unmarried daughter

iv) A child who is infirm by reason of any physical or mental abnormality or injury and is wholly dependent on the earnings of the insured person, so long as the infirmity continues

v) Dependent parents

Insurable Employment: An employment in a factory or establishment to which this Act applies

Insured Person: A person who is or was an employee in respect of whom contributions are or were payable under this Act and who is entitled to any benefit under the ESIC Scheme

Sickness: A condition that requires medical treatment and attendance and necessitates abstention from work on medical grounds

Contribution: The sum of money payable to the "Corporation" by the principal employer in respect of an employee and includes any amount payable by or on behalf of the employee in accordance with the provisions of this Act

Employment Injury: A personal injury to an employee caused by accident or an occupational disease arising out of and in the course of his employment, being an insurable employment, whether the accident occurs or the occupational disease is contracted within or outside the territorial limits of India. For example, an insured person, if deployed abroad, or if travelling abroad in course of his employment meets with an accident, he shall be eligible to receive the benefits to which he is entitled under the Act.

Permanent Partial Disablement: Such disablement of a permanent nature as reduces the earning capacity of an employee in every employment that he was capable of undertaking at the time of the accident resulting in the disablement. For example, loss of the index finger of the right hand may result in a permanent partial disability. The Part II of the second schedule of the Act lists the partial disablements and prescribes the percentage of partial disablement.

Permanent Total Disablement: Such disablement of a permanent nature as incapacitates an employee for all work that he was capable of performing at the time of the accident resulting in such disablement. Part I of Schedule 2 contains a list of all injuries considered to be of permanent total nature. If two or more permanent partial disablements (as per Part 2) combine to constitute injury amounting to 100 per cent or more, the same will constitute permanent total disablement. For example, loss of both hands will constitute total permanent disablement.

Temporary Disablement: A condition resulting from an employment injury, which requires medical treatment and renders an employee, as a result of such injury, temporarily incapable of doing the work that he was doing prior to or at the time of the injury

Wages: All remuneration paid or payable, in cash to an employee, if the terms of the contract of employment, express or implied, were fulfilled and includes any payment to an employee in respect of any period of authorized leave, lock-out, strike that is not illegal or lay-off and other additional remuneration, if any, paid at intervals not exceeding two months

Wage does not include:

a) Any contribution paid by the employer to any pension fund or provident fund
b) Travelling allowance or the value of any travelling concession
c) Any sum paid to the person employed to defray special expenses entailed on him by the nature of his employment
d) Any gratuity payable on discharge

Table 10.1 illustrates the components that are to be reckoned as wages for the purpose of the Act.

10.2.3 Administration

There is elaborate administrative machinery for the implementation of the provisions of the most comprehensive of all social security legislations.

ESI CORPORATION. This social-security programme is administered by a corporate body called the Employee State Insurance Corporation. It comprises members representing interest groups that include employee, employers, the central and state government, besides representatives of parliament and the medical profession. The corporation is headed by the Union Minister of Labour as its chairman, where as the Director General, appointed by the central government, functions as its CEO. A standing committee constituted from amongst the members of the corporation, acts as an executive body. The medical benefit council, constituted by the central government, is yet another statutory body that advises the corporation on matters related to effective delivery of services to the beneficiary population.

ESI Corporation

Provisions of the ESI Act are administered by a corporate body called the Employee State Insurance Corporation. It comprises members representing interest groups that include, employees, employers, the central and state governments, besides representatives of parliament and the medical profession. The corporation is headed by the Union Minister of Labour.

Table 10.1

Wages for ESI contributions.

To be Deemed as Wages	Not to be Deemed as Wages
• Basic pay • Dearness Allowance • House Rent Allowance • City Compensatory Allowance • Overtime Wages (but not to be taken into account for determining the coverage of employee) • Payment for day of rest • Production Incentive • Bonus other than statutory bonus • Night-shift Allowance • Heat, Gas and Dust Allowance • Payment for unsubstituted holidays • Meal/Food Allowance • Suspension Allowance • Lay-off Allowance • Children Education Allowance (not being reimbursement for actual tuition fees)	• Contribution paid by the employer to any pension/provident of under ESI Act • Sum paid to defray special expenses entailed by the nature of employment—daily allowance paid for the period spent on tour • Gratuity payable on discharge • Pay in lieu of notice of retrenchment compensation • Benefits paid under the ESI Scheme • Encashment of leave • Payment of Inam, which does not form part of the term of employment • Washing allowances for livery • Conveyance amount towards reimbursement for duty-related journey

The Corporation is vested with the following powers:

- To promote measures for the improvement of health and welfare of the insured employees and for the rehabilitation and re-employment of those who have been disabled or injured
- To appoint inspectors for purposes of the Act
- To determine the amount of contribution payable in respect of employees of a factory or establishment that has not furnished or maintained any particulars, registers or records

ESI Scheme Financing

ESI scheme is a self-financing health-insurance scheme. Contributions are raised from covered employees and their employers as a fixed percentage of wages. As of now, covered employees contribute 1.75 per cent of the wages, whereas as the employers contribute 4.75 per cent of the wages. Employees earning less than INR 50 a day as daily wage are exempted from payment of their share of contribution.

FINANCE. Like most social-security schemes the world over, ESI is a self-financing health-insurance scheme. Contributions are raised from covered employees and their employers as a fixed percentage of wages. As of now, covered employees contribute 1.75 per cent of the wages, whereas the employers contribute 4.75 per cent of the wages. Employees earning less than INR 50 a day as daily wage are exempted from payment of their share of contribution. The state government, as per the provision of the Act, contributes 1/8 of the expenditure on medical benefit within a per capita ceiling of INR 1000 per insured person per annum. Any additional expenditure incurred by the state government, over and above the ceiling, and not falling within the shareable pool, is borne by the state governments concerned. The responsibility for payment of all contributions is that of the employer with a right to deduct the employees' share of contribution from employees' wages relating to the period in respect of which the contribution is payable.

CONTRIBUTION PERIODS AND BENEFIT PERIOD. Workers, covered under the ESI Act, are required to pay contribution towards the scheme on a monthly basis. Contribution period means a six-month time span from 1 April to 30 September and 1 October

Table 10.2

Contribution and benefit periods.

Contribution Period	Corresponding Benefit Period
1 April to 30 September	1 January to 30 June of the following year
1 October to 31 March	1 July to 31 December

to 31 March. Thus, in a financial year, there are two contribution periods of six months' duration. Cash benefits under the scheme are generally linked with the contribution paid. The benefit period starts three months after the closure of a contribution period (see Table 10.2).

10.2.4 Benefits in Detail

Employees covered under the scheme are entitled to medical facilities for self and dependants. They are also entitled to cash benefits in the event of specified contingencies resulting in loss of wages or earning capacity, as mentioned above. The insured women are entitled to maternity benefit for confinement. Where death of an insured employee occurs due to employment injury or occupational disease, the dependants are entitled to family pension. In this section, we examine the various benefits that the insured employees and their dependants are entitled to, the duration of benefits and the contributory conditions.

MEDICAL BENEFIT. Full medical facilities for self and dependants are admissible from day one of entering insurable employment. The primary, outpatient, in-patient and specialist services are provided through a network of panel clinics, whereas ESI dispensaries and hospitals and super specialty services are provided through a large number of advanced, empanelled medical institutions on referral basis. The eligibility criteria for availing the medical benefits are the following:

- Facilities are admissible from day one of entering insurable employment for self and dependants such as spouse, parents and children—own or adopted
- For self and spouse on superannuation, subject to having completed five years in insurable employment on superannuation or in case of having suffered permanent physical disablement during the course of insurable employment
- The rate of contribution for superannuated/disabled is INR 120 per annum payable in lump sum at the local office for availing full medical care for self and spouse

SICKNESS BENEFIT. Sickness benefit in cash is payable under three types of conditions as mentioned below:

Sickness Benefit: Sickness benefit is payable to an insured person in cash, in the event of sickness resulting in absence from work and duly certified by an authorized insurance medical officer/practitioner.

- The benefit becomes admissible only after an insured has paid contribution for at least 78 days in a contribution period of 6 months.
- Sickness benefit is payable for a maximum of 91 days in 2 consecutive contribution periods [one year].
- Payment is to be made by the local office within 7 days of certificate of sickness at a **standard rate**, which is not less than 50 per cent of the wages.

[The logic behind fixing of 78 and 91 days of contribution is based on actuarial studies.]

Extended Sickness Benefit: Extended sickness benefit is payable to insured persons for the period of certified sickness in case of the specified, 34 long-term diseases that need prolonged treatment and absence from work on medical advice.

- For entitlement to this benefit, an insured person should have been in insurable employment for at least 2 years. He/she should also have paid contribution for a minimum of 156 days in the preceding 4 contribution periods or say 2 years.
- ESI is payable for a maximum period of 2 years on the basis of proper medical certification and authentication by the designated authority.
- Amount payable in cash as extended sickness benefit is payable within 7 days following the submission of complete claim papers at the local office concerned.

Enhanced Sickness Benefit: This cash benefit is payable to insured persons in the productive age group for undergoing sterilization operation—either vasectomy or tubectomy.

- The contribution is the same as for the normal sickness benefit.
- Enhanced sickness benefit is payable to the IPs for 14 days for tubectomy and for 7 days in case of vasectomy.
- The amount payable is double the standard sickness benefit rate that is equal to full wages.

MATERNITY BENEFIT. Maternity benefit is payable to insured women in case of confinement or miscarriage or sickness related thereto.

- For claiming this, the insured woman should be paid for at least 70 days in 2 consecutive contribution periods, i.e., 1 year.
- The benefit is normally payable for 12 weeks, which can be further extended up to 16 weeks on medical grounds.
- The rate of payment of the benefit is equal to wage or double the standard sickness benefit rate.
- The benefit is payable within 14 days of duly authenticated claim papers.

DISABLEMENT BENEFIT (CASH). Disablement benefit is payable to insured employees suffering from physical disablement due to employment injury or occupation disease.

- An insured person should be an employee on the date of the accident. Temporary disablement benefit at 70 per cent of the wages is payable till temporary disablement lasts and is duly certified by an authorized insurance medical officer.
- In case of permanent disablement, the cash benefit is payable for life.
- The amount payable is worked out on the basis of earning capacity determined by a medical board.
- Disablement benefit is payable within one month of submission of the complete claim papers.

DEPENDANT'S BENEFITS (CASH). Dependant's benefit (family pension) is payable to dependants of a deceased, insured person where death occurs due to employment or occupational disease.

- A widow can receive this benefit on a monthly basis for life or till remarriage.
- A son or daughter can receive this benefit till 18 years of age.
- Other dependants like parents, including a widowed mother, can also receive the benefit under certain conditions.
- The rate of payment is about 70 per cent of the wages shareable among dependants in a fixed ratio.

- The first instalment is payable within a maximum of three months following the death of an insured person, and thereafter, on a regular monthly basis.

FUNERAL EXPENSES. Funeral expenses are payable in case of death, subject to a maximum of INR 2,500.

BENEFITS NOT TO BE COMBINED. An employee shall not be entitled to receive for the same period:

a) Both sickness benefit and maternity benefit

b) Both sickness benefit and disablement benefit for temporary disablement

c) Both maternity benefit and disablement benefit for temporary disablement

The employee shall be entitled to choose any one of the aforesaid benefits, at his option.

10.2.5 Obligations of Employers

1. The employer should get his factory or establishments registered with the ESI Corporation within 15 days after the Act becomes applicable to it, and obtain the employer's code number.
2. The employer should obtain the declaration form from the employees covered under the Act and submit the same along with the return of declaration forms to the ESI office. He should arrange for the allotment of insurance numbers to the employees and their identity cards.
3. The employer should deposit the employees' and his own contributions to the ESI account in the prescribed manner; whether he has sufficient resources or not, his liability under the Act cannot be disputed. He cannot justify non-payment of ESI contribution due to non-availability of finance.
4. The employer should furnish a Return of Contributions along with the *challans* of monthly payment, within 30 days of the end of each contribution period.
5. The employer should not reduce the wages of an employee on account of the contribution payable by him (employer).
6. The employer should cause to be maintained the prescribed records/registers namely the register of employees, the inspection book and the accident book.
7. The employer should report to the ESI authorities of any accident in the place of employment, within 24 hours or immediately in case of serious or fatal accidents. He should make arrangements for first-aid and transportation of the employee to the hospital. He should also furnish to the authorities such further information and particulars of an accident as may be required.
8. The employer should inform the local office and the nearest ESI dispensary/hospital, in case of death of any employee, immediately.
9. The employer must not put to work any sick employee and must allow him leave, if he/she has been issued the prescribed certificate.
10. The employer should not dismiss or discharge any employee during the period he/she is in receipt of sickness/maternity/temporary disablement benefit, or is under medical treatment, or is absent from work as a result of illness duly certified or due to pregnancy or confinement.

Most organizations in the organized sector nowadays provide adequate benefits to those in their employment. A number of these organizations have also facilitated some kind of medical, accident and life insurance to the employees. The PSUs have elaborate schemes for the treatment of their employees. A sizeable number of these employees, however, are above the salary limit of INR 10,000 per month. It is those employees in the unorganized sector, the contractual employees, earning less than INR 10,000 per month whom the Act aims to protect from risks in working life, which may impact their earning. From an employee relation point of view, the organization must address this insecurity of the individual employee and benchmark the provisions of the ESI Act as the minimum that can be provided to the employees. Without this security, the organization will not be able to harness the full potential of the human resources that it employs.

10.3 Maternity Benefit Act, 1961

Prior to the enactment of the Maternity Benefit Act of 1961, there were in force several central and state maternity benefit Acts in the country. However, there was no uniformity in their provisions for all women workers in the country. It is true that its object was achieved by the enactment of the Employees' State Insurance Act, 1948, which superseded the provisions of several Maternity Benefit Acts. But the ESI did not cover all women workers in the country. The Maternity Benefit Act of 1961 was, therefore, passed to provide uniform maternity benefit for women workers in certain industries not covered by the Employees' State Insurance Act, 1948. The Act is amended by the Amendment Act No. 29 of 1995. The Amendment Act has come into force with effect from 1 February 1996.

10.3.1 Objectives

1. To provide for maternity benefit to women workers in certain establishments
2. To regulate the employment of women workers in such establishments for a certain period before and after child birth

10.3.2 Coverage

The Act extends to the whole of India and is applicable to:

- Every factory, mine or plantation (including those belonging to the government)
- An establishment engaged in the exhibition of equestrian, acrobatic and other performances, irrespective of the number of employees
- To every shop or establishment wherein 10 or more persons are employed or were employed on any day of the preceding 12 months.

The state government may extend the Act to any other establishment or class or establishments; industrial, commercial, agricultural or otherwise. However, the Act does not apply to any such factory/other establishments to which the provisions of the Employees' State Insurance Act are applicable. But, where the factory/establishment is governed under the Employees' State Insurance Act, and the woman employee is not qualified to claim maternity benefit under Section 50 of that Act, because her wages exceed the stipulated amount, such women will be covered under the provisions of Maternity Benefit Act.

> The Maternity Benefit Act, 1961 was enacted after the enactment of the ESI Act, 1948. Prior to this enactment, there were several such enactments from different state governments and the central government. The Enactment of 1961 brought uniformity in such provisions and also sought to provide coverage to women left outside the coverage of ESI Act, 1948.

10.3.3 Provisions

CONDITIONS AND ELIGIBILITY

- Ten weeks before the date of her expected delivery, she may ask the employer to give her light work for a month. At that time, she should produce a certificate that she is pregnant.
- She should give written notice to the employer about seven weeks before the date of her delivery that she will be absent for six weeks before and after her delivery. She

should also name the person to whom payment will be made in case she cannot take it herself.

- She should take the payment for the first six weeks before she goes on leave. She will get payment for the 6 weeks after child-birth within 48 hours of giving proof that she has had a child.
- A woman worker is eligible for maternity benefit when she is expecting a child and has worked for her employer for at least 80 days in the 12 months immediately preceding the date of her expected delivery
- The maximum period for which any woman shall be entitled to maternity benefit shall be 12 weeks in all, whether taken before or after childbirth. However she cannot take the benefit for more than six weeks before her expected delivery.

Prior to the amendment of 1989, a woman employee could not avail of the six weeks' leave preceding the date of her delivery; she was entitled to only six weeks' leave following the day of her delivery. However, by the above amendment, the position has changed. Now, in case a woman employee does not avail of 6 weeks' leave preceding the date of her delivery, she can avail of that leave following her delivery, provided the total leave period, i.e. preceding and following the day of her delivery does not exceed 12 weeks.

CASH BENEFITS

- Leave with average pay for six weeks before the delivery
- Leave with average pay for six weeks after the delivery
- A medical bonus of INR 250 if the employer does not provide free medical care to the woman. This was later amended to INR 1,000 with a proviso that the government can periodically increase it periodically subject to an ultimate limit of INR 20,000.
- An additional leave with pay up to one month if the woman shows proof of illness due to the pregnancy, delivery, miscarriage or premature birth
- In case of miscarriage, six weeks leave with average pay from the date of miscarriage

NON-CASH BENEFITS/PRIVILEGE

- Light work for ten weeks (six weeks plus one month) before the date of her expected delivery, if she asks for it
- Two nursing breaks in the course of her daily work until the child is 15 months old
- No discharge or dismissal while she is on maternity leave
- No change to her disadvantage in any of the conditions of her employment while on maternity leave
- Pregnant women discharged or dismissed may still claim maternity benefit from the employer

Exception: Women dismissed for gross misconduct lose their right under the Act for Maternity Benefit

LEAVE FOR MISCARRIAGE AND TUBECTOMY OPERATION

- Leave with wages at the rate of maternity benefit, for a period of six weeks immediately following the day of her miscarriage or her medical termination of pregnancy
- Entitled to leave with wages at the rate of maternity benefit for a period of two weeks immediately following the day of her tubectomy operation

10.4 The Workmen's Compensation Act, 1923

The Workmen's Compensation Act is the first piece of legislation towards social security. It deals with compensation for workers who are injured in the course of duty. The scheme of the Workmen's Compensation Act is not to compensate the worker in lieu of wages. The general principle is that a worker who suffers an injury in the course of his employment, which results in a disablement, should be entitled to compensation and in the case of a fatal injury, his dependants should be compensated. Under the Workmen's Compensation Act, it is the employer who is responsible to pay compensation (as opposed to the Employees' State Insurance. For those establishments to which the Employees' State Insurance Act applies, the liability to pay compensation is on the ESI Corporation).

The meaning of "compensation" in this Act is limited to compensation granted under the Act for employment injuries sustained during the course of work. It is also limited to specifically monetary compensation other than a salary, travel allowance, and any other form of remuneration that could be paid under normal circumstances of employment. To get an overall understanding of the Act, it is useful to look at the "Statement of Objects and Reasons" published with the Act when it was first passed in 1923. To quote, "... the growing complexity of industry in this country with the increasing use of the machinery and consequent danger to workmen, along with the comparative poverty to workmen themselves renders it advisable that they should be protected, as far as possible from hardship arising out of accidents. An additional advantage of a legislation of this type is that by increasing the importance for employers of adequate safety devises, it reduces the number of accidents to workmen in a manner that cannot be achieved by official inspection. Further, the encouragement given to employers to provide adequate medical treatment for their workmen should mitigate the effects of such accidents as does occur. The benefits so conferred added to the increased sense of security, which he will enjoy, should render industrial life more attractive and thus increase the available supply of labour. At the same time, a corresponding increase in the efficiency of the average workmen may be expected."[1]

While these were the official objects and reasons, the reality in India today is that the protection offered by the Act does not act as an incentive for workers, most of whom are unaware of it and who simply join work to earn a livelihood. At the time the framing of the bill, two criteria were followed in determining whom the Act would apply to:[1]

1. Those industries that were more or less organized
2. Workmen whose occupations were hazardous

Nowadays, the government (state or central) may extend the application of this Act to other establishments of an industry that may not be organized.

10.4.1 Scope and Coverage

The Act extends to the whole of India.

ESTABLISHMENTS COVERED. All establishments hiring 20 workers and above must compulsorily register themselves under the Employees' State Insurance Act (ESI Act). The Workmen's Compensation Act is applicable only to those establishments that do not come within the purview of the ESI Act.

Also, if employers fail to register themselves under the ESI Act, they will be held responsible to pay compensation under the Workmen's Compensation Act.

However, the Workmen's Compensation Act will only apply to those persons considered "workers" and those considered "employers", as defined under the Act.

ELIGIBILITY. The Act will apply only to persons recognized as a "workman" under the Act.

However, with amendment to the Act in the year 2000, the eligibility has been made more inclusive. In addition, various judicial rulings have forever been expanding the people who are eligible to claim benefits under the Act. The following list would give an indication of the eligibility:

- The only requirement is that the worker should be employed in an activity, which has to be either listed in schedule II of the Act, *or* any duty having connection with the specified activity mentioned in the schedule.
- Schedule III of the Act contains a list of diseases and persons in occupations where infection is possible. They can claim compensation under this Act. They are "workmen" for the purposes of this Act.
- In addition to persons employed in the capacity mentioned in Schedule II, a driver, a mechanic, cleaner, or person employed in any other capacity in connection with a motor vehicle are also considered "workers" under this Act.
- In case a part of the work of an establishment is contracted out to a contractor, and a worker employed by the contractor for this purpose is injured, then the principal employer and not the contractor (who is the worker's immediate employer) is responsible to pay compensation as though the worker was directly employed by him. However, this principal employer holds the right to be indemnified by the person who would normally pay for the compensation of an injured/deceased worker, i.e., the contractor.

The Employer: Defined in this Act as a body of person/s whom the worker has entered into a contract of apprenticeship or service with, the term "employer" also extends to his agent, legal representative of a dead employer, or a temporary employer on to whom the worker has been lent on hire basis.

EMPLOYER'S LIABILITY FOR COMPENSATION. As per Section 3 of the Act, the employer is liable to pay compensation if the worker is injured by an accident that:

1. Arises out of (i.e., while engaged in) work
2. Occurs in the course of his employment (i.e., during work hours)
3. Causes an injury that results in disablement of the worker

If these three conditions are met, the employer of an establishment covered by the Act is bound to pay compensation. While the second condition is easy to prove, the first condition has been difficult to establish in certain cases. (See Box 10.1.)

BOX 10.1 **FOR CLASS DISCUSSION**

A bus was on its last trip for the day. Some assailants entered the bus, sprayed chilli powder on the passengers and shot the conductor dead. It occurred during work hours, but could such an act be termed as an injury "arising out of the course of work"?

In this particular case, it was argued—successfully—that such an incident is a contingency that can arise during the course of duty. The occupants were exposed to that particular risk by reason of their employment.

The above argument could be extended to almost all situations where the workman was present, either at the workplace, or during duty hours, or both. What, then, could be the purpose of laying down the three conditions when the interpretation could be so broad as to defeat the very purpose of defining the same?

DISABLEMENT. The definition of "disablement" is very important in this Act, as it determines the extent of compensation that can be claimed by the worker injured in the course of his employment.

Under the Act, there are four types of eventualities, which can be compensated:

1. **Death**
2. **Permanent Total Disablement:** Disablement that incapacitates a worker from all kinds of work
3. **Permanent Partial Disablement:** Disablement that reduces the capacity to work in any employment similar to that the worker was performing at the time of the accident
4. **Temporary Disablement:** This may be total or partial disablement, of temporary nature, which reduces the earning capacity of the worker in any similar employment for the period of disablement.

Figure 10.2 presents a schematic representation of the various kinds of injuries (including death) defined in the Act. (Also see Box 10.2.)

Total disability (i.e. 100 per cent disability) has a different meaning under the Workmen's Compensation Act as compared to its meaning in normal language. According to the Act, disability is determined with reference to the work that the worker was doing immediately before accident took place, and if the resulting injury leaves him incapable of performing any work of a similar nature, then his disability is considered as 100 per cent.

If the injury suffered by the worker produces a disease, which aggravates a pre-existing disease thereby causing a death or disability, it is still compensable (i.e. compensation can be paid).

The employer cannot defend himself by saying that the worker already had an existing disease. For example, a worker has a pre-existing heart condition, which due to the strain or over exertion of work causes his death, the employer is still liable to pay compensation. All that is required is that the accident suffered during the course of and arising out of the work immediately led to his death injury. In legal terminology, the injury suffered by the workmen at work should be the "proximate cause" of his death, or that there should be a "close causal connection" between the accident and the injury.

COMPENSATION NOT PAYABLE. An employer is not liable to pay compensation under following circumstances:

1. Where the disablement does not last for more than three days
2. Where the disablement has arisen out of the following:
   a) Drugs or drink
   b) Disobedience
   c) Disregard for the safety measures prescribed

Figure 10.2

Classification of injuries (including death).

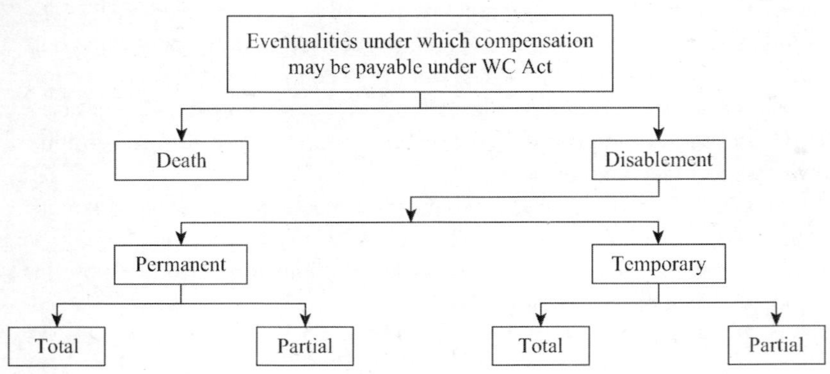

BOX 10.2 FOR CLASS DISCUSSION

Discuss as to the nature of the following kinds of disablements:

Manmohan, a machinist in an engineering shop, got his fingers cut off by accident. This injury has reduced his capacity to work in any such employment.

Gursharan is a helper with the public-health-engineering department. While cleaning an overhead tank, he slipped and fell, fracturing his hand. He could not work for one month.

Binu George lost both his eyesight and his legs when the bus that he was driving met with an accident. He can no longer work as a driver or do any work of a similar nature.

An accident left a worker—a porter—with a defect in his leg, making him incapable of performing his work as a porter. He could, however, do some other work.

The grey area in this section is that there is no definition whatsoever that defines what is "drink", "drugs", "disobedience" or "disregard to safety measures". The employers may take advantage of this section and evade paying the compensation. However, being under the influence of drugs or alcohol is not a defence in the case of death or total disablement resulting from injury. Second, in the case of disobedience, such disobedience should be "wilful".

OCCUPATIONAL DISEASE. An occupational disease, while in service, is a disease that inflicts workers in that particular occupation in which s/he was employed in and resulting from exposure to a hazardous working atmosphere, particular to that employment. If a worker contracts such a disease, then the employer is liable to pay compensation, provided that the worker was employed by him for a continuous period of six months.

An occupational disease that is contracted in the course of employment will fall within the meaning of an "accident" for the purposes of this Act. In the case of such a disease being contracted, the employer will be liable to pay compensation to the affected worker.

The occupational diseases for which compensation is payable are specified in a list attached to the Act—specifically, Part A of Schedule III.

Some examples of occupational diseases are as follows:

- Skin diseases caused by physical, chemical or biological agents
- Bronchopulmonary disease caused by flax, hemp and sisal dust (Byssinosis)
- Occupational asthma caused by recognized sensitizing agents inherent to the work process

10.4.2 Compensation

The compensation to be paid by the employer for injuries caused depends on the extent of the disablement suffered by the worker; more severe disablements naturally receive higher compensation. The guiding principle in the payment of compensation is: the higher the age of the injured worker, the lower the compensation. Compensation, and its payment, thereof, has been categorized as under:

1. Death
2. Disablement
    a) Permanent total disablement
    b) Permanent partial disablement
    c) Temporary disablement:
        i) Temporary total disablement
        ii) Temporary partial disablement

THE BASIS OF CALCULATION. Wages are the basis for the amount of compensation paid. Two workers earning different salaries, therefore, will get different amounts of compensation even though the injury they suffered might be identical. Compensation under this Act is calculated on the basis of the monthly wage received by the worker. According to this Act, it is the amount of wages that would be payable for a month's service, i.e., irrespective of whether the worker is paid on a daily, weekly or piece-rate basis.

Wages: The term "wage" is defined as the privilege or benefit that is measurable in terms of either money, other than any travel allowance, or provident fund or any other special benefit claimable by the worker, during the course of his employment.

DEPENDANT. A "dependant" is defined under the Act in Section 2(d). This definition is of vital value as it determines who will be eligible to receive the compensation, in case the worker dies in the course of his employment.

QUANTUM OF COMPENSATION. The Act prescribes the manner in which "compensation" is to be computed and paid in the event of death or disablement resulting from accidents arising out of and in the course of employment.

Death: In case of death of an employee, the compensation due to the dependants is an amount equal to 50 per cent of the monthly salary of the deceased worker multiplied by the relevant factor or an amount of INR 80,000, whichever is more. The minimum compensation in the case of death in no circumstances can be less than INR 80,000.

The *relevant factor* is mentioned in the Schedule IV of the Act. The factor depends on the age of the deceased person, i.e., the number of years the person could have worked for, if he did not die on the job. Box 10.3 illustrates how the compensation is calculated in case of the death of an employee.

PERMANENT TOTAL DISABLEMENT. Where there is total permanent disablement resulting from the injury suffered, the worker is entitled to be paid 60 per cent of his monthly salary, multiplied by the relevant factor, or an amount of INR 90,000, whichever is more. The minimum compensation in the case of total permanent disablement cannot be less than INR 90,000. Box 10.4 illustrates the computation of the compensation payable to an employee in case of permanent total disability.

Permanent Partial Disablement: In the case of partial disablement of the worker, the amount he is entitled to is the percentage of that for total permanent disablement, the

BOX 10.3 **COMPENSATION IN CASE OF DEATH**

Thirty-five-year-old Budhan Majhi, a fitter in a State-owned steel plant, met with an accident and died while at work (i.e., in the course of employment). At the time of his death, he drew a monthly wage of INR8,000. As per Schedule IV of the Act, the relevant factor applicable to his case would be 197.06. Thus, the amount of compensation payable to his dependants will be arrived at in the following way:

i) 50 per cent of the current salary = INR 4,000
ii) Total compensation payable = 50 per cent of current salary × relevant factor
= 2000* × 197.06
= INR 3,04,120

**Where the monthly wage of a worker is more than INR 4,000, it is taken to be only INR 4,000 for calculating compensation in the case of either death or permanent disablement. In this case, therefore, even though the basic pay was INR 8,000 per month, for the purpose of computing compensation, it has been reckoned as INR 4,000 (maximum permissible under the Act) and 50 per cent of INR 4,000 is INR 2,000.*

BOX 10.4 COMPENSATION IN CASE OF PERMANENT TOTAL DISABILITY

Laldhari Mahato, a rigger of 35 years of age, meets with an accident and suffers permanent total disablement while at work (i.e., in the course of employment). At the time, he drew a monthly wage of INR 3,500. As per Schedule IV of the Act, the relevant factor applicable to his case would be 197.06. The amount of compensation payable will be arrived at as follows:

i) 60 per cent of the current salary = INR 2,100
ii) Total compensation payable = 2,100 × 197.06
= 4,13,826

percentage being given in the schedule of the Act. Schedule I, Part II, to the Act contains a list of injuries said to result in permanent partial disablement and the corresponding loss in earning capacity. Table 10.3 highlights the loss of earning capacity for various types of injuries.

The compensation is calculated on the lines given in Box 10.2 for permanent total disablement, substituting the percentage of disability suffered and the appropriate "relevant factor" obtained from Schedule IV, as per the age of the concerned worker. For example, had the worker needed "amputation through the shoulder joint", loss in his earning capacity would have been to the extent of 90 per cent. The compensation in this case would have to be computed as under:

Compensation for partial permanent disability = 90 per cent of (compensation for total permanent disability) = 90 per cent of (60 per cent × salary × relevant factor) = 90 per cent of INR 413,826.

Temporary Disablement: In case of temporary disablement, payments equal to 25 per cent of the workers' wages shall be made at fortnightly intervals. In case the disablement lasts for more than 28 days, the employer should make the payment on the 16th day from the day of the disablement.

If the period of disablement lasts for less than 28 days, the payment shall be made after the expiry of 3 days. This wait for 3 days is to ascertain how long the temporary disablement will last—less than/equal to 28 days or more.

In case the employer makes any payment to the worker before the payment of this half-monthly or lump sum amount, it shall be deducted from this. This provision envisages a situation where an application is made when the worker is still undergoing treatment and recovering.

In the case of temporary disablement, where half-monthly wages is to be paid, there is provision for review of such amount, by the commissioner. Either party, supported by an attested certificate of a medical examiner, can apply for the review to the commissioner.

The review might lead to the increase, decrease or the end of the half-monthly wages, depending on the condition of the worker. In case the temporary disablement leads to a permanent disablement, then the review has the power to call for the lump sum compensation to be paid to the worker. The lump sum the worker is entitled to excludes any amount that s/he has already received in half-monthly payments.

Table 10.3

The loss of earning capacity in case of permanent partial disablement.

Description of Injury	Per cent Loss of Earning Capacity
Amputation through the shoulder joint	90
Loss of all toes of one foot through a metatarsophalangeal joint	20
Loss of one eye, without complications, the other being normal	40

NOTICE OF ACCIDENT TO THE EMPLOYER. In the case of an accident or an accident leading to death, a notice must be sent to the employer or any other person who is employed to supervise work in the same establishment as soon as is practicable after the occurrence of the accident.

The notice from the aggrieved party can be served to the employers either by sending the notice by registered post to the residence or the office of the employer, or by entering such notice into the notice book, maintained at the premises of the office.

THE COMMISSIONER'S POWER IN CASE OF AN ACCIDENT RESULTING IN DEATH. Anyone can report to the labour commissioner in case of a worker being killed in an accident. If the employer feels that he is responsible to do so, he must deposit the compensation with the commissioner within 30 days after the notice is served. If he does not feel so, he must inform the commissioner of the grounds under which he claims such exemption. On claiming such exemption, the commissioner may inform the dependants of the deceased worker, leaving it open to them, whether they would want to claim compensation or not.

In case the commissioner is aware of a fatal accident, he has the power to send a notice to the employer (i.e., without receiving any application), requiring him to submit a statement within a month's time.

10.5 The Payment of Gratuity Act, 1972

It is a beneficient piece of social-security legislation that aims at providing a scheme for providing gratuity to employees engaged in factories, mines, oil fields, plantations, ports, railways, shops and other establishments. The gratuity was to be paid in the event of superannuation, retirement, resignation, death or total disablement due to accident or disease.

10.5.1 Scope, Coverage and Definitions

The main purpose of the Payment of Gratuity Act is to provide a sum of payment to an employee as a token of gratitude for having served the organization. This payment is intended to help the employee provide for his/her needs after severance of his/her relationship with the employer.

An employee is eligible for receiving gratuity payment only after s/he has completed five years of continuous service. S/he is said to be in continuous service, when s/he has provided uninterrupted service during that period, till his/her:

- Superannuation, or
- Retirement, or
  resignation, or
- Death or disablement due to accident or disease.

This condition of five years is not necessary if the termination of the employment of an employee is due to death or disablement. However, interruption on account of sickness, accident, leave, lay-off, strike, lockout, cessation of work not due to any fault of the employee will not be considered as a break in service (Section 4).

Employee: Any person (other than an apprentice) employed on wages, in any establishment, factory, mine, oilfield, plantation, port, railway company or shop, to do any skilled, semi-skilled, or unskilled, manual, supervisory, technical or clerical work, whether the terms of such employment are express or implied, and whether or not such person is employed in a managerial or administrative capacity; but does not include any such person who holds a post under the central government or a state government, and is governed by any other Act or by any rules providing for payment of gratuity.

Retirement: Termination of the service of an employee otherwise than on superannuation

Superannuation: In relation to an employee, it means the attainment by the employee of such age as is fixed in the contract or conditions of service on the attainment of which the employee shall vacate the employment

In case of death or disablement, there is no minimum eligibility period. The amount of gratuity payable shall be at the rate of 15 days' wages based on the rate of wages last drawn, for every completed year of service. The maximum amount of gratuity payable is INR 3,50,000.
Wages: Under this Act, it means all emoluments that are earned by an employee (in cash) while on duty or on leave in accordance with the terms and conditions of his employment. It includes dearness allowance but does not include any bonus, commission or house rent.

10.5.2 The Calculation of Gratuity

For every completed year of service, or part thereof, in excess of six months, the employer shall pay gratuity to an employee at the rate of 15 days' wages based on the rate of wages last drawn by the employee concerned. Further, a month will be taken to comprise 26 days, i.e., 30 days in a month adjusted for 4 weekly offs.

In the case of a piece-rated employee, daily wages shall be computed on the average of the total wages received by him for a period of three months immediately preceding the termination of his employment, and, for this purpose, the wages paid for any overtime work shall not be taken into account.

The amount of gratuity payable to an employee shall not exceed INR 3,50,000.

For the purpose of computing the gratuity payable to an employee who is employed, after his disablement, on reduced wages, his wages for the period preceding his disablement shall be taken to be the wages received by him during that period, and his wages for the period subsequent to his disablement shall be taken to be the wages as so reduced.

Nothing in this section shall affect the right of an employee to receive better terms of gratuity under any award or agreement or contract with the employer.

An example of gratuity calculation under the Act is given in Box 10.5.

10.5.3 Gratuity Not Payable

The gratuity of an employee, whose services have been terminated for any act, wilful omission or negligence causing any damage or loss to, or destruction of, property belonging to the employer, shall be forfeited to the extent of the damage or loss so caused.

The gratuity payable to an employee may be wholly or partially forfeited if:

i) The services of the employee have been terminated for his riotous or disorderly conduct or any other act of violence on his part, or

ii) The services of the employee have been terminated for any act, which constitutes an offence involving moral turpitude, provided that such offence is committed by him in the course of his employment.

BOX 10.5 **THE CALCULATION OF GRATUITY**

Dattatreya Bakshi joined the National Bank as a teller on 22 August 1975. On attaining the age of superannuation on 31 December 2008, he was released from the services of the bank. On the date of his superannuation, his basic pay, as an accountant, was INR 11,500 and his dearness allowance was INR 3,700. His gratuity was calculated as follows:

Monthly wage = INR 11,500 + INR 3,700 = INR 15,200
Completed years of service = 33
Gratuity = 15 days of wage for every completed year of service
Gratuity payable = INR 15,200 × 15/26 × 33 = INR 2,89,385

Note:

i) The factor 15/26 means 15 days' wage in a month comprising 26 working days (i.e. 30 days less 4 weekly off days).

ii) Maximum gratuity payable as per the Act is INR 3,50,000. However, if the employer so desires, the maximum limit can be raised by him.

10.5.4 Obligations of the Employer

a) The employer is usually required to submit a notice of opening of an establishment to the controlling authority of the area in Form A containing names and addresses of the establishment, employer, number of persons employed, nature of business, etc.

b) The employer shall display conspicuously a notice at or near the main entrance of the establishment in bold letters in English and in a language understood by the majority of employees.

c) It is the duty of the employer to determine the amount of gratuity as soon as it becomes payable. Failure to do so shall render him liable to pay the interest at the prevailing rate from the time taken.

d) The employer should obtain insurance in the prescribed manner for his liability for the payment of gratuity under the Act or establish approved gratuity fund in the prescribed manner.

10.5.5 The Process for Receiving Payment

1. A person who is eligible for payment of gratuity under this Act or any person authorized, in writing, to act on his behalf shall send a written application to the employer, for the payment of gratuity.
2. As soon as gratuity becomes payable, the employer shall, whether an application has been made or not, determine the amount of gratuity and give notice in writing to the person to whom the gratuity is payable and also to the controlling authority specifying the amount of gratuity so determined.
3. The employer shall arrange to pay the amount of gratuity within 30 days from the date it becomes payable to the person to whom the gratuity is payable. If the amount of gratuity payable under Sub-section (3) is not paid by the employer within the period specified in Sub-section (3), the employer shall pay, from the date on which the gratuity becomes payable to the date on which it is paid, simple interest at a rate not exceeding the rate notified by the central government from time to time for repayment of long-term deposits. No such interest shall be payable if the delay in the payment is due to the fault of the employee and the employer has obtained permission in writing from the controlling authority for the delayed payment on this ground.

10.6 Employees' Provident Funds and Miscellaneous Provisions Act, 1952

The Employees' Provident Funds and Miscellaneous Provisions Act, 1952 was enacted to provide a kind of social security to the industrial workers. It purports to be a social measure, inducing employees to save a portion from their present earning for future.

10.6.1 Objectives

The Employees' Provident Funds and Miscellaneous Provisions Act mainly provides retirement or old-age benefits, such as provident fund, superannuation, pension, invalidation pension, family pension and deposit linked insurance.

Provision for terminal benefit of restricted nature was made in the Industrial Disputes Act, 1947, in the form of payment of retrenchment compensation. But this benefit is not available to a worker on retirement, on reaching the age of superannuation or voluntary retirement.

The Employees' Provident Funds and Miscellaneous Provisions Act is intended to provide wider terminal benefits to the industrial workers. For example, the Act provides for payment of terminal benefit on reaching the age of superannuation, voluntary retirement and retirement due to incapacity to work. In industrially advanced nations, provisions have been made for old age and survivor's pension. Due to prevailing conditions in India at the time of enactment, institution of a pension scheme along the above lines was thought to be not feasible. The Workmen's Compensation and ESI Acts did not cover normal superannuation. Any kind of gratuity scheme that depended solely on the employer would generate too meagre an amount for any long-term relief. Under the circumstances, the EPF& MP Act (1952) was thought to be most appropriate as it would institute compulsory and contributory fund in which both the employer and the employee would contribute. The fund was thought to also promote a habit of savings amongst employees.

10.6.2 Scope and Coverage

The Act extends to the whole of India, except the state of Jammu and Kashmir.

It applies to every establishment of the following nature:

- A factory engaged in any industry specified in Schedule I (of this Act) and in which 20 or more persons are employed
- Any other establishment employing 20 or more persons or class of such establishments which the central government may, by notification in the official gazette, specify in this behalf

Employees employed through a contractor in such establishments are also covered.

The central government may, through notification in the gazette, bring any establishment, or a class of establishments, that employ 20 or more persons under the Act.

Once the Act applies to any establishment, it continues to be applicable even if the number of employees falls below 20 subsequently. There is no provision in the Act that deals with the cessation of its application.

Section 16 of the Act exempts certain establishments from the application of this Act. These are:

- An establishment registered under the Co-Operative Societies Act, 1912 employing less than 50 workers and without the aid of power
- Any establishment belonging to or under the control of the central government or a state government or establishments set up under a state or central Act and whose employees are entitled to the benefits of contributory provident fund or old-age pension in accordance with a rule framed by the respective government or the Act creating the establishment
- Any newly set up establishment, from the date of set up to three years therefrom.

Section 17 of the Act empowers the appropriate government to exempt certain establishments from the provisions of this Act provided, in its opinion, the provisions of the rules of a similar scheme within the organization (rates of contribution, etc.) are not less favourable than those provided for in the Act.

10.6.3 Definitions

A few important definitions in the Act will be useful to our understanding of the main provisions:

Establishment: A factory engaged in any industry specified in Schedule 1 (of the Act) and in which 20 or more persons are employed. Any other establishment employing 20 or more persons that the central government may, by notification, specify in this behalf. Any establishment employing even less than 20 persons can be covered voluntarily under Section 1(4) of the Act.

Basic Wages: All emoluments that are earned by an employee while on duty or on leave or on holidays with wages in either case in accordance with the terms of the contract of employment and which are paid or payable in cash to him but does not include :

i) The cash value of any food concession

ii) Any dearness allowance (that is to say all cash payments by whatever name called paid to an employee on account of a rise in the cost of living), house-rent allowance, overtime allowance, bonus commission or any other similar allowance payable to the employee in respect of his/her employment or of work done in such employment

iii) Any presents made by the employer

Contribution: A contribution payable in respect of a member under a scheme or the contribution payable in respect of an employee to whom the insurance scheme applies
Employee: Any person who is employed for wages in any kind of work, manual or otherwise, in or in connection with the work of an establishment and who gets his wages directly or indirectly from the employer and includes any person

i) employed by or through a contractor in or in connection with the work of the establishment;

ii) engaged as an apprentice (but not as an apprentice as defined under the Apprentices Act, 1961 or under the standing orders of the establishment)

Superannuation: In relation to an employee who is a member of the Pension Scheme, it means the attainment by the said employee of the age of 58 years.

10.6.4 Provisions

Section 5 of the Act empowers the central government to create an Employee Provident Fund Scheme for the establishment of the fund. The Act provides for three schemes, namely:

- EPF (Employee Provident Fund Scheme, 1952)
- EPS & F (Employee Pension Scheme and Fund, 1995)
- EDLI (Employees Deposit Linked Insurance Scheme and Fund, 1976)

Sections 6, 6A and 6C make provisions for the rates of contributions to the Provident Fund, the Pension Fund and the Employee Deposit Linked Insurance (EDLI). Various sub-sections of Section 5 provide for the administrative wherewithal for the administration and institutional framework for the schemes.

THE PAYMENT OF CONTRIBUTION. The Act is applicable to employees of establishments covered by the Act whose wage is INR 6,500 per month or below. However, employees with wage more than this ceiling may also join the scheme if the employees and the employer agree and with the approval of the government (PF Commissioner or an officer so authorized in this regard).

- The employer shall pay the contribution payable to the EPF, EDLI and Employees' Pension Fund in respect of the member of the Employees' Pension Fund employed by him directly by or through a contractor.
- It shall be the responsibility of the principal employer to pay the contributions payable to the EPF, EDLI and Employees' Pension Fund by himself in respect of the employees directly employed by him and also in respect of the employees employed by or through a contractor.
- Over the years, there have been many amendments to the Act and currently, contributions under various schemes stand as under the following heads:
- **Provident Fund:**

  For most of the establishments, the rate of contribution has been raised to 12 per cent of wages, i.e.,

  Employee contribution = 12 per cent

Let us suppose the wage of an employee is INR 6,200. His contribution to PF, therefore, would be 12 per cent of INR 6,200, i.e., INR 744. The employer's contribution, too, would be INR 744. However, if an employee with wage of INR 8,000 has voluntarily joined the scheme, the contribution from both will be INR 960 each.

An employee can voluntarily contribute more than 12 per cent to the fund, but the employer's contribution shall remain limited to 12 per cent of wage.

- **Pension Fund:**

  Employee contribution = Nil

  Employer's contribution = 8.33 per cent out of the 12 per cent contribution of employer made to the provident fund (calculated with a maximum wage ceiling of INR 6,500) shall be transferred to this fund. The balance 3.67 per cent remains with the provident fund.

  For example, in the above example, the employer's total contribution to PF was INR 744. Therefore, 8.33 per cent of INR 6,200, i.e., INR 517 gets diverted to the pension fund, whereas the balance 3.67 per cent (12 – 8.33), i.e., INR 227 remains with the provident fund.

  In addition, the government contributes up to 1.16 per cent of wage (up to a maximum wage limit of INR 6,500) to the pension fund.

- **Employee Deposit Linked Insurance Fund:**

  There is no contribution from the employee in this fund. The employer must contribute 0.5 per cent on the wage (subject to a maximum wage ceiling of INR 6,500) to the fund and another 0.01 per cent as administrative expenses for running the scheme.

BENEFITS UNDER THE SCHEMES. These are schemes under social security and, hence, the benefits under the scheme focus on providing sustenance during old age or an eventuality when the earning capacity diminishes or ceases.

Provident Fund Scheme: An account of each contributing member is maintained by the PF Organization. Interest is calculated on the basis of the rate declared every year by the central government in consultation with the Board of Trustees. The fund with accruing interest becomes payable at the time of superannuation or death.

Pension Fund Scheme: Provides for members to avail of pension on superannuation or retirement and on disablement.

EDLI: EDLI provides life-insurance benefits to employees who are members of the Provident Fund Scheme.

PENAL PROVISIONS. For violating certain provisions of this Act, an employer is liable to be arrested without warrants.

Defaults by the employer in paying contributions or inspection/administrative charges attract imprisonment up to three years and fines up to INR. 10,000.

For any retrospective application, all dues have to be paid by the employer with damages up to 100 per cent of arrears.

SUMMARY

Employees' State Insurance Act:

- Employees' State Insurance Corporation (ESIC) was constituted under the Employees' State Insurance Act, 1948, and Employees' State Insurance (Central) Rules, 1950.
- The Act is applicable to all factories including those under the government other than seasonal factories.
- The Act was intended to provide certain benefits to employees in case of sickness, maternity and "employment injury" and to make provisions for certain other matters in relevant thereto.
- The ESI schemes through its hospitals and clinics have provided curative healthcare to workers all over India and have recently entered the area of occupational health.

- The ESI scheme is administered by the ESIC, an autonomous body that consists of Minister for Labour, Ministry of Health, five representatives of the central government, one representative each from the states and one representative from all the union territories, five representatives of employees and five of employers, two of medical profession and three Members of Parliament, and the Director General of Corporation.
- The ESI Corporation's main function is to frame policies.
- The benefits under the ESI Act include:
  - **Sickness Benefit:** At the rate of 7/12th of the daily average wage, benefit is given to the employee for a maximum period of 91 days in one year. In diseases such as tuberculosis, leprosy, fracture and malignancy, the sickness benefits are extended to one year at half the rate of sickness benefits.
  - **Maternity Benefit:** The benefit is given at the rate of full wages for a period of 84 days in case of pregnancy and 6 weeks in case of miscarriage or MTP.
  - **Disablement Benefit:** In cash, 72 per cent of the wages is given to the temporary disabled person during the period of disablement. In case of permanent disablement, the payment is made at the same rate for the whole of his life in the form of pension.
  - **Dependent Benefit:** Widow or legitimate or adopted child (up to the age of 18 years or till the daughter gets married) of the diseased person gets the cash payment may be in the form of pension.
  - **Funeral Benefit:** An amount of INR 2,500 is paid to the eldest surviving member for the funeral purpose.
  - **Medical Benefit:** All members of the worker gets the medical cover including the outdoor treatment, domiciliary treatment facilities by the panel system, specialist services, ambulance services, and indoor services.

The Maternity Benefit Act:

- This Act is a central legislation, which provides maternity benefits and is applicable to factories covered under the Factories Act, 1948.
- It also applies to shops and establishments in which 10 or more workers are employed or were employed on any day of the preceding 12 months.
- The provisions of this Act do not apply to any factory or establishment to which the provisions of Employee State Insurance Act, 1948 apply.
- The main provisions of the Act are as follows:
  - No employer shall knowingly employ a woman in any establishment during the six weeks immediately following the day of her delivery or her miscarriage. Also, no woman shall work in any establishment during the six weeks immediately following the day of her delivery or her miscarriage.
  - Every woman shall be entitled to, and her employer shall be liable for, the payment of maternity benefit at the rate of the average daily wage for the period of her actual absence immediately preceding and including the day of her delivery and for the six weeks immediately following that day. The "average daily wage" means the average of the woman's wages payable to her for the days on which she has worked during the period of three calendar months immediately preceding the date from which she absents herself on account of maternity, or one rupee a day, whichever is higher.
  - No woman shall be entitled to maternity benefit unless she has actually worked in an establishment of the employer from whom she claims maternity benefit, for a period of not less than 160 days in the 12 months immediately preceding the date of her expected delivery.
  - The maximum period for which any woman shall be entitled to maternity benefit shall be 12 weeks, that is to say, not exceeding 6 weeks up to and including the day of her delivery and 6 weeks immediately following that day.
  - No deduction from the normal and usual daily wages of a woman entitled to maternity benefit shall be made by reason only of (i) the nature of work assigned to her by virtue of the provisions of the Act; or (ii) breaks for nursing the child allowed to her under the provisions of the Act.
  - If a woman works in any establishment, after she has been permitted by her employer to make herself absent for any period, during such authorized absence, she shall forfeit her claim to the maternity benefit for such period.

The Workmen's Compensation Act:

- The Workmen's Compensation Act is an act for payment of compensation for injury by accident or occupational disease arising out of and in course of employment.
- It extends to the whole of India.
- Compensation is something that constitutes an equivalent or recompense; specifically payment to an unemployed or injured person or his dependents.
- Section 3 of the Act makes the employer liable to pay compensation for injury caused to a workman by accident arising out of and in the course of his employment.
- The object of the Act is to ensure financial assistance and to relieve the workman and his family members of the hardship they may suffer on account of a personal injury that may be caused to a workman in an accident arising out of and in the course of his employment.

- Any payment or allowance that the workman may have received from the employer towards his medical treatment shall not be deemed to be payment or allowance received by him by way of compensation.
- In case of death, the minimum amount of compensation fixed is INR 80,000 and INR 90,000 in case of permanent total disablement.
- The existing wage ceiling for computation of maximum amount of compensation is INR 4,000.
- Under the Act, the state governments are empowered to appoint commissioners for workmen's compensation for (i) the settlement of disputed claims, (ii) the disposal of cases of injuries involving death, and (iii) the revision of periodical payments.

The Payment of Gratuity Act:

- The Act provides for the payment of gratuity to workers employed in every factory, shop and establishment or educational institution employing 10 or more persons on any day of the proceeding 12 months.
- All the employees irrespective of status or salary are entitled to the payment of gratuity on the completion of five years of service.
- In case of death or disablement, there is no minimum eligibility period.
- Gratuity is payable at the rate of 15 days' wages for every year of completed service or part thereof in excess of 6 months.
- The maximum amount of gratuity payable is INR 3.5 lakhs.
- Any person to whom the gratuity amount is payable shall make a written application to the employer. The employer is required to determine the amount of gratuity payable and give notice in writing to the person to whom the same is payable and to the controlling authority, thereby specifying the amount of gratuity payable.
- The employer is under obligation to pay the gratuity amount within 30 days from the date it becomes payable. Simple interest at a specified rate is payable on the expiry of the said period. If there is a dispute as regards the amount of gratuity payable or with regards the person to whom it is payable, the employer shall deposit the said amount payable with the controlling authority.
- If the gratuity is not paid within the prescribed time, the controlling authority shall, after due inquiry, determine the amount payable and direct the employer to deposit the said amount.
- If an employer agrees to provide more benefits than the benefits flowing from the Act, he can always have a private scheme.
- Gratuity can be forfeited for any employee whose services have been terminated for any act, wilful omission or negligence causing damage or destruction to the property belonging to the employer.
- It can also be forfeited for any act that constitutes an offence involving moral turpitude.
- Where services have not been terminated on any of the above grounds, the employer cannot withhold gratuity due to the employee.

The Employees' Provident Funds and Miscellaneous Provisions Act, 1952:

- A piece of social welfare legislation
- A beneficent measure, enacted for the purpose of institution of provident fund for employees in factories and other establishments.
- It is an effective old-age and survivorship benefit.
- The provisions are intended for a better future of the industrial worker on his retirement and also for his dependants in the event of his death in the course of employment.

KEY TERMS

- confinement 201
- continuous service 212
- contribution 197
- delivery 204
- disablement 195
- employment injury 196
- gratuity 196
- insurable employment 198
- insured person 198
- maternity benefit 202
- occupational disease 199
- permanent partial disablement 199
- permanent total disablement 199
- retirement 195
- sickness 195
- superannuation 201
- temporary disablement 199
- wages 197
- workmen's compensation 206

REVIEW QUESTIONS

1. Which establishments are covered under the ESI Act? Indicate whether the following would be covered: petrol pump, cinema theatre, automobile workshop, casual workers employed for housekeeping in an establishment.
2. Who are required to be insured under the ESI Act? Does the Act apply to an apprentice?
3. What components of wages are covered for ESI contribution? Does conveyance allowance form part of wages within the ambit of Section 2(22) of the Act?
4. Explain the benefits provided under the ESI Act.
5. Is an insured person who ceases to be in an insurable employment on account of permanent disablement eligible to receive any benefits under the Act?
6. Does a conviction of an insured person under the ESI Act disentitle him to any benefits admissible under the Act?
7. Is a retired insured person eligible to receive any benefits under the ESI Act?
8. Can a person, who was not an insured person at the time of his retirement but who remained an insured person at some stage of his employment, claim medical benefits?
9. Is it permissible for any person to draw a benefit of the same kind under the ESI Act and also under any other Act?
10. What are the objectives of the Maternity Benefit Act, 1961?
11. What establishments are covered under the Maternity Benefit Act?
12. Is there any justification for denying the benefits of the Maternity Benefit Act to women workers on the ground that they are not regular employees but they are on the muster roll?
13. What are the restrictions placed by the Maternity Benefit Act on the employment of women?
14. To whom is maternity benefit payable in case of death of a woman?
15. What are the restrictions placed by the Maternity Benefit Act on the termination of employment of a woman?
16. What is the time for payment of maternity benefit?
17. What is the period for which a woman is entitled to maternity benefit and what is the rate of the benefit?
18. Is a woman, who is entitled to maternity benefit, also entitled to any medical bonus?
19. Can a woman claim the maternity benefit from her employer if she works elsewhere during the period for which she has been permitted to make herself absent under the provisions of the Act?
20. Is it permissible under the Act to exempt any establishment for the provisions of the Maternity Benefit Act?
21. Is a woman entitled to any leave with wages for illness in addition to the period of absence allowed to her under the provisions of the Maternity Benefit Act?
22. Is a woman entitled to any leave with wages for miscarriage?
23. Define the following terms used in the Workmen's Compensation Act, 1923:
    a) Partial disablement
    b) Total disablement
    c) Workman
    d) Dependent
24. Define the term "out of and in the course of employment" with examples. If a person has an accident while travelling to work , would it be covered under this definition?
25. How is the amount of compensation payable to an injured workman calculated under the Workmen's Compensation Act, 1923?
26. State the rules regarding the notice of accident for making a claim under the Act.
27. Under what circumstances is an employer not liable to pay compensation under the Workmen's Compensation Act?
28. When is lump sum compensation payable under the Workmen's Compensation Act?
29. Define the following terms as used in the Payment of Gratuity Act , 1972:
    a) Continuous service
    b) Completed year of service
    c) Employee
    d) Employer
30. When does gratuity become payable and what is the basis of the calculation of gratuity?
31. What are the rules regarding nomination by an employee under the Payment of Gratuity Act?
32. What are the rights and obligations of the employers under the Payment of Gratuity Act?
33. Which establishments are covered by the PF&MP Act?
34. Would the PF&MP Act continue to apply to an establishment that has closed its manufacturing activities and does not employ a single employee?
35. Is the PF&MP Act applicable to a factory that is closed down but is employing a few employees to look after the assets of the establishment?
36. Is the PF &MP Act applicable to charitable institutions?

37 Compute the contributions to be made by the employer and the employee (whose wage is INR 7,500) towards provident fund, pension fund and EDLI? Is this employee eligible to be covered under the Act?

QUESTIONS FOR CRITICAL THINKING

1 It is not the intent of the ESI Act but its implementation in terms of medical facilities and treatment available to its members that would fulfil the constitutional provisions of socio-economic justice. Discuss.

2 Do you think the restriction placed on discharge or dismissal of a woman during pregnancy on account of absence is appropriate? Should it prevail irrespective of whether the absence was authorized or unauthorized?

3 In IT and ITES sector, attrition is the highest averaging around 12–13 per cent. Why do you think the social-security cover under the gratuity scheme does not help employers retain talent even for the five-year period that makes an employee eligible for the benefit?

4 Most of the social-security legislations have ceased to be relevant in the new economy. These legislations mostly covered employees in the organized sector, who don't need them. Critically examine the above statement with reference to the coverage and provisions of the major pieces of social-security legislations in India.

5 There is a need for rationalization of various social-security legislations so as to avoid contradictions and duplication. Examine the above with regard to the ESI Act, the Workmen's Compensation Act and the Maternity Benefit Act. Suggest an outline for a coherent legislation covering the provisions of these three Acts.

DEBATE

1 The Workmen's Compensation Act is biased against the employer as it covers accidents beyond the control of the management.

2 In terms of employee relations management, the provision of gratuity is a good retention strategy.

CASE ANALYSIS

Mr Sawant's Liability

Mr Sawant has employed a driver whose wages are reimbursed by the company. Mr Sawant has an Act-only policy covering his private car. While driving the vehicle after dropping Mr Sawant at his office, the vehicle collides with a truck and the driver dies on the spot. Being an old car, Mr Sawant had nothing much to lose and that is why he had not taken a comprehensive policy. However, the family of the driver lost their income source.

Is Mr Sawant liable to pay compensation to the dependants of the driver? Specifically state the relevant provisions of the Act under which he is liable.

If the post-mortem reported an unacceptable level of alcohol in the driver, will Mr Sawant be liable to pay compensation? Why or why not?

The Provident Fund Scheme at Metallica Structurals

Metallica Structurals Private Limited is a company in the construction business. The annual turnover is INR 25 billion and it has 500 employees on its rolls, most of them being engineers and technicians. Due to a competitive market, the firm does its best to retain top talent and, therefore, most of the employees draw fixed salary of more than INR 10,000 per month. The Managing Director, Mr Shashikant, one day, while going through the morning correspondence, saw a letter addressed to him by the Metallica Diploma Engineers' Association. Amongst other things, the letter mentioned a "demand" from its members to become a member of the Provident Fund Scheme. Mr Shashikant remembered having told by a consultant that Metallica was not obliged to make any contributions under provident fund.

Going through the provisions of the relevant Act, can you suggest a line of argument that Mr Shashikant may take while discussing the issue with the Diploma Engineers?

NOTES

1 V. G. Goswami, *Labour and Industrial Law*, eighth edition (Allahabad: Central Law Agency, 2004), p. 384.

chapter eleven

CHAPTER OUTLINE

LEARNING OBJECTIVES

After reading this chapter, you will be able to:

- Appreciate the need for and limitations of wage legislations in India
- List the major pieces of legislations related to wages in India
- Understand the main provisions related to these legislations
- Prepare a check-list for compliance to these provisions

Strike for Higher Bonus

About 1,000 employees of Reliable Industries (RT) working at its plants in Hyderabad threatened to go on strike just before the festival season in September, 2008, demanding a hike in bonus offered by the management. The management had offered INR 33,000 as bonus. All three labour unions affiliated with different political parties gave notice to the management of the company and the Labour Commissioner in this regard. Hydrocarbons Limited was earlier a PSU, but later, the government divested its holding and sold it off to RI, a conglomerate in the hydrocarbons and petrochemicals, and merged with it. Before the merger, the employees worked for the government-owned Hydrocarbons India Limited (HIL). Union leaders said RI's bonus offer of INR 33,000 was not acceptable to them, since the previous year, it was INR 40000.

The unions questioned the Reliable management on fixing different amounts of bonus for employees working in plants located in different parts of the country. Union leaders said the company's (RIL's) profit is more than INR 120 billion. The leaders accused the management of not providing them with production data-sheet and computation sheet despite repeated demand. They said these demands were raised in a meeting between local management of the company and the union leaders the previous month.

The workers have requested RIL management not to deposit any bonus money into their accounts without a discussion and an agreement as to the quantum of bonus.

Wage Legislation

Wages are miserably low and employment too scarce and insecure in the rural and in the unorganized sectors to mitigate poverty and deprivation; while in the organized sector, the wages are rising and employment is secure.

The opening vignette concerning employees threatening to go on strike over bonus issues raises a few questions. What is bonus? Is it a right of the workers? Or is it a form of coercion through industrial action? From where does the right originate? Are all wage earners entitled to a "bonus"? Who decides the "amount" of bonus to be paid? Is it negotiable? Does a loss-making company have an obligation to pay bonus to its employees? Do employees have a right to a portion of profits of the company? In a free market, is there a need for the government to regulate the wages of labour? Why and how could the wages be regulated keeping in mind the capacity of an industry to pay? What is the objective of the State in such regulation?

In answering such questions, we will explore the legislations related to wages and bonus (a contentious issue and frequently in news) in this chapter.

11.1 The History of Wage Legislation

Article 43 of the Constitution of India states "the State shall endeavour to secure by suitable legislation or economic organization or in any other way, to all workers—agricultural, industrial or otherwise, work, a living wage, conditions of work ensuring decent standard of life and full enjoyment of leisure and social and cultural opportunities".

The 15th Indian Labour Conference (1957) resulted in the formulation of the following norms as a guide for all wage-fixing authorities, including minimum wage committees, wage boards, and judicatures:

In calculating the minimum wage, the standard working-class family should be taken to comprise three consumption units for one earner; the earnings of women, children and adolescents should be disregarded.

i) Minimum food requirements should be calculated on the basis of a net intake of 2,700 calories.

ii) Clothing requirements should be estimated at a per capita consumption of 18 yards, which would give for the average worker's family of four, a total of 72 yards.

iii) In respect of housing, the norm should be the minimum rent charged by the government in any area for houses provided under the subsidized Industrial Housing Scheme for low-income groups.

iv) Fuel, lighting and other "miscellaneous" items of expenditure should constitute 20 per cent of total minimum wage.

Fair Wage: The wage that is above the minimum wage, but below the living wage. Between the lower limit set by the minimum wage and the upper limit set by the living wage, the actual fair wage must be determined in the light of the following factors:

- The productivity of labour
- The prevailing rates of wages in the same/similar occupation in the same or neighbouring locations
- The level of national income and its distribution
- The place of industry in the national economy of the country

Living Wage: This must provide not merely for bare sustenance but also for the preservation of efficiency of the worker and must include provision for some measure of education, medical requirements and amenities.

According to the report of the Committee on Fair Wages, 1954, for the purpose of determination of fair wages, the Wage Board should take into consideration factors like the degree of skill required to work, the fatigue involved, the training and experience of the worker, the responsibility undertaken, the mental and physical requirements for the work, the disagreeableness or otherwise of work and the hazard involved in the work. The board is required to make due allowance for a fair return on capital, remuneration to management and a fair allocation to reserves and depreciation.

11.1.1 The Need for Wage Legislation

The main objectives of State regulation of wages have been:

a) The prevention of sweating in industries deploying illiterate and unorganized workers

b) Promoting industrial peace

c) Speeding up the pace of economic recovery

d) Preventing inflationary pressure and maintaining economic stability

e) Facilitating the achievement of the national-income-distribution policy and the programme of economic development

f) Narrowing the gap between marginal productivity of labour and the actual level of wages as the average

11.1.2 The Regulation of Wages

Wage regulation through legislations has been executed mainly through the following:

i) Prescribing minimum wages (Minimum Wages Act,1948)

ii) Regulating the payment of wages (Payment of Wages Act, 1936)

iii) Compulsory conciliation and arbitration of wage disputes (Industrial Disputes Act, 1947)

iv) Setting up of wage boards

v) The payment of bonus (Payment of Bonus Act, 1965)

11.2 The Payment of Wages Act, 1936

The Payment of Wages Act, 1936 was enacted to regulate the payment of wages to workers employed in industries and to ensure a speedy and effective remedy against illegal deductions and/or unjustified delay caused in the payment of wages to them. The Payment of Wages Act, 1936 is a central legislation, which applies to the persons

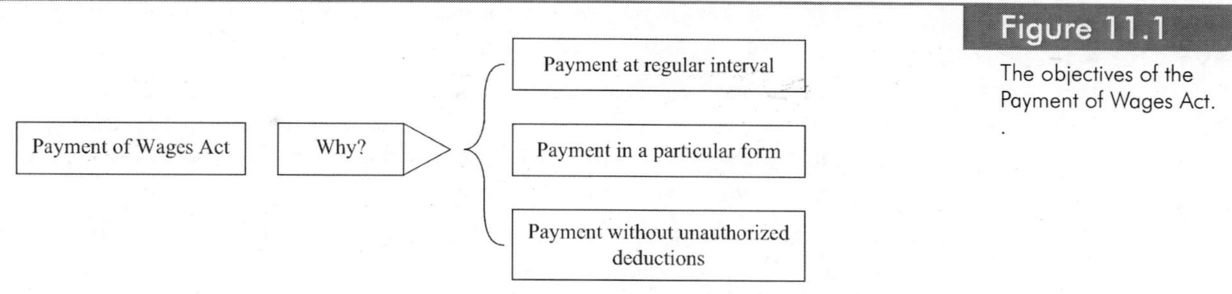

Figure 11.1

The objectives of the Payment of Wages Act.

employed in factories, industries and other establishments. The establishments where it is applicable include:

- Factory
- Railway
- Industrial or other establishment such as:
  - Tramway, motor transport service
  - Air transport service
  - Dock, wharf, jetty
  - Mine, quarry, oil field
  - Plantation
  - Workshops in which articles are produced, adapted or manufactured
  - Construction
  - Any other covered through notification

Figure 11.1 captures the three-pronged objectives of the Act.

11.2.1 Coverage

It covers every person who is employed in any of the establishments (defined in the Act) and drawing an average wage of up to INR 6,500 per month (as amended with effect from 6 September 2005).

11.2.2 Important Terms

A few important definitions are quoted verbatim from the Act:

The term "wages" means all remuneration (whether by way of salary, allowances or otherwise) expressed in terms of money or capable of being so expressed, which would, if the terms of employment express or implied were fulfilled, be payable to a person employed in respect of his employment or of work done in such employment, and includes—

a) Any remuneration payable under any award or settlement between the parties or order of a court

b) Any remuneration to which the person employed is entitled in respect of overtime work or holidays or any leave period

Wage: The term "wages" means all remuneration (whether by way of salary, allowances or otherwise) expressed in terms of money or capable of being so expressed, which would, if the terms of employment express or implied were fulfilled, be payable to a person employed in respect of his employment or of work done in such employment.

c) Any additional remuneration payable under the terms of employment (whether called a bonus or by any other name)

d) Any sum, which by reason of the termination of employment of the person employed, is payable under any law contract or instrument, which provides for the payment of such sum whether with or without deductions but does not provide for the time within which the payment is to be made

e) Any sum to which the person employed is entitled under any scheme framed under any law, but does not include—

   i) Any bonus (whether under a scheme of profit-sharing or otherwise) which does not form part of the remuneration payable under the terms of employment or which is not payable under any award or settlement between the parties or order of a court

   ii) The value of any house-accommodation or of the supply of light, water, medical attendance or other amenity or of any service excluded from the computation of wages by a general or special order of the state government

   iii) Any contribution paid by the employer to any pension or provident fund and the interest that may have accrued thereon

   iv) Any travelling allowance or the value of any travelling concession

   v) Any sum paid to the employed person to defray special expenses entailed on him by the nature of his employment

   vi) Any gratuity payable on the termination of employment in cases other than those specified in Sub-clause (d).

11.2.3 Provisions

The Act prescribes certain benefits:

Pay Day: Wages must be paid on a working day and not on a holiday. When there are less than 1,000 persons employed, the wages shall be paid before the expiry of the seventh day of the following month. When there are more than 1,000 workers, the wages are to be paid before the expiry of the 10th day of the following month.

Wage Period: The period to be fixed for paying wages to an employed person must not exceed one month. That means, an employer can choose to pay wages to a person employed by him for a period of every week or every fortnight, but not for a period of every two months or every three months.

- Wage Periods: Not to exceed one month
- Time: Before expiry of 10th/7th day following wage period (> / < 1,000)
- Termination: Second working day on which employment is terminated
- Working Day: Wages to be paid on a working day
- Medium: Payment in currency, not kind. cheque/bank transfer on written consent
- Only authorized "deductions" from wages are permitted

Terminal Wage: When the employment of any person is terminated, the wages earned by him must be paid before the expiry of the second working day from the day of termination.

Mode of Payment: Wages must be paid in current coin or currency notes or in both and not in kind. It is, however, permissible for an employer to pay wages by cheque or by crediting them in the bank account if so authorized in writing by an employed person.

Deductions from Wages: The Act prohibits all kinds of deductions except those that are authorized by or under the Act (Section 7). Authorized deductions include fine, deduction for amenities and services supplied by the employer, advances paid, over-payment of wages, loan, granted for house-building or other purposes, income tax payable, in pursuance of the order of the court, provident fund contributions, cooperative societies, premium for life insurance, contribution to any fund constituted by employer or a trade union, recovery of losses, ESI contribution, etc.

Deduction for Fines (Section 8):

i) No fine shall be imposed on any employed person save in respect of such acts and omissions on his part as the employer, with the previous approval of the state government or of the prescribed authority, specified by notice under Sub-section (2).

ii) A notice specifying such acts and omissions shall be exhibited in the prescribed manner on the premises in which the employment is carried on or in the case of person employed upon a railway (otherwise than in a factory), at the prescribed place or places.

iii) No fine shall be imposed on any employed person until s/he has been given an opportunity of showing cause against the fine, or otherwise, than in accordance with such procedure as may be prescribed for the imposition of fines.

iv) The total amount of fine that may be imposed in any one wage period shall not exceed 3 per cent of the wages payable during that period.

Absence Without Reasonable Cause: Absence for whole or any part of the day—if ten or more persons are absent without reasonable cause, there should be deduction of wages up to eight days (Section 9).

Deduction for Damage or Loss: For default or negligence of an employee resulting in loss. Show-cause notice has to be given to the employee before effecting any deduction.

Other authorized deductions can be:

- Deduction for amenities and services
- Recovery of advances and interests
- Deduction for overpayment of wages, etc.

All authorized deductions that can be made from the wages are defined in the Act. The employer cannot make arbitrary deductions. (See Box 11.1.)

Kinds of Deductions

Fines
Deduction for absence from duty
Deduction for damage to or loss of goods entrusted to custody
Deduction for house accommodation
Deduction for amenities
Deduction for recovery of advances/loans
Deduction for income tax payable
Statutory deduction (court or magistrate or competent authority)
And so on....

11.2.4 The Enforcement Machinery

The central government is responsible for the administration of the Act in railways, mines, oilfields and air transport services, while state governments are responsible in factories and other industrial establishments. In respect of major ports, state governments have appointed officers of the Central Industrial Machinery as inspectors for enforcing the Act.

11.2.5 Penal Provisions

In respect of any contravention to the provisions of the Act including unauthorized deductions and delayed payments, the Act provides for various penal provisions against the defaulting employer.

11.3 The Minimum Wages Act, 1948

The need for a country to have minimum-wage-fixing machinery was stressed by the International Labour Organization way back in 1928. Twenty years later, our country passed the Minimum Wages Act in 1948. The reason given by the government for passing

BOX 11.1 FOR CLASS DISCUSSION

What is the responsibility of an employer in respect of wages remaining unpaid on account of death of an employed person when the whereabouts of the employed person are not known?

Is deducting some amount or union levies from wages of employees and paying the same to the union valid?

A group of 10 employees were absent for 2 days without intimation, in connection with a new order for deployment of manpower and specific job allocation. What is the maximum amount that may be deducted on account of such absence from duty?

the Act was that the workers' organizations in the country were poorly developed and, consequently, their bargaining power also was very poor. A tripartite committee—The Committee on Fair Wage—was set up in 1948 to provide guidelines for wage structures in the country. The report of this committee was a major landmark in the history of formulation of wage policies in India. Its recommendations set out the key concepts of the living wage, minimum wage and fair wage besides setting out guidelines for wage fixation.

Article 39 of the Constitution states that the State shall direct its policy towards securing that:

a) The citizens, men and women equally, shall have the right to an adequate means of livelihood, and

b) There is equal pay for equal work for both men and women

11.3.1 Objectives, Scope and Coverage

As the name suggests, the Minimum Wages Act aims at establishing a mechanism for fixing minimum wage rates in various kinds of employments.

It extends to the whole of India. It applies to any person who directly, or through a contractor, employs one or more employees in any of the "scheduled" employment for which minimum wages have been fixed under this Act.

11.3.2 Important Terms

Wages: All remuneration capable of being expressed in terms of money, which would, if the terms of the contract of employment express or implied were fulfilled, be payable to a person employed in respect of his employment or of work done in such employment and includes house-rent allowance but does not include—

i) The value of (a) any house accommodation, supply of light, water, medical attendance, or (b) any other amenity or any service excluded by general or special order of the appropriate government

ii) Any contribution paid by the employer to any person, fund or provident fund or under any scheme of social insurance

iii) Any travelling allowance or the value of any travelling concession

iv) Any sum paid to the person employed to defray special expenses entailed on him by the nature of his employment

v) Any gratuity payable on discharge of employees or for the payment of wages

Employee: Any person who is employed for hire or reward to do any work, skilled or unskilled, manual or clerical, in a scheduled employment in respect of which minimum rates of wages have been fixed; and includes an out-worker to whom any articles or materials are given out by another person to be made up, cleaned, washed, altered, ornamented, finished, repaired, adapted, or otherwise processed for sale for the purposes of the trade or business of that other person where the process is to be carried out either in the home of the out-worker or in some other premises not being premises under the control and management of that other person; and also includes an employee declared to be an employee by the appropriate government; but does not include any member of the armed forces of the union

Cost of Living Index Number: In relation to employees, in any scheduled employment in respect of which minimum rates of wages have been fixed, the index number ascertained and declared by the competent authority by notification in the official gazette is to be the cost of living index number applicable to employees in such employment

11.3.3 Main Provisions

The Act prescribes the minimum rates of wages payable to employees for different scheduled employments for different classes of work and for adults, adolescents, children and apprentices depending upon different localities. The employer is required to pay to every employee stipulated in the schedule of employment, at a rate not less than minimum rates of wages as fixed by notification by not making deduction other than prescribed.

FIXATION OF MINIMUM RATES OF WAGES. The appropriate government is empowered to fix minimum rates of wages and to review at such intervals not exceeding five years the minimum rates so fixed and revise them if required. The government can also fix minimum wages for (a) time work (b) piece work at piece rate (c) piece work for the purpose of securing to such employees on a time-work basis (d) overtime work done by employees for piece work or time-rate workers.

The government has to take into account many factors before notifying any changes in minimum wage. The live case in Box 11.2 shows the different interest groups that must be addressed before arriving at a decision. Often, wages in an industry are arrived at through the collective bargaining between the employers' group and the employees' group.

Notice that in the case presented in Box 11.2, there are many contextual issues that come into play with minimum-wage notification. More often than not, it becomes a collective bargaining issue rather than a simple process of notifying a revision based on economic data. The Act has built in provisions for consultation, as we will see later in the chapter.

MINIMUM RATES OF WAGES

1. Any minimum rate of wages fixed or revised by the appropriate government may consist of—
    i) A basic rate of wages and a special allowance, e.g., cost-of-living allowance
    ii) A basic rate of wages with or without a cost-of-living allowance and cash value of concessions for the supply of essential-commodities allowance

BOX 11.2 MINIMUM WAGE NOTIFICATION: A REAL-LIFE CASE

On 14 March 2008, the Tamil Nadu government proposed a draft minimum wage notification of a daily rate of Rs 101.52 for tea-plantation workers. Reacting to the draft, management sources stated that this wage "would be a death knell for the plantations in the State".

Expressing concern over the proposed hike and its adverse impact on plantations, the United Planters Association of Southern India (UPASI) said, "If the state government does not give up the present proposal of fixing the minimum wage above the prevailing rate negotiated between the trade unions and the planters' associations, it would signal the end of collective bargaining."

The apex body of the plantation industry in South India has not only appealed to the state government to retrace its steps, but has sought the Centre's intervention in dissuading the Tamil Nadu government from going ahead with the proposed wage plan.

"The extra wage burden arising from the minimum wages proposed by the state government will add Rs 7–8 per kg to the cost of production, thereby making the entire industry terminally sick. The plight of the small growers could be worse; they may even be wiped out," sources pointed out.

The current notified wage is much higher than the minimum wage of Rs 76.65 in Karnataka as on March 2008.

Source: L. N. Revathy, "Tea Plantations Upset over Minimum Wage Proposal", *The Hindu Business Line*, 2 April 2008.

BOX 11.3 **FOR CLASS DISCUSSION**

Is an employer, who is not paying basic wages and cost-of-living allowance separately as fixed under the Act, but who is paying wages more than the minimum prescribed rates under the Act, committing any illegality?

Can attendance bonus be treated as part of the minimum wage fixed under the Act?

Can the supply of essential commodities at concessional rates form part of the minimum wage?

iii) An all-inclusive rate, i.e., basic wage, cost-of-living allowance and cash value of concessions on essential commodities

The questions based in Box 11.3 are based on case laws. The purpose is only to show that you can, in most cases, guess the correct interpretation on an approach based on common sense and understanding of the spirit of the enactment.

THE PROCEDURE FOR FIXING AND REVISING MINIMUM RATES OF WAGES. For fixing the minimum wages, the appropriate government may follow one of the following two procedures:

- **Committee Procedure:** The appropriate government may appoint a committee comprising representatives of employers and employees and independent members (not exceeding 1/3 of the committee's strength). The recommendations of the committee are published in the official gazette and come into effect after expiry of three months.
- **Notification Procedure:** In this procedure, the government notifies the proposed revision in the official gazette. A minimum of two months' period is provided for persons likely to be affected by the proposal to react and send their representations. The government should also consult the Advisory Board.

There are two basic procedures for determining the minimum wages:

1. **Committee Procedure:** A tripartite committee comprising employers' and employees' representatives and independent members
2. **Notification Procedure:** Notification of proposed changes by the government. The final revision based on consideration of objections by affected parties.

The exhibit in Box 11.4[1] is an extract from an actual notification issued by the Tamil Nadu government revising the minimum wages for the leather and manufacturing industry.

BOX 11.4 **LABOUR AND EMPLOYMENT (J1) DEPARTMENT G.O.(2D) NO. 30**

Dated: 27.03.2007

Read:

1. G.O.(2D) No.28, Labour and Employment Department dated 3.4.2003
2. From the Commissioner of Labour, Chennai-6, Letter No.Z1/58373/2002, dated 14.9.2004.
3. From the Commissioner of Labour, Chennai – 6, Letter No.Z1/58515/2002 dated 19.01.2006.

ORDER

In the Government Order first read above, a preliminary Notification containing proposals to revise further the minimum rates of wages for employment in Tanneries and Leather Manufactory was issued and objection and suggestion were invited from the persons likely to be affected by such revision.

1. After examining the objection and suggestion with regard to the Preliminary Notification, the Government have decided to confirm the preliminary Notification.
2. The appended Notification will be published in the **Tamil Nadu Government Gazette** both in English and Tamil. The Secretary to Government, Tamil Development Culture and Religious Endowments (Translation) Department, Secretariat, Chennai-600 009

is requested to send the Tamil translation of the Notification to the Works Manager, Government Central Press, Chennai – 600079.

(BY ORDER OF THE GOVERNOR)

APPENDIX

Notification

In exercise of the powers conferred by clause (b) of sub-section (1) of section 3 and sub-section (2) of section 5 of the Minimum Wages Act, 1948 (Central Act XI of 1948) and in supersession of the Labour and Employment Department Notification No.II(2)/LE/868/2000, published at pages 398 and 399 of Part II-Section 2 of the **Tamil Nadu Government Gazette,** dated the 9th August, 2000, the Governor of Tamil Nadu after consultation with the Advisory Board, hereby revises the minimum rates of wages payable to the classes of employees in the employment in Tanneries and Leather Manufactory in the State of Tamil Nadu specified in column (1) of the Schedule below, as specified in the corresponding entries in column (2) thereof, the draft proposal of the same having been previously published as required by clause (b) of sub-section (1) of section 5 of the said Act.

3. This Notification shall come into force with effect on and from the date of its publication in the **Tamil Nadu Government Gazette.**

// TRUE COPY //

SECTION OFFICER

THE SCHEDULE (Abridged)

EMPLOYMENT IN TANNERIES AND LEATHER MANUFACTORY

Classes of Employee

LIMEYARD

(1) Helpers 57.00
(2) Flashers 58. 00
(3) Scudders 58.00
(4) Goat Skin Knifers 58.00

TANNING AND DYEING DEPARTMENT

(1) Helpers 57.00
(2) Drum Boys 57.00
(3) Shavers 60.00
(4) Splitters 60.00
(5) Shaving Learners 57.00
(6) Bamming Helpers 57.00

EXPLANATIONS

(i) The employees shall be paid dearness allowance in addition to the minimum wages specified above. For calculation of dearness allowance, the base shall be taken as 2174 (base 1960 = 100) being the All India Average of Consumer Price Index Number for the year 2000. For further raise of one point over and above 2174 points, an increase of 2.5 paise shall be paid per day.

(ii) Where the nature of work is the same or work of similar nature is done, no distinction in payment of wages should be made as between men and women workers.

(iii) Where piece rate workers are employed in any Tannery and Leather Manufactory, the Wages paid to each of them for a normal working day shall not be less than the minimum rates of wages fixed for that category.

(iv) To arrive at daily wages, the monthly wages shall be divided by 26.

(v) To arrive at the monthly wage, the daily wages plus the daily Dearness Allowance would be multiplied by 30.

(vi) Wherever the existing wages are higher than the minimum wages fixed herein, the same shall be continued to be paid.

TRUE COPY

SECTION OFFICER

The exhibit in Box 11.4 is based on Notification Procedure for the leather and tannery industry in Tamil Nadu. Read it carefully to notice how every provision of the Act has been taken care of and also the "process" that has been followed. Likewise, notifications under the Minimum Wages Act, 1948 can also be notified in the official gazette through the Committee Process. It might be a good idea to look for such a notification and compare the difference.

WORKING HOURS AND OVERTIME. Overtime hours are to be reckoned in terms of working hours in a normal working day and the payment for every hour or for part of an hour so worked in excess shall be at the overtime rate, double the ordinary rate. In case the Factories Act applies, then it should be at whichever rate is higher.

THE PROCEDURE FOR MAKING CLAIMS UNDER THE ACT. The procedure for making a claim is as follows:

a) An employee having any claim under the Act has to make an application to the authority appointed under the Act.

b) Such application can be made by the employee himself/herself, or any legal practitioner or any official of a registered trade union.

c) Application has to be made within six months from the date on which the claim amount became payable.

d) In appropriate case, the authority can, over and above directing the payment of the difference between minimum wages payable and wages actually paid, award compensation up to 10 times the amount of the difference.

e) The amount directed to be paid by the authority can be recovered as if it were a fine imposed by a magistrate.

f) Every direction of the authority will be final (Section 20).

11.4 The Payment of Bonus Act, 1965

"Bonus" is one of the most contentious issues in the area of wage legislations. Starting from its first use during the early 1920s, bonus has neither satisfied the employee, nor the employer. Starting as an ex gratia payment, over the years, it has acquired the form of obligatory payment through the enactment of legislation (Payment of Bonus Act, 1965) in this regard. The opening vignette describes a typical "situation" relating to payment of bonus and the complexities of the issues surrounding it.

Interestingly, the term "bonus" is not defined in the Payment of Bonus Act, 1965.

The *Meriam-Webster Dictionary* defines "bonus" as "something in addition to what is expected or strictly due" or "money or an equivalent given in addition to an employee's usual compensation".

In common parlance, bonus is regarded as an ex gratia payment made by the employer to his workers to provide encouragement for the extra effort by them in the production process. Sometimes, it also represents a desire of the management to share its gains with the workers, who are vital to the production process and who contribute to the income and profits of the enterprise.

The payment of "bonus" started in the cotton mills of Bombay during the closing period of the First World War. End of the war and declining profits, however, led to discontinuation of this practice. The Second World War started in 1939 and industrial units, including, cotton textile, again started making profits, and the practice started once again. Wartime bonus came to be regarded as payment made to the workers out of the extraordinary profits earned during the war. Although several employers paid bonus voluntarily, there being no statutory provision, many disputes on the issue arose and were referred to adjudication. The adjudication took the view that profits were made possible by the cooperation, both of labour and capital. Labour, therefore, had a right to share in increased profits. The claim to bonus was accepted chiefly on grounds of broad principles of justice, equity and good conscience with a view to keeping labour contented. This position continued until the Bombay High Court laid down that payment of bonus could be demanded by workers as a right, that is to say, a payment that should be made by the employer as extra-remuneration for work done by the employee under a contract, express or implied.

11.4.1 Labour Appellate Tribunal (LAT) Formula

A dispute relating to payment of bonus by the cotton mills of Bombay was decided by the Industrial Court, Bombay.

In its decision, the LAT laid down the main principles involved in the grant of bonus to workers. These principles are known as the LAT formula. According to the formula, the following prior charges were to be deducted gross profits of a company:

i) Provisions for depreciation

ii) Reserve for rehabilitation (of machinery and equipment)

iii) Return of 6 per cent on the paid-up capital

iv) Return on the working capital at a rate lower than the return on paid-up capital

The balance, if any, was called "available surplus", and the workmen were to be given a reasonable share out of it by way of bonus for the year.

11.4.2 Bonus Commission

The formula laid down by the labour appellate tribunal was followed all over the country by industrial tribunals in awarding bonus, although demands for its revision continued to be made from time to time. The main point on which this revision was sought centred on the provisions for rehabilitation, accepted by the LAT as a prior charge. The Government of India appointed a Bonus Commission in 1961 to consider all issues of employers and employees in totality and give its recommendations. The recommendations of the Commission were accepted by the government with minor changes and promulgated as an Ordinance in 1964. This Ordinance was the basis of the Payment of Bonus Act, 1965.

11.4.3 Objectives

The object of the Payment of Bonus Act has been articulated comprehensively by the Supreme Court as follows[2]:

- Impose statutory liability upon employer covered by the Act to pay bonus to employees
- Define the principles of bonus payment
- To provide limits for maximum and minimum bonus payable and linking the same to principles of "set-off" and "set-on"
- Provide machinery for enforcement of the liability of employer

Objectives of the Act

- Impose statutory liability upon employer to pay bonus to employees
- Define the principles of bonus payment
- Provide limits for maximum and minimum bonus payable and linking the same to principles of "set-off" and "set-on"
- Provide machinery for enforcement of the liability of employer

11.4.4 Applicability

- The Payment of Bonus Act extends to the whole of India.
- It is applicable to every factory and to every establishment wherein 20 or more workers are employed on any day during an accounting year.

- The appropriate government can extend its provisions to any establishment employing less than 20 but more than 10 employees.
- For the purpose of calculating the number of employees for applicability of the Act, part-time employees are also included.
- Every employee, not drawing more than INR 10,000 per month,[3] who has worked for not less than 30 days in an accounting year shall be eligible for bonus.
- Bonus is to be paid within eight months from the expiry of the accounting year.
- Once the Act is applicable, it continues to apply even if the number of employees falls below 20.
- The Act is applicable to government companies and corporations owned by the government, which produces goods or renders services in competition with the private sector.

The Act is ***not*** applicable to:

- Government employees
- Employees of local bodies, universities, public-sector insurance employees and LIC employees, employees of RBI and public-sector financial institutions, charitable hospitals, social-welfare organizations and defence employees
- Any not-for-profit institution

The meaning of "establishment" has not been defined in the Act. However, "establishment", under Labour Laws, has wide connotation. It may include any office or a fixed place where business is carried out.

The Act applies to an establishment in the public sector only if the establishment in the public sector sells the goods or renders services in competition with an establishment in the private sector, and the income from such sale or services or both is not less than 20 per cent of the gross income of the establishment. Basically, the intent appears to be to make the Act applicable only to institutions established for the purpose of profit.

Establishment in the public sector means an establishment owned, controlled or managed by—(a) a government company as defined in Section 617 of the Companies Act (b) a corporation in which not less than 40 per cent of its capital is held (whether singly or taken together) by the government; or the Reserve Bank of India; or a corporation owned by the government or the Reserve Bank of India.

"Corporation" means any corporate body established by or under any central or state Act, but does not include a company or a cooperative society.

Where an establishment consists of different departments or undertakings or has branches, whether situated in the same place or in different places, all such departments or undertakings or branches shall be treated as parts of the same establishment for the purpose of computation of bonus under this Act.

11.4.5 Important Terms

The Payment of Bonus Act comprises a few terms that may require some accounting and taxation knowledge. These are: "available surplus", "allocable surplus", "prior charges", "set-off" and "set-on". Instead of reproducing the definitions from the Act, we have tried to explain the concept behind these terms. As a manager, you are expected to have a broad overview of the concepts and a basic understanding of the process of bonus calculations, applicability or non-applicability of the Act to certain establishments and employees, the obligations of an employer, etc. You can always seek the help of legal and accounting professionals, should the need arise.

ACCOUNTING YEAR. Different business entities may have different accounting periods. The Act, therefore, defines the accounting periods with precision mainly because the bonus calculations are based on the financial results of an entity.

In Relation to a Corporation: The year ending on the day on which the books and accounts of the corporation are to be closed and balanced.

In Relation to a Company: The period in respect of which any profit-and-loss account of the company laid before it in the annual general meeting is made up, whether that period is a year or not.

In Any Other Case: The year commencing on the 1st day of April; or, if the accounts of an establishment maintained by the employer are closed and balanced on any day other than the 31st day of March, then, at the option of the employer, the year ending on the day on which its accounts are closed and balanced. An option, once exercised by the employer, shall not again be exercised, except with the previous permission in writing of the prescribed authority and upon such conditions as that authority may think fit.

GROSS PROFIT, PRIOR CHARGES, AVAILABLE SURPLUS, ALLOCABLE SURPLUS. Simply stated, bonus has to be distributed from the allocable surplus in the accounts of a company/establishment. The allocable surplus is a percentage of available surplus (usually 60 per cent). The available surplus is arrived at after deducting prior charges from the gross profit. A simplified version has been shown in Figure 11.2.

With a simplified process in place, let us now try to understand the terms in greater detail.

Step 1: The starting point would be the financial statements (P&L and balance sheet) at the end of the accounting year. The first step is to determine the gross profit. Section 4 of the Act

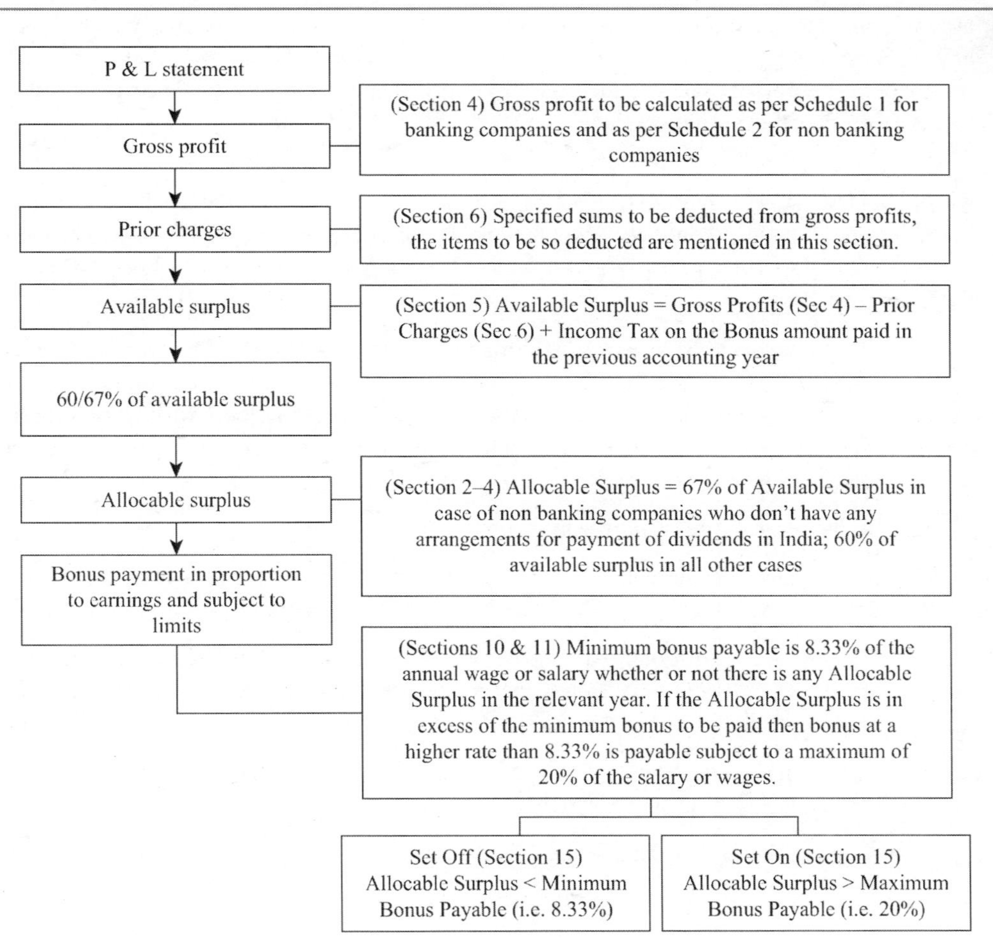

Figure 11.2 Flow chart for the payment of bonus.

gives the method of calculating the gross profit as per Schedules 1 and 2 of the Act. Schedule 1 prescribes the method for banking companies, whereas Schedule 2 provides the method for other companies.

Step 2: It is the process through which available surplus (Section 5) is arrived at. From the gross profit calculated through Section 4, certain specified sums are to be deducted as prior charges. These prior charges are mentioned in Section 6 of the Act; for example, depreciation as permissible under the Income Tax Act, development rebate or allowance that the employer is entitled to deduct from his income under the Income Tax Act, any direct tax liability within the provisions of Section 7 or any other amount specified in Schedule 3. These would depend upon the category of the employer namely:

- Company other than a banking company
- Banking company
- Corporation
- Cooperative Society
- Any other not falling in the above categories

Step 3: To this amount (gross profits – prior charges), the following *difference* is added: Direct tax on gross profits for the previous accounting year – direct tax on gross profits in last accounting year – amount of bonus paid or liable to pay during the last accounting year.

In effect, this means that the tax paid on the amount of bonus gets added to arrive at available surplus.

Step 4: Allocable surplus will be an amount equivalent to 60 per cent or 67 per cent of the available surplus. It would be 67 per cent in case of non-banking companies, which do not have provisions for payment of dividends out of their profit in India. For all other companies, it is 60 per cent. For all practical purposes, therefore, 60 per cent of available surplus is to be reckoned as allocable surplus.

MINIMUM AND MAXIMUM BONUS. It is from the allocable surplus that bonus is to be paid to the employees, proportionate to their wages. A minimum of 8.33 per cent of the annual salary or wages or INR 100, whichever is higher, is to be paid as bonus. This has a few noteworthy points:

1. The employee must have worked for a minimum of 30 days in the relevant accounting year to be eligible for bonus payment. However, the employee would be considered to have worked on days he has been laid off, been on leave with wages, absent due to temporary disablement arising out of and in course of employment or on maternity leave.
2. Salary/wage of the employee must be INR 10,000 or less.
3. Even though the salary may be more than INR 3,500 for the purpose of bonus calculation, the maximum salary is to be reckoned as INR 3,500 only. (See Box 11.5.)
4. An employee is disqualified for payment of bonus if s/he has been dismissed from service for: a) fraud or b) riotous or violent behaviour within premises of establishment or c) theft, misappropriation or sabotage of any property of establishment.
5. Where an employee has not worked for all the working days in an accounting year, his bonus will be proportionately reduced.
6. Payment of bonus must be made within eight months of the closing of the accounting year.
7. Most importantly, even if the establishment does not have any allocable surplus, or suffers losses, minimum bonus is payable. Minimum bonus, thus, has

> BOX 11.5 **CALCULATING THE MINIMUM BONUS**
>
> If the monthly wage of an employee is, say, INR 8,000, then in a year when minimum bonus is to be paid, he shall be paid only 8.33 per cent of his annual wage calculated at the rate of INR 3,500 per month.
>
> However, if the wage of another employee is INR 2,200 (a hypothetical situation, since the minimum wage in majority of cases is more than this) the bonus will be paid at the rate of 8.33 per cent of INR 2,200 × 12 (actual monthly wage × 12).

been made a statutory right of employees through this legislation. There are a few exceptions, as in the case of new establishments, which are mentioned in Section 16.

Where the allocable surplus in an accounting year exceeds the minimum amount to be paid as bonus, the employer is bound to pay an amount in proportion to the salary or wage earned by the employee subject to a maximum of 20 per cent of such salary or wage (Section 11).

SET-ON AND SET-OFF OF ALLOCABLE SURPLUS. Where, for any accounting year, the allocable surplus exceeds the amount of maximum bonus payable to the employees in the establishment under Section 11, the excess shall, subject to a limit of 20 per cent of the total salary or wage of the employees employed in the establishment in that accounting year, be carried forward for being set-on in the succeeding accounting year and so on up to and inclusive of the fourth accounting year to be utilized for the purpose of payment of bonus in the manner illustrated in Schedule 4. What this means is that if the allocable surplus in a year is more than 20 per cent (maximum limit) of the wages and salaries, then the amount in excess of 20 per cent shall be carried forward to be utilized in a year when the allocable surplus is either nil or less than the minimum limit (8.33 per cent). The amount so carried forward, however, cannot be more than 20 per cent of salaries and wages. The 20-per-cent figure occurs twice and this, at times, may be confusing on first reading. To illustrate this, suppose the 20 per cent of salaries and wages in a year is INR 200,000. The allocable surplus is INR 500,000. This would mean that INR 200,000 would be distributed for the relevant accounting year (being maximum limit for bonus payment). Out of the excess of INR 300,000, only INR 200,000 can be carried forward for being set-on (cap of 20 per cent).

> **Maximum and Minimum**
>
> Minimum Bonus Payable in an Accounting Year = 8.33 Per Cent of Annual Wage or Salary
> Maximum Bonus Payable in an Accounting Year = 20 Per Cent of Annual Wage or Salary
> The principle behind fixing a minimum and maximum limit for payment of bonus is that the rate of bonus should not fluctuate widely from year to year.

Where, for any accounting year, there is no available surplus, or the allocable surplus in respect of that year falls short of the amount of minimum bonus payable to the employees in the establishment under Section 10, and there is no amount or sufficient amount carried forward and set-on under Sub-section (1), which could be utilized for the purpose of payment of the minimum bonus, then such minimum amount or the deficiency, as the case may be, shall be carried forward for being set-off in the succeeding accounting year and so on up to and inclusive of the fourth accounting year in the manner illustrated in Schedule 4.

Where in any accounting year, any amount has been carried forward and set-on or set-off under this section, then, in calculating bonus for the succeeding accounting year, the amount of set-on or set-off carried forward from the earliest accounting year shall first be taken into account.

Table 11.1 has been adapted from Schedule 4 of the Act for the purpose of complete understanding. To understand the table, the following assumptions are to be made:

For an establishment, in any accounting year, the minimum bonus payable is INR 104,167, i.e., 8.33 per cent of the annual wage bill. The maximum limit works out to INR 250,000, i.e., 20 per cent of the wage bill. The allocable surplus (60 or 67 per cent of the available surplus) has been assumed for each of the 10 years.

Table 11.1 "Set-on" and "set-off".

Year	Allocable Surplus (INR)	Amount Payable as Bonus (INR)	Set-on or Set-off to be carried Forward (INR)	Total Set-on or Set-off Carried Forward (INR)	Explanation
1.	104,167	104,167	Nil	Nil	The allocable surplus equal to minimum limit (8.33per cent). No carry forward
2.	635,000	250,000	Set-on = 250,000	Set-on: 250,000 (Year 2)	250,000 is the maximum bonus payable in column 2. 250,000 (i.e., 20 per cent maximum over the maximum limit of 20 per cent) only out of the balance 385,000 (635,000−250,000) can be carried forward to be set-on
3.	220,000	250,000 (including 30,000 from year 2 carry forward of 250,000)	Nil	Set-on: 220,000 (Year 2)	The allocable surplus is 220,000. To this, add 30,000 from the carry forward amount of year 2 to make the bonus payable at the maximum of 20 per cent, i.e., 250,000. The carry forward amount from year 2 (i.e., 250,000) is reduced by 30,000 to 220,000.
4.	3,75,000	250,000	Set-on = 125,000	Set-on: 220,000 (Year 2) 125,000 (Year 4)	Note that in subsequent years, the carried-forward amount from an earlier year gets set-off first.
5.	140,000	250,000 (Including 1,10,000 out of INR 220,000 from year 2)	Nil	Set-on: 110,000 (Year 2) 125,000 (Year 4)	Carry forward amount of 220,000 from year 2 gets reduced by 110,000 and balance carried forward from year 2 also remains at 110,000 (220,000-110,000)
6.	310,000	250,000	Set-on = 60,000	Set-on: Nil (Year 2) 125,000(Year 4) 60,000 (Year 6)	The carry forward of 110,000 from year 2 lapses after the fourth accounting year

(Continued)

7.	100,000	250,000 (Includes 125,000 from year 4 and 25,000 from year 6)	Nil	Set-on: 35,000 (Year 6)	Carried forward amounts to the extent of 150,000 (125,000 from year 4 and 25,000 from year 6) used to arrive at the maximum bonus of 250,000 payable.
8.	Nil (Due to loss)	104,167	Set-off = 69,167 (104,167 – 35000)	Set-off: 69,167 (Year 8)	Minimum bonus of 8.33 per cent (104,167) must be paid. The balance remaining after adjusting the carried forward amount from year 6 is carried forward to be set-off in subsequent accounting years.
9.	10,000	104,167	Set-off = 94,167 (104,167 – 10,000)	Set-off: 69,167 (Year 8) 94,167 (Year 9)	Minimum bonus to be paid. The deficit carried forward to be set-off in subsequent accounting years.
10.	215,000	104,167	Nil	Set-off: 52,501 (Year 9)	Minimum bonus = 104,167. Carried forward of year 8 set-off against the amount of allocable surplus remaining after paying minimum bonus (215,000−104,167 = 1,10,833). From 1,04,833, the carried forward amount of year 8, i.e. 69,167 is set-off, leaving 41,666 (104,833−69,167 = 41,666). The remaining C/F amount from year 9, i.e. 94,167 is now adjusted, leaving an amount of 52,501 to be carried forward to be set-off in future accounting years (94,167−41,666 = 52,501)

A FEW DEFINITIONS AND PROVISIONS. Although most definitions, terms and provisions have been explained in the text above, a few are once again explained in terms of the Act:

Employee: Any person (other than an apprentice) employed on a salary or wage not exceeding INR 10,000 per month in any industry to do any skilled or unskilled manual, supervisory, managerial, administrative, technical or clerical work for hire or reward, whether the terms of employment be express or implied

Salary or Wage: All remuneration (other than remuneration in respect of overtime work) capable of being expressed in terms of money, which would, if the terms of employment, express or implied, were fulfilled, be payable to an employment or of work done in such employment and includes dearness allowance (that is to say, all cash payments, by whatever name called, paid to an employee on account of a rise in the cost of living, but does not include—

i) Any other allowance that the employee is, for the time being, entitled to
ii) The value of any house accommodation or such of light, water, medical attendance or other amenity or of any service of any concessional supply of food grains or other articles
iii) Any travelling concession
iv) Any bonus (including incentive, production and attendance bonus)
v) Any contribution paid or payable by the employer to any pension fund or provident fund or for the benefit of the employees under any law for the time being in force
vi) Any retrenchment compensation or any gratuity or other retirement benefit payable to the employees or any ex gratia payment made to him
vii) Any commission payable to the employee

Proportionate Reduction in Bonus in Certain Cases: Where an employee has not worked for all the working days in an accounting year, the minimum bonus of INR 100 or, as the case may be, of INR 60, if such bonus is higher than 8.33 per cent of his salary or wage for the days he has worked in that accounting year, shall be proportionately reduced.

Computation of Number of Working Days: For the purposes of Section 13 (proportionate reduction in bonus in certain cases), an employee shall be deemed to have worked in an establishment in any accounting year also on the days on which:

i) He has been laid off under an agreement or as permitted by standing orders under the Industrial Employment (Standing Orders) Act, 1946 (20 of 1946), or under the Industrial Disputes Act, 1947 (14 of 1947) or under any other law applicable to the establishment
ii) He has been on leave with salary or wage
iii) He has been absent due to temporary disablement caused by accident arising out of and in the course of his employment
iv) The employee has been on maternity leave with salary or wage, during the accounting year

Adjustment of Customary or Interim Bonus Against Bonus Payable Under the Act: Where in any accounting year: (a) an employer has paid any *puja* bonus or other customary bonus to an employee; or (b) an employer has paid a part of the bonus payable under this Act to an employee before the date on which such bonus becomes payable; then, the employer shall be entitled to deduct the amount of bonus so paid from the amount of bonus payable by him to the employee under this Act in respect of that accounting year and the employee shall be entitled to receive only the balance.

Deduction of Certain Amounts from Bonus Payable Under the Act: Where in any accounting year, an employee is found guilty of misconduct causing financial loss to the employer, then it shall be lawful for the employer to deduct the amount of loss from the amount of bonus payable by him to the employee under this Act in respect of that accounting year only, and the employee shall be entitled to receive the balance, if any.

Separate Establishment: If profit and loss accounts are prepared and maintained in respect of any such department or undertaking or branch, then such department or undertaking or branch is treated as a separate establishment.

Disqualification and Deduction of Bonus: On dismissal of an employee for fraud, or riotous or violent behaviour while in the premises of the establishment, or theft, misappropriation or sabotage of any property of the establishment, or misconduct of causing financial loss to the employer to the extent that bonus can be deducted for that year.

The situation described in the chapter-opening vignette is not an isolated case but almost a normal occurrence in the industrial relations scenario. The point of contention is no longer the provisions of the Act, but the difficult area of arriving at a mutually accepted available surplus. In the absence of detailed computations being made available, the contention from one side is the lack of transparency in the calculation of available surplus (and deduction of prior charges), whereas the other side maintains that the employees take a short-term view and do not have a "buy-in" in the future challenges facing the company. A lack of rigid criteria and, at places, of transparency and credibility of calculations, the employees rely on previous reported profits and bonus paid to demand bonus in the current year. For the employees, it is a legitimate expectation that if the reported profits show a growth, there should be a corresponding growth in the rate of bonus payment. Another contentious issue is that larger number of the workforce is now outside the purview of the Act on account of a higher salary/wage. There is a pressure from these set of "employees" for some sort of ex gratia payment, causing potential for industrial strife. In fact, in many cases (especially in the PSUs), these employees wait for the announcement of statutory bonus before raising the issue for collective bargaining on ex gratia and, if need be, industrial action.

SUMMARY

The Payment of Wages Act, 1936

- The Payment of Wages Act, 1936 has been enacted with the intention of ensuring timely payment of wages to the workers and for the payment of wages without unauthorized deductions.
- The salary in factories/establishments employing less than 1,000 workers is required to be paid by the 7th of every month, and in other cases, by the 10th day of every month.
- A worker, who either has not been paid wages in time or from whose wages unauthorized deductions have been made, can file a "claim" either directly or through a trade union or through an inspector under this Act, before the authority appointed under the Payment of Wages Act.
- The power for hearing and deciding claims under this Act has been vested at present with the Presiding Officer of a Labour Court.

The Minimum Wages Act, 1948

- The need for a country to have minimum wage-fixing machinery was stressed by the International Labour Organization long back in 1928. Twenty years later, our country passed the Minimum Wages Act, 1948.
- The reason given by the government for passing the Act was that workers' organizations in the country were poorly developed and, consequently, their bargaining power also was very poor.
- A tripartite committee, The Committee on Fair Wage, was set up in 1948 to provide guidelines for wage structures in the country. Its recommendations set out the key concepts of the "living wage", "minimum wages" and "fair wage" besides setting out guidelines for wage fixation.
- Article 39 of the Constitution states that the State shall direct its policy towards securing:
  - that the citizen, men and women equally shall have the right to an adequate livelihood and
  - that there is equal pay for equal work for both men and women
- The Act prescribes the minimum rates of wages payable to employees for different scheduled employment for different classes of work and for adults, adolescents, children and apprentices depending upon different localities.
- An employer is required to pay to every employee stipulated in the schedule of employment, at a rate not less than minimum rates of wages as fixed by notification by not making deductions other than prescribed.
- The appropriate government is empowered to fix minimum rates of wages and to review at such intervals not exceeding five years the minimum rates so fixed, and revise if required.
- The government can also fix minimum wages for (a) time work (b) piece work at piece rate (c) piece work for the purpose of securing to such employees on a time-work basis (d) overtime work done by employees for piece work or time-rate workers.
- For fixing the minimum wages, the appropriate government may follow one of the following two procedures:
  - Committee Procedure
  - Notification Procedure

The Payment of Bonus Act, 1965

- The Payment of Bonus Act, 1965 gives to the employees a statutory right to a share in the profits of his employer.
- Prior to the enactment of the Act, some employees used to get bonus, but that was so if their employers were pleased to pay the same.
- The Act enables the employees to get a minimum bonus equivalent to one month's salary or wages (8.33 per cent of annual earnings), whether the employer makes any profit or not.
- But the Act also puts a ceiling on the bonus and the maximum bonus payable under the Act is equivalent to about two-and-a-half months' salary or wage (20 per cent of annual earnings).
- Employees drawing salary or wage exceeding INR. 10,000 per month are not entitled to get any bonus under the Act (w.e.f. 1 April 2006).

KEY TERMS

- maximum bonus 237
- minimum bonus 237
- minimum wage 223
- set-off 233
- set-on 233
- wage period 226
- wages 223

REVIEW QUESTIONS

1 What is the object of the Payment of Wages Act, 1936?

2 To which establishments is the Act applicable?

3 Are all wages covered or protected by the Act?

4 Are overtime wages to be taken into account for deciding the applicability of the Act?

5 Can any employer fix a period longer than one month for paying wages to a person employed by him?

6 What are the requirements of the Act in respect of the time of payment of wages?

7 What are the requirements of the Act in respect of the method of payment of wages?

8 What is the provision of the Act regarding deductions from the wages payable to an employed person?

9 What is the objective of the Minimum Wages Act, 1948?

10 Which employments are intended to be benefited by fixation of minimum rates of wages?

11 What is the procedure the government has to follow for fixing and revising minimum wages?

12 Is the task of the government over once it fixes minimum rates of wages payable to employees employed in a scheduled employment?

13 What is the obligation of the employer in respect of payment of wages under the Minimum Wages Act, 1948?

14 What is the objective of the Payment of Bonus Act, 1965?

15 To which establishments is the Act applicable? Are the establishments in public sector covered by the Act?

16 Who are entitled to be paid bonus under The Payment of Bonus Act, 1965?

17 What is to be included in and excluded from a salary or wage for the purpose of calculating bonus?

18 What is the amount of minimum bonus payable by the employer to his employees every year?

19 What is the meaning of available surplus and allocable surplus and what is the connection between allocable surplus and bonus?

20 What is the principle of set-on and set-off of allocable surplus?

QUESTIONS FOR CRITICAL THINKING

1 Are the provisions of Section 9(2) of the Payment of Wages Act permitting deduction in wages for the participation in illegal strike affected by the provisions of Section 26 of the Industrial Disputes Act providing for penalty for illegal strikes? Do an Internet search for relevant case laws on the matter and discuss it in the class.

DEBATE

1. The Payment of Wages Act is of limited use, i.e., only with regard to organized labour. It is, therefore, unsuccessful in establishing standards and norms with regard to payment of wages across the country.
2. The object of the Minimum Wages Act is not fully served as the wage levels are mostly decided on the basis of collective bargaining.
3. More than focusing on minimum wages, the government needs to introduce a nation-wide, legally binding, employment-guarantee programme, in terms of the right to work under the Directive Principles of State Policy.
4. Should contract workers be brought within the purview of the Bonus Act, 1965? Discuss points in favour of and against of this amendment from the employer's perspective.

CASE ANALYSIS

Periodicity of Payments

Girdhar is in a dilemma. When he was appointed at the construction site of Ketak Building and Construction Company, he was told that his deployment and location would change with the projects the company undertakes, and payment would be dependent on the completion of the allotted job at the site, not on a daily or a monthly basis. Girdhar was desperate for a job and agreed to these terms in writing. He has been working for over eight years now and the payment continues to be erratic with long gaps. In the initial years, when he did not have a family to look after, the aperiodicity of payment was not a matter of concern to him. Over the last few years, he has been repeatedly taking up the matter with the supervisor, who dismissed his request saying that this is the way the company makes payment. "Take it or leave" was a warning note that still rings out in Girdhar's ears.

Girdhar's plight has worsened since the time he has been asked to travel to local shops to make small purchases or snacks for the supervisors deployed on the site. Many a time, he has to travel by local transport. The reimbursement of the expenses is also accumulated in the register, and the payment is made along with his salary. One day, Girdhar refused to go to the central market of the site area, which resulted in an altercation with the supervisor. An exchange of abuses led to his dismissal. Girdhar is now seeking help of some union leaders belonging to another construction company to collect his past dues. When the appointment letter was shown to the union officials, they informed him of a provision of notice period of one month stipulated in the letter.

1. Discuss the grounds on which Girdhar can claim his dues with specific reference to the Act.
2. What could the arguments be from the employer's side?

Eligibility for Bonus

A group of 31 workers were employed during maintenance shut-down period of one month inside the factory premises. Once Unit 1 maintenance activity was completed, the same set of workers was deployed in another unit for a period of 40 days. The practice of engaging the same set of 31 workers for unskilled work with regard to maintenance activities carried on for over 8 months. After a gap of 10 days, 28 of the 31 workers were deployed at the head office for stock-taking audit and cleaning activities, which extended for 95 days. When the regular workers were given bonus, these workers also raised a demand for bonus. The General Manager (HR) informed the workers that they are not entitled to bonus as they have not completed the minimum eligibility period for the grant of bonus.

The workers approached the local union leader who took up the case with the employer. His contention was that the spirit of the Bonus Act makes the employees eligible for bonus and it was not for them to decide their place of deployment. Just to avoid bonus payment, the employer has been frequently deploying these workers on different assignments.

1. Are they entitled to "bonus"? Why? Prepare a detailed report quoting relevant provisions of the Act, and also relevant case laws on the subject.
2. Would they be entitled to a differential bonus for the work period inside the factory premises and the period of work activity in the head office?

NOTES

1. http://www.tn.gov.in/gorders/labour/labemp
2. Jalan Trading Company Private Limited vs Mills Mazdoor Union, AIR (19) SC 9611
3. Introduced retrospectively from 1 April 2006 through an Ordinance in October, 2007

chapter twelve

CHAPTER OUTLINE

LEARNING OBJECTIVES

After reading this chapter, you will be able to:

- Get a comprehensive overview of the institutional framework for the maintenance of industrial relations—preventive and reactive
- Understand the main reasons for industrial disputes
- See the trend of industrial relations in India in recent times
- Relate the IR concepts to real-life situations
- Appreciate the changing paradigms of industrial conflict from the employee-relations-management perspective

The Loco Operators

The loco operators of the traffic department in a steel plant are classified as a "critical category" of workmen. Their job involves the movement of raw materials and intermediate products from one shop to another, quickly and without spillage. Any delay on their part may lead to large production and other losses. To operate a loco, a minimum crew size was agreed to, through a tripartite agreement with the plant union. The agreement was signed six years back, but today, none of the loco drivers insisted on the minimum crew size. In case of need, they would multi-task. One day, O. P. Garg, the manager in the traffic department, got a report that one of the loco operators had refused to operate his loco, since the shunting operator was absent, thus reducing the minimum crew requirement. This led to a huge loss, since the hot metal that was to be transported from melting shop to the rolling mills was left at the shipping bay to cool off. There were reports of loco operators insisting on minimum crew strength throughout the day. The operators insisted that it was unsafe for them to operate without minimum strength and also that the absence of minimum crew increased the job burden on them. Garg recommended strict disciplinary action against the erring operators. As a result, "charge sheets" were served on all the loco operators. Immediately, the plant control reported that the entire traffic operations in the plant had come to a standstill. Workers had refused to work and had assembled in the local union office. Next day, the refusal to work had spread to other shops too and the union had served a strike notice for the entire plant. Demonstrations and gate meetings were held throughout the plant, demanding action against managers who had indulged in unfair treatment of employees, and with it, a host of other issues like safety, incentives, officiating allowance, etc. Garg reported to the general manager that all these pressure tactics by the loco operators was a manifestation of the distribution of overtime within the traffic department. This was an operational issue that was being discussed for the past few months, and by insisting on minimum crew strength, the operators and the union had just created a bargaining issue, since this had ceased to be of any significance over the past three to four years. Whatever the objective facts, the steel plant was now facing a serious industrial relations "situation". Garg was of the opinion that the management should retaliate, as negotiating on this issue will send a wrong signal. Suspending the erring loco operators and declaring a "lockout" in the traffic department were some of the "options" he suggested to the GM.

Industrial Relations: Institutional Framework for the Prevention and Settlement of Industrial Disputes

Industrial disputes issues are some of the most contentious and potentially divisive issues in many parts of the world. It is important to establish the power of prediction through a comprehensive understanding of the issues of industrial relations, particularly those covering the theoretical aspects of industrial conflict and its management in organizations, Industrial disputes are essentially symptoms of industrial unrest and reflect a lack of cooperative spirit and harmonious relations in industry. Elaborate preventive and reactive measures are put in place to minimize the debilitating social-economic-political fallouts of industrial disputes. Disputes and conflicts, to an extent, are unavoidable. The effort, therefore, is to prevent it from becoming dysfunctional, i.e., when the outcome has the potential to damage the parties to the conflict.

Situations like these are not very uncommon in an industrial set-up. Working "as per rules", raising the stakes, collective refusal to work, putting pressure on the other side and resolving conflict through the use of power are what happen at the workplace very often. The loco-operator case highlights the facets that an industrial conflict may have. This chapter will explore the issues underlying such conflicts and disputes at the workplace.

12.1 Industrial Conflict

Conflict, in some form or the other, at a workplace is inevitable. We generally get to hear of only those kinds of conflicts at workplaces that make headlines. In Chapters 12, 13 and 14, we shall be taking a look at the perspectives, causes, types and measures for resolving these conflicts.

12.1.1 The IR Perspective

Industrial conflict can occur at various levels—between two employees, between two groups of employees, between members of a group, between employees and employers as a group or individually. It has different implications for individual behaviour and work-group behaviour. Industrial conflict is generally attributed to inter-group conflict; between management and workers (unions) or between two worker groups or even between two groups of employers. Whenever there are differences between the goals of separate groups or even several individuals in a group, conflict occurs.

It needs to be understood that all conflicts are not dysfunctional. It also needs to be appreciated that conflict is inherent in the industrial structure. Industrial peace and harmony are, however, the objectives of every business organization. A conflict of interests between the various groups is essentially the progeny of a capitalist economic organization. In a situation where wants of both parties are unlimited, and resources limited, a kind of "distributive bargaining" would lead to a "win-lose" situation, which would lead to a conflict. This, if not prevented or resolved in time, is likely to result in industrial action, which may result in production and other losses. The conflict occurs due to different orientations and perceptions of interests by the three main players—the owners, the workers and the union. The pursuit of divergent objectives by each causes friction severe enough to lead to industrial actions like strikes/lockouts.

At the organizational level, industrial conflict can occur due to the interactions: (i) within individual players in the organization—between union leaders and managers and (ii) between the groups represented by the management and union leaders

These groups, organized and unorganized, manifest their conflict in various forms—some may be overt in the form of protests and strikes, while others may be in the form of undercurrent of resistances. The ultimate manifestation of industrial conflict is a strike on the part of workers, and lockout on the part of managers/employer.

The origin of conflict is perceptual differences based on each party's area or focus of interest. However, Japanese firms adopting espirit-de-corps, whereby workers resort to demonstrations in support of their demands after working hours lest it affect production, can be considered an exception. Truly, such a situation can be achieved only if the management brings about a culture of trust and empowerment that creates a strong sense of belongingness and organizational citizenship.

12.1.2 The ER Perspective

Organizational performance is based upon the cooperation between labour and capital. However, cooperation is provoked from the pursuit of self-interests as well. Thus, owners of capital offer employment, wages, welfare amenities to labour, who in turn offer their services, the quantity and quality of which is determined by the motivation and morale of the workforce. A fair degree of give-and-take would be the foundation on which a base for cooperation can be developed. How this mutual trust and sense of belongingness are developed within the organization would determine the state of employee relations in the industry.

The common thread between the IR and the ER perspective is how relationships are built within the organization, how production is carried out and how costs and profits are shared between labour and capital. The employee relations approach to conflict resolution is to focus on systemic, structural and processual aspects, creating an environment of cooperation, so as to promote the organizational-citizenship behaviour as mentioned in the paragraph above.

12.2 The Big Picture

We have come to that part of human relations, where relationships are sought to be managed between different groups at a macro-level or at the aggregate level. Conflict is a reality, and this has been realized by all the parties of industrial relations. It is axiomatic that the slate of industrial relations can never be clean. Indeed, quite a few scholars and management practitioners believe that the path to growth is only through effectively resolving conflicts. Nevertheless, it is vital that both preventive and other measures be there in place to ensure that such conflicts do not get dysfunctional and, in turn, cause losses to individuals, society, polity and economy. We, in India, also have an elaborate framework in place, both statutory and non-statutory, to prevent and resolve conflicts that may become dysfunctional. The big picture is given in Figure 12.1. As students and practitioners, it is advisable to completely understand the overall scheme of things in the total industrial relations framework. We shall, thereafter, take each of the components for a detailed treatment. In this manner, one will be able to understand the relationship of each component to the over all framework.

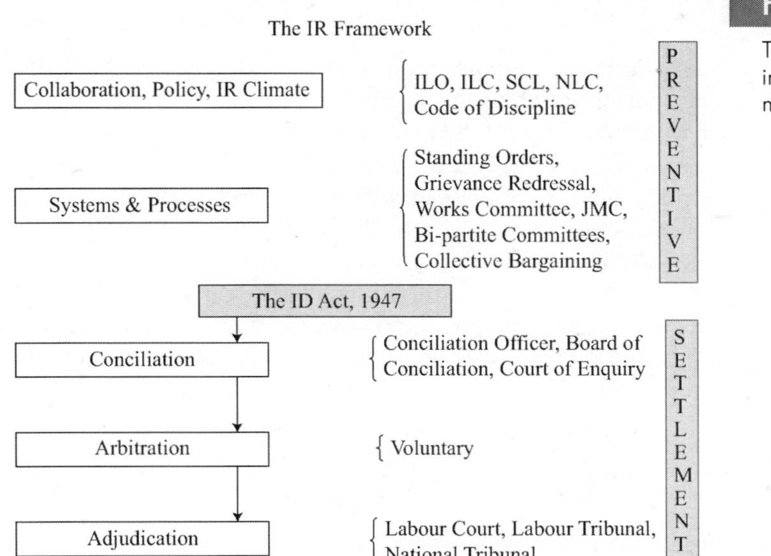

Figure 12.1 The "big picture" of industrial relationship machinery.

The top half of Fig. 12.1 (above the box labelled "The ID Act, 1947"), together, are what we can term as preventive measures, systems and processes for the maintenance of industrial peace or a productive industrial relations climate. The bottom half comprise measures that take effect when a conflict or dispute has arisen. These are mostly statutory measures and covered under the Industrial Disputes Act, 1947.

In this chapter and Chapter 13, we shall discuss, first of all, the nature, concept and causes of industrial disputes. Thereafter, we shall discuss the provisions of the Industrial Disputes Act, 1947. In Chapter 14, we shall discuss the preventive measures, systems and processes. Keep the "big picture" (Figure 12.1) in mind when we are discussing each of the components ,and where it is placed in the larger scheme of things.

12.3 Industrial Dispute Under the ID Act

There are many perspectives and definitions of industrial dispute. For the purpose of clarity, simplicity and relevance, we would consider the definition as provided in the ID Act, 1947.

According to Section 2(k) of the Industrial Disputes Act, 1947, "industrial dispute" is defined as, "Any disputes or differences between employers and employers, or employers and workmen, or workmen and workmen which is connected with the employment or non-employment or the terms of employment or with the conditions of labour, of any person". It is surprising that the definition includes differences between employers and employers also as an industrial dispute. Can you think of an example?

12.4 Industrial Dispute: Concept

Seen from the perspective of the definition stated above, various terms can be associated with "industrial dispute"—"labour dispute" or even "trade dispute", which basically are terms used to identify differences between the employers and the workers. A dispute, to become an industrial dispute, should satisfy the following:

i) There must be a dispute or a difference (a) between employers and employees; (b) between employers and workmen and (c) between workmen and workmen.

ii) It should be connected to employment or non-employment or terms of employment or with the conditions of labour (not managers or supervisors).

iii) A relationship between the employer and the workman should exist and it should be the result of the contract and the workman actually employed.

Thus, industrial dispute is related to an existing industry and must entail a real dispute. The persons or parties to the dispute are connected through an employment relationship, and have a direct or substantial interest. The requirement at (ii) eliminates issues between supervisors/managers and the top management. This marks the differentiation of the definition of "industrial disputes" viewed from an industrial relations perspective as it takes cognizance to the definition prescribed in the ID Act and the employee relations perspective, which would embody all disputes relating to the employee–employer relationship irrespective of the level of the employee concerned. It should also be noted that the subject-matter of an industrial dispute must be specific, i.e., that which affects the relationship of employers and workers. This establishes the form and type of dispute, and the resolution of the same becomes easier to operationalize.

12.5 Forms of Industrial Action

Industrial action is a term that has not been defined in any of the industrial laws but it means action that may follow if disputes of conflicts cannot be resolved through negotiations. "Strikes" and "lockouts" are forms of industrial action. In general, a strike is a form of protest by the workers or their representatives while a lockout is an industrial action taken by the employer. A strike is stoppage of work initiated or supported by a trade union when a group of employees act together as a last resort to bring pressure on an employer, to resolve a grievance or constrain him to accept such terms and conditions of service as the employees want to enjoy. If, however, an employer closes down his factory or place where his workers are employed, or if he refuses to continue in his employ a person or persons, because he wants to force them to agree to his terms and conditions of service during the pendency of a dispute, the resulting situation is a lockout.

In both "strike" and "lockout", there is an element of demand and coercion. These are the ultimate weapons in the hands of the two parties.

In the ID Act, 1947, a strike has been defined as:

"... a cessation of work by a body of persons employed in an industry acting in combination; or a concerted refusal of any number of persons who are or have been so employed to continue to work or to accept employment; or a refusal under a common understanding of any number of such persons to continue to work or to accept employment". By defining and making provisions to go on strike under certain circumstances, the ID Act, 1947 recognizes the right to go on a strike (and to declare a "lockout").

For trade unions, a strike is the most powerful weapon for forcing the management to accept their demands. Various kinds of strikes (a form of industrial action arising out of non-settlement of disputes or non-resolution of conflicts) are described below.

12.5.1 Different Forms of Strike

Strikes can be classified in several ways, although it has not been done in any of the Acts.

One such classification divides strikes into two categories—primary and secondary (see Table 12.1).

PRIMARY STRIKES. Primary strikes include the following.

i) **Economic Strike:** Most of the strikes of workers are for more facilities and increase in wage levels. In economic strike, the employees demand increase in wages, travelling allowance, house-rent allowance, dearness allowance and other facilities such as increase in privilege leave and casual leave. Pilots of an airline may go on a strike on the issue of parity in pay with expatriate pilots of the same airline.

Table 12.1

Types of industrial actions and disputes.

Types of Industrial Action	Types of Disputes
Primary Strikes	
Economic	
General	
Stay-In	Rights
Slow Down	Interest
Secondary Strikes	Grievance
Sympathetic	Recognition
Boycott	
Picketing	
Gherao	
Bandh	
Employers	
Lockout	
Bandh	

ii) **General Strike:** It means a strike by members of all or most of the unions in a region or an industry. It may be a strike of all the workers in a particular region of industry to force demands common to all the workers. It may also be an extension of the sympathetic strike to express generalized protest by the workers. The Federation of Insurance Employees may strike work across the insurance industry to mark their protest against policies of the government towards opening up the sector for FDI.

iii) **Stay-in Strike:** In this case, workers do not make themselves absent from their place of work when they are on strike. They keep control over production facilities, but they do not work. Such a strike is also known as "pen-down" or "tool-down" strike. The employees would show up for work, mark their attendance, but will not start the work.

iv) **Slow-down Strike:** This is a variation on the stay-in strike. The rate of output is reduced to a level much below the normal output rate. Employees remain on their jobs under this type of strike. They do not stop work, but restrict the rate of output in an organized manner. They adopt go-slow tactics to put pressure on the employers.

v) **Work to Rule:** Employees are not formally on strike and continue to work strictly as per the rules prescribed. Strict adherence to rules in some businesses can have a retarding effect on productivity and the quality of service. It is a form of slow-down movement.

Please refer to Box 12.1 to understand what a "go slow" in real life is. Often, there is an absence of a clear demarcation between strategies such as "go-slow" and "work to rule". You may see that the union has described the situation as work according to rules. They have explained it away by saying that workers who were not taking "scheduled" breaks are now being asked to take those breaks, which is strictly as per "rules".

BOX 12.1 **GO-SLOW AT NEW MANGALORE PORT**

Port workers at New Mangalore have adopted a go-slow attitude in work over the issue of payment of money to them. While the Dock Workers' Union at the port claims that the port workers are working as per the rule, the Association of New Mangalore Port Stevedores has said that these workers are seeking the payment of "speed money" in cash rather than in cheque. The association urged the authorities concerned to bring normalcy in the operations at the port.

In a letter to the port users, the President of the Association of New Mangalore Port Stevedores said port labourers are being paid "speed money" apart from their wages and official incentives. These labourers are drawing a huge salary and other benefits and an equal amount of unofficial "speed money". These labourers are adopting a go-slow attitude since Friday, seeking "speed money" in cash rather than in cheque. It is difficult to pay such amounts in cash, the letter said.

When contacted, the General Secretary of Dock Workers' Union said: "There is no strike. We are working as per rule." He said that earlier, some labourers were working without taking the scheduled breaks as they were getting more incentives for working that extra time. Now, they are taking those breaks.

However, he agreed with the fact that this go-slow attitude has brought down the output. The productivity might have come down by 100–150 tonnes per shift. The work-to-rule has not affected the operation, he said.

Source: Bureau, "Go Slow on New Mangalore Port on Payment," *The Hindu Business Line*, 6 May 2008.

SECONDARY STRIKES. Secondary Strikes include the following.

i) **Sympathetic Strike:** When workers of one unit or industry go on strike in sympathy with workers of another unit or industry who are already on strike, it is called a sympathetic strike.

ii) **Boycott:** The workers may decide to boycott the company in two ways—first, by not using its products; and second, by making an appeal to the public in general. In the former case, the boycott is known as primary and in the latter secondary.

iii) **Picketing:** When workers are dissuaded from work by stationing certain men at the factory gates, such a step is known as picketing. If picketing does not involve any violence, it is perfectly legal.

iv) **Gherao:** *Gherao* in Hindi means to surround. The workers may gherao the members of the management by blocking their exits and forcing them to stay inside their cabins. The main object of gherao is to inflict physical and mental duress on the person being gheraoed. This started as a political pressure tactics in West Bengal in the 1960s, and, thereafter, has been used by trade unions in the industry as a means of putting pressure on the management.

v) **Bandh:** In Hindi, it means "closed", and it is a form of protest used by political activists in countries like India and Nepal. During a bandh, a large chunk of a community declares a general strike, usually lasting one day. Often bandh means that the community or political party declaring a bandh expect the general public to stay in their homes and strike work. Also, all the shopkeepers are expected to keep their shops closed and the transport operators like buses and cabs are supposed to stay off the road and not carry any passengers. All this is expected to be voluntary, but in many instances, people are terrorized and coerced into participating in a bandh. There have been instances of large metropolitan cities coming to a standstill. Bandhs are powerful means for civil disobedience. Because of the huge impact that a bandh has on the local community, it is much feared as a tool of protest. A bandh is not the same as a "hartal", which simply means a strike—during a bandh, any business activity (and sometimes even traffic) in the area affected will be forcibly prevented by the strikers. In recent years, the courts have taken a very serious view towards bandh, which is considered a tool that causes misery to the general public.

MANAGEMENT ACTIONS TO COUNTER STRIKES. The management uses its own methods to counter the workers. Some of the industrial actions in the management armoury are:

1. **Employers' Association:** The employers may form their unions to collectively oppose the working class and put pressure on the trade unions.
2. **Lockout:** An employer may close down the place of employment temporarily. Such a step is technically known as lockout. It is the reverse of a strike and is a very powerful weapon in the hands of an employer to pressurize the workers to return to the place of work. According to the Industrial Disputes Act, 1947, "lockout means the closing of a place of employment or the suspension of work, or the refusal by an employer to continue to employ any number of persons employed by him (please refer to Box 12.2). Here, the management has tried to put counter-pressure on the union and the workmen against alleged "illegal strike" by the union. Notice that, just like strike, lockout also has an element of "demand".
3. **Termination of Service:** The employers may resort to suspension or disciplinary action leading to termination of services of those workers who are on strike. The list of employees so suspended/dismissed may be circulated to other employers so as to act as a deterrent and also restrict their chances of getting employment with other employers.

Procedures for avoiding strikes, lockouts and other forms of coercive action, in connection with industrial disputes between trade unions and employers are generally laid down in the form of a clause or clauses in an agreement between the two. At the same time, it is also laid down that there shall be no stoppage of work and no coercive act on the part of either party, to a dispute till the procedures outlined in the agreement have been gone through and the two parties have been unable to come to a compromise or reach a settlement. As we will see later, there are elaborate provisions and guidelines, both statutory and non-statutory, which are meant to prevent conflicts and disputes from getting dysfunctional. Yet, they do! Box 12.3 provides a glimpse of the extent to which they do! And please notice that all the 430 disputes in the box resulted in some form of industrial action (temporary work stoppages due to a strike or a lockout). Many actions fail to make it to the labour statistics due to a variety of reasons (for example, you may, as an ER manager, be reluctant to book production loss to man/woman-made disputes. It may have a bearing on your annual appraisal). Thus, industrial-disputes reporting is anything but simple.

BOX 12.2 **LOCKOUT DECLARED BY APOLLO TYRES**

On 6 December 2008, recession-hit Tyre major, Apollo Tyres, declared a "lockout" in its Kalamassery unit in Kerala. The unit employs 1,100 persons. According to the management, this unit was a high-cost centre in terms of cost of production. To overcome this challenge, management had been trying its best to improve the utilization of equipments and machinery in sections such as curing and extrusion. Cooperation of the union had been sought to overcome the challenge. But the unions, according to the management, had taken a negative and non-cooperative attitude. There was reluctance to even give agreed output in terms of long-term settlement signed earlier. The immediate provocation for the lockout, according to management, was the "illegal strike" resorted to by the union after months of non-cooperative and confrontationist attitude.

BOX 12.3 **INDUSTRIAL DISPUTES AND INDUSTRIAL ACTION: FY 2006**

Industrial Disputes: 430 industrial disputes were reported involving 1.81 million workers and resulting in total loss of 20.32 million man-days, INR.1730.07 (in 173 cases reported) were lost by workers as wages and production loss of INR 3813.82 million was reported (in 99 cases). Out of these disputes, 80 (18.60 per cent) were in central sphere and 350 (81.40 per cent) in the state sphere. The private sector accounted for 342 (79.53 per cent) industrial disputes and the public sector only 88 (20.47 per cent) disputes were reported. There has been a declining trend in the number of disputes, workers involved and man-days lost over the previous year 2005. The declining trend indicates comparatively better working condition and cordial industrial relations during the year 2006.

Among the states, West Bengal accounted for the highest number of disputes, i.e., 173 (40.23 per cent). The manufacturing sector among the industry groups reported 259 (60.23 per cent) of the disputes and "Wages and Allowances" was the cause which accounted for 18.37 per cent of disputes reported during the year 2006.

Strikes and Lockouts: Out of 430 industrial disputes reported during 2006, 243 (56.51 per cent) were strikes and 187 (43.49 per cent) were lockouts. The private sector accounted for 63.79 per cent (155) of the strikes. Amongst the states, Tamil Nadu accounted for the highest number of strikes, i.e., 50 (20.58 per cent) and West Bengal reported the highest number of lockouts, i.e., 144 (77.01 per cent). There has been an increase in the number of strikes and decline in the number of lockouts during 2006 as compared to the year 2005.

Others: The number of work-stoppages due to reasons other than industrial disputes during the year 2006 was 182. Out of the total, 178 were lockouts and 4 were strikes. Here, too, there has been a declining trend in the number of disputes, workers involved and man-days lost, which indicates better management of the economy and availability of raw materials, power and sufficient demand for the products, etc. during the year.

Adapted from "Statistics on Industrial Disputes, Closures, Retrenchment and Lay-Offs in India During the Year 2006", Labour Bureau, Government of India (http://labourbureau.nic.in/reports.htm).

12.6 Types of Disputes

Industrial disputes may be raised on any of the following issues:

i) Fairness of the Standing Orders

ii) Interpretation of Standing Orders and "settlements" and "rules"

iii) Retrenchment of workers following the closing down of a factory, lays-offs, discharge or dismissal, reinstatement of dismissed employees and compensation for them

iv) Coverage of benefits to particular employees, dependants, non-payment of personal allowance to seasonal employees; the demand of employees for medical relief for their parents

v) Wage, fixation of wages and minimum rates, modes of payment and the right of an employee to choose one of the awards when two awards on wages have been given

vi) Lockout and claim for damages by an employer because employees resorted to an illegal strike

vii) Payment of bonus, gratuity, provident fund, pension and travelling allowance

viii) Disputes between rival unions

ix) Disputes between employers and employees

12.6.1 The Classification of Disputes

It is sometimes convenient to put the myriad of dispute under certain categories. It will help in providing some structure to the study of disputes and will automatically throw light on the genesis of disputes. The Industrial Disputes Act, 1947 does not provide for any such classification, nor do any of the employment-related statutes in India. Academics and practising managers have attempted to classify disputes in different categories. One such categorization classifies disputes into:

DISPUTES OF RIGHTS. These relate to the application or interpretation of an existing agreement or contract of employment. This kind of dispute, if unresolved through negotiations, is very amenable to resolution through arbitration or adjudication.

DISPUTES OF INTEREST. These relate to claims by employees or proposals by a management about the terms and conditions of employment. These are mostly disputes that can be resolved through discussions and negotiations, give and take. However, in the event of a dispute not getting resolved through negotiation, these too may be left for resolution through arbitration/adjudication.

Another common scheme of classification is based on the terms of employment. These are:

i) **Interest Disputes:** Arising out of deadlocks in negotiations for a collective agreement

ii) **Grievance Disputes:** Arising from day-to-day workers' grievance or complaints

iii) **Disputes Relating to Discipline:** Arising from acts of interference with the exercise of right to organize, or acts, also termed as "unfair labour practices"

iv) **Recognition Disputes:** Disputes over the right of a trade union to represent a particular class or category of workers for purposes of collective bargaining

12.7 Severity of Effects

Manifestations of industrial unrest or conflict cause stoppage of work and/or disruption of production. Continued and prolonged industrial unrest has serious consequences for the employees, employers and also for the economy at large.

From the point of view of the employer, an industrial dispute resulting in stoppage of work means a stoppage of production at the expense of fixed costs, which will yield no returns. It may lead to a dip in sales turnover, leading to a fall in profits, and loss of prestige and credibility in business. In some cases, it may also result in destruction of property, personal injury and physical intimidation or inconvenience. An establishment prone to industrial unrest would also be a barrier in attracting the best available manpower. Investment climate suffers and, thus, modernization, expansion and technological upgradation become that much more difficult.

For the employee, an industrial dispute entails loss of income, as invariably, a strike or any form of protest leads to the deduction in wages. In India, the ability of trade unions to provide for the needs of striking workers is very limited. The threat of loss of employment in case of failure to settle the dispute advantageously, or the threat of reprisal action by employers also exists.

Prolonged stoppages of work have also an adverse effect on the national productivity and national income. In some cases, it may also result in political action disrupting amicable social relations.

12.8 Causes of Industrial Dispute

The disputes between the management and the workers may arise on account of the following factors:

1. **Economic Cause:** These causes may be classified as:

- Demand for increase in wages on account of increase in all-India consumer price index for industrial workers
- Demand for better social-security benefits
- Demand for higher bonus
- Demand for certain allowances such as:
  - House-rent allowance
  - Medical allowance
  - Night-shift allowance
  - Conveyance allowance
- Demand for paid holidays
- Mode or terms and conditions of employment
- Reduction of working hours
- Better working conditions
- Violation of a registered agreement or settlement or award
- Demarcation or role clarity about a job or function

2. **Political Causes:** As in India, various political parties control trade unions in India. In many cases, their leadership vests in the hands of persons who are more interested in achieving their political interests rather than the interests of the workers.
3. **Personnel Causes:** Sometimes, industrial disputes arise because of personnel problems like dismissal, retrenchment, layoff, transfer, promotion, etc.
4. **Indiscipline:** Industrial disputes also take place because of indiscipline and violence on the part of the workforce. The managements, to curb indiscipline and violence, resort to disciplinary action. In some cases, they may resort to lockouts as well.
5. **Managements:** Generally, they are not willing to talk over any dispute with their employees or their representatives. It may also be on account of the management's unwillingness to recognize a particular trade union. Even when the representative trade unions have been recognized by employers, officials are not delegated to negotiate with the workers or representatives.
6. **Absence of Grievance Redress Machinery or Procedure:** This results in the accumulation of grievances creating a climate of unrest among workers.
7. **Government Machinery:** The machinery provided by the government for the resolution of industrial conflicts may be inadequate and slow.
8. **Miscellaneous Causes:** Some of the other causes of industrial disputes can be:
   - Workers' resistance to rationalization
   - Automation, the introduction of new machinery
   - Change of place

   Often, unemployment results from the implementation of rationalization schemes and the installation of new machines because of which fewer persons would be employed. Capital-intensive, rather than labour-intensive, industries are set up, which further aggravates the problem of unemployment and creates dissatisfaction among the workers.

   - Non-recognition of trade union
   - Misinformation campaigns and rumours

BOX 12.4 FOR CLASS DISCUSSION

Nandigram in East Midnapur district of West Bengal is one of the seven SEZs sanctioned in West Bengal. The proposed SEZ (now scrapped) was to develop a mega-chemical hub. The choice of this mega-chemical hub in the Haldia region was the result of a long exercise undertaken by the Government of India where this venue was chosen along with four other sites in the country. With the existing petroleum refinery of the IOC, the petrochemical plant at Haldia in the joint sector and the huge facility of Mitsubishi chemicals, this decision to have the mega-chemical hub located here made business sense. The Haldia petrochemicals have led to 700 units in the downstream providing an employment to over 1 lakh people. The Government of West Bengal had signed a Memorandum of Understanding with the Indian Oil Corporation to be an anchor investor for the project, while the Salim group would have been the promoter for building the infrastructure.

The Chief Minister of West Bengal had stated no progress on the project would take place until consultations were held with elected representatives in the panchayat and the people of the area. As there had been no survey done and consultations held, the question of land acquisition did not arise before these processes took place.

The demand was that land acquisition would only take place if a credible plan for improving the quality of life and livelihood could be put forth. This was the overall approach of the left.

To add to the unrest, a number of other political forces had come together at Nandigram. There were cases of legitimate protests and also cases of planned violence disrupting the peace at Nandigram. The compelling reason for any such project in the state will be premised on the question of employment generation and improving the lot of the poor and disadvantaged sections. The Left Front had anticipated the need for such a project on the eve of the last elections. Therefore, the Left Front election manifesto had clearly stated: "Industrial parks have been decided to be set up in the task of modernizing the traditional labour-intensive industries, and to make them competitive. Parks will be set up for foundry, jute, rubber, garments, textile, iron and steel, chemicals polymer, light engineering, and food" and "a minimum of four big industrial taluka and special economic zones will be set up in the state".

The industrial conflict here was with regard to the nature of the industry and the manner in which it took place. The difference in perception was with regard to the private corporate's way of viewing industries and that of the Left. Will this have an effect on workplace IR?

- Working conditions and working methods
- Lack of proper communication
- Behaviour of supervisors
- Inter-trade-union rivalry, etc.

9. **Non-Industrial factors:** There could be many causes that are rooted in historical, political and socio-economic factors and the attitudes of workers and their employers. Some of the causes of dispute could be—no improvement in the standard of living of employees who put forward demands for higher wages, or persons displaced on account of an industrial activity on land acquired from them. Refer to Box 12.4.

12.9 Measures to Improve Industrial Relations

These are a few measures required for a healthy industrial relationship—

Progressive Management Outlook: There should be progressive outlook of the management of each industrial enterprise in relation to—

- Obligations and responsibilities to the owners of the business, the employees, the consumers and the nation
- The rights of workers and proactive approach towards addressing issues of concern, or an employee relations approach

Strong and Stable Union: The union must be strong and stable to represent the majority of workers and negotiate with the management about the terms and conditions of service.

An Atmosphere of Mutual Trust: Through a systemic approach at developing an atmosphere of mutual cooperation, confidence and respect have to be created. While the management adopts a progressive outlook and recognizes the rights of workers, the labour unions are to take pains and persuade their members to work for the common objectives of the organization. Both the management and the unions must repose faith in collective bargaining and other peaceful methods of settling disputes.

Collaboration: The employers must recognize the right of collective bargaining of the trade unions (not only in letter but in spirit). In any organization, there must be a great emphasis on mutual accommodation rather than conflict or uncompromising competitive attitude. Competitive attitude is likely to foster union militancy. The approach must be of mutual "give and take" for creating "win-win" situations.

Fair Implementation of Agreements: One must sincerely adhere to the terms of settlements reached with the trade unions in letter and spirit.

Workers' Participation in Management: The participation of workers in the management of the industrial unit should be encouraged by making effective use of workers' committees, joint consultation and other methods. This will improve communication between managers and workers, which may, in the long run, increase productivity and lead to greater effectiveness.

Measures to Improve IR

- Progressive management outlook
- Strong and stable union
- An atmosphere of mutual trust
- Collaboration
- Fair implementation of agreements
- Workers' participation in management
- Sound personnel policies
- The government's role

Sound HRM Systems, Policies: As far as practicable, the following measures regarding HRM-related policies would have a bearing on healthy IR:

- Consultation in formulation of policies
- Clarity in statement of objectives, procedures, rules and regulation
- Uniformity in implementation of the policies

The Government as an Honest Broker: The government should play an active role for promoting industrial peace. It should facilitate collective bargaining through measures aimed at creating "bargaining agents" in each industrial unit. It should intervene to settle disputes if the management and the workers are unable to settle their disputes. This will ensure industrial harmony.

12.10 Industrial Disputes: A Historical Perspective

An overall assessment of industrial peace or unrest can be made through a series of hard data over a period of time. The Labour Bureau, Government of India publishes annual data on the following:

i) Number of work stoppages and lockouts

ii) Man-hours lost due to industrial disputes

iii) Production loss due to industrial disputes

In a broader context, strikes or lockouts or collective work stoppages are taken as indicators of good or bad industrial relation. Taking an ER or employee relations perspective would include the number of grievances not settled attrition rate of the company, career growth opportunities, etc. Comparisons of the number of work stoppages or man-days lost would be meaningful

Industrial disputes resulting in work stoppages. **Table 12.2**

	1961	1971	1981	1991	2003	2004	2005
No. of Disputes	1357	2752	2589	1810	552	477	456
No. of Workers Involved ('000)	511860	138937	1588004	1342022	1816	2072	2914
Man-days Lost ('000)	4918755	16545636	36583564	26428090	30256	23866	29665
Wages Lost					66.14	108.16	116.12
(Rs. in Crores)					(191)	(160)	(146)
Value of Production Loss (Rs. In Crores)					418.49	355.60	345.07
					(149)	(131)	(121)

Source: Various issues of the *Handbook of Labour Statistics* and the annual report of the Ministry of Labour.

only if compared against the workable population of the country. Further, statistics published by the labour ministry take into consideration only the organized sector. A large part of industrial activity in India is also in the unorganized sector. Table 12.2 shows the trends in industrial disputes over the years. The table includes end-of-decade figures for earlier years.

It is interesting to note that even though the number of work stoppages has reduced, the the impact in terms of number of workers involved and wage loss have has grown over the years. The intensity as well as frequency, both, account for the dynamics of the industrial relations environment. Table 12.3 traces the nature and underlying causes of industrial disputes in the organized sector in India over a period of time, since the early part of the twentieth century.

An analysis of labour statistics indicates:

- An upward trend in disputes begins after 1965 induced by inflationary pressure
- The decade of the 1970s influenced by inter-union rivalry and politically provoked disputes
- Marked reduction in the 1980s as labour found it difficult to protest with a change in the balance of power, more so with the advent of the New Economic Policy
- Labour-intensive industries like plantations, coal, textiles, railways and banking have accounted for 20–30 per cent of work stoppages in India
- Work stoppages were fewer in the public sector than the private sector

For an understanding and appreciation of the industrial relations scenario in the current phase of economic growth in the country, a detailed analysis of the industrial conflicts in the current decade is more important. The socio-economic environment today is markedly different. The *Pocketbook of Labour Statistics,* published by the Labour Bureau, Government of India, is a very useful source for analysing trends. The analysis in the following paragraphs is based on these annual publications.

The number of industrial disputes in the country has shown a slow but steady fall over the past 10 years. In 1998, the total number of disputes was 1,097, which fell by more than half to 440 in 2006. This significant decline is attributed to the serious attempts made by industries to improve relations with their workers on a one-to-one basis. This is the paradigm shift from an industrial relations approach to an employee relations approach. However, a deeper look at the data reveals that the number of man-days (i.e., the industrial unit of production equal to the work one person can produce in a day) lost due to disputes has not

Table 12.3 Causes of industrial disputes.

Period	Characteristics	Reasons	Outcome
Prior to 1920	No signs of industrial unrest		
1920–1930	Frequent strikes involving textile workers of Bombay, railway workers and jute workers of Bengal	Wages affected by trade depression—wage and bonus issues, growing cohesion among workers, no effective organization to address demands of workers	Appointment of Industrial Disputes Enquiry Committee in 1921 to study the Bombay strike
1930–1940	Decline in number of strikes but intensity stronger—Kanpur textile industry strike most eventful	Wage and bonus issues	
1940–1950	Pre–World War II period strikes affected by price rise but post-War period notorious years in the history of industrial unrest affecting cotton, woollen and silk mills. In 1949, intense industrial unrest in railways and post and telegraph	Higher wages, leave and conditions of work	Two Ordinances: 1. Defence of India rules prohibiting strikes and lockouts and compel employers and workers to observe certain terms and conditions 2. 1942—prohibiting a person from going on strike without giving 15 days' notice 3. ID Act, 1948
1950–1960	General strike in Bombay textile mills started on 14 August 1950 continuing till 17 October 1950. Cotton textile mills affected the most	Rise in cost of living and rising expectations of workers post-Independence, growing communist influence among workers	Code of Discipline evolved in 1958
1960–1970	Reduction in industrial disputes	Adjudication machinery functioning well	Industrial Truce Resolution of 1962
1970–1980	Emergency period—declining trend in number of disputes but reversed during post-Emergency—worst-hit states West Bengal and Maharashtra	Outburst of excesses suffered by workers during emergency period and rejection of routine grievances	
1980–1990	Relative peace	Economic pressure	
1990s	Aggressive employer, clamour for labour-market flexibility and labour-law reforms	Liberalization	Amendments proposed in labour laws but not enacted, stalemate

come down as significantly. The country, on an average, lost 25.4 million man-days of work annually between 1998 and 2006. The most recent statistics relating to man-days lost and the number of disputes is given in Table 12.4.

The decline in the number of industrial disputes has been consistent since 1998, as shown in Table 12.4 and Fig. 12.2. Following this, a decline of 2.3 per cent has been registered

Table 12.4

Industrial disputes (*in numbers*).

Year	Number of Disputes				Workers involved ('000)				Man days lost (in millions)			
	Strikes	Lockouts	Total		Strikes	Lockouts	Total		Strikes	Lockouts	Total	
2001	372	302	674	*−12.6*	489	199	688	*−51.5*	5.56	18.2	23.77	*−17.4*
2002	295	284	579	*−14.1*	900	179	1079	*56.8*	9.66	16.92	26.58	*11.8*
2003	255	297	552	*−4.7*	1011	805	1816	*68.3*	3.2	27.04	30.25	*13.8*
2004	239	230	469	*−15.0*	1742	141	1883	*3.7*	3.9	10.4	14.3	−52.7
2005*	243	215	458	−2.3	2111	184	2295	*21.9*	7.3	16.0	23.3	62.9

Note: Monthly data are provisional. *Figures for 2005 are not strictly comparable with those for 2004 in view of the incomplete coverage of the former. Figures in italics are percentage change over the previous year. Source: *Indian Labour Journal, Labour Bureau,* various issues and *Ministry of Labour and Employment, 2004–2005*

in 2005 over the previous year. Although there has been a decline in the number of strikes, the country still witnessed some major strikes between 2004 and 2006, like those in Honda, Escorts, Apollo, and S Kumar's factories and in SBI.

Interestingly, the number of workers involved and man-days lost has risen substantially in 2005, which can be attributed to greater worker participation in disputes and prolonged nature of industrial disputes, as compared to those in 2004. Nevertheless, a declining number of industrial disputes exhibit relative improvement in labour relations as compared to the yester years, which could be conducive to faster industrial growth. There have been 222 disputes in which 51,127 workers have been affected and 10,496,911 man-days have been lost due to the reasons other than industrial disputes during 2005. These reasons may include shortage of raw material, shortage of power, financial stringency, wages-and-allowances indiscipline or violence, and non-implementation of labour enactments, etc.

In February 2006, there have been 17 industrial disputes due to which more than 1,67,000 man-days were lost. This was slightly lesser than approximately 1,73,000 man-days lost in February 2005 due to a larger number of workers involved. Interestingly, the number of industrial disputes has shown sudden increase in a month's time; it increased to 17 in February 2006 as against 4 in January 2006. Similarly, the number of workers involved and the man-days lost due to these disputes has also shown substantial increase during such a short span of time.

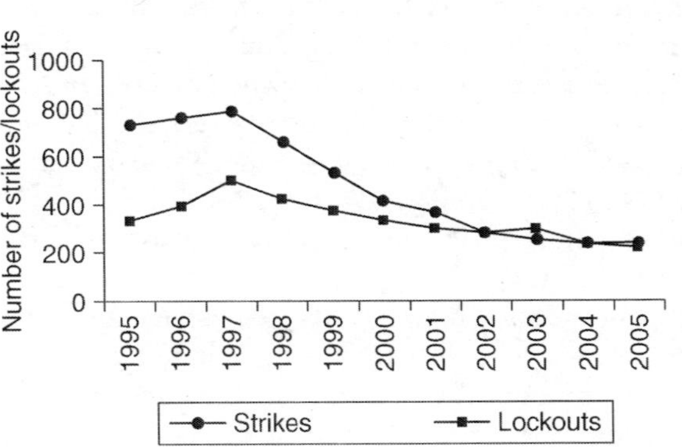

Figure 12.2

The number of strikes and lockouts from 1995 to 2005.

12.10.1 Sector-wise Trends

The numbers of strikes reported during 2005 were 227 (56 in public and 171 in private sector) and 229 lockouts (1 in public and 228 in private sector). The numbers (456) of disputes reported during 2005 were less by 4.4 per cent as compared to the year 2004 (477). The percentage share of public sector in the number of disputes, workers involved and man-days lost was 12.5, 70.0 and 7.8 per cent respectively of the all-India total numbers of disputes, workers involved and man-days lost. Similarly, private sector constituted 87.5, 30.0 and 92.2 per cent respectively.

12.10.2 Spatial Trends

On an all-India basis, the state sphere had the highest percentage of disputes and man-days lost (i.e. 89.9 per cent and 92.6 per cent), whereas, central sphere constituted less number of disputes and man-days lost (i.e., 10.1 per cent and 7.4 per cent). The large number of workers involved in strikes and lockouts, i.e., 69.9 per cent, were in the central sphere as compared to the state sphere. In the Central Sphere, the ***Banks*** accounted for the highest time loss (1.49 million man-days) followed by Industry group ***Coal Mines*** with 0.50 million man-days.

12.10.3 A State-wise Comparison

West Bengal accounted for the highest time loss during 2005 (19.22 million man-days) followed by Kerala (3.62 million man-days), Rajasthan (1.93 million man-days), Maharashtra (1.43 million man-days), Andhra Pradesh (1.01 million man-days) and Tamil Nadu (0.66 million man-days). In the central sphere, Andhra Pradesh had the highest number of disputes (13) and workers involved were 0.93 millions and the number of man-days lost (0.94 million man-days) were the highest in Maharashtra. There was only one lockout reported in the central sphere, involving 64,721 workers and resulting, thereby, 0.19 million man-days. Out of 229 lockouts, as many as 223 or 97.38 per cent were pure lockouts (i.e., lockouts originating and terminating as lockouts). These lockouts caused a time loss of 18.26 million man-days or 96.78 per cent of the total time loss caused by all lockouts in the country. The state of West Bengal accounted for the highest number of pure lockouts, i.e., 181 resulting in a time loss of 15.86 million man-days or 86.85 per cent of the total time loss caused by pure lockouts during the year 2005.

12.10.4 Industry-wise Trends

Amongst the industry group, the manufacturing sector accounted for the highest number of disputes (290 or 63.60 per cent of the total disputes) with a time loss of 19.33 million man-days or 65.15 per cent of the total time loss. Within this industry division, "manufacturing of textiles" accounted for the highest time loss (13.54 million man-days or 70.03 per cent of the total time loss) in the manufacturing division during the year 2005.

The industries facing intense agitation from the workers have been textiles, engineering, chemicals and food products, where indiscipline and violence, wage rates and personnel issues have been the primary causes of strikes and lockouts. In terms of industry-wise permanent closures and workers affected, the manufacturing sector has recorded the highest number along with other industries like "other community, social and personal services". Similarly, in terms of the number of units affecting retrenchment and workers affected thereby, the only industry, which has registered positive numbers, is "health and social".

It is apparent that both, the employers and employees, hold their respective strong grounds in order to justify their stand in industrial matters. This calls for an urgent need to rationalize labour laws in terms of regulating working hours and wages of contract labour and establishing machinery for a dispute resolution. Some states like Andhra Pradesh, Madhya Pradesh and Maharashtra have proposed to seek relaxation in provisions of the central laws through state enactments. Even though labour reform in India remains a contentious issue, a significant change in India's industrial sector after 2002 was witnessed in a dramatic 50 per cent fall in instances of strikes and lockouts.

12.10.5 Cause-wise Trends

As regards the causes of industrial disputes, they can be broadly classified into two categories: economic and non-economic causes. The economic causes will include issues relating to compensation like wages, bonus, allowances, and conditions for work, working hours, leave and holidays without pay, unjust layoffs and retrenchments. The non-economic factors will include victimization of workers, ill-treatment by staff members, sympathetic strikes, political factors, indiscipline, etc.

- **Wages and Allowances:** Since the cost of living index is increasing, workers generally bargain for higher wages to meet the rising cost of living index and to increase their standards of living. In 2002, 21.4 per cent of disputes were caused by the demand for higher wages and allowances. This percentage was 20.4 per cent during 2003 and during 2004 increased up to 26.2 per cent. In 2005, wages and allowances accounted for 21.8 per cent of the disputes.
- **Personnel and Retrenchment:** The personnel and retrenchment have also been an important factor that accounted for disputes. During the year 2002, disputes caused by personnel were 14.1 per cent, while those caused by retrenchment and layoffs were 2.2 per cent and 0.4 per cent respectively. In 2003, a similar trend could be seen, wherein 11.2 per cent of the disputes were caused by personnel, while 2.4 per cent and 0.6 per cent of the disputes were caused by retrenchment and layoffs. In 2005, only 9.6 per cent of the disputes were caused by personnel, and only 0.4 per cent was caused by retrenchment.
- **Indiscipline and Violence:** The number of disputes caused by indiscipline has shown an increasing trend. In 2002, 29.9 per cent of the disputes were caused because of indiscipline, which rose up to 36.9 per cent in 2003. Similarly, in 2004 and 2005, 40.4 per cent and 41.6 per cent of disputes were caused due to indiscipline, respectively. During the year 2003, indiscipline accounted for the highest percentage (36.9 per cent) of the total time loss of all disputes, followed by cause-groups wage and allowance and personnel with 20.4 per cent and11.2 per cent respectively. A similar trend was observed in 2004, where indiscipline accounted for 40.4 per cent of the disputes.
- **Bonus:** Bonus has always been an important factor in industrial disputes; 6.7 per cent of the disputes were because of bonus in 2002 and 2003 as compared to 3.5 per cent and 3.6 per cent in 2004 and 2005 respectively.
- **Leave and Working Hours:** Leaves and working hours have not been very important causes of industrial disputes. During 2002, 0.5 per cent of the disputes were because of leave and hours of work, while this percentage increased to 1 per cent in 2003. During 2004, only 0.4 per cent of the disputes were because of leaves and working hours.
- **Miscellaneous:** The miscellaneous factors include inter/intra-union rivalry, charter of demands, workload issues, Standing orders/rules/service, conditions/safety measures, non-implementation of agreements and awards, etc.

Table 12.5 gives cause-wise break-up (based on the classification adopted by the Ministry of Labour since 1992) of the number of industrial disputes during the period 2002–2005. In terms of time lost on account of industrial disputes, "Wages and Allowances" and "Bonus" accounted for 31.35 per cent of the total time loss due to industrial disputes. Amongst the non-monetary causes, indiscipline accounted for the highest time loss, i.e., 47.84 per cent followed by personnel, i.e., 1.87 per cent of the total time loss during the year 2005. The single most important cause "indiscipline" was responsible for 72.93 per cent (167) lockouts to the

Table 12.5

A cause-wise analysis of the number of labour disputes.

Cause Group	2002	2003	2004	2005
Wages & allowances	21.3	20.4	26.2	21.8
Personnel	14.1	11.2	13.2	9.6
Retrenchment	2.2	2.4	0.2	0.4
Lay off	0.4	0.6	–	0.2
Indiscipline	29.9	36.9	40.4	41.6
Violence	0.9	1	0.9	0.4
Leave and Hours of work/shift working	0.5	1	0.4	–
Bonus	6.7	6.7	3.5	3.6
Inter/Intra-union rivalry	0.4	0.6	0.4	0.4
Non-implementation of agreements	3.1	1	1.1	0.9
Charter of demands	10.5	8.8	5.7	7.1
Workload	0.5	0.4	0.7	1.1
Standing orders, service rules, safety measures	1.8	1	2.4	0.2

Source: Compiled from *Pocket Book of Labour Statistics, 2006*

total number of lockouts, which alone accounted for 74.28 per cent of the total time loss due to lockouts during the year 2005. Three all-India strikes took place on 22 March 2005, 31 March 2005 and 29 September 2005 in nationalised banks, Life Insurance Corporation of India and in other various industries due to the causes of "Wages and Allowances" and "Charter of Demands" in which 1.83 million workers were involved and accounted for a time loss of 1.83 million man-days during the year 2005. During the year 2005, 239 disputes were reported, which were caused by reasons other than industrial disputes. Out of these, 235 (98.33 per cent) cases were of lockouts and 4 (1.67 per cent) cases of strikes, which accounted for 99.44 per cent and 0.56 per cent of time loss respectively.

12.11 Machinery to Deal with Industrial Disputes

These days not only the employers and workers, but also the government and the public at large are equally concerned about disputes, since conflicts, if not resolved in time, take the form of strikes or lockouts resulting in the loss of profit, wages, production and supply of goods. There are various ways to cope with industrial conflicts, which have been discussed in the following section.

12.11.1 Statutory and Non-statutory Measures

In India, the various measures of conflict resolution can be broadly categorized into statutory measures, non-statutory measures and government-sponsored guidelines. Statutory measures relate to the various types of machinery set up by the government under the Industrial Disputes Act, 1947 (like Labour Courts and Industrial and National Tribunals) for specific conflicts which the government refers to the respective authorities. Moreover, the formation of Works Committees is also statutorily provided for, to see that the conflict is resolved in time. Several non-statutory measures like the code of discipline, workers' participation in management and collective bargaining, which are voluntary in nature, are supported by the government, and they help in resolving the conflict. These non-statutory measures encourage a resolution through negotiation between the two parties and, thus, by their very nature, speed up the process and cut short the long procedures. Also, intervention by a third party can be considerably minimized or done away with altogether. The government labour departments both at the central and the states have a considerable role to play in maintaining industrial harmony. We shall examine the various methods in some detail.

12.12 The Industrial Disputes Act, 1947

The diverse and conflicting interests of the workmen and employers, the growing labour consciousness and ever-expanding complex industrial spectra entail frequent friction of the opposite interests resulting in strikes and lockouts, paralysing the industrial world. This necessitates amicable settlements to put an end to the dispute already in existence or to prevent an apprehended dispute. The Industrial Disputes Act, 1947 was an outcome of this need to create a preventive as well as settlement machinery for minimizing industrial unrest.

The Industrial Disputes Act, 1947 is a special legislation, which applies to workmen drawing wages not exceeding a specified amount per month and governs the service conditions of such persons. This Act deals with the prevention and the settlement of conflicts in pursuance of industrial peace and harmony.

The Act provides for a special machinery of conciliation officers, work committees, courts of inquiry, Labour Courts, Industrial Tribunals and National Tribunals defining their powers, functions and duties and also the procedure to be followed by them.

12.12.1 Objectives

The Industrial Disputes Act, 1947 is formulated to make provisions for the investigation and the settlement of industrial disputes and for certain other purposes. It is an Act that aims to ensure specific justice both to the employers and workmen and advance the progress of industry by bringing about harmony and cordial relationships between the parties. Specifically, the object of the Act is to:

i) Promote measures for securing and preserving amity and good relations between employer and employees to minimize the differences, and to get the dispute settled through adjudicatory authorities

ii) Provide suitable machinery for the investigation and the settlement of industrial disputes between employers and employees, between employers and workmen, or between workmen and workmen with a right of representation by a registered trade union or by an association of employers

iii) Prevent illegal strikes and lockouts

iv) Provide relief to workmen in matters of lay-offs, retrenchment, wrongful dismissals and victimization

v) Give the workmen the right of collective bargaining and promote conciliation

vi) In short, ameliorate the conditions of workmen in an industry.

12.12.2 Definitions

It is important to have a clear understanding of how the following terms are defined in the Act.

Appropriate Government: In relation to any industrial dispute concerning any industry carried on by or under the authority of the central government, or by a railway company or concerning any such controlled industry as may be specified in this behalf by the central government or in relation to an industrial dispute specifically mentioned in the Act

Controlled Industry: Any industry the control of which by the union has been declared by any central Act to be expedient in the public interest

Industry: Any business, trade, undertaking, manufacturing or calling of employers and includes any calling, service, employment, handicraft, or industrial occupation or a vocation of workmen. This definition has since been amended but not implemented. The amendment has come about because of a series of interpretations by the Supreme Court over the years. In effect, the position today is that, save for the sovereign functions of the state, all other organizations/enterprise would fall within the meaning of industry unless the government specifically mentions otherwise. However, due to political and other implications, the amended definition has not been put into effect yet.

Industrial Establishment or Undertaking: An establishment or undertaking in which any industry is carried on. There may be certain establishments comprising more than one unit. Maybe, there is "industry" being carried out in one unit but not in other units. So, if the unit is "severable" from the others, it would be a separate industrial establishment. Provided that where several activities are carried on in an establishment or undertaking and only one or some of such activities is or are an industry or industries, then,-if any unit of such establishment or undertaking carrying on any activity, being an industry, is severable from the other unit or units of such establishment or undertaking, such unit shall be deemed to be a separate industrial establishment or undertaking; if the predominant activity or each of the predominant activities carried on in such establishment or undertaking or any unit thereof is an industry and the other activity or each of the other activities carried on in such establishment or undertaking or unit thereof is not severable from and is, for the purpose of carrying on, or aiding the carrying on of such predominant activity or activities, the entire establishment or undertaking or, as the case may be, unit thereof shall be deemed to be an industrial establishment or undertaking.

Lay-off: The failure, refusal or inability of an employer, on account of shortage of coal, power or raw materials or the accumulation of stocks or the break-down of machinery or natural calamity or for any other connected reason, to give employment to a workman whose name is borne on the muster rolls of his industrial establishment and who has not been retrenched

Lockout: The temporary closing of a place of employment, or the suspension of work, or the refusal by an employer to continue to employ any number of persons employed by him

Retrenchment: The termination by an employer of the service of a workman for any reason whatsoever, other than as a punishment inflicted by way of disciplinary action. It does not include—voluntary retirement of the workman; or retirement of the workman on reaching the age of superannuation if the contract of employment between the employer and the workman concerned contains a stipulation in that behalf; or termination of the service of the workman as a result of the non-renewal of the contract of employment between the employer and the workman concerned on its expiry or of such contract being terminated under a stipulation on that behalf contained therein; or termination of the service of a workman on the ground of continued ill health

Strike: A cessation of work by a body of persons employed in any industry acting in combination or a concerted refusal, or a refusal, under a common understanding of any number of persons who are or have been so employed to continue to work or to accept employment

Trade Union: A trade union registered under the Trade Unions Act, 1926 (16 of 1926)

Tribunal: An Industrial Tribunal constituted under Section 7A and includes an Industrial Tribunal constituted before the 10 March 1957, under this Act.

Unfair Labour Practice: Any of the practices specified in Schedule 5

Wages: All remuneration capable of being expressed in terms of money, which would, if the terms of employment, expressed or implied, were fulfilled, be payable to a workman in respect of his employment or of work done in such employment, and includes such allowances (including dearness allowance) as the workman is for the time being entitled to; the value of any house accommodation, or of supply of light, water, medical attendance or other amenity or of any service or of any concessional supply of food grains or other articles; any travelling concession; any commission payable on the promotion of sales or business or both;

but does not include any bonus; any contribution paid or payable by the employer to any pension fund or provident fund or for the benefit of the workman under any law for the time being in force; any gratuity payable on the termination of his service

Workman: Any person, including an apprentice employed in any industry to do any manual, unskilled, skilled, technical, operational, clerical or supervisory work for hire or reward, whether the terms of employment be expressed or implied, and for the purposes of any proceeding under this Act in relation to an industrial dispute, includes any such person who has been dismissed, discharged or retrenched in connection with, or as a consequence of, that dispute; or whose dismissal, discharge or retrenchment has led to that dispute; but does not include any such person in the armed forces, police, managerial, supervisory or administrative capacity and those drawing wages above INR 1,600/ p.m.

12.12.3 The Prohibition of Strike and Lockout

The Act prohibits strikes and lockouts subject to the following terms.

1. No person employed in a public-utility service shall go on strike in breach of contract:
   - Without giving to the employer notice of strike, as hereinafter provided, within six weeks before striking; or
   - Within 14 days of giving such notice; or
   - Before the expiry of the date of strike specified in any such notice as aforesaid; or
   - During the pendency of any conciliation proceedings before a conciliation officer and seven days after the conclusion of such proceedings
2. No employer carrying on any public-utility service shall lockout any of his workmen:
   - Without giving them notice of lockout as hereinafter provided, within six weeks before locking out; or
   - Within 14 days of giving such notice; or
   - Before the expiry of the date of lockout specified in any such notice as aforesaid; or
   - During the pendency of any conciliation proceedings before a conciliation officer and seven days after the conclusion of such proceedings
3. The notice of lockout or strike under this section shall not be necessary where there is already in existence a strike or, as the case may be, lockout in the public-utility service, but the employer shall send intimation of such lockout or strike on the day on which it is declared, to such authority as may be specified by the appropriate government either generally or for a particular area or for a particular class of public-utility services.
4. The notice of strike referred to in Subsection (1) shall be given by such number of persons to such person or persons and in such manner as may be prescribed.
5. The notice of lockout referred to in Subsection (2) shall be given in such manner as may be prescribed.
6. If on any day, an employer receives from any person employed by him any such notices as are referred to in Subsection (1) or gives to any person employed by him any such notices as are referred to in Subsection (2), he shall, within five days thereof, report to the appropriate government or to such authority as that government may prescribe, the number of such notices received or given on that day.
7. No workman who is employed in any industrial establishment shall go on strike in breach of contracts and no employer of any such workman shall declare a lock out:

- during the pendency of conciliation proceedings before a Board and seven days after the conclusion of such proceedings;
- during the pendency of proceedings before (a Labour Court, Tribunal or National Tribunal) and two months, after the conclusion of such proceedings);
- during the pendency of arbitration proceedings before an arbitrator and two months after the conclusion of such proceedings, where a notification has been issued under Subsection 3A (of Section 10A); or
- during any period in which a settlement or award is in operation, in respect of any of the matters covered by the settlement or award

12.12.4 Illegal Strikes and Lockouts

1. A strike or lockout shall be illegal if:
   i) It is commenced or declared in contravention of Section 22 or Section 23; or
   ii) It is continued in contravention of an order made under Subsection (3) of Section 10 [or Subsection (4A) of Section 10A.]
2. Where a strike or lockout in pursuance of an industrial dispute has already commenced and is in existence at the time of the reference of the dispute to a Board (an arbitrator, a Labour Court, Tribunal or National Tribunal), the continuance of such strike or lockout shall not be deemed to be illegal, provided that such strike or lockout was not at its commencement in contravention of the provisions of this Act or the continuance thereof was not prohibited under Subsection (3) of Section 10 [or Subsection (4A) of Section 10A].
3. A lockout declared in consequence of an illegal strike or a strike declared in consequence of an illegal lockout shall not be deemed to be illegal.

12.12.5 Lay-off, Retrenchment and Closure

Lay-off and retrenchment are one of the most controversial propositions of the Industrial Disputes Act. Apprehending the termination of employment to be one of the most important reasons for dispute, the ID Act has tried to lay down the circumstances and procedures for lay-off, retrenchment and closure of undertaking. Before going into the procedures relating to these, let us see what these terms mean.

LAY-OFF. Lay-offs have been defined under Clause 2(KKK) of the ID Act. It means the failure, refusal or the inability of an employer to give employment to a workman whose name is present on the muster rolls of the industrial establishment and who has not been retrenched. The "failure, refusal or inability" can be for arbitrary reasons but must be specifically attributed to any of the following:

Shortage of coal /power/raw materials

Accumulation of stocks

Breakdown of machinery

Natural calamity

Any other "connected" reason

Therefore, a workman who has not been retrenched can be laid-off, provided the above-described conditions are met.

RETRENCHEMENT. Retrenchment has been defined in Section 2 (OO) of the Act. Retrenchment means termination of service by an employer, of a workman, for any reason whatsoever other than:

as punishment inflicted by way of disciplinary action;

retirement on reaching the age of superannuation if such a stipulation exists in the contract of employment;

voluntary retirement;

non-renewal of contract; and

continued ill health.

In effect, this means that termination for any reason except the above shall construe to mean "retrenchment", in which case, it is necessary for the employer to follow the procedure for retrenchment, as laid down in the Act. If the proper procedure is not followed, the termination will be deemed illegal.

CLOSURE. Closure means the permanent closing down of a business. It has been defined in Clause 2 (CC) of the Act.

CHAPTER VB. Till 1976, the provisions for lay-off, retrenchment and closure were identical for all industrial establishments. However, through an amendment in 1976, Chapter VB was added. Its provisions were different from the earlier provisions and covered industrial establishments that were not of a seasonal nature and employed, on average, during the last 12-month period, 300 or more workmen. This was further amended in 1982 to make these provisions applicable to establishments with 100 or more workmen.

THE PROVISIONS FOR LAY-OFF AND RETRENCHMENT IN VA. Let us now look at the procedure for effecting lay-off and retrenchment.

- Lay-off can be for half-a-day, a full day or more than one day but cannot amount to retrenchment.
- Stoppage of work must be notified on the notice board in accordance with the provisions of Standing Orders
- The period of detention after stoppage of work must not exceed two hours.
- The maximum period of lay-off during a year cannot exceed 45 days.
- A lay-off compensation (the sum of 50% of wage and dearness allowance) has to be paid.
- There is no compensation after 45 days if an agreement to that effect is in place.
- If the employers inability to provide employment exceeds 45 days, the employer can retrench after adjusting the compensation paid for lay-off.

THE PROVISIONS FOR LAY-OFF AND RETRENCHMENT IN VB. In the provisions outlined in Chapter VB, the employer prior to effecting lay-off, has to take permission from the appropriate government.

THE PROHIBITION OF LAY-OFF

1. No workman whose name is borne on the muster rolls of an industrial establishment shall be laid off by his employer except with the permission of the appropriate government unless such lay-off is due to shortage of power or to natural calamity,

and in the case of a mine, such lay-off is due also to fire, flood, excess of inflammable gas or explosion.

2. An application for permission shall be made by the employer stating clearly the reasons for the intended lay-off and a copy of such application shall also be served simultaneously on the workmen concerned.
3. Where the workmen of an industrial establishment, being a mine, have been laid off for reasons of fire, flood or excess of inflammable gas or explosion, the employer, shall, within a period of 30 days from the date of commencement of such lay-off, apply to the appropriate government for permission to continue the lay-off.
4. Where an application for permission has been made, the appropriate government after making such enquiry and after giving a reasonable opportunity of being heard to the employer, the workmen concerned by order and for reasons to be recorded in writing, grant or refuse to grant such permission and a copy of such order shall be communicated to the employer and the workmen.
5. Where an application for permission has been made and the appropriate government does not communicate the order granting or refusing to grant permission to the employer within a period of 60 days from the date on which such application is made, the permission applied for shall be deemed to have been granted on the expiration of the said period of 60 days.
6. An order of the appropriate government or the specified authority granting or refusing to grant permission shall be final and binding on all the parties concerned and shall remain in force for one year from the date of such order.
7. The appropriate government review its order granting or refusing to grant permission or refer the matter to a Tribunal for adjudication.
8 The compensation payable for lay-off shall be the same as payable under Chapter VA.

   Explanation: For the purposes of this section, a workman shall not be deemed to be laid-off by an employer if such employer offers any alternative employment (which in the opinion of the employer does not call for any special skill or previous experience and can be done by the workman) in the same establishment from which he has been laid-off or in any other establishment belonging to the same employer, situated in the same town or village, or situated within such distance from the establishment to which he belongs that the transfer will not involve undue hardship to the workman having regard to the facts and circumstances of his case, provided that the wages that would normally have been paid to the workman are offered for the alternative appointment also.

APPLICATION OF SECTIONS 25C TO 25E

1. Sections 25C to 25E (inclusive) shall not apply to industrial establishments to which Chapter VB applies, or to (i) industrial establishments in which less than 50 workmen on an average per working day have been employed in the preceding calendar month; or (ii) industrial establishments that are of a seasonal character or in which work is performed only intermittently
2. If a question arises whether an industrial establishment is of a seasonal character or whether work is performed therein only intermittently, the decision of the appropriate government thereon shall be final.

CONDITIONS PRECEDENT TO THE RETRENCHMENT OF WORKMEN.

No workman employed in any industry who has been in continuous service for not less than one year under an employer shall be retrenched by that employer until:

a) The workman has been given one month's notice in writing indicating the reasons for retrenchment and the period of notice has expired, or the workman has been paid in lieu of such notice wages for the period of the notice

b) The workman has been paid, at the time of retrenchment, compensation that shall be equivalent to 15 days' average pay (for every completed year of continuous service) or any part thereof in excess of 6 months

c) Notice in the prescribed manner is served on the appropriate government (for such authority as may be specified by the appropriate government by notification in the official gazette).

12.12.6 Closure of Undertaking

Closure is when the business of an industrial establishment closes down. The Chapter VB provisions for closure are given below.

SIXTY DAYS' NOTICE TO BE GIVEN OF INTENTION TO CLOSE DOWN ANY UNDERTAKING

1. An employer who intends to close down an undertaking shall serve, at least 60 days before the date on which the intended closure is to become effective, a notice in the prescribed manner, on the appropriate government stating clearly the reasons for the intended closure of the undertaking, provided that nothing in this section shall apply to an undertaking in which (i) less than 50 workmen are employed, (ii) less than 50 workmen were employed on an average per working day in the preceding 12 months, or (iii) an undertaking set up for the construction of building, bridges, roads, canals, dams or for other construction work or project

2. Notwithstanding anything contained in subsection (1), the appropriate government may, if it is satisfied that owing to such exceptional circumstances as accident in the undertaking or death of the employer or the like, it is necessary so to do, by order, direct that provisions of Subsection (1) shall not apply in relation to such undertaking for such period as may be specified in the order.

COMPENSATION TO WORKMEN IN CASE OF CLOSING DOWN OF UNDERTAKINGS

1. Where an undertaking is closed down for any reason whatsoever, every workman who has been in continuous service for not less than one year in that undertaking immediately before such closure shall, subject to the provisions of Subsection (2), be entitled to notice and compensation in accordance with the provisions of Section 25F, as if the workman had been retrenched: provided that where the undertaking is closed down on account of unavoidable circumstances beyond the control of the employer, the compensation to be paid to the workman under Clause (b) of Section 25F, shall not exceed his average pay for three months.
   Explanation: An undertaking that is closed down for reasons of (i) financial difficulties (including financial losses); (ii) accumulation of indisposed stocks; (iii) the expiry of the period of the lease or license granted to it, or (iv) In case where the undertaking is engaged in mining operations, exhaustions of the minerals in the area in which operations are carried on, shall not be deemed to be closed down on account of unavoidable circumstances beyond the control of the employer within the meaning of the proviso to this subsection. Notwithstanding anything contained in subsection (1), where an undertaking engaged in mining operations is closed down by reason merely of exhaustion of the minerals in the area in which such operations are carried on, no workman referred to in that Subsection shall be entitled to any notice or

compensation in accordance with the provisions of Section 25F, if (i) the employer provides the workman with alternative employment with effect from the date of closure at the same remuneration as he was entitled to receive, and on the same terms and conditions of service, as were applicable to him, immediately before the closure; (ii) the service of the workman has not been interrupted by such alternative employment; and (iii) the employer is, under the terms of such alternative employment or otherwise, legally liable to pay to the workman, in the event of his retrenchment, compensation on the basis that his service has been continuous and has not been interrupted by such alternative employment

2. Where any undertaking set up for the construction of buildings, bridges, roads, canals, dams or other construction work is closed down on account of the completion of the work within two years from the date on which the undertaking had been set up, no workman employed therein shall be entitled to any compensation under Clause (b) of Section 25F, but if the construction work is not so completed within two years, he shall be entitled to notice and compensation under that section for every completed year of continuous service or any part thereof in excess of six months.

12.12.7 Last IN–First OUT

Where any workman in an industrial establishment is to be retrenched and he belongs to a particular category of workmen in that establishment, in the absence of any agreement between the employer and the workman in this behalf, the employer shall ordinarily retrench the workman who was the last person to be employed in that category, unless for reasons to be recorded, the employer retrenches any other workman.

12.12.8 Unfair Labour Practices

In 1984, unfair labour practices were introduced in the ID Act. The fifth schedule to the Act lists down the activities, on part of both parties, that would constitute unfair labour practice.

PROHIBITION OF UNFAIR LABOUR PRACTICES

- No employer or workman or a trade union, whether registered under the Trade Unions Act, 1926 (16 of 1926), or not, shall commit any unfair labour practice.
- Penalty for Committing Unfair Labour Practices: Any person who commits any unfair labour practice shall be punishable with imprisonment for a term, which may extend to six months, or with fine, which may extend to INR 1,000 or with both.
- Penalty for Illegal Strikes and Lock-outs: Any workman who commences, continues or otherwise acts in furtherance of a strike, which is illegal under this Act, shall be punishable with imprisonment for a term that may extend to one month, or with fine may extend to INR 50, or with both.
- Any employer, who commences, continues, or otherwise acts in furtherance of a lockout, which is illegal under this Act, shall be punishable with imprisonment for a term that may extend to one month, or with fine, which may extend to INR 1,000, or with both.

12.12.9 Settlement Machinery

Settlement means a settlement arrived at in the course of conciliation proceeding and includes a written agreement between employer and workmen arrived at otherwise than in course of a conciliation proceeding where such agreement has been signed by the parties there to in such manner as may be prescribed and a copy thereof has been sent to the officer authorized in this behalf by the appropriate government and the conciliation officer. The definition envisages two categories of settlement.

1. Settlement arrived at in the course of conciliation
2. Settlement arrived at privately or otherwise than in the course of conciliation

The settlement arrived at in the course of conciliation stand on a higher plane than the settlements arrived at otherwise than in the course of conciliation. The legal effect of both these settlements is not identical. The settlement arrived at otherwise than in the course conciliation binds only the parties to settlement and none else. In any case, it does not stand on a plane higher than the settlements arrived at in the conciliation, and that makes the two distinct and different from each other.

Procedures for Settling Labour Dispute: Collective bargaining, negotiation, conciliation and mediation, arbitration and adjudication are well-known methods for the settlement of industrial disputes.

Collective Bargaining: Collective bargaining is a technique by which disputes as to conditions of employment are resolved amicably, by agreement, rather than by coercion. The dispute is settled peacefully and voluntarily, although reluctantly, between labour and management. The content and scope of collective bargaining also varies from country to country. Broadly speaking, collective bargaining is a process of bargaining between employers and workers, by which they settle their disputes relating to employment or non-employment, terms of employment or conditions of the labour of the workman, among themselves, on the strength of the sanctions available to each side. Occasionally, such bargaining results in an amicable settlement arrived at voluntarily and peacefully, between the parties. But quite often, the workers and employers have to apply sanctions by resorting to weapons of strike and lockouts, to pressurize one another, which makes both the sides aware of the strength of one another, and that finally forces each of them to arrive at a settlement in mutual interest. It is, thus, the respective strength of the parties that determine the issue, rather than the wordy duals, which are largely put on for show, as an element of strength in one party is by the same token an element of weakness in another. The final outcome of bargaining may also depend upon the art, skill and dexterity of displaying the strength by the representatives of one party to the other.

Negotiation: Negotiation is one of the principal means of settling labour disputes. However, due to lack of trust between the employers and workmen or their trade unions or inter-rivalry of the trade unions and the employers being in a commanding position, many a time negotiations fail. Through Amendment in the ID Act in 1982, Chapter II B, reference of certain individual disputes to Grievance Settlement Authority has been inserted. Under this chapter, Section 9C has made it obligatory for the employers to make provision for Grievance Settlement Authority for the settlement of industrial disputes connected with an individual workman employed in an establishment, in which 50 or more workmen are employed or have been employed on any day, in the preceding 12 months. This amendment, however, made over 20 years back, has not seen the light of the day.

Conciliation and Mediation: Through conciliation and mediation, a third party provides assistance with a view to help the parties to reach an agreement. The conciliator brings the rival parties together to discuss with them their differences and assist them in finding out a solution to their problems. A mediator, on the other hand, is more actively involved while assisting the parties to find an amicable settlement. Sometimes, he submits his own proposals for the settlement of their disputes.

Conciliation may be voluntary or compulsory. It is voluntary if the parties are free to make use of the same, while it is compulsory when the parties have to participate irrespective of whether they desire to do so or not. Section 4 of the Act provides for the appointment for conciliation officers and Section 5 for the constitution of Boards of Conciliation. The Board of conciliation is to consist of an independent chairman and two or four members representing the parties in equal number. While the former is charged with the duty of mediating in and promoting the settlement of industrial disputes, the latter is required to promote the settlement of industrial disputes. The Act generally allows registered trade unions or a substantial number of workers/employees, and also in certain cases, an individual workman to raise disputes.

Arbitration: The resort to arbitration procedure may be compulsory or arbitrary. Compulsory arbitration is the submission of disputes to arbitration without consent or agreement of the parties involved in the dispute and the award given by the arbitrator being binding on the parties to the dispute. On the other hand, in case of voluntary arbitration, the dispute can be referred for arbitration only if the parties agree to the same. Section 10 A of the Act, however, provides only for voluntary reference of dispute to arbitration. This system, however, has not been widely practised so far. One of the main reasons for this procedure not gaining popularity is the lack of arbitrators who are able to command respect and confidence of the parties to the dispute. Inter-union rivalry also sometimes makes it difficult in arriving at an agreement on settlement of an arbitrator who is acceptable to all the trade unions in the industry.

Adjudication: If despite efforts of the conciliation officer, no settlement is arrived at between employer and the workman, The Industrial Disputes Act provides for a three-tier system of adjudication, viz., Labour Courts, Industrial Tribunals and National Tribunals under Sections 7, 7A and under Section 7B respectively. Labour Courts have been empowered to decide disputes relating to matters specified in Schedule 2. These matters are concerned with the rights of workers, such as propriety of legality of an order passed by an employer under the Standing Orders, application and interpretation of Standing Orders, discharge or dismissal of workman including reinstatement of grant of relief to workman wrongfully discharged or dismissed, withdrawal of any customary concession or privilege and illegality or otherwise of a strike or lockout.

The industrial tribunal is empowered to adjudicate on matters specified in both the Second and Third Schedule, i.e., both rights and interest disputes. The jurisdiction of the Industrial Tribunal is wider than the Labour Courts. In case of disputes, which, in the opinion of the central government, involve question of national importance or is of such nature that workers in more than one state are likely to be affected, the Act provides for constitution of National Tribunals.

The Act was amended in the year 1956 providing for constituting Labour Courts and national Industrial Tribunals. The subject of labour having been in the Concurrent List of the Constitution of India, both the centre and states have the power to legislate on labour matters. Several states have amended the Central Act, 1947 so as to suit to them, while others have enacted their own Acts.

The main object of the enactment of the Act is to ensure social justice to both the employees and the employers and advance the progress of industry by bringing about the existence of harmony and cordial relationship between the parties so as to bring about industrial peace, which would accelerate procedure activity of the country. The Act provides for the prevention and settlement of industrial disputes. "Industry" means a business, a trade, a manufacture, an undertaking, or service.

12.12.10 Conclusion

Industrial peace and industrial harmony may have the same generic meaning; but looking from the perspective of industrial relations, all attempts are made for industrial peace, emphasizing on the absence of strife and struggle. The concept of industrial harmony is positive and comprehensive and it postulates the existence of understanding cooperation and a sense of partnership between the employers and the employees. This is the ERM perspective and a proactive approach would be to seek industrial harmony. The focus, therefore, has to be on prevention of conflict in an organization.

SUMMARY

- Industrial disputes are those that arise due to any disagreement in an industrial relation.
- The term "industrial dispute" involves various aspects of interactions between the employer and the employees, among the employees as well as between the employers.
- These disputes may take various forms such as protests, strikes, demonstrations, lockouts, retrenchment and dismissal of workers.
- Some of the important causes of an industrial dispute are demands for:
  - Higher wages and allowances
  - Payment of bonus and determination of its rate thereof
  - Higher social-security benefits
  - Good and safer working conditions, including length of a working day, the interval and frequency of leisure and physical work environment
  - Improved labour welfare and other benefits. For example, adequate canteen, rest, recreation and accommodation facility and arrangements for travel to and from distant places.
- Besides, poor personnel management; conflicting legislative measure or government policies; and psychological factors such as denial of opportunity to the worker for satisfying his/her basic urge for self-expression, personal achievement and betterment may also result in labour problems.
- In India, the Industrial Disputes Act, 1947 is the main legislation for the investigation and settlement of all industrial disputes.
- The Act enumerates the contingencies when a strike or lockout can be lawfully resorted to, when they can be declared illegal or unlawful, conditions for laying off, retrenching, discharging or dismissing a workman, circumstances under which an industrial unit can be closed down and several other matters related to industrial employees and employers.
- According to the Act, the term "industrial dispute" means "any dispute or difference between employers and employers, or between employers and workmen, or between workmen and workmen, which is connected with the employment or non-employment, or the terms of employment or with the conditions of labour, of any person". The basic objectives of the Act are to:
  - Provide a suitable machinery for the just, equitable and peaceful settlement of industrial disputes
  - Promote measures for securing and preserving amity and good relations between employers and employees
  - Prevent illegal strikes and lockouts
  - Provide relief to workers against lay-offs, retrenchment, wrongful dismissal and victimization.
  - Promote collective bargaining
  - Ameliorate the conditions of workers
- A strike is a form of industrial action, resorted to by workmen. It is a cessation of work by a body of workmen acting in concert.
- A lockout on the other hand is a coercive action by the management. It is the temporary closing down of a place of work or refusal to employ the workmen.
- Lay-off, retrenchment and closures are the commonest cause for dispute. The ID Act, therefore, provides for a separate procedure to deal with these.

KEY TERMS

- adjudication 253
- arbitration 253
- collective bargaining 253
- conciliation and mediation 271
- closure disputes of interest 253
- disputes of rights 253
- industrial dispute 247
- lay-off 266
- lockout 246
- retrenchment 264
- strike 246

REVIEW QUESTIONS

1 Differentiate the concept of industrial conflict from the industrial relations and employee relations perspective.

2 What are the types and forms of industrial disputes? Give examples to explain.

3 What are the major causes of labour unrest? What have been the major causes of industrial disputes in India in the last decade?

4 Discuss the provisions in the ID Act, 1947 with regard to (i) strikes (ii) layoffs (iii) retrenchment, and (iv) unfair labour practices

QUESTIONS FOR CRITICAL THINKING

1 Pick up any industry or sector and trace the incidents of industrial unrest and conflict. Analyse the trends with regard to causes, and discuss how they could have been prevented or resolved.

2 Suggest ways and means to avoid industrial conflict and disputes in India in the current globalized competitive growth environment.

3 Discuss strategies to deal with resistance to any kind of organizational change through the employee-relations-management approach.

DEBATE

1 Most disputes occur due to managerial negligence.

2 In a competitive industrial environment, conflicts and disputes are unavoidable.

CASE ANALYSIS

Industrial Conflict and Unrest at Toyota Kirloskar Motor Company[1]

The management at Toyota Kirloskar Motor (TKM) Private Limited, on January 8, 2006, declared a lockout of the manufacturing unit at Bidadi, Karnataka. The lockout was in retaliation to a strike by the Toyota Kirloskar Motor Employees Union (TKMEU) three days ago. TKMEU was the recognized union in the plant. The management, in its notice of lockout stated the strike to be illegal since the union did not follow the provisions of the ID Act, 1947, requiring them to give 14 days' notice.

As the name suggests, TKM was a joint venture between Toyota Motor Corporation and the Kirloskar Group with equity in the ratio of 89:11 respectively. The plant had a capacity of producing 60,000 units per annum and Toyota had invested nearly INR 15 billion in the facilities. Of the 2,400 employees, 65% were members of the recognized union (TKMEU). The unit at Bidadi manufactures models such as Innova, Corolla and Camry. The strike by the Union was to demand reinstatement of 3 employees who had been dismissed and 10 employees who had been suspended. The Union also demanded an improvement in the working conditions at the plant. The dismissals and suspensions were carried out on disciplinary grounds. Allegedly, the dismissed employees had assaulted a supervisor. This action by management resulted in a strike call by the Union and three days later, a lockout by the management. The management did not agree to the demand of the Union to reinstate the dismissed employees and revoke suspension of the others. The management, further, made it clear that it would not rehire the dismissed employees under any circumstances.

Alleging strong arm tactics of the union with threats of blowing up LPG cylinders and inciting other non striking workers, intimidating them, obstructing movement of goods to and from the plant, the management said it had no option but to declare an indefinite lockout of the plant.

TKMEU on the other hand alleged that the management was trying to curb legitimate union activities by victimizing those who took active interest in union activities. The working conditions in the plant, they alleged, were inhuman and dictatorial against which it was the legitimate right of the unions to protest. The workers, allegedly, were made to work long hours without adequate compensation.

In response, the employee union said that three employees were dismissed because they were actively participating in trade union activities and the company wanted to suppress the trade union. They further said that working conditions at the plant were inhuman and slave-like. They were often made to stretch their working hours without sufficient breaks and/or compensation.

To resolve the conflict, when the State Labour Authorities called both parties for a conciliatory meeting, the management took a stand that the atmosphere was not conducive for any discussion since the union had vitiated the atmosphere and that they (the management) anticipated violence. TKM appealed for two weeks' time from the labour authorities but was granted three days and was asked again to be present on the 12th January, 2006. TKMEU was clamouring for the intervention of the Government for resolution of the dispute.

The unions canvassed for support and gathered the same from various other trade unions. The production, in the meantime, fell to just 32 vehicles per day from the normal output of around 90 a day. TKM, because of reduced production, was losing out on sales. The skeleton production was being carried out with the help of non striking employees and management staff specially trained for the same.

The state government declared the strike to be illegal on January 21, 2006. The management withdrew the lockout saying that the workers were eager to return to work. However, the management put a condition that before lifting of lockout, workers would have to give an undertaking for "good conduct" so that the atmosphere is strife free and production could go on full stream. Since the strike was declared "illegal", the Union withdrew the strike and the matter was referred to adjudication. But the Union refused to accept the demand for signing undertaking for good conduct.

This conflict had implications for attracting FDI in India. Now, TMC has reservations about investing in a second unit in the state. There has been a spate of such industrial unrest in the auto manufacturing in India, the most notable being the violent conflict at the Honda Motor & Scooters India Limited. Such incidents may mar the perception of India as an attractive FDI destination in the minds of Japanese business, one of the largest investors in India.

Questions:

1. Prepare a report in the light of the "big picture" of the Industrial Relations Framework with special reference to your opinion as to the adequacy or inadequacy of the frame work in dealing with industrial action.

2. Do you think that the "lockout" declared by the Toyota Motors was legal? Why? Do you think the strike by the workman was illegal? Why or why not?

3. How would you interpret the above incident from an employee relations perspective? Do you think that the employee relations perspective has limitations in dealing with such situations?

NOTES

1 The Financial Express, "Signs of Thaw," *The Financial Express*, January 21, 2006, available online at http://www.financialexpress.com/news/sign-of-thaw-toyota-lifts-lockout/99843/ and.

2 BS Bureau, "Lockout at Toyota Car Plant," *Business Standard*, January 2006, available online at http://in.rediff.com/money/2006/jan/09toy.htm.

SUGGESTED READING

Goswami, V. G. *Labour and Industrial Law, Eighth Edition*, Allahabad: Central Law Agency, 2004.

Monappa, *Arun Industrial Relations*, New Delhi: TMH 1985.

The Government of India, *Indian Labour Yearbook*, New Delhi: Labour Bureau, Various Years.

The Government of India, *Report of the National Commission on Labour*, 1969

The Government of India, *Report of the Second National Commission on Labour*, 2002.

The Industrial Disputes Act, 1947 (The Bare Act)

Venkatratnam, C.S. *Industrial Relations*, New Delhi: Oxford University Press, 2006

chapter thirteen

CHAPTER OUTLINE

LEARNING OBJECTIVES

After reading this chapter, you will be able to:

- Understand the machinery available for settlement of industrial disputes
- Understand the processes of conciliation, arbitration and adjudication
- Know the recommendations made by the Second National Commission of Labour on changes required in the settlement machinery

Status Quo Ante?

Amit Biswas is happy today because the matter relating to working hours of the employees of his branch has finally been sorted out. Slightly more than three years ago, the management had signed a "settlement" with the recognized union, increasing the working hours from 7 hours to 8.5 hours (including break). In lieu of the increase, the canteen allowance paid to the employees was increased. The settlement was valid for a period of three years after which it was terminable by either party on giving a three months' notice. On expiry of 2.5 years, the employees indicated that they were not willing to continue with the terms of settlement after expiry, and that they would want to revert to the old timings and working hours. This would disrupt the operations of the branch and, therefore, the management did not agree to what the employees demanded. The earlier settlement was signed through "conciliation" between the two parties by the concerned conciliation officer. This time, too, the conciliation officer was involved in resolving the dispute, and he urged the two parties to discuss and narrow down their differences so that a new "settlement" could be signed. In the mean time, on the expiry of three years, the employees reverted to the earlier work timings, causing inconvenience to the customers and the image of the branch. The situation became really tense, and the parties could not resolve the issue even through the intervention of the conciliation officer, who formally wrote to the government that his efforts had failed. Finally, the matter was "referred" to the Labour Court by the concerned government, wherein the court ruled that till a time a fresh settlement replaces the existing one, the employees are bound by the terms of the settlement in operation. The "earlier" working hours no longer existed and were replaced by the new working hours. Since it was an award of the Labour Court, the employees, too, realized that a fresh settlement had to be signed, and till then, the current working arrangement was to continue.

Industrial Conflict: Settlement Machinery

Industrial conflicts arise despite the existing preventive machinery to assume threatening proportions. There is a 'settlement' machinery in place which attempts to facilitate the 'settlement' of 'disputes' at as early a stage as feasible so as to prevent them from taking a dysfunctional and harmful shape. The Industrial Disputes Act, 1947 lays down the settlement procedure, systems and structure in detail.

Sometimes, negotiations and discussions do not work despite best intentions, as in the above case. The government, as a stakeholder in national progress, cannot sit as a bystander and let disputes assume larger dimensions. There is elaborate machinery in place that is intended to settle a dispute or resolve a conflict that could not be sorted out bilaterally through discussions and negotiations. As a manager, it is important to have a general overview of the settlement machinery, which should be made use of during a conflict that appears going out of hand. The provisions for the settlement of industrial disputes are codified in the Industrial Disputes Act. Recall the "big picture" (Figure 12.1 in Chapter 12). The settlement machinery is outlined in the lower portion of the figure.

13.1 The Settlement of Disputes: An Overview

Cordial industrial relations and lasting industrial peace require an environment of mutual cooperation and trust, resolution of conflicting interests and a collaborative work culture. In case conflicts arise, all attempts need to be made to eliminate the cause of such a conflict. In other words, preventive steps should be taken so that industrial disputes do not occur. Preventive measures seek to create an environment where industrial disputes do not arise. But if preventive machinery fails, then the government should activate the industrial settlement machinery because non-settlement of disputes proves to be harmful not only for the workers, but also for the management and the society as a whole. The registration of an industrial dispute necessitates the identification of a method for its resolution for harmonious industrial relations.

A "process flow" of the settlement process is given in Figure 13.1. Students are advised to refer to this figure, when we discuss the various components and sub-processes of the settlement machinery.

The machinery for the settlement of industrial disputes has been provided under the Industrial Disputes Act, 1947. This machinery comprises:

a) Conciliation

b) Arbitration

c) Adjudication

Box 13.1 contains the ILO recommendation on the principles for constituting voluntary conciliation and arbitration mechanisms. What this recommendation means is that the constituent members of ILO, while legislating for dispute-settlement machinery, must keep these recommendations in mind. As we proceed through the chapter, we will see that the legislative provisions relating to conciliation and arbitration (in Industrial Disputes Act, 1947) are in complete consonance with the ILO recommendations.

Figure 13.1

The process flow of settlement machinery.

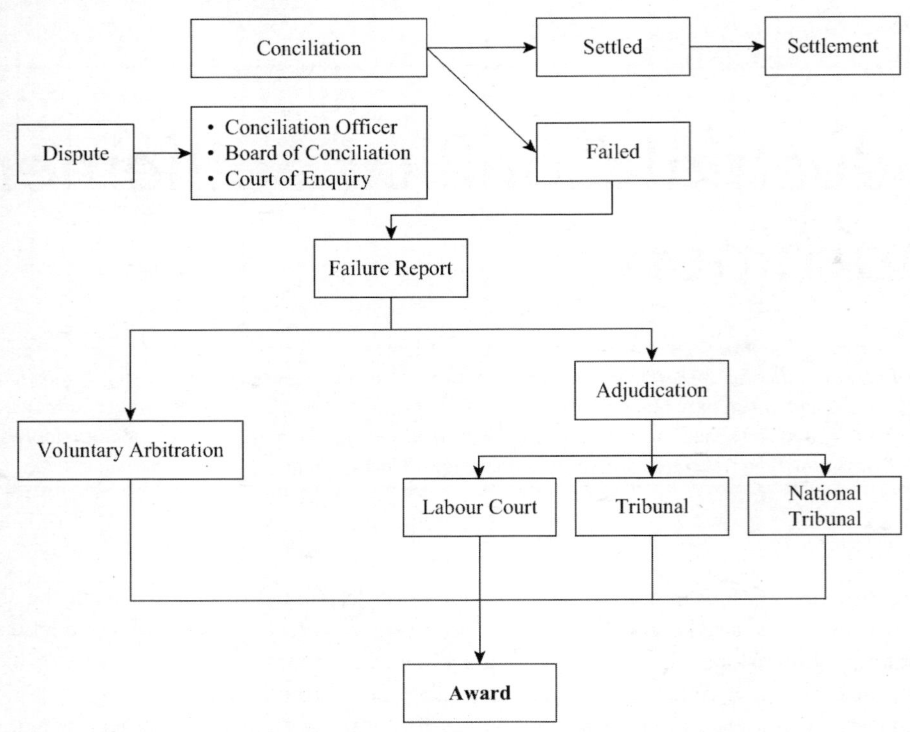

BOX 13.1 **RECOMMENDATION 92 OF ILO CONCERNING VOLUNTARY CONCILIATION AND ARBITRATION (1951): THE GENERAL CONFERENCE OF THE INTERNATIONAL LABOUR ORGANIZATION**

I. Voluntary Conciliation

1. Voluntary conciliation machinery, appropriate to national conditions, should be made available to assist in the prevention and settlement of industrial disputes between employers and workers.
2. Where voluntary conciliation machinery is constituted on a joint basis, it should include equal representation of employers and workers.
3. <The third point seems to be missing!>
   (1) The procedure should be free of charge and expeditious; such time limits for the proceedings as may be prescribed by national laws or regulations should be fixed in advance and kept to a minimum.
   (2) Provision should be made to enable the procedure to be set in motion, either on the initiative of any of the parties to the dispute or ex officio by the voluntary conciliation authority.
4. If a dispute has been submitted to conciliation procedure with the consent of all the parties concerned, the latter should be encouraged to abstain from strikes and lockouts while conciliation is in progress.
5. All agreements that the parties may reach during the conciliation procedure or as a result thereof should be drawn up in writing and be regarded as equivalent to agreements concluded in the usual manner.

II. Voluntary Arbitration

6. If a dispute has been submitted to arbitration for final settlement with the consent of all parties concerned, the latter should be encouraged to abstain from strikes and lockouts while the arbitration is in progress and to accept the arbitration award.

III. General

7. No provision of this Recommendation may be interpreted as limiting, in any way whatsoever, the right to strike.

13.2 Conciliation

Conciliation or mediation signifies third-party intervention in promoting the voluntary settlement of disputes. It is equated with mediation. The International Labour Organization describes "conciliation" as the practice by which the services of a neutral third party are used in a dispute as a means of helping the disputing parties to reduce the extent of their differences and to arrive at an amicable settlement or agreed solution[1]. It is a process of rational and orderly discussion of differences between the parties to a dispute under the guidance of a conciliator. Conciliation has not been defined under any of the Indian Labour Laws, although the ID Act, 1947 has made provisions for conciliation as an important tool for dispute settlement. Conciliation, as a method of dispute resolution, must allow the use of different approaches in differing situations. The conciliator is not a judge and does not have any "powers" to impose an agreement or settlement between the parties. All he can do is to try and narrow down the differences through discussions and suggestions. The conciliator assists the parties to dispute in their negotiations by removing bottlenecks in communication between them. Statutory provision for the conciliation machinery in the country was made for the first time in the Trade Disputes Act of 1929, which provided for the setting up of Boards of Conciliation by the government for settling industrial disputes. On the recommendation of the Royal Commission of Labour, the Trade Disputes Act of 1929 was amended in 1938 to provide for the appointment of conciliation officers. Conciliation machinery, as provided under the Industrial Disputes Act, 1947, comprises conciliation officers and the Board of Conciliation. So, the conciliation machinery comprises the following:

- Conciliation by an officer [Sn.4 & 2(d)]
- A Board (an ad-hoc Board consisting of a Chairman and equal number of workmen and the employer's representatives [Sn.5 & 2(e)]
- Court of Enquiry

The Board is not a permanent body. It is set up only for a particular dispute and will stand dissolved when the issue is settled. A Court of Enquiry assists with the investigation of issues during the conciliation stage. However, the Board of Conciliation and Courts of Enquiry are hardly ever constituted these days.

13.2.1 Conciliation Officers

The ID Act, 1947 provides for the appointment of conciliation officers, permanently or for a limited period, for a specific area or for a specific industry, to which the industrial disputes shall be referred for conciliation. The conciliation officer enjoys the powers of a civil court; he can call and witness parties on oath. Section 4 of the Industrial Disputes Act, 1947 confers power upon the government to appoint conciliation officers by notification in the official gazette, for a specified area or for one or more specified industries for the purpose of mediating in and promoting the settlement of industrial disputes. The conciliation officer examines all facts relevant to the disputed matter, and then helps both parties with discussion on the areas of dispute with the aim of progressively narrowing down the dispute.

DUTIES AND POWERS OF CONCILIATION OFFICERS. The duties and powers of a conciliation officer are given below:

Powers of Conciliation Officer:

- Section 11 (2) of the Industrial Disputes Act, 1947, prescribing the powers of the conciliation officers, states that such officer may, for the purpose of inquiry into existing or apprehended industrial dispute, after giving reasonable notice, enter the premises occupied by an industrial establishment to which the dispute relates.

- Section 11 (4) permits a conciliation officer to enforce the attendance of any person for the purpose of examination of such person or call for and inspect any document that he has ground for considering to be relevant to the industrial dispute or to be necessary for the purpose of verifying the implementation of any award, or carrying out duty imposed on him under this Act, and for the aforesaid purposes, the conciliation officer shall have the same powers as are vested in a civil court under the Code of Civil Procedure, 1908 (5 of 1908), in respect of enforcing the attendance of any person and examining him or of compelling the production of documents.
- Section 11 (6) allows all conciliation officers, members of a Conciliation Board or Court of Enquiry and the Presiding Officers of a Labour Court, Tribunal or National Tribunal to be deemed public servants within the meaning of Section 21 of the India Penal Code.

Duties of Conciliation Officers

- May intervene as a mediator if disputants fail to arrive at a settlement on their own
- Must intervene in case of a strike notice in a public-utility service
- Investigate and facilitate the resolution of disputes
- Help arriving at a settlement
- In case of failure, send a "failure report" to the appropriate government
- Conciliate in cases of "notice of change"

Duties of Conciliation Officers: Section 12 of the Industrial Disputes Act, 1947 prescribes the duties of conciliation officers:

- If the employer and the workmen fail to arrive at a settlement through negotiations, the conciliation officer may intervene as a mediator, endeavour to reconcile the differences of opinion and help the labour and management in achieving a successful settlement. Intervention by the conciliation officer is mandatory in case an industrial dispute has arisen in a public-utility service and a notice of strike or lockout (under Section 22) has been served.
- The conciliation officer shall, for the purpose of bringing about a settlement of dispute, without delay, investigate the dispute and all matters affecting the merits and the right settlement thereof and may do all such things as he thinks fit for the purpose of inducing the parties to come to a fair and amicable settlement of the dispute.
- The conciliation officer shall send a report of proceedings to the government, as to whether the settlement has been achieved or not, within 14 days of the commencement of the conciliation proceedings or within such extended time as may be allowed and in the prescribed manner.
- If a settlement is arrived at as a result of conciliation proceedings, a memorandum of settlement is worked out and it becomes binding on all the parties concerned for a period agreed upon.
- If no settlement is arrived at, the conciliation officer shall, as soon as practicable after the close of investigation, send a full report to the government, setting forth the steps taken by him for ascertaining the facts and circumstances relating to the dispute and for bringing about a settlement thereof, and the reasons on account of which a settlement could not be reached.
- If, on a consideration of the report referred to in Sub-section (4), the appropriate government is satisfied that there is a case for reference to a Board (Labour Court, Tribunal or National Tribunal), it may make such reference. Where the appropriate government does not make such a reference, it shall record and communicate to the parties concerned its reasons thereof.
- A report under this section shall be submitted within 14 days of the commencement of the conciliation proceedings or within such shorter period as may be fixed by the appropriate government.

SETTLEMENT. A conciliation officer helps the parties in dispute to arrive at a "settlement". However, the parties themselves may also arrive at a settlement without the help of a conciliation officer. A settlement basically means a formal agreement and it can either be arrived at bilaterally [Section 18(1) and 18(3)] or through the help of a third party (conciliation officer) in the course of conciliation proceedings [Section 12(3)]. In case of a bipartite settlement, a copy of the settlement may be jointly forwarded by both the parties to the conciliation officer for registration, whereas in case of tripartite settlement, the conciliator is also a signatory in addition to the representatives of the two parties. The terms of a bipartite settlement are binding on the parties to the settlement (the members of a union that is not signatory to the settlement may not be bound by the terms of settlement. Similarly, employees who join the organization after the settlement was signed may not be bound by the terms of settlement). However, a tripartite settlement is binding on all (employers and their successors/heirs, all employees employed in the establishment, even those not belonging to the representative union and future entrants to the organization).

Settlement arrived at, in the course of conciliation proceedings [Section 12(3)] comes into operation:

- On such date as is agreed upon by the parties to the dispute; and
- Where no such date is agreed upon, on the date on which the memorandum of settlement is signed by the parties to the dispute.

The settlement shall be binding:

- For the period agreed upon by the parties; and
- Where no such period is agreed upon, for a period of six months from the date on which the memorandum of settlement is signed.

The settlement shall remain binding for a further period until the expiry of two months from the date on which a notice in writing for termination of the settlement is given by any one party to the other party or parties.

Settlement

- A settlement is an agreement arrived at between two parties regarding a dispute.
- It may be bipartite (S 18-1 or 18-3) or tripartite (S 12-3)
- Settlements under S 18 are binding on the parties to dispute alone.
- Settlements under 12-3 are binding on all.
- Settlements under S 12-3 are arrived at in the course of conciliation.

13.2.2 The Protection of Workmen During Pendency of Conciliation Proceedings

During pendency of any conciliation proceedings before a conciliation officer in respect of any dispute, no employer can alter the conditions of service to the prejudice of the workmen concerned with the dispute or dismiss or punish any such workmen without obtaining written permission of the authority concerned.

13.3 Obligations of Employers

The employers have certain obligations with regards to conciliation proceedings and also the conditions leading to the need for conciliation and the implementation of settlement:

1. Not to make any change in the service condition of the workmen without giving a notice prescribed under Section 9A
2. To assist the conciliation officer in resolving any dispute
3. To implement all agreements, settlements and awards
4. To maintain a muster-roll of the workmen employed in the establishment, even at the time when workmen have been laid-off, and to ensure that the names of the workmen who present themselves for work at the appointed hours are entered therein. This is desirable as it could be a source of future dispute.
5. Not to declare, support or finance an illegal lock-out, in the establishment
6. Not to lay-off or retrench any workman or close down any undertaking, without obtaining prior approval of the government if so required.
7. To pay lay-off, retrenchment and closure compensation and compensation for illegal lock-out to workers, as prescribed under the provisions of the Act.
8. Not to indulge in unfair labour practices

13.4 Obligations of Employees

Similarly, employees and their representatives too have certain obligations:

1. To assist and cooperate with the conciliation officer in resolving any industrial dispute
2. Not to participate in, support or finance an illegal strike
3. To abide by all agreements, settlements and awards
4. Not to indulge in unfair labour practices

13.5 The Board of Conciliation

The Act also empowers the government to appoint a Board of Conciliation for promoting the settlement of disputes where the conciliation officer fails to do so within 14 days. The Conciliation Board is a tripartite ad hoc body consisting of a chairman and two to four other members nominated by the parties to the dispute. The mode and procedure of the functioning of the Board are similar to those of the conciliation officer.

- The chairman shall be an independent person and the other members shall be persons appointed in equal numbers to represent the parties to the dispute and any person appointed to represent a party shall be appointed on the recommendation of that party, provided that if any party fails to make a recommendation as aforesaid within the prescribed time, the appropriate government shall appoint such persons as it thinks fit to represent that party.
- A Board, having the prescribed quorum, may act notwithstanding the absence of the chairman or any of its members or any vacancy in its number, provided that if the appropriate government notifies the Board that the services of the chairman or of any other member have ceased to be available, the Board shall not act until a new chairman or member, as the case may be, has been appointed.

The conciliation machinery can take note of the existing as well as apprehended disputes either on its own or on being approached by any party to the dispute. While conciliation is compulsory in all public-utility services, it is optional in non-public-utility services. In conciliation, the ultimate decision rests with the parties themselves, but the conciliator may offer a solution to the dispute acceptable to both the parties and serve as a channel of communication. The parties may accept the recommendation for settlement of any dispute, or reject it altogether. If conciliation fails, the next stage may be compulsory adjudication. Broadly speaking, the conciliators bring the contending parties to a conference table and endeavour at least to narrow down the differences between them by removing the sources of friction and tension, and help them to find common areas of agreement. They have no power to decide the disputes or pass a final or binding order on the parties. In cases where a settlement is arrived at, they can record the settlement, and in cases of failure of the conciliatory negotiations, they can only send a failure report to the appropriate government. It should be noted that they are required under the Act to conclude their proceedings within 14 days, while Boards are allowed 2 months, unless the parties agree for a further extension of the time limit. A memorandum of settlement will be binding on the parties for six months from the date of its signing or for such period as may be agreed to between the parties. Even after the expiry of such period, the agreement remains in operation until one of the parties, which is unwilling to continue it, gives a notice for its termination.

Settlements can also be arrived at by the parties when a dispute is pending before the Labour Court or Industrial Tribunal. Moreover, such settlements can be included in the awards of the Labour Court/Industrial Tribunal in order to give them a legal status. These are called "consent awards".

13.6 The Performance of Conciliation Machinery

Although conciliation has brought about resolution of a large number of conflicts, it has, however, been subjected to several criticisms:

i) Considerable delays are usually involved in conciliation proceedings.

ii) The parties to the dispute, many times, do not attend conciliation meetings on the prescribed dates.

iii) It is alleged that most conciliation officers lack training and competence in conciliation work.

iv) Conciliation is treated as a preliminary step leading to adjudication through the Labour Courts or Tribunals.

In such a state of affairs, the parties do not feel the urge strongly to arrive at a settlement. The performance of conciliation machinery cannot be said to be satisfactory. It is estimated that only 25 per cent of cases are annually handled. Besides, a very large number of disputes are filed and then withdrawn later on by workers or unions. It means that petty issues are taken up for conciliation. Finally, a substantial number of cases remain pending.

The Second National Commission on Labour stated that "conciliation can be more effective if it is freed from outside influence and the conciliation machinery is adequately staffed. The independent charter of the machinery will alone inspire greater confidence and will be able to evoke more cooperation from the parties. The conciliation machinery should, therefore, be a part of the proposed Industrial Relations Commission. This transfer will introduce important structural, functional and procedural changes in the working of the machinery as it exists today. There is a need for certain other measures to enable offices of the machinery to function effectively. Among these are:

1. Proper selection of personnel
2. Adequate pre-job training
3. Periodic in-service training

Other suggestions that may be considered to facilitate speedy disposal of cases are:

i) The conciliation officer should hold conciliation proceedings in the concerned establishment, instead of calling the parties to his office.

ii) S/he should have the statutory power of enforcing attendance of the parties before them on the prescribed date.

iii) S/he should dispose of the cases within the time limit as far as possible".[2]

The Performance of Conciliation Machinery

- It is treated as a preliminary step, leading to adjudication.
- Considerable delays are usually involved in conciliation proceedings.
- Parties to the dispute, many times, do not attend conciliation meetings on the prescribed dates.
- There is a perception that most conciliation officers lack training and competence in conciliation work.

13.7 Arbitration

Arbitration aims to secure an award on an issue of conflict by referring it to an impartial third party called the "arbitrator". The arbitrator hears both parties involved in the conflict, determines the cause and origin of conflict, understands the differing perceptions and attempts to evolve an amicable solution. The decision of the arbitrator is binding on both the parties.

Arbitration is different from conciliation in the fact that the arbitrator is empowered to decide on a dispute, and his/her decision is binding on both the parties. Unlike conciliation, the arbitrator does not just attempt to reconcile differences, but brings about a settlement through an agreement between the contending parties after hearing both the parties. Arbitration is more judicial than conciliation, and is based on equality and justice. Compromise has no place in arbitration.

Table 13.1

The advantages and disadvantages of arbitration.

Advantages	Disadvantages
If voluntary, acceptability of the settlement by both parties would be greater.	It deprives labour of its right to strike.
If arbitration is established by agreement, it is more flexible.	Judgment is often arbitrary, and can often be biased.
It is more expeditious than other methods of settlement.	It is more directive than participative.
It is more informal.	Delays can affect morale of the parties.
There is a greater chance of implementation.	

Approach: The approach to be followed in arbitration is to base the agreement on the principle of natural justice with "split the difference" approach that is workable and acceptable to both the parties.
Type: Arbitration can be compulsory or voluntary.
Competence for Arbitration: High integrity, impartiality, knowledge of labour laws, deep understanding of the issues of conflict and sensitivity to the issues of concern are few of the competencies required for effective arbitration. The advantages and disadvantages of arbitration as a settlement technique are summarized in Table 13.1.

13.7.1 Compulsory Arbitration

Compulsory arbitration is one where the parties are required to accept arbitration without any willingness on their part. When one of the parties to an industrial dispute feels aggrieved by an act of the other, it may apply to the appropriate government to refer the dispute to adjudication machinery. Under compulsory arbitration, the parties are forced to arbitration by the State, when the parties fail to arrive at a settlement by a voluntary method. Compulsory arbitration leaves no scope for strikes and lockouts; it deprives both the parties of their very important and fundamental rights.

13.7.2 Voluntary Arbitration

Voluntary arbitration is a choice made by the contending parties for arbitration, before referring it for adjudication. Voluntary arbitration became popular as a method of settling differences between workers and the management with the advocacy of Mahatma Gandhi, who had applied it in the textile industry of Ahmedabad. However, voluntary arbitration was lent legal identity only in 1956, when the Industrial Disputes Act, 1947 was amended to include a provision relating to it (Section 10-a). On the failure of conciliation proceedings, the conciliation officer may ask the parties to refer the dispute to a voluntary arbitrator. Voluntary arbitration refers to getting the disputes settled through an independent person, chosen by the parties, involved mutually and voluntarily.

An amendment in 1956 introduced Section 10A in the ID Act, making provision for a joint reference of industrial disputes to voluntary arbitration. But the State, in its efforts to resolve industrial disputes, had to provide for arbitration machinery, which could be done either by creating conditions in which arbitration would succeed. The provision for voluntary arbitration was made because of the lengthy legal proceedings and formalities, and the resulting delays involved in adjudication. It may, however, be noted that an arbitrator is not vested with any judicial powers. It is a quasi-judicial process, where the arbitrator sits in judgement on the proceedings, and after coming to a decision, makes it known to the parties. S/he derives his/her powers to decide the dispute from the agreement that the parties have made between themselves regarding the referring of dispute to the arbitrator. The arbitrator submits his/her award to the government. The government then may publish it within 30 days of its submission. Voluntary arbitration is the next best alternative to conciliation, which is built on a democratic process and is a close substitute to collective bargaining. It not only provides a voluntary method of settling industrial disputes, but is also a quicker way of settling them. It is based on the notion of self-management in industrial relations. Furthermore, it helps to curtail the protracted proceedings that adjudication entails. It demonstrates a collaborative attitude, assists in strengthening the trade-union movement and contributes for building up stable industrial relations. Thus, it is a democratic functioning in the industry and inculcates some degree of union–management accommodation. The main ingredients of voluntary arbitration are:

i) The industrial dispute must exist or be apprehended.

ii) The agreement must be in writing.

iii) The reference to voluntary arbitration must be made before a dispute has been referred to under Section 10 to a Labour Court, Tribunal or National Tribunal.

iv) The name of arbitrator/arbitrators must be specified.

v) The arbitrator or arbitrators shall investigate the dispute and submit to the appropriate government the arbitration award signed by the arbitrator or all the arbitrators, as the case may be.

The principle of voluntary arbitration was incorporated in the Code of Discipline, Industrial Truce Resolution of 1962, and also various Five Year Plans. The National Arbitration Promotion Board (NAPB) was set up by the Government of India in 1967 to strengthen the system of voluntary arbitration in our country. The Board consists of representatives of employer and worker organizations, public-sector undertakings and central/state government officials. Model principles were drawn up by the NAPB by tripartite consent. These principles broadly lay down the circumstances under which individual as well as collective disputes can be referred to voluntary arbitration. In 1972, the Board decided that voluntary arbitration would form the next step for resolving industrial disputes when conciliation failed. Many state governments have set up Arbitration Promotion Boards.

13.7.3 National Arbitration Promotion Board

To make voluntary arbitration more acceptable to the parties and to coordinate efforts for its promotion, the government appointed, in July 1967, a National Arbitration Promotion Board with a tripartite composition. The functions of the Board are:

i) To examine the factors inhibiting arbitration

ii) To evolve principles, norms and procedures for the guidance of the arbitrator and the parties

iii) To advise parties, in important cases, to accept arbitration for resolving disputes so that litigation in courts may be avoided

iv) To look into the cause or causes of delay and expedite arbitration proceedings, wherever necessary

v) To specify, from time to time, the types of disputes that would normally be settled by arbitration in tripartite decisions

vi) To maintain a panel of suitable arbitrators

When V. V. Giri became Labour Minister in 1953, he laid greater emphasis on collective bargaining and voluntary arbitration than on compulsory arbitration. Giri was of the opinion that compulsory adjudication for labour disputes should be the last resort and it should be operationalized only in exceptional circumstances. According to Giri's approach, emphasis should be placed on collective bargaining and the mutual settlement of disputes through voluntary arbitration.

13.7.4 The Evaluation of the Working of Voluntary Arbitration

The system of voluntary arbitration, however, has not been used adequately in our country. There exists general indifference among parties to use voluntary arbitration as a method of settling disputes. Hardly 2 to 3 per cent of the disputes not settled by conciliation are referred to voluntary arbitration. As observed by the NCL, voluntary arbitration has not taken root, in spite of the influential advocacy for it in different policy-making forums. Factors that have contributed to its slow progress are:

i) The easy availability of adjudication in case of failure of negotiations
ii) A dearth of suitable arbitrators who command the confidence of both the parties
iii) The absence of a recognized union, which could bind the workers to common agreements
iv) Legal obstacles
v) The fact that in law, no appeal was competent against an arbitrator's awards
vi) The absence of a simplified procedure to be followed in voluntary arbitration
vii) Cost to the parties, particularly workers

With the growth of collective bargaining and the general acceptance or recognition of representative unions and improved management attitudes, the ground may be provided for the acceptance of voluntary arbitration. Moreover, the success of this enlightened approach depends upon the faith, trust, will and dignity, which employers and employees lend to its implementation. Hence, all the participants in the process, viz., trade unions, employers, personnel executives and the arbitrators themselves have an equal stake in an orderly, efficient and constructive arbitration procedure.

One of the main factors that acts as a hurdle to the maintenance and promotion of industrial peace at present is the increasing resort to adjudication machinery in preference to voluntary arbitration and conciliation. The state governments should take all the necessary measures to encourage settlement of disputes through collective bargaining. Box 13.2 extracts the views of the Second National Commission on Labour on voluntary arbitration. The general thrust in the matter of industrial disputes is to resolve the disputes, as far as possible, through collective bargaining, conciliation and voluntary arbitration.

13.8 Adjudication

The ultimate remedy for the settlement of an unresolved dispute is its reference by the government to adjudication. It is a means of a mandatory settlement of a dispute by Labour Courts or Industrial Tribunal or National Tribunal under the ID Act and corresponding State statutes. Adjudication may be described as a process that involves intervention in the dispute by a third party appointed by the government, with or without the consent of the parties to the dispute, for the purpose of settling the dispute. The reference of dispute to adjudication is voluntary when both parties agree to reference of dispute to adjudication at their own accord, and it is compulsory when reference is made to adjudication by the government without the consent of either or both the parties to the dispute. The Industrial Disputes Act, 1947 provides three-tier adjudication machinery that is set up by the government comprising:

BOX 13.2 **NATIONAL COMMISSION ON LABOUR (SECOND) ON VOLUNTARY ARBITRATION**

6.92 We have, at several places so far, referred to arbitration or adjudication for determining disputes between management and labour. We feel arbitration is the better of the two, for the reason that the procedures will be simple, the proceedings will not be tardy and the decision will be rendered by a person in whom both parties have confidence. We would like the system of arbitration to spread, and over time, become the accepted mode of determining disputes, which are not settled by the parties themselves. In fact, it would be desirable if in every settlement entered into between the parties, (and we would urge that the duration of each settlement be four years), there is a clause providing for arbitration by a named arbitrator or panel of arbitrators of all disputes arising out of interpretation and implementation of the settlement and any other disputes. The law may even lay down that such a provision be deemed to be part of every settlement. By having a named person as an arbitrator during the currency of a settlement, the arbitrator is able to familiarize himself with all aspects of the activity in the establishment and to get to know the parties better; also, the fact that the person will be the arbitrator, for better or for worse, during the entire period of the settlement will, hopefully, make him impartial and also act in the best interests of the establishment.

6.93 Arising out of the above, we would like to suggest that a panel of arbitrators is maintained and updated by the LRC (Labour Relations Commission) concerned, which would contain names of all those who are willing and have had experience and familiarity with labour management relations; the panel may consist of labour lawyers, trade union functionaries, employers, managers, officials of the labour department, both serving and retired, academics, retired judicial officers and so on. Some ground rules could also be framed in consultation with representatives of employers and workers, and these could include procedures for selecting an agreed person from the panel, the cost of arbitration, and so on.

Source: Report of Second National Commission on Labour, 2002, Government of India, para 6.92

i) Labour Courts,

ii) Industrial Tribunals, at the state level, and

iii) National Tribunals at the central level.

The matters under the jurisdiction of Labour Courts and Tribunals have been specified in the ID Act. The National Tribunals are set up by the central government to adjudicate upon a dispute involving any question of national importance, or of such nature that industrial establishments situated in more than one state are likely to be affected by it. The adjudication award is legally binding. The parties to an industrial dispute are required not to resort to work stoppages if the dispute is pending in an adjudication process.

13.8.1 Types of Adjudication

When the government gets a report of the failure of conciliatory proceedings to a dispute, it considers the appropriateness to refer it for adjudication. The reference of a dispute to adjudication is at the discretion of the government. Adjudication can be voluntary or compulsory. When reference to adjudication is made by the parties, it is called voluntary adjudication, and when reference is made by the government without the consent of either or both the parties, it is known as compulsory adjudication.

13.8.2 Labour Courts

One or more Labour Courts may be constituted by the appropriate government for adjudication on industrial disputes relating to any matter specified in Schedule 2 of the ID Act.

ISSUES REFERRED TO LABOUR COURTS. The Labour Courts can deal with disputes relating to:

a) The propriety or legality of an order passed by an employer under the Standing Orders
b) The application and interpretation of Standing Orders
c) Discharge and dismissal of workmen and grant of relief to them
d) Withdrawal of any statutory concession or privilege
e) Illegality or otherwise of any strike or lock-out
f) All matters not specified in the third schedule of Industrial Disputes Act, 1947 (it deals with the jurisdiction of Industrial Tribunals)—
    1. Wages including the period and mode of payment
    2. Compensatory and other allowances
    3. Hours of work and rest intervals
    4. Leave with wages and holidays
    5. Bonus, profit sharing, provident fund and gratuity
    6. Shift working otherwise than in accordance with standing orders
    7. Rules of discipline
    8. Rationalization
    9. Retrenchment
    10. Any other matter that may be prescribed

COMPOSITION. A Labour Court shall consist of one person only, who:

a) Is or has been a judge of a High Court; or
b) Has been, for a period of not less than three years, a District Judge; or
c) Has held any judicial office in India for not less than seven years

No person shall be appointed or continue in the office of the Labour Court, if he is not an independent person, or if he has attained the age of 65.

DUTIES OF LABOUR COURTS. The Duties are:

i) To hold adjudication proceedings expeditiously; and
ii) To submit its award to the appropriate government as soon as practicable on the conclusion of the proceedings

The Labour Court usually deals with matters that arise out of the day-to-day working of an undertaking.

JURISDICTION OF LABOUR COURTS. The matters listed in Schedule 2 of the ID Act and any other matters except those in Schedule 3 are within the jurisdiction of the Labour Courts. In case the appropriate government considers fit, it may refer matters listed in Schedule 3 to the Labour Court in case the dispute concerns more than 100 workers. Schedule 2 lists the following issues:

i) Propriety or legality of an order passed by an employer under the Standing Orders
ii) Application and interpretation of Standing Orders

iii) Discharge or dismissal of workers, including reinstatement of, or grant of relief to, workers wrongfully dismissed

iv) Withdrawal of any customary concession or privilege

v) Illegality or otherwise of a strike or lockout

vi) All matters other than those listed in Schedule 3

13.8.3 The Second National Commission on Labour on Labour Relations Commissions

The Second National Commission on Labour, recognizing adjudication to be the prevalent mode of settlement of industrial disputes, has recommended an "integrated adjudicatory system" comprising labour courts, *lok adalats,* and labour relations commissions.

This system will deal with all matters arising out of employment relations but also trends disputes in matters related to employment. There would be a Central Labour Relations Commission (CLRC) for the central sphere and a State Labour Relations Commission (SLRC) for the state sphere. The National Labour Commission would be above these two and function as an appellate body. These bodies would be autonomous and function as appellate tribunals over the labour courts. These bodies would have members and a presiding officer—a person who is eligible for appointment as a judge in a high court. The commissions would have representatives of employers, workers, economists, leading trade unionists, etc. as members.

The government has, so far, not accepted the recommendations and, therefore, these remain just that—recommendations. Incidentally, the First National Commission on Labour had also recommended an Industrial Relations Commission along similar lines nearly forty years back!

13.8.4 Industrial Tribunals

Industrial Tribunals are appointed by the appropriate government for adjudication in matters listed in Schedule 3 prescribed under the ID Act, which affect the working of a company or industry. The matters dealt with in the Industrial Tribunal are:

a) Wages , including the period and the mode of payment

b) Compensatory and other allowances

c) Hours of work and rest intervals

d) Leave with wages and holidays

e) Bonus, profit sharing, provident fund and gratuity

f) Shift working, other than in accordance with the Standing Orders

g) Classification of grades

h) Rules of discipline

i) Rationalization

j) Retrenchment of workmen and the closure of an establishment

k) Any other matter prescribed

COMPOSITION. A Tribunal shall consist of one or more persons, such as those who

i) Are or have been a judge of a High Court; or

ii) Are or have been, for a period of not less than three years, a District Judge; or

iii) Hold or have held the office of Chairman or any other member of the Labour Appellate Tribunal or any Tribunal for a period of not less than two years

The government may, if it deems fit, also appoint two persons as assessors to advise the Tribunal in the proceedings before it.

The functions and duties of the Industrial Tribunal are judicial and have all attributes of a court of natural justice. It may create new obligations or modify contracts in the interest of industrial peace. The Tribunals are expected to give awards based on the peculiar circumstances of each dispute.

India has 12 central government Industrial Tribunals-cum-Labour Courts.

13.8.5 National Tribunals

These Tribunals are meant for those disputes, which, as the name suggests, involve the questions of national importance or issues that are likely to affect the industrial establishments of more than one state.

The employers and unions use adjudication as a primary measure of resolving disputes. About 90 to 95 per cent of disputes are referred to adjudication machinery on an average, annually. However, the functioning of adjudication machinery has not been very satisfactory, particularly because of the delays involved and the inefficient implementation of the awards.

13.8.6 The Performance of Adjudication Machinery

Adjudication has been the most popular measure of resolving disputes, accounting for more than 90 per cent of the disputes every year.

However, because of the involved process, 50 to 60 per cent of the cases are decided in more than a year, and 25 per cent of the cases take between 6 and 12 months. The state of the implementation of awards (requiring implementation) is also not very commendable, since 30 to 40 per cent of the awards are not implemented by the date of enforcement. Incomplete and abrupt implementation of awards creates suspicion in the minds of workers and shakes their faith in the machinery.

Adjudication is not a democratic method and may create bitterness among the parties. It tends to encourage litigation and irresponsible behaviour among employers and labour. The functioning of the adjudication machinery has, in practice, been unsatisfactory mainly because of procedural delays and delay in implementation of awards. Many employers resort to appeal against implementation of awards that go against them. In rights disputes, this becomes totally unfair for the workman. Delays in implementation erode the faith of workers in the adjudication machinery. Adjudication is preferred more by employers who can afford to spend more on the legal proceedings.

13.9 The Recommendation of the National Commission on Labour on Settlement Machinery

Conciliation: The Second National Commission on Labour observes that "the functioning of The First National Commission on Labour had bemoaned that the functioning of the conciliation machinery was not found satisfactory due to the following reasons:

i) Delay in proceedings

ii) Lack of understanding of the issues involved

iii) Ad-hoc nature of the machinery

iv) Discretion vested in the government as regards reference of disputes

As a result, the recommendation was to put the conciliation machinery under the proposed Industrial Relations Commission and outside the control of the executive.

The Second National Commission, however, has observed that the conciliation machinery has been very effective in resolving "interest disputes" but not so much in cases of "rights disputes". The Commission, therefore, recommends conciliation to be optional in cases of rights disputes and compulsory in cases of interest disputes. Conciliation should also be compulsory in the case of strike or lockout over any issue. Issues not setttled in conciliation must be referred to either voluntary arbitration or compulsory arbitration by arbitrators maintained by the Labour Relations Commission.

The Second Commission also laments the inordinate delays in the implementation of awards of labour courts, especially by large organizations, PSUs and other government organizations. The courts should, therefore, be given powers to issue decrees and initiate contempt proceedings against the non-implementation of awards.

Like the First National Commission, the Second Commission also recommends setting up of Labour Relations Commissions (LRCs). There could be LRCs at the central and the state levels, under a National Labour Relations Commission. The LRCs could entertain appeals on judgements from the labour courts. Further, the NCL recommends the abolition of tribunals. The LRCs would supervise the functioning of labour courts within their respective jurisdictions.

The best way to settle industrial disputes is for the parties to the dispute to talk over their differences on the table and settle them by negotiation and bargaining. A settlement so reached leaves no rancour behind and helps to create an atmosphere of harmony and cooperation. There should be a shift to collective bargaining. Disputes between employers and workers, the Commission observes, have been taking a legalistic turn, mainly because of the emphasis on adjudication through Industrial Tribunals and courts. The procedure for the settlement of disputes, suggested by the Commission, is as under:

- After negotiations have failed and before the notice of a strike/lockout is served, the parties may agree to voluntary arbitration. The IRC (Industrial Relations Commission) will help the parties in choosing a mutually acceptable arbitrator or may provide an arbitrator from among its members/officer, if the parties agree to avail of such services.
- In essential services/industries, in the event of the failure of negotiations and conciliation, arbitration must be compulsorily resorted to. The arbitrator must be from a list of approved arbitrators maintained by the respective LRC.
- Adjudication should be resorted to only after exhausting the above.

SUMMARY

- Broadly speaking, the statutory settlement machinery evolved in our country is of two types. One deals with direct settlement, which is the adjudication process, while the other is through third-party intervention by conciliation and arbitration.
- The administration of the settlement machinery is prescribed in the Industrial Disputes Act, 1947.
- Conciliation machinery prescribed under the ID Act includes conciliation officers and conciliation Boards. While conciliation is compulsory in all public-utility services, it is not so in non-public-utility services.
- In conciliation, the ultimate decision rests with the parties themselves, but the conciliator may offer a solution to the dispute acceptable to both the parties and serve as a channel of communication. The parties may accept his recommendation for the settlement of dispute or reject it altogether.
- Arbitration is another option that aims to secure an award on an issue of conflict by referring it to an impartial third party called the "arbitrator".
- The arbitrator hears both the parties involved in the conflict, determines the cause and the origin of conflict, understands the differing perceptions and attempts to evolve an amicable solution.
- The decision of the arbitrator is binding on both the parties. Arbitration can be compulsory by way of government initiative, or voluntary by the acceptance of both the contending parties.
- Voluntary arbitration was lent legal identity only in 1956, when Industrial Disputes Act, 1947 was amended to include a provision relating to it. On the failure of conciliation proceedings, the conciliation officer may persuade the parties to refer the dispute to a voluntary arbitrator.

Voluntary arbitration refers to getting the disputes settled through an independent person chosen by the parties involved mutually and voluntarily.

- The ultimate remedy for the settlement of an unresolved dispute is its reference by the government to adjudication. It is a means of a mandatory settlement of a dispute by Labour Courts or Industrial Tribunal or National Tribunal under the ID Act and the corresponding State statutes. Labour Courts and Industrial Tribunals are set up by the central government and the state government or the administrations of union territories for dealing with matters that fall in the central and the state sphere, respectively.
- It is open to the central government to refer a matter in relation to which it is the appropriate government to a Labour Court or an Industrial Tribunal constituted by the state government.
- Labour Courts deal with matters pertaining to the discharge and dismissal of workmen, application and interpretation of Standing Orders, propriety of orders passed under Standing Orders, legality of strikes, of lock-outs, etc.
- Industrial Tribunals deal with collective disputes such as wages, hours of work, leave, retrenchment, closure as well as all matters that come under the jurisdiction of Labour Courts.
- The central government may set up a National Tribunal for the adjudication of industrial disputes, which, in its opinion, involve questions of national importance or are of such nature that industrial establishments in more than one state are likely to be interested in such disputes.
- One of the main factors that acts as a hurdle to the maintenance and promotion of industrial peace at present is the increasing resort to adjudication machinery in preference to voluntary arbitration and conciliation. A shift is necessary towards collective bargaining that can work simultaneously with the statutory state machinery.

KEY TERMS

- Board of Conciliation 279
- compulsory arbitration 284
- conciliation officers 276
- Industrial Tribunals 282
- labour courts 283
- National Tribunals 280
- voluntary arbitration 284

REVIEW QUESTIONS

1 What are the legal procedures available for the settlement of disputes in India?

2 Differentiate between the following:

i) Conciliation and arbitration

ii) Voluntary arbitration and compulsory arbitration

3 When is a dispute referred to a National Tribunal?

4 Why is adjudication preferred to conciliation or arbitration? What could be the various advantages and disadvantages of adjudication over conciliation and voluntary arbitration?

5 Discuss the recommendations of the National Commission on Labour with regard to the settlement of disputes.

6 Explain schematically the complete machinery available for the resolution of industrial conflicts. How effective, in your opinion, is the machinery? Give arguments in support of your answer.

QUESTIONS FOR CRITICAL THINKING

1 Despite the time delays in the settlement of disputes, why do employers and unions resort to adjudication? Give suggestions for reversing this trend.

2 The settlement machinery prescribed under the ID Act is no longer relevant in the current fast-paced globally competitive India. Elucidate.

DEBATE

1 The utility of the statutory settlement machinery for industrial disputes prevails only in the industrial relations system. The employee relations management system has no use for it.

2 Which is more important—equitable settlement or prompt settlement?

CASE ANALYSIS

Changes in Shift Timings

Mrityunjay Sahay is the Regional Manager (HR), Northern Region, for an FMCG company with its corporate office at Mumbai. The total employee strength of the company is 5,500, spread all over India. The Northern Region has 1,200 employees spread over 6 Depot Offices located in Patiala, Gurgaon, Jaipur, Gwalior, Delhi and Kanpur. Each Depot has around 150 employees. The Depots mostly comprise warehouse operations, i.e., receipt, storage and dispatch of products. The Depots operate in two overlapping shifts. The Regional Operations Manager wants to introduce three shifts working at the Depots without any addition of manpower. Each Depot has a recognized union. Mrityunjay finds it to be a daunting task. He has approached the unions, but has been warned by them not to press for change. Today, in his morning correspondence, he has received a letter from the Patiala union, announcing their intention to go on a strike if the management went ahead with the proposal to make changes in shift timings.

Questions

1. Can the management introduce the proposed changes? How?
2. Who will be the "appropriate government" in this case? Will the management have to deal with each Depot separately? Or can it deal with it as a single problem? Explain your answer.
3. As per the Industrial Disputes Act, 1947, what should be the role of the conciliation officer? Is he bound to intervene?
4. What role do you see for the "settlement machinery" in resolving the dispute?

Legal or Illegal

You are the Regional Manager (South) of a company, manufacturing and distributing mineral water. The manufacturing units are located in Nanded and Nashik. The company has warehouses in every major city of the country. Each warehouse employs around 30–40 workmen. One morning, you got a call from one of the warehouse managers, informing you that the local union has given a call for a flash strike, and the workers have not been attending to duties since morning.

Questions

1. List down all the points systematically that you will check to determine whether the strike is legal or illegal.
2. Can the management request the government for any help in restoring "normalcy"?

NOTES

1 "Labour Legislation Guidelines", Chapter IV, International Labour Organization (http://www.ilo.org/public/english/dialogue/ifpdial/llg/noframes/ch4.htm#9).

2 Report of the Second National Commission on Labour, Government of India, 2002, para 23.12

SUGGESTED READING

Guidelines on Labour Legislation, ILO Publications, Geneva (www.ilo.org).

Report of the Second National Commission on Labour, Government of India.

Monappa, Arun, Industrial *Relations* (:Tata Mcgraw-Hill Publishing Limited, 1985).

Venkatratnam, C. S., *Industrial Relations* (New Delhi: Oxford University Press,)

International Labour Organization, *Conciliation in Industrial Disputes: A Practical Guide, First Edition* (Geneva: International Labour Organization, 1988).

chapter fourteen

CHAPTER OUTLINE

LEARNING OBJECTIVES

After reading this chapter, you will be able to:

- Identify the various institutions, processes and systems for the prevention of industrial disputes
- Understand the role, genesis and working of these institutions, processes and systems

National Joint Committee for the Steel Industry

The National Joint Committee (for the Steel Industry, NJCS) was constituted in pursuance of the decision taken in the second session of the Industrial Committee on Iron and Steel in October 1969. This Committee arrived at a Memorandum of Agreement on revision of wages and benefits in the steel industry on 27 October 1970. It covered the workers of the then Hindustan Steel Ltd, Tata Iron and Steel Co. (TISCO)—a private sector company, Indian Iron and Steel Co. (IISCO) and the then MISL, now Visvesvaraya Iron and Steel Plant (VISP). The Committee was formed under the aegis of the labour ministry and the then Deputy Chief Labour Commissioner (I) was the Secretary of the Committee.

In February 1971, it was decided that this Committee would continue its work independently without any assistance from the labour ministry and the Committee would raise its own funds including contribution from the workers' representatives. After signing of the first agreement in October 1970, the scope of the Committee was enlarged with a view to deal with the implementation of the agreement, and also the problems of general nature affecting the industry as a whole. Since then, the Committee has notched many milestones.

The NJCS decides and finalizes its own Terms of Reference. The scope of working of the Committee has been widened from time to time and now covers:

i) Negotiations for wage settlement and its implementation
ii) Matters pertaining to and steps to be taken for the increase in production, productivity
iii) Improvement in quality, reduction of cost and wastages, etc.
iv) Review of welfare amenities and facilities
v) Matters/issues demanding immediate attention of the government
vi) Any other matter pertaining to the steel industry and its employees, as may be agreed to in the NJCS, from time to time

The NJCS has now been working for 38 years and has concluded many industry-wide agreements on wide-ranging issues. It is a permanent body and the process of discussion is continuous. It is certain that this bipartite forum for discussion has prevented many a dispute in the industry from turning into dysfunctional conflict affecting the industry and the employees.

Industrial Disputes: Institutional Framework and Preventive Measures

The industrial relations system has, apart from mechanisms for settling industrial disputes, a number of institutions, legislations, systems and processes that help prevent disputes from arising. These measures act as an interface between the parties amongst whom disputes may arise and also act as a safety mechanism.

The opening vignette describes the working of an industry-level bipartite forum where the representatives of the management and the employees engage in continuous discussion on a wide range of issues. The terms of reference are decided by both the parties, with an unstated aim to maintain harmony in the industry. Many flashpoints, which could have otherwise led to conflict, dispute and industrial action, are prevented due to the existence of a forum like NJCS, and a process of collective bargaining and negotiations.

There exist many such institutions, processes, systems and even laws that contribute to the prevention of industrial disputes.

14.1 Harmonious Relations

Howsoever much industrial harmony may be sought as an organizational objective, some conflict is inherent in the industrial structure. Conflict of interests between the various groups can intensify and prolong work stoppages. The three main groups in an industry, namely, owners, managers and workers, develop different orientations and perceptions of their interests. The pursuit of divergent objectives by each causes friction severe enough to, at times, lead to industrial action. A strategic, proactive approach, which brings about some convergence of objectives, on a continuous basis, is necessary to prevent the emergence of conflicts, even if they do arise.

Globalization is now a reality and has come to be reckoned by all sections of the society. The accelerated economic growth witnessed in India today is attributed to the New Economic Policy pursued by the government in the context of a global economic order. Harmonious industrial relations are, therefore, more than ever, a pre-condition for competing. A review of data on work stoppages arising out of industrial disputes reveals a significant improvement in industrial relations scenario in the 1990s as compared to the 1980s. The number of industrial disputes, i.e., strikes and lockouts have shown not only a declining trend but also a steep fall. It cannot be said with any certainty as to the causes of the decline. Most likely, they are a complex interplay of many socio-economic-political factors. Because there is a perceptible change in the figures pre- and post-NEP, this change in policy itself appears to have definitely played a role in the decline of industrial disputes and industrial actions. But these may not be the only reason.

14.2 A Framework of Preventive Measures

A comprehensive framework for industrial relations was presented in a diagrammatic form in Chapter 12 (see Fig. 12.1). The figure presented a clear division between the preventive and settlement aspects of

Figure 14.1

The framework of preventive measures.

Institutions/Fora	Voluntary Codes	Rules/Processes/Systems
• International Labour Organization • Joint Consultative Tripartite Bodies (Indian Labour Conference, Standing Labour Committee) • Industrial Committees, Wage Boards • Bipartite Bodies • Joint Management Councils • Works Committees	• Code of discipline in industry • Code of conduct • Code of efficiency and welfare	• Standing orders • Discipline procedures • Grievance procedure • Collective bargaining • Worker's participation in management • Employee welfare • Empowerment, engagement training and education

disputes. This division, however, is arbitrary and has been used merely to facilitate understanding of the entire machinery. In real life, more often than not, the preventive and settlement measures may interact with each other, operate simultaneously, or be common to both. For example, collective bargaining, as a process, is useful both in preventing disputes and also settling disputes.

Let us make another arbitrary framework to understand all the preventive tools that are in existence for the larger purpose of industrial harmony. These could be studied under three broad heads: (1) Institutions/Bipartite and Tripartite Consultative Bodies (2) Voluntary Codes and (3) Rules/Processes/Systems

Figure 14.1 presents this in a structured form. Please note that these measures are not exhaustive, but cover the most significant of institutions/bodies/processes/systems/rules/codes. A few of these components have been dealt with in detail in other chapters. A few important ones (not all) that have not been covered elsewhere have been discussed below, along with a refresher on those that have been.

14.2.1 Institutions/Consultative Bodies

A few of these institutions and bodies have been briefly discussed in Chapter 2. We will take a look again, especially the objectives of their formation and the current concerns that they have for the maintenance of harmonious industrial relations.

Preamble to the ILO Constitution

- Universal and lasting peace can be established only if it is based upon social justice
- Conditions of labour exist involving such injustice, hardship and privation to large numbers of people as to produce unrest so great that the peace and harmony of the world are imperilled; an improvement of those conditions is urgently required
- The failure of any nation to adopt humane conditions of labour is an obstacle in the way of other nations, which desire to improve the conditions in their own countries

ORIGINS OF THE ILO. The International Labour Organization was founded in the year 1919 in the aftermath of World War I (as a part of Treaty of Versailles, to end WW I). It was felt that lasting peace in the world was possible only if it was based on social justice. ILO was formed at a time when the exploitation of labour was being felt, and talked about, as a result of more than a century of industrialization. However, the need was not only humanitarian and social but also political and economic as there was a realization of economic interdependence of the world. The constitution of ILO was drafted by the Labour Commission set up by the Peace Conference, which first met in Paris and then in Versailles. The Commission, chaired by Samuel Gompers, head of the American Federation of Labour (AFL) in the United States, was composed of representatives from nine countries—Belgium, Cuba, Czechoslovakia, France, Italy, Japan, Poland, the United Kingdom and the United States. It resulted in a tripartite organization, the only one of its kind, bringing together representatives of governments, employers and workers in its executive bodies.[1]

The ILO, at present, has around 177 members. India was one of the founding members and its membership dates to the year 1919.

AIMS AND OBJECTIVES OF THE ILO. The intent for setting up of ILO are best reflected in its Preamble to the Constitution:

"Whereas universal and lasting peace can be established only if it is based upon social justice; and whereas conditions of labour exist involving such injustice, hardship and privation to large numbers of people as to produce unrest so great that the peace and harmony of the world are imperilled; and an improvement of those conditions is urgently required; as, for example, by the regulation of the hours of work including the establishment of a maximum working day and week, the regulation of the labour supply, the prevention of unemployment, the provision of an adequate living wage, the protection of the worker against sickness, disease and injury arising out of his employment, the protection of children, young persons and women, provision for old age and injury, protection of the interests of workers when employed in countries other than their own, recognition of the principle of equal remuneration for work of equal value, recognition of the principle of freedom of association, the organization of vocational and technical education and other measures; whereas also the failure of any nation to adopt humane conditions of labour is an obstacle in the way of other nations, which desire to improve the conditions in their own countries."[2]

The objectives of the ILO were further refined by way of a conference held in the year 1944 at Philadelphia. The outcome of the Philadelphia conference was later incorporated in the Constitution of the ILO as The Philadelphia Declaration. The Philadelphia Declaration, while reaffirming the founding principles of ILO, adds:

a) Labour is not a commodity.

b) Freedom of expression and of association are essential to sustained progress.

c) Poverty anywhere constitutes a danger to prosperity everywhere.

d) The war against want requires to be carried on with unrelenting vigour within each nation, and by continuous and concerted international effort in which the representatives of workers and employers, enjoying equal status with those of governments, join with them in free discussion and democratic decision with a view to the promotion of the common welfare.

The Philadelphia Declaration

a) Labour is not a commodity;
b) Freedom of expression and of association are essential to sustained progress;
c) Poverty anywhere constitutes a danger to prosperity everywhere;
d) The war against want requires to be carried on with unrelenting vigour within each nation, and by continuous and concerted international effort . . .

Further, Part III of the Declaration, incorporated as the annexure to the Constitution, spells out the aims of ILO with clarity:

a) Full employment and the raising of standards of living

b) The employment of workers in the occupations in which they can have the satisfaction of giving the fullest measure of their skill and attainments and make their greatest contribution to the common wellbeing

c) The provision, as a means to the attainment of this end and under adequate guarantees for all concerned, of facilities for training and the transfer of labour, including migration for employment and settlement

d) Policies in regard to wages and earnings, hours and other conditions of work, calculated to ensure a just share of the fruits of progress to all, and a minimum living wage to all employed and in need of such protection

e) The effective recognition of the right of collective bargaining, the cooperation of management and labour in the continuous improvement of productive efficiency, and the collaboration of workers and employers in the preparation and application of social and economic measures

f) The extension of social-security measures to provide a basic income to all in need of such protection and comprehensive medical care

g) Adequate protection for the life and health of workers in all occupations

h) Provision for child welfare and maternity protection

i) The provision of adequate nutrition, housing and facilities for recreation and culture

j) The assurance of equality of educational and vocational opportunity[3].

> **ILO's Strategic Objectives**
>
> Promote and realize standards and fundamental principles and rights at work
>
> Create greater opportunities for women and men to secure decent employment and income
>
> Enhance the coverage and effectiveness of social protection for all
>
> Strengthen tripartism and social dialogue

Through adoption of various "conventions" and "recommendations", the ILO has, over the years, attempted to achieve the above aims. Over the years, a number of these conventions have been ratified by the member states and recommendations implemented. The ILO now articulates its "strategic objectives" as the following:

- Promote and realize standards and fundamental principles and rights at work
- Create greater opportunities for women and men to secure decent employment and income
- Enhance the coverage and effectiveness of social protection for all
- Strengthen tripartism and social dialogue

THE STRUCTURE, THE STANDARDS AND THE PROCESSES AT THE ILO. The ILO, in trying to achieve its strategic objectives, brings together the three parties to the social dialogue, namely, the government, employers and employees to set labour standards and policies. The main instrument of these standards is the ILO "conventions" and "recommendations". In all, the deliberations of ILO, the employers' and employees' organizations have an equal voice with the government's. This tripartism is what sets ILO apart from all other global organizations. It is through tripartism and social dialogue within member nations that ILO helps design and implement policies within member states.

> **Tripartism**
>
> The interaction of government, employers and workers (through their representatives) as equal and independent partners to seek solutions to issues of common concern.

To understand the manner in which ILO goes about setting labour standards (which essentially means "conventions" and "recommendations"), we must first know its structure. The main sub-systems in ILO are:

- The International Labour Conference
- The Governing Body
- The International Labour Office

> **Social Dialogue**
>
> Includes all types of negotiation, consultation or exchange of information between or amongst representatives of governments, employers and workers on issues of common interest relating to economic and social policy.

The International Labour Conference: This is the policy-making and legislative body of ILO. It is here that the conventions and recommendations are finally adopted. In the ILC, each member state is represented by the government, the employers' and the employees' delegates in the ratio of 2:1:1. The delegates may be accompanied by technical advisors. The rights for every delegate are the same, and there is freedom to express views and opinions, across the categories and member states. Therefore, it may so happen that delegates from the same member state may express opposing views or even that members from, say, the workers categories from different member states may express different views. Every delegate has voting rights, and despite diversity of opinions, standards are set through majority opinion.

The Conference, which is often called an international parliament of labour, has several main tasks:

- Debating, voting and adopting the standards in the form of conventions and recommendations. The difference between conventions and recommendations has earlier been explained in Chapter 2
- Supervisions of the application of conventions and recommendations at the national level
- Examination of progress on status of the four fundamental rights, namely: (a) freedom of association and the effective recognition of the right to collective bargaining; (b) the elimination of all forms of forced or compulsory labour; (c) the effective abolition of child labour; and (d) the elimination of discrimination in respect of employment and occupation
- Discussion on issues of importance pertaining to social and labour matters. A report on a central theme is presented by the Director General of the ILO, which is then taken up for discussion. A few examples of such themes are:

- ○ Social insurance and social protection (1993)
- ○ Defending values, promoting change: social justice in a global economy (1994)
- ○ Promoting employment (1995)
- ○ The ILO, standard-setting and globalization (1997)
- ○ Decent work (1999), reducing the decent work deficit: a global challenge (2001)
- ○ A fair globalization: creating opportunities for all (2004)

- Passing of work programmes and budget

The ILO has three main sub-systems:

1. International Labour Conference: This can be equated to the legislative arm of a government
2. The Governing Body: This can be visualized as the executive body
3. International Labour Office: Is the permanent secretariat

The ILC meets every year in the month of June to transact business. International Labour Conference, therefore, can be thought of an international parliament on labour issues. The Conference elects one President and three vice-presidents (one representing each of the three groups, namely, the government, the employers and the employees).

The Governing Body: The Governing Body is the executive body of the International Labour Office (please note that International Labour Office is one of the sub-systems of the International Labour Organization). The Governing Body oversees the functioning of the International Labour Office, which may be thought of as the Secretariat of the International Labour Organization. The Governing Body:

- Decides the agenda of the International Labour Conference
- Helps finalize the draft of Works Programme and Budget of the ILO for submission to the ILC
- Elects the Director-General (of the International Labour Office)

The Governing Body comprises 56 titular members and 66 deputy members. The titular membership is distributed in the ration of 2:1:1 (28 government, 14 employers and 14 employees). Ten of these titular memberships are reserved for States of Chief Industrial Importance, which presently comprise Brazil, China, France, Germany, India, Italy, Japan, the Russian Federation, the United Kingdom and the United States. The other government members are elected by the Conference every three years. The break-up of Deputy Members is—government = 24, employers and employees = 19 each (24 + 19 + 19).

The Governing Body has a Chairperson and two vice-chairpersons. These are elected positions with tenure of one year. The Chairperson is usually chosen from among the government members. The Employer and Worker Vice-Chairpersons are chosen by their respective groups. They can be re-elected in subsequent years.

The International Labour Office: The International Labour Office is the permanent secretariat of the International Labour Organization. It is headed by a Director General, who also functions as the Secretary General of the International Labour Conference. The Director General is elected for a term of five years (renewable by the Governing Body). It functions under the overall supervision of the Governing Body and does all the technical and administrative work pertaining to the functioning of the ILO. The Director General or his Deputy is supposed to attend all the meetings of the Governing Body. The headquarters of the International Labour Office is at Geneva and has around 40 field and regional offices around the world.

Article 10 of the ILO Constitution lays down the roles and function of the International Labour Office:

- Collection and distribution of information on all subjects pertaining to industrial life and labour and with particular reference to matters to be brought before the International Labour Conference for adoption as a Convention
- Prepare the documents on the various items of the agenda for the meetings of the Conference
- Provide assistance to the governments (on their requests) in framing of laws and regulations on the basis of decisions in the Conference

Figure 14.2

The structure of the ILO.

The International Labour Conference: Members in the Ratio of 2:1:1 of Government, Employers and Employees: 1 President + 3 Vice Presidents
(Legislative)

The Governing Body: 56 Titular Members (28+14+14): 66 Deputy Members (28+18+18): 1 Chairperson+ 2 Vice Chairpersons: 10 of the Titular Members from the countries of Chief Industrial Importance
(Executive)

Permanent Secretariat: Works under scrutiny and supervision of the Governing Body: Headed by Director General: DG is also the Secretary General for the ILC: Has a 5 year renewable term
(Secretariat)

- Carry out the duties required of it by the provisions of the ILO Constitution in connection with the effective observation of the Conventions
- Publish, as per directions of the Governing Body may think, papers dealing with problems of industry and employment of international interest

Figure 14.2 gives an overall picture of the sub-systems of the ILO.

Labour Standards: The *ILO Thesaurus* defines[4] "labour standard" as "standards concerning employment and working conditions found acceptable by employers and workers through collective bargaining and by the legislator through labour laws and regulations". ILO standards take the form of ILO "conventions" and "recommendations". Conventions and recommendations, thus, are the principal instruments for setting the labour standards.

Labour Standards

Standards concerning employment and working conditions found acceptable by employers and workers through collective bargaining and by the legislator through labour laws and regulations

An issue of growing concern on labour or related issue is usually taken up for evolving as a labour standard (a convention or a recommendation or both). For example, the issue of child labour could be an area of concern to be focused upon for arriving at an acceptable standard. Developing an ILO standard is a legislative process. A flowchart describing the process is shown in Figure 14.3.

Figure 14.3

The process for setting labour standards.

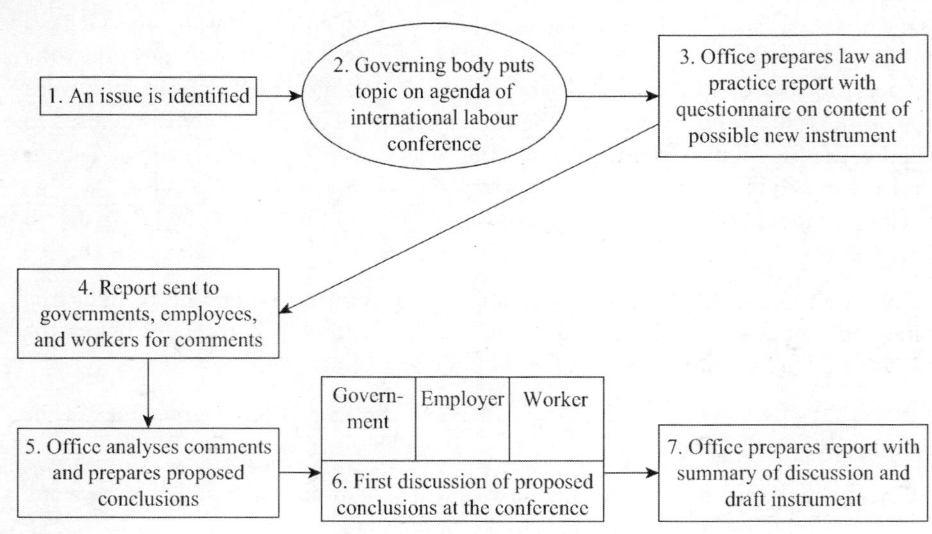

BOX 14.1 **99TH SESSION (JUNE 2010) OF THE INTERNATIONAL LABOUR CONFERENCE**

AGENDA

Standing items

I (a) Reports of the Chairperson of the Governing Body and of the Director-General
(b) Global Report under the Follow-up to the ILO Declaration on Fundamental Principles and Rights at Work*

II Programme and Budget and other questions

III Information and reports on the application of Conventions and Recommendations

Items placed on the agenda by the Conference or the Governing Body

IV Decent work for domestic workers *(standard setting, with a view to the possible adoption of a Convention supplemented by a Recommendation)*

V Elaboration of an autonomous Recommendation on HIV/AIDS in the world of work *(standard setting, second discussion)*

VI A discussion on the strategic objective of employment *(first in the cycle of recurrent discussions to follow up on the 2008 ILO Declaration on Social Justice for a Fair Globalization)*

VII Review of the follow-up to the 1998 ILO Declaration on Fundamental Principles and Rights at Work.

---

*This year the Global Report will be on the effective abolition of child labour

Source: (http://www.ilo.org/wcmsp5/groups/public/—ed_norm/—relconf/documents/meetingdocument/wcms_112359.pdf)

On being brought to notice, the Governing Body decides that the issue be put up to the International Labour Conference for deliberations. An agenda is prepared for the ILC. A sample agenda for the forthcoming meeting in June 2010 is reproduced in Box 14.1.

Next, the International Labour Office prepares a report basically incorporating national laws and practices in the member states pertaining on the issue in focus member. The consolidated report is then sent to all member states, the employers' organizations and the employees' organizations with a view to get their comments for discussion at the International Labour Conference. This is followed by another report, incorporating all views and discussions at the Conference and a draft instrument prepared (convention or a recommendation) to be discussed in the next Conference. The draft is then amended and adopted for action. Discussion on the issue twice in the Conference gives sufficient time for the members to adequately study and discuss the same. A standard needs 2/3 rd majority to be adopted.

Once adopted at the Conference, the member states need it to be submitted to their competent authority for ratification (the parliament in our case). Ratification makes it a legally binding document and thereafter the member states have to create suitable legal provisions to enforce the convention. Once ratified, the implementation comes onto the supervisory radar of the ILO. Recommendations, on the other hand, are not legally binding. The ILO takes into account the realities and, hence, there is enough flexibility in the conventions to allow for implementation suited to national socio-economic practicalities. Examine the issue presented in Box 14.2 to understand the practical constraints that nations face in ratifying a convention.

The ILO, thus, has been one of the most important and influential institutions in enabling worldwide industrial peace. Through the spirit of tripartite consultation on issues, evolving of labour standards, assistance in evolution of legal mechanisms, it has been instrumental in the prevention of conditions leading to industrial strife. It has evolved standards on every conceivable issue relating to labour and brought it up for discussion and consensus. India, too, has benefited by way of being able to put in place suitable labour laws.

> BOX 14.2 **FOR CLASS DISCUSSION**
>
> The general practice in India has been that it ratifies a convention only when the laws are in place for the relevant convention. The government veers around to a position that is prudent and the way for implementation of standards is gradual and progressive. Only after sufficient progress has been made does India consider ratifying a convention after which it becomes legally binding on the country. However, non-ratification of a convention does not prevent it from voting for the said convention.
>
> What are some of the major conventions that India has not ratified? Discuss the possible reasons for non-ratification.

LABOUR STANDARDS AND TRADE/PROTECTIONISM. With the advent of WTO, a debate has begun if trade sanctions could be used by the governments against countries not adhering to "core" ILO standards namely, a) freedom of association b) no forced labour c) no child labour, and d) no discrimination at work (including gender discrimination). All WTO members are committed to the core standards. Does it mean that WTO members could use trade sanctions in furtherance of the core standards? The developing countries have protested saying this argument to be arm-twisting the developing nations who may have comparative advantage in trade because of cheaper labour. The WTO succinctly lists down the debatable issues between labour standards and trade[5]:

"Four broad questions have been raised inside and outside the WTO.

The analytical question: If a country has lower standards for labour rights, do its exports gain an unfair advantage? Would this force all countries to lower their standards (the "race to the bottom")?

The response question: If there is a "race to the bottom", should countries only trade with those that have similar labour standards?

The question of rules: Should WTO rules explicitly allow governments to take trade action as a means of putting pressure on other countries to comply?

The institutional question: Is the WTO the proper place to discuss and set rules on labour—or to enforce them, including those of the ILO?

In addition, all these points have an underlying question: whether trade actions could be used to impose labour standards or whether this would simply be an excuse for protectionism." These are all contentious issues, which have divided the developing and developed nations. In fact, even the trade unions in these countries appear to be divided.

14.2.2 Joint Consultative Tripartite Bodies

The spirit of tripartism that ILO embodies has been incorporated at the national level too, in the form of Indian Labour Conference and Standing Labour Committee. Both of these are tripartite consultative bodies comprising members from the government (central and state), employees' organizations and employers' organization. The two committees have been discussed in Chapter 2. However, the experience with tripartism at the national level has not been as successful as at the ILO, especially after the initial period of their formation. The ILC was effective in its formative years, but in the 1950s, the effectiveness declined and it has been downhill ever since. However, even though the meetings have declined in frequency and the body is not fully representative due to fragmentations within each of the categories, the spirit of tripartism has been persisted with, and matters of importance are still discussed, albeit the results not as spectacular as in late 1940s and early 1950s. There are many reasons for the shortcomings but, in the main, the reasons are:

i) The Government of India treat even the unanimous recommendations of ILC as not binding on the government even though the government is represented in the ILC. This undermined the confidence of the parties in the commitment of the government.

ii) It has become increasingly difficult to find a consensus on the representativeness of members from the three parties, namely, the government, the employers' organizations and the employees' organizations.

iii) The major objective of bringing uniformity in labour legislation in the country has not been completely achieved due to labour being in the Concurrent List on which both the centre and a state could legislate.

THE EVOLUTION OF TRIPARTITE BODIES. The need for consultation on labour matters on the patterns set by the ILO was recommended by the Whitley Commission in 1931. It was recommended that the representatives of employers, labour and the government should meet regularly in conference. The labour members should be elected by registered trade unions and employers' representatives should be elected by their associations. The recommendations could not be implemented till the Second World War, when cooperation of labour was felt to be necessary to foster industrial peace and increase productivity for the war effort.

During the inter-War period, the Government of India adopted a practice of holding consultations on important labour questions, principally those coming up before the legislature or before the International Labour Conference, with the representatives of the then provincial governments, employers and workers. These consultations were, however, held separately with representatives of each group. Accordingly, the Fourth Labour Conference was held in August 1942. It set up permanent tripartite collaboration machinery and constituted Preliminary Labour Conference (later named as the Indian Labour Conference—ILC) and the Standing Labour Advisory Committee (which subsequently dropped the word "Advisory" from its title SLC). Initially, the ILC consisted of 44 members, whereas the SLC was about half the size of the ILC. The pattern of representation was governed by:

i) Equality of representation between the government and the non-government representatives

ii) Parity between employers and workers

iii) Nomination of representatives of organized employers and labourers was left to the concerned organizations

iv) Representation of certain interests (unorganized employers and unorganized workers), where necessary, on an *ad hoc* basis through nomination by the government. The delegates are free to bring one official and one non-official advisor with them.

Representation in ILC

i) Equality of representation between the government and the non-government representatives
ii) Parity between employers and workers
iii) Nomination of representatives of organized employers and labourers was left to the concerned organizations
iv) Representation of certain interests (unorganized employers and unorganized workers), where necessary, on an *ad hoc* basis through nomination by the government. The delegates are free to bring one official and one non-official advisor with them.

The ILC was instituted to advise the Government of India on matters brought to its notice by the government. In the earlier phase of the tripartite, SLC used to deliberate on its own or over matters sent to it by ILC and the latter made the final recommendations. In course of time, both the ILC and SLC have become deliberative bodies, the former being more representative.

The agenda for ILC/SLC meetings was settled by the union labour ministry after taking into consideration the suggestions sent to it by member organizations. These two bodies worked with minimum procedural rules to facilitate free and fuller discussions among the members. The ILC was meant to meet once a year, whereas the SLC was to meet as and when necessary.

The rules and procedures, which characterize the Indian tripartite consultative machinery, are largely in tune with the recommendations of the ILO Committee on consultation and cooperation. (Recommendation No. 113):

i) Use of flexible procedures

ii) Calling a meeting only when necessary with adequate notice of the meeting and the agenda

iii) Reference of certain items to working parties, if necessary

iv) Dispensing with voting procedures in arriving at conclusions to facilitate consultations

v) Maintaining records of discussions in detail and circulating the conclusions reached to all participants

vi) Documentation of references

vii) Provision of an effective secretariat and a small representative steering grant in case of more formal consultative machinery

Extracts from the deliberations of the 42nd Session of ILC (2009) are reproduced in the Box 14.3.

BOX 14.3 **INDIAN LABOUR CONFERENCE; 42ND SESSION; NEW DELHI; EXTRACTS**

Conclusion of the Conference Committee on "All Issues connected with contractualization of Labour" and "Issues related to Migrant Workers"

The Group recognized the need for preventing exploitation of contract labour wherever it exists. There was a consensus that the issue required to be addressed on priority, especially in the wake of economic downturn. Hence, it was felt that the provisions relating to Contract Labour (Regulation and Abolition) Act, 1970 need to be revisited in the context of the following:

- The Employers' Group felt that the Contract Labour has come to stay. Hence, banning of contract labour does not provide solution to the problems relating to contract labour. The inevitability of contract labour needs to be recognized. However, fresh thought has to be given to the protection of working conditions of contract labour. This protection mechanism needs to be clearly defined in the legislation itself so as to ensure that the contract labour is not exploited in terms of appropriate wages, working conditions and social security.
- The Workers' Group unanimously maintained that the Act should be amended to provide for:

  a) Absorption of contract employees in regular jobs after prohibition under Section 10(2);
  b) Insertion in the main Act provision for paying same wages and other benefits for same and similar nature of work.
  c) The ceiling of 20 workers should be deleted.
  d) License should not be given for employment of contract labour in perennial nature of jobs.

- With a view to evolving a strategy paper incorporating amendments to the existing legislation in the context of the views of respective groups, a task force be constituted. Apart from experts, it should consist of representatives from Workers and Employers so as to facilitate intensive interaction. However, this task force should consult all the stakeholders and hold discussion with them. The Task Force should submit its report in six months.

In the context of Inter-State Migrant Workmen (Regulation of Employment and Conditions of Service) Act, 1979, on account of paucity of time, the group could not deliberate at length. It was, however, felt that a tripartite group consisting of representatives from employers, employees and the government should examine the provisions in the Act with a view to facilitating greater social protection to the migrant workers and suggest amendments within six months. In the meanwhile, all efforts should be made for effective implementation of existing provisions.

Excerpted from http://labour.nic.in/lc/42ilc/RecordNoteofDiscussions.pdf.

THE EVALUATION OF ILC AND SLC. According to the National Commission on Labour (1969), these two bodies have immensely contributed to attainment of the objectives set before them. It observed: "The ILC/SLC have facilitated the enactment of central legislation on various subjects to be made applicable to all the states and union territories in order to promote uniformity in labour legislation. Tripartite deliberations helped to reach a consensus on statutory minimum wage fixation (1944); introduction of a health insurance scheme (1945); enactment of the Standing Employment Order Act, 1946; the Industrial Disputes Act, 1947; enactment of the Minimum Wages Act, 1948; Dock Workers' Regulation of Employment Act, 1948; the Employees' State Insurance Act, 1948; Provident Fund Scheme, 1950; the Mines Act, 1952; the Employees' Provident Fund Act, 1952; and the making of legislation concerning payment of bonus, regulation and abolition of contract labour, etc. The tripartite deliberations also facilitated the formulation of comprehensive procedures for the settlement of disputes under the Industrial Disputes Act, 1947. Both the inception of Labour Appellate Tribunal in 1950 and its abolition in 1956 were the result of such deliberations. The range of subjects discussed at the forums of ILC/SLC has been large and has included social, economic and administrative matters concerning labour policy." However, this observation was made in the 1960s and later analysis shows that the effectiveness of these bodies in achieving the objectives set before them has steadily declined. Nevertheless, ILC and SLC remain the main deliberative and consultative bodies for formulation of labour policy in the country. Maybe, time has come for a fundamental shift in making the whole process more relevant to today's political, economic and social reality. Right now, the ILC and SLC appear to be a relic of the past, more a wishful thinking of lofty ideals of tripartism rather than an effective forum promoting social dialogue for policy formulation.

14.2.3 Industrial Committees

The establishment of industrial committees for specific industries was the outcome of the 1944 session of ILC. This committee was essentially tripartite with equal representation of workers and employers. These committees were set up to consider special problems of the industries for which they were constituted. Industrial committees came to be set up for plantations, coal mining, cotton textiles, cement, tanneries, mines other than coal, iron and steel, chemicals, building and construction, road transport, etc. To get a greater insight into the nature and kind of work that these committees do, specimen reports of two such committees set up for the steel and the oil industries is presented in the Box 14.4.

14.2.4 Bipartite Bodies

Two of the most important forms of bipartite bodies are the Works Committee and the Joint Management Councils. Bipartite bodies were envisaged as bodies having equal representation from management and workers to foster discussion and collaboration on issues of mutual interest in day-to-day running of the establishment. The idea for such bipartite bodies has a very long history, stretching into 1920s and has an intuitive appeal. Indeed, the TISCO and a few other progressive employers introduced the bipartite working long before its use became widespread. Bipartite bodies, ideally, are consultative bodies where the parties have an opportunity to discuss work-related issues on a continuous basis, thus preventing conflicts from taking a dysfunctional form. They are not negotiating bodies and issues pertaining to collective bargaining are to be scrupulously kept out of it. The importance of bipartite consultation was recommended by the Royal Commission on Labour and also reiterated in the Industrial Truce Resolution, 1947 and finally found place in the Industrial Disputes Act, 1948. It was further highlighted in both the First and Second Five Year Plan documents.

14.2.5 Works Committee

The ID Act, 1948 requires the employer to constitute a Works Committee consisting of equal representatives of employers and workmen engaged in the establishment in industrial

BOX 14.4 **STUDY GROUP ON IRON & STEEL INDUSTRY**

The Indian Labour Conference set up a study group on **Iron and Steel Industry**.

The group said that the industrial relations are more satisfactory in those plants:

I) "In which the recognized union is strong and is the only union with which management can negotiate matters of collective nature and which is in a position to implement agreements arrived at and takes an objective view of the grievances of employees;
II) Where the rules, regulations, procedures, practices have been either codified or established by convention and made known to the managerial staff and employees;
III) Where a grievance procedure has been established and is used to settle grievances by mutual discussion at different levels and where there is no desire to drag in a third party for help;
IV) Where there is mutual respect and closer association of employers with management at different levels, and where the personnel department is well developed."

The group made the following recommendations for improvements in labour management relations:

a) The union representing a majority of employees should be granted recognition;
b) Closer association should be developed between the management and the employees at all levels in the plant;
c) Grievances should be redressed by mutual discussions;
d) To discuss matters relating to wages, conditions of service, leave, etc. it would be useful if the recognized unions of all the steel plants are federated into one body;
e) Collective bargaining should be preferred both at plant and the industry levels and adjudication should be resorted to when all other methods have failed;
f) A two-way communication system should be developed in the plant, for which bipartite committees may be formed.

Study Group on Oil Industry

This group was set up by the Indian Labour Conference to study industrial relations in the oil-refining and distribution industry. It came across some undesirable events, such as "gheraos" of the management and stay-in strikes. These were held because of the political influence of the unions, greater consciousness among the workers of their rights and delay in decision making.

The group made the following recommendations:

i) Workers should be given a sympathetic treatment by the management;
ii) Collective bargaining should be developed;
iii) Workers should be educated to enable them to understand not only their rights but obligations, too, towards the industry, management and the public;
iv) Adjudication should be resorted to only when negotiation, conciliation and voluntary arbitration have failed;
v) A suitable atmosphere should be created by the government by restricting strikes and lockouts during the period when negotiations are continuing;
vi) Multiplicity of unions should go; and
vii) Mutual faith should be encouraged between the parties for promoting economy in the industry regarding hours of work, overtime work and a weekly holiday

establishments where 100 or more workmen are employed or have been employed on any day in the preceding 12 months. The representatives of the workmen are to be chosen in the prescribed manner from among the workmen engaged in the establishment and in consultation with their trade union, if any, registered under the Indian Trade Unions Act, 1926 (16 of 1926). The Works Committee aims to promote and secure amity and good relations between the employer and workmen and, to that end, to discuss matters of their common concern and resolve differences of opinion. The functions that the Act visualized for the Works Committees were:

- To promote measures for securing and preserving amity and good relations between employers and workmen
- To that end, comment upon matters of common interest or concern
- To endeavour to compose any material difference of opinion between the employer and the workmen in respect of such matters

The Indian Labour Conference in its 17th session held in 1959 discussed the functions of the works committee and approved a list of functions that could be assigned to the works committees and a list of functions that should not be assigned to the works committees. It will be useful to look at the illustrative lists drawn up by the Indian Labour Conference.

Items that works committees, may normally deal with:

- Conditions of work, such as ventilation, lighting, temperature and sanitation, including lavatories and urinals
- Amenities such as drinking water, canteens, dining rooms, crèches, rest rooms, medical and health services, protective equipment
- Adjustment of festival and national holidays
- Administration of welfare and funds
- Educational and recreational activities such as, libraries, reading rooms, cinema shows, sports, games, picnic parties, community welfare and celebrations
- Promotion of thrift and savings
- Implementation and review of decisions reached at meetings of works committees
- Items that the works committees should not normally deal with
- Wages and allowances
- Bonus and profit-sharing schemes
- Rationalization and matters connected with the fixation of workloads
- Matters connected with the fixation of the standard labour force
- Programmes of planning and development
- Matters connected with retrenchment and lay-off
- Victimization for trade-union activities
- Provident fund, gratuity schemes and other retiring benefits
- Quantum of leave, and national and festival holidays
- Incentive schemes
- Housing and transport service

According to a recent assessment, the system has proved its capacity to render substantial help in composing differences between the parties, although, owing to lack of earnest effort, the Committees are not functioning effectively in some units. The decision to demarcate the functions of works committees, as distinct from those of trade unions is necessary for successful functioning of the committees. Works committees need to be strengthened and made an active agency for the democratic administration of labour matters.

14.2.6 Joint Management Councils

The Industrial Policy Resolution adopted by the government in 1956 declared that in a socialist democracy, labour was a partner in the common task of development, and should be asked to participate in it with enthusiasm. A tripartite committee that visited the UK, Sweden, France, Belgium, West Germany and Yugoslavia came to an agreement on the constitution, functions and administration of joint councils. The committee recommended the setting up of JMCs in all undertakings. An all-India seminar held in Delhi in 1957 worked out a model agreement that the management and workers could enter into to set up these JMCs. The scheme was to be voluntary and consultative in nature. Joint management councils were to deal with all matters except matters falling within the area of collective bargaining such as wages, bonus, hours of work, etc.

These Joint Management Councils were envisaged to provide a greater sense of participation and infuse a spirit of cooperation between workers and management. The continuous interaction was supposed to keep friction and tension to a minimum level and create a cooperative atmosphere that facilitated negotiations.

The National Commission on Labour (1966–1969), which reviewed the working of the JMCs, observed that there was not much support for the institutions of the JMCs. The Commission held the view that "when the system of recognition of trade unions becomes an accepted practice, both management and unions would themselves gravitate towards greater cooperation and set up JMCs". The tripartite committee, which approved the draft model agreement regarding the establishment of JMC unanimously, agreed on the criteria that should be followed in selecting the undertakings in which Joint Councils should be established:

- The undertaking should have well-established strong trade unions.
- There should be willingness among the parties, viz. employers, and workers or the unions to try out the experiment in a spirit of cooperation.
- The size of the undertakings in terms of employment should be at least 500 workers.

The Committee further suggested that in choosing enterprises, the following criteria should be kept in mind:

- The employer in the private sector should be a member of one of the leading employers' organizations. Likewise, the trade union should be affiliated to one of the central federations.
- The undertaking should have a fair record of industrial relations.

14.3 Ethical Code: Code of Discipline

A Code of Discipline in industry, which applies both to the public and to the private sector, has been accepted voluntarily by all the central organizations of employers and workers and has been in operation since the middle of 1958. The need for a code was felt in the light of the fact that despite there being many legislations in place, industrial peace had not resulted to the extent it was desired. The code was to be a voluntary agreement between employers and employees to observe certain discipline that would contribute to industrial peace. The idea had a moral appeal to all the parties concerned and a consensus emerged in the late 1950s through deliberations in the 15th Session of the Indian Labour Conference (1957) to lay down a few general principles, namely:

- No strike/lockout without notice
- No unilateral action to be taken
- No resort to go-slow tactics
- No deliberate damage to property
- No acts of violence, instigation, coercion, intimidation to be resorted to
- Full utilization of dispute-resolution machinery
- Speedy implementation of awards and settlements

These general principles were later discussed and evolved into a full fledged Code of Discipline in Industry. And the code was accepted by the major trade unions and the employers' organizations.

The "Code" has the following structure:

1. Part 1: Duties and responsibilities of the three parties
2. Part 2: Obligations common to management and unions
3. Part 3: Obligations of management
4. Part 4: Obligations of unions

The Code also lays down the criteria for "recognition" of a union as a representative body in an enterprise and lists down the rights of a recognized union. It was hoped that by voluntary acceptance of this Code, there would be a lasting industrial peace. However, the Code has lost its relevance today in practical terms, even though the government had set up a mechanism to monitor the implementation of the Code. Discuss the issue raised in Box 14.5.

14.3.1 Standing Orders

One of the most proactive measures to prevent an industrial conflict is setting up of clear and satisfactory terms and conditions of employment. In this context, Standing Orders play a significant role as it governs the rules and regulations that govern the conditions of employment of workers. The Standing Orders in one way specifies the duties and responsibilities on the part of both employer and employees and makes each other clear of the expectations and the restrictions in terms of rules and procedures, which are standardized across the organization.

The purpose of having Standing Orders at plant and unit level is to regulate industrial relations. They define with sufficient precision the conditions of employment under the employers, who are liable to make the said conditions known to the workers. These orders regulate conditions of employment in terms of attendance, leave, hours of work, shift timings, grievances, misconduct, disciplinary action, etc. These are the very issues that have the potential to escalate into industrial conflicts. The standardization of norms prevents

BOX 14.5 **FOR CLASS DISCUSSION**

The Code of Discipline in Industry is now almost forgotten in practice, both by the trade unions and the employers' organizations. The attempt was more of moral exhortation rather than a practical and enforceable code. The attempts at creating institutions and instruments for preventive IR in India were mostly moralistic during the days when the nation was being created. Unlike the evolution at ILO, the institutions and instruments in India have not evolved with the changing times.

Do your own research to compare and contrast the preventive machinery in India with those of ILO.

ambiguity that can lead to misconceptions and raise issues of conflicting concerns. The provisions of the Standing Orders have been explained in Chapter 10.

14.3.2 Grievance Procedure

A grievance is a sign of an employee's discontentment with his job or his relationship with his colleagues. Grievances generally arise out of the day-to-day working relations in an organization. An employee or a trade union protests against an act or policy of the management that they consider as violating employee's rights.

Till the enactment of the Industrial Employment (Standing Orders) Act, 1946, the settlement of day-to-day grievances of workers in India did not receive much attention. Clause 15 of the Model Standing Orders in the Schedule of the Industrial Employment (Standing Orders) Act, 1946, specified that "all complaints arising out of the employment, including those relating to unfair treatment and wrongful action on the part of the employer or his agent, shall be submitted to the manager or other person specified on his behalf with the right of appeal to the employer".

The Industrial Disputes Act, 1947, through an amendment in 1982, provides for the establishment of a Grievance Settlement Authority (9C) in all industrial establishments employing 50 or more workmen. This, however, has not yet been given effect to.

Grievance procedure is a formal communication between an employee and the management designed for the settlement of a grievance. The grievance procedures differ from organization to organization. An organization may follow either of the two policies: (1) open-door policy or (2) step-ladder policy.

OPEN-DOOR POLICY. Under this policy, the aggrieved employee is free to meet the top executives of the organization and get his grievances redressed. Such a policy works well only in small organizations. However, in bigger organizations, top-management executives are usually busy with other concerned matters of the company. Moreover, it is believed that the open-door policy is suitable for executives; operational employees may feel shy to go to the top management.

STEP-LADDER POLICY. Under this policy, the aggrieved employee has to follow a step-by-step procedure for getting his grievance redressed. In this procedure, whenever an employee is confronted with a grievance, he presents his problem to his immediate supervisor. If the employee is not satisfied with the superior's decision, then he discusses his grievance with the departmental head. The departmental head discusses the problem with joint grievance committees to find a solution. However, if the committee also fails to redress the grievance, then it may be referred to chief executive. If the chief executive also fails to redress the grievance, then such a grievance is referred to voluntary arbitration, where the award of arbitrator is binding on both the parties.

GRIEVANCE PROCEDURE IN INDIAN INDUSTRY. The 15th Session of the Indian Labour Conference held in 1957 emphasized the need of an established grievance procedure for the country, which would be acceptable to unions as well as to management. In the 16th Session of the Indian Labour Conference, a model for grievance procedure was drawn up. This model helps in the creation of grievance machinery. According to it, workers' representatives are to be elected for a department or their union is to nominate them. Management has to specify the persons in each department who are to be approached first and the departmental heads who are supposed to be approached in the second step. The Model Grievance Procedure specifies the details of all the steps that are to be followed while redressing grievances (see Figure 14.4). These steps are:

Step 1: In the first step, the grievance is to be submitted to the departmental representative, who is a representative of management. S/he has to give his answer within 48 hours.

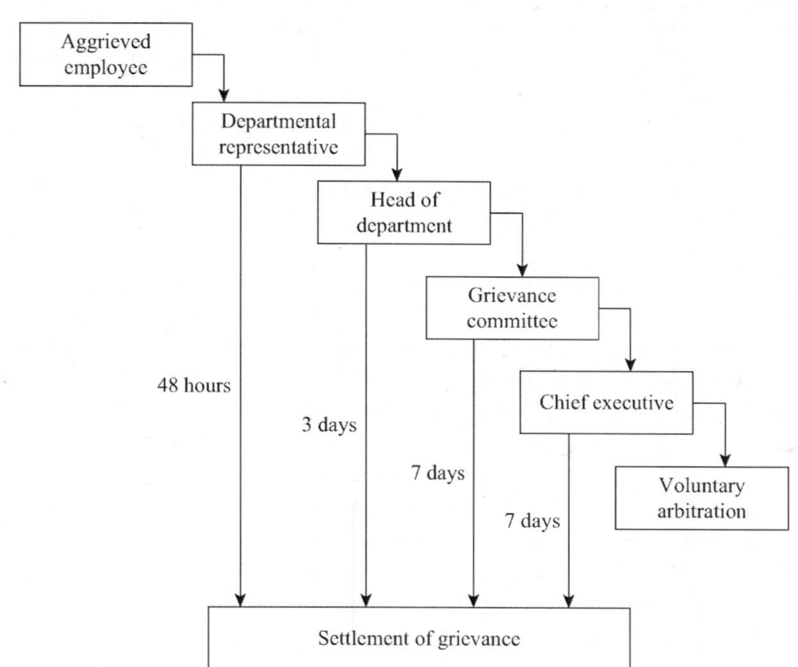

Figure 14.4
The model grievance procedure.

Step 2: If the departmental representative fails to provide a solution, the aggrieved employee can take his grievance to head of the department, who has to give his decision within 3 days.

Step 3: If the aggrieved employee is not satisfied with the decision of the departmental head, s/he can take the grievance to the Grievance Committee. The Grievance Committee makes its recommendations to the manager within seven days in the form of a report. The final decision of the management on the report of Grievance Committee must be communicated to the aggrieved employee within three days of the receipt of report. An appeal for revision of the final decision can be made by the worker if s/he is not satisfied with it. The management must communicate its decision to the worker within seven days.

Step 4: If the grievance still remains unsettled, the case may be referred to voluntary arbitration.

14.3.3 Collective Bargaining

The ILO refers to collective bargaining as "all negotiations which take place between one or more employers or employers' organizations on the one hand, and one or more workers' organizations on the other, for determining working conditions and terms of employment or for regulating relations between employers and workers".[6]

The collective bargaining, therefore, comprises:

- Negotiations
- Between organizations of workers and employers (it is not individual)
- Subject matter is working conditions, terms of employment, relationship between employers and employees

As the term suggests, "collective" means a group, i.e., it must involve a group of employees or trade unions on their behalf who would "bargain" on behalf of the workers they represent.

Since it is bargaining, the parties move to a position different from where they started through negotiations and discussions. The term itself implies flexibility in the process. The fundamental assumption is that solution for mutual gain is possible through discussions and negotiations, thus abjuring violence or precipitate action.

Collective bargaining is a process of joint decision-making that advocates industrial democracy. It establishes a culture of bipartism and joint consultation in industry and an involved adaptable method of adjustment to economic and technical changes in an industry. It helps in establishing industrial peace without disrupting either the existing arrangements or the production activities.

Collective bargaining is a means where both parties find ways for joint regulation through mutual consent. As a term, "collective bargaining" is said to have been coined by Sydney and Beatrice Webb. It emerged through a natural process of resolving industrial conflicts and growth of trade unions. Mahatma Gandhi guided a collective-bargaining process in the textile mills of Ahmedabad in the 1920s.

ILO, in 1949, adopted a convention on "Right to Organize and Collective Bargaining" (see Box 14.6). The right to collective bargaining is a fundamental right. The Indian Constitution (Article 19c) also guarantees freedom of association as a fundamental right. India, however, has still not ratified the ILO Convention on Collective Bargaining (C98). The right to collective bargaining has not been extended to employees of the government whose wages are determined through Pay Commissions and not through bargaining. However, for the industry at large, the right to collectively bargain exists. An important precondition for collective bargaining is the existence of strong and representative trade unions, duly recognized by the management. The collective-bargaining process is weak in India because of fragmentation of trade unions, and also the absence of legislation on a pan-India basis making it mandatory to recognize a trade union. A representative union in a position will have rights to bargain.

It is easy to see how strengthening the collective bargaining could go a long way in prevention of industrial unrest.

THE CONCEPT OF COLLECTIVE BARGAINING. Collective bargaining, as a concept, can be viewed from three perspectives—the "market" perspective, the "rule–making" perspective and the "business" perspective. The market perspective views collective bargaining as the means by which labour is bought and sold in the marketplace. In this context, collective bargaining is perceived as an economic and an exchange relationship. This concept focuses on the substantive content of collective agreements, i.e., on the pay, hours of work, and fringe benefits, which are mutually agreed between employers and trade-union representatives on behalf of their members.

The "rule–making" perspective, on the other hand, regards collective bargaining as an institutional system or rule-making process, which determines the relation between management and trade-union representatives. Here, collective bargaining is seen as a political and power relationship.

The "business" or "employee relations" perspective of collective bargaining views the institution as a participative decision-making between the employees and employers, on matters in which both parties have vital interests.

In collective bargaining, the employer does not deal with workers directly, but he deals with a collective authorized institution. It can be thought of as an institutional mechanism for:

a) Fixing up the price of labour services

b) Establishing a system of industrial jurisprudence

c) Providing a machinery for the representation of individual and group interests

CONDITIONS FOR THE SUCCESS OF COLLECTIVE BARGAINING. The success of collective bargaining depends upon the following factors:

BOX 14.6 **CONVENTION 98: RIGHT TO ORGANISE AND COLLECTIVE BARGAINING CONVENTION, 1949**

Article 1

1. Workers shall enjoy adequate protection against acts of anti-union discrimination in respect of their employment.
2. Such protection shall apply more particularly in respect of acts calculated to—
   (a) make the employment of a worker subject to the condition that he shall not join a union or shall relinquish trade union membership;
   (b) cause the dismissal of or otherwise prejudice a worker by reason of union membership or because of participation in union activities outside working hours or, with the consent of the employer, within working hours.

Article 2

1. Workers' and employers' organisations shall enjoy adequate protection against any acts of interference by each other or each other's agents or members in their establishment, functioning or administration.
2. In particular, acts which are designed to promote the establishment of workers' organisations under the domination of employers or employers' organisations, or to support workers' organisations by financial or other means, with the object of placing such organisations under the control of employers or employers' organisations, shall be deemed to constitute acts of interference within the meaning of this Article.

Article 3

Machinery appropriate to national conditions shall be established, where necessary, for the purpose of ensuring respect for the right to organise as defined in the preceding Articles.

Article 4

Measures appropriate to national conditions shall be taken, where necessary, to encourage and promote the full development and utilisation of machinery for voluntary negotiation between employers or employers' organisations and workers' organisations, with a view to the regulation of terms and conditions of employment by means of collective agreements.

Article 5

1. The extent to which the guarantees provided for in this Convention shall apply to the armed forces and the police shall be determined by national laws or regulations.
2. In accordance with the principle set forth in paragraph 8 of Article 19 of the Constitution of the International Labour Organisation the ratification of this Convention by any Member shall not be deemed to affect any existing law, award, custom or agreement in virtue of which members of the armed forces or the police enjoy any right guaranteed by this Convention.

Article 6

This Convention does not deal with the position of public servants engaged in the administration of the State, nor shall it be construed as prejudicing their rights or status in any way.

Source: http://www.ilo.org/ilolex/english/convdisp1.htm.

i) The union participating in the collective-bargaining process must be strong, democratic and enlightened. The weak and fragmented state of the unions, smallness and instability of their membership, rivalries, company-formed and dominated trade unions are some of the reasons for the undeveloped state of collective bargaining. Collective bargaining cannot become fully effective, if management continues to regard the union as an alien, outside force.

ii) One of the principles for establishing and promoting collective bargaining is to give voluntary recognition to trade unions as one of the contracting parties. It may also have the positive benefit of improving industrial relations, production and productivity.

iii) There should be willingness to give and take by both the parties, and genuine interest on the part of both to reach an agreement and to make collective bargaining work. The trade unions should refrain from putting forward exaggerated demands. Both the parties must realize that collective-bargaining negotiations are, by their very nature, a part of the compromise process. An emphasis on accommodation rather than conflict is necessary.

iv) The whole atmosphere of collective bargaining gets vitiated, relations become bitter and strained and negotiations more difficult, if one or both the parties engage in unfair practices. Both the union and the management, therefore, must desist from committing unfair practices and must have a healthy regard for their mutual rights and responsibilities. Trust and openness are very essential for meaningful discussion.

v) Collective bargaining usually takes place when there are differences between the parties on certain issues. But in order to make the collective-bargaining process more successful, it is essential on the part of the representative of employers and unions to hold meetings at regular intervals to consider matters of common interest. Such an on-going process would enable them to understand one another's problems better and make it easier to find solutions to questions on which their interests conflict.

vi) Effective collective bargaining presupposes an intelligent understanding of both management and union of the needs, aspirations, objectives and problems of the other party. Union leaders must have full knowledge of the economics of the plant or the industry concerned. Management must have a developed awareness of the nature of the union as a political institution operating in an economic environment.

vii) The effectiveness of collective bargaining cannot be attained without maturity of leadership on both sides of the bargaining table. The negotiators should have such qualities as experience, skill, intelligence, resourcefulness, honesty and technical know-how. They must have the capacity to distinguish between basically important and trivial issues. They must know when it is wise or necessary to compromise and when it may be fatal to concede to the demands.

viii) Intelligent collective bargaining demands specialized training. The increasingly technical complexity of the collective-bargaining agenda requires expert professional advice, experience and skill on the part of the negotiators.

ix) Both management and the union often find it difficult to locate the men on the other side of the table, who are authorized to negotiate. For proper negotiations, it is necessary to know the persons empowered to act for the company and the union respectively.

14.4 Managing Discipline

Organization discipline is concerned with standards of attitudes, behaviour and performance. It is derived from the total approach to ER that is adopted, especially from the perspective, culture and behaviour of the organization as a whole and the style of operations management adopted. It is developed, and the effectiveness of operations and actions in the field of organization discipline are reflected in the priority and quality of management and supervisory staff training in the field, as well as the extent, nature and frequency of issues concerning disciplinary actions and grievances raised.

Effective organization discipline, therefore, reflects the strategic approach and the style of ER adopted in its pursuit. Specific policy issues can then be addressed under the headings of attitudes and behaviour and performance. The direction and management of organization discipline is devised and defined by senior managers, operated by those with departmental, divisional and functional responsibilities, and accepted by all those who work in and for the organization. Operationally, it is a process with two key factors:

- Discipline—strategies and activities for the maintenance of standards and remedial action where necessary
- Grievances—strategies that enable employees to raise questions, issues and problems with the organization, so that these may be resolved

It is, therefore, necessary to consider organization discipline from the point of view of:

- **The stated or explicit**—the ways that rules and regulations are laid down, stated standards and levels of performance, the content of discipline and grievance procedures are documented and communicated to employees
- **The actual**—the ways in which the rules are applied in practice, standards and levels of performance are valued, monitored and maintained, and discipline and grievance procedures are applied
- **The implicit**—wider considerations, especially the aura of ER, and whether this is positive or negative, based on harmony and progress, or fear and conflict

14.4.1 Disciplinary Procedures

To understand the disciplinary procedure, we must first understand what "indiscipline" is. Indiscipline can best be understood in its context. Indiscipline has not been defined anywhere, though an absence of discipline has often been referred to as indiscipline!

INDISCIPLINE. All disciplinary procedures must state the circumstances in which they become applicable. Different contexts in which indiscipline may be considered are:

1. **Performance-related:** This requires a clear statement by the manager or supervisor of where and why the performance is falling short, followed by another clear statement of reasons attributing to it. This is then subject to regular monitoring, evaluation and review and is concluded with a clear statement to the employee that either performance is now satisfactory or performance is still unsatisfactory, in which case, further action is to be taken. Care must be taken to consider the skill and motivation aspects of performance gaps.
2. **Misconduct:** Misconduct includes workplace issues and misdemeanours. Misconduct has not been defined in any law or rule books, although most organizations list down an elaborate description of the acts and behaviours that may be construed to be misconduct. Misconducts may include negligence, unacceptable behaviour, failure to follow procedures, failure to act in the organization's best interests, insubordination, rudeness to colleagues and bad time-keeping. It may include persistent absenteeism (although very great care is to be taken to keep documents available for scrutiny). Misconduct may also include victimization, bullying and harassment.
3. **Attitudes and Demeanour:** Attitudes and demeanour are harder to pin down. It is, however, quite legitimate both to make provision for dealing with negative, poor and sloppy attitudes and also those where individuals place their own priorities above

those of the organization. Other matters include attitudes to others—for example, where someone engages in a constant or persistent attitude of blame or denigration towards others.

CLARIFYING MISCONDUCT: GROSS AND SEVERE OR MINOR. The law requires organizations to have and make known to staff what constitutes serious and gross misconduct. The usual form of presentation of this is a list. This list need not be exhaustive. It should give clear and wide-ranging examples. The usual matters covered under this heading are:

- Theft, fraud, sale of confidential information, other dishonesty
- Vandalism, violence, attacks on staff, equipment and premises
- Sexual misconduct
- Serious or gross negligence and inattention to duties and the organization's interests
- Using foul and abusive language, swearing in front of customers and clients
- Dishonesty in dealings with staff, customers, clients and the public
- Failure to follow safety procedures, endangering life and/or equipment

Serious and gross misconduct may also arise as the result of persistent misconduct. This includes persistently bad time-keeping, persistent absenteeism, persistent insubordination and rudeness.

All organizations have their own interpretation and variations; there may also be specific operational requirements underpinned by instant recourse to gross misconduct.

FOLLOW PRINCIPLES OF NATURAL JUSTICE. All disciplinary procedures, and the activities that they support, must include the following rights:

- The right of the individual to know the case against him/her and to confront the accuser
- The right of the individual to respond to the case and present his/her own point of view
- The right to representation at each stage, either by the representative of a recognized trade union or any other person of the individual's choice
- The right to receive in writing a definitive statement of the conclusion and outcome of the case at each stage
- The right of appeal against the conclusion and the outcome at each stage

PROCEDURE

Step 1. Warnings: Minimum standards require of at least two warnings (and many organizations have three or four). These may either be written or oral; when oral, they are normally confirmed in writing. The general aim is to ensure that the employee is aware that an aspect of their conduct, behaviour or performance is unacceptable and giving cause for concern. The warning must confirm this and state the remedial action that is necessary.

For poor performance, this normally includes a restatement of the standards of activity that are necessary and acceptable. For shortfalls in behaviour and conduct, this normally includes a restatement of what the required standard are and why they are necessary. For both performance and conduct, warnings will normally include a date in the future on which a review of progress is to be carried out.

Step 2. Recording Outcome of Warning: Warnings are recorded on the individual's personnel file (or equivalent) for set periods of time. Time periods are stated in the procedure and notified to the individual in each case. It is normal for warnings for minor offences to be kept on file for periods of between three months and two years. Records of more serious offences may be retained for longer periods. The most serious offences are kept on file for life. There are no rules governing this. The only requirement is to be fair and reasonable. The organization must balance its need to set and maintain standards with the requirement of individuals not to have their career or their prospects irreparably harmed by relatively minor incidents.

Step 3. Show-Cause Notice for Serious Misconduct: For matters of serious misconduct, it is acceptable and legitimate to issue a show-cause notice. This is confirmed to the individual in writing and stated clearly that in case he fails to show causes for his/her misconduct, disciplinary action would be initiated against him/her. Organizations must indicate the kind of offences that constitute serious misconduct (although the list need not be exhaustive). These normally include persistently bad time-keeping, persistently poor performance, rudeness and insubordination.

For gross misconduct, it is acceptable and legitimate to move straight to suspension. Organizations must again indicate the kind of offences that constitute gross misconduct (although the list, again, need not be exhaustive). These normally include vandalism, violence, arson, sabotage, theft, dishonesty, sexual misconduct, sale and publication of confidential information, other breaches of the criminal law and harassment, persecution and victimization of members of staff.

Step 4. Issue of Charge Sheet and Constitution of Inquiry Committee: A charge sheet listing out the charges with reference to the clause under which it is termed "misconduct" along with any documents to support the charges are issued in writing to the employee with due receipt acknowledgement obtained. Disciplinary authority (not less than appointing authority) constitutes an Inquiry and appoints an inquiry officer and presiding officer to defend the case on behalf of management.

Step 5. Disciplinary Hearings: For all disciplinary hearings, employees must be informed of the following:

- They must be notified, either orally or in writing, that they are required to attend a disciplinary hearing. The words "disciplinary hearing" must be used. They must be informed of all the rights indicated above, including the rights to be accompanied and represented.
- They must be informed of the case against them, who has brought it and why. They must be given the opportunity to face their accuser. They must be informed of the nature of the case, whether it potentially constitutes a minor offence, repeat offence, serious misconduct or gross misconduct.
- They must be asked to give their explanation of the events and situation.
- They must be allowed time (but not to excess) to prepare their case. They must be allowed to call witnesses and gain access to documents and papers that affect their case.

Procedures must be operated as follows, whatever the level of misconduct alleged and whatever the stage that is being used:

- Individuals facing discipline by their organizations must be allowed representation. Where a trade union is recognized, and where the individual is a member, representation is normally through that union. Where there is no union or where the employee is not a member, they may be accompanied by a colleague of their choice. This must always be allowed.
- Individuals must always be told that they are facing discipline in advance of the hearing. This notification may give an indication of the range of outcomes. It must never prejudge the issue.

- Individuals facing discipline are entitled to hear the charges against them and to face their accuser/accusers in person. They are entitled to respond to the charges and to call witnesses and evidence in support of their case.
- Individuals who have been disciplined must be afforded the opportunity to appeal. They must be notified of the person/official to whom the appeal should be made, and the deadline by which it should be made.
- Individuals facing discipline must be notified in writing of the outcome of the case. A copy of this should be placed in their personal file. When a warning is issued, a copy of this should be given to the employee, and a copy placed on his/her file. This applies to both oral and written warnings. It should state what the warnings were for, any remedial action necessary, what is to happen if there is any repeat and how long it is to remain current.

SUMMARY

- A strategic proactive approach that brings about some convergence of objectives is necessary to prevent the emergence of conflicts, and if they do arise, a method needs to be devised to avoid an escalation that can affect morale and productivity of the workforce.
- The declining trends in industrial action have generally been attributed to the preventive steps taken by employers to reduce conflicts at the workplace. The preventive machinery of the government has also played a significant role in this regard.
- The preventive machinery includes the following:
    - Tripartite and Bipartite Consultative Bodies, Voluntary Codes and Systems/Processes
    - ILO is the ultimate tripartite body that has the aim of laying down the labour standards through tripartism and social dialogue
    - Joint consultative tripartite and bipartite bodies like ILC, SLC, Industrial Committees and Central Implementation and Evaluation Committees are the tripartite bodies at the national level shaping the policy and encouraging consultation amongst partners.
    - Code of Discipline in Industry is a voluntary measure from the partners to ensure industrial peace.
    - The ID Act, 1948 requires the employer to constitute a Works Committee consisting of equal representatives of employers and workmen engaged in the establishment in industrial establishments where 100 or more workmen are employed.
- The functions that the Act visualized for the Works Committees were:
    - To promote measures for securing and preserving amity and good relations between employers and workmen
    - To that end, comment upon matters of common interest or concern
    - To endeavour to compose any material difference of opinion between the employer and the workmen in respect of such matters
- An all-India Seminar held in Delhi in 1957 worked out a model agreement that the management and workers could enter into to set up these JMCs. The scheme was to be voluntary and consultative in nature. Joint management councils were to deal with all matters except matters falling within the area of collective bargaining such as wages, bonus and hours of work.
- One of the most proactive measures to prevent an industrial conflict is setting up of clear and satisfactory terms and conditions of employment. In this context, Standing Orders play a significant role as it governs the rules and regulations that govern the conditions of employment of workers.
- Grievance procedure is a formal communication between an employee and the management designed for the settlement of a grievance. The grievance procedures differ from organization to organization. A model grievance procedure has been recommended.
- A Code of Discipline in Industry, which applies both to the public and to the private sector, has been accepted voluntarily by all the central organizations of employers and workers and has been in operation since the middle of 1958. The Code lays down specific obligations for the management and the workers with the object of promoting constructive cooperation between their representatives at all levels, avoiding stoppages as well as litigation, securing settlement of disputes and grievances by mutual negotiations, conciliation and voluntary arbitration, facilitating the free growth of trade unions and eliminating all forms of coercion and violence in industrial relations.

- Collective bargaining is a process of joint decision-making that advocates industrial democracy. It establishes a culture of bipartism and joint consultation in industry and an involved adaptable method of adjustment to economic and technical changes in an industry. It helps in establishing industrial peace without disrupting either the existing arrangements or the production activities.

KEY TERMS

REVIEW QUESTIONS

1. Give an overview of the preventive measures that are in place to ensure that industrial peace is maintained.
2. Describe the structure of ILO.
3. What are labour standards? What is the process involved in establishing a labour standard?
4. Describe in detail the overall preventive measures, systems, and structure that has been put in place to ensure that a healthy climate of relationships prevail in the Indian industry.
5. Describe in detail the structure, objectives and performance of the ILC and the SLC. Is it right to say that the SLC is a mere Secretariat of the ILC? Why or why not?
6. What is collective bargaining? What are the matters that can be taken up for collective bargaining?
7. Critically examine the various theories of collective bargaining.
8. Schematically explain the Model Grievance Procedure. Do you think it is of any value in the era of computers and intranet? Suggest an alternative grievance procedure for a modern business organization.
9. Employee relations management is just another name for proactive concepts like employee involvement and employee engagement. Do you agree?

QUESTIONS FOR CRITICAL THINKING

1. Critically examine the contributions and shortcomings of various tripartite bodies in the prevention of industrial conflicts. In the light of fundamental changes in the working of industry since 1991, how do you think the institutions can be strengthened?
2. How effective has the Code of Discipline been in preventing industrial conflict? Please do a survey of literature on Code of Discipline to find out the manner in which it has ceased to be effective? What could be the reasons for its decline as a moral force in industrial relations?
3. Do the government employees in India have the right for collective bargaining? From where does the right to collective bargaining come to the employees in India?

DEBATE

1. The preventive measures for maintaining IR is only a set of good intentions. The actual maintenance of industrial relations is situational.
2. The settlement machinery has proved to be far more effective in maintaining industrial peace rather than the utopian "preventive measures".
3. The WTO, under the garb of providing a level playing field, is using labour standards to negate the comparative advantage of developing nations.

CASE ANALYSIS

Union Problems at Alloy Steel Plants

Alloy Steels Plant is a manufacturer of different grades of special steels. The annual capacity is 100,000 MT per annum. The total employee strength in the plant is around 7,000. The plant is located in a state where the trade-union activity is very vigorous. The ASP has had a history of labour strife for the past four to five years. It has three very strong unions and the management is really hard pressed to arrive at a consensus with the three unions, even though one of these unions is the recognized union. Every issue relating to production and productivity is linked by the union to either the terms of employment or the economic issues. Management wanted to separate the two issues (operational and employment related). As per the ID Act, 1947, a Works Committee has been constituted with representatives from the workmen and the management. The subject matters for discussion are all the issues that are not covered by the collective bargaining. However, invariably, the discussions veer off to discussing matters like deployment, overtime payments, disciplinary issues and inter-union issues. Management, despite numerous attempts to focus completely on production issues, finds itself to be in a position of helplessness, due to the strength of the unions.

Questions:

1. Can you suggest a concrete way in which management can tackle the separation of the two issues?
2. Why do you think this is happening at ASP?

Clean Clothes Campaign

The Clean Clothes Campaign (CCC) is the garment industry's alliance of labour unions and non-governmental organizations. Started in 1989, this alliance comprises unions and NGOs from 13 European nations.

The Clean Clothes Campaign educates and mobilizes consumers, lobbies companies and governments, and offers direct solidarity support to workers as they fight for their rights and demand better working conditions.

A partner network of around 200 unions and NGOs in garment-producing countries, CCC attempts to identify local problems and objectives, and to help develop campaign strategies to support workers in achieving their goals.

CCC claims to base its campaign on the principles that "all workers—regardless of sex, age, country of origin, legal status, employment status or location, or any other basis—have a right to good and safe working conditions, where they can exercise their fundamental rights to associate freely and bargain collectively, and earn a living wage, which allows them to live in dignity". It believes that minimum standards related to these rights are derived from the ILO conventions, the ILO Declaration on Fundamental Principles and Rights at Work adopted in 1998, as well as on the Article.

The CCC pressures retailers and manufacturers to adopt the Code of Labour Practices and ensure that the principles are upheld. It lobbies governments to be responsible consumers themselves by committing to the ethical procurement of government uniforms and workwear.

Questions

1. The national governments of the garment-exporting countries allege that campaigns like CCC are merely a pressure group of interested parties (trade unions and governments in Europe and other developed nations) bent upon lowering the comparative advantage of the developing countries, which they enjoy because of lower labour costs. Do your own research on this to bring out a balanced report on labour standards and comparative advantage in developing countries.
2. What position should the ILO take to see that in implementing the standards, there is a consensus rather than branding clothes from a few countries as "unclean" because of violation of standards?

NOTES

1 "About the History—Origins of ILO", http://www.ilo.org/global/About_the_ILO/Origins_and_history/lang--en/index.htm.

2 The Preamble, The Constitution of ILO, http://www.ilo.org/ilolex/english/constq.htm.

3 Constitution of the ILO, http://www.ilo.org/ilolex/english/constq.htm.

4 ILO, *ILO Thesaurus*, s.v. "labour standard, " (Geneva: ILO, 2005), available at http://www.ilo.org/public/libdoc/ILO-Thesaurus/english/tr4113.htm)

5 UNDERSTANDING THE WTO: CROSS-CUTTING AND NEW ISSUES - Labour standards: consensus, coherence and controversy (http://www.wto.org/english/thewto_e/whatis_e/tif_e/bey5_e.htm).

6 ILO, *ILO Thesauru*, (Geneva: Bureau of Information and Library Services, 2005), (http://www.ilo.org/public/libdoc/ILO-Thesaurus/english/tr1009.htm).

SUGGESTED READING

1 Mamoria, Mamoria and Gankar, *Dynamics of Industrial Relations, 15th Edition* (Mumbai: Himalaya Publishing House, 1983).

2 Mathur, K. and N. R. Sheth, *Tripartism in Labour Policy: The Indian Experience* (New Delhi: Shriram Center for IR, 2006).

3 National Commission on Labour (1969), Government of India, New Delhi.

4 Venkatratnam, C. S., *Industrial Relations*, (New Delhi: Oxford University Press, 2006).

chapter fifteen

CHAPTER OUTLINE

LEARNING OBJECTIVES

After going through this chapter, you will be able to:

- Understand the concepts of minimum wage, fair wage and living wage
- Trace the evolution of wage administration in India
- Schematically understand the dynamics of various internal and external factors in the determination of wages
- Know the various methods that are employed for wage determination in India
- Appreciate the challenges faced in evolving a national wage policy

The Power Project

Manohar Satpathy, the newly appointed General Manager (HR) for a green-field power project in Jharkhand, has been charged with the responsibility of, amongst other things, designing a wage structure for the employees that will eventually be recruited and positioned at different skill positions. Manohar, through years of experience in HRM, knows the complexity of the task and also the crucial role the wage structure will play in attracting and retaining skilled manpower. The new generation of power plants uses high degrees of automation and control, and requires highly skilled technicians with varied experiences. Manohar's training in this field led him to a systematic thought process of first examining the structure proposed by the Project Consultant, the minimum wage notification in the area, the wages paid by industry in the same area, lowest and highest wages paid in the area, what competitors are paying in the same industry, designing of scales according to hierarchical levels, and also internal equity based on job evaluation, components of wage and projected labour cost as a percentage of total cost for expected return on investment. He would also have to see if any agreements are in place between the employer's association and the employees' association at a regional/state level. Then, there would be strategic decisions whether the company wants to lead the market in terms of wages or wants to be in line with the market, or even pitch for a wage level slightly lower than the market. What percentage of wages would be fixed and what would be productivity linked? Manohar has his job cut out for him and he knows that the wage structure and a fair administration of the same would be of critical importance for the project to take off successfully.

Wage Determination, Wage Administration and Employee Relations

Our Constitution accepts the responsibility of the State to create an economic order in which every citizen finds employment and receives a "fair wage". One of the earliest decisions taken by the government of free India was to set up a committee to define fair wage, and indicate the economic and legal means for ensuring a fair wage to every employed citizen. An examination of this question established the integral relation between quantum of the fair wage and the capacity to pay the wage, and the need to balance and constantly upgrade both to ensure a fair standard of life, social security and social justice.
Report of the Second National Commission on Labour, Chapter XII-III (para 12.132)

Wage administration is a process that is influenced by many factors, internal to the unit as well as the larger external environment.

15.1 The Context and Concepts of Wage

The Oxford English Dictionary defines "wage" as "regular payment to an employee for his or her work". "Salary", on the other hand, is defined as "fixed regular (usually monthly) payment to an employee". The various Labour Laws have their own definitions of what constitutes "wages". For our purpose, we will consider wage to be a regular payment to an employee for his/her work. In addition, we will restrict our treatment of the subject to the organized sector only.

Wage is basically the price that an organization is willing to pay for having a particular job carried out as also the price at which an employee is willing to sell his/her labour. In a perfect market, the price determination would take place through an interaction of the market forces.

However, we all know that the above is not entirely true in an industrial environment, more so in India, where the government has a welfare orientation and improving the lot of working class is enshrined in our Constitution also. Employees, being the weaker of the employer–employee pair, need support of the State to strengthen their negotiating power in wage determination. Over the years, therefore, the government, through various mechanisms like legislations, Wage Boards, commissions and committees, has stepped in favour of the employees. Since a majority of disputes between employers and employees have wages as a cause, the judicial pronouncements of higher courts have also influenced, in many instances, policies relating to wages in industries. Of late, national-level sectoral bargaining between employers and national trade unions in select industries (e.g. banks and steel) has also emerged.

15.1.1 Minimum Wage, Fair Wage and Living Wage

How does the State intervene to prevent exploitation of labour, where the bargaining power is unequal? There is also the constitutional responsibility for the State to strive for the payment of "fair wages" to all its employed citizens. The determination of that number, which can be construed as "fair wage", is a complex issue that has vexed the minds of many a committee formed for this

"Wage" may be defined as "regular payment to an employee for his or her work". "Salary", on the other hand, is defined as "fixed regular (usually monthly) payment to an employee".

WAGE

Wage is basically the price that an organization is willing to pay for having a particular job carried out as also the price at which an employee is willing to sell his/her labour. In a perfect market, the price determination would take place through an interaction of the market forces.

purpose. Should there be a certain floor level of wages to be paid by the employer to the employee? What could be the basis for such determination? Should it be adequate only for taking care of the basic requirements of food, shelter and clothing? Or should it be something more? Should it be uniform across the country irrespective of price variations across regions? These questions led the government to constitute Committee on Fair Wages (CFW), which proposed the following three "levels" (we will learn more when we discuss the evolution):

- Minimum Wage
- Fair Wage
- Living Wage

Figure 15.1 titled "Different levels of wages" explain the thinking behind the proposed levels. The consensus so far is on the definitions of the three levels. "Fair wage" is a level between the "living wage" and "minimum wage". Living wage must take into account the capacity of the employer to pay while a uniform minimum wage for the entire country for all classes of industrial workers has not been determined. In fact, the issue of having such uniformity itself is debatable. In the absence of a single number, The Minimum Wages Act, 1948 prescribes procedures for establishing statutory "minimum wages" for different regions and different categories of employees. The Indian Labour Conference (15th Session, 1957) prescribed norms for the calculation of "need-based minimum wage" by way of defining the components of food, clothing, shelter and other essentials that must be taken into account for calculating the minimum wage.

Figure 15.1

Different levels of wages.

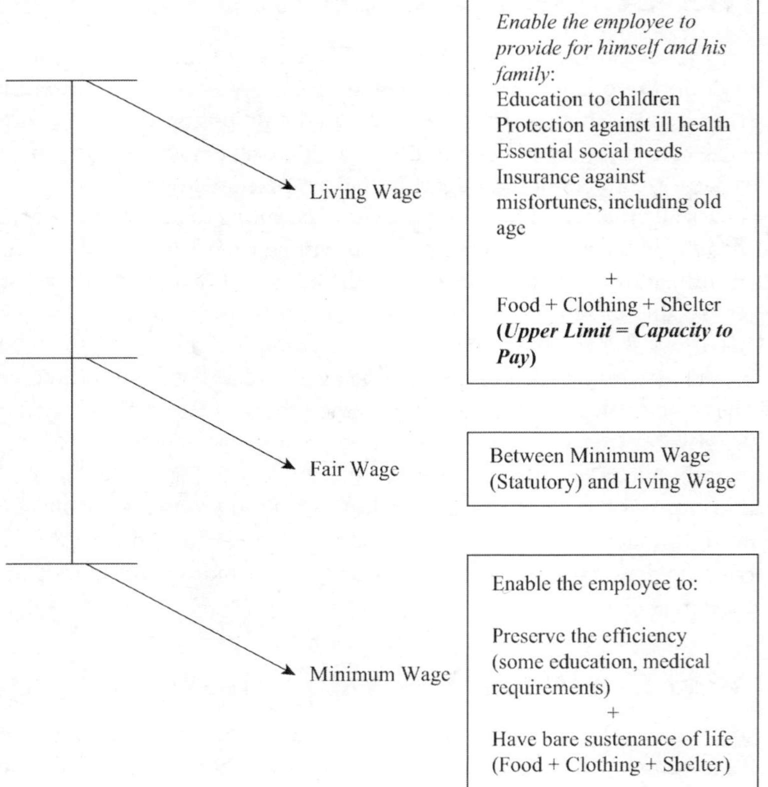

The minimum wage, thus, could be calculated with the following guidelines:

- The standard working-class family should be taken to consist of three consumption units.
- Minimum food requirement should be calculated on the basis of a net intake of 2,700 calories.
- Total annual clothing requirement @ 18 yards per capita = 18 × 4 = 72 Yards.
- Housing should be the minimum rent charged by the government in any area provided under the Subsidized Industrial Housing Scheme for Low Income.
- Fuel, lighting and other miscellaneous items of expenditure should constitute 20 per cent of total minimum wage.

"Fair wage" is a level between the "living wage" and "minimum wage". Living wage must take into account the capacity of the employer to pay, while a uniform minimum wage for the entire country for all classes of industrial workers has not been determined.

The Determination of Minimum Wage

- Standard working-class family = 3 consumption units
- Minimum food requirement = Net intake of 2,700 calories
- Total annual clothing requirement = 18 yards per capita = 72 Yards
- Housing = Minimum rent charged by the government in any area under the Subsidized Industrial Housing Scheme for Low Income
- Fuel, lighting and other miscellaneous items = 20 per cent of total minimum wage.

15.2 The Evolution of Wage Administration in India

Wage administration in India comprises a mix of methods that take into account various internal and external factors. The following tools/methods have been used in combination over a period of time for wage administration:

- Legislation
- Recommendation of expert committees/commissions
- Wage Boards
- Job evaluation
- Collective bargaining

These are not mutually exclusive but used in combination in different circumstances.

15.2.1 Legislation

The first direct intervention by the State towards regulation of wages was the enactment of The Payment of Wages Act, 1936. Prior to this, disputes relating to wages were largely handled within the provisions of The Trade Disputes Act, 1929, and the machinery therein for settling disputes. The Payment of Wages Act made provisions that regulated the time and the mode of payment of wages. The Defence of India Rules (1942) provided further avenues for the resolution of disputes through adjudication and conciliation, which were later incorporated in the ID Act, 1947.

A specific initiative was taken by the government in 1946 to give guidance to legislative and other measures over a period of time. It suggested evolving legislative and administrative measures to bring about the following:

- Statutory determination of minimum wages in "sweated" industry
- Standardization of wages and terms of employment in major industries
- Defining and pr omoting "fair wages", ensuring the welfare of workers as well as keeping in mind the capacity to pay

The Minimum Wages Act was enacted in 1948. The Act set out procedures for determining the minimum wage in certain scheduled employments. The Payment of Bonus Act, 1965 was another piece of legislation related to wages. We have discussed this in detail in Chapter 11.

An initiative was taken by the government in 1946 to give guidance to legislative and other measures. It suggested evolving legislative and administrative measures to bring about the following:

- Statutory determination of minimum wages in "sweated" industry
- Standardization of wages and terms of employment in major industries
- Defining and promoting "fair wages", ensuring the welfare of workers as well as keeping in mind the capacity to pay

15.2.2 Policy Recommendations and Resolutions

The Industrial Truce Resolution (1947): To bring a halt to or slow down the deteriorating condition of IR in the country, the Government of India convened a tripartite meeting in December of 1947, where The Industrial Truce Resolution (1947) was taken out, in which, amongst other things, the three parties resolved to ensure fair wages to labour, fair return on capital to industry and provision for expansion and running of the industry. With the shaping of direction towards a socialistic pattern of society, these measures purported to prevent excessive profits.

The Industrial Policy Resolution (IPR - 1948): The IPR reiterated the earlier direction of the government and put forth the following objectives:

- The determination of statutory minimum wages for "sweated" industry and
- The encouragement of "fair wage" agreements in industry

This paved the way for the CFW, a tripartite committee, which was to study the matter of fair wage and recommend criteria for the determination of fair wages.

Tripartite Committee on Fair Wages: Besides defining the three levels of wages, the CFW examined and gave its views on many related issues:

- Fair wage must be pegged somewhere between living wage and minimum wage, giving weight to factors such as productivity of labour, prevailing wage rates in similar jobs in nearby areas, national income and the pattern of its distribution and the nature of the industry in terms of its contribution to the national economy.
- Collective bargaining on wages, where both parties had bargaining power, would be very close to the level of fair wages. Where this was not the case, there may be distortions in wage levels and this fact must be kept in mind.
- Collective bargaining on wages had so far not taken roots across the industries and, therefore, it was likely that the workers were not getting wages commensurate with their effort and contribution.
- While determining the capacity of an industry to pay, rather than considering individual establishments, the profit-making capacity of a particular industry in the entire region (state) must be taken into account (industry-cum-region basis).
- The level of wages must consider enabling an industry to produce with efficiency.
- Wage differentials among different occupations must be based on criteria such as skill requirement, effort and strain, the number of years of experience required to perform, training requirements for the job, responsibilities and accountabilities of the job and conditions of the workplace.
- Wage-fixation machinery could go into effecting all the above.

Wage Board

A wage board is a tripartite body, which has representation of employers and labour besides independent members. Wage Board was envisaged as machinery for wage fixation in specified industries, and also as a means for implementing many wage-related policies and principles laid down by the various committees and commissions.

15.2.3 Wage Boards

In the above context, the Government of India, through the First and Second Five Year Plan, recommended setting up of Wage Boards to meet the aspirations of labour, and also to give effect to principles mentioned in the above paragraphs.

Wage Board is a tripartite body, which has representation of employers and labour besides independent members. The representatives of the employers and employees were to be nominated by their respective organizations, whereas the government nominated others. Wage Board was envisaged as machinery for wage fixation in specified industries and also a means for implementing many wage-related policies and principles laid down by the various committees and commissions. The Wage Boards, till early 1970s, served a pivotal role in the wage administration in important industries. Some of the industries for which these Boards were set up were:

- Cotton Textile
- Jute
- Plantation
- Mines
- Iron and Steel
- Chemicals
- Sugar
- Cement
- Railways
- Post and Telegraph
- Ports and Docks

The number of Wage Boards declined from 19 in the late 1960s to only 2 in the late 1990s (one for journalists and the other for non-journalist newspaper employees)[1].

The Wage Boards function industry-wise with broad terms of reference, which include recommending the minimum wage, differentials, cost-of-living compensation, regional wage differentials, hours of work, etc.

Although the Wage Boards are set up by the government, another reason for their establishment could also be pressure created by the trade unions; industrial federations on the one hand, and the employers' formal or informal consent on the other. The demands for the Wage Boards are backed either by threatened or actual strikes. Pressure has been used in the case of appointment of Wage Boards for the jute industry by the jute workers' association and for the coal-mining industry by the trade union. The formation of Wage Boards in other industries has been the result of similar demands and pressures on the part of the trade unions, such as plantations, iron and steel, engineering, sugar and electricity.

The functioning of the Board comprises three steps, namely:

- Systematic information-gathering on wage rates in the industry, differentials, paying capacity of the industry
- Public-hearing of the points of view of each of the parties
- Private discussions with parties where proposals and counter-proposals are made and heard

The Wage Boards, despite the long time that they took in submitting their reports, served a useful purpose when the collective bargaining in the industry had not taken roots. Gradually, with the emergence of strong plant/unit-level trade unions, the utility of Wage Boards came down. The increased union militancy of the 1970s enabled these plant-level unions to bargain very good wage agreements. Also, during this period, sectoral bargaining at the national level was going on in industries in which the government was the dominant player . These industries included iron and steel, docks and ports, banks, coal, etc. What this means is that a single employer body (representing all units in the industry), the administrative ministry and federations of national trade unions representing the industry negotiated a long-term settlement on wages.

15.2.4 Job Evaluation

Job evaluation is a scientific method to determine the "relative" worth of a job in comparison to other jobs within an organization. Job evaluation helps establish internal equity within the organization, also enabling inter-organization comparisons. The fundamental concept is based on the assumption that every job comprises a few factors that an employer is willing to

Job Evaluation

Job evaluation is a scientific method to determine the "relative" worth of a job in comparison to other jobs within an organization. Job evaluation helps establish internal equity within the organization, also enabling inter-organization comparisons.

compensate; for example, skill requirement, responsibility, effort, hazard and working conditions could be a few of these factors. The aim is to isolate the compensable factors for each job, determine the extent of requirement of the compensable factors and then determine the amount to be compensated per unit of the compensable factors. Job descriptions and job analyses are the major inputs to job evaluation. We will not go into details here, since this would have been covered in the HRM.

15.3 Components and Determinants of Wage

15.3.1 Components of Wage

Traditionally, the wage comprised the following:

- Basic
- Dearness Allowance
- Bonus
- Incentives
- Other Benefits and Allowances

Few of these components form the fixed part of the wage, whereas others may vary. The recent trend is for the employer to increase the variable portion linked to productivity and efficiency, and keep the fixed part as low as possible. An employee, on the other hand, may prefer a higher portion of his/her wages as fixed in order to have stability of income.

Basic wage remains fixed over a period of time for a prescribed level of output. Basic wage, many times, is the reference figure for various allowances and, hence, a high basic serves the purpose of affecting the other allowances too, besides remaining stable over time. In the organized sector, the statutory minimum wage is losing its relevance, but it remains the floor price of the job since a wage below the stator minimum is out of consideration.

Dearness allowance was introduced to compensate the employees from erosion in income due to the rise in prices. DA has been a contentious issue and the cause of many disputes and even industrial action. Typically, DA is linked to some price index, and compensates employees for the rise in inflation through "neutralization" of increase in the index, thus protecting income. A few establishments pay DA according to a fixed system, whereas others use a variable system or a moving system linked to consumer price index. Yet other organizations use a mixed system. The issue of DA has been a major issue mainly for the PSU and government employees and a matter of examination by various committees and even the higher judiciary. The report of the second NCL laments the considerable delay in conducting a survey to construct the index numbers. The delay, according to the report, defeats the very purpose of linking DA to the price index since consumption pattern of the population undergoes changes, many varieties of items go out of the market and prices for them are not available.[2]

A minimum bonus to employees who fall within the eligibility criteria is obligatory 8.33 per cent of annual wages (basic + DA) on pro-rata basis is payable to all employees. The issue of bonus payment has been discussed in detail in Chapter 11. Pertinent to this chapter is the fact that the payment of bonus has remained a contentious issue and, on the balance, it has satisfied neither the employer nor the employees. The payment of bonus has been the reason for many disputes resulting in industrial action. A bonus amount, between 8.33 per cent and 20 per cent is negotiable, provided the allocable surplus is above the minimum amount. Mostly, statutory bonus is used to further negotiate an ex-gratia amount for employees who are not covered under the Payment of Bonus Act.

The assumption behind wage incentives is that increasing the earnings of an employee will improve his efficiency or, rather the other way round, the anticipation of higher earnings will motivate him or her to greater effort and efficiency. Used correctly, incentives may benefit both, the employees and the management, by increasing earnings for the employee and by improving productivity for the management. More and more employers are trying to link part of the wages to some parameter of performance, e.g., quality, output and reduction in rejects. While we do not have the data, the trend in the new-economy companies is to have a substantial portion of wage as a variable component, contingent upon achieving a predefined standard of performance. For the employer, this makes sense in a fiercely competitive and dynamic environment. This should work for employees also, since economic needs are important. However, for an incentive scheme to work, the following must be kept in mind:

- The "standards" of performance must be clear and simple and understood by all.
- The linkage of performance to incentive payment must be clear and simple, and understood well by the employees.
- The "standards" of performance must be accepted by the employees.
- The incentive must be seen as motivating.
- Payment must be prompt and calculation must be transparent and unambiguous.
- There must be a provision to "appeal".

15.3.2 Determinants of Wage

In the chapter-opening case, "The Power Project", Mr Satpathy tries to systematically map the factors that he would have to take into account while determining a wage structure for the project. Whether green field or brown field or an operating organization, the factors that come into play are similar in the organized industry. Figure 15.2, "Dynamics of wage determination", captures all the variables that interact to determine the wage, wage levels and wage structure in an organization. In the case of Mr Satpathy, what would be

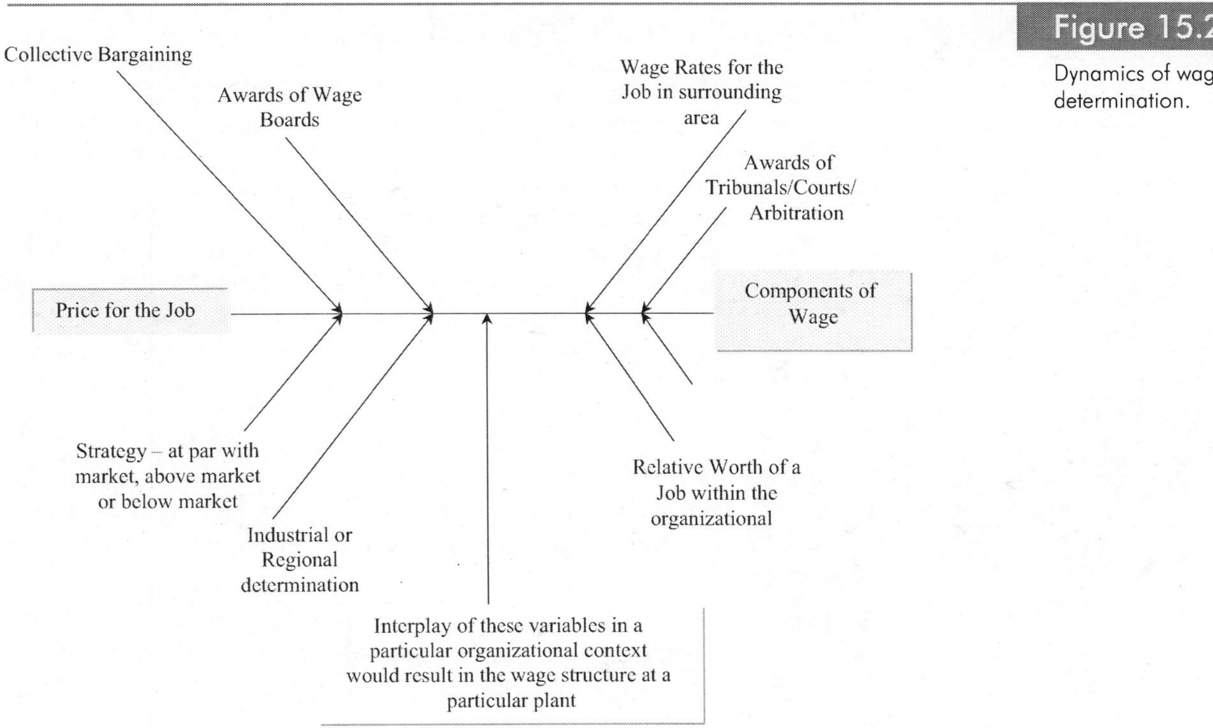

Figure 15.2
Dynamics of wage determination.

the most important variables in play? How would the variables change in case of a public sector company and a private sector company? Would the location of the industrial establishment—industrial hub vis-a-vis an industrially backward and remote region—make a difference?

15.4 Wage Structure

The term "wage structure" signifies the relationship of wage rates for the entire job within the company, industry or labour market areas. The internal wage structure of an organization or company is, thus, established by the relative grading or positioning of jobs within it (i.e., the company) in terms of pay, and it may, therefore, be defined in terms of job or labour grades with either a flat wage rate or a range of rates for each grade that may be applicable to a number of jobs in various departments or units. Organizations may maintain two paralleled wage/salary structure, one for the hourly rated and the other for salaried employees. In setting up a wage structure, necessary information to be used is usually derived from some kind of "job evaluation" system or method.

15.4.1 The Purpose of Wage Structure

The primary objective of wage administration is to establish and maintain a fair and equitable wage structure. This means that the chances of favouritism in respect of compensation to workers or employees should be eliminated and efforts should be made to provide compensation to individuals in accordance with the requirements of their jobs.

An internally consistent relationship amongst jobs is the very essence of a wage structure. It is important for both the management and the employees. The management must be able to justify its reasons for structuring jobs in a particular order. The other input for the wage structure comes from inputs from the surrounding region or industry or trade or skill. Together, these two (internal alignment of jobs and external input) form the basis for a wage structure.

15.5 Towards a Wage Policy

The term "wage policy" in a country like India refers to legislation or government action calculated to affect the level or structure of wages, or both, for the purpose of attaining specific objectives of social and economic policy. The social objectives that a wage policy may be instrumental in attaining may include the elimination of exceptionally low wages, the establishment of "fair" labour standards and the protection of wage-earners from the effect of rising prices. Another aim of wage policy is to increase the economic welfare of the community as a whole. In developing economies, objectives of the wage policy should be established, and the level and structure of wages should be conducive to accelerated economic development. The objectives of the wage policy in an under-developed or developing economy have, thus, been summarized as follows:

a) To abolish malpractices and abuses in wage payment

b) To set minimum wages for workers whose bargaining position is weak because they are either unorganized or inefficiently organized, and this should be accompanied by separate measures to promote the growth of trade unions and collective bargaining

c) To obtain for the workers a just share in the fruits of economic development supplemented by appropriate measures to keep workers' expenditure on consumption goods in step with available supplies so as to minimize inflationary pressure

d) To bring about a more efficient allocation and utilization of manpower through wage differentials and, where appropriate, systems of payments by results

Although the Government of India has not formulated a "wage policy", recommendations of committees like CFW, Pay Commissions, NLC, ILC, ILO Conventions, Truce Resolutions and Five Year Plans have guided the policymakers and the executive from time to time. With progressive opening up of the economy and competitive pressures, the possibility of a rigid wage policy in the organized sector appears remote. The National Commission on Labour points towards evolving a productivity-linked wage for the organized sector. The productivity-linked wage will then have the structure of: total wage = basic wage + variable component (depending on productivity). Basic principles of productivity-wage reform should include the following:

- Wages should aim at providing an adequate standard of living to workers.
- Wage increase must take into account the company's capacity to pay.
- The wage must reflect the value of the job.
- There must be a variable component to accommodate business cycles.
- Wage increase must be commensurate with productivity growth:[3]

But the above is a tall ask since the unions are in no mood yet to discuss the issue, let alone accept it.

SUMMARY

- Wage is basically the price that an organization is willing to pay for having a particular job carried out as also the price at which an employee is willing to sell his/her labour.
- In a perfect market, the price determination would take place through the interaction of the market forces.
- In India, the government has a welfare orientation and improving the lot of working class is enshrined in our Constitution also. Over the years, therefore, the government, through various mechanisms such as legislations, Wage Boards, commissions and committees, has stepped in favour of the employees.
- There is constitutional responsibility for the State to strive for payment of "fair wages" to all its employed citizens.
- The government constituted Committee on Fair Wages (CFW), which proposed the following three "levels":
    - Minimum Wage
    - Fair Wage
    - Living Wage
- The Indian Labour Conference (15th Session, 1957) prescribed norms for the calculation of "need-based minimum wage" by way of defining the components of food, clothing, shelter and other essentials that must be taken into account for calculating the minimum wage. The following tools/methods have been used in combination over a period of time for wage administration:
    - Legislation
    - Recommendation of expert committees/commissions
    - Wage Boards
    - Job evaluation
    - Collective bargaining

  Traditionally, the wage comprised the following:
    - Basic
    - Dearness Allowance
    - Bonus
    - Incentives
    - Other Benefits and Allowances
- The interplay of a number of internal and external variables determines the wage structure in a particular organizational context.
- The term "wage structure" signifies the relationship of wage rates for the entire job within the company, industry or labour market areas. The primary objective of wage administration is to establish and maintain a fair and equitable wage structure.
- The term "wage policy" in a country like India refers to legislation or government action calculated to affect the level or structure of wages, or both, for the purpose of attaining specific objectives of social and economic policy.

- Although the Government of India has not formulated a "wage policy", recommendations of committees such as CFW, Pay Commissions, NLC, ILC, ILO Conventions, Truce Resolutions and Five Year Plans have guided the policymakers and the executive from time to time.
- The National Commission on Labour points towards evolving a productivity-linked wage for the organized sector. The productivity-linked wage will then have the structure of: total wage = basic wage + variable component (depending on productivity).

KEY TERMS

- fair wage 324
- job evaluation 325
- living wage 324
- minimum wage 324
- salary 323
- wage 323
- wage board 325
- wage structure 329

REVIEW QUESTIONS

1 Trace the evolution of wage administration in India.

2 Describe the concept behind "wage levels". Do you think the government has been able to discharge its obligation on fair wages? Explain your answer.

3 Schematically explain the determinants of wage in an industrial unit. Explain the purpose of wage structure.

4 Discuss the evaluation and development of wage policy in India.

5 For what purposes have wage boards been constituted? Do you think they can serve any useful purpose today? Why?

6 State the main objectives of the regulation of wages.

7 Discuss the composition and functions of a Wage Board.

QUESTIONS FOR CRITICAL THINKING

1 What do you think to be the main disadvantages of a productivity-linked wage? What reservations can the employees have to this?

2 Do you think that the Indian State has focused more on the minimum wage and not enough on linking wage to productivity?

DEBATE

1 It is best to let the market forces decide the wage in the industry. The organized sector does not need any State-sponsored policy on wages. Discuss.

CASE ANALYSIS

TISCO

The Steel Industry in India has a standing bipartite committee that negotiates and settles long-term agreements on wages for all the integrated steel plants in the country. Due to this mechanism, with participation from all the steel-plant managements and major national trade unions, there has been no strike in the steel industry on wage-related issues for more than 30 years now. SAIL is one of the major steel producers with 4 integrated steel plants with a combined capacity of 12 million tonnes per annum. SAIL also has a subsidiary at Burnpur, which, because of obsolete machinery and processes, was incurring a loss and had been referred to the Bureau of Industrial Finance and Restructuring (BIFR). Experts felt that with some investment, IISCO could be turned around into a profit-making company. Normally, the wage agreements were signed every four to five years, and in the year 1995, another revision was due. SAIL had made record profits, and it was hoped that the wage issue would be settled soon. However, there was a directive from the government (as majority stakeholder in SAIL and IISCO) that the loss-making units will have to forego the wage revision. The employees of IISCO were very agitated by this stand of the government and started putting pressure on their management as well as the national trade unions. SAIL agreed to "loan" the money to IISCO for effecting the wage agreement, but the government did not agree. The unions threatened to boycott the meeting, creating further pressure on SAIL, since SAIL was under pressure from its own 1,50,000 strong labour force.

- What kind of negotiation process is this?
- Debate the stand of the government and the trade unions.
- Is there a way out of this impasse?

NOTES

1 Report of Second National Commission on Labour, Chapter XVII-III, para 12.156, p. 13–46.

2 Report of NCL, para 12.164, p. 13–49.

3 Report of 2nd NCL, para 12.306, p. 14–01.

SUGGESTED READING

Subramaniam, K. N., *Wages in India* (New Delhi: Tata Mcgraw-Hill, 1979).

The Report of the Second National Commission on Labour, 2002, Government of India.

The Report of the First National Commission on Labour, 1969, Government of India.

chapter sixteen

CHAPTER OUTLINE

LEARNING OBJECTIVES

After reading this chapter, you will be able to:

- Understand the meaning of labour administration
- Trace the evolution of labour administration in India
- Form an overall understanding of the forces that have helped shape the labour policy in India
- Have a clear idea of the labour administrative machinery, subordinate organizations and voluntary arrangements
- Appreciate the role that ILO has played in setting standards for labour administration
- Know the recommendations made by the National Commission on Labour

The Central Industrial Relations Machinery

There are approximately 150,000 establishments in the central sphere. The inspecting officers of CIRM (Central Industrial Relations Machinery) inspect these establishments under different labour enactments through routine inspections and special drives for inspections under the crash-inspection programmes and taskforce inspections to secure benefits of the beneficial legislations to workers. Special emphasis is given to the enforcement of beneficial enactments such as Contract Labour (Regulation and Abolition) Act and Minimum Wages Act and Building and Other Construction Workers (Regulation of Employment and Conditions of Service) Act, 1996 in the unorganized sector. Prosecutions are launched against persistent defaulters and in respect of major violations. During the year 2001–2002, CIRM officers carried out 34,968 inspections, rectified 3,60,712 irregularities, launched 16,040 prosecutions and secured 7,475 convictions of defaulting employers.

Another important function of the CIRM is the enforcement of labour laws in the establishments for which the central government is the appropriate government. The machinery enforces the following labour laws and rules framed thereunder:

1. Payment of Wages Act, 1936 and rules made thereunder for mines, railways, air transport services and docks, wharves and jetties
2. Minimum Wages Act, 1948 and rules
3. Contract Labour (Regulation and Abolition) Act, 1970 and rules
4. Equal Remuneration Act, 1976 and rules
5. Inter-State Migrant Workmen (RE&CS) Act, 1979 and rules
6. Child Labour (Prohibition and Regulation) Act, 1986 and rules
7. Payment of Gratuity Act, 1972 and rules
8. Labour laws (Exemption from Furnishing Returns and Maintaining Registers by Certain Establishments) Act 1988
9. Building and Other Constructions Workers (RE&CS) Act, 1996 and rules
10. Chapter VI-A of the Indian Railway Act; Hours of Employment Regulations for Railways Employees
11. Industrial Employment (Standing Orders) Act, 1946 and rules
12. Maternity Benefit Act, 1961 (Mines and Circus Rules, 1963); and rules
13. Payment of Bonus Act, 1965

Labour Administration

Labour administration means public-administration activities to translate national labour policy into action.

The Central Industrial Relations Machinery (also known as the Office of Chief Labour Commissioner—Central) is one of the many agencies of the government that ensures that some of the policies concerning labour are implemented. There are many such agencies, each charged with specific responsibilities for ensuring compliance of the labour policies. In this chapter, we will try to understand the contours of the policies and the myriad network of organizations that help put these policies into action.

16.1 An Introduction to Labour Administration

Labour administration is primarily concerned with the affairs of labour and administration of social policy. The meeting of experts on labour administration held in Geneva in October 1973 felt that to effectively deal with the vital aspects related to labour administration, there should be central, specialized units for each of the following:

a) Labour protection (working conditions, terms of employment and service, wages, safety, etc.)

b) Labour inspection

c) Labour relations

d) Employment of manpower, including training

e) Social security

Labour administration is not simply the responsibility of the Department of Labour. Many agencies and government departments such as Chambers of Commerce, Factory and Mines Inspectorate, Social Insurance Directorate and the Department of Human Resource Development and Education are involved in it. In some countries, the organizations of employers and workers are also involved in the administration of labour matters. But it is primarily the responsibility of the Department of Labour to lay down, develop and apply sound labour policies, coordinate various recommendations received from various departments, which have a bearing on labour affairs. The formulation of policy decisions are based on consultation with other interests (particularly of employers' and workers' organizations) and of research and field investigation. Most of the labour-policy proposals may emanate from the Minister of Labour himself or from his department. The Department of Labour is the body that receives most such proposals and initiates the preparatory process. In some cases, Labour Courts, arbitration bodies and different ad hoc commissions can be regarded as forming part of the labour-administration machinery, although they are usually outside the Department of Labour. These bodies are either bipartite or tripartite in character.

16.1.1 The Concept of Labour Administration

The Labour Administration Convention No.150, 1978 of ILO defines "labour administration" as "public administration activities in the field of labour policy". According to the same Convention, the term "system of labour administration" covers "all public administration bodies responsible for and/or engaged in

Labour administration concerns itself with translating the labour policy into action. Effective labour administration machinery must be able to address the following:

- Labour protection (working conditions, terms of employment and service, wages, safety, etc.)
- Labour inspection
- Labour relations
- Employment of manpower, including training
- Social security

"System of labour administration" covers "all public administration bodies responsible for and/or engaged in labour administration—whether they are ministerial departments or public agencies, including parastatal and regional or local agencies, and any other form of decentralized administration—and any institutional framework for the coordination of the activities of such bodies and for consultation with and participation by employers and workers and their organizations – *ILO Convention on LA (1978)*

The broad areas covered under labour administration today, whether statutory or non-statutory, include—contracts and terms of employment, wages, working conditions, industrial relations, social security, employment and unemployment, training, employment of children and women, organizations of workers and employers, information and research, and industrial disputes and work stoppages.

labour administration—whether they are ministerial departments or public agencies, including parastatal and regional or local agencies, and any other form of decentralized administration—and any institutional framework for the coordination of the activities of such bodies and for consultation with and participation by employers and workers and their organizations".[1]

In brief, labour administration involves the entire range of activities from preparing ground work, actual preparation, networking, cooperating and coordinating, facilitating dialogue, checking, reviewing and monitoring labour policies and programmes, the preparation and enforcement of labour laws and regulations, and establishment and enforcement of standards in the field of labour. An important feature of labour administration is the involvement of employers' and workers' organizations in various areas and at various levels of labour administration.

A robust system of labour administration would:

- Be capable of responding to changing economic and social conditions
- Justify the confidence of both employers and workers
- Make a vital contribution to the improvement of working conditions and at the same time to national development
- Develop participation through social dialogue and tripartism
- Acquire credibility on account of the fairness of labour policies
- Make known and apply uniformly the laws and regulations
- Demonstrate elements of transparency through openness in decision-making
- Make available the services in labour administration without discrimination

In brief, labour administration contributes to the creation of an environment in the realm of employment that has elements of "participation", "credibility", "transparency" and "responsibility".

16.2 Scope of Labour Administration

The scope or fields of activities under labour administration have expanded during the course of time. Initially confined to the enforcement of a few labour laws or regulations, labour administration has come to cover within its fold a wide variety of subjects. Substantial enlargement of the number and contents of labour laws and regulations all the more necessitated the establishment of a network of labour-administration agencies. State regulation of labour matters became necessary also from many other considerations. The broad areas covered under labour administration today, whether statutory or non-statutory, include—contracts and terms of employment, wages, working conditions, industrial relations, social security, employment and unemployment, training, employment of children and women, organizations of workers and employers, information and research, and industrial disputes and work stoppages. The specific fields of labour-administration activities include—quantum of wages including minimum wages, protection of wages, fringe-benefits, bonus, hours of work, holidays, leave, physical working conditions, occupational safety and health, maternity protection, workmen's compensation, provident fund and pension, gratuity, sickness benefit, medical benefit, unemployment benefit, employment policy, employment exchange, training, vocational guidance, labour-welfare measures, collective bargaining, industrial actions including strikes and lock-outs, workers' participation in management, trade unions, employers' organizations, unfair labour practices, tripartite forums, employment of children and women, collection and dissemination of information relating to labour, labour surveys, and so on. The degree of emphasis, activities undertaken and the extent of intervention vary from country to country.

Labour administration is confined not only to the national ministerial departments or departments of state or local government. It also covers the role of other agencies including workers' and employers' organizations and non-governmental agencies, including workers' and employers' organizations and non-governmental (parastatal) agencies at various levels. The fields of labour-administration activities essentially depend on the nature of labour policy, labour laws and regulations and practices operating in particular countries at particular times.

Of the agencies involved in labour administration, the national ministerial labour department has to play the most significant role. The International Labour Conference suggests the following main functions of such a department:

1. It should be required to provide the government with all useful information or to advise it with regard to the elaboration of the government's labour policy and, where necessary, the preparation of laws and regulations.
2. It should be entrusted with the administration of labour laws and regulations, the implementation of the government's labour policy and the handling of labour questions.
3. It should participate at the highest level and on an accepted and reciprocal basis with other government departments in elaboration of policies concerning such objectives as eradication of unemployment, industrial peace and other questions relating to labour.
4. It should have at its disposal competent and adequate staff and administrative resources such as will enable it to perform its functions efficiently and impartially.

> Of the agencies involved in labour administration, the national ministerial labour department has to play the most significant role. The Department of Labour should:
>
> - Provide the government. with relevant information to aid policy formulation
> - Administer the Labour Laws and labour policy
> - Participate at the highest level on the elaboration of policies and handling of labour questions
> - Be staffed with competent personnel for effective and impartial functioning

16.3 The Evolution of Labour Administration in India

The sole administration of matters pertaining to labour administration, during the late nineteenth century, was enforcement through magistrates. There were just a handful of laws in existence then (e.g. Fatal Accidents, 1855; Workmen's Breach of Contract Act, 1859; Employers and Workmen (Disputes) Act, 1860, etc.) and no "policy" on other aspects of labour prior to 1919. In general, labour administration during the period was piecemeal and ad hoc with the primary responsibility vesting with the local magistrate. There was a general lack of coordination between the central and provincial governments in matters relating to labour administration.

For the first time, the Government of India Act, 1919 defined in some detail the distribution of legislative and administrative powers between the central and provincial governments. Generally, the central government could enact labour laws relating to mines, railways, major ports, seamen and international and inter-provincial emigration and the provincial governments could deliberate on labour matters pertaining to factories, plantations, public works, inland vessels, labour disputes, labour welfare and housing, but under the control of the central government.

Between and at a time when the Whitley Commission submitted its report to the Government of India in 1931, the matters pertaining to labour were handled by the Department of Industries and Labour. This department, however, dealt with many issues, labour being just one of them. The Department was headed by a Member of Executive Council. In the year 1920, few positions of Labour Commissioners were created in the industrially active provinces of Madras and Bengal and a labour office in Mumbai. Subsequently, a labour office was set up in Bombay in 1921.

The Government of India Act, 1935 laid emphasis on provincial autonomy, thereby expanding the role of provincial government's role in matters pertaining to labour. Labour Commissioners were appointed in almost all the provinces under the popular governments. This gave a fillip to labour administration and a number of labour laws were enacted (Factories Act, 1934; Payment of Wages Act, 1936; Mines Act, 1935). These enactments required the creation of suitable enforcement machinery, both at central as well as provincial levels. The Second World War and the Defence of India Rules led to the creation of elaborate machinery for handling industrial disputes and conflicts, which later came to be incorporated under the ID Act, 1947.

Labour administration came to be further strengthened following the recommendations of the Investigation Committee. There was a spate of labour laws enacted prior to or after the attainment of Independence. In 1949, the Government of India ratified ILO's Labour Inspection Convention (No.81), 1947 and ensured the incorporation of its provisions in labour laws of the country. The run up to the current state is covered elsewhere in this chapter.

16.4 Labour Policy in India

Labour Policy

The term "labour policy" includes the treatment of labour under constitutional, legislative and administrative Acts, rules and practices, and various precepts laid down in the successive Five Year Plans. The labour policy derives its philosophy and content from the Directive Principles of State Policy as laid down in the Constitution and has been evolving in response to the specific needs of the situation and to suit the requirements of planned economic development and social justice.

The term "labour policy" conjures up different things to different people. It is not a formal document put together by an agency of the State. It is not a ready reckoner, which one might look up for a quick recap. Neither does it originate from one source, nor can a date be mentioned when the "labour policy" was finally put in place. Partly, these relate to goals of policy and in part to the means and instruments of implementation. There are, however, constraints in setting goals as well as on means and instruments. The term "labour policy" includes the treatment of labour under constitutional, legislative and administrative Acts, rules and practices, and various precepts laid down in the successive Five Year Plans. The labour policy derives its philosophy and content from the Directive Principles of State Policy as laid down in the Constitution and has been evolving in response to the specific needs of the situation and to suit the requirements of planned economic development and social justice.

"Labour policy in India draws inspiration and strength partly from the ideas and declarations of important national leaders during the Freedom struggle, partly from the debates in the Constituent Assembly, partly from the provisions of the Constitution, and partly from International Conventions and Recommendations. It has also been significantly influenced by the deliberations of the various sessions of the Indian Labour Conference and the recommendations of various National Committees and Commissions, such as, the Royal Commission on Labour; the National Commission on Labour, 1969; the National Commission on Rural Labour, 1991, and the like"[2].

According to the Constitution of India, the enactment and administration of labour laws is the responsibility of both the union and state governments, which means that on the subject of Labour, both the state government and the central government can legislate. Matters relating to labour are distributed amongst three lists contained in one of the Schedules to the Constitution. The distribution of subjects in the three lists is as follows:

i) Union List

1. Participation in international conferences, associations and other bodies and implementing decisions made thereat
2. Port quarantine, including hospitals connected therewith, seamen's and marine hospitals
3. Regulation of labour and safety in mines and oilfields
4. Industrial disputes concerning union employees

BOX 16.1 **FOR CLASS DISCUSSION**

In India, 94 per cent workers out of the total workforce of 457.5 million belong to the unorganized/informal sector. These workers work as agricultural labourers, landless labourers, factory workers, domestic help, construction workers, etc. Currently the number of scheduled employments in the central sphere is around 45, whereas the number is approximately 1200 in the state sphere. The labour administration machinery is largely geared towards administration and enforcement of standards and laws in the organized sector. The unorganized sector has largely been neglected which has seen all kinds of NGOs stepping in. Discuss alternatives or some other models of cooperation between the public and the administration to promote a more meaningful administration of the labour laws and labour standards.

5. Union agencies and institutions for:
    i) Professional, vocational or technical training; and
    ii) The promotion of special studies or research;
6. Enquiries, surveys and statistics for the purpose of any of the matters in this list

ii) Concurrent List

1. Economic and social planning
2. Trade unions, industrial and labour disputes
3. Social security and social insurance; employment and unemployment
4. Welfare of labour, including conditions of work, provident fund, employers' liability, workmen's compensation, invalidity and old-age pensions, and maternity benefits
5. Vocational and technical training of labour
6. Factories
7. Inquiries and statistics for purposes of any of the matters specified in the Concurrent and the State List

iii) State List

1. Public order
2. Public health and sanitation, hospitals and dispensaries
3. Relief of the disabled and unemployable

According to the Constitution of India, the enactment and administration of Labour Laws is the responsibility of both the union and state governments, which means that on the subject of labour, both the state government and the central government can legislate.

The first comprehensive approach to a labour policy was spelled out by the interim government in 1946, when a host of issues were set out on which reforms were to be brought about through legislations and other measures over a period of time. A few of these issues were:

- Minimum wages in industry, plantations and agriculture
- Determination and agreements on fair wages
- Regulating hours of work, weekly rest periods, spread-over, holidays, privileged leave or earned leave for workers in unorganized sectors like shops and establishments and other sectors not yet brought under legislative protection
- Improvement of working conditions in factory with special emphasis on health and safety. Similar provisions to be brought in for other sectors.
- Training and apprenticeship schemes on a large scale to increase productivity on the one hand and earning capacity and promotional avenues on the other
- Adequate housing for workers subject to the availability of resources
- Medical and health insurance schemes for the working class
- Revision of the Workmen's Compensation Act
- A central law for maternity benefits to secure benefits for those other than factory workers the extended scale of benefits provided under the Health Insurance Scheme
- Extension to other classes of workers of the right, within specified limits, to leave with allowance during periods of sickness
- Provision of crèches and canteens
- Welfare of the coal-mining labour and welfare of the mica-mining labour
- Strengthening of the inspection staff and the inspectorate of mines

Initial Approach to a Comprehensive Policy

- Minimum wage
- Fair wage
- Regulating working conditions in all sectors
- Training and apprenticeship
- Housing
- Health, accident, sickness insurance
- Coverage of Workmen's Compensation Act
- Central law for maternity benefit with wider coverage
- Increasing coverage of leave with wages in case of sickness
- Creches and canteens
- Welfare of coal and mica workers
- Strengthening of labour inspectorates

Elements of the Current Labour Policy

- State as catalyst of "change" and welfare programmes.
- Recognition of the right to peaceful direct action
- Mutual settlement, collective bargaining and voluntary arbitration
- Intervention by the State in favour of the weaker party to ensure fair treatment to all concerned
- Primacy to the maintenance of industrial peace
- Evolving partnership between the employer and employees in a constructive endeavour
- Ensuring fair wage standards and provisions of social security
- Cooperation for augmenting production and increasing productivity
- Adequate enforcement of legislation
- Enhancing the status of the worker in industry
- Tripartite consultation

The National Commission on Labour (2002) has tried to trace the making of the National Labour Policy and has summarized in its report the main elements of labour policy operating in the country especially with respect to industry, during the last 20 years:

i) Recognition of the State, the custodian of the interests of the community, as the catalyst of "change" and welfare programmes

ii) Recognition of the right of workers to peaceful, direct action if justice is denied to them

iii) Encouragement to mutual settlement, collective bargaining and voluntary arbitration

iv) Intervention by the State in favour of the weaker party to ensure fair treatment to all concerned

v) Primacy to the maintenance of industrial peace

vi) Evolving partnership between the employer and the employees in a constructive endeavour to promote the satisfaction of economic needs of the community in the best possible manner

vii) Ensuring fair wage standards and provisions of social security

viii) Cooperation for augmenting production and increasing productivity

ix) Adequate enforcement of legislation

x) Enhancing the status of the worker in industry

xi) Tripartite consultation

The thrust of the recent labour policy is more towards creating a climate of healthy industrial relations and promoting an industrial culture conducive to the improvement in efficiency, productivity and real wages.

16.5 Labour Laws

Under the Constitution, the legislative powers in different fields of government activity are shared by the central and state governments, in accordance with the lists, which form a part of the Constitution—the Union List, the Concurrent List and the State List. The parliament has exclusive powers to make laws on matters enumerated in the Union List. The state legislatures have powers to legislate for the state, or any part thereof on any matter enumerated in the State List. Both the parliament and the state legislatures have powers to make laws with respect to matters enumerated in the Concurrent List. To avoid a possible conflict, certain safeguards are provided for subjects on which both the centre and the state can legislate. Labour is a subject that is included in the Concurrent List.

At the time of Independence, only a handful of laws existed concerning labour. Post-Independence, legislative support for matters relating to labour as the weaker section of the society was given partly by:

i) Strengthening the then existing legislation through suitable amendments

ii) Overhauling a few of them

iii) Supplementing it by new statutes where none had existed before

Important labour legislations that evolved through all these processes since Independence could be divided into the following main groups:

(i) Legislation about employment and training such as the Dock Workers Regulation of Employment Act, 1948; the Employment Exchanges (Compulsory Notification of Vacancies) Act, 1959; the Apprentices Act, 1961; the Tea District Emigrant Labour Act, 1932, and so on

(ii) Legislation on working conditions: This covers the Factories Act, 1948; the Plantations Labour Act, 1951; the Mines Act, 1952; the Motor Transport Workers' Act, 1961; and legislation relating to safety of workers, like the Indian Dock Labourers' Act, 1934. There have been Acts like the Children (Pledging of Labour) Act, 1933; the Employment of Children Act, 1938; the Madras Bidi Industrial Premises (Regulation of Conditions of Work) Act, 1958; the Kerala Bidi and Cigar Industrial Premises (Regulation of Conditions of Work) Act, 1961, and so on

(iii) Legislation on labour management relations such as the Trade Unions Act, 1926; the Industrial Employment (Standing Orders) Act, 1946; the Industrial Disputes Act, 1947; and legislation enacted in some states like the Bombay Industrial Relations Act, 1946; the UP Industrial Disputes Act, 1947; the Madhya Pradesh Industrial Relations Act, 1960, and so on

(iv) Legislation on wages, earning and social security, which covers the Payment of Wages Act, 1935; the Employees' State Insurance Act, 1948; the Coal Mines Provident Fund and Bonus Act, 1948; the Minimum Wages Act, 1948; the Employees' Provident Fund Act, 1952; the Assam Tea Plantations Service and Miscellaneous Provisions Act; the Payment of Bonus Act, 1965; the Workmen's Compensation Act, 1923; and the Maternity Benefit Acts (central and states)

(v) Legislation on welfare like the Mica Mines Labour Welfare Fund Act, 1946; the Coal Mines Labour Welfare Fund Act, 1947; the UP Sugar and Power Alcohol Industries Labour Welfare and Development Fund Act, 1950; the Bombay Labour Welfare Fund Act, 1953; the Assam Tea Plantation Employees' Welfare Fund Act, 1959; the Iron Ore Mines Labour Welfare Cess Act, 1961

(vi) Miscellaneous Legislation—The Industrial Statistics Act, 1942; the Collection of Statistics Act, 1953; the Industrial Development and Regulation Act, 1951; the Companies Act, 1954 and so on.

The list of legislations mentioned above is illustrative and not exhaustive.

The enforcement and implementation of these laws required the creation of elaborate administrative machinery, both at the central as well as the state level.

Classification of Labour Legislations

1. Employment and training
2. Working conditions
3. Labour management relations
4. Welfare
5. Wages, earnings and social security
6. Other miscellaneous

16.6 Voluntary Arrangements

Voluntary arrangements that are evolved in tripartite discussions have added to the benefits, which are expected to accrue to labour. In this category fall the recommendations of the Indian Labour Conference, the Standing Labour Committee and Industrial Committees. The benefits that workers got out of the Wage Board awards so far are also a result of tripartite discussions. Unanimous recommendations of Wage Board translate into a decision to implement them. The Code of Discipline, which provides for the recognition of unions and setting up of a grievance procedure, has also been the result of a tripartite discussion. The arrangements for housing in plantations were evolved out of an agreement in the Industrial Committee on Plantations. The introduction of the workers' education scheme, the setting up of fair-price shops in industrial establishments and the agreement on guidelines for the introduction of rationalization are some other important matters, which have emerged out of tripartite agreements.

The evolution of labour policy, during the Five Year Plans, has been based upon and is linked with the programme of the over-all economic development of the country. The Planning Commission sought to give a concrete shape to the legitimate needs and aspirations of the working classes, which included fair wages, suitable working and living conditions, social security, etc. With the acceptance of a socialistic pattern of society as the legitimate goal of economic development, there was a corresponding shift in the labour policy. This was reflected in the experiment of workers' participation in management through the machinery of joint consultation. Another important shift in the labour policy was the emphasis on collective bargaining in the promotion of healthy industrial relations. The plans also laid stress on the administrative aspects of the enforcement and implementation machinery. Emphasis was also laid on voluntary approach to the solution of labour problems as witnessed by the promulgation of the Code of Discipline in Industry, Code of Conduct, Industrial Truce Resolution and the various recommendations of the tripartite bodies like the Indian Labour Conference, and the Standing Labour Committee.

16.7 Labour Administrative Machinery of the Government

"The main responsibility for labour administration of the Government of India vests in the Ministry of Labour. The Ministry presently consists of the main Ministry (Secretariat), and four attached offices, ten subordinate offices, four autonomous organizations, a number of adjudication bodies and one arbitration body. Labour administration in India is mostly rooted in labour laws. There are only a few activities that are not based on laws. They are mostly in the field of workers' education and craftsmen training other than apprenticeship training, etc."[3]

16.7.1 Ministry of Labour

The main Ministry of Labour (Secretariat) is the centre for consideration and decision of all questions relating to labour so far as the Government of India is concerned. It is the central administrative machinery "for the formulation of labour policy, enforcement of labour laws and for the promotion of labour welfare[4]." It guides, controls and coordinates the activities of all organizations and agencies involved in labour administration at the centre or in the states. The main subjects include:

i) Labour policy (including wage policy) and legislation
ii) Safety, health and welfare of labour
iii) Social security for labour
iv) Policy relating to special target groups such as women and child labour
v) Industrial relations and the enforcement of labour laws in the central sphere
vi) Adjudication of industrial disputes through central government, Industrial Tribunals, Labour Courts and National Industrial Tribunals
vii) Workers' education
viii) Labour and employment statistics
ix) Emigration of labour for employment abroad
x) Employment services and vocational training
xi) Administration of central labour and employment services
xii) International cooperation in matters relating to labour and employment

16.7.2 Attached Offices

The offices attached to the Ministry of Labour are:

Office of Chief Labour Commissioner (Central), Also Known as the Central Industrial Relations Machinery (CIRM): The CIRM came into being in the year 1945 on recommendations of the Royal Commission on Labour. All of its tasks can be categorized under three major heads namely, enforcement, conciliation and quasi-judicial. It is responsible for:

a) Prevention, investigation and settlement of industrial disputes in the central sphere
b) Implementation of labour laws in industries and establishments in respect of which the central government is the appropriate government (please refer to the list provided in the chapter vignette for the list of labour laws for which CIRM is responsible).
c) Enforcement of settlements and awards
d) Verification of the membership of trade unions affiliated to the central organizations of workers for the purposes of giving them representation in national and

international conferences and committees, and determining their representative character for recognition under the Code of Discipline

e) Investigation into breaches of Code of Discipline

Directorate General, Factory Advice Service and Labour Institutes: This functions as a technical arm of the Ministry in regard to matters concerned with safety, health and welfare of workers in factories and ports and docks. It assists the central government in the formulation and reviews of policy and legislation on occupational safety and health in factories and ports.
Labour Bureau: This is responsible for

a) Collection, compilation and dissemination of labour statistics
b) Construction and maintenance of Working Class Consumer Price Index Numbers for selected centres and all-India basis for industrial workers
c) Construction of CPI numbers for agricultural and rural workers
d) Maintenance of up-to-date data relating to working conditions of industrial workers
e) Undertaking research into specific problems concerning labour with a view to supplying data and information needed for the formulation of labour policy
f) Publishing reports, pamphlets and brochures on various aspects of labour
g) Bringing out regular publications of *Indian Labour Journal* (monthly), *Indian Labour Year Book* and *Pocket Book of Labour Statistics*.

Directorate General, Employment and Training: This is responsible for "laying down the policies, standards, norms and guidelines in the area of vocational training throughout the country and also for coordinating employment services[5]". Employment service and vocational training are operated through a countrywide network of employment exchanges, industrial training institutes and a number of other specialized institutions both at the central and in the states/union territories.

16.7.3 Subordinate Offices

The Subordinate Offices under the Ministry of Labour are—The Directorate General of Mines Safety and nine offices of Welfare Commissioners. The Directorate General of Mines Safety is located in Dhanbad. It is entrusted with the responsibility of enforcing the Mines Act, 1952 and the Rules and Regulations framed under it. The organization also enforces the Indian Electricity Act, 1910 as applicable to mines and oil-fields, and Maternity Benefit Act, 1961 in mines.

16.7.4 The Autonomous Organizations

The Autonomous Organizations are:

i) Employees' State Insurance Corporation
ii) Employees' Provident Fund Organization
iii) Central Board for Workers' Education
iv) V. V. Giri National Labour Institute

Employees' State Insurance Corporation: The organization administers various benefits under the Act, for instance, sickness benefit, maternity benefit, disablement benefit, dependants' expenses, funeral benefit, which are cash benefits, and medical benefit. The medical benefit has been made available to the family members of the insured employees and also to superannuated employees.
Employees' Provident Fund Organization: This is responsible for the enforcement of the Employees' Provident Funds and Miscellaneous Provisions Act, 1952 and the schemes framed under it. The schemes framed and in operation under the Act are: (i) Employees'

Provident Funds Scheme, 1952, (ii) Employees' Deposit lined Insurance Scheme, 1976, and (iii) Employees' Pension Scheme, 1995. The Employees' Family Pension Scheme, 1971 has been merged in the Employees' Pension Scheme, 1995.

V. V. Giri National Labour Institute: This institute was established in 1974 with the objectives of undertaking training, education and research, either on its own or through collaboration.

The Central Board of Workers' Education: Established in 1958, the objective of the Board was to help make the workers aware of their rights and responsibilities through constant training and education. CBWE is a tripartite body with representations from employers, workers and academics. The headquarter of the CBWE is in Nagpur. The Board has Education Officers, whose job is to design and deliver courses for the workers.

16.7.5 Adjudication Bodies

Seventeen Central Government Industrial Tribunal-cum-Labour Courts (CGIT) set up under the Industrial Disputes Act, 1947 were functioning in the country. Of these, two are located in Mumbai and Dhanbad, and one each in Asansol, Bengaluru, Bhubaneshwar, Chandigarh, Chennai, Hyderabad, Kolkata, Kanpur, Lucknow, Jabalpur, Jaipur, New Delhi and Nagpur.

16.7.6 Labour Administration Machinery of the State Government

Labour administration of the state governments is on a pattern similar to central labour administration with slight variations relating to implementing agencies and the requirements of state enactments and non-statutory labour programmes. The main organizations for labour administration in the states comprise:

i) Department of Labour and Employment (Secretariat)
ii) Office of Labour Commissioner
iii) Chief Inspectorate of Factories
iv) Chief Inspectorate of Boilers
v) Office of Chief Inspector, Shops and Establishments
vi) Directorate, Employment and Training
vii) Directorate, Medical Services (ESI Scheme)
viii) Social Security Directorate
ix) Adjudication Authorities

16.8 The Role of ILO in Labour Administration

From its very inception, ILO has given attention to the subject of labour inspection and labour administration. It assists countries in the formulation and development of labour administration and improvement of labour inspection and employment services.

Many conventions and recommendations of ILO deal with labour inspection and labour administration. A particular mention may be made of Labour Inspection Convention (No.81), 1947; Labour Inspection (Agriculture) Convention (No.129), 1969 and Labour Administration Convention (No.150), 1978. The relevant recommendations are: Labour Inspection Recommendation (No.81), 1947; Labour Inspection (Mining and Transport) Recommendation (No.82), 1947; Labour Inspection (Agriculture) Recommendation (No.133) and Labour Administration Recommendation (No.158), 1978. Besides, many other conventions and recommendations also contain provisions relating to labour inspection and administration.

Other contributions of ILO in the field of labour administration and inspection include:

i) Helping Member States in the establishment of efficient labour inspectorates to ensure the implementation and enforcement of labour laws

ii) Identifying gaps in such laws and proposing remedial measures

iii) Advising employers and workers on compliance with relevant laws and regulations

iv) Rendering help to associate employers and workers and their organizations with the efforts of labour inspection services

v) Strengthening the links between labour inspectorates and the various competent bodies concerned with the prevention of occupational accidents and diseases

16.9 Recommendations of the Second National Commission on Labour, 2002

The National Commission on Labour, in the year 2002, submitted its report to the government. The Commission devoted an entire chapter to labour administration (Chapter XI). This chapter details the current status of labour administration in the country and has put forth recommendations for toning up the same. A few of the recommendations pertaining to law, industrial relations and labour administration organization are listed below. Readers are advised to refer to the NCL report[6] to get a thorough understanding of the state of labour administration.

Labour Laws:

- It is necessary to have a clear and unambiguous definition of the "appropriate government".
- There is a need to have uniformity in the definition of the term "workman", which appears in many labour laws.
- Labour laws (Exemption from Furnishing Returns and Maintaining Registers by Certain Establishments) Act, 1988 should be made applicable to all establishments, and the penalty prescribed under the respective laws should be enhanced to make it at par with the labour laws (Exemption from Furnishing Returns and Maintaining Registers by Certain Establishments) Act, 1988.
- The employer should be required to maintain registers and display notices at the work-spot and not elsewhere.
- The procedure for prosecution for non-payment of wages and payment of less than minimum rates of wages should be simplified.
- To make enforcement effective, there should be commensurately deterrent punishment under all enactments.
- Laws like Payment of Wages Act and Minimum Wages Act should contain a provision for recovery officers to be appointed by the labour department.
- Provisions to grant exemptions from various laws, in case of extreme emergency or hardship, should vest with the appropriate government, and should be exercised by officers not below the rank of the Joint Secretary.
- Minimum Wages Act should apply to all establishments and not be confined only to certain scheduled employments.
- Criminal cases under labour laws should be tried by Labour Courts, as is being done in Madhya Pradesh.

Dispute Resolution:

- In rights disputes over dismissal, denial of regularization, promotion, etc., conciliation should be optional. The party should have the right to approach Labour Courts and the Labour Relations Commission straightaway. However, conciliation should be compulsory in case of industrial disputes related to interests—disputes involving wages, allowances, fringe benefits, etc. Conciliation proceedings should also be compulsory in the case of strikes and lockouts over any issue.

- Industrial disputes not settled in conciliation should go for either voluntary arbitration or mediation by arbitrators maintained by the Labour Relations Commission or adjudication. In the case of essential services, the dispute should go for compulsory arbitration. In other cases, it should go for adjudication. Arbitrators should be chosen from eminent persons in industry, conciliators, trade unionists and labour judiciary.
- All employing ministries should be advised to implement awards or sanction prosecution within one month of the matter being referred to them, failing which it should be deemed that the sanction has been given.

Qualification of Presiding Officers:

- Qualifications for the appointment of presiding officers of Labour Courts should be relaxed to enable conciliation officers to be considered for the appointment.
- Labour Courts should be given powers to issue decrees or initiate contempt proceedings for non-implementation or non-compliance of awards.

Labour Relations Commission:

- A central labour relations commission should be set up for central-sphere establishments, and state labour relations commission should be set up for establishments in the state sphere. Above the central and state labour relations commissions, there will be the national labour relations commission to hear appeals against the decisions of the two other commissions. The national LRC, central LRC and the state LRCs will be autonomous and independent. These commissions will function as appellate tribunals over the Labour Courts. They will be charged with the responsibility of superintendence of the work of Labour Courts.

Voluntary Resolution of Disputes:

- Voluntary resolution of disputes should be encouraged over legalistic approach of settlement of disputes through adjudication.
- There should be a legislative framework for voluntary dispute settlement. A basic prerequisite is to place a system of recognition of negotiating agency on the statute.
- The responsibility of conducting verification of trade-union membership for the recognition of trade unions should be vested in the central labour relations commission and the state labour relations commission.
- The works committee required to be constituted under Section 3 of the Industrial Disputes Act should be substituted by an industrial relations committee to promote in-house dispute settlement.

ILC:

- The Indian Labour Conference should be an effective forum for review, consultation and formulation or evolution of perspectives and policies. It must be made as representative as possible. Some means must be found to include representatives from the unorganized sector and from central organizations that are not affiliated to central trade-union federations. The ILC can be used as a sounding board for proposals of legislations. Suggested functions of the Indian Labour Conference would include review of labour situation, consideration of conventions and recommendations of the ILO for adoption, sounding board for legislative proposals, etc. The Standing Labour Committee should prepare the agenda for ILC. There should be a Director General of the ILC having specific functions. The ILC should set up tripartite Standing Committees to consider and review problems, legislations and implementation into main areas.

There are many other recommendations relating to areas such as safety and occupational health, unorganized sector, infrastructure and competence and cadre-building of central and state labour departments.

SUMMARY

- Labour administration refers to those parts of the government machinery, to those public authorities, which are directly concerned with the social and labour policy of a country. It also includes certain boards, institutes, centres or other bodies that are not an integral part of government machinery but to which the government has delegated certain specific areas of labour and social policy.
- What used to be a government tool mainly for the preparation and implementation of labour legislation and for the settlement of labour disputes is gradually evolved into something much broader, extending its concern to employment policy, training, special problems of the unorganized, the expansion of social-security schemes, and other matters.
- Labour policy of the government is forever evolving. The National Labour Policy is the outcome of deliberation of many bodies—the Vision of Founding Fathers conveyed through the Constitution, judicial pronouncements, plan documents, ILO conventions ratified by the country and many other sources.
- The labour policy finds expression by way of legislation and execution of the same through administrative machinery.
- The National Commission on Labour (2002) has recommended many actions for strengthening the labour administration in the country.

KEY TERMS

- Labour Administration 335
- Labour Legislation 340
- Labour Policy 334

REVIEW QUESTIONS

1 Discuss the scope and limitations of labour administration.

2 What is the role of labour administration in the formulation of labour policy?

3 What role does labour administration play in enforcing labour laws?

4 Discuss the role and functions of government machinery in labour administration.

5 What role does ILO play in labour administration?

6 Discuss the practicality of implementing the recommendations of NCL on labour administration. Why do you think the government has not been able to implement any of the major recommendations?

QUESTIONS FOR CRITICAL THINKING

1 What, in your opinion, have been the substantive changes in the labour policy today as compared to the period just after Independence?

2 The existing framework of labour administration is grossly inadequate to meet the challenges of today, considering that the business and industry have transformed completely. Discuss.

DEBATE

1 Legislative provisions with regard to labour have been ineffective on account of weak labour administration machinery.

CASE ANALYSIS

Self-certification[7]

In the year 2002, the Government of Kerala asked the IT companies operating in the state to file self-certified returns to the labour machinery in respect of compliances under various labour-related legislations, and vouchsafing that they are complying with the law applicable to industrial establishments. This facility for self-certification would free the information technology companies from routine inspections by the departments concerned. Only in the event of any complaint about the flouting of the laws and regulations would an information technology company be inspected by the officials for verification.

Questions:

1. Discuss the pros and cons of this move by the Kerala government. Examine it from the points of view of the employer and the employees.
2. Why has the IT sector been singled out for this treatment? Do you think this measure could be extended to the other sectors?

Undue Favours

The Swastik Foundries Private Limited is a medium-sized steel foundry on the Delhi–Mathura Road, a few kilometres away from Faridabad (Haryana). It employs around 350 workmen and the foundry has been operating profitably ever since there was a boom in the steel industry since 2003–04. The employees had been putting pressure on the management for a wage increase and an understanding had been reached on a number of issues after a series of discussions with the representatives of the employees. A few issues still remained which the management thought could be settled with the help of the Assistant Labour Commissioner who was also the designated Conciliation Officer for the area. A few employees, however, were opposed to the general understanding reached in the discussions and were determined to oppose it. The management had not recognized any union but was discussing the issues with employees who claimed to represent majority.

The general practice in the past was that after settling most of the issues in-house, the management and the representatives of the employees (with a letter of authority signed by a majority of workmen) would approach the ALC only for signing the settlement in his presence so that the settlement became binding on all. The ALC would normally accept the list in good faith and help both the parties sign the settlement.

From time to time the factory management also kept the office of the ALC in good humour whenever they needed transportation, office supplies or other help. The ALC had a very large number of industries within his jurisdiction and the office had limited resources. It was always a tall ask for his office to maintain a regular inspection visits to all these industries. Often, even though it was improper, he was forced to depend on the management of these industries for resources.

After signing the settlement, the disgruntled employees lodged a complaint with the Labour Commissioner alleging that the ALC had signed the settlement without proper verification of the "representation" of the employees. They alleged that the ALC had accepted undue "favours" from the management in signing the settlement.

Questions:

1. Is the complaint justified?
2. What precautions could the ALC have taken here?

NOTES

1 International Labour Standards Concerning Labour Administration, Labour Administration Convention, 1978, Article 1 (a) and (b).

2 Report of National Commission on Labour (2002), Chapter XI, Para 11.5, p. 3.

3 National Commission on Labour (2002) Report, Chapter XI, Para 11.8, p. 4.

4 'Ministry of Labour at a Glance in the New Millenium, Government of India (http://labour.nic.in/glance/molglance.html#ORGANISATIONAL)

5 The Citizen's Charter, Ministry of Labour & Employment, Government of India (http://labour.nic.in/main/cit_charter.htm)

6 NCL Report (2002), Volume 2 on Recommendations.

7 Government of Kerala, Labour and Rehabilitation Department Notification No G.O.(Ms) No.55/2002/LBR Dated, Thiruvananthapuram, 27th July, 2002; http://www.kerala.gov.in/dept_labour/itenabledservices.pdf

SUGGESTED READING

1 Khan, Muinuddin (Ed.), *Labour Administration: Profile on India* (Bangkok: International Labour Organisation, Asian and Pacific Regional Centre for Labour Administration, June 1992)

2 Report of Second National Commission on Labour, 2002, Government of India.

3 Saini, D. S., *Labour Administration: An Introduction* (New Delhi: Oxford University, 1994).

4 Venkatratnam, C. S., *Industrial Relations* (New Delhi: Oxford University Press, 2006).

part IV

skills

chapter seventeen

CHAPTER OUTLINE

LEARNING OBJECTIVES

After going through this chapter, you will be able to:

- Understand the genesis of conflict situations
- Gain an understanding of different ways to classify types of negotiations
- Understand and explain the "process" of negotiation and the steps involved in it
- Identify the knowledge, skills and attitudes required for effectiveness in negotiations
- Understand the concept of integrative and distributive outcomes of a negotiation

Due Diligence

Raghav Ahluwalia, Assistant Manager (Shift Operations—Electrical Maintenance), in a firm manufacturing wiring harness for automobiles is in a hurry. He must allocate the jobs at the beginning of the shift and then rush to the office of the Superintendent (Operations) for a meeting that the Superintendent wants to have with a group of electricians. Raghav vaguely knows that overtime is the main topic that is to be discussed. Although he was informed of the meeting the earlier day, he thought he need not make any special preparation since most of the facts were in his head and he knew all of the electricians personally. The hostility, therefore, that he faced from his own employees when the meeting started took Raghav by surprise. The electricians alleged that Raghav favoured a select few employees for overtime and was not fair in the allocation of duties. Knowing this not to be true (but unable to refute since he did not have data with him), Raghav quickly flared up. Raghav was caught completely unawares as regards the issue and as regards the mood of the employees. The meeting, thereafter, degenerated into an ugly exchange of name-calling, and facts involved in the issue flew out of the window. The Superintendent some how pacified all of them and decided to hold the meeting the next day at the same time.

When the electricians left, the Superintendent asked Raghav why he had come unprepared for the meeting when he knew the agenda. And being in charge of shift operations, how could he fail to keep track of the pulse of his people? He asked Raghav to come the next day for the meeting fully prepared, especially with the following:

- Complete deployment chart for the last two months
- Employee-wise breakup of overtime payments made to the employees during the two-month period
- Rules regarding normal deployment and overtime deployment
- An assessment of what the electricians truly want
- Complete figures of the budgeted and actual costs at the shop floor
- An assessment of the opinion-makers amongst the electricians
- What, as a shop-floor-in-charge, are we willing to agree to without compromising on discipline
- Any other detail that he thinks they may need to discuss
- Our own demands from the electricians

Negotiation Essentials for Employee Relations

A "people's manager" increases his/her effectiveness manifold by mastering negotiation skills, and examining his/her basic attitude towards negotiation. Negotiation is rated as one of the key competencies required for professionals, entrepreneurs and managers. The good news is that this is a learnable skill.

Raghav, like many of us, assumed that he would be able to handle any issue on the fly, based on his experience and his competence. The meeting did not go as expected and ended on a worrisome note. The situation escalated into something that, perhaps, neither party wanted. Yet, both of them had reached a place neither of them wanted to! Instead of solving a problem, both parties ended up making the problem even more complicated, a situation that may require even more time and energy to solve than it would have required that day. And, more importantly, Raghav may now carry a defensive attitude towards the meeting the next day, and also a feeling of concealed hostility towards the electricians. This may complicate issues further. Because of a lack of proper appreciation of the subtleties, a seemingly solvable problem became even more complicated.

Conflict and negotiations are what we face every day. What some of us do not do is to examine our attitudes towards conflicts and realize that every negotiating situation may involve understanding of issues, root cause(s), preparation and skills. More so, as an HRM professional (or aspiring to be one), this competence may differentiate a mediocre from the brilliant.

For Raghav's sake, therefore, let us examine these two inter-related concepts in a bit more detail.

17.1 Conflict and Negotiations

Conflict is as natural a part of our lives as learning. However, the word "conflict" has taken a negative connotation and subconsciously, majority of us believe that it is something best avoided, brushed under the carpet or, if inevitable, done away with as quickly as possible. However, if we reflect for a moment, we will realize that:

- Conflict is a necessary part of human life. We can avoid it but cannot wish it away. Conflict is a reality that must be accepted.
- All conflict is not "bad". "How" we resolve the conflicts determine the value of the outcome.
- Sometimes, a conflict may become "dysfunctional", in which case, the outcome may be harmful to the parties to the conflict. The negative connotation to conflict probably has its origins in these dysfunctional conflicts. The lack of skills and understanding results in the formation of a vicious circle.
- Successful resolution of conflict is the way to progress. If we view "conflict" as a "problem", then successful solution to that problem will certainly result in progress.
- As a "people's manager" (or any other manager), a substantial part of our energy will be necessarily directed towards conflicts. Competence to successfully resolve conflicts, therefore, is a sine quo non for an effective "people's manager".

- Conflict is a necessary part of human life.
- The manner of resolving a conflict determines the value of the outcome.
- A conflict may become "dysfunctional", harming the parties.
- The lack of skills and understanding results in the formation of a vicious circle.
- Conflict, when viewed as a "problem-solving exercise", will result in progress when solved.
- Competence to successfully resolve conflicts is a sine quo non for an effective "people's manager".

Before we proceed, it is obligatory on our part to define what a "conflict" is. And since the book has a practical focus, we will restrict ourselves to an operational definition of a conflict and not go into details that have perhaps been discussed in text books on organization behaviour.

Conflict is about perception. When two persons (or groups) look at an issue from their own perspectives (because of a large number of reasons, ranging from inadequate communication, roles, organizational structure, personality, different emotional states, etc.) and the there is a difference in the two perspectives, then there is an existence of a "potential" conflict situation. Actual conflict may not have surfaced at this stage, but the conditions for one arising are there. The moment one person (or group) acknowledges that the difference in perception of the other person (or group) is going to negatively affect the interests of the first person (or group), a conflict surfaces.[1]

The important things to keep in mind, at this stage, would be:

- That different people (or groups), most likely, will have a different perception of an issue.
- The difference in this perception could be due to variables such as different goals, roles, individual level variables, emotional state, clarity of communication, etc. It is a near impossibility to have congruence on all the variables.
- The difference in perceptions is a necessary condition for a potential conflict, not a sufficient one.
- Conflict will arise only when either party believes that this difference may be prejudicial to their interests.
- Before a difference takes the shape of conflict, there is a window of opportunity as to how the two parties frame the issues regarding the different perspectives.

When a person (or a group) acknowledges that differences in perception of the other person (or group) is going to negatively affect the interests of the first person (or group), a conflict surfaces.

To be an effective negotiator, it is essential to understand what a negotiation is all about. And the starting point would be to check our understanding of conflict itself. This may shape the all-important attitude towards conflict and negotiation (see Box 17.1).

17.1.1 Approaches to Resolve Conflict

The books on organizational behaviour have dealt with various approaches to resolving conflicts. The basic approach, however, is dependent to a large extent towards our attitude towards conflict itself. From an employee relations point of view, we would sum up the various approaches under two broad categories, namely:

- Avoidance
- Approach

There are two basic "attitudes" to solving a conflict, "avoidance" and "approach". **"Approach"** means that more often than not, individuals with this attitude would like to confront (or approach) the problem to solve it. **"Avoidance",** as the name suggests, means that individuals avoid the conflicting situation as a means of solving it.

People approach a conflict situation with the above basic approaches. These approaches are based, mostly, on the basic attitude that we hold towards conflict. The "approach" attitude means more often than not we would like to resolve the conflict (or problem) by approaching the problem and solving it. The "avoidance" approach, on the other hand, may lead us to resolve the conflict, more often than not, by avoiding the conflict situation. Of course, the approaches depend on many situational factors and, in many situations, the "avoidance" approach may be the better option. More often, however, it is the attitude of "approach" that is more effective in most situations. A persistent pattern of avoidance points to certain lacunae, which may be rooted in fear or lack of confidence in the ability to solve a problem. We need to, therefore, find out our basic approach towards the resolution of conflicts and to examine the basic competence that may be required to resolve conflicts, and then evaluate whether it is effective or needs a deeper examination. Such instruments are available in many books on organization behaviour. Many times, if we reflect on our own experiences at problem-solving, we may, with fair accuracy, determine our dominant preference for resolving a conflict.

BOX 17.1 **FOR CLASS DISCUSSION**

Mantosh is a lathe operator, Gr-II, in the machining shop of an automobile-manufacturing company. Due to increasing pressure for operational efficiency in a fiercely competitive market, the management is continuously striving to increase the availability of manpower on the shop floor. Unplanned leave is discouraged. The annual leave calendar is planned in advance to ensure that the process does not suffer for want of availability of skilled manpower. Mantosh, like other workmen, has a creditable attendance record but of late, due to increasing pressure at home front (his son is to take the plus-2 exam in the coming year, and the marriage of his daughter has been fixed). Although he had planned for leave to be with his son during the period nearing his exam, he had not provided for his daughter's marriage. Knowing the process of taking leave, he was apprehensive that the supervisor may refuse to grant him leave for as long as he required (around three weeks). This anticipation was causing anxiety and mild negative feeling towards the supervisor/company policies. Mantosh sought a meeting with his supervisor.

When Mantosh narrated the issue to his supervisor, the supervisor took some time to think. He, then, said:

1. Daughter's marriage is very important for the girl's father. No questions about it.
2. Your presence for the smooth conduct of marriage is an absolute must. No questions.
3. We must, therefore, find a workable solution.

The supervisor paused and then asked if Mantosh agreed. Mantosh was relieved, and readily accepted the statement of the problem.

The supervisor then posed that the issue before ***them*** was to find a solution where Mantosh could be present for the marriage with the following proviso:

1. This should cause minimal or no disruption of work.
2. This should not affect the discipline at the shop floor and quoted as precedent for granting unplanned leave to others. Perceived equity is important.

The supervisor paused again and asked Mantosh if they have defined the problem correctly.

What, do you think, will happen here? What did the supervisor do? In how many different ways could this conversation have gone and with what consequences? Even though there is a conflict here, has the "framing of issues" been done properly? Will it result in a constructive search for a solution? What would have happened had the supervisor used his "authority" and refused point blank citing company policy? What if he had accommodated Mantosh's request completely? Do you think that by framing of issues, chances of a solution to the satisfaction of both have increased?

Box 17.2 describes typical situations that people face in their work lives. Similar situations occur in our daily lives too. All these situations describe a problem or a conflict and different ways that have been used in each to resolve the conflict or the problem. Most of us use a mix of these approaches in different situations. However, we may sometimes adopt one or two of these ways as predominant ways of handling the conflicts/problems that we face in life. Sensitizing ourselves to a variety of ways to approach a conflict and our own predisposition towards it may be the starting point of our exploration of knowledge, skills and attitude required for effective conflict resolution and negotiations.

Based on the "attitudes" of "avoidance" and "approach", following styles may be adopted in different situations:

- Resignation
- Avoidance
- De-fusion
- Compromise
- Problem-solving or Negotiation
- Confrontation

Resignation: Tapasya has pre-judged the demands of the situation and her own abilities (or the lack of them) to meet them. Analysing the situational factors, Tapasya has determined that there is no way she could resolve the conflict effectively in her favour and, therefore, accepts the probable outcome as a fait accompli. She has resigned to the "fact" that she cannot do anything to influence the situation and, therefore, is willing to accept the outcome, whatever they may be.

BOX 17.2 **FOR CLASS DISCUSSION**

1. Tapasya Roongta has just taken over as a regional training manager with one of the largest telcos in the country. There is a budget meeting to be held today for the HRM function of which training is a part. Because of intense demand on the training function, there is a pressure on Tapasya to meet the annual targets. There would be need to seek substantial increase in budget provisions for her function. However, Tapasya feels that her being the only woman sectional head in the HRM team puts her at a disadvantage. In the past, her seeking support has met with little response. Her being new to the position too adds to the disadvantage, she feels. There would be little point in her making efforts to get the budget allocation that she wants, since in all probability, it will be rejected. Tapasya decides not to expend her energy in a lost cause and keeps quiet during the meeting.
2. Radhe Shyam, an associate working with a BPO Gurgaon, came late to office for two days in the last week. Abhay Mazumdar, the supervisor of Radhe Shyam noticed this late-coming on both the days. He was in two minds, whether to call Radhe Shyam and ask him why he was late, or may be not to bother! Every one is entitled to come late once in a while. Let it go for the time being. He will intervene if this becomes a problem. Any way, the moment he will ask, Radhe Shyam may flare up and create a scene. Asking him may not be worth the trouble.
3. Ravikesh Shrivastava, the programme director for a management course in one of the premier B-schools was aghast when few students entered his room in a very agitated mood. They had a whole list of grievances regarding the seating arrangement, ventilation in the classroom, non-availability of books in the library, and finally very unhygienic conditions in the canteen. They wanted the issues resolved right then or they threatened to march to the room of the CEO. Alarmed, Ravikesh asked them to sit down, tell everything in a calm manner and then give him 48 hours to revert to them. After stating the whole thing, the students left and Ravikesh heaved a sigh of relief and patted himself on the back for defusing a potentially ugly situation. The next day, the students may most likely be out of steam and the situation may resolve itself or may require minimal interference from his side.
4. Bimal Bhasin, a team leader with Software Solutions limited, has been called by his project manager for a planned Performance Review Meeting. Despite the high-sounding name, Bimal knows what these meetings are all about. These meetings are about haggling target dates for the various milestones of the ongoing Macrosoft projects. Bimal can either discuss each of the milestones threadbare, or quickly settle the whole issue by tactically accepting a few milestones that he thinks are important for his boss (but whose feasibility is not certain) and make the boss relax a bit on the other milestones in lieu of his accepting the critical ones. While this may not be the most effective solution, it will at least save time and keep both of them reasonably satisfied.
5. Tarika Chopra is the front-desk executive at the Miramar Hospital. She considers herself very efficient and is prompt with her service to patients, replying to their queries, directing them to the appropriate section of the hospital, etc. There have been no complaints against her so far. The Lobby Manager, while strolling in the lobby, saw Tarika's table unmanned. He immediately had her paged and after 10 minutes, Tarika reported to the Lobby Manager. The Lobby Manager read her the riot act, telling her in no uncertain terms that her desk should be "manned", "all the time". Tarika meekly mumbled that she had taken a 10-minute toilet break to which the Lobby Manager replied that appropriate breaks are built into the duty hours, and there is no provision for unscheduled breaks. Tarika went back to her desk full of resentment.

Do these hypothetical situations remind you of similar situations that you face in everyday worklife? Would you handle such hypothetical situations in the same ways? Could there be alternative ways? Each of these situations highlights a distinct approach. Can you try and identify what these approaches are, especially on the approach-avoidance dimension?

Avoidance: Abhay Mazumdar, for example, has decided not to confront the problem but to ignore (avoid) it since, in his opinion, the cost of confrontation may not be worth the benefit arising out of such confrontation. Abhay may be right, but could it also be that for Abhay, getting into an unpleasant situation is uncomfortable? If that be the case, may this not develop into a pattern and the "preferred approach" for handling potential conflict? In certain situations, avoiding the situation may be the best approach, but it may not be so all the time or even most of the time. Why? Because, avoiding a conflict does not solve it. At best, Abhay has postponed the immediate show down. The problem may come back later to haunt Abhay, with greater intensity. Remember the "hot stove" principles of maintaining discipline? Every act of indiscipline must be confronted as soon as practicable!

De-fusion: Ravikesh has been able to take out the sting from the situation. His focus was to postpone the problem so that the emotional content becomes manageable. The conflict has not been resolved. It has not been addressed rather. For the time being, however, the conflict has been shifted with the hope that gaining time may help resolve the problem later (if the problem does not disappear of its own). This approach may be very useful some times. But is it always so? Or, does it even happen most of the time? It is a fact that problems or conflicts don't vanish with time. For the present, they may go under the surface to emerge later in another form. What Ravikesh has used is called "de-fusion". The crisis or the problem has been defused for the present. Ravikesh will cross the bridge when he comes to it, no sooner.

Compromise: Bimal has decided that keeping both parties happy is more important for him than discussing the issues threadbare and arriving at the best possible solution. Give and take and be happy and the problem be dammed! Well, as we noted earlier, both parties may leave with some face-saving and satisfaction at not having lost everything, the problem remained largely unaddressed. Bimal has decided to "compromise", an outcome in which we win some, and we lose some, but the deadlock is broken. Some progress is better than no progress or one-sided progress.

Engagement or Problem-solving: In the example of Mantosh, the lathe operator, the boss has listened to Mantosh and tried to bring all the issues to the fore and got an agreement of both the parties on the statement of problem. The intent, thereafter, is to arrive at a mutually satisfying solution.

Confrontation: In direct contrast, Tarika's boss has confronted the situation head on. He did not flinch from calling a spade a spade. There was no need for him to look for mitigating factors where everything was in white and black. He used his positional power to "resolve" the issue. In all likelihood, Tarika would be very careful in leaving her duty post. But, if you reflect for a moment, do you think the resolution was resolved to Tarika's satisfaction? What would Tarika do with her simmering resentment? Could this cause a problem in future? Was there a better way to confront the issue head on so that Tarika did not leave with as much resentment, and at the same time, her boss made it a point to let her know that her absence had been noticed?

Figure 17.1 gives an idea of various approaches that people adopt in handling conflicts or potential conflict situations that they face. The approaches have been mapped along the approach avoidance continuum. Each of these are not discrete approaches, but often there

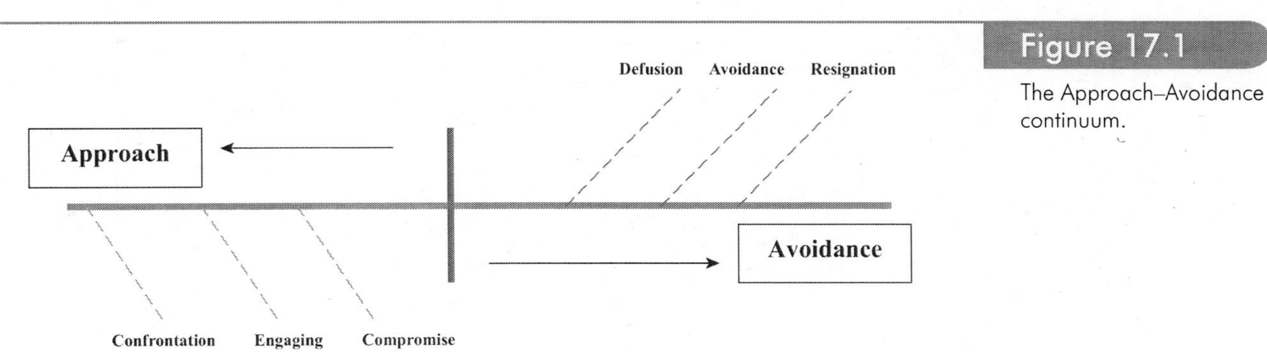

Figure 17.1
The Approach–Avoidance continuum.

is a subtle blend of various approaches with one of them being the dominant and the preferred one in a majority of conflict situations. It is important to know one's fundamental orientation to viewing and handling conflicts. Sensitizing oneself to this may be the first, and in the opinion of others, one of the most important steps in viewing conflicts in a proper perspective.

Conflicts will remain as long as humanity. It makes sense to acquire necessary competence to effectively handle conflicts. It is important to understand that any one of the above approaches may not be the best approach in all situations. Like an experienced golfer, however, we must learn to recognize the different terrain where shots are taken, and to match the appropriate club to each terrain. It is futile to "confront" the boss when you find that he has "lost it". It is better to avoid him at this moment and wait for a more opportune time. It will be harmful for you to "avoid" a conflict when you witness an act of indiscipline.

17.1.2 The Dual Concern Model of Conflict Resolution

Contemporary theorists provide another useful framework in which to view the resolution of conflicts meaningfully[2]. They classify the approaches based on two dimensions namely:

- Cooperativeness (or, concern for others)
- Assertiveness (or, concern for self)

Based on these two dimensions, we can visualize the conflict resolution behaviours or approaches in five categories as shown in Fig. 17.2. Notice that it is more or less similar to the approaches that we discussed in the text above. Sometimes, these five categories are also referred to as negotiating styles or negotiating behaviours, depending upon the context in which these are being discussed. These five categorization, prior to the actual discussion, may be viewed as the "intent", whereas during the discussion, these may be referred to as styles or behaviours. Remember that intent does not always translate into behaviour.

Figure 17.2

The dual concern model. Source: Adapted from Dan Pruitt, "Strategic Choice in Negotiation", in Jefrey Z Lubins. (ed.), *Negotiation Theory and Practice* (Cambridge, MA: Harvard Law School Program on Negotiation, 1991), pp. 27–46.

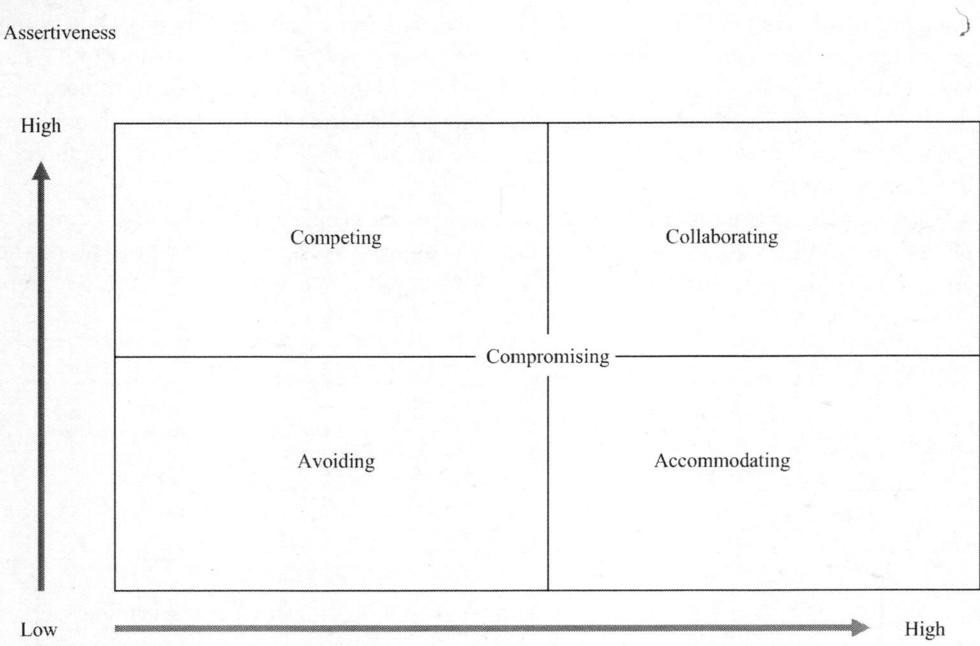

17.1.3 Is "Conflict" Desirable?

We have now gained a perspective on conflict from different angles. But another question remains, which may have a bearing on our fundamental orientation towards conflicts. Can "conflict" serve any useful purpose? Should we encourage "conflict" or discourage it? What is more likely to yield an effective solution—a uniform view on the problem or a diverse view on the problem? Is it possible that the richer the "data" on a problem, more the chances of finding an effective solution? What is better for an organization—a homogenous group of employees or a diverse group?

Once we accept "conflict" as a fact of life, then the right question to ask, perhaps, is not whether conflict is good or bad for the organization, but whether the outcome of conflict resolution is effective or ineffective or, whether the outcomes of the conflict are functional or dysfunctional for the organization. More and more research is pointing out that the presence of conflict is desirable in an organization. Our substantial experience in employee relations makes us believe that absence of conflict in an organization may be symptomatic of decay. In Chapter 12, it had been mentioned that the slate of industrial relations is never "clean", and, within limits, this may be desirable. Research also indicates that diversity in a team or an organization has the potential to give more effective solutions.

Conflict is constructive when it improves the quality of decisions, stimulates creativity and innovation, encourages interest or curiosity among members, provides the medium through which problems can be aired and tension released, and fosters an environment of self-evaluation and change.[3]

Many organizations, today, make efforts to create functional conflicts within the organization. It is believed that in today's fiercely competitive business organizations, the presence of functional conflict and also the competence to ensure that outcomes of conflicts remain functional are critical. And that competence is what we call "negotiation".

17.2 Negotiation

The run up to this point has been to prepare you to smoothly slip into the domain of negotiations from the area of conflict. With the above background on conflict, we are now ready to look at negotiations. What then, you may ask, is negotiation? Is it not the same as "compromise"? Is it not "give and take"? What has negotiation to do with day-to-day work of employee relations? Does negotiation not only take place during commercial deals or with trade unions or international treaties? Is it always necessary to negotiate to resolve a conflict? Is there a "best way" to negotiate? Can good negotiation be learned? Are some people inherently effective as negotiators? In the rest of the chapter, we shall attempt to answer a few of these questions, once again, from a practising manager's standpoint.

Researchers and scholars, who have studied negotiation, have all defined negotiations differently. From a managerial perspective, negotiation is the competence that is required to resolve conflicts or solve people-related problems. We may put very crudely that while conflict may be a situation, negotiation is the art and science of resolving those conflicts. The "approaches" to conflict that we studied earlier in this chapter can also be seen as approaches to negotiation. From a theoretical point of view, one of the broadest definitions of negotiation has been proposed as "a process in which two or more parties exchange goods or services and attempt to agree on the exchange rate for them".[4] Another simple definition that has been proposed is "a way to resolve issues without resorting to actions that hurt or destroy relationships". Not every interaction between two parties is a negotiation. However, every negotiation requires an interaction between at least two parties who have a relationship and who are motivated to negotiate. That is, each party must need or at least perceive that he or she wants or needs something that the other party has or controls. Furthermore, both parties must be able to propose options, make decisions and deliver on their agreement. [5] Negotiation, therefore, has the following features:

> **Negotiation**
>
> Negotiation is "a process in which two or more parties exchange goods or services and attempt to agree on the exchange rate for them". Another simple definition may be "a way to resolve issues without resorting to actions that hurt or destroy relationships".

1. Two or more parties
2. Something of value or interest to the parties
3. Desire to engage in interaction
4. At least some desire to accommodate
5. Authority to honour the agreement/settlement

17.3 Employee Relations and Negotiations

In Box 17.2, various situations have been mentioned. All these situations required negotiation. However, when we think of negotiation in the context of employee relations, the picture that readily comes to mind is that of union–management negotiations. However, this function involves a wide variety of situations requiring negotiations, ranging from structured to unstructured, formal to informal, one-to-one versus team negotiations, dispute resolution to wage settlement.

17.3.1 Situations Requiring Negotiation

Let us take a look at some of the specific situations that may require negotiations. This list is not exhaustive and, also, it may vary with the nature, culture and practices followed in the organizations.

Informal Situations:

Allocation of work

Problem-solving meetings

Target-setting

Performance counselling

One-to-one discipline meetings

Routine meetings with employees or their representatives

Bipartite committee meetings (canteen committee, sports committee)

Formal Situations

Performance-review discussion

Appraisal interviews

Selection interviews

Budgetary meetings

Agenda-based meetings with unions or employees

Grievance meetings

Works committee meetings

Joint council meetings

Pre-decided bipartite meetings

Unstructured Situations

Problem-solving meetings

Target-setting

Performance counselling

Grievance meetings

One-to-one discipline meetings

Routine meetings with employees or their representatives

Bipartite committee meetings (canteen committee, sports committee, etc.)

Structured Situations

Performance-review discussion

Appraisal interviews

Selection interviews

Budgetary meetings

Agenda-based meetings with unions or employees

Works committee meetings

Joint council meetings

Pre-decided bipartite meetings

In fact, in the area of employee relations, it is difficult to imagine an activity that does not require negotiations. You can try and imagine the various activities that you perform and try to identify a few that do not require at least some negotiations. The competence for effective negotiation, therefore, becomes the differentiator for a people's manager. It is important to know the process and skill requirement for an effective negotiation. To approach in an orderly way, it may be useful to use some mental classification, since each may require a different approach and style.

The case in Box 17.3 illustrates the point that preparation for a negotiations meeting must take into account the nature of the meeting. As we will learn later, preparation is one of the most significant steps in the negotiations process. And an assessment of the negotiating situation is one input that must be considered while preparing. Just like in the chapter-opening case, this case also ignores the effort needed to prepare for the negotiation. What, in your view, would be the outcome of this meeting?

17.4 Integrative and Distributive Negotiation Strategies

How do we decide to bargain? Is it maximizing our own gains from a fixed pool of resources? We are, after all, in the negotiations to ensure that we get the maximum. How does it matter that every rupee that we gain is at the cost of the other party? Negotiation, after all, is a game of power, and yielding any ground to the other party may be seen as a sign of weakness. The whole strategy, therefore, must be focused towards taking as much from the kitty as we can. An example of this kind of negotiation could be a wage negotiation. The firm has fixed resources. The labour may like to negotiate as much from it as they can. The more they can manage to take, the more will it add to the income of the members. Management, on the other hand, would like to give as less as they can manage and, thus, save on costs. The gain of one will be a loss to the other. This is what we call the classical zero-sum game. The gain and the loss add up to zero. This is the win-lose bargaining. One party wins at the cost of the other. This kind of bargaining is termed "distributive bargaining" (also sometimes known as "pure bargaining"). Both parties view their own goals to be in direct conflict with those of the other side. In this strategy, it is important to decide one's BATNA (best alternative to no agreement). This means, prior to entering into negotiation, the party must decide what the minimum gain that they would settle for is. Below this point, it would be better not to have a settlement. This point is also known as a reservation point as is shown below in Figure 17.3.

BOX 17.3 **FOR CLASS DISCUSSION**

Amandeep Grover, Manager (HR) in a specialty chemical firm, manufacturing refrigerant gases, had called his Assistant Manager for a Performance Review Discussion. The Performance Review Discussion was an elaborate process and an essential component of the company's Performance Management System. Amandeep had been involved in the development of the PMS and had also been part of the team that trained the other managers of the company in its use. The Performance Review Discussion was a formal process where the boss and the subordinate jointly reviewed the performance of the previous year, discuss shortfalls, agree upon strengths and weaknesses and identified the training and development needs. At the end of the review, both are supposed to discuss next year's plan and arrive at a mutually agreed set of objectives, tasks and targets. The whole process, if done faithfully, takes about an hour's time. Although that day's meeting had been fixed in advance, Amandeep thought he would be able to handle it because of his long experience and thorough knowledge of the system. Moreover, he thought, he knew his subordinates well and had kept a tab of their performances throughout the year. There should be no difficulty in making his subordinate agree to the performance targets that Amandeep had in mind. He was busy attending a phone call when the Assistant Manager walked in with a bunch of typed statements and his "performance diary". After finishing his call, Amandeep asked his subordinate to start speaking, while he (Amandeep) started looking at his mail box. Having finished looking at the mail box, he asked the subordinate to stop and "told" him the targets that had come from the Head (Corporate HR) and, consequently his targets have been formulated accordingly. The Assistant Manager listened to Amandeep quietly and then said, "Boss, it seems you have not been listening to me. I had come prepared for the meeting and had hoped to go through the process systematically. However, since you asked me, I started explaining my achievements and shortfalls, for which I had brought along all supporting documents. I feel by passing on the targets to me, you have not given any heed to the difficulties that I have been trying to explain to you. If you pass on these targets without even going through the process, then it may not be possible for me to accept. I cannot accept something that I cannot deliver. Sorry." Amandeep was irritated and told his subordinate not to educate him on the "process", and that it was he who had been one of the architects of the new PMS. The Assistant Manager kept quiet thereafter, and did not participate in the target-setting exercise.

People have "expectations" from the process, if the process has been defined. The PRD is a structured process and a formal process, and, thus, it may create an expectation. The outcome of this process has to be recorded. If, in the beginning itself, the expectations of one party are belied, the outcome may lack commitment of both parties.

Another kind of bargaining that is fast gaining ground is what is called "integrative bargaining". This bargaining strategy is especially relevant in complex situations involving many issues, and where the long-term relationship between the parties is important. This approach emerged out of management–union negotiations, where long-term relationships

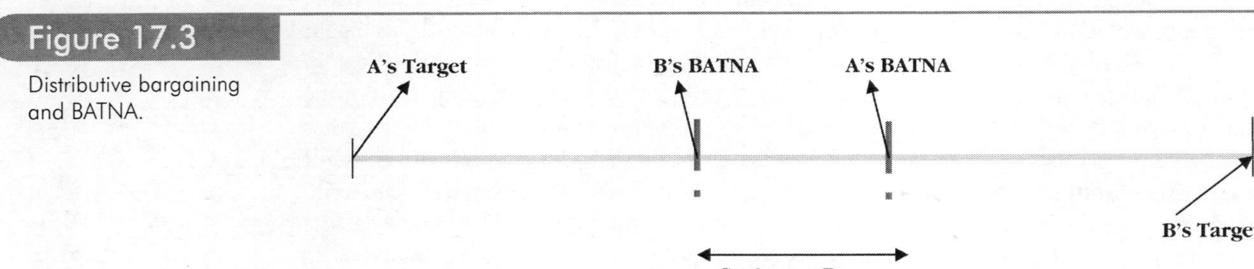

Figure 17.3
Distributive bargaining and BATNA.

are important. In fact, in most of the areas in employee relations, it is the integrative bargaining that finds favour. The concept here is to work towards a win-win solution. The gain or loss need not be at the cost of another party; rather, the strategy is that of joint problem-solving (JPS), where, if need be, the size of the pie itself can be increased so that both parties get a feeling that they have got what they wanted. Both parties collaborate to find a mutually satisfying solution. A typical example would be the labour agreeing to increase productivity so that they are able to get a wage increase that their members would want. Under the distributive bargaining, both management and labour would have fought for the largest piece of a fixed pie. The case of Mantosh, the lathe operator, is a case in point where both the parties have jointly identified the problem and agreed to find a mutually satisfying solution. Notice that the solution may go beyond the mere adherence to rules and practices. Both parties have defined the objectives and identified the constraints. The endeavour now would be to find more than one solution to the problem (unlike the distributive bargaining that could have ensued had each party stuck to their stands, one of them winning at the cost of another).

Distributive bargaining involves distributing a pie of fixed size; the gain of one is at the cost of another. It is a win-lose game. Integrative bargaining, on the other hand, tries to find a mutually satisfying solution through joint problem solving, if need be, by increasing the size of the pie itself.

In real life, the strategies are not cut and dried. Often, one has to employ a mix of strategies in most of the situations because the other party may not be using your strategy, or at some stage of negotiation, it may become necessary to make a tactical change.

Distributive bargaining can be employed where the relationship is not very important, for example, one-off situations involving parties we are not likely to deal with again. Bargaining for best price of a product in a shop may be one such situation. Distributive bargaining is based on "power", whereas integrative bargaining is based on cooperation. Many negotiators use this strategy, so one must be prepared to use this strategy too. Integrative Bargaining is possible only if both parties are prepared to use it.

BATNA

Best Alternative to No Agreement **(BATNA)** means, prior to entering into negotiation, the party must decide what is the minimum gain that they would settle for. Below this point, it would be better not to have a settlement. This point is also known as a reservation point.

Integrative bargaining is especially useful in complex cases involving a large number of issues. Instead of looking at one issue at a time sequentially and closing it (based on individual BATNAS), integrative bargaining looks at issues in totality and arrives at many possible settlements. A structured approach in these cases is to prioritize and classify issues that may be termed as vital, must-have, nice-to-have or trivial/ tradable, etc. and then take each block at a time. To establish goodwill and set the tone for joint problem-solving, probably it may be a good idea to settle one or two trivial issues.

Table 17.1 gives the difference between integrative and distributive bargaining. (Note: Although there is a subtle difference, we have used the terms "negotiation" and "bargaining" interchangeably).

Table 17.1

The difference between distributive and integrative bargaining. Reproduced with permission from Michael R. Carrell and Christina Heavrin, "Integrative Bargaining", in *Negotiating Essentials: Theory, Skills and Practice* (Delhi: Pearson Education, 2008), p. 97.

Factor	Distributive Bargaining	Integrative Bargaining
Number of Issues	One (or with several issues, one at a time)	Several
Technique	Win-Lose	Win-Win
General Strategy	Maximize share of a fixed pie	Expand the pie by creating value and claiming a share
Relationship	One time only	Continuing, long term
Interests	Keep interests hidden	Share interests with other party
Possible Options	One expressed option (one for each issue)	Many options—create new options for maximum mutual gain
Information	Keep information hidden	Share information with other party

17.5 The Basic Negotiation Process

There are as many process outlines for negotiations as there are books. More or less, however, identify the following as the major processes involved in the negotiations process:

- Preparation
  - Define issues
  - Set objectives
  - Formulate BATNA
  - Analyse situation
  - Plan strategy
- Opening
  - Set ground rules
  - Initial offer
  - Decide on approach
- Bargaining
  - Implement strategy
  - Observe strategy
  - Analyse and reorient strategy, if needed
- Closing
  - Check coverage
  - Document
  - Get an agreement

For simpler negotiations (informal), the logical flow would be similar, but many of the above steps may either not be required or get merged with other steps.

17.5.1 Preparation

Preparation is perhaps the most crucial but least cared for part of the negotiation process. In fact, maximum time and effort must be devoted to this phase, as the foundation for a successful negotiation depends to a very large extent on this phase. Refer to the chapter-opening case. How would have Raghav fared with the negotiation had he prepared along the lines suggested by his boss? Apart from getting a good grip on what lies ahead, a thorough preparation also gives confidence, which shows during the actual negotiation. It acts as a framework against which to evaluate progress towards the achievement of goals. Preparation would include investigation and clarity on the following:

Issues
What are you negotiating about?
What are the key issues?
Set aside the issues that have already been decided.
Ask where and how your issues conflict and coincide.
(The answer to these questions will have a major impact on strategy)

Objectives
What are the essential, desirable and tradable objectives?
What would be the BATNA (for each objective and for all the issues taken together?)

Analyse Situation
How important is long-term relationship?
Should we negotiate in team?
If yes, who would be the members and what would be their roles?
Even with scant information, estimate of their objective.
The power balance (alternative suppliers, etc.).
Who needs the deal more?
Personality, political situation, probable strategy, to the extent available
Decide on IB (JPS) or DB (PB).

Strategy
Emphasize early tasks (atmospherics, communicating initial position, learning their position).
Whether or not you will make the first offer
Your initial offer—what or how much? What atmosphere do you want? Where will be your concession?
Support arguments for each of the objectives.
What-if analyses

With this kind of preparation, you can imagine how much could be accomplished even before the negotiation has started. The negotiator will feel a sense of control that will be reflected in the actual negotiation process.

17.5.2 Opening

Opening must set the tone of the process. Depending upon the strategy (JPS or PB), the atmospherics may be different. One must take into account past relationships, the relative power balance, issues at hand before making an opening. This is also the time to agree upon the ground rules like who would be the spokesperson, how long will each discussion last, how frequently breaks would be taken, form of final agreement (verbal or written). This, perhaps, is also an opportunity to assess what strategy the other party favours, and tailor one's own strategy accordingly. In management–union relations, this is also the time for the unions to play to their constituencies. This is the time when there may be outbursts due to past irritants and also a gambit for demonstrating power. One should expect this and keep one's cool, as most likely, this would pass after running its course. This is primarily "posturing" and may serve a useful purpose as a safety valve for pent-up emotions.

Whether or not one is transparent in putting forth the issues is a matter of assessment and strategy. There are proponents of both the views, each with relative advantages and disadvantages.

In a formal union–management meeting, there is a tendency for the representatives to be present in large numbers. While this may be necessary from the union's point of view, it is not always conducive to speedy closure of issues. In fact, the inability to properly address this issue sometimes derails the whole discussion. It is desirable for both parties to have a prior discussion with a smaller group from both sides. In a multi-union situation, the group size often gets unwieldy and attention must be paid for the creation of a shadow negotiation team that meets separately from time to time, and then reports to the larger group, and then participates in the discussion. This arrangement helps steer the negotiation towards the desired end. In a union–management meeting, it is important for the management not to "gloat" over minor "victories" and allow the union to take the lead in announcing the progress to their constituents. It will be very wise to remember that negotiators representing their constituencies have to sell the settlement to their constituencies and provide them some leeway in taking lead in communicating the progress to the larger group.

Opening gambit sets the tone. In a union–management meeting, it is expected that after theatrics, both parties will get down to the business of negotiating. Both parties need each other in the long run.

17.5.3 Bargaining

It is the tactical heart of the negotiation process, the penultimate step before the closure. It is here that the parties get to the substantive issues and try to narrow down their differences. This is not a straight process, but there may be many cyclical rounds. Negotiations involving large and complex issues may have many mini-negotiation processes during the bargaining phase. It is here that the two parties engage in pure bargaining or joint problem-solving. Literature on negotiations suggests many tactics that are deployed to settle issues, especially in pure bargaining situation. In integrative bargaining, efforts are on to forge agreements on smaller issues thus strengthening the movement towards final settlement. Tradable objectives may get exchanged for desirable objectives or essential objectives.

It is at this stage that the negotiator must be aware of their BATNA. BATNA must be determined "before" entering into negotiations. BATNA will prevent us from coming to a sub-standard deal. Many times, the negotiators get emotionally involved with the process, having invested time and energy, that they may ignore their BATNA for a chance at closure. It should be absolutely clear that one should not have a deal below the BATNA and be ready to end the negotiation rather than accept something else. Normally, even if the situation changes during the negotiations or sops are offered, the pre-determined BATNA should not change.

17.5.4 Closing

This is the final step when the end is in sight—all major issues have been settled and minor ones remain. This is the time for drafting the terms of settlement and see if any points have been left out. A written document is not necessary as there is no binding, but it is advisable to document everything in as much detail as possible, taking care to mention dates when various provisions would take effect, period of validity, method of resolving issues, relation to interpretation of provisions, method of terminating the provisions, etc. In labour–management negotiations, the period for which the settlement will be valid must be mentioned clearly, as also what the status of the provisions on expiry of the period of settlement or premature termination would be.

Once again, under Indian conditions, in relation to labour–management settlement, largely it is advisable to go for a tripartite settlement, i.e., through the good offices of a conciliation officer. However, the pros and cons of doing so should be carefully examined before taking a final decision.

17.6 Essential Skills

As we have seen above, negotiation appears to be a complex process. It involves almost all the soft skills, from listening, verbal and non-verbal communication, awareness of one's emotional state, ability to think clearly in highly emotional situations, ability to work under pressure and ability to withstand pressure, planning and strategizing abilities. These are the generic skills that are required in most situations involving human relations. However, there are a few skills that may be needed to be an above-average negotiator. These skills are a combination of two or more "basic" soft skills.

- During negotiation, one has to keep on moving forward, even in the face of incomplete information. Most of the time, negotiators have to decide whether to remain in negotiation or call the bluff. This is a very tough call and is stressful. The negotiator, therefore, must have the ability to feel comfortable with ambiguity and uncertainty.

- During the initial phases, theatrics and posturing are important for positioning oneself. An above-average negotiator must have the ability to look at the theatrics of the other party as just that and be able to insulate oneself. To understand that such theatrics are not meant as personal attack and, therefore, not get rattled by sudden show of hostility. He should be able to make an assertive transition. This would involve heightened sensitivity to the emotions in play and an acute sense to read non-verbal behaviour. In the end, he should be able to separate the emotional and the substantive part of the process.

- Ability to motivate oneself under pressure and adverse situations would also go a long way in ensuring the tenacity and persistence required to go till the end, not throwing in the towel mid-way. A basic belief in one's ability to find a solution is important, and this belief comes only with meticulous preparation, emotional detachment and patience.
- Cultural sensitivity: With increasing diversity, changing profile of the working population and increased interface with people from other nationalities and cultures. A basic knowledge and sensitivity to the do's and dont's of other cultures may be necessary to prevent embarrassment or a breakdown in the process.

SUMMARY

- Conflict, though inevitable in human and organizational life, has acquired a negative connotation. The negative connotation is there perhaps because we do not understand the nature of conflict, we are oblivious of our attitudes towards it and also lack the skills needed to resolve it.
- Conflict is about perception. When two persons (or groups) look at an issue from their own perspectives (because of a large number of reasons, ranging from inadequate communication, roles, organizational structure, personality, different emotional state, etc.) and the there is a difference in the two perspectives, then there is an existence of a "potential" conflict situation. Actual conflict may not have surfaced at this stage but the conditions for one arising are there.
- The moment one person (or group) acknowledges that the difference in perception of the other person (or group) is going to negatively affect the interests of the first person (or group), a conflict surfaces.
- Research suggests that "functional conflicts" enhances group and organizational performance. Many organizations try to induce functional conflict within the organization.
- There are two basic attitudes to resolve a conflict—avoidance and approach. Within these attitudes, there are a number of styles/strategies for resolving a conflict, namely: resignation, avoidance, de-fusion, compromise, engaging and confrontation.
- This approach can also be understood in terms of two concerns that individuals have while resolving a conflict (The Dual Concern Model). These concerns are for the self and for the others, also understood as assertiveness and cooperativeness. These two concerns yield five different styles or strategies; namely, avoidance, accommodation, compromise, competition and collaboration.
- From a managerial perspective, negotiation is the competence that is required to resolve conflicts or solve people-related problems.
- While conflict may be a situation, negotiation is the art and science of resolving those conflicts.
- Negotiation has the following features:
  1. Two or more parties
  2. Something of value or interest to the parties
  3. Desire to engage in interaction
  4. At least some desire to accommodate
  5. Authority to honour the agreement/settlement
- From an employee relations perspective, negotiations may be required in different settings and situations—formal, informal, structured, unstructured, one-on-one or groups.
- The two major strategies in use for negotiation are called distributive bargaining and integrative bargaining.
- Distributive bargaining is based on power and the objective is to take as large a share of the total pie as possible. One party gains at the cost of the other party.
- Integrative bargaining, on the other hand is a win-win strategy where both parties treat negotiation as a joint problem-solving to ensure gains for both.
- Integrative bargaining is gaining ground and is the preferred approach in situations that are complex, or where long-term relationship between the parties is important.
- The negotiations process generally follows certain steps (although it is not always linear). These steps are: preparation, opening, bargaining and closing. Preparation for

negotiations is the most important step of the whole process and needs maximum time and effort.

- Negotiation requires almost all the basic "soft skills".
- In addition to these, there are a few skills that may be a combination of a few basic soft skills, e.g., ability to move forward in the face of ambiguity and incomplete information, ability to think clearly in emotionally charged situations, separate emotional and substantive components, ability to motivate oneself during adverse conditions and cultural sensitivity.

KEY TERMS

REVIEW QUESTIONS

1 Discuss the various approaches to resolving a conflict. Which approach, in your view, is more likely to yield a functional outcome to a conflict?

2 Describe the Dual Concern Model of conflict resolution. Describe a situation where each of the strategies of the Dual Concern Model would be the most appropriate one.

3 Is it desirable to have conflicts within organizations? Why? Explain with examples. What is a "functional conflict"?

4 Compare integrative and distributive bargaining with suitable examples. Elaborate characteristics of the two.

5 What are the steps in the negotiation process? Describe the steps.

6 Imagine a situation where you have been involved in a negotiation. Bring out all the skills that you used in the negotiations process. Which, in your view, was the most critical skill? Why?

QUESTIONS FOR CRITICAL THINKING

1 Do you agree that "power" plays the decisive role in the outcome of conflict resolution? Support your answer with suitable examples.

2 In certain situations, "avoidance" may be a preferred approach for resolving a conflict. Do you agree? Explain, with the help of suitable examples.

3 "Integrative bargaining" cannot work everywhere. It is not a fact that integrative bargaining will always result in better outcomes for both parties. Critically examine this assertion and give your opinion. Support your opinion through arguments and suitable examples.

4 Negotiations must take the natural flow. Any attempt to "structure" the process may result in resistance from the other party. Do you agree with this? What can one do to ensure that the other party does not object?

DEBATE

1 Integrative bargaining is just a jargon. After all, ultimately it is "power" that will settle the issue.

2 In the Indian context, confrontation may not be the best approach to tackle discipline problems at the workplace.

CASE ANALYSIS

Read the briefs of different roles and then answer the questions at the end.

I Zenith Systems: Brief of the Procurement Manager

Zenith Systems is one of the middle-sized IT companies located at Bengaluru. It meets its consumables requirements mostly through locally developed vendors. Printer cartridge is one of the consumables that are procured on a regular basis. The procurement budget is fixed at the beginning of the FY every year based on requisitions received from all the department and section heads. Based on budget and requirement schedule, orders are released at appropriate time, keeping the lead time in mind. It is 10 September 2007. The company is in the process of finalizing procurement for the October–December quarter.

There is a regular requirement of printer cartridges and the orders are placed on a regular basis. Recently, there have been some changes in the market and the vendors have not been very firm about the price. This quarter, the budget for cartridges is INR 1,00, 000 and the requirement for the quarter is 1,000 at a minimum. The company policy is not to carry inventory of more than 20 per cent, i.e., 200 units against a monthly requirement of 1,000. It is the 10th day of the last month of the quarter and the stock is sufficient for only 20 days. The quoted price for the last two orders was Rs 100 per unit for delivery on site.

Your appraisal, to a large extent, depends on your ability to maintain budget, and keeping carrying cost and order costs to the minimum, i.e., you should adhere to the budget, not exceed the prescribed inventory level and not resort to placing frequent orders.

The administration manager has received complaints from the last two lots and wants to be present during the negotiations.

You are to finalize and place an order with the regular vendor who is coming to meet you today. He has been a reliable supplier and you do not foresee much problem. There are several other vendors for this low-cost, low-technology item. But you have a time deadline, and you are not too sure of their quality, cost and delivery schedules.

The Sales Manager of National Officeware (supplier) is coming to see you. He is bringing along people from his operations and the finance team.

II Zenith Systems: Brief of the Administration Manager

Zenith Systems is one of the middle-sized IT companies located at Bengaluru. It meets its consumables requirements mostly through locally developed vendors. Printer cartridge is one of the consumables which are procured on a regular basis. The procurement budget is fixed at the beginning of the FY every year based on requisitions received from all the department and section heads. Based on budget and requirement schedule, orders are released at appropriate time keeping the lead time in mind. It is 10 September 2007. The company is in the process of finalizing procurement for the October–December quarter.

You are the Administration Manager at Zenith Systems. Your job is to consolidate the requirement for office consumables from all the user departments, and send it to procurement section for centralized procurement. The job also requires collecting a systematic feedback on product performance. Printer cartridges are a regular office consumable and the purchase procedure is streamlined so that there is no disruption in supplies. The product quality is OK. However, in the last two quarters, there have been complaints from a few users that there is smudging of ink from the cartridge on to the paper. You had passed on this feedback to the Procurement Manager, but once again, there have been complaints.

If there is a repeat, the matter may get reported to higher-ups, and you may be pulled up. This time, therefore, you want to be present, when the order is being finalized with the supplier. You must ensure that quality parameter is stipulated explicitly in the order. There should be penal provisions in case of repeat complaint from users.

You don't care who the supplier is as long as the delivery and quality parameters are met. Therefore, your limited agenda is to ensure zero-defect and the availability of next-quarter requirement on or before 1 October. You have requested the Procurement Manager to call you while finalizing the order. He has just called.

III National Officeware: Brief of the Sales Manager

National Officeware is a company that manufactures and sells printer cartridges. The company caters mainly to the IT companies that have mushroomed in Bengaluru recently. In a fiercely competitive market, the company has been able to establish itself as one of the better suppliers of cartridges in terms of committed deliveries, competitive price and superior product quality. The company has long-term relationships with many clients, and the order position appears very promising. The company has been in the process of expansion to meet the growing demand for its products from new customers. It has held the price for almost a year now. To meet the growth and modernization demands, the management has taken a decision to be firm on prices in line with the market prices of similar products.

You are the Sales Manager for National Officeware. You have been with the company for three years now, and during this time, the customer base has grown manifold. You have a 100 per cent retention record, i.e., once a customer, always a customer. Zenith is one of your oldest clients with per quarter orders of 1,000 plus. Normally, they place order 15–20 days before the end of the quarter since the lead time for making a delivery is only 20 days. The price at which door delivery of the last order was made was INR 100 per unit. There was a tacit understanding that the price was likely to remain firm for the financial year. Zenith is an old and reliable client and you would like to retain them. The Purchase Manager of Zenith has also raised a quality issue and wants you to be able to address it during the meeting. It is something to do with smudging of ink. You are not fully aware of the reasons for this problem, so you have asked one of the operations executives to accompany you.

You are aware that the company, in keeping with the market trend, intends to follow aggressive pricing policy. You have been told that your performance will now be assessed on the basis of net sales realization and not on the basis of gross sales. It will be an achievement for you to sell at a price so that there is a profit of up to 5 per cent. You intend to discuss the costing structure with the Finance Executive, and ask him to accompany you to the meeting with Zenith so that an immediate closure of the order can be made.

The Finance Executive and the Operations Executive are on their way to meet you.

IV National Officeware: Brief of the Finance Executive

National Officeware is a company that manufactures and sells printer cartridges. The company caters mainly to the IT companies that have mushroomed in Bengaluru recently. In a fiercely competitive market, the company has been able to establish itself as one of the better suppliers of cartridges in terms of committed deliveries, competitive price and superior product quality. The company has long-term relationships with many clients and the order position appears very promising. The company has been in the process of expansion to meet the growing demand for its products from new customers. It has held the price for almost a year now. To meet the growth and modernization demands, the management has taken a decision to be firm on prices in line with the market prices of similar products.

You have been called by the Sales Manager of the company. He wants to discuss the pricing of the printer cartridge with you and then accompany him to a meeting at Zenith Computers. The last price at which the cartridge was supplied was INR 100 per unit. The Financial Controller has asked you not to suggest a price below total cost + margin (3–5 per cent). You have prepared a cost sheet:

Fixed Cost: INR 40 per unit

Variable Cost: INR 60 per unit

Margin: INR 3–INR 5 per unit

Transportation a nd Packaging Cost (Extra): INR 0.50 per unit

Minimum Order Size: Lots of 600

Volume Discount: INR 2 per unit, if minimum order is more than 2 lots, i.e., more than 1,200 units

You are leaving to meet the Sales Manager.

V National Officeware: Brief of the Operations Executive

National Officeware is a company that manufactures and sells printer cartridges. The company caters mainly to the IT companies that have mushroomed in Bengaluru recently. In a fiercely competitive market, the company has been able to establish itself as one of the better suppliers of cartridges in terms of committed deliveries, competitive price and superior product quality. The company has long-term relationships with many clients and the order position appears very promising. The company has been in the process of expansion to meet the growing demand for its products from new customers. It has held the price for almost a year now. To meet the growth and modernization demands, the management has taken a decision to be firm on prices in line with the market prices of similar products.

You are the Operations Executive at National Officeware, handling the printer cartridge line. You have been called by the Sales Manager of the company to discuss i) a customer complaint regarding smudging of the printer cartridge and ii) readiness to ship products, i.e., a feasible delivery schedule.

You are aware of the quality complaint. It is due to occasional malfunctioning of an imported coil in the heat treatment assembly. An order has been placed for the replacement of the coil but it would take at least four weeks for the line to start defect-free operation. No commitment can be made for 100 per cent defect-free supplies till the middle of next month.

To meet the increasing demand, some layout change is going on in the factory and the production schedule may be affected in the coming days. The management has also decided now to accept the delivery of orders only in lots of 600. Orders below this number may be sold only through wholesalers and retailers. There are 600 units in finished goods inventory (which may have defectives). WIP inventory is zero. Manufacturing lead time is normally 20 days per lot. Due to possible layout change at the shop-floor, there can be no firm commitment on delivery for the coming three weeks, since the plant is producing at 60 per cent of capacity, and orders to be serviced have piled up. By the middle of October, firm commitment can be given regarding quality and delivery.

The Operations Manager has told you not to commit anything that the department cannot be sure of. However, orders lost on account of production will affect your performance evaluation and the company will lose business. You are leaving to meet the Sales Manager.

Questions:

1. Prepare a negotiation strategy for each of the role players. In a few cases, the role players may have to negotiate internally, and then with the external customer/supplier.
2. What strategy (integrative or distributive) would you follow if you were the:

   Procurement Manager (Zenith)

   Administration Manager (Zenith)

   Sales Manager (National)

   Finance Executive (National)

Give reasons in support of your approach.

NOTES

1 Adapted from Stephen P. Robbins, Timothy A. Judge and Seema Sanghi, "Conflict and Negotiation", *Organization Behavior, 12th Edition* (Delhi: Pearson Education, 2007), p. 554.

2 Adapted from Dean Pruitt and Jeffery Z. Rubin, *Social Conflict: Escalation, Stalemate and Settlement* (New York: Random House, 1986); Dean Pruitt and Sung Hee Kim, *Social Conflict: Escalation, Stalemate and Settlement, 3rd Edition* (New York: Mcgraw-Hill, 2004), pp. 40–47.

3 Stephen P. Robbins and Seema Sanghi, "Conflict and Negotiation" in , *Organization Behavior, 11th Edition* (Delhi: Pearson Education, 2006), p. 408.

4 James A. Wall, Jr., *Negotiation: Theory and Practice* (Glenview, IL: Scot Foresman, 1985).

5 Michael R. Carrell and Christina Heavrin, "An Introduction to Negotiation" in *Negotiating Essentials: Theory, Skills and Practice* (Delhi: Pearson Education, 2008), p. 13.

chapter eighteen

CHAPTER OUTLINE

LEARNING OBJECTIVES

After going through this, chapter you will be able to:

- Understand what "soft skills" means
- Understand the meaning of emotional intelligence and what constitutes emotional intelligence
- Design a "framework" or an approach for identifying detailed soft-skill requirements
- Identify the typical "soft skills" that are essential for the specialized role of employee relations/HR manager

From Engineer to HR Manager

Ravinder Luthra, a B. Tech. (industrial engineering), on obtaining his degree in 2004, joined an organization manufacturing optical devices as Graduate Engineer Trainee.

On completion of general orientation and "on-the-job" training, Ravinder was posted as Assistant Manager in the Production Planning and Control Department of the plant. He was a quick learner and very soon, he was noticed by the top management for his excellent analytical inputs. His industrial engineering background landed him a special assignment of carrying out job analysis and job evaluation for the entire operations area. Ravinder completed the assignment within the assigned time, and his report was appreciated for its analytical depth. Ravinder was a hard task master, and expected his team members to maintain the same standards of performance as his own. Based on his performance, he was offered a posting in the HR department as Deputy Manager (HRM). It was a tricky decision for him.

After a discussion with the Head of HRM, Ravinder decided to take the offer. With his technical background, good grasping power and analytical mind, he should not face any problem. Moreover, HR was a generalist profile and it should not take him much time learning the ropes.

About eight months after joining the HR department, the HR Manager called Ravinder to ask how things were going. Ravinder replied that everything was under control and that he had been able to streamline the HRIS in record time. There was no unrest on the shop floor and that he had been able to support the Line Manager in maintaining tight discipline. The HR Manager asked Ravinder to sit down and then told him that there appeared to be some gap. There were serious complaints against him from the shop-floor workmen, alleging that Ravinder did not have time to listen to their grievances—that he was forever busy with his PC and no one was supposed to meet him during this time; that he had very little patience to listen to problems of workmen and asked them to mail their grievances to him. The Shift In-charge has alleged that Ravinder was good at analytical work but of no use to him in people management.

Soft Skills for Employee Relations

India has a large pool of qualified persons, but there is a serious shortage of employable persons. The shortage is largely on account of deficient soft skills. In the area of employee relations, these skills assume greater significance since the role mainly envisages interface with a cross-section of employees which, in turn, requires people skills.

Employee relations, like any other function dealing with the management of people, besides requiring "technical skills", also requires certain "other" skills. In some measure, these "other" skills are common to all functions. However, because the employee relations manager is to concern himself mainly with people-related issues, the relative importance of these skills become even more. For want of any universally accepted set of skills, all such skills are clubbed under an umbrella term called "soft skills", essentially distinct from the technical or "hard skills" required for a job. This chapter tries to define "soft skills" and develop a "framework" for the identification of these skills.

18.1 What are Soft Skills?

It is hard to find a universally accepted and rigorous definition of "soft skills". As a "construct", "soft skills" is not well-defined. Although we "understand" it, this understanding is expressed in loose terms. The following definition is a creditable attempt to define "soft skills" with precision. Even though it appears complex, at least the boundaries of the term have been traced and supplemented with examples.

"Soft skills tend to be skills by which the individual interacts with, interprets, structures, coordinates or otherwise informs the social and physical environments within which physical, societal and or personal product may be generated"[1].

Soft skills are deployed for efficient use of hard or technical skills as well as for the achievement of personal and interpersonal goals. These skills are difficult to define, observe, quantify or measure. These skills largely relate to how people understand themselves and how they relate to others. Unlike technical skills which are acquired through formal education, soft skills are largely learnt from life experiences. These are difficult to change later unless one becomes aware of deficit in specific areas and works towards reducing the deficit.

Examples of soft skills would include listening, influencing, communicating, negotiating, counselling, empathizing, asserting, teaming, resolving conflicts, solving problems, managing emotions (in self and others), etc.

In a practising manager's term, "soft skills" are those skills that are needed on the job, in addition to the technical skills required. These "skills" are said to be the differentiator between effective and not-so-effective managers.

Managers whose roles require excessive interaction with people may need one set of "soft skills" whereas those in roles that require interface, largely in the technological domain, may require another set of soft skills. A few soft skills may be common across roles, for example, the ability to motivate oneself.

Soft Skills

Soft skills tend to be skills by which the individual interacts with, interprets, structures, coordinates or otherwise informs the social and physical environments within which physical, societal and/or personal product may be generated.

18.2 Emotional Intelligence and Competence

Daniel Goleman, in his book, *Working with Emotional Intelligence*,[2] cites the findings of a national survey of American employers, which indicated that employers are now looking for entry-level workers, with specific technical skills less important than the underlying ability to learn on the job. The employers listed the following skills as desirable in employees:

1. Listening and oral communication
2. Adaptability and creative responses to setbacks and obstacles
3. Personal management, confidence, motivation to work toward goals, a sense of wanting to develop one's career and take pride in accomplishments
4. Group and interpersonal effectiveness, cooperativeness and teamwork, skills at negotiating disagreements
5. Effectiveness in the organization, wanting to make a contribution, leadership potential

Skills that employers look for in new hires:
Listening and oral communication

- Adaptability and creative responses to setbacks and obstacles
- Personal management, confidence, motivation to work toward goals, a sense of wanting to develop one's career and take pride in accomplishments
- Group and interpersonal effectiveness, cooperativeness and teamwork, skills at negotiating disagreements
- Effectiveness in the organization, wanting to make a contribution, leadership potential

Of the five desired traits, just one was academic: competence in reading, writing, and math.

The model introduced by Daniel Goleman focuses on emotional intelligence as a wide array of competencies and skills that drive leadership performance. Goleman's model outlines five main pillars of emotional intelligence:

Self-Awareness: The ability to read one's emotions—recognizing a feeling as it happens. The ability to monitor feelings from moment to moment is crucial to psychological insight and self-understanding. People with greater certainty about their feelings are better pilots of their lives.

BOX 18.1 **FOR CLASS DISCUSSION**

Suditi Bhadauria, the Training and Development Manager for Genesis Technological Services Limited (a 4,000 strong BPO), was looking at a mail from the VP (Operations), wherein he had asked her to probe and find out specific areas where there may be need for building competence of the team leaders. His concern was an increasing discontent amongst the team members and a very high rate of attrition. The exit interviews had indicated that the leaving employees were satisfied with the systems and policies of the company and that the working conditions were better than what prevailed in the industry. Genesis' compensation was above the industry average. Most of the employees, however, pointed out disappointment with the environment within teams. Lack of perceived equity in job allocation, shift rotation, recognition criteria, performance evaluation, incentives, etc. were mentioned as the main reasons for the decision to quit. What the VP was telling Suditi was that the "systemic" factors could be ruled out. The "problem" most likely was with people handling skills at the TL level. Suditi was to probe and pin-point the specific areas where training and development interventions could help build the required competencies.

Suditi proceeded with the job systematically. She studied the job analysis of the TLs, talked to the team members, process leads (to whom TLs reported) through semi-structured interviews. She could identify various deficient competencies, which she proceeded to map into a "framework" that placed these skills from the "basics" to "advanced" or from "simple" to "complex". The next logical step for her was to design suitable "interventions" for the people whose primary task was to manage "people".

Will Suditi succeed? Did she follow the correct approach? Don't you think a short duration "General Management" module would have helped? Isn't "people management" an inborn trait? Aren't some people naturally competent in managing people? Can people be "trained" in these difficult-to-identify-and-define competencies?

Managing Emotions: Handling feelings so that they are appropriate is an ability that builds on self-awareness. Mere self-awareness is not enough; the ability to handle it and use it to advantage is another distinct ability. The awareness of anger and what to do with that anger are both necessary, although, often, an awareness of the emotion itself provides a handle on the emotion.
Motivating Oneself: Marshalling emotions in the service of a goal is essential for paying attention, for self-motivation, for mastery and for creativity. Emotional self-control—delaying gratification and stifling impulsiveness—underlies accomplishment of every sort.
Recognizing Emotions in Others (Empathy): The ability that builds on emotional self-awareness is the fundamental "people skill".
Handling Relationships: The art of relationships, for the mot part, involves the skill in managing emotions in others.[3]

Five pillars of emotional intelligence:

- Self-awareness
- Managing emotions
- Motivating oneself
- Empathy
- Handling relationship

Goleman includes a set of emotional competencies within each construct of EI. Emotional competencies are not innate talents, but rather learned capabilities that must be worked on and developed to achieve outstanding performance. He posits that individuals are born with a general emotional intelligence that determines their potential for learning emotional competencies[4].

Although criticized by a few as mere pop-psychology, Goleman's framework is an excellent guide for aspiring managers and managers to look at comprehensive range of "soft skills". This is because these emotional competencies are the building blocks of what we call "soft skills". And, once again, the good news is that these competencies can be learned. Goleman has made broad brush strokes, covering all walks of life (including that of an ER manager), but we need to get a closer look at the specific requirements from the role of an ER manager.

18.3 A "Framework"

There are scores of "soft skills" loosely defined. If we try to randomly list down the soft-skill requirements for a position, we may get hopelessly lost and may end up with a list with which we can do little. A rational approach could be to look at the requirements of each role and then break it down into technical and other skill requirements. Many of the "soft skills" are a combination of one or more "basic" skills. We are using "skill" here in this text to cover all the KSA (knowledge, skills, abilities) requirement of a role. The detailed mapping would lie in the realm of job analysis or training-needs identification. Our approach here is to just suggest an approach and to identify the soft skills required for an HR/ER role.

Broadly, we can say that communication may be a crucial skill for an HR role (as also for many other roles). Now communication is such a broad area that unless we break it down further, it may not be of any practical use. Table 18.1 illustrates how we can deconstruct

Table 18.1 The constituent component of soft skills.

	Basic	Intermediate	Advanced
• Communicating	• Attention • Comprehending • Paraphrasing • Verbalizing • Planning What to Speak • Components of Non Verbal Communication • Principles of Verbal Communication • Giving names to different feelings/emotion	• Listening • Validating • Communicating Verbally Deciphering Non Verbal Communication • Using Non-Verbal Communication Receiving Feedback • Giving Feedback • Planning a whole Communication	• Counselling • Reading emotions in self • Reading emotions in others • Persuasive presentation • conducting team meetings • Designing structured communication–with team and others • Negotiating–one on one as well as in teams • Handling emotions and stress in communication

communication into its constituents, especially from the point of view of an HR/ER role. As is evident, proficiency at the basic level is essential to learn the skills of the next two levels. For each of the soft skills, therefore, we can identify the constituent building blocks and then identify customized intervention to build up the deficient component, with the objective of building competence in communication for the HR role. For an HR role, written communication may not be as crucial as verbal and non-verbal communication. It is beyond the scope of this text book to cover all the skills up to the basic level. What we will, therefore, do is to suggest an approach (to identify skills by breaking down a larger grouping into actionable skills) and then list the major soft-skills requirement for this role. Breaking these skills down into the constituent components as suggested in Table 18.1 is an analytical method which would help break down skills other than communication into actionable parts.

18.4 The Role of an ER Manager/Professional

Soft-skills (or any other skills) requirement will flow from the role requirements. While the role of an ER manager may vary from organization to organization, there would be certain aspects that would be common to all. We will look at the role in a unionized organization and a non-unionized organization.

- **Communication**

  Structured Communication

  Planning a meeting

  Ability to hold productive meetings

  Ability to prioritize agenda

  Sensitivity in choosing points for discussion

  Articulation of points in a "sensitive" manner

  Ability to steer discussion on controversial topics

  Manage to handle emotional outbursts of others

  Using one's own emotional expressions to advantage

  Persuasive Presentations

  Unstructured Communication

  One-to-One Communication

  Ability to listen as per situational requirements (empathetic, task-oriented, evaluative)

  Ability to paraphrase and summarize

  Steering a conversation in the desired direction

  Two-Way Communication

  Ability to fulfil emotional and substantive concerns of the group

  Summarize the outcome

  Facilitate consensus (if required)

  Handle undue pressure

  Handling "difficult" members

- **Relationships**

  Ability to give and receive feedback

Fostering "trust" in relationships

Ability to define and maintain boundaries

- **Line Managers**

  Ability to give "factual" assessment of state of the affairs

  Maintain professional integrity

  Withstand pressure

  Creating an alliance and commonality of objectives

  Ability to establish professional credibility

- **Staff**

  Sensing communication requirements (in terms of frequency, content and feelings)

- **Union Office Bearers**

  Ability to maintain neutrality in multi-union situation

  Conveying professional competence

  Ability to withstand undue pressure

  Determination of the level of transparency with dealings

  Ability to assess inter- and intra-union dynamics and power play

  Ability to assess essential and tradable demands

  Intelligence gathering

  Building coalitions within unions

  Negotiations

- **Discipline**

  Ability to convey (through words and through Acts) the non-negotiability of discipline

  Ability to convey explicitly the transparency and equity in the administration of discipline

- **Systems Information**

  Ability to assess information requirement of all stakeholders

  Ability to decide the "need to know" and the "nice to know" requirements

  Ability to assess vital and sensitive information and the establishment of information integrity

- **PMS**

  Skill of persuasion, ensuring a "buy in" to the system

  Coaching, counselling skills

  Giving and receiving feedback

  Training managers and staff in the process

  Ability to prevent distortions in process and outcomes

- **Image of the Self**

  An HR or ER manager is always watched by the employees and fellow managers. It is absolutely critical for this manager to be able to see how others perceive him. Caesar's wife, after all, must be above all suspicion! The HR/ER manager, must never, ever, indulge in acts that are less than 100 per cent honest, short-circuit systems, take advantage of systems or processes or help themselves to something extra. This goes a long way in establishing credibility and, in our opinion; this skill/sensitivity goes on to enhance the image of the HR/ER manager more than any other skill. This is non-negotiable.

18.5 Conclusion

We can go on adding to this list since this is not an exhaustive one. In fact, there can never be one that covers all the roles and all situations. However, we have tried to draw on our long years of experience in industry to map the essential skills that may be required. We have tried to draw the requirements from what the HR or ER manager actually does rather than approach it from the generic skills, for example, inter-personal skills and communication skills. In our opinion, the above approach is based on common sense and can be applied to specific situations to yield a very accurate list of requirements. From the discussion presented in this chapter, it may appear as though the terms "skills" and "tasks" have been mixed. While this may be true in the present context, a painstaking exercise to distinguish and deconstruct these terms would yield the same end result.

SUMMARY

- "Soft skills" is not a very precise construct and has been defined variously depending on the point of view adopted to explain the term.
- In a practising manager's term, soft skills are those skills that are needed on the job, in addition to the technical skills required. These skills are said to be the differentiator between successful and not-so-successful managers. Examples of soft skills could include planning, preparing, organizing, communicating, observing, describing, identifying, empathizing, learning, intuition, sense of timing, attitude, tool development, skill transfer, process development, creativity, ingenuity, design, sense of aesthetics, endurance, etc.
- Daniel Goleman has defined five pillars of emotional intelligence, which, in turn, are made up of emotional competencies. These "pillars" are: self-awareness, the ability to manage emotions, empathy, self-motivation and the ability to handle relationships.
- The emotional competencies that constitute emotional intelligence are called soft skills. Surveys of employers have found that soft skills are the most important competencies that they desire in employees.
- A systematic way of identifying the soft-skills requirement for the role of an ER or HR manager could be made if we moved backwards from the role requirements to the different levels of soft skills. Using this framework, the soft-skills requirements (up to the first level) of an HR/ER manager has been identified.

KEY TERMS

- emotional intelligence 372
- empathy 373
- self-awareness 372
- soft skills 371
- structured communication 374
- unstructured communication 374

REVIEW QUESTIONS

1 What is your understanding of soft skills? List down your own soft-skills requirements (even though you may be a student).

2 What is emotional intelligence? What is emotional competence? What are the pillars of emotional intelligence as described by Daniel Goleman?

3 Describe an approach to map the exact soft-skills requirements of a particular role. Use an example to explain the approach.

4 List down the role requirement of an HR executive (in a non-union environment). Break down the requirements to identify the advanced-level soft skills required for the role.

QUESTIONS FOR CRITICAL THINKING

1 People are born with their soft skills. What, then, would be the use of training people in these skills? Give your arguments in support, with appropriate examples.

2 Soft-skills requirements are common across all jobs. All jobs need communication, motivation, etc. Do you agree with this view? Why or why not?

DEBATE

1 Soft skills do not really matter as much as it is made out to. Unless a person fulfils the functional or technical requirements of a job, he/she will not be hired. A scientist, after all, does not need soft skills to make progress in their research.

2 "Employee relations" is more about instincts than about skills or knowledge. The more experience you have in dealing with people, the better your instincts.

CASE ANALYSIS

Problematic Pay-slip

Anil Sharma is the manager of the ammonium sulphate plant in a fertilizer company. The shop employs about 500 people. The manager of the shop reports to Deputy General Manager (Operations). The manager of the shop is the disciplinary authority for all the workmen under his control.

One day, while going through the production reports in the morning, Anil heard loud noises outside his office. He tried to ignore it for a while but the noise only became louder. When he stepped out of his room to locate the source of the commotion, he saw that all the workmen had stopped work to gather around Bhrigav, a fitter, who was shouting at the top of his voice. Chandan, the HR officer, and Dileep, the Section Officer, were standing closest to Bhrigav, trying to restrain him at which his voice got even louder. It appeared that Bhrigav was agitated about some acts of people in the time office on account of which he had faced problems with his pay-slip for three months in a row.

Anil called Bhrigav and Chandan inside his room and asked for an explanation of the scene that he had witnessed. Chandan said that despite sending Bhrigav's leave regularization to the time office through regular monthly attendance statements, Bhrigav was marked absent as reflected in Bhrigav's pay-slip for the month. At this point, Bhrigav intervened to shout loudly that the people in the time office belonged to the rival union and not updating his leave regularization was just another way of deliberately harassing him. At this point, Bhrigav suddenly grabbed hold of Chandan's collar and threatened him, saying, "I think you are also involved in this game. Your actions always tend to favour the other union. If this thing is not sorted out within two days, there will be hell to pay!" With this Bhrigav stormed out of the room in a huff.

Questions

1. As Anil, what will be your immediate action and why?
2. What skills will Anil need to get to the root of the problem quickly?
3. How will Anil ensure that not only is justice done but also "seen to be done"? Do you think it is important? Why?
4. Why does Bhrigav have a negative opinion of Chandan? What could have led to such an opinion? Do you think Chandan himself was responsible for his image? What could he have done to prevent this?

HR Challenges at Infosys

The globalization is truly globalizing the employment practices in India, like many other functions. The downturn in global economy in 2008 affected the Indian industry in no time. One of the greatest challenges during these times is for the HR or ER professional, when he has to navigate his way through the opposing needs of the business and the employee. Here is an excerpt from an interview given by Nandita Gurjar, Head of HR at Infosys Technologies[5]:

How do priorities for an employee-friendly organization change during a downturn when compared to an upturn?

Whether in good times or downturns, it's never "cool" for HR. There is always enough work, though there are some shifting priorities. As an organization, employees are our utmost concern and at Infosys, during a downturn or an upturn, the larger realities remain the same; i.e., keeping the employee engaged. The focus is now shifting from recruitment to allocation of benched employees and ensuring that they are not on the bench for too long.

What are the new HR strategies aimed at coming to terms with the situation?

Instead of reacting in a knee-jerk fashion to what business wants, we are of the opinion that the principle of HR cannot change. We are not a hiring and firing organization. The management has come up with the philosophy of keeping the flock together for the next two years. We should also ensure that people who stay back don't feel like trapped employees.

1. What should be the soft-skill requirement for an ER manager during such downturns?
2. Can you use the "framework" to map out a few of the soft skills required during such times?

NOTES

1 Glenn P. Costin, Legitimate Subjective Observation [LSO]: The Evaluation of Soft Skills in the Workplace: A Concurrent Session Briefing Paper The National Training Framework - Training Partnerships and Regional Development, Albury Convention Centre and Performing Arts Centre, May 2002, http://www.dsf.org.au//papers/93/SoftSkills

2 Daniel Goleman, *Working with Emotional Intelligence* (<place of publication?>: Bantam Books, <date of publication?>).

3 Adapted from Daniel Goleman, *Emotional Intelligence: Why It Can Matter More Than IQ* (London: Bloomsbury Publishing Plc, 1996), p. 43.

4 Yvonne Stys and Shelley L. Brown, "A Review of the Emotional Intelligence Literature and Implications for Corrections", Research Branch Correctional Service of Canada, March 2004, p. 15 (http://www.csc-scc.gc.ca/text/rsrch/reports/r150/r150_e.pdf).

5 Excerpted from an interview with Nandita Gurjar, "Managing Employee Psyche Tough in a Slowdown", *The Hindu Businessline,* 23 March 2009.

SUGGESTED READING

1 Goleman, Daniel, *Emotional Intelligence: Why It Can Matter More Than IQ* (London: Bloomsbury Publishing Plc, 1996).

2 Stys, Yvonne and Shelley L. Brown, "Literature and Implications for Corrections", Research Branch Correctional Service of Canada, March 2004.

glossary

A

AFL-CIO: The American Federation of Labour and the Congress of Industrial Organizations, commonly the AFL-CIO, is a national trade union centre. It is the largest federation of unions in the United States. It was formed in 1955 with the merger of two large federations named the AFL and the CIO.

Agency Shop: A shop that requires non-union workers to pay a fee to the union for its services in negotiating their contract.

AITUC: The All India Trade Union Congress is the oldest trade union federation in India. At the time of its founding in 1920, it was affiliated to the Indian National Congress. Later (1947), the Indian National Congress formed its own trade union federation. AITUC is now affiliated to the Communist Party of India. It is a central trade union.

Allocable Surplus (Payment of Bonus Act, 1965): Allocable surplus is an amount equivalent to 60 per cent or 67 per cent of the available surplus. It is 67 per cent in case of non-banking companies which do not have provisions for payment of dividends out of their profit in India. For all other companies, it is 60 per cent.

Approach: The "approach" attitude to resolving conflicts means we would like to resolve the conflict (or problem) by approaching the problem and solving it.

Appropriate Government: Many acts refer to the term *appropriate government*. The term denotes the jurisdiction of a particular government in relation to the various provisions of the Act. For example, the "appropriate government" for dealing with Industrial Disputes under the ID Act would be the central government in case of a mine.

Automation: It is the use of control systems or computers used to control industrial machinery or processes replacing human operators. Automation greatly reduces the need for human sensory and mental requirements.

Available Surplus (Payment of Bonus Act, 1965): From the gross profit calculated through Section 4, certain specified sums are to be deducted as prior charges. These prior charges are mentioned in Section 6 of the Act; for example, depreciation as permissible under the Income Tax Act, development rebate or allowance that the employer is entitled to deduct from his income under the Income Tax Act, any direct tax liability within the provisions of Section 7 or any other amount specified in Schedule 3.

Avoidance: The "avoidance" approach is based on fear and conflict is sought to be resolved more often than not by avoiding the conflict situation.

B

Bharatiya Mazdoor Sangh: The Bharatiya Mazdoor Sangh is a CTU organization. Although it claims to be an apolitical organization, there appears to be a strong influence of the RSS/BJP ideology.

Board of Conciliation: A tripartite ad hoc body appointed by the appropriate government for promoting the settlement of disputes where the conciliation officer fails to do so within 14 days. The Conciliation Board consists of a chairman and two to four other members nominated by the parties to the dispute.

Bonus: In common parlance, bonus is regarded as an ex gratia payment made by the employer to his workers to provide encouragement for the extra effort by them in the production process. Sometimes, it also represents a desire of the management to share its gains with the workers, who are vital to the production process and who contribute to the income and profits of the enterprise.

Business Theory of Unions: This was proposed by Samuel Gompers. According to this, the primary objective of the union is to protect the economic interest of the workers.

C

Central Trade-union Organizations: A central trade-union (CTU) organization may be defined as a federation of trade unions. Its strength is the combined membership of all registered unions is taken into account and to qualify as a CTU, the activities must be spread over at least 4 states and in 4 industries and have a combined membership of 500,000. Verification of membership is done by the central government, once in 4 years.

Chaebol: A South Korean term for a conglomerate of many companies clustered around one parent company. The companies usually hold shares in each other and are often run by one family. They also have strong ties with the government in power.

Check-off: This refers to the situation when the employer deducts union dues from pay and hands over the same to the union.

CITU: The Centre for Indian Trade Unions is a CTU with political links with the Communist Party of India (Marxist).

Closed Shop: An organization that employs only those people who are already union members directly from the union.

Closure (ID Act, 1947): The permanent closing down of an industrial establishment.

Collective Bargaining: A process where the collective of employees, through their representatives, bargain with the employer for having their demands met.

Committee Procedure (for fixing and revising minimum wages according to the Minimum Wages Act): The appropriate government may appoint a committee comprising representatives of employers and employees and independent members (not exceeding 1/3 of the committee's strength). The recommendations of the committee are published in the official gazette and come into effect after expiry of three months.

Compulsory Arbitration: When the concerned parties are required to accept arbitration without any willingness on their part. Within the context of the ID Act, 1947, compulsory arbitration amounts to adjudication.

Conciliation Officers: Appointed permanently or for a limited period, for a specific area or for a specific industry, to whom the industrial disputes are referred to by the appropriate government.

Confinement: Labour resulting in the issue of a living child, or labour after 26 weeks of pregnancy resulting in the issue of a child whether alive or dead.

Conflict Approach: An approach that assumes conflict to be inherent in organizations and, managing an organization assumes managing such conflicts. Pluralism and social action are two important sub-categories within the conflict approach.

Conflict: When two persons (or groups) look at an issue from their own perspectives (because of a large number of reasons, ranging from inadequate communication, roles, organizational structure, personality, different emotional states, etc.) and the there is a difference in the two perspectives, then there is an existence of a "potential" conflict situation. Actual conflict may not have surfaced at this stage, but the conditions for one arising are there. The moment one person (or group) acknowledges that the difference in perception of the other person (or group) is going to negatively affect the interests of the first person (or group), a conflict surfaces.

Continuous Service: For the purpose of eligibility for payment of gratuity under the Payment of Gratuity Act, an employee is said be in continuous service if they, for a period of time, have been in uninterrupted service, including service that may be interrupted on account of sickness, accident, leave, absence from duty without leave, etc.

Contract Labour: A workman is deemed to be employed as "contract labour" in or in relation to the work of the establishment, if they are hired for such work by or through a contractor, with or without the knowledge of the principal employer.

Contribution: The sum of money payable to the Corporation by the principal employer in respect of an employee and includes any amount payable by or on behalf of the employee in accordance with the provisions of the ESI Act.

Contributions Period and Benefit Period: Workers, covered under the ESI Act, are required to contribute towards the ESI scheme on a monthly basis. Contribution period means a six-month time span from 1 April to 30 September and 1 October to 31 March. Thus, in a financial year, there are two contribution periods of six months' duration. Cash benefits under the scheme are generally linked to the contribution paid. The benefit period starts three months after the closure of a contribution period.

Craft Union: A trade union that comprises workers who are engaged in a particular craft or skill but who are not all working for the same employer, e.g. Welder's Union, Cabin Crew Association.

D

Deductions from Wages (Payment of Wages Act, 1936): The Act prohibits all kinds of deductions except those that are authorized by or under the Act (Section 7). Authorized deductions include fine, deduction for amenities and services supplied by the employer, advances paid, over-payment of wages, loan, granted for house-building or other purposes, income tax payable, in pursuance of the order of the court, provident fund contributions, cooperative societies, premium for life insurance, contribution to any fund constituted by employer or a trade union, recovery of losses, ESI contribution, etc.

Direct Action: Pressure tactics used by unions, e.g. strikes and agitations, in order to have their demands met.

Disablement: Under the Workmen's Compensation Act, disablement determines the extent of compensation that can be claimed by the worker injured in the course of his employment. Under the Act, there are four types of eventualities that can be compensated—death, permanent total disablement, permanent partial disablement and temporary disablement.

Disintermediation: In the current context, it means the removal of an employee's role between the customer and the product or service. ATMs, for example, enable the customer to avail of the service without going through a bank teller.

Disputes of Interest: These relate to claims by employees or proposals by a management about the terms and conditions of employment. These are mostly disputes that can be resolved through discussions and negotiations, give and take. However, in the event of a dispute not getting resolved through negotiation, these too may be left for resolution through arbitration/adjudication.

Disputes of Rights: These relate to the application or interpretation of an existing agreement or contract of employment. This kind of dispute, if unresolved through negotiations, is very amenable to resolution through arbitration or adjudication.

Disputes Relating to Discipline: These arise from acts of interference either with the exercise of right to organize or with acts termed as "unfair labour practices".

Distributive Bargaining: A kind of bargaining where the gain of one party is at the cost of the other party. The "share in the pie" is to be distributed between the bargaining parties.

E

Emotional Intelligence: Consists of abilities such as being able to motivate one and persist in the face of frustrations; to control impulses and delay gratification; to regulate one's moods and keep distress from swamping the ability to think; to empathize and to hope.

Employee Empowerment: A strategy and philosophy that enables employees to make decisions about their jobs. Employee empowerment helps employees own their work and take responsibility for their results.

Employee Engagement: A combination of commitment to the organization and its values plus a willingness to help out colleagues (organizational citizenship). It goes beyond job satisfaction and is not simply motivation. Engagement is something the employee has to offer: it cannot be "required" as part of the employment contract.

Employee Involvement: Creating an environment in which people have an impact on decisions and actions that affect their jobs. Employee involvement is not the goal nor is it a tool, as practised in many organizations. Rather, employee involvement is a management and leadership philosophy about how people are most enabled to contribute to continuous improvement and the ongoing success of their work organization.

Employee Participation: Employee participation is part of a process of empowerment in the workplace whereby employees are involved in decision-making processes, rather than simply acting on orders.

Employee Relations: This lays emphasis on the individual employee rather than the workforce as a whole. Its purpose today is to build partnerships between the employer and the employee.

Employees Deposit Linked Insurance (EDLI) Scheme: EDLI provides life-insurance benefits to employees who are members of the Provident Fund Scheme.

Employees' Pension Scheme and Fund: Provides for members to avail of pension on superannuation or retirement and on disablement.

Employees' Provident Fund and Miscellaneous Provisions Act, 1952: The Employees' Provident Funds and Miscellaneous Provisions Act, 1952 was enacted to provide a kind of social security to industrial workers. It purports to be a social measure, inducing employees to save a portion from their present earning for future.

Employees' Provident Fund Scheme: A scheme under the provisions of the EPF & MP Act, 1952. Under this scheme, an account of each contributing member is maintained by the provident fund organization. Interest is calculated on the basis of the rate declared every year by the central government in consultation with the Board of Trustees. The fund with accruing interest becomes payable at the time of superannuation or death.

Employees' State Insurance Act, 1948: The Employees' State Insurance Act, 1948, is a piece of social-welfare legislation enacted primarily with the object of providing certain benefits to employees in case of sickness, maternity and employment injury and also to make provision for certain others matters.

Employers' Organizations: Voluntary bureaucratic institutions that place reliance on specialization (industry or sector) to fulfil organization objectives.

Employment Injury: A personal injury to an employee caused by accident or an occupational disease arising out of and in the course of his/her employment, being an insurable employment, whether the accident occurs or the occupational disease is contracted within or outside the territorial limits of India.

Equity Concept: Based on an ethical stance that all employees should be treated equally, and that the same fundamental terms and conditions of employment are to apply to all.

ESI Corporation: The social-security programme under the ESI Act is administered by a corporate body called the Employees' State Insurance Corporation. It comprises members representing interest groups that include employee, employers, the central and state government, besides representatives of parliament and the medical profession.

F

Factory: As defined in the Factories Act, 1948, a "factory" means any premises (i) wherein 10 or more workers are working, or were working on any day of the preceding 12 months, and in any part of which manufacturing process is being carried on with the aid of power or (ii) wherein 20 or more workers are working, or were working on any day of the preceding twelve months, and in any part of which manufacturing process is being carried out without the aid of power but does not include a mine subject to the operation of The Mines Act, 1952, or mobile unit of armed forces, a railway running shed or a hotel, restaurant or eating place.

Fair Wage: A level of wage somewhere between minimum and living wages.

Flexibility Concept: According to the concept of the "flexible workforce", where everyone concerned is trained to be available for any work that the organization may require of them.

G

Globalization: It refers to economic integration of national economies into the international economy through trade, foreign direct investment, capital flows, migration, and the spread of technology.

Gratuity: A lump sum payment made by the employer as a mark of recognition of the service rendered by the employee when he retires or leaves service.

Grievance Disputes: Arising from day-to-day workers' grievance or complaints.

H

Hazardous Process: Defined in Section 2(cb) of the Factories Act, 1948, it implies such processes that may be carried out in an industry specified in Schedule 1 of the Act and the process may cause one of the following two (or both):

i. Cause material impairment to the health of the persons engaged in or connected with it
ii. Result in pollution of the general environment

HMS: The Hind Mazdoor Sabha is a CTU organization with no apparent political affiliation. It was initially formed with socialist leanings.

Human Capital: Human resource deployed in productive work.

I

ILO Conventions: An instrument through which the ILO sets the International Labour Standards. These are matters pertaining to conditions of conditions of labour and employment and are adopted in the International Labour Conference. Once adopted and ratified by the member countries, conventions take the form of international treaty and becomes enforceable.

ILO Recommendations: Also adopted by the International Labour Conference, recommendations too are instruments for setting International Labour Standards. However, as the name suggests, these are only recommendatory in nature.

Industrial Action: Industrial action is a term that has not been defined in any of the industrial laws but it means action that may follow if disputes of conflicts cannot be resolved through negotiations. "Strikes" and "lockouts" are forms of industrial action.

Industrial Democracy: This approach compares democracy in the government (wherein the "state" is prevented from inflicting injury to individual citizens by means of elected representatives and people's power) to an industrial setting where, through unions, the workers protect themselves from the power and influence of the owners, as the individual workers are no match for the owners in these aspects.

Industrial Dispute: Has been defined under the Industrial Disputes Act, 1947. Stated simply, it is à dispute between the employer and (a group of) employees on matters relating to employment or conditions of employment. The ID Act also includes disputes between employees and employees, or employers and employers, which are also considered industrial disputes.

Industrial Disputes Act, 1947: One of the most important pieces of legislations, it concerns itself, in the main, in providing for prevention and settlement of industrial disputes between employers and employees, employees and employees and employers and employers.

Industrial Relations: Looks at the relationship between the management and the workers, particularly groups of workers represented by a union. Its purpose is to maintain industrial peace.

Industrial Tribunals: The tribunals appointed by the appropriate government for adjudication in matters listed in Schedule 3 prescribed under the ID Act, which affect the working of a company or an industry.

Industry Union: In this form of organization, workers in the same industry are organized into the same union, irrespective of their skills.

Insurable Employment: An employment in a factory or establishment to which the ESI Act applies.

Insured Person: A person who is or was an employee in respect of whom contributions are or were payable under this Act and who is, by reason thereof, entitled to any benefit under the ESIC Scheme.

Integrative Bargaining: It is a kind of joint problem solving where both parties try to arrive at a solution that is mutually satisfying. The effort is to find novel solution, maybe increase the size of the pie itself.

International Labour Conference: The policy-making and legislative body of the ILO. It is here that the conventions and recommendations are finally adopted. In the ILC, each member state is represented by the government's, the employers' and the employees' delegates in the ratio of 2:1:1.

International Labour Office: The permanent secretariat of the International Labour Organization. It is headed by a Director General, who also functions as the Secretary General of the International Labour Conference.

International Labour Organization: An international tripartite body founded in 1919 in the aftermath of World War I (as a part of Treaty of Versailles, to end WW I). The main aim of ILO was to promote the conditions of labour throughout the world.

INTUC: Indian Trade Union Congress is the trade-union wing of the Indian National Congress. It is a CTU.

J

Job Evaluation: A scientific method to determine the "relative" worth of a job in comparison to other jobs within an organization. Job evaluation helps establish internal equity within the organization, also enabling inter-organization comparisons.

L

Labour Administration: Involves the formulation of labour policy and the enforcement of labour laws for the promotion of labour welfare.

Labour Courts: Constituted by the appropriate government for adjudication on industrial disputes relating to any matter specified in Schedule 2 of the ID Act.

Labour Legislation: Under the Constitution, the legislative powers in different fields of government activity are shared by the central and state governments, in accordance with the lists that form a part of the Constitution—the Union list, the Concurrent List and the State List. The parliament has exclusive powers to make laws on matters enumerated in the Union List. The state legislatures have powers to legislate for the state or any part thereof on any matter enumerated in the State List. Both the parliament and the state legislatures have powers to make laws with respect to matters enumerated in the Concurrent List. To avoid a possible conflict, certain safeguards are provided for subjects on which both centre and state can legislate. Labour is a subject that is included in the Concurrent List.

Labour Policy: Includes the treatment of labour under constitutional, legislative and administrative Acts, rules and practices, and various precepts laid down in the successive Five Year Plans.

Lay-off (ID Act, 1947): The failure, refusal or inability of an employer, on account of shortage of coal, power or raw materials or the accumulation of stocks or the break-down of machinery or natural calamity or for any other connected reason, to give employment to a workman whose name is borne on the muster rolls of his industrial establishment and who has not been retrenched.

Living Wage: Enables the employee to provide for himself/herself and his/her family, education to children, protection against ill health, essential social needs, insurance against misfortunes, including old age, in addition to the basic sustenance needs. The upper limit should take the capacity to pay into consideration.

Managerial Trade Unionism: A trend whereby the managers in an establishment have organised themselves along the lines of trade unions for the purpose of bargaining with the management. This trend started mainly in the large PSUs and a few large private sector establishments.

Manufacturing Process: It has a precise meaning under the Factories Act, 1948 where it has been defined under section 2(k) as any process for:

- Making, altering, repairing, ornamenting, finishing, packing, oiling, washing, cleaning, breaking-up, demolishing, or otherwise treating or adapting any article or substance with a view to its use, sale, transport, delivery or disposal; or
- Pumping oil, water sewage or any other substance; or
- Generating, transforming or transmitting power; or
- Composing types of printing letter press, lithography, photogravure or other similar process or book-binding; or
- Constructing, reconstructing, repairing or refitting, finishing or breaking-up of ships or vessels; or
- Preserving or restoring any article in the cold storage.

Maternity Benefit Act, 1961: The Maternity Benefit Act of 1961 was, passed to provide uniform maternity benefit for women workers in certain industries not covered by the Employees' State Insurance Act, 1948.

Maternity Benefit: Every woman shall be entitled to, and her employer shall be liable for, the payment of maternity benefit, which is the amount payable to her at the rate of the average daily wage for the period of her actual absence.

Maximum Bonus (Payment of Bonus Act, 1965): Where the allocable surplus in an accounting year exceeds the minimum amount to be paid as bonus, the employer is bound to pay an amount in proportion to the salary or wage earned by the employee subject to a maximum of 20 per cent of such salary or wage.

Minimum (Payment of Bonus Act, 1965): A minimum of 8.33 per cent of the annual salary or wages or INR 100, whichever is higher, is to be paid as bonus.

Minimum Wage: The Minimum Wages Act lays down the mechanism for determination of minimum wages for all kinds of employment. The concept of minimum wage in India was outlined in a recommendation of a tripartite committee on fair wages set up in 1948. As per the Act, the government notifies the minimum wages in different kinds of employment.

Mode of Payment (Payment of Wages Act, 1936): Wages must be paid in current coin or currency notes or in both and not in kind. It is, however, permissible for an employer to pay wages by cheque or by crediting them in the bank account if so authorized in writing by an employed person.

Mutual Insurance: In exchange for the fees that the members pay to the union, the union renders certain services, which are more functional in nature.

National Tribunals: Meant for those disputes that involve the questions of national importance or issues that are likely to affect the industrial establishments of more than one state.

Negotiation: A way to resolve issues without resorting to actions that hurt or destroy relationships.

Neo-Unitary Approach: A variant of the Unitary Approach, Neo-Unitary Approach, appears to have emerged in some organizations since the 1980s. It builds on existing unitary concepts but is more sophisticated in the ways it is articulated and applied within enterprises. Its main aim seems to be to integrate employees, as individuals, into the companies in which they work

Notification Procedure (for fixing and revising minimum wages according to the Minimum Wages Act): In this procedure, the government notifies the proposed revision in the official gazette. A minimum of two months' period is provided for persons likely to be affected by the proposal to react and send their representations. The government should also consult the Advisory Board.

Occupational Disease: An occupational disease while in service, is a disease that inflicts workers in that particular occupation in which s/he was employed, resulting from exposure to a hazardous working atmosphere, particular to that employment. If a worker contracts such a disease, then the employer is liable to pay compensation, provided that the worker was employed by him for a continuous period of six months.

Occupier: As defined in the Factories Act, it means a person who has the ultimate control of the factory.

Open Shop: An organization that does not discriminate based on union membership in employing or keeping workers. Where a union is active, the open shop allows workers to be employed who do not contribute to a union or the collective bargaining process.

Organized Labour: In the context of industrial relations, organized labour would comprise employees under enterprise/ industry/organizations to which most of the labour laws apply.

Overtime: No adult worker shall be required or allowed to work in a factory for more than nine hours in any day or for more than forty-eight hours in a week. Work in excess of that shall be treated as overtime. Where a worker works in a factory for more than nine hours in any day or for more than forty-eight hours in any week, he shall, in respect of overtime work, be entitled to wages at the rate of twice his ordinary rate of wages.

P

Participation Rate: The proportion of people in the labour force out of total cohort population.

Pay Day (Payment of Wages Act, 1936): Wages must be paid on a working day and not on a holiday. When there are less than 1,000 persons employed, the wages shall be paid before the expiry of the seventh day of the following month. When there are more than 1,000 workers, the wages are to be paid before the expiry of the 10th day of the following month.

Permanent Partial Disablement: Disablement that reduces the capacity to work in any employment similar to that the worker was performing at the time of the accident.

Permanent Total Disablement: Disablement that incapacitates a worker from all kinds of work.

Philadelphia Declaration: The objectives of the ILO were further refined by way of a conference held in the year 1944 at Philadelphia. The outcome of the Philadelphia conference was later incorporated in the Constitution of the ILO as the Philadelphia Declaration.

Picketing: The action taken by unionists to prevent willing employees from attending work after a strike has been called. This activity is usually carried out at the gate or entrance but may also be done at any other location near or far from the factory or a section of it.

Pluralism: The existence of more than one ruling principle. The pluralist approach to IR accepts conflict as inevitable but containable through various institutional arrangements.

Post-capitalist Society: An open society in which political, economic and social power is increasingly dispersed and in which the regulation of industrial and political conflict are of necessity dissociated.

Preferential Union Shop: Wherein additional recognition by agreement is accorded by the management to give first chance to union members in recruitment.

Premises and Precincts: It is a term used in the definition of "factory" under the Factories Act, 1948. Though not spelt out clearly in the Act itself, through various interpretations under judicial rulings, premises corresponds to building whereas precincts correspond to a delineated area.

Preventive Machinery: Has not been defined anywhere in any Act. However, it comprises: (i) provisions in law that reduce the scope of conflict (health, safety, wages, etc.); (ii) institutions that provide for periodic and structured consultations (Indian Labour Conference, Standing Labour Committee, Industrial Committees, Works Committee, etc.); (iii) pre-emptive procedures and systems (grievance, standing orders, etc.); and (iv) voluntary codes (Code of Discipline).

Principal Employer: The manager or occupier of a factory or head of the department of a government/local authority who employ contract labour.

Psychological Contract: Represents the mutual beliefs, perceptions, and informal obligations between an employer and an employee. It sets the dynamics for the relationship and defines the detailed practicality of the work to be done. It is distinguishable from the formal written contract of employment, which, for the most part, only identifies mutual duties and responsibilities in a generalized form.

R

Radical Approach: Mainly Marxist, wherein industrial conflict is an inevitable but small part of class struggle between labour and capital or the proletariat and the bourgeoisie. Industrial conflict and organized labour are but a means for larger transformation.

Radicalism: Views commercial and industrial harmony as impossible until the labour controls the means of production, and benefit from the generation of wealth.

Ratification: Once adopted at the International Labour Conference, the member states need it to be submitted to their competent authority for ratification (the parliament in our case). Ratification makes it a legally binding document and thereafter the member states have to create suitable legal provisions to enforce the convention.

Rationalization (of manpower): Strictly, it means bringing the manpower requirements of a firm to optimum levels. In practice, however, it largely means measures to reduce redundant manpower through redeployment, voluntary separation schemes, outsourcing, etc.

Recognition Disputes: Disputes over the right of a trade union to represent a particular class or category of workers for purposes of collective bargaining.

Recognition (of a trade union): A trade union may be recognised (by the management) as representing the body of employees in the whole establishment provided it has a majority of employees supporting it. There is no central legislation for the recognition of trade unions though a few state governments, either through legislation or rules framed for recognition, have provision for recognition of a union based on membership verification.

Reformist Unions: Aim at the preservation of the capitalist economic structure through the maintenance of employer–employee relationship. They do not seek to change the existing social, economic or political structure of the State or the business strategy of the industrial unit.

Registration (of a trade union): Under the Trade Unions Act, 1926, there is provision of registration of Trade Unions with the Registrar of Trade Unions. Any seven or more members of a Trade Union may apply for registration of the Trade Union under this Act by subscribing their names to the rules of the Trade Union and by complying with the provisions of this Act with respect to registration.

Registration under Contract Labour (R&A) Act: Every establishment that intends to employ contract labour, is required to get registration as a Principal Employer from the appropriate government.

Regulatory Union: A union whose main aim is to protect workers' rights. They function on the ideology of economic and social justice, and regulate any decision or policy that violates the "rights" of workers.

Retirement: Termination of the service of an employee other than on superannuation.

Retrenchment (ID Act, 1947): The termination by an employer of the service of a workman for any reason whatsoever, other than as a punishment inflicted by way of disciplinary action. It does not include—voluntary retirement of the workman; or retirement of the workman on reaching the age of superannuation if the contract of employment between the employer and the workman concerned contains a stipulation in that behalf; or termination of the service of the workman as a result of the non-renewal of the contract of employment between the employer and the workman concerned.

Revolutionary Theory: This theory proposes that the means of production must belong to the workers. Trade unions are instruments for a revolution in which the capitalists must be destroyed and the workers (proletariat) must take over the industry and, in turn, the government. Trade unions were a means towards the achievement of a classless society. With this approach, trade unions were regarded as a component in the larger political process for the establishment of a classless society.

Revolutionary Unions: Aim at destroying the present structure and replacing it with a new order that is regarded as preferable to the working class. They could be anarchist or political in nature.

S

Salary: Fixed, regular (usually monthly) payment to an employee.

Set-off: Where, for any accounting year, there is no available surplus, or the allocable surplus in respect of that year falls short of the amount of minimum bonus payable to the employees in the establishment under Section 10 of Payment of Bonus Act, and there is no amount or sufficient amount carried forward and set-on under Sub-section (1), which could be utilized for the purpose of payment of the minimum bonus, then such minimum amount or the deficiency, as the case may be, shall be carried forward for being set-off in the succeeding accounting year and so on up to and inclusive of the fourth accounting year.

Set-on: Where, for any accounting year, the allocable surplus exceeds the amount of maximum bonus payable to the employees in the establishment under Section 11 of the Payment of Bonus Act, the excess shall, subject to a limit of 20 per cent of the total salary or wage of the employees employed in the establishment in that accounting year, be carried forward for being set-on in the succeeding accounting year and so on up to and inclusive of the fourth accounting year to be utilized for the purpose of payment of bonus.

Settlement Machinery: Once an industrial dispute arises, the ID Act (1947) has provisions for three-tier machinery—conciliation, arbitration and adjudication—for the settlement of the dispute.

Shop Stewards: Members who occupy an official position in the union hierarchy and who are also employees of an organization.

Shops and Establishments Act, 1953: These are laws pertaining to conditions of employment of employees in the unorganized sectors mainly. These are "state" government legislations and vary from state to state.

Sickness: A condition that requires medical treatment and attendance and necessitates abstention from work on medical grounds.

Sit-in Strike: Not only work stoppage but also refusal by strikers to vacate the premises.

Social Action Theory: Emphasizes the individual responses of the social actors, such as managers, employees and union representatives to given situations, focusing on understanding particular actions in industrial relations situations rather than on just observing explicit industrial relations behaviour. This contrasts with systems theory, which regards behaviour in industrial relations as reflecting the impersonal processes external to the system's social actors over which they have little or no control.

Social Security: Social security, in the context of employment relations aims at access to health care and income security, in cases of old age, loss of employment, sickness, disability, work injury, maternity or loss of a main income earner.

Socio-psychological Theory: Proposes that members join a Union primarily for meeting their socio-psychological needs like security, esteem, companionship, etc.

Soft Skills: Skills by which the individual interacts with, interprets, structures, coordinates or otherwise informs the social and physical environments within which physical, societal and/or personal product may be generated.

Sole Bargaining Agent: A provision making it binding for a recognized union alone to bargain on behalf of all the employees.

Spread-over: The periods of work of an adult worker in a factory shall be so arranged that inclusive of his intervals for rest, they shall not spread over more than ten and a half hours in any day.

Strike: Refers to a collective refusal to work by the workers with a view to bring pressure on the management to accede to a demand; this is the meaning in its simplest form, although an elaborate definition has been given in the Industrial Disputes Act, 1947

Subsistence Worker/Employment: Subsistence workers are those who hold a self-employment job, and in this capacity, produce goods or services that are predominantly consumed by their own household, and constitute an important basis for its livelihood.

Superannuation: In relation to an employee, it means the attainment by the employee of such age as is fixed in the contract or conditions of service at the attainment of which the employee shall vacate the employment.

Systems Model: An industrial relations system, at any one time in its development, is regarded as comprising certain actors, certain contexts, an ideology that binds industrial relations systems together and a body of rules created to govern the actors at the workplace and work community.

T

Temporary Disablement: This may be total or partial disablement, of temporary nature, which reduces the earning capacity of the worker in any similar employment for the period of disablement.

Terminal Wage (Payment of Wages Act, 1936): When the employment of any person is terminated, the wages earned by him must be paid before the expiry of the second working day from the day of termination.

Thatcherism: Margaret Thatcher's political and economic philosophy of reduced state intervention, free markets, and entrepreneurialism.

The Contract Labour (Regulation and Abolition) Act, 1970: Seeks to regulate the employment of contract labour in certain establishments and to provide for its abolition under certain circumstances.

The Factories Act, 1948: Is an Act that consolidates all laws regulating labour in factories with the aim of protecting workers employed in factories against industrial and occupational hazards.

The Governing Body: Is the executive body of the International Labour Office (please note that International Labour Office is one of the sub-systems of the International Labour Organization). The Governing Body oversees the functioning of the Labour Organization. The Governing Body: a) decides the agenda of the International Labour Conference; b) helps finalize the draft of Works Programme and Budget of the ILO for submission to the ILC; and c) Elects the Director-General (of the International Labour Office).

The Minimum Wages Act, 1948: The Minimum Wages Act aims at establishing a mechanism for fixing minimum wage rates in various kinds of employments.

The Payment of Bonus Act, 1965: The object of the Payment of Bonus Act aims to impose statutory liability upon the employer to bonus to the employees and goes on to define the principles of payment of bonus.

The Payment of Gratuity Act, 1972: It is a beneficent piece of social-security legislation that aims at providing a scheme for providing gratuity to employees engaged in factories, mines, oil fields, plantations, ports, railways, shops and other establishments. The gratuity was to be paid in the event of superannuation, retirement, resignation, death or total disablement due to accident or disease.

The Payment of Wages Act, 1936: The Payment of Wages Act, 1936 was enacted to regulate the payment of wages to workers employed in industries and to ensure a speedy and effective remedy against illegal deductions and/or unjustified delay caused in the payment of wages to them. The Payment of Wages Act, 1936 is a central legislation, which applies to the persons employed in factories, industries and other establishments.

The Standing Orders Act, 1946: An act that purports to statutorily lay down the conditions of employment of industrial employees. It also provides for the process for laying down and certifying these conditions of work known as "Standing Orders".

Trade Union Congress: A federation of trade unions in the United Kingdom, representing the majority of trade unions.

Trade Unions: Are associations of workers united as a single, representative entity for the purpose of improving the workers' economic status and working conditions through collective bargaining with employers.

Tripartism: Consultations involving the three actors of industrial relations, namely, the employer, the employee and the State with a view to having a consensual approach on issues affecting the three parties.

Tripartite Bodies: All bodies that have representation from employees, employers and the government.

Trusteeship: An approach to industrial relations credited mainly to Mahatma Gandhi. A business enterprise has the inherent responsibility to its consumers, workers, shareholders and the community. The responsibilities are mutual. A business enterprise is meant for good for all and not just for profits. The enterprise, in effect, must act as trustee to the interests of all. According to Gandhi, conflicts are inevitable in an industrializing society, but labour and capital must learn to peacefully coexist for mutual benefit and for the community at large.

U

Union Security: Comprises the tools and methods that trade unions use to keep "free riders" from enjoying the benefits of collective bargaining by the unions. It usually takes the form of an agreement between the union and the employer about the extent to which Union may force membership or to collect dues and fees from the members.

Union Shop: Employs non-union workers as well, but sets a time limit within which new employees must join a union.

Unitarism: Assumes that the objectives of all involved are the same or compatible, and concerned only with the well-being of the organization and its products, services, clients and customers.

Unitary Approach: An approach to IR that advocates every work organization is an integrated and harmonious whole, existing for a common purpose. That the labour and management are working towards a common objective.

Unorganized Labour: In the context of Industrial Relations, unorganized labour would comprise labour to which most of the labour laws do not apply and also who lack any kind of formal representative body.

V

Voluntary Arbitration: A choice made by the contending parties for arbitration, before referring it for adjudication.

Wage Board: A tripartite body, which has representation of employers and labour besides independent members. It was envisaged as machinery for wage fixation in specified industries, and also as a means for implementing many wage-related policies and principles laid down by the various committees and commissions.

Wage Period (Payment of Wages Act, 1936): The period to be fixed for paying wages to an employed person must not exceed one month. That means an employer can choose to pay wages to a person employed by him for a period of every week or every fortnight, but not for a period of every two months or every three months.

Wage Structure: Signifies the relationship of wage rates for the entire job within the company, industry or labour market areas.

Wage: Regular payment to an employee for his or her work. Wage is basically the price that an organization is willing to pay for having a particular job carried out as also the price at which an employee is willing to sell his/her labour.

Wages: Usually means compensation in exchange of labour. The compensation though mostly financial, need not necessarily be so. *Different* labour legislations have defined "wages" differently. Under the Payment of Wages Act, 1936, the term *wages* means all remuneration (whether by way of salary, allowances or otherwise) expressed in terms of money or capable of being so expressed, which would, if the terms of employment express or implied were fulfilled, be payable to a person employed in respect of his employment or of work done in such employment.

Weekly Holiday: No adult worker shall be required or allowed to work in a factory on the first day of the week (Sunday) unless given a full day's holiday on one of the three days immediately before or after the said day. This section also specifies that this substitution should not result in any worker working for more than ten days consecutively without a holiday for a whole day.

Wildcat Strike or Walk-Out: Usually by a small section of workers who may defy even their own union leaders, and could be in response to a small shop-floor issue or an argument between a manager and a single employee.

Worker: Defined under the Factories Act, 1948, *worker* means a person employed, directly or through any agency (including a contractor) with or without the knowledge of the principal employer, whether for remuneration or not, in any manufacturing process, or in cleaning any part of the machinery or premises used for a manufacturing process, or the subject of the manufacturing process but does not include any member of the armed forces of the union.

Workers Participation in Management: An approach to involve the participation of workers in the management of the industrial unit through making effective use of workers' committees, joint consultation and other methods. This may improve communication between managers and workers, which may, in the long run, increase productivity and lead to greater effectiveness.

Workers' Organizations: Institutions or/and associations of employees formed and maintained for the specific purpose of negotiating concessions and benefits from the employers.

Work-in Strike: The workers do not stop work but continue the production in defiance of management, who may have stopped production or declared a closure. It is thus the opposite of a usual strike—not a withdrawal of work but a continuation of work to defy management.

Workmen's Compensation Act, 1923: The Workmen's Compensation Act is the first piece of legislation towards social security. It deals with compensation for workers who are injured or contract occupational disease in the course of duty.

Workmen's Compensation: Provides cover for medical care and compensation for employees who are injured in the course of employment, in exchange for mandatory relinquishment of the employee's right to sue his or her employer for negligence at workplace.

Work-to-Rule and Go-Slow: Under these methods, unions may not officially stop work but work only at a slower pace or specifically refuse to do certain tasks, which have the effect of reducing the total output, or disrupting the work process.

EMPLOYEE RELATIONS MANAGEMENT

P. N. Singh & Neeraj Kumar

PART I: CONTEXT

Chapter 1: Industrial Relations: Evolution and Growth

- The term *industrial relations* is generally associated with relations between the employer and the employee in a unit or industry.
- Mass production post industrial revolution, coupled with a laissez faire approach led to employers adopting a mechanistic approach to work and labour as a commodity and a factor of production
- Trade unions emerged out of a necessity to restore some balance in the relationship between powerful capital and weak labour.
- Conflicting interests and ideological orientations conveyed an adversarial and strife-torn relationship.
- The State sought to gain the cooperation of the two partners in industry supporting economic growth and development through an improvement in the quality of work life.

A **definition** of IR must take the following into account:
- IR is about relationships.
- The origin is in the relationship of employment.
- Employer–employee relationship pertains to all kinds of organizations.
- There are actors other than the employer and the employees who influence the relationship.
- The relationships are shaped by the actors, structures, rules, law, technology, etc.
- The impact of social, economic, political and technological features of the context on the shaping of these relationships.

Scope of IR
- Management–union relationship
- Employer–employee relationship
- Relationships amongst various groups of employees
- Effects of extraneous factors (State, socio-political-economic factors) on workplace relationships

Objectives of IR will be different at enterprise/unit, industry and national levels.

Features of IR
- Arises out of an employment relationship
- Sets complex rules and regulations for the participants to ensure industrial peace and harmony
- Hinges on a cooperative spirit between all partners
- Comprise employees and their organizations, employers and their associations, and the government as participants.

The **maintenance of sound IR** needs
- Strong, well-organized and democratic unions for balance of power
- Strong employers' organization
- Belief in cooperative collective bargaining
- Sound HR policies
- Sound preventive systems
- Management support to IR function
- Well-trained IR staff/supervisors
- Systematic effort at building a collaborative culture

Approaches to IR
- The unitary approach
- The systems approach
- The conflict approach
- Weber's social action approach
- The Gandhian approach

Chapter 2: Industrial Relations in India

Forces shaping the IR system in India
- The colonial history
- The government's role in IR—preventive and regulatory
- India being a founder member of ILO
- The political movement for Freedom and labour participation
- "Worker-centric" State policies
- The protection of domestic industries—import substitution
- Multiplicity of TUs and political affiliation of TUs
- Labour in concurrent list

Basic characteristics of the IR system in India
- Overall control through the regulatory provisions
- Regulated primarily through legislations
- Though the laws promulgated are extensive, they are confounded with serious ambiguities and gaps.
- Unionization largely restricted to organized sector
- Most unions have political affiliations.
- Multiplicity of unions and external leadership.
- State intervention has continued to prevail since the time of Independence, although in the last decade, it has shown a declining trend.
- Marked difference in the labour management relations in i) different states, ii) organized and unorganized sectors, iii) public and private enterprises, and iv) multinationals and domestic companies
- There is no national IR policy.
- Collective bargaining is more a matter of optional practice with no statutory backing.
- The changes brought in by the new economic policy have resulted in changes in the IR structure.
- The heterogeneity of the emerging workforce has made it difficult to establish standards or uniform IR practices in the Indian industry.

Tripartism: Consultations amongst the three actors of IR namely employer, employee and the State, has since the beginning years, has been a cornerstone of the IR Policy in India. To give shape to this element of policy, a number of bodies and for a were created. Tripartism, therefore, is an important feature of the IR System and Policy in India.

Important tripartite bodies in India
- Indian Labour Conference (ILC)

STUDY CARD ISBN 978-81-317-2601-3

- Standing Labour Committee (SLC)
- Committee on Conventions
- The Industrial Committees

India and the ILO: India is one of the founding members of the ILO. The ILO activities have impacted IR in India in two important ways:

- Ratification of the ILO conventions formed the basis for many labour legislations
- The requirement of the ILO to have representation from non-government delegates helped to organize the employee and employer groups

Core conventions of the ILO: The ILO has made a total of eight conventions as Core Conventions or Human Rights Conventions. India has ratified four of these conventions, namely

- Forced Labour Convention (No. 29)
- Equal Remuneration Convention (No. 100)
- Abolition of Forced Labour Convention (No. 105)
- Discrimination (Employment Occupation) Convention (No. 111)

Phases of IR in India since Independence

- The protective phase (1947–56)
- The consolidation phase (1956–65)
- The conflict-ridden phase (1965–1977)
- The directionless phase (1977–80)
- The productivity-, efficiency-, quality-orientation phase (1981–90)
- The competitive phase (post 1990)

Chapter 3: Industrial Relations in Major Industrialized Economies: A Comparative Study

- In most industrialized countries, the initial primary goal of the IR system was to maintain labour peace and, more generally, industrial stability.
- In many countries, the IR system began to be institutionalized only in the post-war period, coinciding with independence for some of the countries.

To appreciate the IR framework in major economies, following factors must be taken into account

- Globalization
- Impact of information technology
- Changing demographic profile of workers
- Restructuring of industrial enterprises
- Emergence of knowledge economies and knowledge workers
- Outsourcing of non-core activities
- Uncertainty in trade union movement

These factors, across the industrialized world, affect

- Decentralization of bargaining
- A movement towards increased flexibility in wages, labour deployment, and workplace practices

IR in the UK

- **Early 20th century:** IR was largely shaped around the challenges of the staple industry. This resulted in an industry-level collective bargaining to take care of the twin problems.
- **Post war period:** In the post war period, bargaining took place more and more at the industry level leaving little scope for bargaining at the enterprise level.
- **Post 1979 and Thatcherism:** The Employment Relations Act (1979) and Margaret Thatcher's economic and political philosophy of reduced state intervention, free market and entrepreneurism were reactions to the era of industrial chaos and strong-arm tactics of the trade unions.

Characteristics of trade unions in Britain

- The tradition of voluntarism
- The representation of workers through trade-union officers at workplaces in the form of shop stewards
- The organization of trade-union membership being on occupational rather than industrial lines

IR in the European Union

- The European Commission has been attempting a pooling of research on the IR structures, processes, laws and practices in member countries with a view to bring in gradual uniformity on larger policy matters pertaining to IR.

Trade unions in the EU

- There is a distinct movement towards trade-union organization at the pan-EU level. Though some diversity prevails at national levels, efforts are on at some sort of integration. The ETUC is a step in that direction.
- Unions in most of the member countries are organized on a sectoral or occupational basis.
- Blue-collar unions are losing influence and the white-collar unions gaining significance.

IR in the USA

IR in the USA parallels the development of trade unions, organized labour and labour legislations, as it does elsewhere.

Legislation: The major pieces of labour legislation governing the relationship issues were

- The Norris La Guardia Act, 1932
- The Wagner Act, 1935
- The Taft Hartley Act, 1947
- The Landrum Griffin Act, 1959

Trade unions in the USA

The American Federation of Labour and Congress of Industrial Organizations, commonly known as the AFL-CIO, is a national trade-union centre. It is the largest federation of unions in the United States. It was formed in 1955 with the merger of two large federations named AFL and CIO.

IR legislations in Australia

- Both Federal and State Governments can legislate on Labour matters in Australia.
- The oldest piece of legislation in Australia is the Conciliation and Arbitration Act, 1904.
- The Conciliation and Arbitration Act, 1904, was replaced by the Industrial Relations Act, 1988. The IR Act, 1988, required the federal trade unions to register themselves with a registrar to be able to take assistance of

the arbitration process and other legal rights fl owing from the Act.

- The most significant instrument of the workplace-relationship-reform process was the Workplace Relations Act 1996 (WR Act) with the objective to the settlement of conflicts and disputes at the workplace itself.

IR in China

- Historically, the main characteristics of the IR system included State ownership of industrial enterprises, the implicit guarantee of employment for workers, centralized wage structure, a rigid labour market with little inter-enterprise or inter-regional mobility, and the absence of price- or efficiency-driven controls over the industry.
- Post 1978, the Chinese system is in a state of ferment, more particularly since 1983.
- The Chinese government enacted a new labour law in 1994 that essentially sought to create a new IR system within the socialist market economy, but the implementation of this law has not been uniform.

IR in Japan

- The Japanese IR system is an institutionalized one and has historically included workplace-focused enterprise unions, lifetime-employment systems, broad-based training, and seniority-based wages.
- One of the key outcomes of the Japanese IR system, is the simultaneous achievement of stability in labour-market terms and considerable functional flexibility in workplace-level IR
- The recession of the 1990s led to the questioning of the lifetime-employment concept, with severe declines in job security on an unprecedented scale.
- There was evidence of a sudden and dramatic increase in outsourcing within Japan, termed "work commissioning".
- This resulted in an increase in wage flexibility, resulting in reducing the power of the trade unions.

IR in South Korea

- Prior to 1990 conflict prevention and conflict avoidance became the stated objective, and all actions purported to achieve that as part of the overall goal of maintaining stability in IR for economic development (e.g., in particular, the government's efforts to control wage costs), and political control.
- Legal changes mandated the formation of enterprise unions, although it was made mandatory for these enterprise unions to be a part of FKTU, a union confederation created under the mandate of the government.
- Competitive forces forced employers to demand restructuring in the IR system.
- The Asian Currency Crisis hastened the process for fundamental changes with tripartite involvement in the policy.
- The IR system in Korea is still in the transition phase.

IR in Singapore

- Singapore's IR system is well known for its distinctive tripartite features, and is considered both functional and flexible.
- The State provided funds and training on development issues so as to lay the foundation for "responsible" unionism.
- To ensure that disputes did not result in strikes, the legislation provided for secret ballots on strikes, a notice period, and withdrawal of strikes once the dispute was under mediation or conciliation proceedings.
- At the workplace level, a few contentious issues that impacted the operational flexibility and efficiency were kept out of the bargaining (transfers, promotions, termination, hiring, etc.). Besides reducing scope for disputes, this also provided to the employer flexibility and substantial control over the operational decisions.

Emerging international trends in IR

- Decline in union membership and union density
- Consolidation and merger of trade unions
- Variations in collective bargaining practices
- A shift in the relationship from the employers' organizations and trade unions to the employer and an individual employee
- Organization restructuring and the emergence of "atypical" forms of employment

Chapter 4 Changing Characteristics of Industry and Workforce in India

Result of changes in technology

- Mechanization
- Automation
- Information-based services
- Disintermediation

This, in turn, is forcing

- Rationalization of manpower
- Labour substitution in the case of automation

Major forces driving industrial change

- Computerization
- Automation
- Rationalization
- Globalization

Effect of industrial change on the labour market

- Changed occupational structure
- Changed nature of work
- Integrated job markets leading to a global occupational structure
- Improved education facilitating economic growth

Participation rate: The proportion of people in the labour force out of total cohort population

- In 1999–2000, 7.32 per cent of the labour force, i.e. 26.58 million, were unemployed.
- A large proportion of those employed are in subsistence employment.
- Only 8 per cent of those employed are in the organized sector.
- The education and the skill profile of the current work force is poor.

Main changes in labour demographics

- The decline in participation rates across age groups
- The entry of the younger age groups into the labour force

- More active participation of older people in the labour force
- A reduction in differentials between male and female participation
- Relatively low education and skill levels
- An attitudinal change towards technical and vocational courses

Major trends in the unorganized sector

- Ninety-three per cent of employees in the unorganized sector
- The absence of an institutionalized IR system
- Labor regulations not for smaller establishments
- Social security out of reach
- The absence of unions does not provide any opportunity for collective bargaining.

Trends in industry

- Profit and market leadership are the prime drivers, not social objectives.
- Changes in market and technology are throwing up newer competency requirements.
- There are large employment opportunities in the private sector.
- Public-sector employment faces stagnation and decline.
- More opportunities are there in tertiary sectors.

Chapter 5 Trade Unionism and Trade Unions

Trade unionism, developed as an effort of the labour to organize during the Industrial Revolution era, promoted the Factory System of production and a laissez-faire approach of the state towards participants of the Factory System.

Basic theories explaining trade unionism

- Revolutionary – ownership based
- Industrial – democracy, rights based
- Business – economic power
- Socio-psychological belongingness

Reasons for joining a trade union

- To attain economic security
- To be able to improve bargaining power
- For the ventilation of worker grievances
- For an information medium
- To protect unexpected economic needs
- To satisfy social needs
- For securing power

Tools of trade unionism

- Mutual insurance
- Collective bargaining
- Legal enactment
- Direct action

Link between politics and trade unions

- The politically committed members account for 15–20 per cent of total membership in a union, but their influence is high.
- Political parties and unions function in close cooperation, but there is an essential difference between the two.
- The TUs in India are fragmented due to their allegiance to different political parties.

Rights of Trade Unions: The International Labour Organization (ILO) recognized the right of association through the Freedom of Association and Protection of the Right to Organize Convention (Convention No. 87). Many countries have not ratified this convention.

Major objectives of trade unions

- Ensure security of workers
- Obtain better economic returns
- Improve working conditions
- Power to influence management
- Power to influence the government

Brad areas of trade union functions

- Organizational
- Economic
- Political-legal
- Welfare

Specific trade union functions

- Protect economic interests of the members
- Influence social relationships at the workplace
- Influence policies at the national level
- Collective action for sectional interest
- Collaboration for productivity and gain-sharing
- Enhancing professional status
- Research
- Communication, welfare and education

Features of an effective trade union

- Internally democratic
- Have a strong leadership and large followership
- Exhibit a responsibility towards their worker members
- Committed to promote industrial peace and harmony
- Inclined towards collective bargaining that is collaborative and not competitive
- Possess financial security
- Adaptable to change
- Trade unions may be classified on the basis of purpose and the purpose of membership.

On the basis of purpose

- Regulatory
- Reformist
- Revolutionary

On the basis of membership

- Craft
- Industry
- Staff

Chapter 6 Trade Unions in India

- Indian trade unions are very fragmented.
- Early splits in Indian trade unions tended to be on ideological grounds.
- Recent fragmentations have centered on personalities and, occasionally, on regional and caste considerations.
- Trade-union activities are restricted to industrial areas.
- The AITUC was formed in 1920 on a national basis.

Phases in the grwoth of trade unions

- The first post-Independence growth phase
- The second post-Independence growth phase (1960s–1980s)
- The pre-liberalization era (1980–1991)
- The post liberalization era

Union security: is gained through membership that is sought by providing benefits of collective bargaining only to those who remain their members. The union derives its meaning and strength from the number of members it has. The unions (and management), therefore, look for measures that enhance security, i.e., maintaining a healthy membership in comparison to others. Free riders are discouraged. Union security can be achieved through practices such as:

- Recognition (by management) as the sole bargaining agent
- Maintenance of membership (preferential shop, agency shop, closed shop, open shop, union shop)
- Check-off system

Central trade union organizations: At present there are nine CTUOs (Central Trade Union Organizations) with different political affiliations or leanings.

Major problems faced by trade unions in India

- Outside or political leadership
- Multiplicity of unions and inter-union rivalry
- Small size of the unions
- Low membership
- Uneven growth
- Poor financial position
- Low level of knowledge of labour legislation
- Fear of victimization

Trade unionism in India today

- Unionization according to industry/region/state
- 70,000 registered TUs, many not registered
- 2 per cent of the workforce unionized
- PSUs: Industry-level collective bargaining in coal/steel; enterprise level elsewhere
- Private sector: Plant-level collective bargaining
- Union density according to the size of industry
- Craft unions in the government transport sector
- Low unionization in SMEs
- Twin battle against inter-union competition and assertive management
- Unionization in India under recession

The Trade Unions Act, 1926

- Enacted mainly in deference to the ILO convention, in recognition of the right of workers to organize and also to strengthen the bargaining power of the workers.
- The Act aims to provide for the registration of trade unions and, in certain respects, to define the law relating to registered trade unions.

Objectives of the Act

- Lay down conditions governing the registration of TUs
- Define obligations of a registered TU
- Prescribe rights and liabilities of a registered trade union

Managerial trade unionism: In India, we have unions in the executive cadre as well, such as civil services, doctors, electricity board, bank officers, merchant navy officers, etc. These associations among white-collared workers are more pronounced in the public sector.

PART II: PARADIGM SHIFT

Chapter 7 From Industrial Relations to Employee Relations

Drivers for the Shift in Focus in IR

- Changing political ideologies dictated by concerns for economic growth
- Trying to achieve sustained competitive advantage through people
- Changing characteristics of workforce
- Fast-paced changes in technology reducing dependence on industrial workforce
- The declining credibility of unions

ER includes

- Relations between managers and individual workers
- Collective relations between managers and workers
- The role of the government in the regulation of these relationships

Features of the employee–employer relationship

- Individualized
- Proactive
- Development-oriented rather than maintenance driven
- Flexible rather than standardized
- Informal rather than institutionalized

Principles underlying the shift towards ER

- The recognition of individual differences in needs and aspirations
- Trusting the employees' competence and the ability to perform and, thus, empowering them
- Providing support through coaching, counselling and mentoring
- Facilitating individual development
- Creating a collaborative work environment
- Promoting a healthy work-life balance
- A transparent and open communication system
- Mutual trust and respect as a core value

Chapter 8 Employee Relations Management at Work

- The ER perspective in management could be explained through unitarism, pluralism and radicalism.

Changes brought about by ER at the workplace

- Large-scale changes in people-related strategies and processes
- Human resources management and development becoming an area of strategic concern
- The recognition that core-competence-building and the design of the organization are key differentiators and the sources of competitive advantage

- The motivation of the employees for higher productivity, problem-solving and creativity is a necessity
- Trade unions have to look beyond the economic demands and the organized sectors and focus on larger economic and social issues.
- The government must strive to be more nimble in responding to the changes, and at the same time, protect the interests of all concerned in the productive endeavour.
- ER strategy must be supportive of, and complementary to, the wider aims and objectives of the organization. Where staff has a very strong group identity, ER may evolve to harness the group commitment to the organization's purpose. Labour-intensive organizations may adapt a "safety valve" framework for managing ER.

Factors affecting the ER policy of an organization
- Equity
- Flexibility
- Employee participation in management

ER strategies must draw from findings in the following areas of organization behaviour
- Leadership
- Communication
- Decision making
- Power and authority
- Management of conflicts

Forces driving organizations towards an ER orientation
- Technological changes
- Globalization of operations and markets
- Advances in managerial expertise
- Advances in the understanding of human behaviour
- Changes in aspiration and expectations in work situations
- Changes in organization structures
- Specific initiatives such as privatization, cost-cutting measures, and restructuring for gaining competitive advantage

PART III: LEGISLATIONS AND ADMINISTRATION

Chapter 9: Labour Legislations in a Changing Context

- Labour legislation in India comprises both central and state legislations.
- There could be many bases for classification e.g. purpose, period of enactment, legislative body that has enacted the law, etc.
- On the basis of purpose, legislations can be categorized into groups pertaining to the regulation of working conditions, social security, wage and bonus, IR and conflict prevention.

Regulation of working conditions
- The Factories Act, 1948
- The Shops and Establishment Acts, 1953
- The Contract Labour (Regulation and Abolition Act), 1979

Social security
- The Employees' State Insurance Act, 1948
- The Workmen's Compensation Act, 1923
- The Payment of Gratuity Act, 1972
- The Employees' Provident Fund and Miscellaneous Provisions Act, 1952

Wage and bonus
- The Payment of Wages Act, 1936
- The Minimum Wages Act, 1948
- The Payment of Bonus Act, 1965

IR and conflict prevention
- The Industrial Disputes Act, 1947
- The Industrial Employment (Standing Orders) Act, 1946
- The Trade Unions Act, 1926

The Factories Act, 1948

Objectives of the Factories Act
- To protect health, safety and welfare of the workmen
- Regulate hours of work, weekly off s and annual leave
- Regulate the employment of women and young persons

Factory: A pictorial representation of the definition of factory is given below.

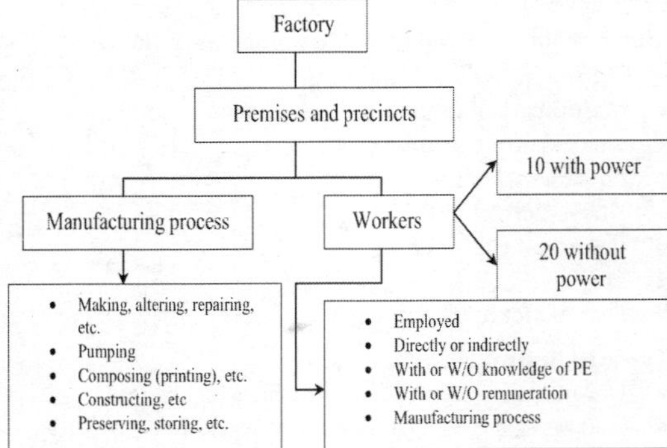

Worker: Under Factories Act, a worker means
- A person employed
- Directly or by or through any agency
- With or without the knowledge of the principal employer (PE)
- He may be employed with or without remuneration

A **worker must be employed** in
- the manufacturing process, or
- in cleaning some parts of machinery or premises used for the manufacturing process, or
- in some other kind of work incidental to or connected with the manufacturing process.

Occupier: An "occupier" refers to a person who has the ultimate control of the factory. In case of a partnership, any one partner shall be deemed as the "occupier". In case of a company, any one of the directors, and in case of a factory owned by the central or state government, the person appointed to manage the affairs of the factory shall be deemed as the "occupier".

Provisions relating to health

Section 11–Cleanliness
Section 12–Disposal of waste and effluents
Section 13–Ventilation and temperature
Section 14–Dust and fume
Section 15–Artificial humidification
Section 16–Over-crowding
Section 17–Lighting
Section 18–Drinking water
Section 19–Latrines and urinals
Section 20–Spittoons

Provisions relating to safety

Section 21–Fencing of machinery
Section 23–Employment of young persons on dangerous machines
Section 24–Striking gear and devices for cutting off power
Section 25–Self-acting machines
Section 26–Casing of new machinery
Section 27–Prohibition of employment of women and children near cotton openers
Section 28–Hoists and lifts
Section 29–Lifting machines, cranes, chains, ropes and lifting tackles
Section 30–Revolving machinery
Section 31–Pressure plant
Section 32–Floors, stairs and means of access
Section 33–Pits, sumps, opening in floors, etc.
Section 34–Excessive weights
Section 35–The protection of eyes
Section 36–Precaution against dangerous fumes
Section 36 A–Precautions regarding the use of portable light
Section 37–Explosive or inflammable dust, gas, etc.
Section 38–Precautions in case of fire
Section 39–Power to require specification of defective part or tests of stability
Section 40–Safety of buildings and machinery
Section 40 A–The maintenance of buildings
Section 40 B–Safety officers
Section 41–Grants rule-making power to states

Provisions relating to welfare

Section 42–Washing facilities
Section 43–Facilities for storing and drying clothing
Section 44–Facilities for sitting
Section 45–First-Aid appliances
Section 46–Canteens
Section 47–Shelters, rest rooms and lunch rooms
Section 48–Crèches
Section 49–Welfare officers
Section 50

Hazardous process: A new chapter added (4 A). "Hazardous process" has been defined in Section 2(cb) of the Act. In essence, it implies such processes that may be carried out in an industry specified in Schedule 1 of the Act and the process may cause one of the following two (or both): (i) material impairment to the health of the persons engaged in or connected with it, and (ii) pollution of the general environment.

Working hours: Not more than 48 in a week. Not more than 9 hours in a day. Rest interval of half an hour after 5 hours' work

Weekly off: First week of the day to be treated as weekly off. If the worker is made to work on weekly holiday, a compensatory off must be given within three days before or three days after the weekly off. No worker to work continuously for more than 10 days.

Spread-over: The total time spread in a factory including working hours and rest intervals. Spreadover cannot be more than 10.5 hours normally.

Women: The employment of women in any factory is restricted to timings between 6 a.m. and 7 p.m. Women are not to be deployed on night shifts.

Extra wages for overtime: Where a worker works in a factory for more than nine hours in any day or for more than forty-eight hours in any week, he shall in respect of overtime work, be entitled to wages at the rate of twice his ordinary rate of wages.

The Shops and Establishments Act, 1953: An act to guide states in enacting their own rules to provide statutory obligation and rights to employees and employers in the unorganized sector of employment, i.e., shops and establishments. Every State has enacted its own rule.

The Contract Labour (Regulation and Abolition) Act, 1970: This Act seeks to regulate the employment of contract labour in certain establishments and to provide for its abolition under certain circumstances.

Objectives of the Contract Labour (Regulation and Abolition) Act, 1970

- Abolish the system of contract labour wherever possible and practicable
- Improve service conditions of contract labour where abolition of the contract labour was not possible
- Regulate the working conditions of the contract labour so as to place it at par with labour employed directly
- Ensure timely payment of wages and provision of essential amenities

Registration and licensing: Every "principal employer" has to get his establishment registered under the Act if he intends to employ (or has employed) 20 or more contract labour in the establishment. Similarly, every contractor employing 20 or more contract labour must obtain a licence before commencing work in a particular establishment.

Principal employer: The manager or occupier of a factory or head of the department of a government/local authority who may employ contract labour in his establishment.

Contract labour: A workman is deemed to be employed as "contract labour" in or in relation to work of the establishment, if he/she is hired for such work by or through a contractor, with or without knowledge of the principal employer.

Duties and obligations of a contractor

- Obtain a licence
- Grievance handling of contract labour

- Administrative control over labour without interference from the principal employer.
- Should not employ more labour than what has been allowed in the licence
- Shall pay wages in the presence of the PE's representative
- Submit half-yearly returns to the licensing officer
- Pay taxes as per statutory provisions

Duties and obligations of a principal employer

- Get registration as a PE
- Ensure that the contractor is paying wages to his workmen
- Ensure that minimum wages are paid
- Pay wages in full to the contract workmen in case the contractor fails to pay the same, which he can recover from the contractor
- Ensure that the contractor has paid the PF and ESI dues
- Ensure provision of amenities as provided for in the Act
- File annual returns to RO

Contract labour may be engaged for the following reasons

- For seasonal/occasional requirement/temporary increase of work
- Need of expertise in a particular job
- Economic and financial feasibility

Areas where contract labour should not be engaged

- All such jobs as notified by the appropriate government
- All processes, operations and other work incidental to, or necessary for, the industry, trade, business, manufacture, or occupation are carried on in the establishment for jobs of perennial nature, that is to say, of sufficient duration
- Jobs done ordinarily through regular workmen in the establishment

Advisory boards: Constituted by the Appropriate Government (State or Central). The Central and State Contract Labour Boards are tripartite bodies comprising members from employers, employees and the government. It is constituted to advise the respective governments on matters arising out of the administration of the Act as are referred to them.

Guidelines for the prohibition/abolition of contract labour deployment

- Work is of perennial nature
- Work is incidental to or necessary for the work of the establishment
- There is sufficient work to employ sufficient number of whole-time workers
- Where a particular work is ordinarily being done through regular workmen
- Where conditions of work and benefits for the contract labour are not alright

Chapter 10 Social-security Legislations

The social-security legislations in India derive their strength and spirit from the Directive Principles of the State Policy as contained in the Constitution of India.

Major social-security acts

- The Employees' State Insurance Act, 1948
- Employees' Provident Funds and Miscellaneous Provisions Act, 1952
- The Workmen's Compensation Act
- The Maternity Benefit Act
- The Payment of Gratuity Act

Two-pronged thrust of social security

- Those relating to the medical facilities, compensation benefits and insurance coverage to the employees in case of accidents, incapacity, illness
- Those relating to the provident fund and gratuity provisions

The Employees' State Insurance Act, 1948

The Act aims to provide security (financial and medical) to employees (and their dependents) during contingencies that may affect their earning capacities, temporarily or permanently.

Benefits under the ESI Act

- Sickness benefit
- Maternity benefit
- Disablement benefit
- Dependant's benefit
- Medical benefit
- Funeral expenses

Eligibility and coverage

- The Act extends to the whole of India
- It applies to non-seasonal, power-using factories or manufacturing units employing 10 or more persons, and, non-power using establishments employing 20 or more persons.
- Employees drawing wages only up to INR 10,000 a month, are entitled to health insurance cover under the ESI Act.

ESI corporation: This social-security programme is administered by a corporate body called the Employees' State Insurance Corporation. It comprises members representing interest groups that include employee, employers, the central and state government, besides representatives of parliament and the medical profession.

Scheme financing: ESI scheme is a self-financing health insurance scheme.

- Employees' Contribution = 1.75% of wages
- Employers' Contribution = 4.75% of wages
- No contribution from employees earning less than INR 50 per day

Contribution periods and benefit period: Contribution towards the scheme are payable on a monthly basis. Contribution period means a six-month time span from 1 April to 30 September and 1 October to 31 March. Thus, in a financial year, there are two contribution periods of six months' duration. Cash benefits under the scheme are generally linked with the contribution paid. The benefit period starts three months after the closure of a contribution period Medical benefit: Full medical facilities for self and dependants are admissible from day one of entering insurable employment.

Sickness benefit

- Payable to an insured person in cash, in the event of sickness resulting in absence from work
- Admissible only after contribution for at least 78 days in a contribution period of 6 months
- Payable for a maximum of 91 days in 2 consecutive contribution periods [one year]
- Payment is to be made at a **standard rate,** which is not less than 50 per cent of the wages.
- **Extended sickness benefit:** Payable for the period of certified sickness in case of the specified, 34 long-term diseases that need prolonged treatment and absence from work
- **Enhanced sickness benefit:** Payable to insured persons in the productive age group for undergoing sterilization operation

Maternity benefits: Maternity benefit is payable to insured women in case of confinement or miscarriage or sickness related thereto.

Disablement benefit (CASH): Disablement benefit is payable to insured employees suffering from physical disablement due to employment injury or occupation disease.

Dependant's benefit (CASH): Dependant's benefit (family pension) is payable to dependants of a deceased, insured person where death occurs due to employment or occupational disease.

Funeral expenses: Funeral expenses are payable in case of death, subject to a maximum of INR 2,500.

The Maternity Benefit Act, 1961

- The ESI did not cover all women workers in the country as far as Maternity Benefit was concerned.
- The Maternity Benefit Act of 1961 was, passed to provide uniform maternity benefit for women workers in certain industries not covered by the Employees' State Insurance Act, 1948.

The Workmen's Compensation Act, 1923

- The Workmen's Compensation Act is the first piece of legislation towards social security.
- It deals with compensation for workers who are injured in the course of duty.
- Under the Workmen's Compensation Act, it is the employer who is responsible to pay compensation (as opposed to the Employees State Insurance. For those establishments to which the Employees' State Insurance Act applies, the liability to pay compensation is on the ESI Corporation).
- The employer is liable to pay compensation if the worker is injured by an accident that
  - Arises out of (i.e., while engaged in) work
  - Occurs in the course of his employment (i.e., during work hours)
  - Causes an injury that results in disablement of the worker

Compensation due in case of

- Death
- Permanent total disablement
- Permanent partial disablement
- Temporary disablement

No liability of the employer

- Where the disablement does not last for more than three days
- Where the disablement has arisen out of the following
  - Drugs or drink
  - Disobedience
  - Disregard for the safety measures prescribed

Occupational disease: An occupational disease that is contracted in the course of employment will fall within the meaning of an "accident" for the purposes of this Act. In the case of such a disease being contracted, the employer will be liable to pay compensation to the affected worker. The occupational diseases for which compensation is payable are specified in a list attached to the Act (Part A of Schedule III)

The Payment of Gratuity Act, 1972

- It is a beneficent piece of social-security legislation that aims at providing a scheme for providing gratuity to employees engaged in factories, mines, oil fields, plantations, ports, railways, shops and other establishments.
- The gratuity was to be paid in the event of superannuation, retirement, resignation, death or total disablement due to accident or disease.
- The main purpose of the Payment of Gratuity Act is to provide a sum of payment to an employee as a token of gratitude for having served the organization. This payment is intended to help the employee provide for his/her needs after severance of his/her relationship with the employer.
- An employee is eligible for receiving gratuity payment only after s/he has completed five years of continuous service. S/he is said to be in continuous service, when s/he has provided uninterrupted service during that period, till their
  - superannuation, or
  - retirement, or
  - resignation, or
  - death or disablement due to accident or disease.

Applicability: To all employees in an establishment, factory, mine, oilfield, plantation etc employed for wages. No ceiling limit of salary/wages for eligibility. Managerial and supervisory employees are also eligible.

Calculation: For every completed year of service, or part thereof, in excess of six months, the employer shall pay gratuity to an employee at the rate of 15 days' wages based on the rate of wages last drawn by the employee concerned. Further, a month will be taken to comprise 26 days, i.e.30 days in a month adjusted for 4 weekly offs.

Maximum Payable: The amount of gratuity payable to an employee shall not exceed INR 350,000.

When not Payable: The gratuity payable to an employee may be wholly or partially forfeited if

- the services of the employee have been terminated for his riotous or disorderly conduct or any other act of violence on his part, or
- the services of the employee have been terminated for any act, which constitutes an offence involving moral turpitude, if offence is committed by him in the course of his employment.

The Employees' Provident Funds and Miscellaneous Provisions Act, 1952

The Employees' Provident Funds and Miscellaneous Provisions Act mainly provides retirement or old-age benefits, such as provident fund, superannuation, pension, invalidation pension, family pension and deposit-linked insurance.

ESI applicable to

- A factory engaged in any industry specified in Schedule I (of this Act) and in which 20 or more persons are employed
- Any other establishment employing 20 or more persons or class of such establishments which the central government may, by notification in the official gazette, specify in this behalf
- The Act is applicable to employees of establishments covered by the Act whose wage is INR 6,500 per month or below
- Employees with wage more than this ceiling may also join the scheme if the employees and the employer agree and with the approval of the government (represented by either the PF Commissioner or an officer so authorized in this regard)

Schemes under the Act

- EPF (Employee Provident Fund Scheme, 1952)
- EPS & F (Employee Pension Scheme and Fund, 1995)
- EDLI (Employees Deposit Linked Insurance Scheme and Fund, 1976)

The PF Scheme

- Employees: 12% on Basic + DA
- Employer:
  - 3.67% on Basic + DA
  - Administrative Charges: 1.10% on Basic +DA

Employees' Pension Scheme, 1995

- Employee: Not required
- Employer: 8.33% on Basic + DA
- NB: Where the pay of the member exceeds INR 6,500 per month, the contribution payable by the employer will be limited to the amt. payable on his pay of INR 6,500 only.

Employees Deposit Linked Insurance Scheme

- Employees: Not required
- Employer:
  - 0.5% on Basic + DA
  - Administrative Charges: 0.01% on Basic +DA
- Where the monthly pay of an employee is more than INR 6,500 the contribution payable in respect of him by the employer is limited to the amts payable on a monthly pay of INR 6,500 only.

Chapter 11 Wage Legislation

Major wage-related legislations

- The Minimum Wages Act, 1948
- The Payment of Wages Act, 1936
- The Payment of Bonus Act, 1965

The Payment of Wages Act, 1936

The Payment of Wages Act, 1936 was enacted to:

- Regulate the payment of wages
- To ensure a speedy and effective remedy against illegal deductions and/or unjustified delay in the payment of wages

Applicability: The Act is applicable to persons employed in factories, industries and other establishments. It covers every person who is employed in any of the establishments and drawing an average wage of up to INR 6,500 per month

Wages: The term wages means all remuneration (whether by way of salary, allowances or otherwise) expressed in terms of money or capable of being so expressed.

Pay day: Wages must be paid on a working day and not on a holiday. When there are less than 1,000 persons employed, the wages shall be paid before the expiry of the seventh day of the following month. When there are more than 1,000 workers, the wages are to be paid before the expiry of the 10th day of the following month.

Wage period: The period to be fixed for paying wages to an employed person must not exceed one month.

Terminal wage: When the employment of any person is terminated, the wages earned by him must be paid before the expiry of the second working day from the day of termination.

Mode of payment: Wages must be paid in current coin or currency notes or in both and not in kind. It is, however, permissible for an employer to pay wages by cheque or by crediting them in the bank account if so authorized in writing by an employed person.

Deductions from wages: The Act prohibits all kinds of deductions except those that are authorized by or under the Act (Section 7).

Absence without reasonable cause: Absence for whole or any part of the day-if ten or more persons are absent without reasonable cause, there should be deduction of wages up to eight days.

The Minimum Wages Act, 1948

The Minimum Wages Act aims at establishing a mechanism for fixing minimum wage rates in various kinds of employments

Employee: Any person who is employed for hire or reward to do any work, skilled or unskilled, manual or clerical, in a scheduled employment in respect of which minimum rates of wages have been fixed

The appropriate government is empowered to fix minimum rates of wages and to review at intervals not exceeding five years

Minimum wages determined by the government

- Time work
- Piece work at piece rate
- Piece work for the purpose determining equivalence on a time rate basis

- Overtime work done by employees for piece work or time-rate workers.

Components: Any minimum rate of wages fixed or revised by the appropriate government may consist of:

- A basic rate of wages + a special allowance (e.g., cost-of-living allowance)
- A basic rate of wages + cash value of concessions for the supply of essential-commodities allowance
- An all-inclusive rate, i.e., basic wage + cost-of-living allowance + cash value of concessions on essential commodities

There are two basic procedures for the determination of wages.

Committee procedure: A tripartite committee comprising employers' and employees' representatives and independent members

Notification procedure: Notification of proposed changes by the government. The final revision based on consideration of objections by affected parties.

The Payment of Bonus Act, 1965

Objectives of the Act

- Impose statutory liability upon employer to pay bonus to employees
- Define the principles of bonus payment
- Provide limits for maximum and minimum bonus payable
- Provide machinery for enforcement of the liability of employer

Applicable to

- Whole of India
- Every factory and to every establishment wherein 20 or more workers are employed
- Every employee, not drawing more than INR 10,000 per month, who has worked for not less than 30 days in an accounting year shall be eligible for bonus.
- Government companies and corporations owned by the government, which produces goods or renders services in competition with the private sector.

Not applicable to

- Government employees
- Employees of local bodies, universities, public-sector insurance employees and LIC employees, employees of RBI and public-sector financial institutions, charitable hospitals, social-welfare organizations and defence employees
- Any not-for-profit institution
- Once the Act is applicable, it continues to apply even if the number of employees falls below 20.
- Bonus is to be paid within eight months from the expiry of the accounting year.

Chapter 12 Industrial Relations: Institutional Framework for the Prevention and Settlement of Industrial Disputes

- Conflict can happen at different interfaces amongst employees, between two groups of employees, between employees and managers, employee groups and managers, federation of employee groups and employer groups
- The ultimate manifestation of industrial conflict is a strike on the part of workers, and lockout on the part of managers/employer. There may be many other ways in which conflict finds expression in an organizational context.
- The employee relations approach to conflict resolution is to focus on systemic, structural and procedural aspects, creating an environment of cooperation it is vital that both preventive and other measures be there in place to ensure that such conflicts do not get dysfunctional
- In the Indian context, there exists an elaborate preventive and settlement machinery, outlined in the figure below:

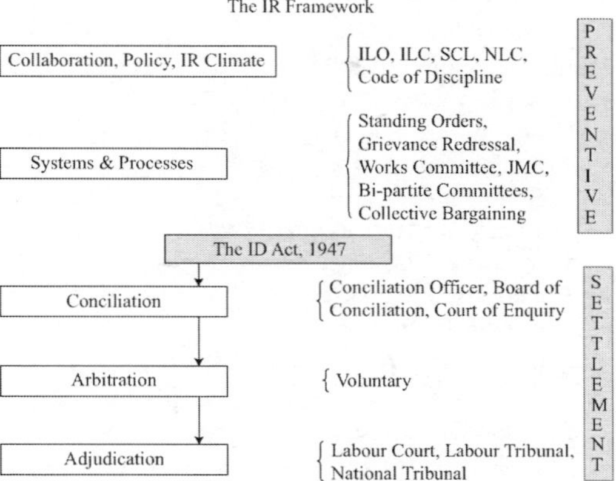

Industrial dispute: Under the Industrial Disputes Act, 1947, an "Industrial Dispute" means a dispute (i) between employers and workmen or, (ii) between workmen and workmen or (iii) between workmen and workmen and the dispute must be connected to employment or non-employment or terms of employment or with the conditions of labour

Industrial action is a term that has not been defined in any of the industrial laws but it means action that may follow if disputes of conflicts cannot be resolved through negotiations. "Strikes" and "lockouts" are forms of industrial action. In both "strike" and "lockout", there is an element of demand and coercion. These are the ultimate weapons in the hands of the two parties.

Strike under ID Act, 1947: A cessation of work by a body of persons employed in an industry acting in combination; or a concerted refusal of any number of persons who are or have been so employed to continue to work or to accept employment; or a refusal under a common understanding of any number of such persons to continue to work or to accept employment

- Strikes can be classified in many ways, one of them being a classification into "primary" and "secondary"
- Primary strikes include economic strike, general strike, stay-in strike, slow-down strike, work to rule etc.
- Secondary strikes include sympathetic strike, boycott, picketing, gherao, *bandh*, etc.

Classification of disputes: Disputes can be classified in several ways. One such classification is:

Disputes of rights: These relate to the application or interpretation of an existing agreement or contract of employment. This kind of dispute, if unresolved through negotiations, is very amenable to resolution through arbitration or adjudication.

Disputes of interest: These relate to claims by employees or proposals by a management about the terms and conditions of employment. These are mostly disputes that can be resolved through discussions and negotiations, give and take.

Classification of disputes based on the terms of employment

- Interest disputes
- Grievance disputes
- Disputes relating to discipline
- Recognition disputes

Measures to improve IR

- Progressive management outlook
- Strong and stable union
- An atmosphere of mutual trust
- Collaboration
- Fair implementation of agreements
- Workers' participation in management
- Sound personnel policies
- The government's role

Trends: An analysis of labour statistics indicates:

- An upward trend in disputes begins after 1965, induced by inflationary pressure.
- The decade of the 1970s was influenced by inter-union rivalry and politically provoked disputes.
- Marked reduction in the 1980s as labour found it difficult to protest with a change in the balance of power, more so with the advent of the New Economic Policy.
- Labour-intensive industries like plantations, coal, textiles, railways and banking have accounted for 20-30 per cent of work stoppages in India.
- Work stoppages were fewer in the public sector than the private sector.

Machinery to deal with industrial disputes

- There are statutory and non-statutory machinery purported to prevent and settle industrial disputes
- The Industrial Disputes Act, 1947 is one of the most important piece of statutory measures for prevention and settlement of Industrial Disputes.

Prohibition of strikes and lockouts: The ID Act prohibits strikes and lockouts subject to the following terms. No person employed in a public-utility service shall go on strike in breach of contract

- Without giving to the employer a notice of 14 days notice of strike, as hereinafter provided, within six weeks before striking
- Within 14 days of giving such notice
- Before the expiry of the date of strike specified in any such notice as aforesaid
- During the pendency of any conciliation proceedings before a conciliation officer and seven days after the conclusion of such proceedings

- Same restrictions apply to an employer for declaring a lockout in a public-utility service
- In non-public-utility service industry, employees are prohibited to strike in breach of contract. If a conciliation is pending before a Board (and seven days thereafter) or dispute is under arbitration or adjudication (and two months after the award) employees are prohibited from going on a strike.

Lay-off: Lay-off has been defined under Clause 2(KKK) of the ID Act. It means the failure, refusal or the inability (for specified causes only) of an employer to give employment to a workman whose name is present on the muster rolls of the industrial establishment and who has not been retrenched.

Retrenchment: Retrenchment has been defined in Section 2 (OO) of the Act. Retrenchment means termination of service by an employer, of a workman, for any reason whatsoever other than

- as punishment inflicted by way of disciplinary action, or
- retirement on reaching the age of superannuation, or
- voluntary retirement, or
- non-renewal of contract, or
- continued ill health.

Closure: Closure means the permanent closing down of a business. It has been defined in Clause 2 (CC) of the Act. Elaborate procedures have been laid down for employers to follow in case they resort to lay-off, retrenchment or closure and relief provided to employees in case they have been subjected to the above.

Chapter VA and VB: The procedure for lay-off, retrenchment and closure are different for industrial establishments employing upto 100 employees (Chapter VA). For establishments employing more than 100 workmen, the procedure is more elaborate and, in most cases, needs approval of the appropriate government (Chapter VB).

Settlement: Settlement means a settlement arrived at in the course of conciliation proceeding and includes a written agreement between employer and workmen arrived at otherwise than in course of a conciliation proceeding where such agreement has been signed by the parties and a copy sent to the Conciliation Officer.

Collective bargaining: Collective bargaining is a technique by which disputes as to conditions of employment are resolved amicably, by agreement, rather than by coercion. The dispute is settled peacefully and voluntarily, although reluctantly, between labour and management.

Chapter 13 Industrial Conflict: Settlement Machinery

- The machinery for the settlement of industrial disputes has been provided under the Industrial Disputes Act, 1947. This machinery comprises conciliation, arbitration and adjudication

Process Flow of Settlement Machinery

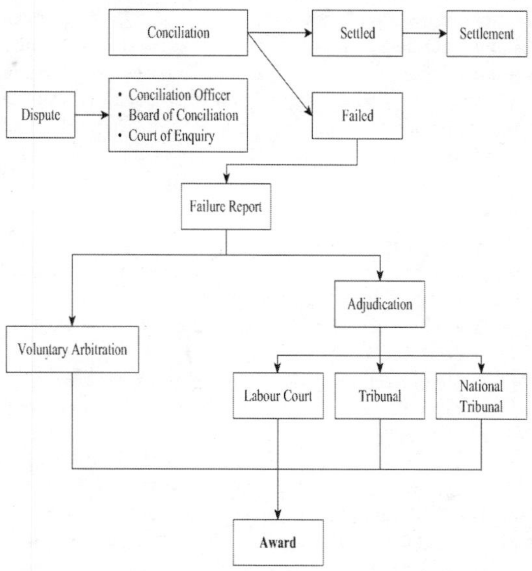

Conciliation: The International Labour Organization describes "conciliation" as the practice by which the services of a neutral third party are used in a dispute as a means of helping the disputing parties to reduce the extent of their differences and to arrive at an amicable settlement or agreed solution

The Conciliation machinery

- Conciliation Officer
- Board of Conciliation
- Court of Enquiry (to assist Conciliation with investigation of issues)

Duties of conciliation officers

- May intervene as a mediator if disputants fail to arrive at a settlement on their own
- Must intervene in case of a strike notice in a public-utility service
- Investigate and facilitate the resolution of disputes
- Help arriving at a settlement
- In case of failure, send a "failure report" to the appropriate government
- Conciliate in cases of "notice of change"

The board of conciliation

- The Act also empowers the government to appoint a Board of Conciliation for promoting the settlement of disputes where the conciliation officer fails to do so within 14 days. The Conciliation Board is a tripartite ad hoc body consisting of a chairman and two to four other members nominated by the parties to the dispute.
- The conciliation machinery can take note of the existing as well as apprehended disputes either on its own or on being approached by any party to the dispute. While conciliation is compulsory in all public-utility services, it is optional in non-public-utility services.

Settlement: A settlement is an agreement arrived at between two parties regarding a dispute. It may be bipartite (S 18-1 or 18-3) or tripartite (S 12-3). Settlements under S18 are binding on the parties to dispute alone. Settlements under 12-3 are binding on all. Settlements under S12-3 are arrived at in the course of conciliation.

Arbitration: Arbitration aims to secure an award on an issue of conflict by referring it to an impartial third party called the "arbitrator". The arbitrator hears both parties involved in the conflict, determines the cause and origin of conflict, understands the differing perceptions and attempts to evolve an amicable solution. The decision of the arbitrator is binding on both the parties. An amendment in 1956 introduced Section 10A in the ID Act, making provision for a joint reference of industrial disputes to voluntary arbitration.

Adjudication: The ultimate remedy for the settlement of an unresolved dispute is its reference by the government to adjudication.

The three-tier adjudication machinery under the Industrial Disputes Act, 1947

- Labour Court
- Industrial Tribunal at the state level
- National Tribunal at the national level

Chapter 14 Industrial Disputes: Institutional Framework and Preventive Measures

- A strategic proactive approach that brings about some convergence of objectives is necessary to prevent the emergence of conflicts, and if they do arise, a method needs to be devised to avoid an escalation that can affect morale and productivity of the workforce.

International labour organization: Formed in 1919, India was one of the ILO's founding members. It is a body that comprises all three parties of a social dialogue namely, Government, employers and employees. Its objective was the amelioration of the conditions of labour worldwide as it constituted a danger to world peace. The objectives were further clarified in the Philadelphia Convention of 1944. Part III of the constitution of the ILO spells out the aims.

Strategic objectives of the ILO

- Promote and realize standards and fundamental principles and rights at work
- Create greater opportunities for women and men to secure decent employment and income
- Enhance the coverage and effectiveness of social protection for all
- Strengthen tripartism and social dialogue

The structure of the ILO

Legislative: The International Labour Conference: Members in the Ratio of 2:1:1 of Government, Employers and Employees: 1 President + 3 Vice Presidents

Executive: The Governing Body: 56 Titular Members (28 + 14 + 14): 66 Deputy Members (28 + 18 + 18): 1 Chairperson + 2 Vice Chairpersons: 10 of the Titular Members from the countries of Chief Industrial Importance

Secretariat: Permanent Secretariat: Works under scrutiny and supervision of the Governing Body: Headed by Director General: DG is also the Secretary General for the ILC: Has a 5-year renewable term

Making labour standards

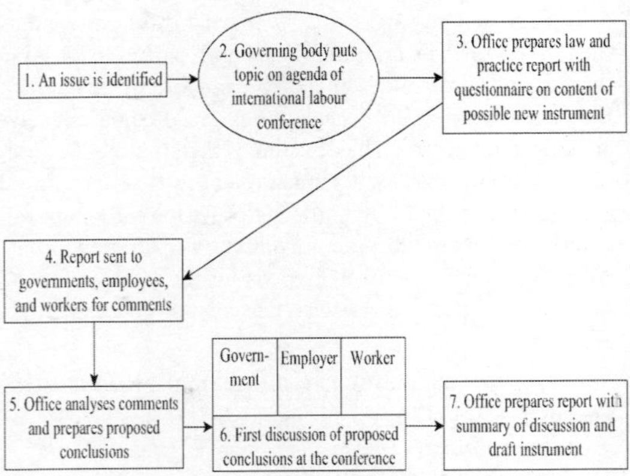

ILC and SLC: Set up in the fourth Labour Conference in 1942.

- It set up permanent tripartite collaboration machinery and constituted Preliminary Labour Conference (later named as the Indian Labour Conference—ILC) and the Standing Labour Advisory Committee (which subsequently dropped the word "Advisory" from its title SLC). Initially, the ILC consisted of 44 members, whereas the SLC was about half the size of the ILC. The pattern of representation was governed by:
  - Equality of representation between the government and the non-government representatives
  - Parity between employers and workers
  - Nomination of representatives of organized employers and labourers was left to the concerned organizations
- These two bodies are roughly patterned on the two ILO bodies namely International Labour Conference and the Governing Body.

Industrial committees: The establishment of industrial committees for specific industries was the outcome of the 1944 session of ILC. Industrial committees came to be set up for plantations, coal mining, cotton textiles, cement, tanneries, mines other than coal, iron and steel, chemicals, building and construction, road transport, etc.

Bipartite bodies: Bipartite bodies were envisaged as bodies having equal representation from management and workers to foster discussion and collaboration on issues of mutual interest in day-to-day running of the establishment. Two of the most important forms of bipartite bodies are the works committee and the joint management councils.

Ethical code or Code of Discipline: The code was to be a voluntary agreement between employers and employees to observe certain discipline that would contribute to industrial peace. The Code has lost its relevance today in practical terms

Standing orders: One of the most proactive measures to prevent an industrial conflict is setting up of clear and satisfactory terms and conditions of employment. In this context, Standing Orders play a significant role as it governs the rules and regulations that govern the conditions of employment of workers. The Standing Orders in one way specifies the duties and responsibilities on the part of both employer and employees and makes each other clear of the expectations and the restrictions in terms of rules and procedures, which are standardized across the organization.

Grievance procedure

- A grievance is a sign of an employee's discontentment with his job or his relationship with his colleagues. Grievances generally arise out of the day-to-day working relations in an organization.
- An employee or a trade union protests against an act or policy of the management that they consider as violating employee's rights.
- Clause 15 of the Model Standing Orders in the Schedule of the Industrial Employment (Standing Orders) Act, 1946, provides for processing grievances.
- The Industrial Disputes Act, 1947, through an amendment in 1982, provides for the establishment of a Grievance Settlement Authority (9C) in all industrial establishments employing 50 or more workmen. This, however, has not yet been given effect to.

Collective bargaining: The ILO refers to collective bargaining as "all negotiations which take place between one or more employers or employers' organizations on the one hand, and one or more workers' organizations on the other, for determining working conditions and terms of employment or for regulating relations between employers and workers". Collective bargaining comprises negotiations between organizations of workers and employers (it is not individual) regarding working conditions, terms of employment, relationship between employers and employees.

Chapter 15 Wage Determination, Wage Administration and Employee Relations

Wage is basically the price that an organization is willing to pay for having a particular job carried out as also the price at which an employee is willing to sell his/her labour.

Three levels of wages (proposed by the CFW)

- Minimum wage
- Fair wage
- Living wage

Basis for the calculation of the minimum wage

- The standard working-class family should be taken to consist of three consumption units.
- Minimum food requirement should be calculated on the basis of a net intake of 2,700 calories.
- Total annual clothing requirement @ 18 yards per capita = 18 X 4 = 72 yards.
- Housing should be the minimum rent charged by the government in any area provided under the subsidized industrial housing scheme for low income.

- Fuel, lighting and other miscellaneous items of expenditure should constitute 20 per cent of total minimum wage.

Methods of wage administration

- Legislation
- Recommendation of expert committees/commissions
- Wage boards
- Job evaluation
- Collective bargaining
- These are not mutually exclusive but used in combination in different circumstances.

Policy recommendations and resolutions

- **The Industrial Truce Resolution (IPR - 1947):** The three parties resolved to ensure fair wages to labour, fair return on capital to industry and provision for expansion and running of the industry. With the shaping
- **The Industrial Policy Resolution (IPR - 1948):** Reiterated the earlier direction of the government and put forth the following objectives:
- The determination of statutory minimum wages for "sweated" industry
- Encouragement of "fair wage" agreements in industry
- **Tripartite Committee on Fair Wages:** Defined the three levels of wages

Wage boards: were envisaged as machinery for wage fixation in specified industries and also a means for implementing many wage-related policies and principles laid down by the various committees and commissions. The Wage Boards, till early 1970s, served a pivotal role in the wage administration in important industries.

Job evaluation: This is a scientific method to determine the "relative" worth of a job in comparison to other jobs within an organization. Job evaluation helps establish internal equity within the organization, also enabling inter-organization comparisons.

Components of wage

- Basic
- Dearness allowance
- Bonus
- Incentives
- Other benefits and allowances

Determinants of wage

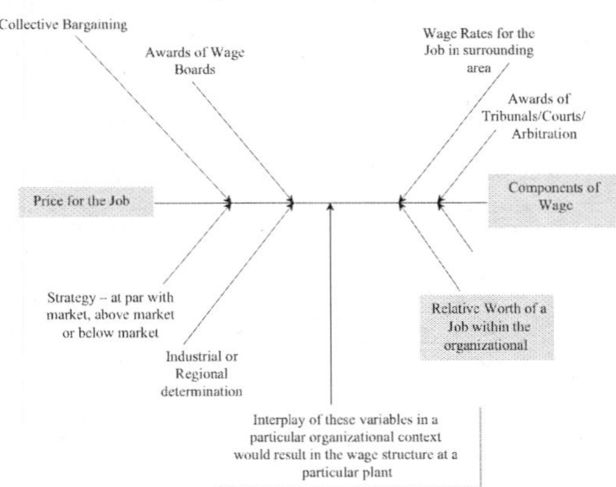

Chapter 16 Labour Administration

- Labour administration is primarily concerned with the affairs of labour and administration of social policy.
- The Labour Administration Convention No.150, 1978 of ILO defines "labour administration" as "public administration activities in the field of labour policy" and the term "system of labour administration" covers "all public administration bodies responsible for and/or engaged in labour administration—whether they are ministerial departments or public agencies.
- The meeting of experts on labour administration held in Geneva in October 1973 recommended central, specialized units for each of the following:
  - Labour protection (working conditions, terms of employment and service, wages, safety, etc.)
  - Labour inspection
  - Labour relations
  - Employment of manpower, including training
  - Social security
- It is primarily the responsibility of the Department of Labour (Central or State) to lay down, develop and apply sound labour policies, coordinate various recommendations received from various departments, which have a bearing on labour affairs.

The role of the Department of Labour

- Provide the government with relevant information to aid policy formulation
- Administer the labour laws and labour policy
- Participate at the highest level on the elaboration of policies and handling of labour questions
- Be staffed with competent personnel for effective and impartial functioning

Labour policy: The term *labour policy* includes the treatment of labour under constitutional, legislative and administrative Acts, rules and practices, and various precepts laid down in the successive Five Year Plans. The labour policy derives its philosophy and content from the Directive Principles of State Policy.

- Labour, as a subject, is in the Concurrent List i.e. on matters relating to labour, both Centre and State can legislate.
- Thrust of the recent labour policy is more towards creating a climate of healthy industrial relations and promoting an industrial culture conducive to the improvement in efficiency, productivity and real wages.

PART IV: SKILLS

Chapter 17: Negotiation Essentials for Employee Relations

- Conflict is a natural part of our lives; all conflict is not bad. How we resolve conflicts determines the value of the outcome. Successful resolution of conflict is the way to progress.
- Sometimes, a conflict may become "dysfunctional", in which case, the outcome may be harmful to the parties to the conflict.

Two ways of resolving conflict

- Avoidance
- Approach

Based on these two methods, the following **styles of conflict resolution** may be adopted in different situations:

- Resignation
- Avoidance
- De-fusion
- Compromise
- Engagement or Problem solving
- Confrontation

The dual concern model of conflict resolution

- Cooperativeness
- Assertiveness

Negotiation: Negotiation is "a process in which two or more parties exchange goods or services and attempt to agree on the exchange rate for them". Another simple definition may be "a way to resolve issues without resorting to actions that hurt or destroy relationships".

Features of negotiation

- Two or more parties
- Something of value or interest to the parties
- Desire to engage in interaction
- At least some desire to accommodate
- Authority to honour the agreement/settlement

Situations requiring negotiation

- Informal
- Formal
- Unstructured
- Structured

Two kinds of bargaining

Distributive bargaining: Distributive bargaining involves distributing a pie of fixed size; the gain of one is at the cost of another. It is a win-lose game.

Integrative bargaining: The concept here is to work towards a win-win solution. The gain or loss need not be at the cost of another party; rather, the strategy is that of joint problem-solving (JPS), where, if need be, the size of the pie itself can be increased so that both parties get a feeling that they have got what they wanted.

Best alternative to no agreement (BATNA): BATNA means, prior to entering into negotiation, the party must decide what is the minimum gain that they would settle for. Below this point, it would be better not to have a settlement. This point is also known as a reservation point.

The basic negotiation process

- **Preparation:** Define issues; set objectives; formulate BATNA; analyse situation; plan strategy
- **Opening:** Set ground rules; initial offer; decide on approach;
- **Bargaining:** Implement strategy; observe strategy; analyse and reorient strategy, if needed
- **Closing:** Check coverage; document; get an agreement

Chapter 18: Soft Skills for Employee Relations

Soft skills: Soft skills tend to be skills by which the individual interacts with, interprets, structures, coordinates or otherwise informs the social and physical environments within which physical, societal and/or personal product may be generated.

Desirable skills in employees

- Listening and oral communication
- Adaptability and creative responses to setbacks and obstacles
- Personal management, confidence, motivation to work toward goals, a sense of wanting to develop one's career and take pride in accomplishments
- Group and interpersonal effectiveness, cooperativeness and teamwork, skills at negotiating disagreements
- Effectiveness in the organization, wanting to make a contribution, leadership potential

Five pillars of emotional intelligence

- Self-awareness
- Managing emotions
- Motivating oneself
- Empathy
- Handling relationship

INDEX